THE DORIS LESSING READER

THE
DORIS LESSING
READER

Doris Lessing

JONATHAN CAPE
THIRTY-TWO BEDFORD SQUARE LONDON

First published 1989
This collection © Doris Lessing 1989
Jonathan Cape Ltd, 32 Bedford Square, London WC1B 3SG

A CIP catalogue record for this book
is available from the British Library

ISBN 0-224-02649-6

The following were first published by Jonathan Cape
© Doris Lessing:

The Habit of Loving, 1957; *A Man and Two Women*, 1963; *The Story of a Non-Marrying Man*, 1972; *Briefing for a Descent into Hell*, 1971; *The Summer Before the Dark*, 1973; *Shikasta*, 1979; *The Marriages Between Zones Three, Four and Five*, 1980; *The Good Terrorist*, 1985; *A Small Personal Voice*, 1966.

The Grass is Singing, 1950, *Going Home*, 1957 and *The Golden Notebook*, 1962, are reproduced by permission of Michael Joseph Ltd © Doris Lessing; *Martha Quest*, 1952, *A Proper Marriage*, 1954 and *In Pursuit of the English*, 1960, are reproduced by permission of Grafton Books Ltd © Doris Lessing.

Typeset at The Spartan Press Ltd,
Lymington, Hants
Printed in Great Britain by
Mackays of Chatham PLC

For dearest Chloe,
with my love

Contents

Preface

The idea of this *Reader* was first sparked, when I stood on a platform in San Francisco to talk about books, as we writers do so often these days, since, clearly – and more and more – reading a book has to be seasoned by actually seeing the author, before it is reckoned to be finally palatable.

One young man stood up to say he hoped I wasn't wasting time writing realism, obviously a waste of my and every other writer's talents, but intended to go on writing, volume after volume, the *Canopus in Argos: Archives* series. A middle-aged woman then said that for her part she thought all science fiction, space fiction, or any other form of fantasy boring, and while she read everything I wrote that was 'real', she could not read a paragraph of *Canopus*, before having to put the book down. These two began an at first tart, then increasingly amiable, discussion, while the audience joned in on one side or the other, and I sat and listened. Then a third, another man, said he could not see these difficulties, he read realism and fantasy with equal pleasure, and hoped I would continue to write both. And anyway, what was all this about the 'realistic' novel being realistic: it was an invention and a convention which we had all agreed to see as 'real'.

This third reader, it goes without saying, cheered me up, seeing the matter in the same way as I do.

Sitting where a writer does, who tends to see 'a body of work' rather more as a river or a stream, sometimes one current uppermost and sometimes another, but always the same, from the same source, the divisions made by reviewers do often seem artificial, particularly when pronouncements are then authoritatively made about 'space fiction' – which I think *Canopus* is or, perhaps, allegory – as being an 'escape from reality'.

This criticism is made, obviously, by people who have never read science fiction or space fiction, for it is there that is to be found the sharpest, and, often, the most prophetic criticisms of the societies we live in. Even odder is the idea that only scenes and characters dealt with in this mode: 'A young woman, aged twenty-eight, sat in a poorly furnished room in an English provincial town, on the 1st of December 1988' – can be real, or realistic. What has happened to the uses of the imagination, presumed by this way of thought to be so earthbound, so tied by factual detail, that analogies cannot be made from situations in space, other planets, other realms of reality, to our own?

What has happened, is something like this. For centuries, no, millennia, human beings told each other stories, but they were nearly all in the shape of myth, fable, animal stories, parables, epics full of out-size events and people. They were never 'realistic'. Our kind of realism was born about four centuries ago, out of – on the one hand – religious tales and religious theatre, centred on churches and – on the other – adventure stories of knights and maidens and heroes and villains, used by Cervantes, for instance, as a jumping-off point for Don Quixote. Our kind of realism is an infant, for four centuries is nothing at all, compared to the millennia-long history of the other mode, and the succession of the old story-tellers, who would have regarded our 'realisms' as poorly furnished. But 'realism' is what we are used to now, is what is 'taught' in schools and colleges (though I am told things are getting better) and so realism is what a large part of the reading public think story-telling is. Because they have forgotten, have not been told about, that many thousands of years long history.

What has happened is an impoverishment of the imagination, of the uses of the mind. Once, a story beginning, 'The cunning Jackal, pausing to admire his reflection in the waters of the river, went to the Tiger, and said "Oh, great Tiger, I have come to . . ."' would at once have had an audience making comparisons with their own state. Not now. There is a strong, and always I think increasing, need for a reader to identify with the 'hero' or 'heroine' of a tale, but these days they need to be supported by a mass of the most down-to-earth detail and description.

The selection in this book has been made from the joint points of view of author and publisher, but predominantly to show that divisions between 'imaginative' and 'realistic' writing are much exaggerated, and that to emphasise them means to lose the advantages of both. Also, to try and show, by a chronological selection, that there is not all that much difference between the ways of writing of an author in early life, or in middle or late life. I'm damned if I can see much difference between some parts of *The Grass is Singing*, my first novel, and some parts of *Shikasta*. Every writer carries a cargo of characters and impressions and ideas, and these modify and develop and change, but very seldom does something completely new come in.

It is a strange business, reading rapidly right through half a lifetime's work, to make selections that will strike a reader in a certain way. Soon you stop worrying about how this will, or will not, strike the reader – 'Why put this story in rather than that?' 'Why emphasise this part of a novel rather than another?' 'If I wrote this story now, how would I do it?' 'What on earth could have happened to me so strongly that I had to write this story, with so much emotion?' – because you can no longer remember the – obviously – powerful emotion that fuelled it.

There is a kind of roughness in some early work, almost always, that goes with the vitality of youthful confidence. And, too, an elderly writer may admire the honest naïvety of a youthful self.

DORIS LESSING
London, 1989

PART I

The Habit of Loving

In 1947 George wrote again to Myra, saying that now the war was well over she should come home and marry him. She wrote back from Australia, where she had gone with her two children in 1943 because there were relations there, saying she felt they had drifted apart; she was no longer sure she wanted to marry George. He did not allow himself to collapse. He cabled her the air fare and asked her to come over and see him. She came, for two weeks, being unable to leave the children for longer. She said she liked Australia; she liked the climate; she did not like the English climate any longer; she thought England was, very probably, played out; and she had become used to missing London. Also, presumably, to missing George Talbot.

For George this was a very painful fortnight. He believed it was painful for Myra, too. They had met in 1938, had lived together for five years, and had exchanged for four years the letters of lovers separated by fate. Myra was certainly the love of his life. He had believed he was of hers until now. Myra, an attractive woman made beautiful by the suns and beaches of Australia, waved goodbye at the airport, and her eyes were filled with tears.

George's eyes, as he drove away from the airport, were dry. If one person has loved another truly and wholly, then it is more than love that collapses when one side of the indissoluble partnership turns away with a tearful goodbye. George dismissed the taxi early and walked through St James's Park. Then it seemed too small for him, and he went to Green Park. Then he walked into Hyde Park and through to Kensington Gardens. When the dark came and they closed the great gates of the park he took a taxi home. He lived in a block of flats near Marble Arch. For five years Myra had lived with him there, and it was here he had expected to live with her again. Now he moved into a new flat near Covent Garden. Soon after that he wrote Myra a very painful letter. It occurred to him that he had often received such letters, but had never written one before. It occurred to him that he had entirely underestimated the amount of suffering he must have caused in his life. But Myra wrote him a sensible letter back, and

George Talbot told himself that now he must finally stop thinking about Myra.

Therefore he became rather less of a dilettante in his work than he had been recently, and he agreed to produce a new play written by a friend of his. George Talbot was a man of the theatre. He had not acted in it for many years now; but he wrote articles, he sometimes produced a play, he made speeches on important occasions and was known by everyone. When he went into a restaurant people tried to catch his eye, and he often did not know who they were. During the four years since Myra had left, he had had a number of affairs with young women round and about the theatre, for he had been lonely. He had written quite frankly to Myra about these affairs, but she had never mentioned them in her letters. Now he was very busy for some months and was seldom at home; he earned quite a lot of money, and he had a few affairs with women who were pleased to be seen in public with him. He thought about Myra a great deal, but he did not write to her again, nor she to him, although they had agreed they would always be great friends.

One evening in the foyer of a theatre he saw an old friend of his he had always admired, and he told the young woman he was with that that man had been the most irresistible man of his generation – no woman had been able to resist him. The young woman stared briefly across the foyer and said, 'Not really?'

When George Talbot got home that night he was alone, and he looked at himself with honesty in the mirror. He was sixty, but he did not look it. Whatever had attracted women to him in the past had never been his looks, and he was not much changed: a stoutish man, holding himself erect, grey-haired, carefully brushed, well dressed. He had not paid much attention to his face since those days many years ago when he had been an actor; but now he had an uncharacteristic fit of vanity and remembered that Myra had admired his mouth, while his wife had loved his eyes. He took to taking glances at himself in foyers and restaurants where there were mirrors, and he saw himself as unchanged. He was becoming conscious, though, of a discrepancy between that suave exterior and what he felt. Beneath his ribs his heart had become swollen and soft and painful, a monstrous area of sympathy playing enemy to what he had been. When people made jokes he was often unable to laugh; and his manner of talking, which was light and allusive and dry, must have changed, because more than once old friends asked him if he were depressed, and they no longer smiled appreciatively as he told his stories. He gathered he was not being good company. He understood he might be ill, and he went to the doctor. The doctor said there was nothing wrong with his heart, he had thirty years of life in him yet – luckily, he added respectfully, for the British theatre.

George came to understand that the word 'heartache' meant that a person could carry a heart that ached around with him day and night for, in his case, months. Nearly a year now. He would wake in the night, because of the pressure of pain in his chest; in the morning he woke under a weight of grief. There seemed to be no end to it; and this thought jolted him into two actions. First, he wrote to Myra, a tender, carefully phrased letter, recalling the years of their love. To this he got, in due course, a tender and careful reply. Then he went to see his wife. With her he was, and had been for many years, good friends. They saw each other often, but not so often now the children were grown-up; perhaps once or twice a year, and they never quarrelled.

His wife had married again after they divorced, and now she was a widow. Her second husband had been a member of Parliament, and she worked for the Labour Party, and she was on a Hospital Advisory Committee and on the Board of Directors of a progressive school. She was fifty, but did not look it. On this afternoon she was wearing a slim grey suit and grey shoes, and her grey hair had a wave of white across the front which made her look distinguished. She was animated, and very happy to see George; and she talked about some deadhead on her hospital committee who did not see eye to eye with the progressive minority about some reform or other. They had always had their politics in common, a position somewhere left of centre in the Labour Party. She had sympathized with his being a pacifist in the First World War – he had been for a time in prison because of it; he had sympathized with her militant feminism. Both had helped the strikers in 1926. In the thirties, after they were divorced, she had helped with money when he went on tour with a company acting Shakespeare to people on the dole, or hunger-marching.

Myra had not been at all interested in politics, only in her children. And in George, of course.

George asked his first wife to marry him again, and she was so startled that she let the sugar tongs drop and crack a saucer. She asked what had happened to Myra, and George said: 'Well, dear, I think Myra forgot about me during those years in Australia. At any rate, she doesn't want me now.' When he heard his voice saying this it sounded pathetic, and he was frightened, for he could not remember ever having to appeal to a woman. Except to Myra.

His wife examined him and said briskly: 'You're lonely, George. Well, we're none of us getting any younger.'

'You don't think you'd be less lonely if you had me around?'

She got up from her chair in order that she could attend to something with her back to him, and she said that she intended to marry again quite soon. She was marrying a man considerably younger than herself, a doctor who was in the progressive minority at her hospital. From her voice George understood that she was both proud and ashamed of this marriage, and that was why she was hiding her face from him. He congratulated her and asked her if there wasn't perhaps a chance for him yet? 'After all, dear, we were happy together, weren't we? I've never really understood why that marriage ever broke up. It was you who wanted to break it up.'

'I don't see any point in raking over that old business,' she said, with finality, and returned to her seat opposite him. He envied her very much, looking young with her pink and scarcely lined face under that brave lock of deliberately whitened hair.

'But dear, I wish you'd tell me. It doesn't do any harm now, does it? And I always wondered . . . I've often thought about it and wondered.' He could hear the pathetic note in his voice again, but he did not know how to alter it.

'You wondered,' she said, 'when you weren't occupied with Myra.'

'But I didn't know Myra when we got divorced.'

'You knew Phillipa and Georgina and Janet and Lord knows who else.'

'But I didn't care about them.'

She sat with her competent hands in her lap and on her face was a look he remembered seeing when she told him she would divorce him. It was bitter and full of hurt. 'You didn't care about me either,' she said.

'But we were happy. Well, I was happy . . .' he trailed off, being pathetic against all his knowledge of women. For, as he sat there, his old rake's heart was telling him that if only he could find them, there must be the right words, the right tone. But whatever he said came out in this hopeless, old dog's voice, and he knew that this voice could never defeat the gallant and crusading young doctor. 'And I did care about you. Sometimes I think you were the only woman in my life.'

At this she laughed. 'Oh, George, don't get maudlin now, please.'

'Well, dear, there was Myra. But when you threw me over there was bound to be Myra, wasn't there? There were two women, you and then Myra. And I've never never understood why you broke it all up when we seemed to be so happy.'

'You didn't care for me,' she said again. 'If you had, you would never have come home from Phillipa, Georgina, Janet *et al* and said calmly, just as if it didn't matter to me in the least, that you had been with them in Brighton or wherever it was.'

'But if I had cared about them I would never have told you.'

She was regarding him incredulously, and her face was flushed. With what? Anger? George did not know.

'I remember being so proud,' he said pathetically, 'that we had solved this business of marriage and all that sort of thing. We had such a good marriage that it didn't matter, the little flirtations. And I always thought one should be able to tell the truth. I always told you the truth, didn't I?'

'Very romantic of you, dear George,' she said drily; and soon he got up, kissed her fondly on the cheek, and went away.

He walked for a long time through the parks, hands behind his erect back, and he could feel his heart swollen and painful in his side. When the gates shut, he walked through the lighted streets he had lived in for fifty years of his life, and he was remembering Myra and Molly, as if they were one woman, merging into each other, a shape of warm easy intimacy, a shape of happiness walking beside him. He went into a little restaurant he knew well, and there was a girl sitting there who knew him because she had heard him lecture once on the state of the British theatre. He tried hard to see Myra and Molly in her face, but he failed; and he paid for her coffee and his own and went home by himself. But his flat was unbearably empty, and he left it and walked down by the Embankment for a couple of hours to tire himself, and there must have been a colder wind blowing than he knew, for next day he woke with a pain in his chest which he could not mistake for heartache.

He had flu and a bad cough, and he stayed in bed by himself and did not ring up the doctor until the fourth day, when he was getting lightheaded. The doctor said it must be the hospital at once. But he would not go to the hospital. So the doctor said he must have day and night nurses. This he submitted to until the cheerful friendliness of the nurses saddened him beyond bearing, and he asked the doctor to ring up his wife, who would find someone to look after him and would be sympathetic. He was hoping that Molly would come herself to nurse him, but when she arrived he did not mention it, for she was busy with preparations for her new marriage. She promised to find him someone who would not wear a uniform and make jokes. They naturally had many friends in common; and she rang up an old flame of his in the theatre who said she knew of a girl who was looking for a secretary's job to tide her over a patch of not working, but who didn't really mind what she did for a few weeks.

So Bobby Tippett sent away the nurses and made up a bed for herself in his study. On the first day she sat by George's bed sewing. She wore a full dark skirt and a demure printed blouse with short frills at the wrist, and George watched her sewing and already felt much better. She was a small, thin, dark girl, probably Jewish, with sad black eyes. She had a way of letting her sewing lie loose in her lap, her hands limp over it; and her eyes fixed themselves, and a bloom of dark introspection came over them. She sat very still at these moments, like a small china figure of a girl sewing. When she was nursing George, or letting in his many visitors, she put on a manner of cool and even languid charm; it was the extreme good manners of heartlessness, and at first George was chilled: but then he saw through the pose; for whatever world Bobby Tippett had been born into he did not think it was the English class to which these manners belonged. She replied with a 'yes' or a 'no' to questions about herself; he gathered that her parents were dead, but there was a married sister she saw sometimes; and for the rest she had lived around and about London, mostly by herself, for ten or more years. When he asked her if she had not been lonely, so much by herself, she drawled, 'Why, not at all, I don't mind being alone.' But he saw her as a small, brave child, a waif against London, and was moved.

He did not want to be the big man of the theatre; he was afraid of evoking the impersonal admiration he was only too accustomed to; but soon he was asking her questions about her career, hoping that this might be the point of her enthusiasm. But she spoke lightly of small parts, odd jobs, scene painting and understudying, in a jolly good-little-trouper's voice; and he could not see that he had come any closer to her at all. So at last he did what he had tried to avoid, and sitting up against his pillows like a judge or an impresario, he said: 'Do something for me, dear. Let me see you.' She went next door like an obedient child, and came back in tight black trousers, but still in her demure little blouse, and stood on the carpet before him, and went into a little song-and-dance act. It wasn't bad. He had seen a hundred worse. But he was very moved; he saw her now above all as the little urchin, the gamin, boy-girl and helpless. And utterly touching. 'Actually,' she said, 'this is half of an act. I always have someone else.'

There was a big mirror that nearly filled the end wall of the large, dark room. George saw himself in it, an elderly man sitting propped up on pillows watching the small doll-like figure standing before him on the carpet. He saw her turn her head towards her reflection in the darkened mirror, study it, and then she began to dance with her own reflection, dance against it, as it were. There were two small, light figures dancing in George's room; there was something uncanny in it. She began singing, a little broken song in stage cockney, and George felt that she was expecting the other figure in the mirror to sing with her; she was singing at the mirror as if she expected an answer.

'That's very good, dear,' he broke in quickly, for he was upset, though he did not know why. 'Very good indeed.' He was relieved when she broke off and came away from the mirror, so that the uncanny shadow of her went away.

'Would you like me to speak to someone for you, dear? It might help. You know how things are in the theatre,' he suggested apologetically.

'I don't maind if I dew,' she said in the stage cockney of her act; and for a moment her face flashed into a mocking, reckless, gamin-like charm. 'Perhaps I'd better change back into my skirt?' she suggested. 'More natural-like for a nurse, ain't it?'

But he said he liked her in her tight black trousers, and now she always wore them, and her neat little shirts; and she moved about the flat as a charming feminine boy, chattering to him about the plays she had had small parts in and about the big actors and producers she had spoken to, who were, of course, George's friends or, at least, equals. George sat up against his pillows and listened and watched, and his heart ached. He remained in bed longer than there was need, because he did not want her to go. When he transferred himself to a big chair, he said: 'You mustn't think you're bound to stay here, dear, if there's somewhere else you'd rather go.' To which she replied, with a wide flash of her black eyes, 'But I'm resting, darling, resting. I've nothing better to do with myself.' And then: 'Oh aren't I aw*ful*, the things wot I sy?'

'But you do like being here? You don't mind being here with me, dear?' he insisted.

There was the briefest pause. She said: 'Yes, oddly enough I do like it.' The 'oddly enough' was accompanied by a quick, half-laughing, almost flirtatious glance; and for the first time in many months the pressure of loneliness eased around George's heart.

Now it was a happiness to him because when the distinguished ladies and gentlemen of the theatre or of letters came to see him, Bobby became a cool, silky little hostess; and the instant they had gone she relapsed into urchin charm. It was proof of their intimacy. Sometimes he took her out to dinner or to the theatre. When she dressed up she wore bold, fashionable clothes and moved with the insolence of a mannequin; and George moved beside her, smiling fondly, waiting for the moment when the black, reckless, freebooting eyes would flash up out of the languid stare of the woman presenting herself for admiration, exchanging with him amusement at the world; promising him that soon, when they got back to the apartment, by themselves, she would again become the dear little girl or the gallant, charming waif.

Sometimes, sitting in the dim room at night, he would let his hand close over the thin point of her shoulder; sometimes, when they said good night, he bent to kiss her, and she lowered her head, so that his lips encountered her demure, willing forehead.

George told himself that she was unawakened. It was a phrase that had been the prelude to a dozen warm discoveries in the past. He told himself that she knew nothing of what she might be. She had been married, it seemed – she dropped this information once, in the course of an anecdote about the theatre; but George had known women in plenty who after years of marriage had been unawakened. George asked her to marry him; and she lifted her small sleek head with an animal's startled turn and said: 'Why do you want to marry me?'

'Because I like being with you, dear. I love being with you.'

'Well, I like being with you.' It had a questioning sound. She was questioning herself? 'Strainge,' she said in cockney, laughing. 'Strainge but trew.'

The wedding was to be a small one, but there was a lot about it in the papers. Recently several men of George's generation had married young women. One of them had fathered a son at the age of seventy. George was flattered by the newspapers, and told Bobby a good deal about his life that had not come up before. He remarked for instance that he thought his generation had been altogether more successful about this business of love and sex than the modern generation. He said, 'Take my son, for instance. At his age I had had a lot of affairs and knew about women; but there he is, nearly thirty, and when he stayed here once with a girl he was thinking of marrying I know for a fact they shared the same bed for a week and nothing ever happened. She told me so. Very odd it all seems to me. But it didn't seem odd to her. And now he lives with another young man and listens to that long-playing record thing of his, and he's engaged to a girl he takes out twice a week, like a schoolboy. And there's my daughter, she came to me a year after she was married, and she was in an awful mess, really awful . . . it seems to me your generation are very frightened of it all. I don't know why.'

'Why my generation?' she asked, turning her head with that quick listening movement. 'It's not my generation.'

'But you're nothing but a child,' he said fondly.

He could not decipher what lay behind the black, full stare of her sad eyes as she looked at him now; she was sitting cross-legged in her black glossy trousers before the fire, like a small doll. But a spring of alarm had been touched in him and he didn't say any more.

'At thirty-five, I'm the youngest child alive,' she sang, with a swift sardonic glance at him over her shoulder. But it sounded gay.

He did not talk to her again about the achievements of his generation.

After the wedding he took her to a village in Normandy where he had been once, many years ago, with a girl called Eve. He did not tell her he had been there before.

It was spring, and the cherry trees were in flower. The first evening he walked with her in the last sunlight under the white-flowering branches, his arm around her thin waist, and it seemed to him that he was about to walk back through the gates of a lost happiness.

They had a large comfortable room with windows which overlooked the cherry trees and there was a double bed. Madame Cruchot, the farmer's wife, showed them the room with shrewd, noncommenting eyes, said she was always happy to shelter honeymoon couples, and wished them a good night.

George made love to Bobby, and she shut her eyes, and he found she was not at all awkward. When they had finished, he gathered her in his arms, and it was then that he returned simply, with an incredulous awed easing of the heart, to a happiness which – and now it seemed to him fantastically ungrateful that he could have done – he had taken for granted for so many years of his life. It was not possible, he thought, holding her compliant body in his arms, that he could have been by himself, alone, for so long. It had been intolerable. He held her silent breathing body, and he stroked her back and thighs, and his hands remembered the emotions of nearly fifty years of loving. He could feel the memoried emotions of his life flooding through his body, and his heart swelled with a joy it seemed to him he had never known, for it was a compound of a dozen loves.

He was about to take final possession of his memories when she turned sharply away, sat up, and said: 'I want a fag. How about yew?'

'Why, yes, dear, if you want.'

They smoked. The cigarettes finished, she lay down on her back, arms folded across her chest, and said, 'I'm sleepy.' She closed her eyes. When he was sure she was asleep, he lifted himself on his elbow and watched her. The light still burned, and the curve of her cheek was full and soft, like a child's. He touched it with the side of his palm, and she shrank away in her sleep, but clenched up, like a fist; and her hand, which was white and unformed, like a child's hand, was clenched in a fist on the pillow before her face.

George tried to gather her in his arms, and she turned away from him to the extreme edge of the bed. She was deeply asleep, and her sleep was unsharable. George could not endure it. He got out of bed and stood by the window in the cold spring night air, and saw the white cherry trees standing under the white moon, and thought of the cold girl asleep in her bed. He was there in the chill moonlight until the dawn came; in the morning he had a very bad cough and could not get up. Bobby was charming, devoted, and gay. 'Just like old times, me nursing you,' she commented, with a deliberate roll of her black eyes. She asked Madame Cruchot for another bed, which she placed in the corner of the room, and George thought it was quite reasonable she should not want to catch his cold; for he did not allow himself to remember the times in his past when quite serious illness had been no obstacle to the sharing of the dark; he decided to forget the sensualities of tiredness, or of fever, or of the extremes of sleeplessness. He was even beginning to feel ashamed.

For a fortnight the Frenchwoman brought up magnificent meals, twice a day, and George and Bobby drank a great deal of red wine and of calvados and made jokes with Madame Cruchot about getting ill on honeymoons. They returned from Normandy rather earlier than had been arranged. It would be better for George, Bobby said, at home, where his friends could drop in to see him. Besides, it was sad to be shut indoors in springtime, and they were both eating too much.

On the first night back in the flat, George waited to see if she would go into the study to sleep, but she came to bed in her pyjamas, and for the second time, he held her in his arms for the space of the act, and then she smoked, sitting up in bed and looking rather tired and small and, George thought, terribly young and pathetic. He did not sleep that night. He did not dare move out of bed for fear of disturbing her, and he was afraid to drop off to sleep for fear his limbs remembered the habits of a lifetime and searched for hers. In the morning she woke smiling, and he put his arms around her, but she kissed him with small gentle kisses and jumped out of bed.

That day she said she must go and see her sister. She saw her sister often during the next few weeks and kept suggesting that George should have his friends around more than he did. George asked why didn't the sister come to see her here, in the flat? So one afternoon she came to tea. George had seen her briefly at the wedding and disliked her, but now for the first time he had a spell of revulsion against the marriage itself. The sister was awful – a commonplace, middle-aged female from some suburb. She had a sharp, dark face that poked itself inquisitively into the corners of the flat, pricing the furniture, and a thin acquisitive nose bent to one side. She sat, on her best behaviour, for two hours over the teacups, in a mannish navy blue suit, a severe black hat, her brogued feet set firmly side by side before her; and her thin nose seemed to be carrying on a silent, satirical conversation with her sister about George. Bobby was being cool and well mannered, as it were deliberately tired of life, as she always was when guests were there, but George was sure this was simply on his account. When the sister had gone, George was rather querulous about her; but Bobby said, laughing, that of course she had known George wouldn't like Rosa; she *was* rather ghastly; but then who had suggested inviting her? So Rosa came no more, and Bobby went to meet her for a visit to the pictures, or for shopping. Meanwhile, George sat alone and thought uneasily about Bobby, or visited his old friends. A few months after they returned from Normandy, someone suggested to George that perhaps he was ill. This made George think about it, and he realized he was not far from being ill. It was because he could not sleep. Night after night he lay beside Bobby, after her cheerfully affectionate submission to him; and he saw the soft curve of her cheek on the pillow, the long dark lashes lying close and flat. Never in his life had anything moved him so deeply as that childish cheek, the shadow of those lashes. A small crease in one cheek seemed to him the signature of emotion; and the lock of black glossy hair falling across her forehead filled his throat with tears. His nights were long vigils of locked tenderness.

Then one night she woke and saw him watching her.

'What's the matter?' she asked, startled. 'Can't you sleep?'

'I'm only watching you, dear,' he said hopelessly.

She lay curled up beside him, her fist beside her on the pillow, between him and her. 'Why aren't you happy?' she asked suddenly; and as George laughed with a sudden bitter irony, she sat up, arms around her knees, prepared to consider this problem practically.

'This isn't marriage; this isn't love,' he announced. He sat up beside her. He did not know that he had never used that tone to her before. A portly man, his elderly face flushed with sorrow, he had forgotten her for the moment, and he was speaking across her from his past, resurrected in her, to his past. He was dignified with responsible experience and the warmth of a lifetime's responses. His eyes were heavy, satirical, and condemning. She rolled herself up against him and said with a small sad smile, 'Then show me, George.'

'Show you?' he said, almost stammering. 'Show you?' But he held her, the obedient child, his cheek against hers, until she slept; then a too close pressure of his shoulder on hers caused her to shrink and recoil from him away to the edge of the bed.

In the morning she looked at him oddly, with an odd sad little respect, and said, 'You know what, George. You've just got into the habit of loving.'

'What do you mean, dear?'

She rolled out of bed and stood beside it, a waif in her white pyjamas, her black hair ruffled. She slid her eyes at him and smiled. 'You just want something in your arms, that's all. What do you do when you're alone? Wrap yourself around a pillow?'

He said nothing; he was cut to the heart.

'My husband was the same,' she remarked gaily. 'Funny thing is, he didn't care anything about me.' She stood considering him, smiling mockingly. 'Strange, ain't it?' she commented and went off to the bathroom. That was the second time she had mentioned her husband.

That phrase, the habit of loving, made a revolution in George. It was true, he thought. He was shocked out of himself, out of the instinctive response to the movement of skin against his, the pressure of a breast. It seemed to him that he was seeing Bobby quite newly. He had not really known her before. The delightful little girl had vanished, and he saw a young woman toughened and wary because of defeats and failures he had never stopped to think of. He saw that the sadness that lay behind the black eyes was not at all impersonal; he saw the first sheen of grey lying on her smooth hair; he saw that the full curve of her cheek was the beginning of the softening into middle age. He was appalled at his egotism. Now, he thought, he would really know her, and she would begin to love him in response to it.

Suddenly, George discovered in himself a boy whose existence he had totally forgotten. He had been returned to his adolescence. The accidental touch of her hand delighted him; the swing of her skirt could make him shut his eyes with happiness. He looked at her through the jealous eyes of a boy and began questioning her about her past, feeling that he was slowly taking possession of her. He waited for a hint of emotion in the drop of her voice, or a confession in the wrinkling of the skin by the full, dark, comradely eyes. At night, a boy again, reverence shut him into ineptitude. The body of George's sensuality had been killed stone dead. A month ago he had been a man vigorous with the skilled harbouring of memory; the long use of his body. Now he lay awake beside this woman, longing – not for the past, for that past had dropped away from him, but dreaming of the future. And when he questioned her, like a jealous boy, and she evaded him, he could see it only as the locked virginity of the girl who would wake in answer to the worshipping boy he had become.

But still she slept in a citadel, one fist before her face.

Then one night she woke again, roused by some movement of his. 'What's the matter *now*, George?' she asked, exasperated.

In the silence that followed, the resurrected boy in George died painfully.

'Nothing,' he said. 'Nothing at all.' He turned away from her, defeated.

It was he who moved out of the big bed into the narrow bed in the study. She said with a sharp, sad smile, 'Fed up with me, George? Well I can't help it, you know. I didn't ever like sleeping beside someone very much.'

George, who had dropped out of his work lately, undertook to produce another play, and was very busy again; and he became drama critic for one of the big papers and was in the swim and at all the first nights. Sometimes Bobby was with him, in her startling, smart clothes, being amused with him at the whole business of being fashionable.

Sometimes she stayed at home. She had the capacity for being by herself for hours, apparently doing nothing. George would come home from some crowd of people, some party, and find her sitting cross-legged before the fire in her tight trousers, chin in hand, gone off by herself into some place where he was now afraid to try and follow. He could not bear it again, putting himself in a position where he might hear the cold, sharp words that showed she had never had an inkling of what he felt, because it was not in her nature to feel it. He would come in late, and she would make them both some tea; and they would sit hand in hand before the fire, his flesh and memories quiet. Dead, he thought. But his heart ached. He had become so used to the heavy load of loneliness in his chest that when, briefly, talking to an old friend, he became the George Talbot who had never known Bobby, and his heart lightened and his oppression went, he would look about him, startled, as if he had lost something. He felt almost lightheaded without the pain of loneliness.

He asked Bobby if she weren't bored, with so little to do, month after month after month, while he was so busy. She said no, she was quite happy doing nothing. She wouldn't like to take up her old work again?

'I wasn't ever much good, was I?' she said.

'If you'd enjoy it, dear, I could speak to someone for you.'

She frowned at the fire but said nothing. Later he suggested it again, and she sparked up with a grin and: 'Well, I don't maind if I dew . . .'

So he spoke to an old friend, and Bobby returned to the theatre, to a small act in a little intimate review. She had found somebody, she said, to be the other half of her act. George was very busy with a production of *Romeo and Juliet*, and did not have time to see her at rehearsal, but he was there on the night *The Offbeat Revue* opened. He was rather late and stood at the back of the gimcrack little theatre, packed tight with fragile little chairs. Everything was so small that the well-dressed audience looked too big, like oversize people crammed in a box. The tiny stage was left bare, with a few black and white posters stuck here and there, and there was one piano. The pianist was good, a young man with black hair falling limp over his face, playing as if he were bored with the whole thing. But he played very well. George, the man of the theatre, listened to the first number, so as to catch the mood, and thought, Oh Lord, not again. It was one of the songs from the First World War, and he could not stand the flood of easy emotion it aroused. He refused to feel. Then he realized that the emotion was, in any case, blocked; the piano was mocking the song; 'There's a Long, Long Trail' was being played like a five-finger exercise; and 'Keep the Home Fires Burning' and 'Tipperary' followed in the same style, as if the piano were bored. People were beginning to chuckle, they had caught the mood. A young blond man with a moustache and wearing the uniform of 1914 came in and sang fragments of the songs, like a corpse singing; and then George understood he was supposed to be one of the dead of that war singing. George felt all his responses blocked, first because he could not allow himself to feel any emotion from that time at all – it was too painful; and then because of the five-finger exercise style, which contradicted everything, all pain or protest, leaving nothing, an emptiness. The show went on; through the twenties, with bits of popular songs from that time, a number about the General Strike, which reduced the whole thing to the scale of marionettes without passion, and then on to the thirties. George saw it was a sort of potted history, as it were – Noel Coward's falsely heroic view of his time parodied. But it wasn't even that. There was no emotion, nothing. George did not know what he was supposed to feel. He looked curiously at the faces of the people around him and saw that the older people looked puzzled, affronted, as if the show were an insult to them. But the younger people were in the mood of the thing. But what mood? It was the parody of a parody. When the Second World War was evoked by 'Run Rabbit Run' played like *Lohengrin*, while the soldiers in the uniforms of the time mocked their own understated heroism from the other side of death, then George could not stand it. He did not look at the stage at all. He was waiting for Bobby to come on, so he could say that he had seen her. Meanwhile he smoked and watched the face of a very young man near him; it was a pale, heavy, flaccid face, but it was responding, it seemed from a habit of rancour, to everything that went on on the stage. Suddenly, the young face lit into sarcastic delight, and George looked at the stage. On it were two urchins, identical it seemed, in tight black glossy trousers, tight crisp white shirts. Both had short black hair, neat little feet placed side by side. They were standing together, hands crossed loosely before them at the waist, waiting for the music to start. The man at the piano, who had a cigarette in the corner of his mouth, began playing something very sentimental. He broke off and looked with sardonic enquiry at the urchins. They had not moved. They shrugged and rolled their eyes at him. He played a marching song, very loud and pompous. The urchins twitched a little and stayed still.

Then the piano broke fast and sudden into a rage of jazz. The two puppets on the stage began a furious movement, their limbs clashing with each other and with the music, until they fell into poses of helpless despair while the music grew louder and more desperate. They tried again, whirling themselves into a frenzied attempt to keep up with the music. Then, two waifs, they turned their two small white sad faces at each other, and, with a formal nod, each took a phrase of music from the fast flood of sound that had already swept by them, held it, and began to sing. Bobby sang her bad stage-cockney phrases, meaningless, jumbled up, flat, hopeless; the other urchin sang drawling languid phrases from the upperclass jargon of the moment. They looked at each other, offering the phrases as it were, to see if they would be accepted. Meanwhile, the hard, cruel, hurtful music went on. Again the two went limp and helpless, unwanted, unaccepted. George, outraged and hurt, asked himself again: What am I feeling? What am I supposed to be feeling? For that insane nihilistic music demanded some opposition, some statement of affirmation, but the two urchins, half-boy, half-girl, as alike as twins (George had to watch Bobby carefully so as not to confuse her with 'the other half of her act') were not even trying to resist the music. Then, after a long, sad immobility, they changed roles. Bobby took the languid jaw-writhing part of a limp young man, and the other waif sang false-cockney phrases in a cruel copy of a woman's voice. It was the parody of a parody of a parody. George stood tense, waiting for a resolution. His nature demanded that now, and quickly, for the limp sadness of the turn was unbearable, the two false urchins should flash out in some sort of rebellion. But there was nothing. The jazz went on like hammers; the whole room shook – stage, walls, ceiling – and it seemed the people in the room jigged lightly and helplessly. The two children on the stage twisted their limbs into the wilful mockery of a stage convention, and finally stood side by side, hands hanging limp, heads lowered meekly, twitching a little while the music rose into a final crashing discord and the lights went out. George could not applaud. He saw the damp-faced young man next to him was clapping wildly, while his lank hair fell all over his face. George saw that the older people were all, like himself, bewildered and insulted.

When the show was over, George went backstage to fetch Bobby. She was with 'the other half of the act', a rather good-looking boy of about twenty, who was being deferential to the impressive husband of Bobby. George said to her: 'You were very good, dear, very good indeed.' She looked smilingly at him, half-mocking, but he did not know what it was she was mocking now. And she had been good. But he never wanted to see it again.

The revue was a success and ran for some months before it was moved to a bigger theatre. George finished his production of *Romeo and Juliet* which, so the critics said, was the best London had seen for many years, and refused other offers of work. He did not need the money for the time being, and besides, he had not seen very much of Bobby lately.

But of course now she was working. She was at rehearsals several times a week, and away from the flat every evening. But George never went to her theatre. He did not want to see the sad, unresisting children twitching to the cruel music.

It seemed Bobby was happy. The various little parts she had played with him – the urchin, the cool hostess, the dear child – had all been absorbed into the hard-working female who cooked him his meals, looked after him, and went out to her theatre giving him a friendly kiss on the cheek. Their relationship was most pleasant and amiable. George lived beside this good friend, his wife Bobby, who was doing him so much credit in every way, and ached permanently with loneliness.

One day he was walking down the Charing Cross Road, looking into the windows of bookshops, when he saw Bobby strolling up the other side with Jackie, the other half of her act. She looked as he had never seen her: her dark face was alive with animation, and Jackie was looking into her face and laughing. George thought the boy very handsome. He had a warm gloss of youth on his hair and in his eyes; he had the lithe, quick look of a young animal.

He was not jealous at all. When Bobby came in at night, gay and vivacious, he knew he owed this to Jackie and did not mind. He was even grateful to him. The warmth Bobby had for 'the other half of the act' overflowed towards him; and for some months Myra and his wife were present in his mind, he saw and felt them, two loving presences, young women who loved George, brought into being by the feeling between Jackie and Bobby. Whatever that feeling was.

The Offbeat Revue ran for nearly a year, and then it was coming off, and Bobby and Jackie were working out another act. George did not know what it was. He thought Bobby needed a rest, but he did not like to say so. She had been tired recently, and when she came in at night there was strain beneath her gaiety. Once, at night, he woke to see her beside his bed. 'Hold me for a little, George,' she asked. He opened his arms and she came into them. He lay holding her, quite still. He had opened his arms to the sad waif, but it was an unhappy woman lying in his arms. He could feel the movement of her lashes on his shoulder, and the wetness of tears.

He had not lain beside her for a long time, years it seemed. She did not come to him again.

'You don't think you're working too hard, dear?' he asked once, looking at her strained face; but she said briskly, 'No, I've got to have something to do, can't stand doing nothing.'

One night it was raining hard, and Bobby had been feeling sick that day, and she did not come home at her usual time. George became worried and took a taxi to the theatre and asked the doorman if she was still there. It seemed she had left some time before. 'She didn't look too well to me, sir,' volunteered the doorman, and George sat for a time in the taxi, trying not to worry. Then he gave the driver Jackie's address; he meant to ask him if he knew where Bobby was. He sat limp in the back of the taxi, feeling the heaviness of his limbs, thinking of Bobby ill.

The place was in a mews, and he left the taxi and walked over rough cobbles to a door which had been the door of stables. He rang, and a young man he didn't know let him in, saying yes, Jackie Dickson was in. George climbed narrow, steep, wooden stairs slowly, feeling the weight of his body, while his heart pounded. He stood at the top of the stairs to get his breath, in a dark which smelled of canvas and oil and turpentine. There was a streak of light under a door; he went towards it, knocked, heard no answer, and opened it. The scene was a high, bare, studio sort of place, badly lighted, full of pictures, frames, junk of various kinds. Jackie, the dark, glistening youth, was seated cross-legged before the fire, grinning as he lifted his face to say something to Bobby, who sat in a chair, looking down at him. She was wearing a formal dark dress and jewellery, and her arms and neck were bare and white. She looked beautiful, George thought, glancing once, briefly, at her face, and then away; for he could see on it an emotion he did not want to recognize. The scene held for a moment before they realized he was there and turned their heads with the same lithe movement of disturbed animals, to see him standing there in the doorway. Both faces froze. Bobby looked quickly at the young man, and it was in some kind of fear. Jackie looked sulky and angry.

'I've come to look for you, dear,' said George to his wife. 'It was raining and the doorman said you seemed ill.'

'It's very sweet of you,' she said and rose from the chair, giving her hand formally to Jackie, who nodded with bad grace at George.

The taxi stood in the dark, gleaming rain, and George and Bobby got into it and sat side by side, while it splashed off into the street.

'Was that the wrong thing to do, dear?' asked George, when she said nothing.

'No,' she said.

'I really did think you might be ill.'

She laughed. 'Perhaps I am.'

'What's the matter, my darling? What is it? He was angry, wasn't he? Because I came?'

'He thinks you're jealous,' she said shortly.

'Well, perhaps I am rather,' said George.

She did not speak.

'I'm sorry, dear, I really am. I didn't mean to spoil anything for you.'

'Well, that's certainly *that*,' she remarked, and she sounded impersonally angry.

'Why? But why should it be?'

'He doesn't like – having things asked of him,' she said, and he remained silent while they drove home.

Up in the warmed, comfortable old flat, she stood before the fire, while he brought her a drink. She smoked fast and angrily, looking into the fire.

'Please forgive me, dear,' he said at last. 'What is it? Do you love him? Do you want to leave me? If you do, of course you must. Young people should be together.'

She turned and stared at him, a black strange stare he knew well.

'George,' she said, 'I'm nearly forty.'

'But darling, you're a child still. At least, to me.'

'And he,' she went on, 'will be twenty-two next month. I'm old enough to be his mother.' She laughed, painfully. 'Very painful, maternal love . . . or so it seems . . . but then how should I know?' She held out her bare arm and looked at it. Then, with the fingers of one hand she creased down the skin of that bare arm towards the wrist, so that the aging skin lay in creases and folds. Then, setting down her glass, her cigarette held between tight, amused, angry lips, she wriggled her shoulders out of her dress, so that it slipped to her waist, and she looked down at her two small, limp, unused breasts. 'Very painful, dear George,' she said, and shrugged her dress up quickly, becoming again the formal woman dressed for the world. 'He does not love me. He does not love me at all. Why should he?' She began singing:

> He does not love me
> With a love that is trew . . .

Then she said in stage cockney, 'Repeat; I could 'ave bin 'is muvver, see?' And with the old rolling derisive black flash of her eyes she smiled at George.

George was thinking only that this girl, his darling, was suffering now what he had suffered, and he could not stand it. She had been going through this for how long now? But she had been working with that boy for nearly two years. She had been living beside him, George, and he had had no idea at all of her unhappiness. He went over to her, put his arms around her, and she stood with her head on his shoulder and wept. For the first time, George thought, they were together. They sat by the fire a long time that night, drinking, smoking and her head was on his knee and he stroked it, and thought that now, at last, she had been admitted into the world of emotion and they would learn to be really together. He could feel his strength stirring along his limbs for her. He was still a man, after all.

Next day she said she would not go on with the new show. She would tell Jackie he must get another partner. And besides, the new act wasn't really any good. 'I've had one little act all my life,' she said, laughing. 'And sometimes it's fitted in, and sometimes it hasn't.'

'What was the new act? What's it about?' he asked her.

She did not look at him. 'Oh, nothing very much. It was Jackie's idea, really . . .' Then she laughed. 'It's quite good really, I suppose . . .'

'But what is it?'

'Well, you see . . .' Again he had the impression she did not want to look at him. 'It's a pair of lovers. We make fun . . . it's hard to explain, without doing it.'

'You make fun of love?' he asked.

'Well, you know, all the attitudes . . . the things people say. It's a man and a woman – with music of course. All the music you'd expect, played offbeat. We wear the same costume as for the other act. And

then we go through all the motions . . . It's rather funny, really . . .'
she trailed off, breathless, seeing George's face. 'Well,' she said,
suddenly very savage, 'if it isn't all bloody funny, what is it?' She turned
away to take a cigarette.

'Perhaps you'd like to go on with it after all?' he asked ironically.

'No. I can't. I really can't stand it. I can't stand it any longer,
George,' she said, and from her voice he understood she had nothing to
learn from him of pain.

He suggested they both needed a holiday, so they went to Italy. They
travelled from place to place, never stopping anywhere longer than a
day, for George knew she was running away from any place around
which emotion could gather. At night he made love to her, but she
closed her eyes and thought of the other half of the act; and George
knew it and did not care. But what he was feeling was too powerful for
his old body; he could feel a lifetime's emotions beating through his
limbs, making his brain throb.

Again they curtailed their holiday, to return to the comfortable old
flat in London.

On the first morning after their return, she said: 'George, you know
you're getting too old for this sort of thing – it's not good for you; you
look ghastly.'

'But, darling, why? What else am I still alive for?'

'People'll say I'm killing you,' she said, with a sharp, half angry, half
amused, black glance.

'But, my darling, believe me . . .'

He could see them both in the mirror; he, an old pursy man, head
lowered in sullen obstinacy; she . . . but he could not read her face.

'And perhaps *I'm* getting too old?' she remarked suddenly.

For a few days she was gay, mocking, then suddenly tender. She was
provocative, teasing him with her eyes; then she would deliberately
yawn and say, 'I'm going to sleep. Good night, George.'

'Well of course, my darling, if you're tired.'

One morning she announced she was going to have a birthday party;
it would be her fortieth birthday soon. The way she said it made George
feel uneasy.

On the morning of her birthday she came into his study where he had
been sleeping, carrying his breakfast tray. He raised himself on his
elbow and gazed at her, appalled. For a moment he had imagined it
must be another woman. She had put on a severe navy blue suit, cut like

a man's; heavy black-laced shoes; and she had taken the wisps of black hair back off her face and pinned them into a sort of clumsy knot. She was suddenly a middle-aged woman.

'But, my darling,' he said, 'my darling, what have you done to yourself?'

'I'm forty,' she said. 'Time to grow up.'

'But, my darling. I do so love you in your nice clothes. I do so love you being beautiful in your lovely clothes.'

She laughed, and left the breakfast tray beside his bed, and went clumping out on her heavy shoes.

That morning she stood in the kitchen beside a very large cake, on which she was carefully placing forty small pink candles. But it seemed only the sister had been asked to the party, for that afternoon the three of them sat around the cake and looked at one another. George looked at Rosa, the sister, in her ugly straight, thick suit, and at his darling Bobby, all her grace and charm submerged into heavy tweed, her hair dragged back, without make-up. They were two middle-aged women, talking about food and buying.

George said nothing. His whole body throbbed with loss.

The dreadful Rosa was looking with her sharp eyes around the expensive flat, and then at George and then at her sister.

'You've let yourself go, haven't you, Bobby?' she commented at last. She sounded pleased about it.

Bobby glanced defiantly at George. 'I haven't got time for all this nonsense any more,' she said. 'I simply haven't got time. We're all getting on now, aren't we?'

George saw the two women looking at him. He thought they had the same black, hard, inquisitive stare over sharp-bladed noses. He could not speak. His tongue was thick. The blood was beating through his body. His heart seemed to be swelling and filling his whole body, an enormous soft growth of pain. He could not hear for the tolling of the blood through his ears. The blood was beating up into his eyes, but he shut them so as not to see the two women.

To Room Nineteen

This is a story, I suppose, about a failure in intelligence: the Rawlingses' marriage was grounded in intelligence.

They were older when they married than most of their married friends: in their well-seasoned late twenties. Both had had a number of affairs, sweet rather than bitter; and when they fell in love – for they did fall in love – had known each other for some time. They joked that they had saved each other 'for the real thing'. That they had waited so long (but not too long) for this real thing was to them a proof of their sensible discrimination. A good many of their friends had married young, and now (they felt) probably regretted lost opportunities; while others, still unmarried, seemed to them arid, self-doubting, and likely to make desperate or romantic marriages.

Not only they, but others, felt they were well matched: their friends' delight was an additional proof of their happiness. They had played the same roles, male and female, in this group or set, if such a wide, loosely connected, constantly changing constellation of people could be called a set. They had both become, by virtue of their moderation, their humour, and their abstinence from painful experience people to whom others came for advice. They could be, and were, relied on. It was one of those cases of a man and a woman linking themselves whom no one else had ever thought of linking, probably because of their similarities. But then everyone exclaimed: Of course! How right! How was it we never thought of it before!

And so they married amid general rejoicing, and because of their foresight and their sense for what was probable, nothing was a surprise to them.

Both had well-paid jobs. Matthew was a sub-editor on a large London newspaper, and Susan worked in an advertising firm. He was not the stuff of which editors or publicized journalists are made, but he was much more than 'a sub-editor', being one of the essential background people who in fact steady, inspire and make possible the people in the limelight. He was content with this position. Susan had a talent for commercial drawing. She was humorous about the advertisements she was responsible for, but she did not feel strongly about them one way or the other.

Both, before they married, had had pleasant flats, but they felt it unwise to base a marriage on either flat, because it might seem like a submission of personality on the part of the one whose flat it was not. They moved into a new flat in South Kensington on the clear understanding that when their marriage had settled down (a process they knew would not take long, and was in fact more a humorous concession to popular wisdom than what was due to themselves) they would buy a house and start a family.

And this is what happened. They lived in their charming flat for two years, giving parties and going to them, being a popular young married couple, and then Susan became pregnant, she gave up her job, and they bought a house in Richmond. It was typical of this couple that they had a son first, then a daughter, then twins, son and daughter. Everything right, appropriate, and what everyone would wish for, if they could choose. But people did feel these two had chosen; this balanced and sensible family was no more than what was due to them because of their infallible sense for *choosing* right.

And so they lived with their four children in their gardened house in Richmond and were happy. They had everything they had wanted and had planned for.

And yet . . .

Well, even this was expected, that there must be a certain flatness . . .

Yes, yes, of course, it was natural they sometimes felt like this. Like what?

Their life seemed to be like a snake biting its tail. Matthew's job for the sake of Susan, children, house, and garden – which caravanserai needed a well-paid job to maintain it. And Susan's practical intelligence for the sake of Matthew, the children, the house and the garden – which unit would have collapsed in a week without her.

But there was no point about which either could say: 'For the sake of *this* is all the rest.' Children? But children can't be a centre of life and a reason for being. They can be a thousand things that are delightful, interesting, satisfying, but they can't be a wellspring to live from. Or they shouldn't be. Susan and Matthew knew that well enough.

Matthew's job? Ridiculous. It was an interesting job, but scarcely a reason for living. Matthew took pride in doing it well; but he could hardly be expected to be proud of the newspaper: the newspaper he read, *his* newspaper, was not the one he worked for.

Their love for each other? Well, that was nearest it. If this wasn't a centre, what was? Yes, it was around this point, their love, that the whole extraordinary structure revolved. For extraordinary it certainly was. Both Susan and Matthew had moments of thinking so, of looking in secret disbelief at this thing they had created: marriage, four children, big house, garden, charwomen, friends, cars . . . and this *thing*, this entity, all of it, had come into existence, been blown into being out of nowhere, because Susan loved Matthew and Matthew loved Susan. Extraordinary. So that was the central point, the wellspring.

And if one felt that it simply was not strong enough, important enough, to support it all, well whose fault was that? Certainly neither Susan's nor Matthew's. It was in the nature of things. And they sensibly blamed neither themselves nor each other.

On the contrary, they used their intelligence to preserve what they had created from a painful and explosive world: they looked around them, and took lessons. All around them, marriages collapsing, or breaking, or rubbing along (even worse, they felt). They must not make the same mistakes, they must not.

They had avoided the pitfall so many of their friends had fallen into – of buying a house in the country *for the sake of the children*; so that the husband became a weekend husband, a weekend father, and the wife always careful not to ask what went on in the town flat which they called (in joke) a bachelor flat. No, Matthew was a full-time husband, a full-time father, and at nights, in the big married bed in the big married bedroom (which had an attractive view of the river) they lay beside each other talking and he told her about his day, and what he had done, and whom he had met; and she told him about her day (not as interesting, but that was not her fault) for both knew of the hidden resentments and deprivations of the woman who has lived her own life – and above all, has earned her own living – and is now dependent on a husband for outside interests and money.

Nor did Susan make the mistake of taking a job for the sake of her independence, which she might very well have done, since her old firm, missing her qualities of humour, balance, and sense, invited her often to go back. Children needed their mother to a certain age, that both parents knew and agreed on; and when these four healthy wisely brought-up children were of the right age, Susan would work again, because she knew, and so did he, what happened to women of fifty at the height of their energy and ability, with grown-up children who no longer needed their full devotion.

So here was this couple, testing their marriage, looking after it, treating it like a small boat full of helpless people in a very stormy sea. Well, of course, so it was . . . The storms of the world were bad, but not too close – which is not to say they were selfishly felt: Susan and Matthew were both well-informed and responsible people. And the inner storms and quicksands were understood and charted. So everything was all right. Everything was in order. Yes, things were under control.

So what did it matter if they felt dry, flat? People like themselves, fed on a hundred books (psychological, anthropological, sociological) could scarcely be unprepared for the dry, controlled wistfulness which is the distinguishing mark of the intelligent marriage. Two people, endowed with education, with discrimination, with judgment, linked together voluntarily from their will to be happy together and to be of use to others – one sees them everywhere, one knows them, one even is that thing oneself: sadness because so much is after all so little. These two, unsurprised, turned towards each other with even more courtesy and gentle love: this was life, that two people, no matter how carefully chosen, could not be everything to each other. In fact, even to say so, to think in such a way, was banal, they were ashamed to do it.

It was banal, too, when one night Matthew came home late and confessed he had been to a party, taken a girl home and slept with her. Susan forgave him, of course. Except that forgiveness is hardly the word. Understanding, yes. But if you understand something, you don't forgive it, you are the thing itself: forgiveness is for what you *don't* understand. Nor had he *confessed* – what sort of word is that?

The whole thing was not important. After all, years ago they had joked: Of course I'm not going to be faithful to you, no one can be faithful to one other person for a whole lifetime. (And there was the word *faithful* – stupid, all these words, stupid, belonging to a savage old world.) But the incident left both of them irritable. Strange, but they were both bad-tempered, annoyed. There was something unassimilable about it.

Making love splendidly after he had come home that night, both had felt that the idea that Myra Jenkins, a pretty girl met at a party, could be even relevant was ridiculous. They had loved each other for over a decade, would love each other for years more. Who, then, was Myra Jenkins?

Except, thought Susan, unaccountably bad-tempted, she was (is?) the first. In ten years. So either the ten years' fidelity was not important, or she isn't. (No, no, there is something wrong with this way of thinking, there must be.) But if she isn't important, presumably it wasn't important either when Matthew and I first went to bed with each other that afternoon whose delight even now (like a very long shadow at sundown) lays a long, wand-like finger over us. (Why did I say sundown?) Well, if what we felt that afternoon was not important, nothing is important, because if it hadn't been for what we felt, we wouldn't be Mr and Mrs Rawlings with four children, etc., etc. The whole thing is *absurd* – for him to have come home and told me was absurd. For him not to have told me was absurd. For me to care, or for that matter not to care, is absurd . . . and who is Myra Jenkins? Why, no one at all.

There was only one thing to do, and of course these sensible people did it: they put the thing behind them, and consciously, knowing what they were doing, moved forward into a different phase of their marriage, giving thanks for past good fortune as they did so.

For it was inevitable that the handsome, blond, attractive, manly man, Matthew Rawlings, should be at times tempted (oh, what a word!) by the attractive girls at parties she could not attend because of the four children; and that sometimes he would succumb (a word even more repulsive, if possible) and that she, a good-looking woman in the big well-tended garden at Richmond, would sometimes be pierced as by an arrow from the sky with bitterness. Except that bitterness was not in order, it was out of court. Did the casual girls touch the marriage? They did not. Rather it was they who knew defeat because of the handsome Matthew Rawlings's marriage body and soul to Susan Rawlings.

In that case why did Susan feel (though luckily not for longer than a few seconds at a time) as if life had become a desert, and that nothing mattered, and that her children were not her own?

Meanwhile her intelligence continued to assert that all was well. What if her Matthew did have an occasional sweet afternoon, the odd affair? For she knew quite well, except in her moments of aridity, that they were very happy, that the affairs were not important.

Perhaps that was the trouble? It was in the nature of things that the adventures and delights could no longer be hers, because of the four children and the big house that needed so much attention. But perhaps she was secretly wishing, and even knowing that she did, that the wildness and the beauty could be his. But he was married to her. She was married to him. They were married inextricably. And therefore the gods could not strike him with the real magic, not really. Well, was it Susan's fault that after he came home from an adventure he looked harassed rather than fulfilled? (In fact, that was how she knew he had been *unfaithful*, because of his sullen air, and his glances at her, similar to hers at him: What is it that I share with this person that shields all delight from me?) But none of it by anybody's fault. (But what did they feel ought to be somebody's fault?) Nobody's fault, nothing to be at fault, no one to blame, no one to offer or to take it . . . and nothing wrong, either, except that Matthew never was really struck, as he wanted to be, by joy; and that Susan was more and more often threatened by emptiness. (It was usually in the garden that she was invaded by this feeling: she was coming to avoid the garden, unless the children or Matthew were with her.) There was no need to use the dramatic words, unfaithful, forgive, and the rest: intelligence forbade them. Intelligence barred, too, quarrelling, sulking, anger, silences of withdrawal, accusations and tears. Above all, intelligence forbids tears.

A high price has to be paid for the happy marriage with the four healthy children in the large white gardened house.

And they were paying it, willingly, knowing what they were doing. When they lay side by side or breast to breast in the big civilized bedroom overlooking the wild sullied river, they laughed, often, for no particular reason; but they knew it was really because of these two small people, Susan and Matthew, supporting such an edifice on their intelligent love. The laugh comforted them; it saved them both, though from what, they did not know.

They were now both fortyish. The older children, boy and girl, were ten and eight, at school. The twins, six, were still at home. Susan did not have nurses or girls to help her: childhood is short; and she did not regret the hard work. Often enough she was bored, since small children can be boring; she was often very tired; but she regretted nothing. In another decade, she would turn herself back into being a woman with a life of her own.

Soon the twins would go to school, and they would be away from home from nine until four. These hours, so Susan saw it, would be the preparation for her own slow emancipation away from the role of hub-of-the-family into woman-with-her-own-life. She was already planning for the hours of freedom when all the children would be 'off her hands'. That was the phrase used by Matthew and by Susan and by their friends, for the moment when the youngest child went off to school. 'They'll be off your hands, darling Susan, and you'll have time to yourself.' So said Matthew, the intelligent husband, who had often enough commended and consoled Susan, standing by her in spirit during the years when her soul was not her own, as she said, but her children's.

What it amounted to was that Susan saw herself as she had been at twenty-eight, unmarried; and then again somewhere about fifty, blossoming from the root of what she had been twenty years before. As if the essential Susan were in abeyance, as if she were in cold storage. Matthew said something like this to Susan one night: and she agreed that it was true – she did feel something like that. What, then, was this essential Susan? She did not know. Put like that it sounded ridiculous, and she did not really feel it. Anyway, they had a long discussion about the whole thing before going off to sleep in each other's arms.

So the twins went off to their school, two bright affectionate children who had no problems about it, since their older brother and sister had trodden this path so successfully before them. And now Susan was going to be alone in the big house, every day of the school term, except for the daily woman who came in to clean.

It was now, for the first time in this marriage, that something happened which neither of them had foreseen.

This is what happened. She returned, at nine-thirty, from taking the twins to the school by car, looking forward to seven blissful hours of freedom. On the first morning she was simply restless, worrying about the twins 'naturally enough' since this was their first day away at school. She was hardly able to contain herself until they came back. Which they did happily, excited by the world of school, looking forward to the next day. And the next day Susan took them, dropped them, came back, and found herself reluctant to enter her big and beautiful home because it was as if something was waiting for her there that she did not wish to confront. Sensibly, however, she parked the car in the garage, entered the house, spoke to Mrs Parkes the daily woman about her duties, and went up to her bedroom. She was possessed by a fever which drove her out again, downstairs, into the kitchen, where Mrs Parkes was making cake and did not need her, and into the garden. There she sat on a bench, and tried to calm herself, looking at trees, at a brown glimpse of the river. But she was filled with tension, like a panic: as if an enemy was in the garden with her. She spoke to herself severely, thus: All this is quite natural. First, I spent twelve years of my adult life working, *living my own life*. Then I married, and from the moment I became pregnant for the first time I signed myself over, so to speak, to other people. To the children. Not for one moment in twelve years have I been alone, had time to myself. So now I have to learn to be myself again. That's all.

And she went indoors to help Mrs Parkes cook and clean, and found some sewing to do for the children. She kept herself occupied every day. At the end of the first term she understood she felt two contrary emotions. First: secret astonishment and dismay that during those weeks when the house was empty of children she had in fact been more occupied (had been careful to keep herself occupied) than ever she had been when the children were around her needing her continual attention. Second: that now she knew the house would be full of them, and for five weeks, she resented the fact she would never be alone. She was already looking back at those hours of sewing, cooking (but by herself), as at a lost freedom which would not be hers for five long weeks. And the two months of term which would succeed the five weeks stretched alluringly open to her – freedom. But what freedom – when in fact she had been so careful *not* to be free of small duties during the last weeks? She looked at herself, Susan Rawlings, sitting in a big chair by the window in the bedroom, sewing shirts or dresses, which she might just as well have bought. She saw herself making cakes for hours at a time in the big family kitchen: yet usually she bought cakes. What she saw was a woman alone, that was true, but she had not felt alone. For instance, Mrs Parkes was always somewhere in the house. And she did not like being in the garden at all, because of the closeness there of the enemy – irritation, restlessness, emptiness, whatever it was, which keeping her hands occupied made less dangerous for some reason.

Susan did not tell Matthew of these thoughts. They were not sensible. She did not recognize herself in them. What should she say to her dear friend and husband Matthew? 'When I go into the garden, that is, if the children are not there, I feel as if there is an enemy there waiting to invade me.' 'What enemy, Susan darling?' Well I don't know, really . . .' 'Perhaps you should see a doctor?'

No, clearly this conversation should not take place. The holidays began and Susan welcomed them. Four children, lively, energetic, intelligent, demanding: she was never, not for a moment of her day, alone. If she was in a room, they would be in the next room, or waiting for her to do something for them; or it would soon be time for lunch or tea, or to take one of them to the dentist. Something to do: five weeks of it, thank goodness.

One the fourth day of these so welcome holidays, she found she was storming with anger at the twins, two shrinking beautiful children who (and this is what checked her) stood hand in hand looking at her with sheer dismayed disbelief. This was their calm mother, shouting at them. And what for? They had come to her with some game, some bit of nonsense. They looked at each other, moved closer for support, and went off hand in hand, leaving Susan holding on to the windowsill of the living room, breathing deep, feeling sick. She went to lie down, telling the older children she had a headache. She heard the boy Harry telling the little ones: 'It's all right, Mother's got a headache.' She heard that *It's all right* with pain.

That night she said to her husband: 'Today I shouted at the twins, quite unfairly.' She sounded miserable, and he said gently: 'Well, what of it?'

'It's more of an adjustment than I thought, their going to school.'

'But Susie, Susie darling . . .' For she was crouched weeping on the bed. He comforted her: 'Susan, what is all this about? You shouted at them? What of it? If you shouted at them fifty times a day it wouldn't be more than the little devils deserve.' But she wouldn't laugh. She wept. Soon he comforted her with his body. She became calm. Calm, she wondered what was wrong with her, and why she should mind so much that she might, just once, have behaved unjustly with the children. What did it matter? They had forgotten it all long ago: Mother had a headache and everything was all right.

It was a long time later that Susan understood that that night, when she had wept and Matthew had driven the misery out of her with his big solid body, was the last time, ever in their married life, that they had been – to use their mutual language – with each other. And even that was a lie, because she had not told him of her real fears at all.

The five weeks passed, and Susan was in control of herself, and good and kind, and she looked forward to the holidays with a mixture of fear and longing. She did not know what to expect. She took the twins off to school (the elder children took themselves to school) and she returned to the house determined to face the enemy wherever he was, in the house, or the garden or – where?

She was again restless, she was possessed by restlessness. She cooked and sewed and worked as before, day after day, while Mrs Parkes remonstrated: 'Mrs Rawlings, what's the need for it? I can do that, it's what you pay me for.'

And it was so irrational that she checked herself. She would put the car into the garage, go up to her bedroom, and sit, hands in her lap, forcing herself to be quiet. She listened to Mrs Parkes moving around the house. She looked out into the garden and saw the branches shake the trees. She sat defeating the enemy, restlessness. Emptiness. She ought to be thinking about her life, about herself. But she did not. Or perhaps she could not. As soon as she forced her mind to think about Susan (for what else did she want to be alone for?) it skipped off to thoughts of butter or school clothes. Or it thought of Mrs Parkes. She realized that she sat listening for the movements of the cleaning woman, following her every turn, bend, thought. She followed her in her mind from kitchen to bathroom, from table to oven, and it was as if the duster, the cleaning cloth, the saucepan, were in her own hand. She would hear herself saying: No, not like that, don't put that there . . . Yet she did not give a damn what Mrs Parkes did, or if she did it at all. Yet she could not prevent herself from being conscious of her, every minute. Yes, this was what was wrong with her: she needed, when she was alone, to be really alone, with no one near. She could not endure the knowledge that in ten minutes or in half an hour Mrs Parkes would call up the stairs: 'Mrs Rawlings, there's no silver polish. Madam, we're out of flour.'

So she left the house and went to sit in the garden where she was screened from the house by trees. She waited for the demon to appear and claim her, but he did not.

She was keeping him off, because she had not, after all, come to an end of arranging herself.

She was planning how to be somewhere where Mrs Parkes would not come after her with a cup of tea, or a demand to be allowed to telephone (always irritating since Susan did not care who she telephoned or how often), or just a nice talk about something. Yes, she needed a place, or a state of affairs, where it would not be necessary to keep reminding herself: In ten minutes I must telephone Matthew about . . . and at half past three I must leave early for the children because the car needs cleaning. And at ten o'clock tomorrow I must remember . . . She was possessed with resentment that the seven hours of freedom in every day (during weekdays in the school term) were not free, that never, not for one second, ever, was she free from the pressure of time, from having to remember this or that. She could never forget herself; never really let herself go into forgetfulness.

Resentment. It was poisoning her. (She looked at this emotion and thought it was absurd. Yet she felt it.) She was a prisoner. (She looked at this thought too, and it was no good telling herself it was a ridiculous one.) She must tell Matthew – but what? She was filled with emotions that were utterly ridiculous, that she despised, yet that nevertheless she was feeling so strongly she could not shake them off.

The school holidays came round, and this time they were for nearly two months, and she behaved with a conscious controlled decency that nearly drove her crazy. She would lock herself in the bathroom, and sit on the edge of the bath, breathing deep, trying to let go into some kind of calm. Or she went up into the spare room, usually empty, where no one would expect her to be. She heard the children calling 'Mother, Mother,' and kept silent, feeling guilty. Or she went to the very end of the garden, by herself, and looked at the slow-moving brown river; she looked at the river and closed her eyes and breathed slow and deep, taking it into her being, into her veins.

Then she returned to the family, wife and mother, smiling and responsible, feeling as if the pressure of these people – four lively children and her husband – were a painful pressure on the surface of her skin, a hand pressing on her brain. She did not once break down into irritation during these holidays, but it was like living out a prison sentence, and when the children went back to school, she sat on a white stone seat near the flowing river, and she thought: It is not even a year since the twins went to school, since *they were off my hands* (What on earth did I think I meant when I used that stupid phrase?) and yet I'm a different person. I'm simply not myself. I don't understand it.

Yet she had to understand it. For she knew that this structure – big white house, on which the mortgage still cost four hundred a year, a husband, so good and kind and insightful, four children, all doing so nicely, and the garden where she sat, and Mrs Parkes the cleaning woman – all this depended on her, and yet she could not understand why, or even what it was she contributed to it.

She said to Matthew in their bedroom: 'I think there must be something wrong with me.'

And he said: 'Surely not, Susan? You look marvellous – you're as lovely as ever.'

She looked at the handsome blond man, with his clear, intelligent, blue-eyed face, and thought: Why is it I can't tell him? Why not? And she said: 'I need to be alone more than I am.'

At which he swung his slow blue gaze at her, and she saw what she had been dreading: Incredulity. Disbelief. And fear. An incredulous blue stare from a stranger who was her husband, as close to her as her own breath.

He said: 'But the children are at school and off your hands.'

She said to herself: I've got to force myself to say: Yes, but do you realize that I never feel free? There's never a moment I can say to myself: There's nothing I have to remind myself about, nothing I have to do in half an hour, or an hour, or two hours . . .

But she said: 'I don't feel well.'

He said: 'Perhaps you need a holiday.'

She said, appalled: 'But not without you, surely?' For she could not imagine herself going off without him. Yet that was what he meant. Seeing her face, he laughed, and opened his arms, and she went into them, thinking: Yes, yes, but why can't I say it? And what is it I have to say?

She tried to tell him, about never being free. And he listened and said: 'But Susan, what sort of freedom can you possibly want – short of being dead! Am I ever free? I go to the office, and I have to be there at ten – all right, half past ten, sometimes. And I have to do this or that, don't I? Then I've got to come home at a certain time – I don't mean it, you know I don't – but if I'm not going to be back home at six I telephone you. When can I ever say to myself: I have nothing to be responsible for in the next six hours?'

Susan, hearing this, was remorseful. Because it was true. The good marriage, the house, the children, depended just as much on his voluntary bondage as it did on hers. But why did he not feel bound? Why didn't he chafe and become restless? No, there was something really wrong with her and this proved it.

And that word *bondage* – why had she used it? She had never felt marriage, or the children, as bondage. Neither had he, or surely they wouldn't be together lying in each other's arms content after twelve years of marriage.

No, her state (whatever it was) was irrelevant, nothing to do with her real good life with her family. She had to accept the fact that after all, she was an irrational person and to live with it. Some people had to live with crippled arms, or stammers, or being deaf. She would have to live knowing she was subject to a state of mind she could not own.

Nevertheless, as a result of this conversation with her husband, there was a new regime next holidays.

The spare room at the top of the house now had a cardboard sign saying: PRIVATE! DO NOT DISTURB! on it. (This sign had been drawn in coloured chalks by the children, after a discussion between the parents in which it was decided that was psychologically the right thing.) The family and Mrs Parkes knew this was 'Mother's Room' and that she was entitled to her privacy. Many serious conversations took place between Matthew and the children about not taking Mother for granted. Susan overheard the first, between father and Harry, the older boy, and was surprised at her irritation over it. Surely she could have a room somewhere in that big house and retire into it without such a fuss being made? Without it being so solemnly discussed? Why couldn't she simply have announced: 'I'm going to fit out the little top room for myself, and when I'm in it I'm not to be disturbed for anything short of fire'? Just that, and finished; instead of long earnest discussions. When she heard Harry and Matthew explaining it to the twins with Mrs Parkes coming in – 'Yes, well, a family sometimes gets on top of a woman' – she had to go right away to the bottom of the garden until the devils of exasperation had finished their dance in her blood.

But now there was a room, and she could go there when she liked, she used it seldom: she felt even more caged there than in her bedroom. One day she had gone up there after a lunch for ten children she had cooked and served because Mrs Parkes was not there, and had sat alone for a while looking into the garden. She saw the children stream out from the kitchen and stand looking up at the window where she sat behind the curtains. They were all – her children and their friends – discussing Mother's Room. A few minutes later, the chase of children in some game came pounding up the stairs, but ended as abruptly as if they had fallen over a ravine, so sudden was the silence. They had remembered she was there, and had gone silent in a great gale of 'Hush!

Shhhhhh! Quiet, you'll disturb her . . .' And they went tiptoeing downstairs like criminal conspirators. When she came down to make tea for them, they all apologized. The twins put their arms around her, from front and back, making a human cage of loving limbs, and promised it would never occur again. 'We forgot, Mummy, we forgot all about it!'

What it amounted to was that Mother's Room, and her need for privacy, had become a valuable lesson in respect for other people's rights. Quite soon Susan was going up to the room only because it was a lesson it was a pity to drop. Then she took sewing up there, and the children and Mrs Parkes came in and out: it had become another family room.

She sighed, and smiled, and resigned herself – she made jokes at her own expense with Matthew over the room. That is, she did from the self she liked, she respected. But at the same time, something inside her howled with impatience, with rage . . . And she was frightened. One day she found herself kneeling by her bed and praying: 'Dear God, keep it away from me, keep him away from me.' She meant the devil, for she now thought of it, not caring if she were irrational, as some sort of demon. She imagined him, or it, as a youngish man, or perhaps a middle-aged man pretending to be young. Or a man young-looking from immaturity? At any rate, she saw the young-looking face which, when she drew closer, had dry lines about mouth and eyes. He was thinnish, meagre in build. And he had a reddish complexion, and ginger hair. That was he – a gingery, energetic man, and he wore a reddish hairy jacket, unpleasant to the touch.

Well, one day she saw him. She was standing at the bottom of the garden, watching the river ebb past, when she raised her eyes and saw this person, or being, sitting on the white stone bench. He was looking at her, and grinning. In his hand was a long crooked stick, which he had picked off the ground, or broken off the tree above him. He was absent-mindedly, out of an absent-minded or freakish impulse of spite, using the stick to stir around in the coils of a blindworm or a grass snake (or some kind of snake-like creature: it was whitish and unhealthy to look at, unpleasant). The snake was twisting about, flinging its coils from side to side in a kind of dance of protest against the teasing prodding stick.

Susan looked at him thinking: Who is the stranger? What is he doing in our garden? Then she recognized the man around whom her terrors had crystallized. As she did so, he vanished. She made herself walk over to the bench. A shadow from a branch lay across thin emerald grass, moving jerkily over its roughness, and she could see why she had taken it for a snake, lashing and twisting. She went back to the house thinking: Right, then, so I've seen him with my own eyes, so I'm not crazy after all – there *is* a danger because I've seen him. He is lurking in the garden and sometimes even in the house, and he wants *to get into me and to take me over*.

She dreamed of having a room or a place, anywhere, where she could go and sit, by herself, no one knowing where she was.

Once, near Victoria, she found herself outside a news agent that had Rooms to Let advertised. She decided to rent a room, telling no one. Sometimes she could take the train in from Richmond and sit alone in it for an hour or two. Yet how could she? A room would cost three or four pounds a week, and she earned no money, and how could she explain to Matthew that she needed such a sum? What for? It did not occur to her that she was taking it for granted she wasn't going to tell him about the room.

Well, it was out of the question, having a room; yet she knew she must.

One day, when a school term was well established, and none of the children had measles or other ailments, and everything seemed in order, she did the shopping early, explained to Mrs Parkes she was meeting an old school friend, took the train to Victoria, searched until she found a small quiet hotel, and asked for a room for the day. They did not let rooms by the day, the manageress said, looking doubtful, since Susan so obviously was not the kind of woman who needed a room for unrespectable reasons. Susan made a long explanation about not being well, being unable to shop without frequent rests for lying down. At last she was allowed to rent the room provided she paid a full night's price for it. She was taken up by the manageress and a maid, both concerned over the state of her health . . . which must be pretty bad if, living at Richmond (she had signed her name and address in the register), she needed a shelter at Victoria.

The room was ordinary and anonymous, and was just what Susan needed. She put a shilling in the gas fire, and sat, eyes shut, in a dingy armchair with her back to a dingy window. She was alone. She was alone. She was alone. She could feel pressures lifting off her. First the sounds of traffic came very loud; then they seemed to vanish; she might even have slept a little. A knock on the door: it was Miss Townsend the manageress, bringing her a cup of tea with her own hands, so concerned was she over Susan's long silence and possible illness.

Miss Townsend was a lonely woman of fifty, running this hotel with all the rectitude expected of her, and she sensed in Susan the possibility of understanding companionship. She stayed to talk. Susan found herself in the middle of a fantastic story about her illness, which got more and more improbable as she tried to make it tally with the large house at Richmond, well-off husband, and four children. Suppose she said instead: Miss Townsend, I'm here in your hotel because I need to be alone for a few hours, above all *alone and with no one knowing where I am*. She said it mentally, and saw, mentally, the look that would inevitably come on Miss Townsend's elderly maiden's face. 'Miss Townsend, my four children and my husband are driving me insane, do you understand that? Yes, I can see from the gleam of hysteria in your eyes that comes from loneliness controlled but only just contained that I've got everything in the world you've ever longed for. Well, Miss Townsend, I don't want any of it. You can have it, Miss Townsend. I wish I was absolutely alone in the world, like you. Miss Townsend, I'm besieged by seven devils, Miss Townsend, Miss Townsend, let me stay here in your hotel where the devils can't get me . . .' Instead of saying all this, she described her anaemia, agreed to try Miss Townsend's remedy for it which was raw liver, minced, between whole-meal bread, and said yes, perhaps it would be better if she stayed at home and let a friend do shopping for her. She paid her bill and left the hotel, defeated.

At home Mrs Parkes said she didn't really like it, no, not really, when Mrs Rawlings was away from nine in the morning until five. The teacher had telephoned from school to say Joan's teeth were paining her, and she hadn't known what to say; and what was she to make for the children's tea, Mrs Rawlings hadn't said.

All this was nonsense, of course. Mrs Parkes's complaint was that Susan had withdrawn herself spiritually, leaving the burden of the big house on her.

Susan looked back at her day of 'freedom' which had resulted in her becoming a friend to the lonely Miss Townsend, and in Mrs Parkes's remonstrances. Yet she remembered the short blissful hour of being alone, really alone. She was determined to arrange her life, no matter what it cost, so that she could have that solitude more often. An absolute solitude, where no one knew her or cared about her.

But how? She thought of saying to her old employer: I want to back you up in a story with Matthew that I am doing part-time work for you. The truth is that . . . but she would have to tell him a lie too, and which lie? She could not say: I want to sit by myself three or four times a week in a rented room. And besides, he knew Matthew, and she could not really ask him to tell lies on her behalf, apart from his being bound to think it meant a lover.

Suppose she really took a part-time job, which she could get through fast and efficiently, leaving time for herself. What job? Addressing envelopes? Canvassing?

And there was Mrs Parkes, working widow, who knew exactly what she was prepared to give to the house, who knew by instinct when her mistress withdrew in spirit from her responsibilities. Mrs Parkes was one of the servers of this world, but she needed someone to serve. She had to have Mrs Rawlings, her madam, at the top of the house or in the garden, so that she could come and get support from her: 'Yes, the bread's not what it was when I was a girl . . . Yes, Harry's got a wonderful appetite, I wonder where he puts it all . . . Yes, it's lucky the twins are so much of a size, they can wear each other's shoes, that's a saving in these hard times . . . Yes, the cherry jam from Switzerland is not a patch on the jam from Poland, and three times the price . . .' And so on. That sort of talk Mrs Parkes must have, every day, or she would leave, not knowing herself why she left.

Susan Rawlings, thinking these thoughts, found that she was prowling through the great thicketed garden like a wild cat: she was walking up the stairs, down the stairs, through the rooms, into the garden, along the brown running river, back, up through the house, down again . . . It was a wonder Mrs Parkes did not think it strange. But on the contrary, Mrs Rawlings could do what she liked, she could stand on her head if she wanted, provided she was *there*. Susan Rawlings prowled and muttered through her house, hating Mrs Parkes, hating poor Miss Townsend, dreaming of her hour of solitude in the dingy respectability of Miss Townsend's hotel bedroom, and she knew quite well she was mad. Yes, she was mad.

She said to Matthew that she must have a holiday. Matthew agreed with her. This was not as things had been once – how they had talked in each other's arms in the marriage bed. He had, she knew, diagnosed her finally as *unreasonable*. She had become someone outside himself that he had to manage. They were living side by side in this house like two tolerably friendly strangers.

Having told Mrs Parkes, or rather, asked for her permission, she went off on a walking holiday in Wales. She chose the remotest place she knew of. Every morning the children telephoned her before they went off to school, to encourage and support her, just as they had over Mother's Room. Every evening she telephoned them, spoke to each child in turn, and then to Matthew. Mrs Parkes, given permission to telephone for instructions or advice, did so every day at lunchtime. When, as happened three times, Mrs Rawlings was out on the mountainside, Mrs Parkes asked that she should ring back at such and such a time, for she would not be happy in what she was doing without Mrs Rawlings's blessing.

Susan prowled over wild country with the telephone wire holding her to her duty like a leash. The next time she must telephone, or wait to be telephoned, nailed her to her cross. The mountains themselves seemed trammelled by her unfreedom. Everywhere on the mountains, where she met no one at all, from breakfast time to dusk, excepting sheep, or a shepherd, she came face to face with her own craziness which might attack her in the broadest valleys, so that they seemed too small; or on a mountain-top from which she could see a hundred other mountains and valleys, so that they seemed too low, too small, with the sky pressing down too close. She would stand gazing at a hillside brilliant with ferns and bracken, jewelled with running water, and see nothing but her devil, who lifted inhuman eyes at her from where he leaned negligently on a rock, switching at his ugly yellow boots with a leafy twig.

She returned to her home and family, with the Welsh emptiness at the back of her mind like a promise of freedom.

She told her husband she wanted to have an *au pair* girl.

They were in their bedroom, it was late at night, the children slept. He sat, shirted and slippered, in a chair by the window, looking out. She sat brushing her hair and watching him in the mirror. A time-hallowed scene in the connubial bedroom. He said nothing, while she heard the arguments coming into his mind, only to be rejected because every one was *reasonable*.

'It seems strange to get one now, after all, the children are in school most of the day. Surely the time for you to have help was when you were stuck with them day and night. Why don't you ask Mrs Parkes to cook for you? She's even offered to – I can understand if you are tired of cooking for six people. But you know that an *au pair* girl means all kinds of problems, it's not like having an ordinary char in during the day . . .'

Finally he said carefully: 'Are you thinking of going back to work?'

'No,' she said, 'no, not really.' She made herself sound vague, rather stupid. She went on brushing her black hair and peering at herself so as to be oblivious of the short uneasy glances her Matthew kept giving her. 'Do you think we can't afford it?' she went on vaguely, not at all the old efficient Susan who knew exactly what they could afford.

'It's not that,' he said, looking out of the window at dark trees, so as not to look at her. Meanwhile she examined a round, candid, pleasant face with clear dark brows and clear grey eyes. A sensible face. She brushed thick healthy black hair and thought: Yet that's the reflection of a madwoman. How very strange! Much more to the point if what looked back at me was the gingery green-eyed demon with his dry meagre smile . . . Why wasn't Matthew agreeing? After all, what else could he do? She was breaking her part of the bargain and there was no way of forcing her to keep it: that her spirit, her soul, should live in this house, so that the people in it could grow like plants in water, and Mrs Parkes remain content in their service. In return for this, he would be a good loving husband, and responsible towards the children. Well, nothing like this had been true of either of them for a long time. He did his duty, perfunctorily; she did not even pretend to do hers. And he had become like other husbands, with his real life in his work and the people he met there, and very likely a serious affair. All this was her fault.

At last he drew heavy curtains, blotting out the trees, and turned to force her attention: 'Susan, are you really sure we need a girl?' But she would not meet his appeal at all: She was running the brush over her hair again and again, lifting fine black clouds in a small hiss of electricity. She was peering in and smiling as if she were amused at the clinging hissing hair that followed the brush.

'Yes, I think it would be a good idea on the whole,' she said, with the cunning of a madwoman evading the real point.

In the mirror she could see her Matthew lying on his back, his hands behind his head, staring upwards, his face sad and hard. She felt her heart (the old heart of Susan Rawlings) soften and call out to him. But she set it to be indifferent.

He said: 'Susan, the children?' It was an appeal that *almost* reached her. He opened his arms, lifting them from where they had lain by his sides, palms up, empty. She had only to run across and fling herself into them, on to his hard, warm chest, and melt into herself, into

Susan. But she could not. She would not see his lifted arms. She said vaguely: 'Well, surely it'll be even better for them? We'll get a French or a German girl and they'll learn the language.'

In the dark she lay beside him, feeling frozen, a stranger. She felt as if Susan had been spirited away. She disliked very much this woman who lay here, cold and indifferent beside a suffering man, but she could not change her.

Next morning she set about getting a girl, and very soon came Sophie Traub from Hamburg, a girl of twenty, laughing, healthy, blue-eyed, intending to learn English. Indeed, she already spoke a good deal. In return for a room – 'Mother's Room' – and her food, she undertook to do some light cooking, and to be with the children when Mrs Rawlings asked. She was an intelligent girl and understood perfectly what was needed. Susan said: 'I go off sometimes, for the morning or for the day – well, sometimes the children run home from school, or they ring up, or a teacher rings up. I should be here, really. And there's the daily woman . . .' And Sophie laughed her deep fruity *Fräulein*'s laugh, showed her fine white teeth and her dimples, and said: 'You want some person to play mistress of the house sometimes, not so?'

'Yes, that is just so,' said Susan, a bit dry, despite herself, thinking in secret fear how easy it was, how much nearer to the end she was than she thought. Healthy Fräulein Traub's instant understanding of their position proved this to be true.

The *au pair* girl, because of her own common sense, or (as Susan said to herself with her new inward shudder) because she had been *chosen* so well by Susan, was a success with everyone, the children liking her, Mrs Parkes forgetting almost at once that she was German, and Matthew finding her 'nice to have around the house'. For he was now taking things as they came, from the surface of life, withdrawn both as a husband and a father from the household.

One day Susan saw how Sophie and Mrs Parkes were talking and laughing in the kitchen, and she announced that she would be away until teatime. She knew exactly where to go and what she must look for. She took the District Line to South Kensington, changed to the Circle, got off at Paddington, and walked around looking at the smaller hotels until she was satisfied with one which had FRED'S HOTEL painted on windowpanes that needed cleaning. The façade was a faded shiny yellow, like unhealthy skin. A door at the end of a passage said she must knock; she did, and Fred appeared. He was not at all attractive, not in any way, being fattish, and run-down, and wearing a tasteless striped suit. He had small sharp eyes in a white creased face, and was quite prepared to let Mrs Jones (she chose the farcical name deliberately, staring him out) have a room three days a week from ten until six. Provided of course that she paid in advance each time she came? Susan produced fifteen shillings (no price had been set by him) and held it out, still fixing him with a bold unblinking challenge she had not known until then she could use at will. Looking at her still, he took up a ten-shilling note from her palm between thumb and forefinger, fingered it; then shuffled up two half crowns, held out his own palm with these bits of money displayed thereon, and let his gaze lower broodingly at them. They were standing in the passage, a red-shaded light above, bare boards beneath, and a strong smell of floor polish rising about them. He shot his gaze up at her over the still-extended palm, and smiled as if to say: What do you take me for? 'I shan't,' said Susan, 'be using this room for the purposes of making money.' He still waited. She added another five shillings, at which he nodded and said: 'You pay, and I ask no questions.' 'Good,' said Susan. He now went past her to the stairs, and there waited a moment: the light from the street door being in her eyes, she lost sight of him momentarily. Then she saw a sober-suited, white-faced, white-balding little man trotting up the stairs like a waiter, and she went after him. They proceeded in utter silence up the stairs of this house where no questions were asked – Fred's Hotel, which could afford the freedom for its visitors that poor Miss Townsend's hotel could not. The room was hideous. It had a single window, with thin green brocade curtains, a three-quarter bed that had a cheap green satin bedspread on it, a fireplace with a gas fire and a shilling meter by it, a chest of drawers, and a green wicker armchair.

'Thank you,' said Susan, knowing that Fred (if this was Fred, and not George, or Herbert or Charlie) was looking at her, not so much with curiosity, an emotion he would not own to, for professional reasons, but with a philosophical sense of what was appropriate. Having taken her money and shown her up and agreed to everything, he was clearly disapproving of her for coming here. She did not belong here at all, so his look said. (But she knew, already, how very much she did belong: the room had been waiting for her to join it.) 'Would you have me called at five o'clock, please?' and he nodded and went downstairs.

It was twelve in the morning. She was free. She sat in the armchair, she simply sat, she closed her eyes and sat and let herself be alone. She was alone and no one knew where she was. When a knock came on the door she was annoyed, and prepared to show it: but it was Fred himself, it was five o'clock and he was calling her as ordered. He flicked his sharp little eyes over the room – bed, first. It was undisturbed. She might never have been in the room at all. She thanked him, said she would be returning the day after tomorrow, and left. She was back home in time to cook supper, to put the children to bed, to cook a second supper for her husband and herself later. And to welcome Sophie back from the pictures where she had gone with a friend. All these things she did cheerfully, willingly. But she was thinking all the time of the hotel room, she was longing for it with her whole being.

Three times a week. She arrived promptly at ten, looked Fred in the eyes, gave him twenty shillings, followed him up the stairs, went into the room, and shut the door on him with gentle firmness. For Fred, disapproving of her being here at all, was quite ready to let friendship, or at least acquaintanceship, follow his disapproval, if only she would let him. But he was content to go off on her dismissing nod, with the twenty shillings in his hand.

She sat in the armchair and shut her eyes.

What did she *do* in the room? Why, nothing at all. From the chair, when it had rested her, she went to the window, stretching her arms, smiling, treasuring her anonymity, to look out. She was no longer Susan Rawlings, mother of four, wife of Matthew, employer of Mrs Parkes and of Sophie Traub, with these and those relations with friends, schoolteachers, tradesmen. She no longer was mistress of the big white house and garden, owning clothes suitable for this and that activity or occasion. She was Mrs Jones, and she was alone, and she had no past and no future. Here I am, she thought, after all these years of being married and having children and playing those roles of responsibility – and I'm just the same. Yet there have been times I thought that nothing existed of me except the roles that went with being Mrs Matthew Rawlings. Yes, here I am, and if I never saw any of my family again, here I would still be . . . how very strange that is! And she leaned on the sill, and looked into the street, loving the men and women who passed, because she did not know them. She looked at the downtrodden buildings over the street, and at the sky, wet and dingy, or sometimes blue, and she felt she had never seen buildings or sky before. And then she went back to the chair, empty, her mind a blank. Sometimes she talked aloud, saying nothing – an exclamation, meaningless, followed by a comment about the floral pattern on the thin rug, or a stain on the green satin coverlet. For the most part, she wool-gathered – what word is there for it? – brooded, wandered, simply went dark, feeling emptiness run deliciously through her veins like the movement of her blood.

This room had become more her own than the house she lived in. One morning she found Fred taking her a flight higher than usual. She stopped, refusing to go up, and demanded her usual room, Number 19. 'Well, you'll have to wait half an hour then,' he said. Willingly she descended to the dark disinfectant-smelling hall, and sat waiting until the two, man and woman, came down the stairs, giving her swift indifferent glances before they hurried out into the street, separating at the door. She went up to the room, *her* room, which they had just vacated. It was no less hers, though the windows were set wide open, and a maid was straightening the bed as she came in.

After these days of solitude, it was both easy to play her part as mother and wife, and difficult – because it was so easy: she felt an impostor. She felt as if her shell moved here, with her family, answering to Mummy, Mother, Susan, Mrs Rawlings. She was surprised no one saw through her, that she wasn't turned out of doors, as a fake. On the contrary, it seemed the children loved her more; Matthew and she 'got on' pleasantly, and Mrs Parkes was happy in her work under (for the most part, it must be confessed) Sophie Traub. At night she lay beside her husband, and they made love again, apparently just as they used to, when they were really married. But she, Susan, or the being who answered so readily and improbably to the name of Susan, was not there; she was in Fred's Hotel, in Paddington, waiting for the easing hours of solitude to begin.

Soon she made a new arrangement with Fred and with Sophie. It was for five days a week. As for the money, five pounds, she simply asked Matthew for it. She saw that she was not even frightened he might ask what for: he would give it to her, she knew that, and yet it was terrifying it could be so, for this close couple, these partners, had once known the destination of every shilling they must spend. He agreed to give her five pounds a week. She asked for just so much, not a penny more. He sounded indifferent about it. It was as if he were paying her, she thought: *paying her off* – yes, that was it. Terror came back for a moment, when she understood this, but she stilled it: things had gone too far for that. Now, every week, on Sunday nights, he gave her five pounds, turning away from her before their eyes could meet on the transaction. As for Sophie Traub, she was to be somewhere in or near the house until six at night, after which she was free. She was not to cook, or to clean, she was simply to be there. So she gardened or sewed, and asked friends in, being a person who was bound to have a lot of friends. If the children were sick, she nursed them. If teachers telephoned, she answered them sensibly. For the five daytimes in the school week, she was altogether the mistress of the house.

One night in the bedroom, Matthew asked: 'Susan, I don't want to interfere – don't think that, please – but are you sure you are well?'

She was brushing her hair at the mirror. She made two more strokes on either side of her head, before she replied: 'Yes, dear, I am sure I am well.'

He was again lying on his back, his big blond head on his hands, his elbows angled up and part-concealing his face. He said: 'Then Susan, I have to ask you this question, though you must understand, I'm not putting any sort of pressure on you.' (Susan heard the word pressure with dismay, because this was inevitable, of course she could not go on like this.) 'Are things going to go on like this?'

'Well,' she said, going vague and bright and idiotic again, so as to escape: 'Well, I don't see why not.'

He was jerking his elbows up and down, in annoyance or in pain, and, looking at him, she saw he had got thin, even gaunt; and restless angry movements were not what she remembered of him. He said: 'Do you want a divorce, is that it?'

At this, Susan only with the greatest difficulty stopped herself from laughing: she could hear the bright bubbling laughter she *would* have emitted, had she let herself. He could only mean one thing: she had a lover, and that was why she spent her days in London, as lost to him as if she had vanished to another continent.

Then the small panic set in again: she understood that he hoped she did have a lover, he was begging her to say so, because otherwise it would be too terrifying.

She thought this out, as she brushed her hair, watching the fine black stuff fly up to make its little clouds of electricity, hiss, hiss, hiss. Behind her head, across the room, was a blue wall. She realized she was absorbed in watching the black hair making shapes against the blue. She should be answering him. 'Do *you* want a divorce, Matthew?'

He said: 'That surely isn't the point, is it?'

'You brought it up, I didn't,' she said, brightly, suppressing meaningless tinkling laughter.

Next day she asked Fred: 'Have enquiries been made for me?'

He hesitated, and she said: 'I've been coming here a year now. I've made no trouble, and you've been paid every day. I have a right to be told.'

'As a matter of fact, Mrs Jones, a man did come asking.'

'A man from a detective agency?'

'Well, he could have been, couldn't he?'

'I was asking you . . . well, what did you tell him?'

'I told him a Mrs Jones came every weekday from ten until five or six and stayed in Number 19 by herself.'

'Describing me?'

'Well, Mrs Jones, I had no alternative. Put yourself in my place.'

'By rights I should deduct what that man gave you for the information.'

He raised shocked eyes: she was not the sort of person to make jokes like this! Then he chose to laugh: a pinkish wet slit appeared across his white crinkled face: his eyes positively begged her to laugh, otherwise he might lose some money. She remained grave, looking at him.

He stopped laughing and said: 'You want to go up now?' – returning to the familiarity, the comradeship, of the country where no questions are asked, on which (and he knew it) she depended completely.

She went up to sit in her wicker chair. But it was not the same. Her husband had searched her out. (The world had searched her out.) The pressures were on her. She was here with his connivance. He might walk in at any moment, here, into Room 19. She imagined the report from the detective agency: 'A woman calling herself Mrs Jones, fitting the description of your wife (etc., etc., etc.) stays alone all day in Room No. 19. She insists on this room, waits for it if it is engaged. As far as the proprietor knows, she receives no visitors there, male or female.' A report something on these lines, Matthew must have received.

Well of course he was right: things couldn't go on like this. He had put an end to it all simply by sending the detective after her.

She tried to shrink herself back into the shelter of the room, a snail pecked out of its shell and trying to squirm back. But the peace of the room had gone. She was trying consciously to revive it, trying to let go into the dark creative trance (or whatever it was) that she had found there. It was no use, yet she craved for it, she was as ill as a suddenly deprived addict.

Several times she returned to the room, to look for herself there, but instead she found the unnamed spirit of restlessness, a prickling fevered hunger for movement, an irritable self-consciousness that made her brain feel as if it had coloured lights going on and off inside it. Instead of the soft dark that had been the room's air, were now waiting for her demons that made her dash blindly about, muttering words of hate; she was impelling herself from point to point like a moth dashing itself against a windowpane, sliding to the bottom, fluttering off on broken wings, then crashing into the invisible barrier again. And again and again. Soon she was exhausted, and she told Fred that for a while she would not be needing the room, she was going on holiday. Home she went, to the big white house by the river. The middle of a weekday, and she felt guilty at returning to her own home when not expected. She stood unseen, looking in at the kitchen window. Mrs Parkes, wearing a discarded floral overall of Susan's, was stooping to slide something into the oven. Sophie, arms folded, was leaning her back against a cupboard and laughing at some joke made by a girl not seen before by Susan – a dark foreign girl, Sophie's visitor. In an armchair Molly, one of the twins, lay curled, sucking her thumb and watching the grownups. She must have some sickness, to be kept from school. The child's listless face, the dark circles under her eyes, hurt Susan: Molly was looking at the three grownups working and talking in exactly the same way Susan looked at the four through the kitchen window: she was remote, shut off from them.

But then, just as Susan imagined herself going in, picking up the little girl, and sitting in an armchair with her, stroking her probably heated forehead, Sophie did just that: she had been standing on one leg, the other knee flexed, its foot set against the wall. Now she let her foot in its ribbon-tied red shoe slide down the wall, stood solid on two feet, clapping her hands before and behind her, and sang a couple of lines in German, so that the child lifted her heavy eyes at her and began to smile. Then she walked, or rather skipped, over to the child, swung her up, and let her fall into her lap at the same moment she sat herself. She said: 'Hopla! Hopla! Molly . . .' and began stroking the dark untidy young head that Molly laid on her shoulder for comfort.

Well . . . Susan blinked the tears of farewell out of her eyes, and went quietly up the house to her bedroom. There she sat looking at the river through the trees. She felt at peace, but in a way that was new to her. She had no desire to move, to talk, to do anything at all. The devils that had haunted the house, the garden, were not there; but she knew it was because her soul was in Room 19 in Fred's Hotel; she was not really here at all. It was a sensation that should have been frightening: to sit at her own bedroom window, listening to Sophie's rich young voice sing German nursery songs to her child, listening to Mrs Parkes clatter and move below, and to know that all this had nothing to do with her: she was already out of it.

Later, she made herself go down and say she was home: it was unfair to be here unannounced. She took lunch with Mrs Parkes, Sophie, Sophie's Italian friend Maria, and her daughter Molly, and felt like a visitor.

A few days later, at bedtime, Matthew said: 'Here's your five pounds,' and pushed them over to her. Yet he must have known she had not been leaving the house at all.

She shook her head, gave it back to him, and said, in explanation, not in accusation: 'As soon as you knew where I was, there was no point.'

He nodded, not looking at her. He was turned away from her: thinking, she knew, how best to handle this wife who terrified him.

He said: 'I wasn't trying to . . . it's just that I was worried.'

'Yes I know.'

'I must confess that I was beginning to wonder . . .'

'You thought I had a lover?'

'Yes, I am afraid I did.'

She knew that he wished she had. She sat wondering how to say: 'For a year now I've been spending all my days in a very sordid hotel room. It's the place where I'm happy. In fact, without it I don't exist.' She heard herself saying this, and understood how terrified he was that she might. So instead she said: 'Well, perhaps you're not far wrong.'

Probably Matthew would think the hotel proprietor lied: he would want to think so.

'Well,' he said, and she could hear his voice spring up, so to speak, with relief: 'in that case I must confess I've got a bit of an affair on myself.'

She said, detached and interested: 'Really? Who is she?' and saw Matthew's startled look because of this reaction.

'It's Phil. Phil Hunt.'

She had known Phil Hunt well in the old unmarried days. She was thinking: No, she won't do, she's too neurotic and difficult. She's never been happy yet. Sophie's much better: Well Matthew will see that himself, as sensible as he is.

This line of thought went on in silence, while she said aloud:

'It's no point telling you about mine, because you don't know him.'

Quick, quick, invent, she thought. Remember how you invented all that nonsense for Miss Townsend.

She began slowly, careful not to contradict herself: 'His name is Michael' – (*Michael What?*) – 'Michael Plant.' (What a silly name!) 'He's rather like you – in looks, I mean.' And indeed, she could imagine herself being touched by no one but Matthew himself. 'He's a publisher.' (Really? Why?) 'He's got a wife already and two children.'

She brought out this fantasy, proud of herself.

Matthew said: 'Are you two thinking of marrying?'

She said, before she could stop herself: 'Good God, *no!*'

She realized, if Matthew wanted to marry Phil Hunt, that this was too emphatic, but apparently it was all right, for his voice sounded relieved as he said: 'It is a bit impossible to imagine oneself married to anyone else, isn't it?' With which he pulled her to him, so that her head lay on his shoulder. She turned her face into the dark of his flesh, and listened to the blood pounding through her ears saying: I am alone, I am alone, I am alone.

In the morning Susan lay in bed while he dressed.

He had been thinking things out in the night, because now he said: 'Susan, why don't we make a foursome?'

Of course, she said to herself, of course he would be bound to say that. If one is sensible, if one is reasonable, if one never allows oneself a base thought or an envious emotion, naturally one says: Let's make a foursome!

'Why not?' she said.

'We could all meet for lunch. I mean, it's ridiculous, you sneaking off to filthy hotels, and me staying late at the office, and all the lies everyone has to tell.'

What on earth did I say his name was? – she panicked, then said: 'I think it's a good idea, but Michael is away at the moment. When he comes back though – and I'm sure you two would like each other.'

'He's away, is he? So that's why you've been . . .' Her husband put his hand to the knot of his tie in a gesture of male coquetry she would not before have associated with him; and he bent to kiss her cheek with the expression that goes with the words: Oh you naughty little puss! And she felt its answering look, naughty and coy, come on to her face.

Inside she was dissolving in horror at them both, at how far they had both sunk from honesty of emotion.

So now she was saddled with a lover, and he had a mistress! How ordinary, how reassuring, how jolly! And now they would make a foursome of it, and go about to theatres and restaurants. After all the Rawlingses could well afford that sort of thing, and presumably the publisher Michael Plant could afford to do himself and his mistress quite well. No, there was nothing to stop the four of them developing the most intricate relationship of civilized tolerance, all enveloped in a charming afterglow of autumnal passion. Perhaps they would all go off on holidays together? She had known people who did. Or perhaps Matthew would draw the line there? Why should he, though, if he was capable of talking about 'foursomes' at all?

She lay in the empty bedroom, listening to the car drive off with Matthew in it, off to work. Then she heard the children clattering off to school to the accompaniment of Sophie's cheerfully ringing voice. She slid down into the hollow of the bed, for shelter against her own irrelevance. And she stretched out her hand to the hollow where her husband's body had lain, but found no comfort there: he was not her husband. She curled herself up in a small tight ball under the clothes: she could stay here all day, all week, indeed, all her life.

But in a few days she must produce Michael Plant, and – but how? She must presumably find some agreeable man prepared to impersonate a publisher called Michael Plant. And in return for which she would – what? Well, for one thing they would make love. The idea made her want to cry with sheer exhaustion. Oh no, she had finished with all that – the proof of it was that the words 'make love', or even imagining it, trying hard to revive no more than the pleasures of sensuality, let alone affection, or love, made her want to run away and hide from the sheer effort of the thing . . . Good Lord, why make love at all? Why make love with anyone? Or if you are going to make love, what does it matter who with? Why shouldn't she simply walk into the street, pick up a man and have a roaring sexual affair with him? Why not? Or even with Fred? What difference did it make?

But she had let herself in for it – an interminable stretch of time with a lover, called Michael, as part of a gallant civilized foursome. Well, she could not, and would not.

She got up, dressed, went down to find Mrs Parkes, and asked her for the loan of a pound, since Matthew, she said, had forgotten to leave her money. She exchanged with Mrs Parkes variations on the theme that husbands are all the same, they don't think, and without saying a word to Sophie, whose voice could be heard upstairs from the telephone, walked to the underground, travelled to South Kensington, changed to the Inner Circle, got out at Paddington, and walked to Fred's Hotel. There she told Fred that she wasn't going on holiday after all, she needed the room. She would have to wait an hour, Fred said. She went to a busy tearoom-cum-restaurant around the corner, and sat watching the people flow in and out the door that kept swinging open and shut, watched them mingle and merge and separate, felt her being flow into them, into their movement. When the hour was up she left a half crown for her pot of tea, and left the place without looking back at it, just as she had left her house, the big, beautiful white house, without another look, but silently dedicating it to Sophie. She returned to Fred, received the key of No. 19, now free, and ascended the grimy stairs slowly, letting floor after floor fall away below her, keeping her eyes lifted, so that floor after floor descended jerkily to her level of vision, and fell away out of sight.

No. 19 was the same. She saw everything with an acute, narrow, checking glance: the cheap shine of the satin spread, which had been replaced carelessly after the two bodies had finished their convulsions under it; a trace of powder on the glass that topped the chest of drawers; an intense green shade in a fold of the curtain. She stood at the window, looking down, watching people pass and pass and pass until her mind went dark from the constant movement. Then she sat in the wicker chair, letting herself go slack. But she had to be careful, because she did not want, today, to be surprised by Fred's knock at five o'clock.

The demons were not here. They had gone forever, because she was buying her freedom from them. She was slipping already into the dark fructifying dream that seemed to caress her inwardly, like the movement of her blood . . . but she had to think about Matthew first. Should she write a letter for the coroner? But what should she say? She would like to leave him with the look on his face she had seen this morning – banal, admittedly, but at least confidently healthy. Well, that was impossible, one did not look like that with a wife dead from suicide. But how to leave him believing she was dying because of a man – because of the fascinating publisher Michael Plant? Oh, how ridiculous! How absurd! How humiliating! But she decided not to trouble about it, simply not to think about the living. If he wanted to believe she had a lover, he would believe it. And he *did* want to believe it. Even when he had found out that there was no publisher in London called Michael Plant, he would think: Oh poor Susan, she was afraid to give me his real name.

And what did it matter whether he married Phil Hunt or Sophie? Though it ought to be Sophie who was already the mother of those children . . . and what hypocrisy to sit here worrying about the children, when she was going to leave them because she had not got the energy to stay.

She had about four hours. She spent them delightfully, darkly, sweetly, letting herself slide gently, gently, to the edge of the river. Then, with hardly a break in her consciousness, she got up, pushed the thin rug against the door, made sure the windows were tight shut, put two shillings in the meter, and turned on the gas. For the first time since she had been in the room she lay on the hard bed that smelled stale, that smelled of sweat and sex.

She lay on her back on the green satin cover, but her legs were chilly. She got up, found a blanket folded into the bottom of the chest of drawers, and carefully covered her legs with it. She was quite content lying there, listening to the faint soft hiss of the gas that poured into the room, into her lungs, into her brain, as she drifted off into the dark river.

Outside the Ministry

As Big Ben struck ten, a young man arrived outside the portals of the Ministry, and looked sternly up and down the street. He brought his wrist up to eye level and frowned at it, the very picture of a man kept waiting, a man who had expected no less. His arm dropped, elbow flexed stiff, hand at mid-thigh level, palm downwards, fingers splayed. There the hand made a light movement, balanced from the wrist, as if sketching an arpeggio, or saying goodbye to the pavement – or greeting it? An elegant little gesture, full of charm, given out of an abundant sense of style to the watching world. Now he changed his stance, and became a man kept waiting, but maintaining his dignity. He was well dressed in a dark suit which, with a white shirt and a small grey silk bow tie that seemed positively to wish to fly away altogether, because of the energy imparted to it by his person, made a conventional enough pattern of colour – dark grey, light grey, white. But his black glossy skin, setting off this soberness, made him sparkle, a dandy – he might just as well have been wearing a rainbow.

Before he could frown up and down the street again, another young African crossed the road to join him. They greeted each other, laying their palms together, then shaking hands; but there was a conscious restraint in this which the first seemed to relish, out of his innate sense of drama, but made the second uneasy.

'Good morning, Mr Chikwe.'

'Mr Mafente! Good morning!'

Mr Mafente was a large smooth young man, well dressed too, but his clothes on him were conventional European clothes, remained suit, striped shirt, tie; and his gestures had none of the inbuilt, delighting self-parody of the other man's. He was suave, he was dignified, he was calm; and this in spite of a situation which Mr Chikwe's attitude (magisterial, accusing) said clearly was fraught with the possibilities of evil.

Yet these two had known each other for many years; had worked side by side, as the political situation shifted, in various phases of the Nationalist movement; had served prison sentences together; had only recently become enemies. They now (Mr Chikwe dropped the accusation from his manner for this purpose) exchanged news from home, gossip, information. Then Mr Chikwe marked the end of the truce by a change of pose, and said, soft and threatening: 'And where is your great leader? Surely he is very late?'

'Five minutes only,' said the other smiling.

'Surely when at last we have achieved this great honour, an interview with Her Majesty's Minister, the least we can expect is punctuality from the great man?'

'I agree, but it is more than likely that Her Majesty's Minister will at the last moment be too occupied to see us, as has happened before.'

The faces of both men blazed with shared anger for a moment: Mr Chikwe even showed a snarl of white teeth.

They recovered themselves together and Mr Mafente said: 'And where is your leader? Surely what applies to mine applies to yours also?'

'Perhaps the reasons for their being late are different? Mine is finishing his breakfast just over the road there and yours is – I hear that the night before last your Mr Devuli was observed very drunk in the home of our hospitable Mrs James?'

'Possibly, I was not there.'

'I hear that the night before that he passed out in the hotel before some unsympathetic journalists and had to be excused.'

'It is possible, I was not there.'

Mr Chikwe kept the full force of his frowning stare on Mr Mafente's bland face as he said softly: 'Mr Mafente!'

'Mr Chikwe?'

'Is it not a shame and a disgrace that your movement, which, though it is not mine, nevertheless represents several thousand people (not millions, I am afraid, as your publicity men claim) – is it not a pity that this movement is led by a man who is never sober?'

Mr Mafente smiled, applauding this short speech which had been delivered with a grace and an attack wasted, surely, on a pavement full of London office workers and some fat pigeons. He then observed, merely: 'Yet it is Mr Devuli who is recognized by Her Britannic Majesty's Minister?'

Mr Chikwe frowned.

'And it is Mr Devuli who is recognized by those honourable British philanthrophic movements – the Anti-Imperialist Society, the Movement for Pan-African Freedom, and Freedom for British Colonies?

Here Mr Chikwe bowed, slightly, acknowledging the truth of what he said, but suggesting at the same time its irrelevance.

'I hear, for instance,' went on Mr Mafente, 'that the Honourable Member of Parliament for Sutton North-West refused to have your leader on his platform on the grounds that he was a dangerous agitator with left-wing persuasions?'

Here both men exchanged a delighted irrepressible smile – that smile due to political absurdity. (It is not too much to say that it is for the sake of this smile that a good many people stay in politics.) Mr Chikwe even lifted a shining face to the grey sky, shut his eyes, and while offering his smile to the wet heavens lifted both shoulders in a shrug of scorn.

Then he lowered his eyes, his body sprang into a shape of accusation and he said: 'Yet you have to agree with me, Mr Mafente – it is unfortunate that such a man as Mr Devuli should be so widely accepted as a national representative, while the virtues of Mr Kwenzi go unacknowledged.'

'We all know the virtues of Mr Kwenzi,' said Mr Mafente, and his accent on the word *we*, accompanied by a deliberately cool glance into the eyes of his old friend, made Mr Chikwe stand silent a moment, thinking. Then he said softly, testing it: 'Yes, yes, yes. And – *well*, Mr Mafente?'

Mr Mafente looked into Mr Chikwe's face, with intent, while he continued the other conversation: 'Nevertheless, Mr Chikwe, the situation is as I've said.'

Mr Chikwe, responding to the look, not the words, came closer and said: 'Yet situations do not have to remain unchanged?' They looked deeply into each other's face as Mr Mafente enquired, almost mechanically: 'Is that a threat, perhaps?'

'It is a political observation . . . Mr Mafente?'

'Mr Chikwe?'

'This particular situation could be changed very easily.'

'Is that so?'

'You know it is so.'

The two men were standing with their faces a few inches from each other, frowning with the concentration necessary for the swift mental balancing of a dozen factors: so absorbed were they, that clerks and typists glanced uneasily at them, and then, not wishing to be made uneasy, looked away again.

But here they felt approaching a third, and Mr Mafente repeated quickly: 'Is that a threat, perhaps?' in a loud voice, and both young men turned to greet Devuli, a man ten or more years older than they, large, authoritative, impressive. Yet even at this early hour he had a look of dissipation, for his eyes were red and wandering, and he stood upright only with difficulty.

Mr Mafente now fell back a step to take his place half a pace behind his leader's right elbow; and Mr Chikwe faced them both, unsmiling.

'Good morning to you, Mr Chikwe,' said Mr Devuli.

'Good morning to you, Mr Devuli. Mr Kwenzi is just finishing his breakfast, and will join us in good time. Mr Kwenzi was working all through the night on the proposals for the new constitution.'

As Mr Devuli did not answer this challenge, but stood, vague, almost swaying, his red eyes blinking at the passers-by, Mr Mafente said for him: 'We all admire the conscientiousness of Mr Kwenzi.' The *we* was definitely emphasized, the two young men exchanged a look like a nod, while Mr Mafente tactfully held out his right forearm to receive the hand of Mr Devuli. After a moment the leader steadied himself, and said in a threatening way that managed also to sound like a grumble: 'I, too, know all the implications of the proposed constitution, Mr Chikwe.'

'I am surprised to hear it, Mr Devuli, for Mr Kwenzi, who has been locked up in his hotel room for the last week, studying it, says that seven men working for seventy-seven years couldn't make sense of the constitution proposed by Her Majesty's Honourable Minister.'

Now they all three laughed together, relishing absurdity, until Mr Chikwe reimposed a frown and said: 'And since these proposals are so complicated, and since Mr Kwenzi understands them as well as any man with mere human powers could, it is our contention that it is Mr Kwenzi who should speak for our people before the Minister.'

Mr Devuli held himself upright with five fingers splayed out on the forearm of his lieutenant. His red eyes moved sombrely over the ugly façade of the Ministry, over the faces of passing people, then, with an effort, came to rest on the face of Mr Chikwe. 'But I am the leader, I am the leader acknowledged by all, and therefore I shall speak for our country.'

'You are not feeling well, Mr Devuli?'

'No, I am not feeling well, Mr Chikwe.'

'It would perhaps be better to have a man in full possession of himself speaking for our people to the Minister?' (Mr Devuli remained silent, preserving a fixed smile of general benevolence.) 'Unless, of course, you expect to feel more in command of yourself by the time of' – he brought his wrist smartly up to his eyes, frowned, dropped his wrist – 'ten-thirty a.m., which hour is nearly upon us?'

'No, Mr Chikwe, I do not expect to feel better by then. Did you not know, I have severe stomach trouble?'

'You have stomach trouble, Mr Devuli?'

'You did not hear of the attempt made upon my life when I was lying helpless with malaria in the Lady Wilberforce Hospital in Nkalolele?'

'Really, Mr Devuli, is that so?'

'Yes, it is so, Mr Chikwe. Some person bribed by my enemies introduced poison into my food while I was lying helpless in hospital. I nearly died that time, and my stomach is still unrecovered.'

'I am extremely sorry to hear it.'

'I hope that you are. For it is a terrible thing that political rivalry can lower men to such methods.'

Mr Chikwe stood slightly turned away, apparently delighting in the flight of some pigeons. He smiled, and enquired: 'Perhaps not so much political rivalry as the sincerest patriotism, Mr Devuli? It is possible that some misguided people thought the country would be better off without you.'

'It must be a matter of opinion, Mr Chikwe.'

The three men stood silent: Mr Devuli supported himself unobtrusively on Mr Mafente's arm; Mr Mafente stood waiting; Mr Chikwe smiled at pigeons.

'Mr Devuli?'

'Mr Chikwe?'

'You are of course aware that if you agree to the Minister's proposals for this constitution civil war may follow?'

'My agreement to this constitution is because I wish to avert bloodshed.'

'Yet when it was announced that you intended to agree, serious rioting started in twelve different places in our unfortunate country.'

'Misguided people – misguided by your party, Mr Chikwe.'

'I remember, not twelve months ago, that when you were accused by the newspapers of inciting to riot, your reply was that the people had minds of their own. But of course that was when you refused to consider the constitution.'

'The situation has changed, perhaps?'

The strain of this dialogue was telling on Mr Devuli; there were great beads of crystal sweat falling off his broad face, and he mopped it with the hand not steadying him, while he shifted his weight from foot to foot.

'It is your attitude that has changed, Mr Devuli. You stood for one man, one vote. Then overnight you become a supporter of the weighted vote. That cannot be described as a situation changing, but as a political leader changing – *selling out*.' Mr Chikwe whipped about like an adder and spat these two last words at the befogged man.

Mr Mafente, seeing that his leader stood silent, blinking, remarked quietly for him: 'Mr Devuli is not accustomed to replying to vulgar abuse, he prefers to remain silent.' The two young men's eyes consulted; and Mr Chikwe said, his face not four inches from Mr Devuli's: 'It is not the first time a leader of our people has taken the pay of the whites and has been disowned by our people.'

Mr Devuli looked to his lieutenant, who said: 'Yet it is Mr Devuli who has been summoned by the Minister, and you should be careful, Mr Chikwe – as a barrister you should know the law: a difference of political opinion is one thing, slander is another.'

'As, for instance, an accusation of poisoning?'

Here they all turned, a fourth figure had joined them. Mr Kwenzi, a tall, rather stooped, remote man, stood a few paces off, smiling. Mr Chikwe took his place a foot behind him, and there were two couples, facing each other.

'Good morning, Mr Devuli.'

'Good morning, Mr Kwenzi.'

'It must be nearly time for us to go in to the Minister,' said Mr Kwenzi.

'I do not think that Mr Devuli is in any condition to represent us to the Minister,' said Mr Chikwe, hot and threatening. Mr Kwenzi nodded. He had rather small direct eyes, deeply inset under his brows, which gave him an earnest focussed gaze which he was now directing at the sweat-beaded brow of his rival.

Mr Devuli blurted, his voice rising: 'And who is responsible? Who? The whole world knows of the saintly Mr Kwenzi, the hardworking Mr Kwenzi, but who is responsible for my state of health?'

Mr Chikwe cut in: 'No one is responsible for your state of health but yourself, Mr Devuli. If you drink two bottles of hard liquor a day, then you can expect your health to suffer for it.'

'The present health of Mr Devuli,' said Mr Mafente, since his chief was silent, biting his lips, his eyes red with tears as well as with liquor, 'is due to the poison which nearly killed him some weeks ago in the Lady Wilberforce Hospital in Nkalolele.'

'I am sorry to hear that,' said Mr Kwenzi mildly. 'I trust the worst is over?'

Mr Devuli was beside himself, his face knitting with emotion, sweat drops starting everywhere, his eyes roving, his fists clenching and unclenching.

'I hope,' said Mr Kwenzi, 'that you are not suggesting I or my party had anything to do with it?'

'Suggest!' said Mr Devuli. '*Suggest*? What shall I tell the Minister? That my political opponents are not ashamed to poison a helpless man in hospital? Shall I tell him that I have to have my food tasted, like an Eastern potentate? No, I cannot tell him such things – I am helpless there too, for he would say – black savages, stooping to poison, what else can you expect?'

'I doubt whether he would say that,' remarked Mr Kwenzi. 'His own ancestors considered poison an acceptable political weapon, and not so very long ago either.'

But Mr Devuli was not listening. His chest was heaving, and he sobbed out loud. Mr Mafente let his ignored forearm drop by his side, and stood away a couple of paces, gazing sombrely at his leader. After this sorrowful inspection, which Mr Kwenzi and Mr Chikwe did nothing to shorten, he looked long at Mr Chikwe, and then at Mr Kwenzi. During this three-sided silent conversation, Mr Devuli, like a dethroned king in Shakespeare, stood to one side, his chest heaving, tears flowing, his head bent to receive the rods and lashes of betrayal.

Mr Chikwe at last remarked: 'Perhaps you should tell the Minister that you have ordered a bulletproof vest like an American gangster? It would impress him no doubt with your standing among our people?' Mr Devuli sobbed again, and Mr Chikwe continued: 'Not that I do not agree with you – the vest is advisable, yes. The food tasters are not enough. I have heard our young hotheads talking among themselves and you would be wise to take every possible precaution.'

Mr Kwenzi, frowning, now raised his hand to check his lieutentant: 'I think you are going too far, Mr Chikwe, there is surely no need . . .'

At which Mr Devuli let out a great groan of bitter laughter, uncrowned king reeling under the wet London sky, and said: 'Listen to the good man, he knows nothing, no – he remains upright while his seconds do his dirty work, listen to the saint!'

Swaying, he looked for Mr Mafente's forearm, but it was not there. He stood by himself, facing three men.

Mr Kwenzi said: 'It is a very simple matter, my friends. Who is going to speak for our people to the Minister? That is all we have to decide now. I must tell you that I have made a very detailed study of the proposed constitution and I am quite sure that no honest leader of our people could accept it. Mr Devuli, I am sure you must agree with me – it is a very complicated set of proposals, and it is more than possible there may be implications you have overlooked?'

Mr Devuli laughed bitterly: 'Yes, it is possible.'

'Then we are agreed?'

Mr Devuli was silent.

'I think we are all agreed,' said Mr Chikwe, smiling, looking at Mr Mafente who after a moment gave a small nod, and then turned to face his leader's look of bitter accusation.

'It is nearly half past ten,' said Mr Chikwe. 'In a few minutes we must present ourselves to Her Majesty's Minister.'

The two lieutenants, one threatening, one sorrowful, looked at Mr Devuli, who still hesitated, grieving, on the pavement's edge. Mr Kwenzi remained aloof, smiling gently.

Mr Kwenzi at last said: 'After all, Mr Devuli, you will certainly be elected, certainly we can expect that, and with your long experience the country will need you as Minister. A minister's salary, even for our poor country, will be enough to recompense you for your generous agreement to stand down now.'

Mr Devuli laughed – bitter, resentful, scornful.

He walked away.

Mr Mafente said: 'But Mr Devuli, Mr Devuli, where are you going?'

Mr Devuli threw back over his shoulder: 'Mr Kwenzi will speak to the Minister.'

Mr Mafente nodded at the other two, and ran after his former leader, grabbed his arm, turned him around. 'Mr Devuli, you must come in with us, it is quite essential to preserve a united front before the Minister.'

'I bow to superior force, gentlemen,' said Mr Devuli, with a short sarcastic bow, which, however, he was forced to curtail: his stagger was checked by Mr Mafente's tactful arm.

'Shall we go in?' said Mr Chikwe.

Without looking again at Mr Devuli, Mr Kwenzi walked aloofly into the Ministry, followed by Mr Devuli, whose left hand lay on Mr Mafente's arm. Mr Chikwe came last, smiling, springing off the balls of his feet, watching Mr Devuli.

'And it is just half past ten,' he observed, as a flunkey came forward to intercept them. 'Half past ten to the second. I think I can hear Big Ben itself. Punctuality, as we all know, gentlemen, is the cornerstone of that efficiency without which it is impossible to govern a modern state. Is it not, so, Mr Kwenzi? Is it not so, Mr Mafente? Is it not so, Mr Devuli?'

Spies I Have Known

I don't want you to imagine that I am drawing any sort of comparison between Salisbury, Rhodesia, of thirty years ago, a one-horse town then, if not now, and more august sites. God forbid. But it does no harm to lead into a weighty subject by way of the minuscule.

It was in the middle of the Second World War. A couple of dozen people ran a dozen or so organizations, of varying degrees of left-wingedness. The town, though a capital city, was still in that condition when 'everybody knows everybody else'. The white population was about ten thousand; the number of black people, then as now, only guessed at. There was a Central Post Office, a rather handsome building, and one of the mail sorters attended the meetings of the Left Club. It was he who explained to us the system of censorship operated by the Secret Police. All the incoming mail for the above dozen organizations was first put into a central box marked CENSOR and was read, at their leisure, by certain trusted citizens. Of course all this was to be expected, and what we knew must be happening. But there were other proscribed organizations, like the Watchtower, a religious sect for some reason suspected by governments up and down Africa – perhaps because they prophesied the imminent end of the world? – and some fascist organizations, reasonably enough in a war against fascism. There were organizations of obscure aims, and perhaps five members and a capital of five pounds, and there were individuals whose mail had first to go through the process, so to speak, of decontamination, or defusing. It was this last list of a hundred or so people which was the most baffling. What did they have in common, these sinister ones whose opinions were such a threat to the budding Southern Rhodesian State, then still in the Lord Malvern phase of the Huggins/Lord Malvern/Welensky/ Garfield Todd/Winston Field/Smith succession? After months, indeed years, of trying to understand what could unite them, we had simply to give up. Of course, half were on the Left, kaffir-lovers and so on, but what of the others? It was when a man wrote a letter to the *Rhodesia Herald* in solemn parody of Soviet official style – as heavy then as now – urging the immediate extermination by firing squad of our government, in favour of a team from the Labour Opposition, and we heard from our contact in the post office that his name was now on the Black List, that we began to suspect the truth.

Throughout the war, this convenient arrangement continued. Our Man in the Post Office – by then several men, but it doesn't sound so well – kept us informed of what and who was on the Black List. And if our mail was being held up longer than we considered reasonable, the censors being on holiday, or lazy, authority would be gently prodded to hurry things up a little.

This was my first experience of Espionage.

Next was when I knew someone who knew someone who had told him of how a certain Communist Party Secretary had been approached by the man whose occupation it was to tap communist telephones – we are now in Europe. Of course, the machinery for tapping was much more primitive then. Probably by now they have dispensed with human intervention altogether, and a machine judges the degree of a suspicious person's disaffection by the tones of his voice. Then, and in that country, they simply played back records of conversation. This professional had been in the most intimate contact with communism and communists for years, becoming involved with shopping expeditions, husbands late from the office, love affairs, a divorce or so, children's excursions. He had been sucked into active revolutionary politics through the keyhole.

'I don't think you ought to let little Jackie go at all. He'll be in bed much too late, and you know how bad-tempered he gets when he is over-tired.'

'She said to me No, she said. That's final. If you want to do a thing like that, then you must do it yourself. You shouldn't expect other people to pull your chestnuts out of the fire, she said. If he was rude to you, then it's your place to tell him so.'

He got frustrated, like an intimate friend or lover with paralysis of the tongue. And there was another thing, he was listening to events, emotions, several hours old. Sometimes weeks old, as for instance when he went on leave and had to catch up with a month's dangerous material all in one exhausting twenty-four hours. He found that he was getting possessive about certain of his charges; resented his colleagues listening in to 'my suspects'. Once he had to wrestle with temptation because he longed to seek out a certain woman on the point of leaving her husband for another man. Owing to his advantageous position he knew the other man was not what she believed. He imagined how he would trail her to the café which he knew she frequented, sit near her, then lean over and ask: 'May I join you? I have something of importance to divulge.' He knew she would agree: he knew her character well. She was unconventional, perhaps not as responsible as she ought to be, careless for instance about the regularity of meals, but fundamentally, he was sure, a good girl with the potentiality of good wifehood. He would say to her: 'Don't do it, my dear! No, don't ask me how I know, I can't tell you that. But if you leave your husband for that man, you'll regret it!' He would press her hands in his, looking deeply into her eyes – he was sure they were brown, for her voice was definitely the voice of a brown-eyed blonde – and then stride for ever out of her life. Afterwards he could check on the success of his intervention through the tapes.

To cut short a process that took some years, he at last went secretly to a communist bookshop, bought some pamphlets, attended a meeting or two, and discovered that he would certainly become a Party member if it were not that his job, and a very well-paid one with good prospects, was to spy on the Communist Party. He felt in a false position. What to do? He turned up at the offices of the Communist Party, asked to see the Secretary, and confessed his dilemma. Roars of laughter from the Secretary.

These roars are absolutely obligatory in this convention, which insists on a greater degree of sophisticated understanding between professionals, even if on opposing sides and even if at war – Party officials, government officials, top-ranking soldiers and the like – and the governed, ever a foolish, trusting and sentimental lot.

First, then, the roar. Then a soupçon of whimsicality: alas for this badly ordered world where men so well equipped to be friends must be enemies. Finally, the hard offer.

Our friend the telephone-tapper was offered a retaining fee by the Communist Party, and their provisional trust, on condition that he stayed where he was, working for the other side. Of course, what else had he expected? Nor should he have felt insulted, for in such ways are the double agents born, those rare men at an altogether higher level than he could ever aspire to reach in the hierarchies of espionage. But his finer feelings had been hurt by the offer of money, and he refused. He went off and suffered for a week or so, deciding that he really did have to leave his job with the Secret Police – an accurate name for what he was working for, though of course the name it went under was much

blander. He returned to the Secretary in order to ask for the second time
to become just a rank-and-file Communist Party member. This time
there was no roar of laughter, not even a chuckle, but the frank (and
equally obligatory) I-am-concealing-nothing statement of the position.
Which was that he surely must be able to see their point of view – the
Communist Party's. With a toehold in the enemy camp (a delicate way of
describing his salary and his way of life) he could be of real use. To stay
where he was could be regarded as a real desire to serve the People's
Cause. To leave altogether, becoming just honest John Smith, might
satisfy his conscience (a subjective and conditioned organ, as he must
surely know by now if he had read those pamphlets properly) but would
leave behind him an image of the capricious, or even the unreliable. What
had he planned to tell his employers? 'I am tired of tapping telephones, it
offends me!' Or: 'I regard this as an immoral occupation!' – when he had
done nothing else for years? Come, come, he hadn't thought it out. He
would certainly be under suspicion for ever more by his ex-employers.
And of course he could not be so innocent, after so long spent in that
atmosphere of vigilance and watchfulness, as not to expect the
communists to keep watch on himself? No, his best course would be to
stay exactly where he was, working even harder at tapping telephones. If
not, then his frank advice (the Secretary's) could only be that he must
become an ordinary citizen, as far from any sort of politics as possible, for
his own sake, the sake of the Service he had left, and the sake of the
Communist Party – which of *course* they believed he now found his
spiritual home.

But the trouble was that he did want to join it. He wanted nothing more
than to become part of the world of stern necessities he had followed for so
long, but as it were from behind a one-way pane of glass. Integrity had
disfranchised him. From now on he could not hope to serve humanity
except through the use of the vote.

His life was empty. His resignation cut off his involvement, like
turning off the television on a soap opera, with the deathless real-life
dramas of the tapes.

He felt that he was useless. He considered suicide, but thought better
of it. Then, having weathered a fairly routine and unremarkable nervous
breakdown, became a contemplative monk – high Church of England.

Another spy I met at a cocktail party, in the course of chat about this or
that (it was in London, in the late 'fifties), said that at the outbreak of the
Second World War he had been in Greece, or perhaps it was Turkey,

where at another cocktail party, over the canapés, an official from the British Embassy invited him to spy for his country.

'But I can't,' said this man. 'You must know that perfectly well.'

'But why ever not?' inquired the official; a Second Secretary I think he was.

'Because, as of course you must know, I am a Communist Party member.'

'Indeed? How interesting? But surely that is not going to stand in the way of your desire to serve your country?' said the official, trumping ferocious honesty with urbanity.

To cut this anecdote short – it comes from a pretty petty level in the affairs of men – this man went home, spent a sleepless night weighing his allegiances, and decided by morning that of course the Second Secretary was right. He would like to serve his country, which was engaged, after all, in a war against fascism. He explained his decision to his superiors in the Communist Party, who agreed with him, and to his wife and his comrades. Then, meeting the Second Secretary at another cocktail party, he informed him of the decision he had taken. He was invited to attach himself to a certain Army unit, in some capacity to do with the Ministry of Information. He was to await orders. In due course they came, and he discovered that it was his task to spy on the Navy, or rather, that portion of it operating near him. Our Navy, of course. He was always unable to work out the ideology of this. That a communist should not be set to spy on, let's say, Russia seemed to him fair and reasonable, but why was he deemed suitable material to spy on his own side? He found it all baffling, and indeed rather lowering. Then, at a cocktail party, he happened to meet a naval officer with whom he proceeded to get drunk, and they both suddenly understood on a hunch that they were engaged in spying on each other, one for the Navy, one for the Army. Both found this work without much uplift; they were simply not able to put their hearts into it, apart from the fact that they had been in the same class at prep school and had many other social ties. Not even the fact that they weren't being paid, since it was assumed by their superiors – quite correctly of course – that they would be happy to serve their countries for nothing, made them feel any better. They developed the habit of meeting regularly in a café where they drank wine and coffee and played chess in a vine-covered arbour overlooking a particularly fine bit of the Mediterranean where, without going through all the tedium of spying on each other, they gave each other relevant information. They were found out. Their excuse that they were fighting the war on the same side was deemed inadequate. They were both given the sack as spies, and transferred to less demanding work. But until D-Day and beyond, the British Army spied on the British Navy, and vice versa. They probably all still do.

The fact that human beings, given half a chance, start seeing each other's points of view seems to me the only ray of hope there is for humanity, but obviously this tendency must be one to cause anguish to seniors in the Diplomatic Corps, and the employers of your common or garden spy – not the high-level spies, but of that in a moment. Diplomats, until they have understood why, always complain that as soon as they understand a country and its language really well, hey presto, off they are whisked to another country. But diplomacy could not continue if the opposing factotums lost a proper sense of national hostility. Some Diplomatic Corps insist that their employees must visit only among each other, and never fraternize with the locals, obviously believing that understanding with others is inculcated by a sort of osmosis. And, of course, any diplomat who shows signs of going native, that is to say really enjoying the manners and morals of a place, must be withdrawn at once.

Not so the masters among the spies: one dedicated to his country's deepest interests must be worse than useless. The rarest spirits must be those able to entertain two or three allegiances at once; the counter-spies, the double and triple agents. Such people are not born. It can't be that they wake up one morning at the age of thirteen, crying: Eureka, I've got it, I was born to be a double agent! Nor can there be a training school for multiple spies, a kind of top class that promising pupils graduate towards. Yet that capacity which might retard a diplomat's career, or mean death to the small fry among spies, must be precisely the one watched out for by the Spymasters who watch and manipulate in the high levels of the world's thriving espionage systems. What probably happens is that a man drifts, even unwillingly, into serving his country as a spy – like my acquaintance of the cocktail party who then found himself spying on the Senior Service of his own side. Then, whether there through a deep sense of vocation or unwillingly, he must begin by making mistakes; is sometimes pleased with himself and sometimes not; goes through a phase of wondering whether he would not have done better to go into the Stock Exchange, or whatever his alternative was – and then suddenly there comes that moment, fatal to punier men but a sign of his own future greatness, when he is invaded by sympathy for the enemy. Long dwelling on what X is doing, likely to be doing, or thinking, or planning, makes X's thoughts as familiar and as likeable as his own. The points of view of the nation he spends all his time trying to undo, are comfortably at home in a mind once tuned only to those of his own dear Fatherland. He is thinking the thoughts of those he used to call enemies before he understands that he is already psychologically a double agent, and before he guesses that those men who must always be on the watch for such precious material have noticed, perhaps even prognosticated, his condition.

On those levels where the really great spies move, whose names we never hear, but whose existence we have to deduce, what fantastic feats of global understanding must be reached, what metaphysical heights of international brotherhood!

It is of course not possible to do more than take the humblest flights into speculation, while making do with those so frequent and highly publicized spy dramas, for some reason or other so very near to farce, that do leave obscurity for our attention.

It can't be possible that the high reaches of espionage can have anything in common with, for instance, this small happening.

A communist living in a small town in England, who had been openly and undramatically a communist for years, and for whom the state of being a communist had become rather like the practice of an undemanding religion – this man looked out of his window one fine summer afternoon to see standing in the street outside his house a car of such foreignness and such opulence that he was embarrassed, and at once began to work out what excuses he could use to his working-class neighbours whose cars, if any, would be dust in comparison. Out of this monster of a car came two large smiling Russians, carrying a teddy bear the size of a sofa, a bottle of vodka, a long and very heavy roll, which later turned out to be a vast carpet with a picture of the Kremlin on it, and a box of chocolates of British make that had a pretty lady and a pretty dog on it.

Every window in the street already had heads packed behind the curtains.

'Come in,' said he, 'but I don't think I have the pleasure of knowing who . . .'

The roll of carpet was propped in the hall, the three children were sent off to play with the teddy bear in the kitchen, and the box of chocolates was set aside for the lady of the house, who was out doing the week's shopping in the High Street. The vodka was opened at once.

It turned out that it was his wife they wanted: they were interested in him only as a go-between. They wished him to ask his wife, who was an employee of the Town Council, to get hold of the records of the Council's meetings, and to pass these records on to them. Now, this wasn't London, or even Edinburgh. It was a small, unimportant North of England town, in which it would be hard to imagine anything ever happening that could be of interest to anyone outside it, let alone the agents of a Foreign Power. But, said he, these records are open, anyone could go and get copies – you, for instance. 'Comrades, I shall be delighted to take you to the Town Hall myself.'

No, what they had been instructed to do was to ask his wife to procure them minutes and records, nothing less would do.

A long discussion ensued. It was all no use. The Russians could not be made to see that what they asked was unnecessary. Nor could they understand that to arrive in a small suburban street in a small English town in a car the length of a battleship, was to draw the wrong sort of attention.

'But why is that?' they inquired. 'Representatives of the country where the workers hold power should use a good car. Of course, comrade! You have not thought it out from a class position!'

The climax came when, despairing of the effects of rational argument, they said: 'And, comrade, these presents – the bear, the carpet, the chocolates, the vodka – are only a small token in appreciation of your work for our common cause. Of course you will be properly recompensed.'

At which point he was swept by, indeed taken over entirely by, atavistic feelings he had no idea were in him at all. He stood up and pointed a finger shaking with rage at the door: 'How dare you imagine', he shouted, 'that my wife and I would take money. If I were going to spy, I'd spy for the love of mankind, for duty, and for international socialism. Take those bloody things out of here – wait, I'll get that teddy bear from the kids. And you can take your bloody car out of here too.'

His wife, when she came back from the supermarket and heard the story, was even more insulted than he was.

But emotions like these are surely possible only at the lowest possible levels of spy material – in this case so low they didn't qualify for the first step, entrance into the brotherhood.

Full circle back to Our Man in the Post Office, or, rather, the first of three.

After sedulous attendance at a lot of left-wing meetings, semi-private and public – for above all Tom was a methodical man who, if engaged in a thing, always gave it full value – he put his hand up one evening in the middle of a discussion about Agrarian Reform in Venezuela, and said: 'I must ask permission to ask a question.'

Everyone always laughed at him when he did this, put up his hand to ask permission to speak, or to leave, or to have opinions about something. Little did we realize that we were seeing here not just a surface mannerism, or habit, but his strongest characteristic.

It was late in the meeting, at that stage when the floor is well loaded with empty coffee cups, beer glasses and full ash trays. Some people had already left.

He wanted to know what he ought to do: 'I want to have the benefit of your expert advice.' As it happened he had already taken the decision he was asking about.

After some two years of a life not so much double – the word implies secrecy – as dual, his boss in the Central Post Office called him to ask how he was enjoying his life with the Left. Tom was as doggedly informative with him as he was with us, and said that we were interesting people, well-informed, and full of a high-class brand of idealism which he found inspiring.

'I always feel good after going to one of their meetings,' he reported he had said. 'It takes you right out of yourself and makes you think.'

His chief said that he, for his part, always enjoyed hearing about idealism and forward-looking thought, and invited Tom to turn in reports about our activities, our discussions, and most particularly our plans for the future, as well in advance as possible.

Tom told us that he said to his boss that he didn't like the idea of doing that sort of thing behind our backs because, 'say what you like about the Reds, they are very hospitable'.

The chief had said that it would be for the good of his country.

Tom came to us to say that he had told his boss that he had agreed, because he wanted to be of assistance to the National War Effort.

It was clear to everyone that having told us that he had agreed to spy on us, he would, since that was his nature, most certainly go back to his boss and tell him that he had told us that he had agreed to spy. After which he would come back to us to tell us that he had told his boss that . . . and so on. Indefinitely, if his boss didn't get tired of it. Tom could not see that his chief would shortly find him unsuitable material for espionage, and might even dismiss him from being a sorter in the post office altogether – a nuisance for us. After which he, the chief, would probably look for someone else to give him information.

It was Harry, one of the other two post office employees attending Left Club meetings, who suggested that it would probably be himself who would next be invited to spy on us, now that Tom had 'told'. Tom was upset when everybody began speculating about his probable supersession by Harry, or even Dick. The way he saw it was that his complete frankness with both us and his chief was surely deserving of reward. He ought to be left in the job. God knows how he saw the future. Probably that both his boss and ourselves would continue to employ him. We would use him to find out how our letters were slowly moving through the toils of censorship, and to hurry them on, if possible; his chief would use him to spy on us. When I say employ, I don't want anyone to imagine this implies payment. Or, at least, certainly not from our side. Ideology had to be his spur, sincerity his reward.

It will by now have been noticed that our Tom was not as bright as he might have been. But he was a pleasant enough youth. He was rather good-looking too, about twenty-two. His physical characteristic was neatness. His clothes were always just so; he had a small alert dark moustache; he had glossy dark well-brushed hair. His rather small hands were well manicured – this last trait bound to be found offensive by good colonials, whose eye for such anti-masculine evidence (as they were bound to see it), then if not now, was acute. But he was a fairly recent immigrant, from just before the war, and had not yet absorbed the mores.

Tom, in spite of our humorous forecast that he would tell his boss that he had told us, and his stiff and wounded insistence that such a thing was impossible, found himself impelled to do just that. He reported back that his chief had 'lost his rag with him'.

But that was not the end. He was offered the job of learning how to censor letters. He had said to his boss that he felt in honour bound to tell us, and his boss said: 'Oh, for Christ's sake. Tell them anything you damned well like. You won't be choosing what is to be censored.'

As I said, this was an unsophisticated town in those days, and the condition of 'everybody knowing everybody else' was always leading to such warm human situations.

He accepted the offer because: 'My mother always told me that she wanted me to do well for myself, and I'll increase my rating into Schedule Three as soon as I start work on censoring, and that means an increment of fifty pounds a year.'

We congratulated him, and urged him to keep us informed about how people were trained as censors, and he agreed to do this. Shortly after that the war ended, and all the cameraderie of wartime ended as the Cold War began. The ferment of Left activity ended too.

We saw Tom no more, but followed his progress, steady if slow, up the Civil Service. The last I heard he was heading a Department among whose duties is censorship. I imagine him, a man in his fifties, a husband and no doubt a father, looking down the avenues of lost time to those dizzy days when he was the member of a dangerous revolutionary organization. 'Yes,' he must often say, 'you can't tell me anything about them. They are idealistic, I can grant you so much, but they are dangerous. Dangerous and wrong-headed! I left them as soon as I understood what they really were.'

But of our three post office spies Harry was the one whose career, for a while at least, was the most rewarding for idealistic humanists.

He was a silent, desperately shy schoolboy who came to a public meeting and fell madly in love for a week or so with the speaker, a girl giving her first public speech and as shy as he was. His father had died and his mother, as the psychiatrists and welfare workers would say, was 'inadequate'. That is to say, she was not good at being a widow, and was frail in health. What little energy she had went into earning enough money for herself and two younger sons to live on. She nagged at Harry for not having ambition, and for not studying for the examinations which would take him up the ladder into the next grade in the post office – and for wasting time with the Reds. He longed to be of use. For three years he devoted all his spare time to organization on the Left, putting up exhibitions, hiring halls and rooms, decorating ballrooms for fund-raising dances, getting advertisements for our socialist magazine – circulation two thousand, and laying it out and selling it. He argued principle with Town Councillors – 'But it's not *fair* not to let us have the hall, this is a democratic country, isn't it?' – and spent at least three nights a week discussing world affairs in smoke-filled rooms.

At the time we would have dismissed as beyond redemption anyone who suggested it, but I dare say now that the main function of those gatherings was social. Southern Rhodesia was never exactly a hospitable country for those interested in anything but sport and the sundowner, and the fifty or so people who came to the meetings, whether in the Forces, or refugees from Europe, or simply Rhodesians, were all souls in need of congenial company. And they were friendly occasions, those meetings, sometimes going on till dawn.

A girl none of us had seen before came to a public meeting. She saw Harry, a handsome, confident, loquacious, energetic, efficient young man. Everyone relied on him.

She fell in love, took him home, and her father, recognizing one of the world's born organizers, made him manager in his hardware shop.

Which leaves the third, Dick. Now there are some people who should not be allowed anywhere near meetings, debates, or similar intellect-fermenting agencies. He came to two meetings. Harry brought him, describing him as 'keen'. It was Harry who was keen. Dick sat on the floor on a cushion. Wild bohemian ways, these, for well-brought-up young whites. His forehead puckered like a puppy's while he tried to follow wild un-Rhodesian thought. He, like Tom, was a neat, well-set-up youth. Perhaps the Post Office, or at least in Rhodesia, is an institution that attracts the well-ordered? I remember he reminded me of a boiled sweet, bland sugar with a chemical tang. Or perhaps he was like a bulldog, all sleek latent ferocity, with its little bulging eyes, its little snarl. Like Tom, he was one for extracting exact information. 'I take it you people believe that human nature can be changed?'

At the second meeting he attended, he sat and listened as before. At the end he inquired whether we thought socialism was a good thing in this country where there was the white man's burden to consider.

He did not come to another meeting. Harry said that he had found us seditious and un-Rhodesian. Also insincere. We asked Harry to go and ask Dick why he thought we were insincere, and to come back and tell us. It turned out that Dick wanted to know why the Left Club did not take over the government of the country and run it, if we thought the place ill run. But we forgot Dick, particularly as Harry, at the zenith of his efficiency and general usefulness, was drifting off with his future wife to become a hardware-store manager. And by then Tom was lost to us.

Suddenly we heard that 'The Party for Democracy, Liberty and Freedom' was about to hold a preliminary mass meeting. One of us was delegated to go along and find out what was happening. This turned out to be me.

The public meeting was in a side room off a ballroom in one of the town's three hotels. It was furnished with a sideboard to hold the extra supplies of beer and sausage rolls and peanuts consumed so plentifully during the weekly dances, a palm in a pot so tall the top fronds were being pressed down by the ceiling, and a dozen stiff dining-room chairs ranged one by one along the walls. When I arrived, there were eleven men and women in the room, including Dick. Unable to understand immediately why this gathering struck me as so different from the ones in which I spent so much of my time, I then saw it was because there were elderly people present. Our gatherings loved only the young.

Dick was wearing his best suit in dark-grey flannel. It was a very hot evening. His face was scarlet with endeavour and covered with sweat, which he kept sweeping off his forehead with impatient fingers. He was reading an impassioned document, in tone rather like the Communist Manifesto, which began: 'Fellow Citizens of Rhodesia! Sincere Men and Women! This is the Time for Action! Arise and look about you and enter into your Inheritance! Put the forces of International Capital to flight!'

He was standing in front of one of the chairs, his well-brushed little head bent over his notes, which were hand-written and in places hard to read, so that these inflammatory sentiments were being stammered and stumbled out, while he kept correcting himself, wiping off sweat, and then stopping with an appealing circular glance around the room at the others. Towards him were lifted ten earnest faces, as if at a saviour or a Party Leader.

The programme of this nascent Party was simple. It was to 'take over by democratic means but as fast as possible' all the land and the industry of the country 'but to cause as little inconvenience as possible' and 'as soon as it was feasible' to institute a regime of true equality and fairness in 'this land of Cecil Rhodes'.

He was intoxicated by the emanations of admiration from his audience. Burning, passionate faces like these (alas, and I saw how far we had lapsed from fervour) were no longer to be seen at our Left Club meetings, which long ago had sailed away on the agreeable tides of debate and intellectual speculation.

The faces belonged to a man of fifty or so, rather grey and beaten, who described himself as a teacher 'planning the total reform of the entire educational system'; a woman of middle age, a widow, badly dressed and smoking incessantly, who looked as if she had long since gone beyond what she was strong enough to bear from life; an old man with an angelic pink face fringed with white tufts who said he was named after Keir Hardie; three schoolboys, the son of the widow and his two friends; the woman attendant from the Ladies' cloakroom who had unlocked this room to set out the chairs and then had stayed out of interest, since it was her afternoon off; two aircraftmen from the R.A.F.; Dick the convenor; and a beautiful young woman no one had ever seen before who, as soon as Dick had finished his manifesto, stood up to make a plea for vegetarianism. She was ruled out of order. 'We have to get power first, and then we'll simply do what the majority wants.' As for me, I was set apart from them by my lack of fervour, and by Dick's suspicion.

This was in the middle of the Second World War, whose aim it was to defeat the hordes of National Socialism. Communist Russia was twenty-five years old. It was more than a hundred and fifty years since the French Revolution, and even more than that since the American Revolution which overthrew the tyrannies of England. The Independence of India would shortly be celebrated. It was nearly twenty years after the death of Lenin. Trotsky had only just been murdered.

One of the schoolboys, a friend of the widow's son, put up his hand to say timidly that he believed 'there might be books which we could read about socialism and that sort of thing'.

'Indeed there are,' said the namesake of Keir Hardie, nodding his white locks, 'but we needn't follow the writ that runs in other old countries when we have got a brand new one here.'

(It must be explained that the whites of Rhodesia, then as now, are always referring to 'this new country'.)

'As for books,' said Dick, eyeing me with all the scornful self-command he had acquired since leaving his cushion weeks before on the floor of our living room, 'books don't seem to do some people any good, so why do we need them? It is all perfectly simple. It isn't right for a few people to own all the wealth of a country. It isn't fair. It should be shared out among everybody, equally, and then that would be a democracy.'

'Well, obviously,' said the beautiful girl.

'Ah yes,' sighed the poor tired woman, emphatically crushing out her cigarette and lighting a new one.

'Perhaps it would be better if I just moved that palm a little,' said the cloakroom attendant, 'it does seem to be a little in your way perhaps.'

'Never mind about the palm,' said Dick magnificently. 'It's not important.'

And this was the point at which someone asked: 'Excuse me, but where do the Natives come in?' (In those days, the black inhabitants of Rhodesia were referred to as the Natives.)

This was felt to be in extremely bad taste.

'I don't really think that is applicable,' said Dick hotly. 'I simply don't see the point of bringing it up at all – unless it is to make trouble.'

'They do live here,' said one of the R.A.F.

'Well, I must withdraw altogether if there's any likelihood of us getting mixed up with kaffir trouble,' said the widow.

'You can be assured that there will be nothing of that,' said Dick, firmly in control, in the saddle, leader of all, after only half an hour of standing up in front of his mass meeting.

'I don't see that,' said the beautiful girl. 'I simply don't see that at all! We must have a policy for the Natives.'

Even twelve people in one small room, whether starting a mass Party or not, mean twelve different, defined, passionately held viewpoints. The meeting at last had to be postponed for a week to allow those who had not had a chance to air their views to have their say. I attended this second meeting. There were fifteen people present. The two R.A.F. were not there, but there were six white trade unionists from the railways, who, hearing of the new Party, had come to get a resolution passed. 'In the opinion of this meeting, the Native is being advanced too fast towards civilization and in his own interests the pace should be slowed.'

This resolution was always being passed in those days, on every possible occasion. It probably still is.

But the nine from the week before were already able to form a solid bloc against this influx of alien thought – not as champions of the Natives, of course not, but because it was necessary to attend to first things first. 'We have to take over the country first, by democratic methods. That won't take long, because it is obvious our programme is only fair, and after that we can decide what to do about the Natives.' The six railway workers then left, leaving the nine from last week, who proceeded to form their Party for Democracy, Liberty and Freedom. A steering committee of three was appointed to draft a constitution.

And that was the last anyone ever heard of it, except for one cyclostyled pamphlet which was called 'Capitalism is Unfair. Let's Join Together to Abolish it. This means You!'

The war was over. Intellectual ferments of this sort occurred no more. Employees of the post office, all once again good citizens properly employed in sport and similar endeavours, no longer told the citizens in what ways they were being censored and when.

Dick did not stay in the post office. That virus, politics, was in his veins for good. From being a spokesman for socialism for the whites, he became, as a result of gibes that he couldn't have a socialism that excluded most of the population, an exponent of the view that Natives must not be advanced too fast in their own interests, and from there he developed into a Town Councillor, and from there into a Member of Parliament. And that is what he still is, a gentleman of distinguished middle age, an indefatigable server on Parliamentary Committees and Commissions, particularly those to do with the Natives, on whom he is considered an authority.

An elderly bulldog of the bulldog breed he is, every inch of him.

Homage for Isaac Babel

The day I had promised to take Catherine down to visit my young friend Philip at his school in the country, we were to leave at eleven, but she arrived at nine. Her blue dress was new, and so were her fashionable shoes. Her hair had just been done. She looked more than ever like a pink and gold Renoir girl who expects everything from life.

Catherine lives in a white house overlooking the sweeping brown tides of the river. She helped me clean up my flat with a devotion which said that she felt small flats were altogether more romantic than large houses. We drank tea, and talked mainly about Philip, who, being fifteen, has pure stern tastes in everything from food to music. Catherine looked at the books lying around his room, and asked if she might borrow the stories of Isaac Babel to read on the train. Catherine is thirteen. I suggested she might find them difficult, but she said: 'Philip reads them, doesn't he?'

During the journey I read newspapers and watched her pretty frowning face as she turned the pages of Babel, for she was determined to let nothing get between her and her ambition to be worthy of Philip.

At the school, which is charming, civilized, and expensive, the two children walked together across green fields, and I followed, seeing how the sun gilded their bright friendly heads turned towards each other as they talked. In Catherine's left hand she carried the stories of Isaac Babel.

After lunch we went to the pictures. Philip allowed it to be seen that he thought going to the pictures just for the fun of it was not worthy of intelligent people, but he made the concession, for our sakes. For his sake we chose the more serious of the two films that were showing in the little town. It was about a good priest who helped criminals in New York. His goodness, however, was not enough to prevent one of them from being sent to the gas chamber; and Philip and I waited with Catherine in the dark until she had stopped crying and could face the light of a golden evening.

At the entrance of the cinema the doorman was lying in wait for anyone who had red eyes. Grasping Catherine by her suffering arm, he said bitterly: 'Yes, why are you crying? He had to be punished for his crime, didn't he?' Catherine stared at him, incredulous. Philip rescued her by saying with disdain: 'Some people don't know right from wrong even when it's *demonstrated* to them.' The doorman turned his attention to the next red-eyed emerger from the dark; and we went on together to the station, the children silent because of the cruelty of the world.

Finally Catherine said, her eyes wet again: 'I think it's all absolutely beastly, and I can't bear to think about it.' And Philip said: 'But we've got to think about it, don't you see, because if we don't it'll go on and *on*, don't you see?'

In the train going back to London I sat beside Catherine. She had the stories open in front of her, but she said: 'Philip's awfully lucky. I wish I went to that school. Did you notice that girl who said hullo to him in the garden? They must be great friends. I wish my mother would let me have a dress like that, it's *not* fair.'

'I thought it was too old for her.'

'Oh *did* you?'

Soon she bent her head again over the book, but almost at once lifted it to say: 'Is he a very famous writer?'

'He's a marvellous writer, brilliant, one of the very best.'

'Why?'

'Well, for one thing, he's so simple. Look how few words he uses, and how strong his stories are.'

'I see. Do you know him? Does he live in London?'

'Oh no, he's dead.'

'Oh. Then why did you – I thought he was alive, the way you talked.'

'I'm sorry, I suppose I wasn't thinking of him as dead.'

'When did he die?'

'He was murdered. About twenty years ago, I suppose.'

'*Twenty years*.' Her hands began the movement of pushing the book over to me, but then relaxed. 'I'll be fourteen in November,' she stated, sounding threatened, while her eyes challenged me.

I found it hard to express my need to apologize, but before I could speak, she said, patiently attentive again: 'You said he was murdered?'

'Yes.'

'I expect the person who murdered him felt sorry when he discovered he had murdered a famous writer.'

'Yes, I expect so.'

'Was he old when he was murdered?'

'No, quite young really.'

'Well, that was bad luck, wasn't it?'

'Yes, I suppose it was bad luck.'

'Which do you think is the very best story here? I mean, in your honest opinion, the very very best one.'

I chose the story about killing the goose. She read it slowly, while I sat waiting, wishing to take it from her, wishing to protect this charming little person from Isaac Babel.

When she had finished she said: Well, some of it I don't understand. He's got a funny way of looking at things. Why should a man's legs in boots look like *girls*?' She finally pushed the book over at me, and said: 'I think it's all morbid.'

'But you have to understand the kind of life he had. First, he was a Jew in Russia. That was bad enough. Then his experience was all revolution and civil war and . . .'

But I could see these words bouncing off the clear glass of her fiercely denying gaze; and I said: 'Look, Catherine, why don't you try again when you're older? Perhaps you'll like him better then?'

She said gratefully: 'Yes, perhaps that would be best. After all, Philip is two years older than me, isn't he?'

A week later I got a letter from Catherine.

Thank you very much for being kind enough to take me to visit Philip at his school. It was the most lovely day in my whole life. I am extremely grateful to you for taking me. I have been thinking about the Hoodlum Priest. That was a film which demonstrated to me beyond any shadow of doubt that Capital Punishment is a Wicked Thing, and I shall never forget what I learned that afternoon, and the lessons of it will be with me all my life. I have been meditating about what you said about Isaac Babel, the famed Russian short story writer, and I now see that the conscious simplicity of his style is what makes him, beyond the shadow of a doubt, the great writer that he is, and now in my school compositions I am endeavouring to emulate him so as to learn a conscious simplicity which is the only basis for a really brilliant writing style. Love, Catherine. P.S. Has Philip said anything about my party? I wrote but he hasn't answered.

Please find out if he is coming or if he just forgot to answer my letter. I hope he comes, because sometimes I feel I shall die if he doesn't. P.P.S. Please don't tell him I said anything, because I should die if he knew. Love, Catherine.

A Woman on a Roof

It was during the week of hot sun, that June.

Three men were at work on the roof, where the leads got so hot they had the idea of throwing water on to cool them. But the water steamed, then sizzled; and they made jokes about getting an egg from some woman in the flats under them, to poach it for their dinner. By two it was not possible to touch the guttering they were replacing, and they speculated about what workmen did in regularly hot countries. Perhaps they should borrow kitchen gloves with the egg? They were all a bit dizzy, not used to the heat; and they shed their coats and stood side by side squeezing themselves into a foot-wide patch of shade against a chimney, careful to keep their feet in the thick socks and boots out of the sun. There was a fine view across several acres of roofs. Not far off a man sat in a deck chair reading the newspapers. Then they saw her, between chimneys, about fifty yards away. She lay face down on a brown blanket. They could see the top part of her: black hair, a flushed solid back, arms spread out.

'She's stark naked,' said Stanley, sounding annoyed.

Harry, the oldest, a man of about forty-five, said: 'Looks like it.'

Young Tom, seventeen, said nothing, but he was excited and grinning.

Stanley said: 'Someone'll report her if she doesn't watch out.'

'She thinks no one can see,' said Tom, craning his head all ways to see more.

At this point the woman, still lying prone, brought her two hands up behind her shoulders with the ends of a scarf in them, tied it behind her back, and sat up. She wore a red scarf tied around her breasts and brief red bikini pants. This being the first day of the sun she was white, flushing red. She sat smoking, and did not look up when Stanley let out a wolf whistle. Harry said: 'Small things amuse small minds,' leading the way back to their part of the roof, but it was scorching. Harry said: 'Wait, I'm going to rig up some shade,' and disappeared down the skylight into the building. Now that he'd gone, Stanley and Tom went to the farthest point they could to peer at the woman. She had moved, and all they could see were two pink legs stretched on the blanket. They whistled and shouted but the legs did not move. Harry came back with a blanket and shouted: 'Come on, then.' He sounded irritated with them. They clambered back to him and he said to Stanley: 'What about your missus?' Stanley was newly married, about three months. Stanley said, jeering: 'What about my missus?' – preserving his independence. Tom said nothing, but his mind was full of the nearly naked woman. Harry slung the blanket, which he had borrowed from a friendly woman downstairs, from the stem of a television aerial to a row of chimney pots. This shade fell across the piece of gutter they had to replace. But the shade kept moving, they had to adjust the blanket, and not much progress was made. At last some of the heat left the roof, and they worked fast, making up for lost time. First Stanley, then Tom, made a trip to the end of the rood to see the woman. 'She's on her back,' Stanley said, adding a jest which made Tom snicker, and the older man smile tolerantly. Tom's report was that she hadn't moved, but it was a lie. He wanted to keep what he had seen to himself: he had caught her in the act of rolling down the little red pants over her hips, till they were no more than a small triangle. She was on her back, fully visible, glistening with oil.

Next morning, as soon as they came up, they went to look. She was already there, face down, arms spread out, naked except for the little red pants. She had turned brown in the night. Yesterday she was a scarlet and white woman, today she was a brown woman, Stanley let out a whistle. She lifted her head, startled, as if she'd been asleep, and looked straight over at them. The sun was in her eyes, she blinked and stared, then she dropped her head again. At this gesture of indifference, they all three, Stanley, Tom and old Harry, let out whistles and yells. Harry was doing it in parody of the younger men, making fun of them, but he was also angry. They were all angry because of her utter indifference to the three men watching her.

'Bitch,' said Stanley.

'She should ask us over,' said Tom, snickering.

Harry recovered himself and reminded Stanley: 'If she's married, her old man wouldn't like that.'

'Christ,' said Stanley virtuously, 'if my wife lay about like that, for everyone to see, I'd soon stop her.'

Harry said, smiling: 'How do you know, perhaps she's sunning herself at this very moment?'

'Not a chance, not on our roof.' The safety of his wife put Stanley into a good humour, and they went to work. But today it was hotter than yesterday; and several times one or the other suggested they should tell Matthew, the foreman, and ask to leave the roof until the heat wave was over. But they didn't. There was work to be done in the basement of the big block of flats, but up here they felt free, on a different level from ordinary humanity shut in the streets or the buildings. A lot more people came out on to the roofs that day, for an hour at midday. Some married couples sat side by side in deck chairs, the women's legs stockingless and scarlet, the men in vests with reddening shoulders.

The woman stayed on her blanket, turning herself over and over. She ignored them, no matter what they did. When Harry went off to fetch more screws, Stanley said: 'Come on.' Her roof belonged to a different system of roofs, separated from theirs at one point by about twenty feet. It meant a scrambling climb from one level to another, edging along parapets, clinging to chimneys, while their big boots slipped and slithered, but at last they stood on a small square projecting roof looking straight down at her, close. She sat smoking, reading a book. Tom thought she looked like a poster, or a magazine cover, with the blue sky behind her and her legs stretched out. Behind her a great crane at work on a new building in Oxford Street swung its black arm across the roofs in a great arc. Tom imagined himself at work on the crane, adjusting the arm to swing over and pick her up and swing her back across the sky to drop near him.

They whistled. She looked up at them, cool and remote, and went on reading. Again, they were furious. Or rather, Stanley was. His sun-heated face was screwed into rage as he whistled again and again, trying to make her look up. Young Tom stopped whistling. He stood beside Stanley, excited, grinning; but he felt as if he were saying to the woman: 'Don't associate me with *him*,' for his grin was apologetic. Last night he had thought of the unknown woman before he slept, and she had been tender with him. This tenderness he was remembering as he shifted his feet by the jeering, whistling Stanley, and watched the indifferent healthy brown woman a few feet off, with the gap that plunged to the street between them. Tom thought it was romantic, it was like being high on two hilltops. But there was a shout from Harry, and they clambered back. Stanley's face was hard, really angry. The boy kept looking at him and wondered why he hated the woman so much, for by now he loved her.

They played their little games with the blanket, trying to trap shade to work under; but again it was not until nearly four that they could work seriously, and they were exhausted, all three of them. They were grumbling about the weather, by now. Stanley was in a thoroughly bad humour. When they made their routine trip to see the woman before they packed up for the day, she was apparently asleep, face down, her back all naked save for the scarlet triangle on her buttocks. 'I've got a good mind to report her to the police,' said Stanley, and Harry said: 'What's eating you? What harm's she doing?'

'I tell you, if she was my wife!'

'But she isn't, is she?' Tom knew that Harry, like himself, was uneasy at Stanley's reaction. He was normally a sharp young man, quick at his work, making a lot of jokes, good company.

'Perhaps it will be cooler tomorrow,' said Harry.

But it wasn't, it was hotter, if anything, and the weather forecast said the good weather would last. As soon as they were on the roof, Harry went over to see if the woman were there, and Tom knew it was to prevent Stanley going, to put off his bad humour. Harry had grown-up children, a boy the same age as Tom, and the youth trusted and looked up to him.

Harry came back and said: 'She's not there.'

'I bet her old man has put his foot down,' said Stanley, and Harry and Tom caught each other's eyes and smiled behind the young married man's back.

Harry suggested they should get permission to work in the basement, and they did, that day. But before packing up Stanley said: 'Let's have a breath of fresh air.' Again Harry and Tom smiled at each other as they followed Stanley up to the roof, Tom in the devout conviction that he was there to protect the woman from Stanley. It was about five-thirty, and a calm, full sunlight lay over the roofs. The great crane still swung its black arm from Oxford Street to above their heads. She was not there. Then there was a flutter of white from behind a parapet, and she stood up, in a belted, white dressing gown. She had been there all day, probably, but on a different patch of roof, to hide from them. Stanley did not whistle, he said nothing, but watched the woman bend to collect papers, books, cigarettes, then fold the blanket over her arm. Tom was thinking: If they weren't here, I'd go over and say . . . what? But he knew from his nightly dreams of her that she was kind and friendly. Perhaps she would ask him down to her flat? Perhaps . . . He stood watching her disappear down the skylight. As she went, Stanley let out a shrill derisive yell; she started, and it seemed as if she nearly fell. She clutched to save herself, they could hear things falling. She looked straight at them, angry. Harry said, facetiously: 'Better be careful on those slippery ladders, love.' Tom knew he said it to save her from Stanley, but she could not know it. She vanished, frowning. Tom was full of secret delight, because he knew her anger was for the others, not for him.

'Roll on some rain,' said Stanley, bitter, looking at the blue evening sky.

Next day was cloudless, and they decided to finish the work in the basement. They felt excluded, shut in the grey cement basement fitting pipes, from the holiday atmosphere of London in a heat wave. At lunchtime they came up for some air, but while the married couples, and the men in shirt-sleeves or vests, were there, she was not there, either on her usual patch of roof or where she had been yesterday. They all, even Harry, clambered about, between chimney pots, over parapets, the hot leads stinging their fingers. There was not a sign of her. They took off their shirts and vests and exposed their chests, feeling their feet sweaty and hot. They did not mention the woman. But Tom felt alone again. Last night she had asked him into her flat; it was big and had fitted white carpets and a bed with a padded white leather head top. She wore a black filmy négligé and her kindness to Tom thickened his throat as he remembered it. He felt she had betrayed him by not being there.

And again after work they climbed up, but still there was nothing to be seen of her. Stanley kept repeating that if it was as hot as this tomorrow he wasn't going to work and that's all there was to it. But they were all there next day. By ten the temperature was in the middle seventies, and it was eighty long before noon. Harry went to the foreman to say it was impossible to work on the leads in that heat; but the foreman said there was nothing else he could put them on, and they'd have to. At midday they stood, silent, watching the skylight on her roof open, and then she slowly emerged in her white gown, holding a bundle of blanket. She looked at them, gravely, then went to the part of the roof where she was hidden from them. Tom was pleased. He felt she was more his when the other men couldn't see her. They had taken off their shirts and vests, but now they put them back again, for they felt the sun bruising their flesh. 'She must have the hide of a rhino,' said

Stanley, tugging at guttering and swearing. They stopped work, and sat in the shade, moving around behind chimney stacks. A woman came to water a yellow window box just opposite them. She was middle-aged, wearing a flowered summer dress. Stanley said to her: 'We need a drink more than them.' She smiled and said: 'Better drop down to the pub quick, it'll be closing in a minute.' They exchanged pleasantries, and she left them with a smile and a wave.

'Not like Lady Godiva,' said Stanley. 'She can give us a bit of a chat and a smile.'

'You didn't whistle at *her*,' said Tom, reproving.

'Listen to him,' said Stanley, 'you didn't whistle, then?'

But the boy felt as if he hadn't whistled, as if only Harry and Stanley had. He was making plans, when it was time to knock off work, to get left behind and somehow make his way over to the woman. The weather report said the hot spell was due to break, so he had to move quickly. But there was no chance of being left. The other two decided to knock off work at four, because they were exhausted. As they went down, Tom quickly climbed a parapet and hoisted himself higher by pulling his weight up a chimney. He caught a glimpse of her lying on her back, her knees up, eyes closed, a brown woman lolling in the sun. He slipped and clattered down, as Stanley looked for information: 'She's gone down,' he said. He felt as if he had protected her from Stanley, and that she must be grateful to him. He could feel the bond between the woman and himself.

Next day, they stood around on the landing below the roof, reluctant to climb up into the heat. The woman who had lent Harry the blanket came out and offered them a cup of tea. They accepted gratefully, and sat around Mrs Pritchett's kitchen an hour or so, chatting. She was married to an airline pilot. A smart blonde, of about thirty, she had an eye for the handsome sharp-faced Stanley; and the two teased each other while Harry sat in a corner, watching, indulgent, though his expression reminded Stanley that he was married. And young Tom felt envious of Stanley's ease in badinage; felt, too, that Stanley's getting off with Mrs Pritchett left his romance with the woman on the roof safe and intact.

'I thought they said the heat wave'd break,' said Stanley, sullen, as the time approached when they really would have to climb up into the sunlight.

'You don't like it, then?' asked Mrs Pritchett.

'All right for some,' said Stanley. 'Nothing to do but lie about as if it was a beach up there. Do you ever go up?'

'Went up once,' said Mrs Pritchett. 'But it's a dirty place up there, and it's too hot.'

'Quite right too,' said Stanley.

Then they went up, leaving the cool neat little flat and the friendly Mrs Pritchett.

As soon as they were up they saw her. The three men looked at her, resentful at her ease in this punishing sun. Then Harry said, because of the expression on Stanley's face: 'Come on, we've got to pretend to work, at least.'

They had to wrench another length of guttering that ran beside a parapet out of its bed, so that they could replace it. Stanley took it in his two hands, tugged, swore, stood up. 'Fuck it,' he said, and sat down under a chimney. He lit a cigarette. 'Fuck them,' he said. 'What do they think we are, lizards? I've got blisters all over my hands.' Then he jumped up and climbed over the roofs and stood with his back to them. He put his fingers either side of his mouth and let out a shrill whistle. Tom and Harry squatted, not looking at each other, watching him. They could just see the woman's head, the beginnings of her brown shoulders. Stanley whistled again. Then he began stamping with his feet, and whistled and yelled and screamed at the woman, his face getting scarlet. He seemed quite mad, as he stamped and whistled, while the woman did not move, she did not move a muscle.

'Barmy,' said Tom.

'Yes,' said Harry, disapproving.

Suddenly the older man came to a decision. It was, Tom knew, to save some sort of scandal or real trouble over the woman. Harry stood up and began packing tools into a length of oily cloth. 'Stanley,' he said, commanding. At first Stanley took no notice, but Harry said: 'Stanley, we're packing it in, I'll tell Matthew.'

Stanley came back, cheeks mottled, eyes glaring.

'Can't go on like this,' said Harry. 'It'll break in a day or so. I'm going to tell Matthew we've got sunstroke, and if he doesn't like it, it's too bad.' Even Harry sounded aggrieved, Tom noted. The small, competent man, the family man with his grey hair, who was never at a loss, sounded really off balance. 'Come on,' he said, angry. He fitted himself into the open square in the roof, and went down, watching his feet on the ladder. Then Stanley went, with not a glance at the woman. Then Tom who, his throat beating with excitement, silently promised her in a backward glance: Wait for me, wait, I'm coming.

On the pavement Stanley said: 'I'm going home.' He looked white now, so perhaps he really did have sunstroke. Harry went off to find the foreman who was at work on the plumbing of some flats down the street. Tom slipped back, not into the building they had been working on, but the building on whose roof the woman lay. He went straight up, no one stopping him. The skylight stood open, with an iron ladder leading up. He emerged on to the roof a couple of yards from her. She sat up, pushing back her black hair with both hands. The scarf across her breasts bound them tight, and brown flesh bulged around it. Her legs were brown and smooth. She stared at him in silence. The boy stood grinning, foolish, claiming the tenderness he expected from her.

'What do you want?' she asked.

'I . . . I came to . . . make your acquaintance,' he stammered, grinning, pleading with her.

They looked at each other, the slight, scarlet-faced excited boy, and the serious, nearly naked woman. Then, without a word, she lay down on her brown blanket, ignoring him.

'You like the sun, do you?' he enquired of her glistening back.

Not a word. He felt panic, thinking of how she had held him in her arms, stroked his hair, brought him where he sat, lordly, in her bed, a glass of some exhilarating liquor he had never tasted in life. He felt that if he knelt down, stroked her shoulders, her hair, she would turn and clasp him in her arms.

He said: 'The sun's all right for you, isn't it?'

She raised her head, set her chin on two small fists. 'Go away,' she said. He did not move. 'Listen,' she said, in a slow reasonable voice, where anger was kept in check, though with difficulty; looking at him, her face weary with anger: 'If you get a kick out of seeing women in bikinis, why don't you take a sixpenny bus ride to the Lido? You'd see dozens of them, without all this mountaineering.'

She hadn't understood him. He felt her unfairness pale him. He stammered: 'But I like you, I've been watching you and . . .'

'Thanks,' she said, and dropped her face again, turned away from him.

She lay there. He stood there. She said nothing. She had simply shut him out. He stood, saying nothing at all, for some minutes. He thought:

she'll have to say something if I stay. But the minutes went past, with no sign of them in her, except in the tension of her back, her thighs, her arms – the tension of waiting for him to go.

He looked up at the sky, where the sun seemed to spin in heat; and over the roofs where he and his mates had been earlier. He could see the heat quavering where they had worked. 'And they expect us to work in these conditions!' he thought, filled with righteous indignation. The woman hadn't moved. A bit of hot wind blew her black hair softly, it shone, and was iridescent. He remembered how he had stroked it last night.

Resentment of her at last moved him off and away down the ladder, through the building, into the street. He got drunk then, in hatred of her.

Next day when he woke the sky was grey. He looked at the wet grey and thought, vicious: 'Well, that's fixed you, hasn't it now? That's fixed you good and proper.'

The three men were at work early on the cool leads, surrounded by damp drizzling roofs where no one came to sun themselves, black roofs, slimy with rain. Because it was cool now, they would finish the job that day, if they hurried.

PART II

The Grass is Singing

1

MURDER MYSTERY

By Special Correspondent

Mary Turner, wife of Richard Turner, a farmer at Ngesi, was found murdered on the front veranda of their homestead yesterday morning. The houseboy, who has been arrested, has confessed to the crime. No motive has been discovered. It is thought he was in search of valuables.

The newspaper did not say much. People all over the country must have glanced at the paragraph with its sensational heading and felt a little spurt of anger mingled with what was almost satisfaction, as if some belief had been confirmed, as if something had happened which could only have been expected. When natives steal, murder, or rape, that is the feeling white people have.

And then they turned the page to something else.

But the people in the 'district' who knew the Turners, either by sight or from gossiping about them for so many years, did not turn the page so quickly. Many must have snipped out the paragraph, put it among old letters or betweeen the pages of a book, keeping it perhaps as an omen or a warning, glancing at the yellowing piece of paper with closed, secretive faces. For they did not discuss the murder; that was the most extraordinary thing about it. It was as if they had a sixth sense which told them everything there was to be known, although the three people in a position to explain the facts said nothing. The murder was simply not discussed. 'A bad business,' someone would remark; and the faces of the people round about would put on that reserved and guarded look. 'A very bad business,' came the reply – and that was the end of it. There was, it seemed, a tacit agreement that the Turner case should not be given undue publicity by gossip. Yet it was a farming district, where those isolated white families met only very occasionally, hungry for contact with their own kind, to talk and discuss and pull to pieces, all speaking at once, making the most of an hour or so's companionship before returning to their farms, where they saw only their own faces and the faces of their black servants for weeks on end. Normally that murder would have been discussed for months; people would have been positively grateful for something to talk about.

To an outsider it would seem perhaps as if the energetic Charlie Slatter had travelled from farm to farm over the district telling people to keep quiet; but that was something that would never have occurred to him. The steps he took (and he made not one mistake) were taken apparently instinctively and without conscious planning. The most interesting thing about the whole affair was this silent, unconscious agreement. Everyone behaved like a flock of birds who communicate – or so it seems – by means of a kind of telepathy.

Long before the murder marked them out, people spoke of the Turners in the hard, careless voices reserved for misfits, outlaws, and the self-exiled. The Turners were disliked, though few of their neighbours had ever met them, or even seen them in the distance. Yet what was there to dislike? They simply 'kept themselves to themselves'; that was all. They were never seen at district dances, or fêtes, or gymkhanas. They must have had something to be ashamed of; that was the feeling. It was not right to seclude themselves like that; it was a slap in the face of everyone else; what had they got to be so stuck-up about? What, indeed! Living the way they did! That little box of a house – it was forgivable as a temporary dwelling, but not to live in permanently. Why, some natives (though not many, thank heavens) had houses as good; and it would give them a bad impression to see white people living in such a way.

And then it was that someone used the phrase 'poor whites'. It caused disquiet. There was no great money-cleavage in those days (that was before the era of the tobacco barons), but there was certainly a race division. The small community of Afrikaners had their own lives, and the Britishers ignored them. 'Poor whites' were Afrikaners, never British. But the person who said the Turners were poor whites stuck to it defiantly. What was the difference? What was a poor white? It was the way one lived, a question of standards. All the Turners needed were a drove of children to make them poor whites.

Though the arguments were unanswerable, people would still not think of them as poor whites. To do that would be letting the side down. The Turners were British, after all.

Thus the district handled the Turners, in accordance with that *esprit de corps* which is the first rule of South African society, but which the Turners themselves ignored. They apparently did not recognize the need for *esprit de corps*; that, really, was why they were hated.

The more one thinks about it, the more extraordinary the case becomes. Not the murder itself; but the way people felt about it, the way they pitied Dick Turner with a fine fierce indignation against Mary, as if she were something unpleasant and unclean, and it served her right to get murdered. But they did not ask questions.

For instance, they must have wondered who that 'Special Correspondent' was. Someone in the district sent in the news, for the paragraph was not in newspaper language. But who? Marston, the assistant, left the district immediately after the murder. Denham, the policeman, might have written to the paper in a personal capacity, but it was not likely. There remained Charlie Slatter, who knew more about the Turners than anyone else, and was there on the day of the murder. One could say that he practically controlled the handling of the case, even taking precedence over the Sergeant himself. And people felt that to be quite right and proper. Whom should it concern, if not the white farmers, that a silly woman got herself murdered by a native for reasons people might think about, but never, never mentioned? It was their livelihood, their wives and families, their way of living, at stake.

But to the outsider it is strange that Slatter should have been allowed to take charge of the affair, to arrange that everything should pass over without more than a ripple of comment.

For there could have been no planning: there simply wasn't time. Why, for instance, when Dick Turner's farm boys came to him with the news, did he sit down to write a note to the Sergeant at the police camp? He did not use the telephone.

Everyone who has lived in the country knows what a branch telephone is like. You lift the receiver after you have turned the handle the required number of times, and then, click, click, click, you can hear the receivers coming off all over the district, and soft noises like breathing, a whisper, a subdued cough.

Slatter lived five miles from the Turners. The farm boys came to him first, when they discovered the body. And though it was an urgent matter, he ignored the telephone, but sent a personal letter by a native bearer on a bicycle to Denham at the police camp, twelve miles away. The Sergeant sent out half a dozen native policemen at once, to the Turners' farm, to see what they could find. He drove first to see Slatter, because the way that letter was worded roused his curiosity. That was why he arrived late on the scene of the murder. The native policemen did not have to search far for the murderer. After walking through the house, looking briefly at the body, and dispersing down the front of the little hill the house stood on, they saw Moses himself rise out of a tangled ant-heap in front of them. He walked up to them and said (or words to this effect): 'Here I am.' They snapped the handcuffs on him, and went back to the house to wait for the police cars to come. There they saw Dick Turner come out of the bush by the house with two whining dogs at his heels. He was off his head, talking crazily to himself, wandering in and out of the bush with his hands full of leaves and earth. They let him be, while keeping an eye on him, for he was a white man, though mad, and black men, even when policemen, do not lay hands on white flesh.

People did ask, cursorily, why the murderer had given himself up. There was not much chance of escape, but he did have a sporting chance. He could have run to the hills and hidden for a while. Or he could have slipped over the border to Portuguese territory. Then the District Native Commissioner, at a sundowner party, said that it was perfectly understandable. If one knew anything about the history of the country, or had read any of the memoirs or letters of the old missionaries and explorers, one would have come across accounts of the society Lobengula ruled. The laws were strict: everyone knew what they could or could not do. If someone did an unforgivable thing, like touching one of the King's women, he would submit fatalistically to punishment, which was likely to be impalement over an ant-heap on a stake, or something equally unpleasant. 'I have done wrong, and I know it,' he might say, 'therefore let me be punished.' Well, it was the tradition to face punishment, and really there was something rather fine about it. Remarks like these are forgiven from native commissioners, who have to study languages, customs, and so on; although it is not done to say things natives do are 'fine'. (Yet the fashion is changing: it is permissible to glorify the old ways sometimes, providing one says how depraved the natives have become since.)

So that aspect of the affair was dropped, yet it is not the least interesting, for Moses might not have been a Matabele at all. He was in Mashonaland; though of course natives do wander all over Africa. He might have come from anywhere: Portuguese territory, Nyasaland, the Union of South Africa. And it is a long time since the days of the great king Lobengula. But then native commissioners tend to think in terms of the past.

Well, having sent the letter to the police camp, Charlie Slatter went to the Turners' place, driving at a great speed over the bad farm roads in his fat American car.

Who *was* Charlie Slatter? It was he who, from the beginning of the tragedy to its end, personified Society for the Turners. He touches the story at half a dozen points; without him things would not have happened quite as they did, though sooner or later, in one way or another, the Turners were bound to come to grief.

Slatter had been a grocer's assistant in London. He was fond of telling his children that if it had not been for his energy and enterprise they would be running round the slums in rags. He was still a proper cockney, even after twenty years in Africa. He came with one idea: to make money. He made it. He made plenty. He was a crude, brutal, ruthless, yet kindhearted man, in his own way, and according to his own impulses, who could not help making money. He farmed as if he were turning the handle of a machine which would produce pound notes at the other end. He was hard with his wife, making her bear unnecessary hardships at the beginning; he was hard with his children, until he made money, when they got everything they wanted; and above all he was hard with his farm labourers. They, the geese that laid the golden eggs, were still in that state where they did not know there were other ways of living besides producing gold for other people. They know better now, or are beginning to. But Slatter believed in farming with the sjambok. It hung over his front door, like a motto on a wall: 'You shall not mind killing if it is necessary.' He had once killed a native in a fit of temper. He was fined thirty pounds. Since then he had kept his temper. But sjamboks are all very well for the Slatters; not so good for people less sure of themselves. It was he who had told Dick Turner, long ago, when Dick first started farming, that one should buy a sjambok before a plough or a harrow, and that sjambok did not do the Turners any good, as we shall see.

Slatter was a shortish, broad, powerful man, with heavy shoulders and thick arms. His face was broad and bristled; shrewd, watchful, and a little cunning. He had a crop of fair hair that made him look like a convict; but he did not care for appearances. His small blue eyes were hardly visible, because of the way he screwed them up, after years and years of South African sunshine.

Bent over the steering wheel, almost hugging it in his determination to get to the Turners quickly, his eyes were little blue chinks in a set face. He was wondering why Marston, the assistant, who was after all his employee, had not come to him about the murder, or at least sent a note. Where was he? The hut he lived in was only a couple of hundred yards from the house itself. Perhaps he had got cold feet and run away? Anything was possible, thought Charlie, from this particular type of young Englishman. He had a rooted contempt for soft-faced, soft-voiced Englishmen, combined with a fascination for their manner and breeding. His own sons, now grown up, were gentlemen. He had spent plenty of money to make them so; but he despised them for it. At the same time he was proud of them. This conflict showed itself in its attitude towards Marston: half hard and indifferent, half subtly deferential. At the moment he felt nothing but irritation.

Half way he felt the car rock, and, swearing, pulled it up. It was a puncture: no, two punctures. The red mud of the road held fragments of broken glass. His irritation expressed itself in the half-conscious thought, 'Just like Turner to have glass on his roads!' But Turner was now necessarily an object of passionate, protective pity, and the irritation was focused on Marston, the assistant who, Slatter felt, should somehow have prevented this murder. What was he being paid for? What had he been engaged for? But Slatter was a fair man in his own way, and where his own race was concerned. He restrained himself, and got down to mending one puncture and changing a tyre, working in the heavy red slush of the roads. This took him three-quarters of an hour, and by the time he was finished, and had picked the pieces of green glass from the mud and thrown them into the bush, the sweat was soaking his face and hair.

When he reached the house at last, he saw, as he approached through the bush, six glittering bicycles leaning against the walls. And in front of the house, under the trees, stood six native policemen, and among them the native Moses, his hands linked in front of him. The sun glinted on the handcuffs, on the bicycles, on the masses of heavy wet leaves. It was a wet, sultry morning. The sky was a tumult of discoloured clouds: it looked full of billowing dirty washing. Puddles on the pale soil held a sheen of sky.

Charlie walked up to the policemen, who saluted him. They were in fezes, and their rather fancy-dress uniform. This last thought did not occur to Charlie, who liked his natives either one way or the other: properly dressed according to their station, or in loincloths. He could not bear the half-civilized native. The policemen, picked for their physique, were a fine body of men, but they were put in the shade by Moses, who was a great powerful man, black as polished linoleum, and dressed in a singlet and shorts, which were damp and muddy. Charlie stood directly in front of the murderer and looked into his face. The man stared back, expressionless, indifferent. His own face was curious: it showed a kind of triumph, a guarded vindictiveness, and fear. Why fear? Of Moses, who was as good as hanged already? But he was uneasy, troubled. Then he seemed to shake himself into self-command, and turned and saw Dick Turner, standing a few paces away, covered with mud.

'Turner!' he said, peremptorily. He stopped, looking into the man's face. Dick appeared not to know him. Charlie took him by the arm and drew him towards his own car. He did not know he was incurably mad then; otherwise he might have been even more angry than he was. Having put Dick into the back seat of his car, he went into the house. In the front room stood Marston, his hands in his pockets, in a pose that seemed negligently calm. But his face was pale and strained.

'Where were you?' asked Charlie at once, accusingly.

'Normally Mr Turner wakes me,' said the youth calmly. 'This morning I slept late. When I came into the house I found Mrs Turner on the veranda. Then the policemen came. I was expecting you.' But he was afraid: it was the fear of death that sounded in his voice, not the fear that was controlling Charlie's actions: he had not been long enough in the country to understand Charlie's special fear.

Charlie grunted: he never spoke unless necessary. He looked long and curiously at Marston, as if trying to make out why it was the farm natives had not called a man who lay asleep a few yards off, but had instinctively sent for himself. But it was not with dislike or contempt he looked at Marston now; it was more the look a man gives a prospective partner who has yet to prove himself.

He turned and went into the bedroom. Mary Turner was a stiff shape under a soiled white sheet. At one end of the sheet protruded a mass of pale strawish hair, and at the other a crinkled yellow foot. Now a curious thing happened. The hate and contempt that one would have expected to show on his face when he looked at the murderer, twisted his features now, as he stared at Mary. His brows knotted, and for a few seconds his lips curled back over his teeth in a vicious grimace. He had his back to Marston, who would have been astonished to see him. Then, with a hard, angry movement, Charlie turned and left the room, driving the young man before him.

Marston said: 'She was lying on the veranda. I lifted her on the bed.' He shuddered at the memory of the touch of the cold body. 'I thought she shouldn't be left lying there.' He hesitated and added, the muscles of his face contracting whitely: 'The dogs were licking at her.'

Charlie nodded, with a keen glance at him. He seemed indifferent as to where she might be lying. At the same time he approved the self-control of the assistant who had performed the unpleasant task.

'There was blood everywhere. I cleaned it up . . . I thought afterwards I should have left it for the police.'

'It makes no odds,' said Charlie absently. He sat down on one of the rough wood chairs in the front room, and remained in thought, whistling softly through his front teeth. Marston stood by the window, looking for the arrival of the police car. From time to time Charlie looked round the room alertly, flicking his tongue over his lips. Then he lapsed back into his soft whistling. It got on the young man's nerves.

At last, cautiously, almost warningly, Charlie said: 'What do *you* know of this?'

Marston noted the emphasized *you*, and wondered what Slatter knew. He was well in control of himself, but as taut as wire. He said, 'I don't know. Nothing really. It is all so difficult . . .' He hesitated, looking appealing at Charlie.

That look of almost soft appeal irritated Charlie, coming from a man, but it pleased him too: he was pleased the youth deferred to him. He knew the type so well. So many of them came from England to learn farming. They were usually ex-public school, very English, but extremely adaptable. From Charlie's point of view, the adaptability redeemed them. It was strange to see how quickly they accustomed themselves. At first they were diffident, though proud and withdrawn; cautiously learning the new ways, with a fine sensitiveness, an alert self-consciousness.

When old settlers say 'One has to understand the country,' what they mean is, 'You have to get used to our ideas about the native.' They are saying, in effect, 'Learn our ideas, or otherwise get out: we don't want you.' Most of these young men were brought up with vague ideas about equality. They were shocked, for the first week or so, by the way natives were treated. They were revolted a hundred times a day by the casual way they were spoken of, as if they were so many cattle; or by a blow, or a look. They had been prepared to treat them as human beings. But they could not stand out against the society they were joining. It did not take them long to change. It was hard, of course, becoming as bad oneself. But it was not very long that they thought of it as 'bad'. And anyway, what had one's ideas amounted to? Abstract ideas about decency and goodwill, that was all: merely abstract ideas. When it came to the point, one never had contact with natives, except in the master-servant relationship. One never knew them in their own lives, as human beings. A few months, and these sensitive, decent young men had coarsened to suit the hard, arid, sun-drenched country they had come to; they had grown a new manner to match their thickened sunburnt limbs and toughened bodies.

If Tony Marston had been even a few more months in the country it would have been easy. That was Charlie's feeling. That was why he looked at the young man with a speculative frowning look, not condemning him, only wary and on the alert.

He said: 'What do you mean, it is all so difficult?'

Tony Marston appeared uncomfortable, as if he did not know his own mind. And for that matter he did not: the weeks in the Turners' household with its atmosphere of tragedy had not helped him to get his mind clear. The two standards – the one he had brought with him and the one he was adopting – conflicted still. And there was a roughness, a warning note, in Charlie's voice, that left him wondering. What was he being warned against? He was intelligent enough to know he was being warned. In this he was unlike Charlie, who was acting by instinct and did not know his voice was a threat. It was all so unusual. Where were the police? What right had Charlie, who was a neighbour, to be fetched before himself, who was practically a member of the household? Why was Charlie quietly taking command?

His ideas of right were upset. He was confused, but he had his own ideas about the murder, which could not be stated straight out, like that, in black and white. When he came to think of it, the murder was logical enough; looking back over the last few days he could see that something like this was bound to happen, he could almost say he had been expecting it, some kind of violence or ugliness. Anger, violence, death, seemed natural to this vast, harsh country . . . he had done a lot of thinking since he had strolled casually into the house that morning, wondering why everyone was so late, to find Mary Turner lying murdered on the veranda, and the police boys outside, guarding the houseboy; and Dick Turner muttering and stumbling through the puddles, mad, but apparently harmless. Things he had not understood, he understood now, and he was ready to talk about them. But he was in the dark as to Charlie's attitude. There was something here he could not get hold of.

'It's like this,' he said, 'when I first arrived I didn't know much about the country.'

Charlie said, with a good-humoured but brutal irony, 'Thanks for the information.' And then, 'Have you any idea why this nigger murdered Mrs Turner?'

'Well, I have a sort of idea, yes.'

'We had better leave it to the Sergeant, when he comes then.'

It was a snub; he had been shut up. Tony held his tongue, angry but bewildered.

When the Sergeant came, he went over to look at the murderer, glanced at Dick through the window of Slatter's car, and then came into the house.

'I went to your place, Slatter,' he said, nodding at Tony, giving him a keen look. Then he went into the bedroom. And his reactions were as Charlie's had been; vindictiveness towards the murderer, emotional pity for Dick, and for Mary, a bitter contemptuous anger: Sergeant Denham had been in the country for a number of years. This time Tony saw the expression on the face, and it gave him a shock. The faces of the two men as they stood over the body, gazing down at it, made him feel uneasy, even afraid. He himself felt a little disgust, but not much; it was mainly pity that agitated him, knowing what he knew. It was the disgust that he would feel for any social irregularity, no more than the distaste that comes from failure of the imagination. This profound instinctive horror and fear astonished him.

The three of them went silently into the living-room.

Charlie Slatter and Sergeant Denham stood side by side like two judges, as if they had purposely taken up this attitude. Opposite them was Tony. He stood his ground, but he felt an absurd guiltiness taking hold of him, simply because of their pose, standing like that, looking at him with subtle reserved faces that he could not read.

'Bad business,' said Sergeant Denham briefly.

No one answered. He snapped open a notebook, adjusted elastic over a page and poised a pencil.

'A few questions, if you don't mind,' he said. Tony nodded.

'How long have you been here?'

'About three weeks.'

'Living in this house?'

'No, in a hut down the path.'

'You were going to run this place while they were away?'

'Yes, for six months.'

'And then?'

'And then I intended to go on a tobacco farm.'

'When did you know about this business?'

'They didn't call me. I woke and found Mrs Turner.'

Tony's voice showed he was now on the defensive. He felt wounded, even insulted that he had not been called: above all, that these two men seemed to think it right and natural that he should be by-passed in this fashion, as if his newness to the country unfitted him for any kind of responsibility. And he resented the way he was being questioned. They had no right to do it. He was beginning to simmer with rage, although he knew quite well that they themselves were quite unconscious of the patronage implicit in their manner, and that it would be better for him to try and understand the real meaning of this scene, rather than to stand on his dignity.

'You had your meals with the Turners?'

'Yes.'

'Apart from that, were you ever here – socially, so to speak?'

'No, hardly at all. I have been busy learning the job.'

'Get on well with Turner?'

'Yes, I think so. I mean, he was not easy to know. He was absorbed in his work. And he was obviously very unhappy at leaving the place.'

'Yes, poor devil, he had a hard time of it.' The voice was suddenly tender, almost maudlin, with pity, although the Sergeant snapped out the words, and then shut his mouth tight, as if to present a brave face to the world. Tony was disconcerted: the unexpectedness of these men's responses was taking him right out of his depth. He was feeling nothing that they were feeling: he was an outsider in this tragedy, although both the Sergeant and Charlie Slatter seemed to feel personally implicated, for they had unconsciously assumed poses of weary dignity, appearing

bowed down with unutterable burdens, because of poor Dick Turner
and his sufferings.

Yet it was Charlie who had literally turned Dick off his farm; and in
previous interviews, at which Tony had been present, he had shown
none of this sentimental pity.

There was a long pause. The Sergeant shut his notebook. But he had
not yet finished. He was regarding Tony cautiously, wondering how to
frame the next question. Or that was how it appeared to Tony, who
could see that here was the moment that was the crux of the whole
affair. Charlie's face: wary, a little cunning, a little afraid, proclaimed
it.

'See anything out of the ordinary while you were here?' asked the
Sergeant, apparently casual.

'Yes, I did,' blurted Tony, suddenly determined not to be bullied.
For he knew he was being bullied, though he was cut off from them
both by a gulf in experience and belief. They looked up at him,
frowning; glanced at each other swiftly – then away, as if afraid to
acknowledge conspiracy.

'What did you see? I hope you realize the – unpleasantness – of this
case?' The last question was a grudging appeal.

'Any murder is surely unpleasant,' remarked Tony dryly.

'When you have been in the country long enough, you will
understand that we don't like niggers murdering white women.'

The phrase 'When you have been in the country', stuck in Tony's
gullet. He had heard it too often, and it had come to jar on him. At the
same time it made him feel angry. Also callow. He would have liked to
blurt out the truth in one overwhelming, incontrovertible statement;
but the truth was not like that. It never was. The fact he knew, or
guessed, about Mary, the fact these two men were conspiring to ignore,
could be stated easily enough. But the important thing, the thing that
really mattered, so it seemed to him, was to understand the background, the circumstances, the characters of Dick and Mary, the
pattern of their lives. And it was not so easy to do. He had arrived at
the truth circuitously: circuitously it would have to be explained. And
his chief emotion, which was an impersonal pity for Mary and Dick
and the native, a pity that was also rage against circumstances, made
it difficult for him to know where to begin.

'Look,' he said, 'I'll tell you what I know from the beginning, only it
will take some time, I am afraid . . .'

'You mean you know why Mrs Turner was murdered?' The question was a quick, shrewd parry.

'No, not just like that. Only I can form a theory.' The choice of words was most unfortunate.

'We don't want theories. We want facts. And in any case, you should remember Dick Turner. This is all most unpleasant for him. You should remember him, poor devil.'

Here it was again: the utterly illogical appeal, which to these two men was clearly not illogical at all. The whole thing was preposterous! Tony began to lose his temper.

'Do you or do you not want to hear what I have to say?' he asked, irritably.

'Go ahead. Only remember, I don't want to hear your fancies. I want to hear facts. Have you ever seen anything *definite* which would throw light on this murder. For instance, have you seen this boy attempting to get at her jewellery, or something like that. Anything that is definite. Not something in the air.'

Tony laughed. The two men looked at him sharply.

'You know as well as I do this case is not something that can be explained straight off like that. You know that. It's not something that can be said in black and white, straight off.'

It was pure deadlock; no one spoke. As if Sergeant Denham had not heard those last words, a heavy frown on his face, he said at last: 'For instance, how did Mrs Turner treat this boy? Did she treat her boys well?'

The angry Tony, fumbling for a foothold in this welter of emotion and half-understood loyalties, clutched at this for a beginning.

'Yes, she treated him badly, I thought. Though on the other hand . . .'

'Nagged at him, eh? Oh well, women are pretty bad that way, in this country, very often. Aren't they, Slatter?' The voice was easy, intimate, informal. 'My old woman drives me mad – it's something about this country. They have no idea how to deal with niggers.'

'Needs a man to deal with niggers,' said Charlie. 'Niggers don't understand women giving them orders. They keep their own women in their right place.' He laughed. The Sergeant laughed. They turned towards each other, even including Tony, in an unmistakable relief. The tension had broken; the danger was over: once again, he had been bypassed, and the interview, it seemed, was over. He could hardly believe it.

'But look here,' he said. Then he stopped. Both men turned to look at him, a steady, grave, irritated look on their faces. And the warning was unmistakable! It was the warning that might have been given to a greenhorn who was going to let *himself* down by saying too much. This realization was too much for Tony. He gave in; he washed his hands of it. He watched the other two in utter astonishment: they were together in mood and emotion, standing there in perfect understanding; the understanding was unrealized by themselves, the sympathy un-acknowledged; their concerted handling of this affair had been instinctive: they were completely unaware of there being anything extraordinary, even anything illegal. And was there anything illegal, after all? This was a casual talk, on the face of it, nothing formal about it now that the notebook was shut – and it had been shut ever since they had reached the crisis of the scene.

Charlie said, turning towards the sergeant, 'Better get her out of here. It is too hot to wait.'

'Yes,' said the policeman, moving to give orders accordingly.

And that brutally matter-of-fact remark, Tony realized afterwards, was the only time poor Mary Turner was referred to directly. But why should she be? – except that this was really a friendly talk between the farmer who had been her next neighbour, the policeman who had been in her house on his rounds as a guest, and the assistant who had lived there for some weeks. It wasn't a formal occasion, this: Tony clung to the thought. There was a court case to come yet, which would be properly conducted.

'The case will be a matter of form, of course,' said the Sergeant, as if thinking aloud, with a look at Tony. He was standing by the police car, watching the native policemen lift the body of Mary Turner, which was wrapped in a blanket, into the back seat. She was stiff; a rigid outstretched arm knocked horribly against the narrow door; it was difficult to get her in. At last it was done and the door shut. And then there was another problem: they could not put Moses the murderer into the same car with her; one could not put a black man close to a white woman, even though she were dead, and murdered by him. And there was only Charlie's car, and mad Dick Turner was in that, sitting staring in the back. There seemed to be a feeling that Moses, having committed a murder, deserved to be taken by car; but there was no help for it, he would have to walk, guarded by the policemen, wheeling their bicycles, to the camp.

All these arrangements completed, there was a pause.

They stood there beside the cars, in the moment of parting, looking at the red-brick house with its shimmering hot roof, and the thick encroaching bush, and the group of black men moving off under the trees on their long walk. Moses was quite impassive, allowing himself to be directed without any movement of his own. His face was blank. He seemed to be staring straight into the sun. Was he thinking he would not see it much longer? Impossible to say. Regret? Not a sign of it. Fear? It did not seem so. The three men looked at the murderer, thinking their own thoughts, speculative, frowning, but not as if he were important now. No, he was unimportant: he was the constant, the black man who will thieve, rape, murder, if given half a chance. Even for Tony he no longer mattered; and his knowledge of the native mind was too small to give him any basis for conjecture.

'And what about him?' asked Charlie, jerking his thumb at Dick Turner. He meant: where does he come in, as far as the court case is concerned?'

'He looks to me as if he won't be good for much,' said the Sergeant, who after all had plenty of experience of death, crime, and madness.

No, for them the important thing was Mary Turner, who had let the side down; but even she, since she was dead, was no longer a problem. The one fact that remained still to be dealt with was the necessity for preserving appearances. Sergeant Denham understood that: it was part of his job, though it would not appear in regulations, was rather implicit in the spirit of the country, the spirit in which he was soaked. Charlie Slatter understood it, none better. Still side by side, as if one impulse, one regret, one fear, moved them both, they stood together in that last moment before they left the place, giving their final silent warning to Tony, looking at him gravely.

And he was beginning to understand. He knew now, at least, that what had been fought out in the room they had just left was nothing to do with the murder as such. The murder, in itself, was nothing. The struggle that had been decided in a few brief words – or rather, in the silences between the words – had had nothing to do with the surface meaning of the scene. He would understand it all a good deal better in a few months, when he had 'become used to the country'. And then he would do his best to forget the knowledge, for to live with the colour bar in all its nuances and implications means closing one's mind to many things, if one intends to remain an accepted member of society. But, in the interval, there would be a few brief moments when he would see the thing clearly, and understand that it was 'white civilization' fighting to defend itself that had been implicit in the attitude of Charlie Slatter and the Sergeant, 'white civilization' which will never, never admit that a white person, and most particularly, a white woman, can have a human relationship, whether for good or for evil, with a black person. For once it admits that, it crashes, and nothing can save it. So, above all, it cannot afford failures, such as the Turners' failure.

For the sake of those few lucid moments, and his present half-confused knowledge, it can be said that Tony was the person present who had the greatest responsibility that day. For it would never have occurred to either Slatter or the Sergeant that they might be wrong: they were upheld, as in all their dealings with the black-white relationship, by a feeling of almost martyred responsibility. Yet Tony, too, wanted to be accepted by this new country. He would have to adapt himself, and if he did not conform, would be rejected: the issue was clear to him, he had heard the phrase 'getting used to our ideas' too often to have any illusions on the point. And, if he had acted according to his by now muddled ideas of right and wrong, his feeling that a monstrous injustice was being done, what difference would it make to the only participant in the tragedy who was neither dead nor mad? For Moses would be hanged in any case; he had committed a murder, that fact remained. Did he intend to go on fighting in the dark for the sake of a principle? And if so, which principle? If he had stepped forward then, as he nearly did, when Sergeant Denham climbed finally into the car, and had said: 'Look here, I am just not going to shut up about this,' what would have been gained? It is certain that the Sergeant would not have understood him. His face would have contracted, his brow gone dark with irritation, and, taking his foot off the clutch, he would have said, 'Shut up about what? Who has asked you to shut up?' And then, if Tony had stammered out something about responsibility, he would have looked significantly at Charlie and shrugged. Tony might have continued, ignoring the shrug and its implication of his wrongminded-ness: 'If you must blame somebody, then blame Mrs Turner. You can't have it both ways. Either the white people are responsible for their behaviour, or they are not. It takes two to make a murder – a murder of this kind. Though, one can't really blame her either. She can't help being what she is. I've lived here, I tell you, which neither of you has done, and the whole thing is so difficult it is impossible to say who is to blame.' And then the Sergeant would have said, 'You can say what you think right in court.' That is what he would have said, just as if the issue had not been decided – though ostensibly it had never been mentioned – less than ten minutes before. 'It's not a question of blame,' the Sergeant might have said. 'Has anyone said anything about blame? But you can't get away from the fact that this nigger has murdered her, can you?'

So Tony said nothing, and the police car went off through the trees. Charlie Slatter followed in his car with Dick Turner. Tony was left in the empty clearing, with an empty house.

He went inside, slowly, obsessed with the one clear image that remained to him after the events of the morning, and which seemed to him the key to the whole thing: the look on the Sergeant's and Slatter's faces when they looked down at the body; that almost hysterical look of hate and fear.

He sat down, his hand to his head, which ached badly; then got up again and fetched from a dusty shelf in the kitchen a medicine bottle marked 'Brandy'. He drank it off. He felt shaky in the knees and in the thighs. He was weak, too, with repugnance against this ugly little house which seemed to hold within its walls, even in its very brick and cement, the fear and horror of the murder. He felt suddenly as if he could not bear to stay in it, not for another moment.

He looked up at the bare crackling tin of the roof, that was warped with the sun, at the faded gimcrack furniture, at the dusty brick floors covered with ragged animal skins, and wondered how those two, Mary and Dick Turner, could have borne to live in such a place, year in and year out, for so long. Why even the little thatched hut where he lived at the back was better than this! Why did they go on without even so much as putting in ceilings? It was enough to drive anyone mad, the heat in this place.

And then, feeling a little muddle-headed (the heat made the brandy take effect at once), he wondered how all this had begun, where the tragedy had started. For he clung obstinately to the belief, in spite of Slatter and the Sergeant, that the causes of the murder must be looked for a long way back, and that it was they which were important. What sort of woman had Mary Turner been, before she came to this farm and had been driven slowly off balance by heat and loneliness and poverty? And Dick Turner himself – what had he been? And the native – but here his thoughts were stopped by lack of knowledge. He could not even begin to imagine the mind of a native.

Passing his hand over his forehead, he tried desperately, and for the last time, to achieve some sort of a vision that would lift the murder above the confusions and complexities of the morning, and make of it, perhaps, a symbol, or a warning. But he failed. It was too hot. He was still exasperated by the attitude of the two men. His head was reeling. It must be over a hundred in this room, he thought angrily, getting up from his chair, and finding that his legs were unsteady. And he had drunk, at the most, two tablespoons of brandy! This damned country, he thought, convulsed with anger. Why should this happen to me, getting involved with a damned twisted affair like this, when I have only just come; and I really can't be expected to act as judge and jury and compassionate God into the bargain!

He stumbled on to the veranda, where the murder had been committed the night before. There was a ruddy smear on the brick, and a puddle of rainwater was tinged pink. The same big shabby dogs were licking at the edges of the water, and cringed away when Tony shouted at them. He leaned against the wall and stared over the soaked greens and browns of the veld to the kopjes, which were sharp and blue after the rain; it had poured half the night. He realized, as the sound grew loud in his ears, that cicadas were shrilling all about him. He had been too absorbed to hear them. It was a steady, insistent screaming from every bush and tree. It wore on his nerves. 'I am getting out of this place,' he said suddenly. 'I am getting out of it altogether. I am going to the other end of the country. I wash my hands of the thing. Let the Slatters and the Denhams do as they like. What has it got to do with me?'

That morning, he packed his things and walked over to the Slatters' to tell Charlie he would not stay. Charlie seemed indifferent, even relieved; he had been thinking there was no need for a manager now that Dick would not come back.

After that the Turners' farm was run as an overflow for Charlie's cattle. They grazed all over it, even up to the hill where the house stood. It was left empty: it soon fell down.

Tony went back into town, where he hung round the bars and hotels for a while, waiting to hear of some job that would suit him. But his early carefree adaptability was gone. He had grown difficult to please. He visited several farms, but each time went away: farming had lost its glitter for him. At the trial, which was as Sergeant Denham had said it would be, a mere formality, he said what was expected of him. It was suggested that the native had murdered Mary Turner while drunk, in search of money and jewellery.

When the trial was over, Tony loafed about aimlessly until his money was finished. The murder, those few weeks with the Turners, had affected him more than he knew. But his money being gone, he had to do something in order to eat. He met a man from Northern Rhodesia, who told him about the copper mines and the wonderfully high salaries. They sounded fantastic to Tony. He took the next train to the copper belt, intending to save some money and start some business on his own account. But the salaries, once there, did not seem so good as they had from a distance. The cost of living was high, and then, everyone drank so much . . . Soon he left underground work and was a kind of manager. So, in the end, he sat in an office and did paper work, which was what he had come to Africa to avoid. But it wasn't so bad really. One should take things as they came. Life isn't as one expects it to be – and so on; these were the things he said to himself when depressed, and was measuring himself against his early ambitions.

For the people in 'the district', who knew all about him by hearsay, he was the young man from England who hadn't the guts to stand more than a few weeks of farming. No guts, they said. He should have stuck it out.

2

As the railway lines spread and knotted and ramified all over Southern Africa, along them, at short distances of a few miles, sprang up little dorps that to a traveller appear as insignificant clusters of ugly buildings, but which are the centres of farming districts perhaps a couple of hundred miles across. They contain the station building, the post office, sometimes a hotel, but always a store.

If one was looking for a symbol to express South Africa, the South Africa that was created by financiers and mine magnates, the South Africa which the old missionaries and explorers who charted the Dark Continent would be horrified to see, one would find it in the store. The store is everywhere. Drive ten miles from one and you come on the next; poke your head out of the railway carriage, and there it is; every mine has its store, and many farms.

It is always a low single-storied building divided into segments like a strip of chocolate, with grocery, butchery, and bottle-store under one corrugated-iron roof. It has a high dark wooden counter, and behind the counter shelves hold anything from distemper mixture to tooth-brushes, all mixed together. There are a couple of racks holding cheap cotton dresses in brilliant colours, and perhaps a stack of shoe-boxes, or a glass case for cosmetics or sweets. There is the unmistakable smell, a smell compounded of varnish, dried blood from the killing yard behind, dried hides, dried fruit, and strong yellow soap. Behind the counter is a Greek, or a Jew, or an Indian. Sometimes the children of this man, who is invariably hated by the whole district as a profiteer and an alien, are playing among the vegetables because the living-quarters are just behind the shop.

For thousands of people up and down Southern Africa the store is the background to their childhood. So many things centred round it. It brings back, for instance, memories of those nights when the car, after driving endlessly through a chilly, dusty darkness, stopped unexpect-edly in front of a square of light where men lounged with glasses in their hands, and one was carried out into the brilliantly-lit bar for a sip of searing liquid 'to keep the fever away'. Or it might be the place where one drove twice a week to collect mail, and to see all the farmers from miles around buying their groceries, and reading letters from Home with one leg propped on the running-board of the car, momentarily oblivious to the sun, the square of red dust where the dogs lay scattered like flies on meat, and the groups of staring natives – momentarily transported back to the country for which they were so bitterly homesick, but where they would not choose to live again: 'South Africa gets into you,' these self-exiled people would say, ruefully.

For Mary, the word 'Home', spoken nostalgically, meant England, although both her parents were South Africans and had never been to England. It meant 'England' because of those mail-days, when she slipped up to the store to watch the cars come in, and drive away again laden with stores and letters and magazines from overseas.

For Mary, the store was the real centre of her life, even more important to her than to most children. To begin with, she always lived within sight of it, in one of those little dusty dorps. She was always having to run across to bring a pound of dried peaches or a tin of salmon for her mother, or to find out whether the weekly newspaper had arrived. And she would linger there for hours, staring at the piles of sticky coloured sweets, letting the fine grain stored in the sacks round the walls trickle through her fingers, looking covertly at the little Greek girl whom she was not allowed to play with, because her mother said her parents were dagoes. And later, when she grew older, the store came to have another significance: it was the place where her father bought his drink. Sometimes her mother worked herself into a passion of resentment, and walked up to the barman, complaining that she could not make ends meet, while her husband squandered his salary in drink. Mary knew, even as a child, that her mother complained for the sake of making a scene and parading her sorrows: that she really enjoyed the luxury of standing there in the bar while the casual drinkers looked on, sympathetically; she enjoyed complaining in a hard sorrowful voice about her husband. 'Every night he comes home from here,' she would say, 'every night! And I am expected to bring up three children on the money that is left over when he chooses to come home.' And then she would stand still, waiting for the condolences of the man who pocketed the money which was rightly hers to spend for the children. But he would say at the end, 'But what can I do? I can't refuse to sell him drink, now can I?' And at last, having played out her scene and taken her fill of sympathy, she would slowly walk away across the expanse of red dust to her house, holding Mary by the hand – a tall, scrawny woman with angry, unhealthy brilliant eyes. She made a confidante of Mary early. She used to cry over her sewing while Mary comforted her miserably, longing to get away, but feeling important too, and hating her father.

This is not to say that he drank himself into a state of brutality. He was seldom drunk as some men were, whom Mary saw outside the bar, frightening her into a real terror of the place. He drank himself every evening into a state of cheerful fuddled good humour, coming home late to a cold dinner, which he ate by himself. His wife treated him with a cold indifference. She reserved her scornful ridicule of him for when her friends came to tea. It was as if she did not wish to give her husband the satisfaction of knowing that she cared anything for him at all, or felt anything for him, even contempt and derision. She behaved as if he were simply not there for her. And for all practical purposes he was not. He brought home the money, and not enough of that. Apart from that he was a cipher in the house, and knew it. He was a little man, with dull ruffled hair, a baked-apple face, and an air of uneasy though aggressive jocularity. He called visiting petty officials 'sir'; and shouted at the natives under him; he was on the railway, working as a pumpman.

And then, as well as being the focus of the district, and the source of her father's drunkenness, the store was the powerful, implacable place that sent in bills at the end of the month. They could never be fully paid: her mother was always appealing to the owner for just another month's grace. Her father and mother fought over these bills twelve times a year. They never quarrelled over anything but money; sometimes, in fact, her mother remarked dryly that she might have done worse: she might, for instance, be like Mrs Newman, who had seven children; she had only three mouths to fill, after all. It was a long time before Mary saw the connexion between these phrases, and by then there was only one mouth to feed, her own; for her brother and sister both died of dysentery one very dusty year. Her parents were good friends because of this sorrow for a short while: Mary could remember thinking that it was an ill wind that did no one good; because the two dead children were both so much older than she that they were no good to her as playmates, and the loss was more than compensated by the happiness of living in a house where there were suddenly no quarrels, with a mother who wept, but who had lost that terrible hard indifference. That phase did not last long, however. She looked back on it as the happiest time of her childhood.

The family moved three times before Mary went to school; but afterwards she could not distinguish between the various stations she had lived in. She remembered an exposed dusty village that was backed by a file of bunchy gum trees, with a square of dust always swirling and settling because of passing ox-wagons; with hot sluggish air that sounded several times a day with the screaming and coughing of trains. Dust and chickens; dust and children and wandering natives; dust and the store – always the store.

Then she was sent to boarding school and her life changed. She was extremely happy, so happy that she dreaded going home at holiday times to her fuddled father, her bitter mother, and the fly-away little house that was like a small wooden box on stilts.

At sixteen she left school and took a job in an office in town: one of those sleepy little towns scattered like raisins in a dry cake over the body of South Africa. Again, she was very happy. She seemed born for typing and shorthand and book-keeping and the comfortable routine of an office. She liked things to happen safely one after another in a pattern, and she liked, particularly, the friendly impersonality of it. By the time she was twenty she had a good job, her own friends, a niche in the life of the town. Then her mother died and she was virtually alone in the world, for her father was five hundred miles away, having been transferred to yet another station. She hardly saw him: he was proud of her, but (which was more to the point) left her alone. They did not even write; they were not the writing sort. Mary was pleased to be rid of him. Being alone in the world had no terrors for her at all, she liked it. And by dropping her father she seemed in some way to be avenging her mother's sufferings. It had never occurred to her that her father, too, might have suffered. 'About what?' she would have retorted, had anyone suggested it. 'He's a man, isn't he? He can do as he likes.' She had inherited from her mother an arid feminism, which had no meaning in her own life at all, for she was leading the comfortable carefree existence of a single woman in South Africa, and she did not know how fortunate she was. How could she know? She understood nothing of conditions in other countries, had no measuring rod to assess herself with.

It had never occurred to her to think, for instance, that she, the daughter of a petty railway official and a woman whose life had been so unhappy because of economic pressure that she had literally pined to death, was living in much the same way as the daughters of the wealthiest in South Africa, could do as she pleased – could marry, if she wished, anyone she wanted. These things did not enter her head. 'Class' is not a South African word; and its equivalent, 'race',, meant to her the office boy in the firm where she worked, other women's servants, and the amorphous mass of natives in the streets, whom she hardly noticed. She knew (the phrase was in the air) that the natives were getting 'cheeky'. But she had nothing to do with them really. They were outside her orbit.

Till she was twenty-five nothing happened to break the smooth and comfortable life she led. Then her father died. That removed the last link that bound her to a childhood she hated to remember. There was nothing left to connect her with the sordid little house on stilts, the screaming of trains, the dust, and the strife between her parents. Nothing at all! She was free. And when the funeral was over, and she had returned to the office, she looked forward to a life that would continue as it had so far been. She was very happy: that was perhaps her only positive quality, for there was nothing else distinctive about her,

though at twenty-five she was at her prettiest. Sheer contentment put a
bloom on her: she was a thin girl, who moved awkwardly, with a
fashionable curtain of light-brown hair, serious blue eyes, and pretty
clothes. Her friends would have described her as a slim blonde: she
modelled herself on the more childish-looking film stars.

At thirty nothing had changed. On her thirtieth birthday she felt a
vague surprise that did not even amount to discomfort – for she did not
feel any different – that the years had gone past so quickly. Thirty! It
sounded a great age. But it had nothing to do with her. At the same time
she did not celebrate this birthday; she allowed it to be forgotten. She
felt almost outraged that such a thing could happen to her, who was no
different from the Mary of sixteen.

She was by now the personal secretary of her employer, and was
earning good money. If she had wanted, she could have taken a flat and
lived the smart sort of life. She was quite presentable. She had the
undistinguished, dead-level appearance of South African white democracy. Her voice was one of thousands: flattened, a little sing-song,
clipped. Anyone could have worn her clothes. There was nothing to
prevent her living by herself, even running her own car, entertaining on
a small scale. She could have become a person on her own account. But
this was against her instinct.

She chose to live in a girls' club, which had been started, really, to
help women who could not earn much money, but she had been there so
long no one thought of asking her to leave. She chose it because it
reminded her of school, and she had hated leaving school. She liked the
crowds of girls, and eating in a big dining-room, and coming home after
the pictures to find a friend in her room waiting for a little gossip. In the
club she was a person of some importance, out of the usual run. For one
thing she was so much older than the others. She had come to have what
was almost the role of a comfortable maiden aunt to whom one can tell
one's troubles. For Mary was never shocked, never condemned, never
told tales. She seemed impersonal, above the little worries. The
stiffness of her manner, her shyness protected her from many spites and
jealousies. She seemed immune. This was her strength, but also a
weakness that she would not have considered a weakness: she felt
disinclined, almost repelled, by the thought of intimacies and scenes
and contacts. She moved among all those young women with a faint
aloofness that said as clear as words: I will not be drawn in. And she was
quite unconscious of it. She was very happy in the club.

Outside the girls' club, and the office, where again she was a person of some importance, because of the many years she had worked there, she led a full and active life. Yet it was a passive one, in some respects, for it depended on other people entirely. She was not the kind of woman who initiates parties, or who is the centre of a crowd. She was still the girl who is 'taken out'.

Her life was really rather extraordinary: the conditions which produced it are passing now, and when the change is complete, women will look back on them as on a vanished Golden Age.

She got up late, in time for office (she was very punctual) but not in time for breakfast. She worked efficiently, but in a leisurely way, until lunch. She went back to the club for lunch. Two more hours' work in the afternoon and she was free. Then she played tennis, or hockey, or swam. And always with a man, one of those innumerable men who 'took her out', treating her like a sister: Mary was such a good pal! Just as she seemed to have a hundred women friends, but no particular friend, so she had (it seemed) a hundred men, who had taken her out, or were taking her out, or who had married and now asked her to their homes. She was friend to half the town. And in the evening she always went to sundowner parties that prolonged themselves till midnight, or danced, or went to the pictures. Sometimes she went to the pictures five nights a week. She was never in bed before twelve or later. And so it had gone on, day after day, week after week, year after year. South Africa is a wonderful place: for the unmarried white woman. But she was not playing her part, for she did not get married. The years went past; her friends got married; she had been bridesmaid a dozen times; other people's children were growing up; but she went on as companionable, as adaptable, as aloof, and as heart-whole as ever, working as hard enjoying herself as she ever did in office, and never for one moment alone, except when she was asleep.

She seemed not to care for men. she would say to her girls, 'Men! They get all the fun.' Yet outside the office and the club her life was entirely dependent upon men, though she would have most indignantly repudiated the accusation. And perhaps she was not so dependent upon them really, for when she listened to other people's complaints and miseries she offered none of her own. Sometimes her friends felt a little put off, and let down. It was hardly fair, they felt obscurely, to listen, to advise, to act as a sort of universal shoulder for the world to weep on, and give back nothing of her own. The truth was she had no troubles.

She heard other people's complicated stories with wonder, even a little fear. She shrank away from all that. She was a most rare phenomenon: a woman of thirty without love troubles, headaches, backaches, sleep-lessness, or neurosis. She did not know how rare she was.

And she was still 'one of the girls'. If a visiting cricket team came to town and partners were needed, the organizers would ring up Mary. That was the kind of thing she was good at: adapting herself sensibly and quietly to any occasion. She would sell tickets for a charity dance or act as a dancing partner for a visiting full-back with equal amiability.

And she still wore her hair little-girl fashion on her shoulders, and wore little-girl frocks in pastel colours, and kept her shy, naïve manner. If she had been left alone she would have gone on, in her own way, enjoying herself thoroughly, until people found one day that she had turned imperceptibly into one of those women who have become old without ever having been middle-aged: a little withered, a little acid, hard as nails, sentimentally kindhearted, and addicted to religion or small dogs.

They would have been kind to her, because she had 'missed the best things of life'. But then there are so many people who don't want them: so many for whom the best things have been poisoned from the start. When Mary thought of 'home' she remembered a wooden box shaken by passing trains; when she thought of marriage she remembered her father coming home red-eyed and fuddled; when she thought of children she saw her mother's face at her children's funeral – anguished, but as dry and as hard as rock. Mary liked other people's children but shuddered at the thought of having any of her own. She felt sentimental at weddings, but she had a profound distaste for sex; there had been little privacy in her home and there were things she did not care to remember; she had taken good care to forget them years ago.

She certainly did feel, at times, a restlessness, a vague dissatisfaction that took the pleasure out of her activities for a while. She would be going to bed, for instance, contentedly, after the pictures, when the thought would strike her, 'Another day gone!' And then time would contract and it seemed to her only a breathing space since she left school and came into town to earn her own living; and she would feel a little panicky, as if an invisible support had been drawn away from underneath her. But then, being a sensible person, and firmly convinced that thinking about oneself was morbid, she would get into bed and turn out the lights. She might wonder, before drifting off to sleep, 'Is this all? When I get to be old will this be all I have to look back on?' But by morning she would have forgotten it, and the days went round, and she would be happy again. For she did not know what she wanted. Something bigger, she would think vaguely – a different kind of life. But the mood never lasted long. She was so satisfied with her work, where she felt sufficient and capable; with her friends, whom she relied on; with her life at the club, which was as pleasant and as gregarious as being in a giant twittering aviary, where there was always the excitement of other people's engagements and weddings; and with her men friends, who treated her just like a good pal, with none of this silly sex business.

But all women become conscious, sooner or later, of that impalpable, but steel-strong pressure to get married, and Mary, who was not at all susceptible to atmosphere, or the things people imply, was brought face to face with it suddenly, and most unpleasantly.

She was in the house of a married friend, sitting on the veranda, with a lighted room behind her. She was alone; and heard people talking in low voices, and caught her own name. She rose to go inside and declare herself: it was typical of her that her first thought was, how unpleasant it would be for her friends to know she had overheard. Then she sank down again, and waited for a suitable moment to pretend she had just come in from the garden. This was the conversation she listened to, while her face burned and her hands went clammy.

'She's not fifteen any longer: it is ridiculous! Someone should tell her about her clothes.'

'How old is she?'

'Must be well over thirty. She has been going strong for years. She was working long before I began working, and that was a good twelve years ago.'

'Why doesn't she marry? She must have had plenty of chances.'

There was a dry chuckle. 'I don't think so. My husband was keen on her himself once, but he thinks she will never marry. She just isn't like that, isn't like that at all. Something missing somewhere.'

'Oh, I don't know.'

'She's gone off so much, in any case. The other day I caught sight of her in the street and hardly recognized her. It's a fact! The way she plays all those games, her skin is like sandpaper, and she's got so thin.'

'But she's such a nice girl.'

'She'll never set the rivers on fire, though.'

'She'd make someone a good wife. She's a good sort, Mary.'

'She should marry someone years older than herself. A man of fifty would suit her . . . you'll see, she will marry someone old enough to be her father one of these days.'

'One never can tell!'

There was another chuckle, good-hearted enough, but it sounded cruelly malicious to Mary. She was stunned and outraged; but most of all deeply wounded that her friends could discuss her thus. She was so naïve, so unconscious of herself in relation to other people, that it had never entered her head that people could discuss her behind her back. And the things they had said! She sat there writhing, twisting her hands. Then she composed herself and went back into the room to join her treacherous friends, who greeted her as cordially as if they had not just that moment driven knives into her heart and thrown her quite off balance; she could not recognize herself in the picture they had made of her!

That little incident, apparently so unimportant, which would have had no effect on a person who had the faintest idea of the kind of world she lived in, had a profound effect on Mary. She, who had never had time to think of herself, took to sitting in her room for hours at a time, wondering: 'Why did they say those things? What is the matter with me? What did they mean when they said that I am *not like that*?' And she would look warily, appealingly, into the faces of friends to see if she could find there traces of their condemnation of her. And she was even more disturbed and unhappy because they seemed just as usual, treating her with their ordinary friendliness. She began to suspect double meanings where none were intended, to find maliciousness in the glance of a person who felt nothing but affection for her.

Turning over in her mind the words she had by accident listened to, she thought of ways to improve herself. She took the ribbon out of her hair, though with regret, because she thought she looked very pretty with a mass of curls round her rather long thin face; and bought herself tailor-made clothes, in which she felt ill at ease, because she felt truly herself in pinafore frocks and childish skirts. And for the first time in her life she was feeling uncomfortable with men. A small core of contempt for them, of which she was quite unconscious, and which had protected her from sex as surely as if she had been truly hideous, had melted, and she had lost her poise. And she began looking around for someone to marry. She did not put it to herself like that; but, after all, she was nothing if not a social being, though she had never thought of 'society', the abstraction; and if her friends were thinking she should get married, then there might be something in it. If she had ever learned to put her feelings into words, that was perhaps how she would have expressed herself. And the first man she allowed to approach her was a widower of fifty-five with half-grown children. It was because she felt safer with him . . . because she did not associate ardours and embraces with a middle-aged gentleman whose attitude towards her was almost fatherly.

He knew perfectly well what he wanted: a pleasant companion, a mother for his children, and someone to run his house for him. He found Mary good company, and she was kind to the children. Nothing, really, could have been more suitable: since apparently she had to get married, this was the kind of marriage to suit her best. But things went wrong. He underestimated her experience; it seemed to him that a woman who had been on her own so long should know her own mind and understand what he was offering her. A relationship developed which was clear to both of them, until he proposed to her, was accepted, and began to make love to her. Then a violent revulsion overcame her and she ran away; they were in his comfortable drawing-room, and when he began to kiss her, she ran out of his house into the night and all the way home through the streets to the club. There she fell on the bed and wept. And his feeling for her was not one to be enhanced by this kind of foolishness, which a younger man, physically in love with her, might have found charming. Next morning, she was horrifed at her behaviour. What a way to behave: she, who was always in command of herself, and who dreaded nothing more than scenes and ambiguity. She apologized to him, but that was the end of it.

And now she was left at sea, not knowing what it was she needed. It seemed to her that she had run from him because he was 'an old man', that was how the affair arranged itself in her mind. She shuddered, and avoided men over thirty. She was over that age herself; but in spite of everything, she thought of herself as a girl still.

And all the time, unconsciously, without admitting it to herself, she was looking for a husband.

During those few months before she married, people were discussing her in a way which would have sickened her, had she suspected it. It seems hard that Mary, whose charity towards other people's failures and scandals grew out of a genuine, rock-bottom aversion towards the personal things like love and passion, was doomed all her life to be the subject of gossip. But so it was. At this time, too, the shocking and rather ridiculous story of that night when she had run away from her elderly lover was spreading round the wide circle of her friends, though it is impossible to say who could have known about it in the first place. But when people heard it they nodded and laughed as if it confirmed something they had known for a long time. A woman of thirty behaving like that! They laughed, rather unpleasantly; in this age of scientific sex, nothing seems more ridiculous than sexual gaucherie. They didn't forgive her; they laughed, and felt that in some way it served her right.

She was so changed, they said; she looked so dull and dowdy, and her skin was bad; she looked as if she were going to be ill; she was obviously having a nervous breakdown and at her age it was to be expected, with the way she lived and everything; she was looking for a man and couldn't get one. And then, her manner was so odd, these days . . . These were some of the things they said.

It is terrible to destroy a person's picture of himself in the interests of truth or some other abstraction. How can one know he will be able to create another to enable him to go on living? Mary's idea of herself was destroyed and she was not fitted to recreate herself. She could not exist without that impersonal, casual friendship from other people; and now it seemed to her there was pity in the way they looked at her, and a little impatience, too, as if she were really rather a futile woman after all. She felt as she had never done before; she was hollow inside, empty, and into this emptiness would sweep from nowhere a vast panic, as if there were nothing in the world she could grasp hold of. And she was afraid to meet people, afraid, above all, of men. If a man kissed her (which they did, sensing her new mood), she was revolted; on the other hand she went to the pictures even more frequently than before and came out feverish and unsettled. There seemed no connexion between the distorted mirror of the screen and her own life; it was impossible to fit together what she wanted for herself, and what she was offered.

At the age of thirty, this woman who had had a 'good' State education, a thoroughly comfortable life enjoying herself in a civilized way, and access to all knowledge of her time (only she read nothing but bad novels) knew so little about herself that she was thrown completely off her balance because some gossiping women had said she ought to get married.

Then she met Dick Turner. It might have been anybody. Or rather, it would have been the first man she met who treated her as if she were wonderful and unique. She needed that badly. She needed it to restore her feeling of superiority to men, which was really, at bottom, what she had been living from all these years.

They met casually at the cinema. He was in for the day from his farm. He very rarely came into town, except when he had to buy goods he could not get at his local store, and that happened perhaps once or twice a year. On this occasion he ran into a man he had not seen for years and was persuaded to stay the night in town and go to the cinema. He was almost amused at himself for agreeing: all this seemed so very remote from him. His farm lorry, heaped with sacks of grain and two harrows, stood outside the cinema, looking out of place and cumbersome; and Mary looked through the back window at these unfamiliar objects and smiled. It was necessary for her to smile when she saw them. She loved the town, felt safe there, and associated the country with her childhood, because of those little dorps she had lived in, and the way they were all surrounded by miles and miles of nothingness – miles and miles of veld.

Dick Turner disliked the town. When he drove in from the veld he knew so well, through those ugly scattered suburbs that looked as if they had come out of housing catalogues; ugly little houses stuck anyhow over the veld, that had no relationship with the hard brown African soil and the arching blue sky, cosy little houses meant for cosy little countries – and then on into the business part of the town with the shops full of fashions for smart women and extravagant imported food, he felt ill at ease and uncomfortable and murderous.

He suffered from claustrophobia. He wanted to run away – either to run away or to smash the place up. So he always escaped as soon as possible back to his farm, where he felt at home.

But there are thousands of people in Africa who could be lifted bodily out of their suburb and put into a town the other side of the world and hardly notice the difference. The suburb is as invincible and fatal as factories, and even beautiful South Africa, whose soil looks outraged by those pretty little suburbs creeping over it like a disease, cannot escape. When Dick Turner saw them, and thought of the way people lived in them, and the way the cautious suburban mind was ruining *his* country, he wanted to swear and to smash and to murder. He could not bear it. He did not put these feelings into words; he had lost the habit of word-spinning, living the life he did, out on the soil all day. But the feeling was the strongest he knew. He felt he could kill the bankers and the financiers and the magnates and the clerks – all the people who built prim little houses with hedged gardens full of English flowers for preference.

And above all, he loathed the cinema. When he found himself inside the picture-house on this occasion, he wondered what had possessed him that he had agreed to come. He could not keep his eyes on the screen. The long-limbed, smooth-faced women bored him; the story seemed meaningless. And it was hot and stuffy. After a while he ignored the screen altogether, and looked round the audience. In front of him, around him, behind him, rows and rows of people staring and leaning away from each other up at the screen – hundreds of people flown out of their bodies and living in the lives of those stupid people posturing there. It made him feel uneasy.

He fidgeted, lit a cigarette, gazed at the dark plush curtains that masked the exits. And then, looking along the row he was sitting in, he saw a shaft of light fall from somewhere above, showing the curve of a cheek and a sheaf of fairish glinting hair. The face seemed to float, yearning upwards, ruddily gold in the queer greenish light. He poked the man next to him, and said, 'Who is that?' 'Mary,' was the grunted reply, after a brief look. But 'Mary' did not help Dick much. He stared at that lovely floating face and the falling hair, and after the show was over, he looked for her hurriedly in the crush outside the door. But he could not see her. He supposed, vaguely, that she had gone with someone else. He was given a girl to take home whom he hardly glanced at. She was dressed in what seemed to him a ridiculous way, and he wanted to laugh at her high heels, in which she tiptapped beside him across the street. In the car she looked over her shoulder at the piled back of the lorry, and asked in a hurried affected voice: 'What are those funny things at the back?'

'Have you never seen a harrow?' he asked. He dropped her, without regret, at the place where she lived – a big building, which was full of light and people. He forgot her immediately.

But he dreamed about the girl with the young up-tilted face and the wave of loose gleaming hair. It was a luxury, dreaming about a woman, for he had forbidden himself such things. He had started farming five years before, and was still not making it pay. He was indebted to the Land Bank, and heavily mortgaged, for he had had no capital, when he started. He had given up drink, cigarettes, all but the necessities. He worked as only a man possessed by a vision can work, from six in the morning till seven at night, taking his meals on the lands, his whole being concentrated on the farm. His dream was to get married and have children. Only he could not ask a woman to share such a life. First he would have to get out of debt, build a house, be able to afford the little luxuries. Having driven himself for years, it was part of his dream to spoil a wife. He knew exactly what sort of a house he would build: not one of those meaningless block-like buildings stuck on top of the soil. He wanted a big thatched house with wide verandas open to the air. He had even chosen the ant-heaps that he would dig to make his bricks, and had marked the parts of the farm where the grass grew tallest, taller than a big man, for the thatch. But it seemed to him sometimes that he was very far from getting what he wanted. He was pursued by bad luck. The farmers about him, he knew, called him 'Jonah'. If there was a drought he seemed to get the brunt of it, and if it rained in swamps then his farm suffered most. If he decided to grow cotton for the first time, cotton slumped that year, and if there was a swarm of locusts, then he took it for granted, with a kind of angry but determined fatalism, that they would make straight for his most promising patch of mealies. His dream had become a little less grandiose of late. He was lonely, he wanted a wife, and above all, children; and the way things were it would be years before he had them. He was beginning to think that if he could pay off *some* of the mortgage, and add an extra room to his house, perhaps get some furniture, then he could think of getting married. In the meantime he thought of the girl in the cinema. She became the focus of his work and imaginings. He cursed himself for it, for he knew thinking about women, particularly one woman, was as dangerous as drink to him, but it was no good. Just over a month after his visit to town, he found himself planning another. It was not necessary and he knew it. He gave up even persuading himself that it was necessary. In town, he did the little business he had to do quickly, and went in search of someone who could tell him 'Mary's' surname.

When he drove up to the big building, he recognized it, but did not connect the girl he had driven home that night with the girl of the cinema. Even when she came to the door, and stood in the hall looking to see who he was, he did not recognize her. He saw a tall, thin girl, with deeply blue, rather evasive eyes that looked hurt. Her hair was in tight ridges round her head; she wore trousers. Women in trousers did not seem to him females at all: he was properly old-fashioned. Then she said

'Are you looking for me?' rather puzzled and shy; and at once he remembered that silly voice asking about the harrows and stared at her incredulously. He was so disappointed he began to stammer and shift his feet. Then he thought that he could not stand there for ever, staring at her, and he asked her to go for a drive. It was not a pleasant evening. He was angry with himself for his self-delusion and weakness; she was flattered but puzzled as to why he had sought her out, since he hardly spoke now he had got her into the car and was driving aimlessly around the town. But he wanted to find in her the girl who had haunted him, and he had done so, by the time he had to take her home. He kept glancing at her sideways as they passed street lamps, and he could see how a trick of light had created something beautiful and strange from an ordinary and not very attractive girl. And then, he began to like her, because it was essential for him to love somebody; he had not realized how very lonely he had been. And when he left her that night, it was with regret, saying he would come again soon.

Back on the farm, he took himself to task. This would end in marriage if he were not careful, and he simply could not afford it. That was the end of it, then; he would forget her, put the whole thing out of his mind. Besides, what did he know about her? Nothing at all! Except that she was obviously, as he put it, 'thoroughly spoiled'. She was not the kind to share a struggling farmer's life. So he argued with himself, working harder than he had ever done before, and thinking sometimes, 'After all, if I have a good season this year I might go back and see her.' He took to walking ten miles over the veld with his gun after his day's work to exhaust himself. He wore himself out, grew thin and haunted-looking. He fought with himself for two months, until at last one day he found himself preparing to take the car into town, exactly as if he had decided it long ago, and as if all his exhortations and self-discipline had been nothing but a shield to hide from himself his real intention. As he dressed he whistled jauntily, but with a crestfallen undertone; and his face wore a curious little defeated smile.

As for Mary, those two months were a long nightmare. He had come all the way in from his farm after meeting her once for five minutes, and then, having spent an evening with her, had not thought it worth his while to come back. Her friends were right, she lacked something. There was something wrong with her. But she clung to the thought of him, in spite of the fact that she said to herself she was useless, a failure, a ridiculous creature whom no one wanted. She gave up going out in the evenings, and remained in her room waiting for him to call for her. She sat for hours and hours by herself, her mind numb with misery; and at night she dreamed long grey dreams in which she struggled through sand, or climbed staircases which collapsed as she reached the top, letting her slide back to the bottom again. She woke in the mornings tired and depressed, unable to face the day. Her employer, used to her inevitable efficiency, told her to take a holiday and not to come back till she felt better. She left the office, feeling as if she had been thrown out (though he could not have been nicer about her breakdown) and stayed all day in the club. If she went away for a holiday she might miss Dick. Yet what was Dick to her, really? Nothing. She hardly knew him. He was a spare, sunburnt, slow-voiced, deep-eyed young man who had come into her life like an accident, and that was all she could say about him. And yet, she would have said it was for his sake she was making herself ill. All her restlessness, her vague feelings of inadequacy, centred on him, and when she asked herself, in chilly dismay, why it should be he, rather than any of the other men she knew, there was no satisfactory reply.

Weeks after she had given up hope, and had gone to the doctor for a prescription because 'she was feeling tired' and had been told she must take a holiday at once, if she wanted to avoid complete breakdown; when she had reached a stage of misery that made it impossible for her to meet any of her old friends, because of her obsession that their friendship was a cloak for malicious gossip and real dislike of her, she was called to the door again one evening. She was not thinking about Dick. When she saw him it took all her self-control to greet him calmly; if she had shown her emotion he might after all have given her up. By now he had persuaded himself into believing she was a practical, adaptable, serene person, who would need only a few weeks on the farm to become what he wanted her to be. Tears of hysteria would have shocked him, ruined his vision of her.

It was to an apparently calm, maternal Mary that he proposed. He was adoring, self-abasing, and grateful when she accepted him. They were married by special licence two weeks later. Her desire to get married as quickly as possible surprised him; he saw her as a busy and popular woman with a secure place in the social life of the town, and thought it would take her some time to arrange her affairs: this idea of her was part of her attraction for him. But a quick marriage fell in with his plans, really. He hated the idea of waiting about the town while a woman fussed with clothes and bridesmaids. There was no honey-moon. He explained he was too poor really to afford one, though if she insisted he would do what he could. She did not insist. She was very relieved to escape a honeymoon.

Martha Quest

Two elderly women sat knitting on that part of the veranda which was
screened from the sun by a golden shower creeper; the tough stems
were so thick with flower it was as if the glaring afternoon was dammed
against them in a surf of its own light made visible in the dripping,
orange-coloured clusters. Inside this coloured barrier was a darkened
recess, rough mud walls (the outer walls of the house itself) forming two
sides, the third consisting of a bench loaded with painted petrol tins
which held pink and white geraniums. The sun splashed liberal gold
through the foliage, over the red cement floor, and over the ladies. They
had been here since lunchtime, and would remain until sunset, talking,
talking incessantly, their tongues mercifully let off the leash. They were
Mrs Quest and Mrs Van Rensberg; and Martha Quest, a girl of fifteen,
sat on the steps in full sunshine, clumsily twisting herself to keep the
glare from her book with her own shadow.

   She frowned, and from time to time glanced up irritably at the women,
indicating that their gossip made it difficult to concentrate. But then,
there was nothing to prevent her moving somewhere else; and her spasms
of resentment when she was asked a question, or her name was used in the
family chronicling, were therefore unreasonable. As for the ladies, they
sometimes allowed their eyes to rest on the girl with that glazed look
which excludes a third person, or even dropped their voices; and at these
moments she lifted her head to give them a glare of positive contempt; for
they were seasoning the dull staple of their lives – servants, children,
cooking – with a confinement or scandal of some kind; and since she was
reading Havelock Ellis on sex, and had taken good care they should know
it, the dropped voices had the quality of an anomaly. Or rather, she was
not actually reading it: she read a book that had been lent to her by the
Cohen boys at the station, while Ellis lay, like an irritant, on the top step,
with its title well in view. However, there are certain rites in the talk of
matrons, and Martha, having listened to such talk for a large part of her
life, should have learned that there was nothing insulting, or even
personal, intended. She was merely expected to play the part 'young girl'
against their own familiar roles.

At the other end of the veranda, on two deck chairs planted side by side and looking away over the bush and the mealie fields, were Mr Quest and Mr Van Rensberg; and they were talking about crops and the weather and the native problem. But their backs were turned on the women with a firmness which said how welcome was this impersonal talk to men who lived shut into the heated atmosphere of the family for weeks at a time, with no refuge but the farmwork. Their talk was as familiar to Martha as the women's talk; the two currents ran sleepily on inside her, like the movements of her own blood, of which she was not conscious except as an ache of irritation when her cramped position made her shift her long, bare and sunburnt legs. Then, when she heard the nagging phrases 'The Government expects the farmers to . . .' and 'The kaffirs are losing all respect because . . .', she sat up sharply; and the irritation overflowed into a flood of dislike for both her parents. Everything was the same; intolerable that they should have been saying the same things ever since she could remember; and she looked away from them, over the veld.

In the literature that was her tradition, the word *farm* evokes an image of something orderly, compact, cultivated; a neat farmhouse in a pattern of fields. Martha looked over a mile or so of bush to a strip of pink ploughed land; and then the bush, dark green and sombre, climbed a ridge to another patch of exposed earth, this time a clayish yellow; and then, ridge after ridge, fold after fold, the bush stretched to a line of blue kopjes. The fields were a timid intrusion on a landscape hardly marked by man; and the hawk which circled in mile-wide sweeps over her head saw the house, crouched on its long hill, the cluster of grass huts which was the native compound huddled on a lower rise half a mile away; perhaps a dozen patches of naked soil – and then nothing to disturb that ancient, down-peering eye, nothing that a thousand generations of his hawk ancestors had not seen.

The house, raised high on its eminence into the blue and sweeping currents of air, was in the centre of a vast basin, which was bounded by mountains. In front, there were seven miles to the Dumfries Hills; west, seven miles of rising ground to the Oxford Range; seven miles east, a long swelling mountain which was named Jacob's Burg. Behind, there was no defining chain of kopjes, but the land travelled endlessly, without limit, and faded into a bluish haze, like that hinterland to the imagination we cannot do without – the great declivity was open to the north.

Over it curved the cloudless African sky, but Martha could not look at it, for it pulsed with light; she must lower her eyes to the bush; and that was so familiar the vast landscape caused her only the prickling feeling of claustrophobia.

She looked down at her book. She did not want to read it; it was a book on popular science, and even the title stiffened her into a faint but unmistakable resentment. Perhaps, if she could have expressed what she felt, she would have said that the calm factual air of the writing was too distant from the uncomfortable emotions that filled her; perhaps she was so resentful of her surroundings and her parents that the resentment overflowed into everything near her. She put that book down and picked up Ellis. Now, it is hardly possible to be bored by a book on sex when one is fifteen, but she was restless because this collection of interesting facts seemed to have so little to do with her own problems. She lifted her eyes and gazed speculatively at Mrs Van Rensberg, who had had eleven children.

She was a fat, good-natured, altogether pleasant woman in a neat flowered cotton dress, which was rather full and long, and, with the white kerchief folded at the neck, gave her the appearance of a picture of one of her own grandmothers. It was fashionable to wear long skirts and tie a scarf loosely at the neck, but in Mrs Van Rensberg the fashion arranged itself obstinately into that other pattern. Martha saw this, and was charmed by it; but she was looking at the older woman's legs. They were large and shapeless, veined purple under the mask of sunburn, and ended in green sandals, through which her calloused feet unashamedly splayed for comfort. Martha was thinking with repugnance, Her legs are like that because she has had so many children.

Mrs Van Rensberg was what is described as uneducated; and for this she might apologize, without seeming or feeling in the slightest apologetic, when a social occasion demanded it – for instance, when Mrs Quest aggressively stated that Martha was clever and would have a career. That the Dutchwoman could remain calm and good-natured on such occasions was proof of considerable inner strength, for Mrs Quest used the word 'career' not in terms of something that Martha might actually do, such as doctoring, or the law, but as a kind of stick to beat the world with, as if she were saying, 'My daughter will be somebody, whereas yours will only be married.' Mrs Quest had been a pretty and athletic-looking English girl with light-brown hair and blue eyes as candid as spring sunshine; and she was now exactly as she would have been had she remained in England: a rather tired and disappointed but decided matron, with ambitious plans for her children.

Both ladies had been living in this farming district for many years, seventy miles from the nearest town, which was itself a backwater; but no part of the world can be considered remote these days; their homes had the radio, and newspapers coming regularly from what they respectively considered as Home – Tory newspapers from England for the Quests, nationalist journals from the Union of South Africa for the Van Rensbergs. They had absorbed sufficient of the spirit of the times to know that their children might behave in a way which they instinctively thought shocking, and as for the book Martha now held, its title had a clinical sound quite outside their own experience. In fact, Martha would have earned nothing but a good-natured and traditional sigh of protest, had not her remaining on the steps been in itself something of a challenge. Just as Mrs Quest found it necessary to protest, at half-hourly intervals, that Martha would get sunstroke if she did not come into the shade, so she eventually remarked that she supposed it did no harm for girls to read that sort of book; and once again Martha directed towards them a profoundly scornful glare, which was also unhappy and exasperated; for she felt that in some contradictory way she had been driven to use this book as a means of asserting herself, and now found the weapon had gone limp and useless in her hands.

Three months before, her mother had said angrily that Epstein and Havelock Ellis were disgusting. 'If people dug up the remains of this civilization a thousand years hence, and found Epstein's statues and that man Ellis, they would think we were just savages.' This was at the time when the inhabitants of the colony, introduced unwillingly through the chances of diplomacy and finance to what they referred to as 'modern art', were behaving as if they had been severally and collectively insulted. Epstein's statues were not fit, they averred, to represent them even indirectly. Mrs Quest took that remark from a leader in the *Zambesia News*; it was probably the first time she had made any comment on art or literature for twenty years. Martha then had borrowed a book on Epstein from the Cohen boys at the station. Now, one of the advantages of not having one's taste formed in a particular school is that one may look at the work of an Epstein with the same excited interest as at a Michelangelo. And this is what Martha did. She felt puzzled, and took the book of reproductions to her mother. Mrs

Quest was busy at the time, and had never found an opportunity since to tell Martha what was so shocking and disgusting in these works of art. And so with Havelock Ellis.

Now Martha was feeling foolish, even let down. She knew, too, that she was bad-tempered and boorish. She made resolutions day after day that from now on she would be quite different. And yet a fatal demon always took possession of her, so that at the slightest remark from her mother she was impelled to take it up, examine it, and hand it back, like a challenge – and by then the antagonist was no longer there; Mrs Quest was simply not interested.

'Ach,' said Mrs Van Rensberg, after a pause, 'it's not what you read that matters, but how you behave.' And she looked with good-natured affection towards Martha, who was flushed with anger and with sunshine. 'You'll have a headache, my girl,' she added automatically; and Martha bent stubbornly to her book, without moving, and her eyes filled with tears.

The two women began discussing, as was natural, how they had behaved when young, but with reservations, for Mrs Van Rensberg sensed that her own experience included a good deal that might shock the English lady; so what they exchanged were not the memories of their behaviour, but the phrases of their respective traditions, which sounded very similar – Mrs Van Rensberg was a member of the Dutch Reformed Church; the Quests, Church of England. Just as they never discussed politics, so they never discussed – but what did they discuss? Martha often reflected that their years-old friendship had survived just because of what had been left out, everything of import-ance, that is; and the thought caused the girl the swelling dislike of her surroundings which was her driving emotion. On the other hand, since one lady was conservative British and the other conservative Afrikaans, this friendship could be considered as a triumph of tact and good feeling over almost insuperable obstacles, since they were bound, by those same traditions, to dislike each other. This view naturally did not recommend itself to Martha, whose standards of friendship were so high she was still waiting for that real, that ideal friend to present himself.

'*The Friend*', she had copied in her diary, '*is some fair floating isle of palms eluding the mariner in Pacific seas . . .*' And so down the page to the next underlined sentence: '*There goes a rumour that the earth is inhabited, but the shipwrecked mariner has not seen a footprint on the shore.*' And the next: '*Our actual friends are but distant relations of those to whom we pledged.*'

And could Mrs Van Rensberg be considered even as a *distant* relation? Clearly not. It would be a betrayal of the sacred name of friendship.

Martha listened (not for the first time) to Mrs Van Rensberg's long account of how she had been courted by Mr Van Rensberg, given with a humorous deprecation of everything that might be described (though not by Martha, instinctively obedient to the taboos of the time) as Romance. Mrs Quest then offered an equally humorous though rather drier account of her own engagement. These two heavily, though unconsciously, censored tales at an end, they looked towards Martha, and sighed resignedly, at the same moment. Tradition demanded from them a cautionary moral, helpful to the young, the fruit of their sensible and respectable lives; and the look on Martha's face inhibited them both.

Mrs Van Rensberg hesitated, and then said firmly (the firmness was directed against her own hesitation), 'A girl must make men respect her.' She was startled at the hatred and contempt in Martha's suddenly raised eyes, and looked for support towards Mrs Quest.

'That's right,' said Mrs Quest, rather uncertainly. 'A man will never marry a girl he does not respect.'

Martha slowly sat up, closing her book as if it were of no more use to her, and stared composedly at them. She was now quite white with the effort of controlling that hatred. She got up, and said in a low tight voice, 'You are loathsome, bargaining and calculating and . . .' She was unable to continue. 'You are *disgusting*,' she ended lamely, with trembling lips. Then she marched off down the garden, and ran into the bush.

The two ladies watched her in silence. Mrs Quest was upset, for she did not know why her daughter thought her disgusting, while Mrs Van Rensberg was trying to find a sympathetic remark likely to be acceptable to her friend.

'She's so difficult', murmured Mrs Quest apologetically; and Mrs Van Rensberg said, 'It's the age, my Marnie's just as bad.' She did not know she had failed to find the right remark: Mrs Quest did not consider her daughter to be on a level with Marnie, whom she found in altogether bad taste, wearing grown-up clothes and lipstick at fifteen, and talking about 'boys'. Mrs Van Rensberg was quite unconscious of the force of her friend's feeling. She dismissed her strictness with Martha as one of those English foibles; and besides, she knew Marnie to be potentially a sensible woman, a good wife and mother. She continued to talk about Marnie, while Mrs Quest listened with the embarrassment due to a social *gaffe*, saying 'Quite' or 'Exactly,' thinking that her daughter's difficulty was caused by having to associate with the wrong type of child, meaning Marnie herself. But the Dutchwoman was unsnubbable, since her national pride was as deep as the Englishwoman's snobbishness, and soon their conversation drifted back to servants and cooking. That evening, each would complain to her husband – one, with the English inarticulateness over matters of class, that Mrs Van Rensberg was 'really so trying,' while the other, quite frankly, said that these rooineks got her down, they were all the same, they thought they owned the earth they walked on. Then, from unacknowledged guilt, they would ring each other up on the district telephone, and talk for half an hour or so about cooking and servants. Everything would continue as usual, in fact.

In the meantime, Martha, in an agony of adolescent misery, was lying among the long grass under a tree, repeating to herself that her mother was hateful, all these old women hateful, every one of these relationships, with their lies, evasions, compromises, wholly disgusting. For she was suffering that misery peculiar to the young, that they are going to be cheated by circumstances out of the full life every nerve and instinct is clamouring for.

After a short time, she grew more composed. A self-preserving nerve had tightened in her brain, and with it her limbs and even the muscles of her face became set and hardened. It was with a bleak and puzzled look that she stared at a sunlit and glittering bush which stood at her feet; for she did not see it, she was seeing herself, and in the only way she was equipped to do this – through literature. For if one reads novels from earlier times, and if novels accurately reflect, as we hope and trust they do, the life of their era, then one is forced to conclude that being young was much easier then than it is now. Did X and Y and Z, those blithe heroes and heroines, loathe school, despise their parents and teachers who never understood them, spend years of their lives fighting to free themselves from an environment they considered altogether beneath them? No, they did not; while in a hundred years' time people will read the novels of this century and conclude that everyone (no less) suffered adolescence like a disease, for they will hardly be able to lay hands on a novel which does not describe the condition. What then? For Martha was tormented, and there was no escaping it.

Perhaps, she thought (retreating into the sour humour that was her refuge at such moments), one should simply take the years from, let us say, fourteen to twenty as read, until those happier times arrive when adolescents may, and with a perfectly clear conscience, again enjoy themselves? How lucky, she thought, those coming novelists, who would be able to write cheerfully, and without the feeling that they were evading a problem: 'Martha went to school in the usual way, liked the teachers, was amiable with her parents, and looked forward with confidence to a happy and well-spent life'! But then (and here she suffered a twisting spasm of spite against those cold-minded mentors who so persistently analysed her state, and in so many volumes), what would they have to write about?

That defensive spite released her, and it was almost with confidence that she again lay back, and began to consider herself. For if she was often resentfully conscious that she was expected to carry a burden that young people of earlier times knew nothing about, then she was no less conscious that she was developing a weapon which would enable her to carry it. She was not only miserable, she could focus a dispassionate eye on that misery. This detached observer, felt perhaps as a clear-lit space situated just behind the forehead, was the gift of the Cohen boys at the station, who had been lending her books for the last two years. Joss Cohen tended towards economics and sociology, which she read without feeling personally implicated. Solly Cohen was in love (there is no other word for it) with psychology; he passionately defended everything to do with it, even when his heroes contradicted each other. And from these books Martha had gained a clear picture of herself, from the outside. She was adolescent, and therefore bound to be unhappy; British, and therefore uneasy and defensive; in the fourth decade of the twentieth century, and therefore inescapably beset with problems of race and class; female, and obliged to repudiate the shackled women of the past. She was tormented with guilt and responsibility and self-consciousness; and she did not regret the torment, though there were moments when she saw quite clearly that in making her see herself thus the Cohen boys took a malicious delight which was only too natural. There were moments, in fact, when she hated them.

But what they perhaps had not foreseen was that this sternly objective picture of herself merely made her think, no doubt unreasonably, Well, if all this has been said, why do I have to go through with it? If we *know* it, why do we have to go through the painful business of living it? She felt, though dimly, that now it was time to move on to something new, the act of giving names to things should be enough.

Besides, the experts themselves seemed to be in doubt as to how she should see herself. There was the group which stated that her life was already determined when she still crouched sightless in the womb of Mrs Quest. She grew through phases of fish and lizard and monkey, rocked in the waters of ancient seas, her ears lulled by the rhythm of the tides. But these tides, the pulsing blood of Mrs Quest, sang no uncertain messages to Martha, but songs of anger, or love, or fear or resentment, which sank into the passive brain of the infant, like a doom.

Then there were those who said it was the birth itself which set Martha on a fated road. It was during the long night of terror, the night of the difficult birth, when the womb of Mrs Quest convulsed and fought to expel its burden through the unwilling gates of bone (for Mrs Quest was rather old to bear a first child), it was during that birth, from which Martha emerged shocked and weary, her face temporarily scarred purple from the forceps, that her character and therefore her life were determined for her.

And what of the numerous sects who agreed on only one thing, that it was the first five years of life which laid an unalterable basis for everything that followed? During those years (though she could not remember them), events had occurred which had marked her fatally forever. For the feeling of fate, of doom, was the one message they all had in common. Martha, in violent opposition to her parents, was continually being informed that their influence on her was unalterable, and that it was much too late to change herself. She had reached the point where she could not read one of these books without feeling as exhausted as if she had just concluded one of her arguments with her mother. When a native bearer came hastening over the veld with yet another parcel of books from the Cohen boys, she felt angry at the mere sight of them, and had to fight against a tired reluctance before she could bring herself to read them. There were, at this very moment, half a dozen books lying neglected in her bedroom, for she knew quite well that if she read them she would only be in possession of yet more information about herself, and with even less idea of how to use it.

But if to read their books made her unhappy, those occasions when she could visit them at the store were the happiest of her life. Talking to them exhilarated her, everything seemed easy. She walked over to the kaffir store when her parents made the trip into the station; sometimes she got a lift from a passing car. Sometimes, though secretly, since this was forbidden, she rode in on her bicycle. But there was always an uneasiness about this friendship, because of Mrs Quest; only last week, she had challenged Martha. Being what she was, she could not say outright, 'I don't want you to know Jewish shopkeepers.' She launched into a tirade about how Jews and Greeks exploited the natives worse than anyone, and ended by saying that she did not know what to do with Martha, who seemed bent on behaving so as to make her mother as unhappy as possible. And for the first time that Martha could remember, she wept; and though her words were dishonest, her emotion was not. Martha had been deeply disturbed by those tears.

Yesterday, Martha had been on the point of getting out her bicycle in order to ride in to the station, so badly did she need to see the Cohen boys, when the thought of another scene with her mother checked her. Guiltily, she left the bicycle where it was. And now, although she wanted more than anything else to tell them about her silly and exaggerated behaviour in front of Mrs Van Rensberg, so that they might laugh good-naturedly at it, and restore it to proportion, she could not make the effort to rise from under the big tree, let alone get out the bicycle and go secretly into the station, hoping she would not be missed. And so she remained under the tree, whose roots were hard under her back, like a second spine, and looked up through the leaves to the sky, which shone in a bronze clamour of light. She ripped the fleshy leaves between her fingers, and thought again of her mother and Mrs Van Rensberg. She would *not* be like Mrs Van Rensberg, a fat and earthy housekeeping woman; she would *not* be bitter and nagging and dissatisfied, like her mother. But then, who was she to be like? Her mind turned towards the heroines she had been offered, and discarded them. There seemed to be a gap between herself and the past, and so her thoughts swam in a mazed and unfed way through her mind, and she sat up, rubbing her stiffened back, and looked down the aisles of stunted trees, over a wash of pink feathery grass, to the red clods of a field which was invisible from the house.

There moved a team of oxen, a plough, a native driver with his long whip, and at the head of the team a small black child, naked except for a loincloth, tugging at the strings which passed through the nostrils of the leaders of the team. The driver she did not like – he was a harsh and violent man who used that whip with too much zest; but the pity she refused herself flooded out and surrounded the black child like a protective blanket. And again her mind swam and shook, like clearing water, and now, instead of one black child, she saw a multitude, and so lapsed easily into her familiar daydream. She looked away over the ploughed land, across the veld to the Dumfries Hills, and refashioned that unused country to the scale of her imagination. There arose, glimmering whitely over the harsh scrub and the stunted trees, a noble city, set foursquare and colonnaded along its falling, flower-bordered terraces. There were splashing fountains, and the sound of flutes; and its citizens moved, grave and beautiful, black and white and brown together; and these groups of elders paused, and smiled with pleasure at the sight of the children – the blue-eyed, fair-skinned children of the North playing hand in hand with the bronze-skinned, dark-eyed children of the South. Yes, they smiled and approved these many-fathered children, running and playing among the flowers and the terraces, through the white pillars and tall trees of this fabulous and ancient city . . .

It was about a year later. Martha was seated beneath the same tree, and in rather the same position, her hands full of leaves which she was unconsciously rubbing to a green and sticky mess. Her head was filled with the same vision, only more detailed. She could have drawn a plan of that city, from the central market place to the four gates. Outside one of the gates stood her parents, the Van Rensbergs, in fact most of the people of the district, forever excluded from the golden city because of their pettiness of vision and small understanding; they stood grieving, longing to enter, but barred by a stern and remorseless Martha – for unfortunately one gets nothing, not even a dream, without paying heavily for it, and in Martha's version of the golden age there must always be at least one person standing at the gate to exclude the unworthy. She heard footsteps, and turned her head to find Marnie picking her way down the native path, her high heels rocking over the stones.

'Hey,' said Marnie excitedly, 'heard the news?'

Martha blinked her eyes clear of the dream, and said, rather stiffly, 'Oh, hullo.' She was immediately conscious of the difference between herself and Marnie, whose hair was waved, who wore lipstick and nail varnish, and whose face was forced into an effect of simpering maturity, which continually vanished under pressure from her innate good sense. Now she was excited she was like a healthy schoolgirl who had been dressing up for fun; but at the sight of the sprawling and undignified Martha, who looked rather like an overgrown child of eleven, with a ribbon tying her lanky blond hair, and yoked dress in flowered print, she remembered her own fashionable dress, and sat primly on the grass, placed her black heels together, and looked down at her silk-stockinged legs with satisfaction.

'My sister's getting married,' she announced.

There were five sisters, two already married, and Martha asked, 'Who, Marie?' For Marie was next, according to age.

'No, not Marie,' said Marnie with impatient disparagement. 'Marie'll never get herself a man, she hasn't got what it takes.'

At the phrase 'get herself a man,' Martha flushed, and looked away, frowning. Marnie glanced doubtfully at her, and met a glance of such scorn that she blushed in her turn, though she did not know what for.

'You haven't even asked who,' she said accusingly, though with a timid note; and then burst out: 'Man, believe it or not, but it's Stephanie.'

Stephanie was seventeen, but Martha merely nodded.

Damped, Marnie said, 'She's doing well for herself, too, say what you like. He's got a V-8, and he's got a bigger farm than Pop.'

'Doing well for herself' caused Martha yet another internal shudder. Then the thought flashed across her mind: I criticize my mother for being a snob, but despise the Van Rensbergs with a clear conscience, because my snobbishness is intellectual. She could not afford to keep this thought clear in her mind; the difficult, painful process of educating herself was all she had to sustain her. But she managed to say after a pause, though with genuine difficulty, 'I'm glad, it will be nice to have another wedding.' It sounded flat.

Marnie sighed, and glanced down at her pretty fingernails for comfort. She would have so much liked an intimate talk with a girl her own age. Or rather, though there were girls of her own age among the Afrikaans community growing up around her father's farm, she would have liked to be friends with Martha, whom she admired. She would have liked to say, with a giggle, that she was sixteen herself and could get a man, with luck, next year, like Stephanie. Finding herself confronted by Martha's frowning eyes, she wished she might return to the veranda, where the two mothers would be discussing the fascinating details of the courtship and wedding. But it was a tradition that the men should talk to the men, women with the women, and the children should play together. Marnie did not consider herself a child, though Martha, it seemed, did. She thought that if she could return by herself to the veranda, she might join the women's talk, whereas if Martha came with her they would be excluded. She said, 'My mom's telling your mom.'

Martha said, with that unaccountable resentment, 'Oh, she'll have a wonderful time gossiping about it.' Then she added quickly, trying to make amends for her ungraciousness, 'She'll be awfully pleased.'

'Oh, I know your mom doesn't want you to marry young, she wants you to make a career,' said Marnie generously.

But again Martha winced, saying angrily, 'Oh she'd love it if I married young.'

'Would you like it, hey?' suggested Marnie, trying to create an atmosphere where they might 'have a good talk.'

Martha laughed satirically and said, 'Marry young? Me? I'd die first. Tie myself down to babies and housekeeping . . .'

Marnie looked startled, and then abashed. She remarked defiantly, 'Mom says you're sweet on Joss Cohen.' At the sight of Martha's face she giggled with fright. 'Well, he's sweet on you, isn't he?'

Martha gritted her teeth, and ground out, '*Sweet* on!'

'Hell, he likes you, then.'

'Joss Cohen,' said Martha angrily.

'He's a nice boy. Jews can be nice, and he's clever, like you.'

'You make me sick,' said Martha, reacting, or so she thought, to this racial prejudice.

Again Marnie's good-natured face drooped with puzzled hurt, and she gave Martha an appealing look. She stood up, wanting to escape.

But Martha slid down a flattened swathe of long grass, and scrambled to her feet. She rubbed the back of her thighs under the cotton dress, saying, 'Ooh, taken all the skin off.'

Her way of laughing at herself, almost clowning, at these graceless movements, made Marnie uncomfortable in a new way. She thought it extraordinary that Martha should wear such clothes, behave like a clumsy schoolboy, at sixteen, and apparently not mind. But she accepted what was in intention an apology, and looked at the title of the book Martha held – it was a life of Cecil Rhodes – and asked, was it interesting? Then the two girls went together up the native path, which wound under the low scrubby trees, through yellow grass that reached to their shoulders, to the clearing where the house stood.

It was built native style, with mud walls and thatched roof, and had been meant to last two seasons, for the Quests had come to the colony after seeing an exhibition in London which promised new settlers that they might become rich on maize-growing almost from one year to the next. This had not happened, and the temporary house was still in use. It was a long oval, divided across to make rooms, and around it had been flung out projecting verandas of grass. A square, tin-roofed kitchen stood beside it. This kitchen was now rather tumble-down, and the roof was stained and rusted. The roof of the house too had sagged, and the walls had been patched so often with fresh mud that they were all colours, from dark rich red through dulling yellow to elephant grey. There were many different kinds of houses in the district, but the Quests' was original because a plan which was really suitable for bricks and proper roofing had been carried out in grass and mud and stamped dung.

The girls could see their mothers sitting behind the screen of golden shower; and at the point where they should turn to climb the veranda steps, Martha said hastily, 'You go,' and went off into the house, while Marnie thankfully joined the women.

Martha slipped into the front room like a guilty person, for the people on the veranda could see her by turning their heads. When the house was first built, there had been no verandas. Mrs Quest had planned the front of the house to open over the veld 'like the prow of a ship,' as she herself gaily explained. There were windows all around it, so that there had been a continuous view of mountains and veld, lightly intersected by strips of wall, like a series of framed 'views.' Now the veranda dipped over them, and the room was rather dark. There were chairs and settees, and a piano on one side, and a dining table on the other. Years ago, when the rugs and chintzes were fresh, this had been a pretty room, with cream-washed walls and smooth black linoleum under the rugs. Now it was not merely faded, but dingy and overcrowded. No one played the piano. The silver teatray that had been presented to Mrs Quest's grandfather on retirement from his bank stood on the sideboard among bits of rock, nuts and bolts from the ploughs, and bottles of medicine.

When Mrs Quest first arrived, she was laughed at, because of the piano and the expensive rugs, because of her clothes, because she had left visiting cards on her neighbours. She laughed herself now, ruefully, remembering her mistakes.

In the middle of the floor was a pole of tough thornwood, to hold the end of the ridgepole. It had lain for weeks in a bath of strong chemical, to protect it from ants and insects; but now it was riddled with tiny holes, and if one put one's ear to it there could be heard a myriad tiny jaws at work, and from the holes slid a perpetual trickle of faint white dust. Martha stood beside it, waiting for the moment when everyone on the veranda would be safely looking the other way, and felt it move rockingly on its base under the floor. She thought it typical of her parents that for years they had been reminding each other how essential it was to replace the pole in good time, and, now that the secretly working insects had hollowed it so that it sounded like a drum when tapped, remarked comfortingly, 'Well, it doesn't matter, the ridgepole never really rested in the fork, anyway.' And indeed, looking up at the thatch, one could see a clear two inches between the main spine of the roof and its intended support. The roof seemed to be held well enough on the web of light poles which lay under the thatch. The whole house was like this – precarious and shambling, but faithful, for it continued to remain upright against all probability. 'One day it'll fall on our heads,' Mrs Quest would grumble when her husband said, as usual, that they could not afford to rebuild. But it did not fall.

At a suitable moment, Martha slipped into the second room. It was her parents' bedroom. It was a large square, and rather dark, for there were only two windows. The furniture was of petrol and paraffin boxes, nailed together and painted and screened by cretonne. The curtains, originally bought in London, had faded to a yellowish grey. On the thin web of the stuff, which hung limp against the glare, showed a tenacious dark outline of strutting peacocks. There were two large iron beds standing side by side on one wall, a dressing table facing them on the other. Habit had not dulled Martha into blindness of these things, of the shabby neglect of the place. But the family lived here without *really* living here. The house had been built as temporary, and was still temporary. Next year they would go back to England, or go into town. The crops might be good; they would have a stroke of luck and win the sweepstake; they would find a gold mine. For years Mr and Mrs Quest had been discussing these things; and to such conversations Martha no longer listened, for they made her so irritable she could not stand them.

She had seen clearly, when she was about eleven or twelve, that her parents were deluding themselves; she had even reached the stage where she could say, If they really wanted to move, they would. But this cold, exasperated thought had never been worked out, and she still shared her parents' unconscious attitude, although she repudiated their daydreaming and foolishness, that this was not really her home. She knew that to Marnie, to others of their neighbours, this house seemed disgracefully shabby, even sordid; but why be ashamed of something that one has never, not for a moment, considered as home?

When Martha was alone in this room, and had made sure the doors were closed, she moved carefully to the small square mirror that was nailed to the centre of the window, over the dressing table. She did not look at the things on the dressing table, because she disliked them. For many years, Mrs Quest had been describing women who used cosmetics as fast; then she saw that everyone else did, and bought herself lipstick and nail varnish. She had no instinct for them, and they were the wrong colour. Her powder had a musty, floury smell, like a sweet, rather stale cake. Martha hastily put the lid on the box and slipped it into a drawer, so as to remove the smell. Then she examined herself in the mirror, leaning up on her toes, for it was too high: Mrs Quest was a tall woman. She was by no means resigned to the appearance her mother thought suitable. She spent much time, at night, examining herself with a hand mirror; she sometimes propped the mirror by her pillow, and, lying beside it, would murmur like a lover, 'Beautiful, you are so beautiful.' This happened when Mrs Quest had made one of her joking remarks about Martha's clumsiness, or Mr Quest complained that girls in this country matured so early.

She had a broad but shapely face, with a pointed chin, severe hazel eyes, a full mouth, clear straight dark brows. Sometimes she would take the mirror to her parents' bedroom, and hold it at an angle to the one at the window, and examine herself, at this double remove, in profile; for this view of herself had a delicacy her full face lacked. With her chin tilted up, her loose blond hair falling back, her lips carefully parted in an eager, expectant look, she possessed a certain beauty. But it seemed to her that her face, her head, were something quite apart from her body; she could see herself only in sections, because of the smallness of the mirror. The dresses her mother made looked ugly, even obscene, for her breasts were well grown, and the yokes emphasized them, showing flattened bulges under the tight band of material; and the straight falling line of the skirt was spoiled by her full hips. Her mother said that girls in England did not come out until at the earliest sixteen, but better still eighteen, and girls of a nice family wore dresses of this type until coming out. That she herself had not 'come out,' and that her family had not by many degrees reached that stage of *niceness* necessary to coming out, was not enough to deflect her. For on such considerations is the social life of England based, and she was after all quite right in thinking that if only she had married better, or if *only* their farming had been successful, it would have been possible to arrange with the prosperous branch of family that Martha should come out. So Martha's sullen criticisms of her snobbishness had no effect at all; and she would smooth the childish dresses down over Martha's body, so that the girl stood hunched with resentment, and say with an embarrassed coyness, 'Dear me, you are getting a pouter pigeon, aren't you?'

Once, Mrs Van Rensberg, watching this scene, remarked soothingly, 'But, Mrs Quest, Martha has a nice little figure, why shouldn't she show it?' But outwardly the issue was social convention, and not Martha's figure; and if Mrs Van Rensberg said to her husband that Mrs Quest was going the right way to make Martha 'difficult' she could not say so to Mrs Quest herself.

This afternoon was a sudden climax after a long brooding underground rebellion. Standing before the mirror, she took a pair of scissors and severed the bodice from the skirt of her dress. She was trying to make the folds lie like Marnie's, when the door suddenly opened, and her father came in. He stopped, with an embarrassed look at his daughter, who was naked, save for a tiny pair of pink drawers; but that embarrassment was having it both ways, for if Martha was still a child, then one could look at her naked.

He said gruffly, 'What are you doing?' and went to a long cupboard beside his bed, formed of seven petrol boxes, one above another, painted dark green, and covered by a faded print curtain. It was packed with medicine bottles, crammed on top of each other so that a touch might dislodge them into an avalanche. He said moodily, 'I think I'll try that new stuff, I've a touch of indigestion', and tried to find the appropriate bottle. As he held them up to the light of the window, one after another, his eyes fell on Martha, and he remarked, 'Your mother won't like you cutting her dresses to pieces.'

She said defiantly, 'Daddy, why should I wear dresses like a kid of ten?'

He said resentfully, 'Well, you are a kid. Must you quarrel all the time with your mother?'

Again the door swung in, banging against the wall, and Mrs Quest entered, saying, 'Why did you run off, Martha, they wanted to tell you about Stephanie, it really is rude of you –' She stopped, stared, and demanded, 'Whatever are you doing?'

'I'm not wearing this kind of dress any more', said Martha, trying to sound calm, but succeeding only in her usual sullen defiance.

'But, my dear, you've ruined it, and you know how badly off we are,' said Mrs Quest, in alarm at the mature appearance of her daughter's breasts and hips. She glanced at her husband, then came quickly across the room, and laid her hands on either side of the girl's waist, as if trying to press her back into childhood. Suddenly Martha moved backwards, and involuntarily lifted her hand; she was shuddering with disgust at the touch of her own mother, and had been going to slap her across the face. She dropped her hand, amazed at her own violence; and Mrs Quest coloured and said ineffectually, 'My dear . . .'

'I'm sixteen,' said Martha, between set teeth, in a stifled voice; and she looked towards her father, for help. But he quickly turned away, and measured medicine into a glass.

'My dear, nice girls wear clothes like this until –'

'I'm not a nice girl,' broke in Martha, and suddenly burst into laughter.

Mrs Quest joined her in a relieved peal, and said, 'Really my dear, you are ridiculous.' And then, on a more familiar note, 'You've spoiled that dress, and it is not fair to Daddy, you know how difficult it is to find money . . .' She stopped again, and followed the direction of Martha's eyes. Martha was looking at the medicine cupboard. Mrs Quest was afraid that Martha might say, as she had said to her, that there must be hundreds of pounds' worth of medicines in that cupboard, and they had spent more on Mr Quest's imaginary diseases than they had spent on educating her.

This was, of course, an exaggeration. But it was strange that when Martha made these comments Mrs Quest began arguing about the worth of the medicines: 'Nonsense, dear, you know quite well it can't be hundreds of pounds.' She did not say, 'Your father is very ill.' For Mr Quest was really ill, he had contracted diabetes three or four years before. And there was an episode connected with this that neither Martha nor Mrs Quest liked to remember. One day, Martha was summoned from her classroom at school in the city, to find Mrs Quest waiting for her in the passage. 'Your father's ill,' she exclaimed, and then, seeing that Martha's face expressed only: Well, there's nothing new in that, is there?, added hastily, 'Yes, really, he's got diabetes, he must go to the hospital and have tests.' There was a long silence from Martha, who at length muttered, like a sleepwalker, '*I knew it.*' Almost the moment these words were out, she flushed with guilt; and at once she hastened to the car, where her father sat, and both women fussed over him, while Mr Quest, who was very frightened, listened to their reassurances.

When Martha remembered that phrase, which had emerged from her depths, as if it had been waiting for the occasion, she felt uneasy and guilty. Secretly, she could not help thinking, He wanted to be ill, he likes being ill, now he's got an excuse for being a failure. Worse than this, she accused her mother, in her private thoughts, of being responsible.

The whole business of Mr Quest's illness aroused such unpleasant depths of emotion between mother and daughter that the subject was left alone, for the most part; and now Mrs Quest said hastily, moving away to the window, 'You're upsetting your father, he worries about you.' Her voice was low and nagging.

'You mean *you* worry about me,' said Martha coldly, unconsciously dropping her voice, with a glance at her father. In a half-whisper she said, 'He doesn't even notice we're here. He hasn't *seen* us for years . . .' She was astounded to find that her voice shook, she was going to cry.

Mr Quest hastily left the room, persuading himself that his wife and daughter were not quarrelling, and at once Mrs Quest said in a normal voice, 'You're a worry to us. You don't realize. The way you waste money and –'

Martha cut it short, by walking out of the room and into her own. The door did not lock, or even fasten properly, for it hung crooked. It had been formed of planks, by a native carpenter, and had warped in the rainy seasons, so that to shut it meant a grinding push across a lumpy and swelling lintel. But though it did not lock, there were moments when it was invisibly locked, and this was one of them. Martha knew her mother would not come in. She sat on the edge of her bed and cried with anger.

This was the pleasantest room of the house, a big square room, freshly whitewashed, and uncrowded. The walls rose clear to the roof, which slanted down on either side of the ridgepole in a gentle sweep of softly glistening thatch, which had turned a greyish gold with the years. There was a wide, low window that looked directly over a descent of trees to an enormous red field, and a rise on the other side, of fresh parklike bush – for it had never been cut to feed mine furnaces, as had most of the trees on the farm – and beyond this slope rose the big mountain, Jacob's Burg. It was all flooded with evening sunlight. Sunset: the birds were singing to the day's end, and the crickets were chirping the approach of night. Martha felt tired, and lay on her low iron bedstead, whose lumpy mattress and pillows had conformed comfortably to the shape of her body. She looked out past the orange-tinted curtains to the sky, which was flooded with wild colour. She was facing, with dubious confidence, what she knew would be a long fight. She was saying to herself, I won't give in, I won't; though it would have been hard for her to define what it was she fought.

And in fact the battle of the clothes had begun. It raged for months, until poor Mr Quest groaned and went out of the room whenever the subject was raised, which was continuously, since it had become a focus for the silent struggle between the women, which had nothing to do with clothes, or even with 'niceness'.

Mr Quest thought of himself as a peace-loving man. He was tall and lean and dark, of slow speech and movement; he was handsome too, and even now women warmed to him, and to the unconscious look of understanding and complicity in his fine dark eyes. For in that look was a touch of the rake; and at these moments when he flirted a little with Mrs Van Rensberg, he came alive; and Mrs Quest was uneasy, and Martha unaccountably rather sad, seeing her father as he must have been when he was young. His good looks were conventional, even dull, save for his moments of animation. And they were rare, for if Mr Quest was a rake, he did not know it.

When Mrs Quest said teasingly, but with an uneasy undertone, 'Mrs Van Rensberg, poor soul, got quite flustered this afternoon, the way you flirted with her,' Mr Quest said, rather irritated, 'What do you mean, I flirted? I was only talking for politeness' sake.' And he really believed it.

What he liked best was to sit for hours on end in his deck chair on the veranda, and watch the lights and shadows move over the hills, watch the clouds deploying overhead, watch the lightning at night, listen to the thunder. He would emerge after hours of silence, remarking, 'Well, I don't know, I suppose it all means something'; or 'Life is a strange business, say what you like.' He was calm, even cheerful, in his absent-minded way, as long as he was not disturbed, which meant, these days, as long as he was not spoken to. At these moments he became suffused with angry irritation; and now both women were continually appealing for his support, and he would reply helplessly, 'For heaven's sake, what is there to quarrel *for*? There isn't anything to quarrel *about*.' When his wife came to him secretly, talking insistently until he had to hear her, he shouted in exasperation, 'Well, if the child wants to make herself ridiculous, then let her, don't waste your time arguing.' And when Martha said helplessly, 'Do talk to her, do tell her I'm not ten years old any longer,' he said, 'Oh, Lord, do leave me alone, and anyway, she's quite right, you're much too young, look at Marnie, she makes me blush wriggling around the farm in shorts and high heels.' But this naturally infuriated Martha, who did not envisage herself in the style of a Marnie. But the women could not leave him alone, several times a day they came to him, flushed, angry, their voices querulous, demanding his attention. They would not leave him in peace to think about the war, in which he had lost his health, and perhaps something more important than health; they would not leave him to dream tranquilly about the future, when some miracle would transport then all into town, or to England; they nagged at him, as he said himself, like a couple of darned fishwives! Both felt that he let them down, and became irritable against him, so that at such times it was as if this very irritation cemented them together, and against him. But such is the lot of the peacemakers.

A Proper Marriage

When a person dies for his country, then you can say he loves it.
Turgenev, *On the Eve*

1

The skies of Africa being for the most part blue and clear, and eminently suitable for aeroplanes, there were few cities in the subcontinent that did not hastily throw up on their outskirts camps of Nissen huts, hangars, runways and temporary houses, surrounded by fences and barbed wire and as self-contained and isolated as those other towns outside the city, the native locations.

For weeks before anything changed, the local inhabitants would drive out of a Sunday afternoon to watch the building; for weeks nothing was spoken of but that the Air Force was coming. That phrase, together with those others now constantly used by the newspapers, like 'Knights of the Air' and 'our boys', evoked in the minds of the population, which was now after all mostly female, an image of a tall graceful youth fitted neatly into sky-blue cloth. Certain poets were partly responsible for this charming figure – the newspapers are not to blame for everything. Besides, this was the period of the Battle of Britain; a need for heroism, starved so long, was being fed at last; it was as if the gallant youth from 1914 had donned a uniform the colour of the sky and taken wing. Their own young men who had left the colony in search of adventure were mostly dead, and killed in the air. The air was their medium, they felt. Useless to ask a country separated from the sea by hundreds of miles to think of itself as a breeder of sailors; and of that mass of young men who had departed north for land fighting, few had as yet actually fought. When they did, when those deaths and wounds were announced, the shock of it would breed a new image; in the meantime, it was an air war, and it was fitting that this colony should be asked to train airmen.

More than this lay behind their impatience for the moment when 'the boys' should actually arrive. Few of them had not been brought up with the words 'Home' and 'England' continually in their mouths, even if they

had not been born there; it was their own people they were expecting –
and more: themselves, at one remove, and dignified by responsibility
and danger. They knew what to expect: the colony was being fed month
by month in peacetime by immigrants who were certainly of the stock
which produced rather graceful young men, even if they changed in so
few weeks into people like themselves – not charming, not – but the
word 'effeminate' was one the Battle of Britain made obsolete; it was
conceded that the war and the number of deaths in the skies over
London made those more sheltered cousins the equals of any veld
adventurer or horizon conqueror.

But before an aeroplane can be sent into the air with its proper
complement of highly trained young men, there must be so many others
on the ground to provide for the welfare of both. It was this that the
local people had not taken into account.

Suddenly, overnight, the streets changed. They were filled with a
race of beings in thick, clumsy greyish uniforms; and from these ill-
fitting cases of cloth emerged pallid faces and hands which had – to
people who above all always had enough to eat and plenty of sunshine –
a look of incompleteness. It was as if nature had sketched an ideal – that
tall, well-fed charming youth, so easily transformed into a tough hero –
and, being starved of material to complete it with, had struggled into
what perfection it could. That, obscurely, was how they felt; they could
not own these ancestors; their cousins from Home were a race of
dwarfs, several inches shorter than themselves. They were not burnt
and brown, but unhealthily pale. They were not glorious and rebellious
individuals – for, above all, emigrants to the colonies have been that –
but they had the look, as they strayed cautiously and curiously about
the shallow little colonial streets, of a community whose oneness was
only emphasized by the uniform.

In short, they were different.

It never entered their heads to apologize for being different.

They made no effort to become like their hosts.

Worse than anything, the faces of these new guests – a colonial people
instinctively feel themselves as hosts – expressed nothing but a patient
and sardonic criticism. They were unwilling guests.

These groundlings, dumped arbitrarily into the middle of Africa,
strayed about the town, noted the two cinemas, half a dozen hotels, a
score of bars; noted that the amenities usual for ten thousand white
inhabitants were to be stretched to provide for them in their hundreds

of thousands; noted that women would be in short supply for the duration; and, with that calm common sense which distinguishes the British working man, decided to make themselves as comfortable as possible in circumstances fully as bad as they had expected. For a time the grey tide ebbed back from the city into the camps that were surrounded by the high, forbidding fences.

Not before a number of disturbing incidents had occurred. For instance, several innocent men had brought Coloured women into the bars of an evening, and had violently resented being asked to leave. Others were observed offering black men cigarettes on street corners, while talking to them, or even walking with them. It was rumoured that quite a number had actually gone into the homes of the servants of the city, in the native location. But this was not the worst; it was felt that such behaviour was merely the result of ignorance; a short acquaintance with local custom would put things right. No, it was something more indefinable, something inarticulate, an atmosphere like an ironic stare, which, since it was not put into words, could not be answered.

A group of airmen might be walking down the street, hoping that some diversion might offer itself, when their attention was drawn by the sound of a wild and urgent motor horn. An expensive car stood by them, in which a couple, smiling with fervent goodwill, urged they should enter. They climbed, therefore, into the car, and were whisked off to McGrath's Hotel, where drinks were called for all round. The orchestra still played, war or no war, from its bower of ferns. The native waiters came round with trays of beer. All was gilt and imitation marble. And this couple, so eager to be kind, were kindness itself. But why this positively effusive hospitality. Why? They might almost have been guilty about something. They talked about England: Do you remember, do you know, have you ever been to . . . But, but! the colonial's England is not the England that these men longed for, not the pubs and streets they were exiled from. They were kind enough not to point this out.

That *but* was felt like a piece of grit in the mouthful of honey which was this chance to be welcoming hosts. How seldom do colonials, starved in their deepest need to be hosts, get the chance to take to their bosoms not one or two but twenty thousand grateful guests at once? All over the city, in bars and hotel lounges and even in private drawing rooms, could be seen – in that first week or so – a couple, man and wife, entertaining anything up to twenty polite but determinedly inarticulate groundlings, who drank and ate all they could, since the pushed-around are entitled to take what crumbs fate offers them, but certainly did not return that loving approval which is what hosts most essentially ask in return. Yes, this was a fine country; yes, it was a grand town; yes, it was a wonderful achievement for half a century. But. But. But.

The tide receded. It would return. Thousands upon thousands more men were arriving every week from Home. From those first tentative contacts it was clear that there was a situation which should be faced by those whose task it was to administer and guide.

In every city there is a group of middle-aged and elderly women who in fact run it. The extent to which they are formally organized is no gauge of their real power. The way in which they respond to danger is that gauge; and from the frankness with which they express their intentions can be measured the extent of the danger. To students of 'local politics' let there be recommended the activities of the mothers of the city:

About a week after the first grey tide, there occurred a conversation between Mr Maynard and his wife, not on the pillow – they had not shared one for many years – but at the breakfast table.

Mrs Maynard was the leader of the council of matriarchs. She was fitted for it not merely by character. The wives of prime ministers, Cabinet ministers, governors, mayors, because of the necessity that they should be above struggle and party strife, are precluded from certain positions. Far from envying such women, Mrs Maynard rather pitied them. She could have been one had she chosen. As it was, she was the daughter of an English family who for centuries had occupied itself with 'public work'; she was a cousin to the existing Governor, her husband was a third cousin to the Prime Minister of Britain; but he was only a magistrate; she was, so it was hoped it would be considered, not only reliable, but above all independent. Nothing she said would be taken as from the Government or a political party.

She remarked over the sheets of the *Zambesia News*, 'It is quite disgraceful that the authorities are not doing anything about it.'

Mr Maynard laid down his paper and asked, 'About what?'

'Millions of poor boys brought into the country and nothing whatsoever done for them.'

'You exaggerate slightly, I think?'

'Well – fifty thousand, a hundred thousand. One thousand would be bad enough.'

'There are cinemas and canteens in the camps, I believe.'

'You know quite well what I mean.'

Mr Maynard stirred his coffee, and remarked, 'Even in peacetime men outnumber women.' He added, 'I assume you are not suggesting a brothel – the churches wouldn't stand for it.'

She coloured and tightened her lips; this mask of annoyed rectitude vanished as she smiled with dry appreciation. 'Personally I'd rather brothels than – but that isn't what I meant.' She frowned and said, 'We should provide entertainment – something to keep them occupied.'

'My dear Myra, save your trouble. Every woman in the town is already lost. Wait until the pilots arrive.'

'I am thinking of the blacks,' she said, irritated. A short pause. Then, as it were thinking aloud, 'I heard from Edgar that they have no idea at all how to treat natives. Not their fault, of course, poor things. I suggested to him a course of lectures on native policy, that sort of thing, *before* they arrive in the country.'

'So you are not concerned with the morals of our wives and mothers?' He smiled at her, the heavy urbane eyebrows raised.

She returned an equally bland smile. 'I am concerned with both. The first thing should be a dance hall, with canteens, ping-pong –something like that.'

'I have just understood that you intend me to sponsor it – is that it?'

'You would do very well,' she suggested, for the first time with a touch of appeal.

'No,' he said decidedly.

'You've got to do something. Everybody's doing something.'

He continued to stir his coffee, and to look at her. It was a challenge.

It was met. 'We are at war, you know!' she cried out at last, from her real emotions. She was now flushed, indignant, and with a hint of quivering softness about brows and mouth – a reminiscence of a certain striking dark beauty.

He smiled unpleasantly; apparently he felt this to be a victory.

But she did not attempt to quell her emotion. 'Your attitude is extraordinary, extraordinary!' she said, lips quivering. 'Don't you care that we are at war?'

'I care very much. But not enough to run a refined club for the boys,' he added. Then: 'I shall confine myself to keeping the native population in its place. Nothing could be more useful than that, surely?'

They exchanged a long married look, which held dislike, and

respect. The two faces, both heavy, black-browed, commanding, confronted each other from opposite ends of the long table. It was, as always, a deadlock.

'Then I shall ask that old stick Anderson to run it.'

'An admirable choice.'

She rose, and went towards the door. His raised voice followed her: 'As regards the problem of the dear boys and the native women, it is my personal view that – regarded from a long-term point of view, of course – a few thousand more half-caste children would be a good thing. It might force the authorities to provide better amenities for them. As things are, the Coloured community provides more petty criminals than any other section of the population.'

This was designed to annoy. But one of the minor pleasures of power is to exchange in private views which would ruin you if your followers ever had a suspicion you held them. Mrs Maynard let out a short dry chuckle and said, 'There are surely simpler ways of getting better housing for the Coloureds than infecting all our boys with VD.'

Two days later a paragraph in the paper announced that three entertainment centres for the Air Force personnel were to be opened shortly under the experienced patronage of Mr Anderson, late of the Department of Statistics, a well-known public figure.

A second grey tide flowed abruptly over the town. Not quite so grey: the idea of the blue air fed a tinge of blue into those stiff uniforms, and now the hungry expectations of the people were assuaged, for these were the cousins, the welcomed relatives from Home – these, the aviators in person, recognizably the same species as themselves. They were perfectly at ease in drawing rooms, clubs, bars and dance rooms, where they at once appeared in their hundreds; and the city, long accustomed to indulging its young men in whatever follies they might choose to use, found nothing remarkable in their behaviour. They brought with them an atmosphere of dedication to danger, of reckless exuberance which – as every young woman in the city soon had reason to know – was covered by a most charming modesty; and this in its turn was a mask for a cynical nihilism which was more dangerously attractive than even recklessness. If the note of the First World War was idealistic dedication, succeeded by its mirror image, sarcastic anger, then the symbol for this period of the Second War was a cynical young airman sprouting aggressive but flippant moustaches, capable of the most appalling heroism, but prone to surprising lapses into self-pitying but stoic despair, during which moments he would say he hoped he would be killed, because there was no point in living, anyway. The truth of the morale of any army is most likely to be discovered between the sheets.

The danger of this mood, felt like a heightened pulse in the town, was expressed to Mr Maynard at the breakfast table thus:

'It's all very well, but we have to think of our boys up north.'

'I expect they are taking care of themselves in their own way.'

'Have you heard about . . .' Here followed the names of about a dozen young women. 'They are all losing their heads.'

'Provided they don't lose them too far, I daresay all will be well at the armistice.'

Mrs Maynard looked sharply at him, tightened her lips, held his eyes steadily with her own. When this couple had come together in 1919 after years of separation, there had been incidents to overlook on both sides. Not forgiven – no. Mrs Maynard could not forgive him that he had overlooked so easily. Yet what had happened? Nothing – she had never been unfaithful to him. There was simply a photograph of an officer, a cousin, among a bundle of old letters. As for him, he could not forgive that there was nothing to forgive. She had always fulfilled the letter of every agreement. But there burned in this handsome matron's heart a steady flame of romance; he knew it. She had given her heart to the dead and was thus free to deal with life as she felt was right. She had never done anything to be ashamed of.

After a few moments, he smiled and enquired, 'What do you propose to do about it, my dear?'

Mrs Maynard paid a number of visits, received others, was a good deal on the telephone. As a result, many young women got letters from various organizations suggesting that they might spend their time on such and such a form of war work. Strings invisibly tightened. Mrs Talbot, wan and beautiful with her daughter's grief (the fiancé had been killed in the air over London during the Battle of Britain), dropped in to see Martha and suggested she should join the organization of women connected with the civil service.

Martha hardly listened. Such was her naïveté that she thought it odd, even interfering, of Mrs Talbot, who had nothing to do with the Service. She gave Mrs Talbot tea, told her what news there was of Douglas – very little, save that he had just finished leave with the boys in some town in Abyssinia. And that meant – Martha calmly stated it, apparently not noticing Mrs Talbot's indrawn breath – that he was probably having dozens of love affairs. Happening to glance at Mrs Talbot, she frowned slightly, and added that he was perfectly entitled to do so; they did not believe in jealousy. Mrs Talbot was searching for the right words to express her disturbance of mind, when Martha, unaware that any were needed, began talking of something else. Martha's advantage in any such encounter was always her assumption that Mrs Talbot (for instance) was bound to agree with her; any suggestion that her view might not be the right one was met with a critical, almost incredulous stare.

Some days later, Mr Maynard himself came to see Martha. Mrs Maynard had said that she intended to visit personally a number of girls who were not pulling their weight. Mr Maynard had said hastily that he would see to young Matty Knowell himself. It was an instinct of protectiveness which he did not analyse.

As he climbed the stairs to the flat, he heard a child screaming; he had to knock several times before he was heard. Martha admitted him and asked him to sit down, announcing brightly that they would have to shout through the noise, if he didn't mind.

Mr Maynard did mind. He said he was prepared to wait. He disposed his large body on one of the small chairs, and watched. He was adjusting his ideas to the fact that Martha was no longer a girl with a baby, that his godchild-without-the-benefit-of-religion was now a personality. He saw a small lively girl striving energetically against the straps that bound her to a high chair, her cheeks scarlet and tear-stained, her black eyes rebellious. Caroline was small-limbed, dainty, with a fine pointed face – a delightful creature. On the platform before her was a heavy china plate, and on that a squelch of greyish pulp. Martha, planted on her two sturdy legs, faced the child like an antagonist, her own lips set as firmly as Caroline's, who was refusing the food she was trying to push in between them. As the spoon came near, Caroline set up an angry yell, and bright sparks of tears gleamed through squeezed lashes; then the small white teeth closed tight on the metal. Martha was pale with anger, trembling with the contest. She even caught the child's nose until the mouth opened, and thrust in the spoon, leaving a mass of that unpleasant-looking pulp. Caroline choked, then began to cry differently – a miserable, helpless wail. Martha winced, then fumblingly loosened the straps, and caught Caroline up. 'Oh, Lord,' she cried helplessly, 'I don't know what to do!' Caroline was twisting in the embrace; Martha set her on the floor, where she stood holding a chair and yelled defiance at her mother. Martha lifted her, with an impatient movement, and took her out to the veranda, came back and shut the door. Silence. She passed her hand across her eyes, reached for a cigarette, lit it, and sat down. She was now pale, tense and exhausted.

'Is all this really necessary?' enquired Mr Maynard.

Martha laughed unhappily, and said that the book ordered that if a child would not eat it should not be forced, but Caroline had not eaten a mouthful for days.

She took great gulps of smoke, but seemed to be sitting on edge, as if waiting for the slightest sound from Caroline.

'She looks very well on being starved,' observed Mr Maynard.

Martha frowned, and was silent. He was reminding himself of that time – so long ago – when Mrs Maynard was engaged in rearing Binkie. He could recall only his violent distaste of what had seemed an indefinite period of smells and mess; he remembered his puzzled respect of that tidy and fastidious lady his wife, who had apparently found nothing distasteful in soiled napkins and dribbling mouths. Now he looked at the high chair planted in the middle of the room, bathed in sunlight from the window. Scraps of brownish vegetable mush clung to it. There were bits of the stuff on the floor around it. Flies were settling over the plate. 'Can't you remove that unpleasant object?'

Martha looked at him enquiringly, and then at the chair. She shrugged at male queasiness, and remarked, 'If I take the chair out and Caroline sees it, she'll start screaming again.' But she lifted it outside, without incurring any protest, hastily wiped the bits of mess off the floor, and sat down again, still smoking. Mr Maynard observed that she was looking very attractive. She wore a slip of a yellow dress showing brown bare legs, brown well-shaped arms. Her fingernails and toenails were painted. She was scarcely recognizable as the pale plump schoolgirl he had married to her husband. She looked very young, self-contained, hard, unhappy. The dark speculative eyes watched him as if he might turn out to be an enemy.

The shell of bright confidence dissolved as she remarked humorously, 'I believe firmly that children should be removed from their parents at birth in their own interests.'

Mr Maynard's thoughts, which had left the infant Caroline, were thus returned to her. He said that children survived anything, in his experience. And returned to considering the fact which appeared to him to be confirmed by Martha's careful attractiveness, that rumour must be right.

'What are you doing with yourself?'

'Nothing much.'

'Having a good time?' he probed.

She said humorously, in a way which grated out resentment, that since children had to be fed three times a day and put to bed at half past six, there was scarcely much time left to enjoy oneself.

Mr Maynard could not remember being discommoded by Binkie's infancy, so he again dismissed Caroline. 'Do you go out much?'

'No,' she said, biting it off. And then: 'I am reading a lot.'

But he did not take it up. He lay propped on the angles of the slight chair, like a broad solid grey plank, and observed her from his heavily accented eyes. He was convinced that no young woman living alone with a small child would go to the trouble of curling her hair and painting her twenty nails, unless it was for the purpose of attracting a man. He dismissed the reading as he dismissed Caroline, and came direct to his point. 'It is being said that you are having an affair with an officer in the Air Force.'

'I have no doubt of it.' She was flushed with anger. 'If I were, I think I should be perfectly entitled to.'

'I am not arguing the matter from its principles,' he began, regarding this as an admission. 'I am merely suggesting that there are ways of doing things.'

'Hypocrite!' Martha snapped out; then stiffly smiled. Her eyebrows were knitting and reknitting as if, above her gulfs of anger, tendrils of thought attempted to engage.

Mr Maynard coloured slowly; such was the power of Martha on him: she paid no tribute at all to the authority he felt he enshrined. 'My dear young woman, what is the point of infuriating people if an ounce of tact would save you from it?'

It appeared a fresh outburst was imminent; then she laughed and said, 'As a matter of fact, I haven't had any love affairs with anybody.'

'Having acknowledged your rights in the matter –' he began, with humorous conciliation, but was interrupted.

'Do you know what happened?' enquired Martha, poised on the verge of what she meant him to think an amusing story.

'I can't wait to hear.'

'Well, I don't go out at nights much, because of Caroline.'

'Why don't you ask your mother to take her?'

'No,' said Martha quickly. 'Well, I asked the woman across the corridor to watch her. She never wakes at night. There was a dance at McGrath's – an officers' dance, of course,' she added disgustedly.

'Well, why not?'

She hurried past this point. 'So they laid on the girls, as usual. You know how they ring you up and ask you if you'll be one of the girls.'

'I don't see why not. As long as the boys are content to be boys, why shouldn't the girls oblige?'

She giggled. Then: 'Well, you know how they go on – but I suppose if there is one thing we've all had plenty of experience in it is coping with the boys on the tear.'

Mr Maynard coloured again, and shifted his limbs uncomfortably. 'Quite.'

'There were half a dozen at my table – you know, all very *English*.' She paused for words, while Mr Maynard wondered what the word 'English' meant to a girl, certainly English by parentage, who had never been in England.

'I am at a loss.'

'Soft,' said Martha, dismissing it. 'You know, those deprecating types with moustaches.'

'I hardly think it is the right word to use *now*,' he observed.

She looked confused and guilty, but persisted. 'Well then, heroes one and all, I know. But what is heroism, then?'

'Can't we leave that fascinating social question aside for the moment?'

'It's easy enough to let yourself be killed.'

'There are hundreds of thousands of men who are doing everything to see they will *not* be killed – I hope you don't admire them more.'

'I didn't say so,' she said sullenly.

Mr Maynard waited.

'About twelve o'clock I was landed with one of them and he was terribly drunk. I mean, really drunk. He was swaying all over the table. I got a waiter to hold him upright. But all his brothers in arms were dancing or in the bar. I couldn't think of anything to do. So I pushed him into my car and brought him here. Well, I could hardly take him into the men's washrooms, could I?'

'I suppose not.'

'So I brought him here and he was duly sick. Then I put him to bed on that divan there, and went to bed myself. About three in the morning, a vast horde of them burst in to claim him. Very solicitous they were about his condition. It appeared he was due to fly at five. He nearly pranged the morning before, he told me . . .' She tailed off. A note of defiant pity that had appeared in her voice must be disowned, apparently, for she continued, 'They all thought it a hell of a joke.'

This was the end of the story. Martha was scarlet with remembered humiliation. After a pause, Mr Maynard said, 'I don't see what you expect – you want to have it both ways.'

'Why?' she enquired reasonably. She lit a cigarette. 'If you want to construct a story that I am having an affair with the Air Force out of that interesting little incident, then you're welcome.'

'I don't see why I should apologize when you think you're entitled to an affair any time you like.'

'But I didn't!'

'When your practice catches up with your theory, all I want to suggest is a little more discretion.'

'Did you come here to tell me that?' she asked, amazed.

He moved his limbs again, and said, 'Well, no.'

First she appeared angry; then, unexpectedly, moved. She leaned towards him and asked, stammering slightly, 'Why – why do you care what I do?'

And again Mr Maynard, having got through the defences of this armoured young woman, could not face the emotion he had found. He took a quick glance at her direct, enquiring eyes, averted his own, and remarked, 'My dear girl, you can all go to the devil for all I care.'

He was surprised and contrite that her eyes filled with tears. She got up abruptly, went outside, and returned in a few moments with the sleeping child. She sat, holding her in her arms, smoking over the soft nestling head. Mr Maynard saw that ancient symbol, mother and child, through a pale blue fog shot with sunlight. He was extraordinarily moved. Martha seemed to him altogether more amenable, conciliating – safe, in fact – thus disposed.

He remarked, 'A charming picture.'

Martha was first puzzled, then embarrassed. She at once sprang up, and deposited the baby in a receptacle outside the door.

'Why did you do that?' enquired the elderly gentleman. 'I meant it.'

She looked at him sardonically. 'I am so glad you find it so satisfactory.' Then: 'It's against the rules to cuddle a baby out of hours – the book says so.'

At this point the door opened, and Mrs Quest came in. 'Matty, why don't you put your name on the door, I keep telling you –' She saw the magistrate, and greeted him warmly.

'I'm just going,' said Mr Maynard, 'having spent a delightful half hour with your daughter.'

'She's an awful scatterbrain,' said Mrs Quest instinctively, avoiding compliments to her own like a peasant afraid of the evil eye. 'Have you ever seen such a mess as this place is in?' She began to set it to rights forthwith. Martha sat on the arm of a chair, puffing out smoke and looking stubbornly ironical.

'Would you like to come with me to a meeting of that Left group tomorrow night?' enquired Mr Maynard.

Martha brightened. Mrs Quest's face glazed – the pillars were rocking. She looked timidly at Mr Maynard and said, 'You don't mean that batch of Communists – someone said yesterday they have the CID at all their meetings.' She gave a short scandalized laugh.

'Oh, I don't think it's as bad as that,' Mr Maynard soothed. He looked enquiringly at Martha.

Mrs Quest said, 'I'll take Caroline, and you can go with Mr Maynard, it's very kind of him.'

Martha said nothing; she was looking angrily at her mother.

Mr Maynard recognized the existence of one of the female situations which it was his principle to avoid, and said to Martha, 'I'll pick you up tomorrow about eight – see you then, goodbye, ladies.' And departed.

'I really don't see why you don't get a boy,' said Mrs Quest irritably.

'Why should I have a servant when I've nothing else to do?'

'Everyone has one.'

'That's apparently final.'

'Besides, you don't do the housework – I've never seen such a mess.'

'Well, I live in it.' But now appeared that old enemy to decision of character, who pointed out to Martha that this argument was ridiculous, not because she was not entirely in the right, but because it sounded so *banal*. She retreated to the divan which not so long ago had supported the inebriated limbs of the Air Force officer, and watched her mother sweep and tidy the flat.

Mrs Quest, relieved by 'doing something', began to chat good-humouredly about Mr Quest – who was much better these days, he had dropped one of his medicines yesterday – and went on from there to Mr Maynard, who must be misinformed about that Left crowd, because a man in his position couldn't afford to get mixed up with such people.

'Oh, Mother!'

'But everybody knows . . .' This was lost as she bent under a corner table to retrieve fallen papers. Martha sprang forward to take them from her. Mrs Quest gave them up suspiciously. Martha put them into a drawer in such a way that she might have been accusing her mother of looking at them. Mrs Quest, hurt, said she had no intention of prying into Martha's private concerns. This reminding her of nearer preoccupations, she enquired offhand, 'And what's all this I hear of your going out gallivanting in the evenings?'

'I can only imagine.'

'I thought you said you weren't going out – what did you do with Caroline?'

'She was not neglected, if that's what you mean.'

'It's all very well,' cried out Mrs Quest, from the depths of her heart, 'but when I dropped in yesterday, she was quite alone and crying. As I told Mrs Talbot at bridge yesterday, you are really quite irresponsible.'

Martha was now alert with anger. 'I was only out for twenty minutes buying vegetables. And what's it to do with Mrs Talbot?'

'You should get a boy, and then you wouldn't have to go out shopping. It's ridiculous, they'll deliver, anyway.'

'I thought you said it was dangerous to have a boy in a place where there was a small girl, because he was bound to rape her?'

They were now on the verge of a real battle, when Caroline let out the sudden, startled wail of an infant woken too soon. Martha got up, but, seeing that her mother was there before her, sat down, telling herself it was all unimportant and she should learn not to mind.

Mrs Quest brought in the small girl, and sat crooning over her, with an access of tenderness that touched and disarmed Martha; but Caroline was striving like an unwilling captive in the arms that held her. Mrs Quest laughed ruefully and set her down, and she unsteadily staggered back to the veranda, while the two women watched her with the same small, proud smile, in which was a touch of regret.

'She's very small for her age,' said Mrs Quest dubiously. 'I hope you are giving her enough to eat.'

Martha jumped up as if stung. Mrs Quest rose hurriedly, and said she might just as well take Caroline now for a few days, it would give Martha a rest. Martha nearly protested, then allowed herself to slide into apathy – for why not? Then Mrs Quest added that Caroline needed to be fed up a little, and Martha turned away helplessly, silenced by the knowledge that she was certainly a failure, she could no more manage Caroline than Mrs Quest had managed *her*. Grandmothers, she reflected, falling back with relief on the abstraction, are better with their grandchildren than with their own children. And she even dwelt wistfully on a charming picture, Mrs Quest tenderly relaxed with Caroline, a picture that had the same soothing, ideal quality as what Mr Maynard saw when he looked at *her* with the child.

In a few minutes Mrs Quest had left with Caroline, and the flat was empty. Martha was, as always, uncomfortably surprised that as soon as Caroline was away from her it was as if she had never had a child at all; whereas as long as they were together that invisible navel string twanged like a harshly plucked string at every movement or sound the child made. She sat down and consciously tried to pull herself together; she felt herself to be a hopeless failure; she was good for nothing, not even the simple natural function that every female should achieve like breathing: being a mother. As she sat there, her eye came to rest on a half-closed drawer from which papers protruded. She jumped up, and, without reading what she had written, tore them up. It was a letter to Douglas. She had fallen into the habit of writing him long letters about – as she put it – what she really felt. The letters that reached him, however, were amusing accounts of Caroline's development, Alice's struggles with her son, Stella's enjoyable sufferings in childbirth. Pride forbade her to post her 'real' letters, which were in effect passionate complaints that he had ever married her if he intended to leave her at the first opportunity; despairing admissions of incompetence with Caroline; and her hatred of the life she led.

The letters she got from him filled her with dismay she would not acknowledge. The incidents of his army life he found as humorous as she did hers. Besides, he continually urged her broad-mindedly, as was the spirit of their compact, to get out and have a good time; which she interpreted, from a deeper instinct than she would admit to possessing, as the voice of guilt itself.

She was about to sit down and describe the visit of Mr Maynard in terms which would make him sound like an avuncular priest, when the telephone rang.

She approached it with caution. Since that moment three nights before when six or seven young men had burst in to claim their comrade, it had been ringing with suggestions that she might go to this dance or that. She had reacted with stiff coldness. She was hurt that the victim himself had made no sign. She had not told the whole truth to Mr Maynard. Thomas Bryant had collapsed onto the divan in more than alcoholic breakdown. He had wept on her breast like a child – he had lost his nerve, he would never be able to go up again, he wished he had been killed when the aircraft had tipped over on its wing that morning. Martha had cradled him, and felt such a depth of emotion that afterwards she could not bear to think of it. It was terrible to her that weakness should have so strong an appeal. And yet it had been a perfect intimacy – for the few minutes before he went limp into sleep. That he should *not* have rung up seemed to her like a slap in the face. Now she took down the receiver, and a hearty embarrassed voice thanked her for holding his head; it was a jolly good show, he said. Then, after a short pause, he said it was a lovely day; Martha laughed in amazement; encouraged by this sound, he invited her for dinner that night. Martha agreed at once.

She ran off to prepare her dress and herself for the occasion: it was shortly after midday. While she bathed and curled her hair and anointed her body, her whole being was dedicating itself anew. She might have never been the wife of Douglas and the mother of Caroline. Her fantasies of the night ahead centred on the intimate talk, a continuation of that existing intimacy, a complete truthfulness which would sanctify what would follow. This, however, never approached even the threshold of consciousness. At the most she imagined a kiss. But until the kiss, fantasy must sleep. She was crying out for a romantic love affair; she had been waiting for months for just this moment; not for one second had the idea entered her head. There is no such thing as a female hypocrite.

When Thomas Bryant entered the flat at eight that night, she had been dressed and ready for over an hour. This was one of the evenings, she knew, when she was beautiful – though why the spirit of attraction should visit her as it did, she did not know; no man had ever explained it to her.

She welcomed him casually, like an old friend; she saw at once he did not recognize her. He looked uncertainly about the flat, and then at the divan on which he had slept.

'Mrs Knowell?' he enquired formally.

Martha laughed involuntarily; saw his startled shamed look; then hastily covered for him: he remembered nothing of what had happened, and she must not tell him. 'It was a terrible evening, wasn't it – we were all drunk as owls,' she remarked flippantly, and saw the relief on his face.

'I'm very sorry,' he said. 'You must let me make amends.'

She offered him a drink, and he arranged his length carefully on the divan, as if he distrusted it. He was very tall and rather slight, though broad-shouldered. He was fair, with a clear, ruddy English skin, and blue eyes inflamed by flying and late nights. They observed Martha with approval. The boys had told him she was a nice little piece; it was an understatement. He could not remember ever having seen her before; he remembered a crowd of vaguely amiable girls. He had decided to take her out to dinner somewhere where he would not meet his friends, behave pleasantly, take her home early, and take care not to see her again. Something like that was owed to a woman whom he remembered dimly as a maternal and practical presence. Now he changed his plans instantly: he would take his prize among his brother officers.

Martha, examining him, saw that he wore his uniform carelessly; that his whole person expressed a sort of humorous resignation to the absurdity of uniforms and war – a studied, self-conscious repudiation of anything serious, particularly his own death, which, since his training would be complete in a couple of weeks, was not likely to be delayed longer than a few months at most. She felt a pity for him which was betrayed even in the way she handed him a glass of whisky; he might already be a figure on a war memorial.

He tossed it down, and said, 'Let's go.' He stood up. 'Shall we dance instead?'

She said immediately she would love to. Somewhere in her was spreading a shadow of desolation. She felt insulted. She became very gay.

All the way to the camp he asked her minute questions about the make of the car, its performance, how much it cost to run. She thought of cars as objects invented to take one efficiently from one place to another; she had never really believed anyone could be seriously interested in such matters. He was offering her the merest small change of conversation; and she answered politely.

At the gates in the great black fence, the sentry stood aside as the young officer held out a piece of paper. There was a newly built hall, surrounded by ranks of parked cars. They entered the hall. It was already full. A band of uniformed men played from a platform.

Martha looked around and knew all the women present. A year ago, they had been dancing in the arms of the local men; now they were moving with equal compliance in the arms of the Air Force, and using with perfect ease the new language. She saw Alice dancing past. She waved. Alice waved back, then stopped, spoke to her partner, and came over.

The young officer stood aside politely while Alice took Martha's elbow and said, 'Hey, Matty, so we're back in circulation – it's awful, isn't it?' She let out her high giggle, and added, 'I'm browned off with everything. I don't see why we shouldn't – God knows what Willie's up to up north.'

Martha, who had felt a stab of jealous shock on behalf of the absent Willie, now agreed instantly that Douglas always said she must go and enjoy herself. At this Alice suddenly smiled, the women smiled ironically, exchanged a look, and separated.

Thomas Bryant returned to Martha, and edged with her around in the space between the dancers and the tables. She suddenly stopped. She had thought of this as going out with Thomas Bryant; she had imagined being with *him*. She saw a long table, around which sat a dozen young officers, half of whom had rung her during the last week. She looked at Thomas, unconsciously reproachful. He glanced curiously at her face: she was scarlet. He avoided looking at his friends, who had already made a space for them, and led Martha to another small table. They sat. Her back was now to the other table. Glancing at him, she saw him looking over her shoulder at his friends; she turned swiftly, and saw them grinning at him; his face expressed a half-sheepish triumph. She hated him. When he summoned the black waiter and suggested champagne, she said she would drink lemonade. They got up to dance, like two wooden things. He was drinking heavily again. After a few dances, he had sunk into the collective wash of emotion; the whole roomful of people was dancing in the anonymous throb of music. That was what he most wanted, she could see: not to have to think, to let himself go into it, to let his mind flow out and away from the terrible necessity of his days. And he wanted her to be a girl whose face he would not have to remember next day. Well, then, she would. She loosened and danced in the beat of the drums.

Quite soon, a grinning young man tapped Thomas on the shoulder. 'Why don't you come and join us?'

He looked awkwardly at Martha; she said at once, 'Why, we'd love to.'

At the end of that dance she went easily with him to the other table. She disliked him now so much it did not matter what she did. She was now that woman who says, 'So that's what you want me to be – very well, then, I'll show you how well I can do it.' She danced cheerfully with the young men to whom she had been so cold on the telephone. Choosing a moment when Thomas was at the bar, she asked one of his friends to tell him she had a headache – she chose the most casually insulting formula she knew – and left, quickly, to find her car. She was now trembling – with cold, she told herself. It was a cold night, the great stars glittering in their patterns as they had on so many dancing nights.

As she got into the car, she saw two people sitting in the back seat. A young woman, lazily disposed in one corner, supported the head and shoulders of a young officer who lay stretched along the seat. Martha peered through the half-dark and saw that the girl was Maisie. Both were asleep.

She sat for a while, watching the bright soft dresses of the women flowing against the neat close shapes of the men as couples passed up and down the steps in the yellow light that fell from the apertures of the hall. Then she grew impatient, and leaned over and shook Maisie's bare white shoulder.

Maisie woke at once, opening her eyes straight into Martha's, and smiling in her easy friendly way. 'Hey, Martha, have we been asleep?' She looked down at the man, whose face was half buried in her bosom, and yawned. 'I picked your car because I knew you wouldn't mind. Lord, this boy's heavy.'

'Who is he?'

'He's the Air Force.'

'Well, of course.'

'You know, Matty, I like these English boys, don't you? It'll be awfully hard to go back to our own after knowing them. They treat us quite differently, don't they?' A pause, and another yawn. 'I never get any sleep. They read more books. They talk about things. They've got culture, that's what it is.'

Maisie's husband had been killed flying in Persia. That was six months before.

'He's very nice, this one,' she went on reflectively. 'He wants to marry me. Men are funny, aren't they, Matty? I mean, the way they are always wanting to get married. I suppose it's because they are going to get killed.'

'Are you going to marry him?'

'Well, I suppose so, if it's going to make him happy. I don't see the sense in it, myself. I look at it this way: Supposing he doesn't get killed after all – a lot don't, they just finish their turn, and then go to the ground. Well, then, he'll be English, and he'll want to live in England. But I like it here and then we'll be married and have to get divorced.' She shifted herself, with infinite gentleness, into a different position, carefully catching her lower lip between white teeth as his head rolled into the crook of her arm. He opened his eyes, stirred, sat up.

'This is Matty. I told you – she's all right.'

'How do you do?' enquired an educated English voice.

'How do you do?' said Martha.

'Do you mind giving us a lift back to town, Matty? That's why we came into your car. Don hasn't got to fly tomorrow. He's got a weekend pass.'

Martha backed out, and drove through the big gates past the sentry. 'When are you getting married?' she asked.

'Tomorrow,' said the young man promptly, in a tender proprietory tone, to which Maisie responded good-humouredly, 'Oh, you're a crazy kid.'

Martha observed in the mirror that they were once more embraced, and was careful not to speak again. She was feeling cold and lonely and left out. Now she regretted behaving so stiffly with Thomas.

She was able to drive to Maisie's room without having to ask for instructions. She stopped outside another white gate, banked with shrubs whose glossy leaves glinted in the starlight. She waited for them to realize that the car was no longer in motion.

Maisie came unhurriedly out of the embrace, saying, 'Thanks a lot, Matty, do the same for you sometime.' As she got out, linked to her young man, she enquired politely, 'And how's our Douggie?'

'He's doing fine.'

'Did you hear that a crowd of our boys tore Mogadishu to pieces a while back? You know how they are when they get into one of their moods.'

Don politely thanked Martha. 'It's very kind of you.'

'Not at all.'

He bent his head over Maisie's fair gleaming curls as they walked into the house where she had her room. Martha watched them going inside, cheeks laid together, dancing a half-mocking, half-dreamy sliding step.

She wished that her principles would allow her to cry. But this would not do; she efficiently let out the clutch, and drove herself back to the flat, feeling herself to be the only cold, sober, isolated person in a moon-drugged city given over to dancing, love and death. She felt as if she had shut the door against her own release. Then she remembered that tomorrow night she would be taken to a meeting packed full – she hoped against hope – of dangerous revolutionaries. She was enabled to retire to bed alone with philosophy.

At half past seven the following evening Mr Maynard folded his napkin and rose from the dinner table, although the meal had reached only the roast-beef stage and there were guests.

'Spending an evening with your chums?' enquired his wife briskly. The word 'chums' was the one she used to deprecate that group of elderly gentlemen who were Mr Maynard's favourite company, and whom she felt as an irritating but not dangerous comment on her own activities.

'No, I'm dropping down to the Left people'.

The ladies let out arch little cries of dismay. They were Mrs Talbot, pale in clouds of grey chiffon and pearls; Mrs Lowe-Island, her stubby, sunburnt sixty-year-old body upright in pink taffeta; and Mrs Maynard herself – sage-green lace and an amber necklace that fell to her waist.

Mr Maynard was prepared to forgo his pudding, but not his brandy; he sipped it standing. Mrs Lowe-Island, born to be that indispensable lieutenant who must say and do what her superiors find beneath them, cried, 'Now that everything is so serious, and the Huns are attacking us in North Africa, I can't see how anyone can waste time with a bunch of agitators – it's encouraging them.'

Mr Maynard smiled, and set down his brandy glass. Mrs Maynard was absorbed in her pudding, but it was to her that he remarked, 'Even with the Huns at our gate, I feel we might keep a sense of proportion.'

Mrs Maynard took another spoonful, but Mrs Lowe-Island said indignantly, 'They might sweep down over the whole continent in a couple of weeks.'

'I'm sorry you have so little confidence in our armies.'

'Oh – but we know Hitler is quite unscrupulous.'

Mr Maynard laughed. He was on his way to the door.

His wife enquired, 'You are taking that Quest girl?'

'You don't mean that young Mrs Knowell?' exclaimed Mrs Lowe-Island.'

'She's a sweet girl,' said Mrs Talbot reproachfully. 'She's a darling thing – and so artistic!'

Mrs Lowe-Island quivered. Mrs Maynard spooned in the last of her pudding in a way which said that the cook would be spoken to about it in the morning, and firmly rang the bell.

From the door, Mr Maynard saw that in the centre of the living room stood a card table, with fresh packs of cards laid out; while on subsidiary tables here and there were piled dockets of papers, files, lists, pencils: his wife intended to indulge both her passions that evening.

'Who's your fourth?' he asked.

'Mrs Anderson.' The name was merely dropped.

'Ah,' Mr Maynard said, and looked curiously at his wife.

'Mrs Anderson is such a sweet, dear woman,' said Mrs Talbot, fingering her thick pearls. 'Now that her son is in uniform, she's taking such an interest in things. And when she's always so busy, too.'

'Busy,' cackled Mrs Lowe-Island, flushing angrily. 'We could all be busy if we took as much interest in men as she does.'

'Oh!' breathed Mrs Talbot.

Mrs Maynard turned her head slightly, and surveyed the areas of wrinkled burnt skin above the ruched pink taffeta. 'I should say that men took an interest in her,' she observed suddenly, her lips compressed over a laugh. Mrs Talbot and she exchanged a rapid malicious glance.

A short pause, while Mrs Lowe-Island looked from one to the other, smiling sourly. She blundered on: 'I hate to think what she spends on clothes.'

Mrs Maynard now surveyed the small puffed pink sleeves on Mrs Lowe-Island's upper arms, and remarked, 'It is so pleasant to sit through a dull committee with a woman like Mrs Anderson, who is always a thing of beauty. It's a rare talent to dress suitably for one's age – it seems.'

Again, Mrs Lowe-Island appeared puzzled. Mr Maynard enquired, 'So she's already on committees, is she?'

'She is coming to talk things over tonight,' said his wife discouragingly.

'What! In the inner councils already?'

'Her husband is being so efficient with the recreation centres,' said Mrs Talbot.

'I can imagine. And what's she providing – the entertainment?'

Mrs Maynard frowned. 'Mrs Anderson is really very efficient.'

'I was always convinced of it. There's nothing I admire more than that kind of efficiency. The art of living in a small town is one of the most difficult to acquire. Or perhaps it is inborn?' Here he looked full at Mrs Talbot; her eyes veiled themselves, she faintly coloured.

Alert to danger, Mrs Maynard glanced from one to the other, and said energetically, 'Perhaps you and Mrs Talbot might discuss it later – privately. As you usually do,' she said, with a pleasant smile. 'Because you are going to be late for your meeting.'

She saw Mrs Lowe-Island's small black eyes fastened eagerly on Mrs Talbot. Mrs Maynard rose, and laid her hand lightly on Mrs Talbot's shoulder. 'Bless you, dear,' she said. Mrs Talbot's face did not change at all; her shoulder shrank away slightly, then stood firm under the slight pressure.

Mr Maynard was looking warningly at his wife. She met his eyes, and raised her heavy black brows mockingly. Then she allowed her hand to slide away from the grey chiffon shoulder, and went towards the living room. They all followed her.

It was a long, low-ceilinged room, painted white, with pale rose-and-green hangings. It was a room appropriate for tea, cards and gossip; and in the middle of it stood Mrs Maynard, upright, hands on her hips, looking at her card indexes and files.

'Mrs Brodeshaw is probably dropping in later,' she informed Mr Maynard.

'So the Players are extending their scope?'

'Not Mrs Player, Mrs Brodeshaw,' Mrs Lowe-Island said, and stopped. Her stiff bulky little body quivered under the pink taffeta; the tolerant silence was another affront. She looked from one to another discreet face, and dropped into an ingratiating smile.

'I wish success to your councils,' Mr Maynard said, and strode off across the veranda.

'I do think it's odd that Mr Maynard should go to the meetings of those people.'

'So boring, I should have thought,' said Mrs Maynard casually. She seated herself at the card table, split the seal off a pack, and remarked, 'It wouldn't be a bad thing if we could get a representative of the Left League, Book Council, whatever it is.'

'Oh, yes, they are such terribly sweet people, really,' urged Mrs Talbot.

'You keep in touch so cleverly with everything.'

Mrs Lowe-Island flushed again and insisted, 'They tell me they have niggers at their meetings.'

Mrs Maynard half closed her eyes, and remarked, 'Aggie, dear, there are parts of Africa where *Africans* sit in Parliament.'

'But we don't want that to happen *here*.'

'It surely depends *how* it happens?' Her smile at Mrs Lowe-Island was an invitation to allow the mills of thought to begin to turn; but Mrs Lowe-Island snapped, 'I wouldn't sit down in the same room with a kaffir.'

'No one has asked you to yet.'

Mrs Lowe-Island swelled; then the round reddened little face twisted itself into a smile; the small black eyes wavered, uncertain.

'Will you cut?' enquired Mrs Maynard.

'What I think is,' breathed Mrs Talbot, 'everybody should get together and learn to like each other. I mean, when you meet anybody, you like them *really* – I don't see why people should dislike each other, and all this bickering . . .'

'Bless you, dear. Would you like a higher chair? Your pearls are getting mixed up with the cards.'

Mr Maynard, having looked at his watch and discovered he was late, amended his pace very slightly, and made his way under the moon-filled branches of the trees which lined the avenues that led towards young Mrs Knowell.

His mind was working comfortably along two different channels. He was thinking that in the 'Left Club' or 'Socialist League' – his contempt for the organization was demonstrated by the fact that he could never remember, or rather, refused to use, its proper name – were some very able men, who, if the Government had any sense, would be made use of in this national emergency. For the purposes of his dissatisfaction he chose to think of the Government as some clearly defined machinery with which he had nothing to do. Besides, he was an amateur, a looker-on, a dropper-in; he was not implicated. Therefore he turned over in his mind the names of the men in question like a woman fingering silks she had no intention of buying. But there rose the vague thought, One might have a word with old Thompson-Jones.

At the same time, he was conscious of a steady chagrin which he defined as due to Martha. He was a handsome man; many women had found him so; Martha was an attractive young woman; there was nothing in the laws of nature to prevent her from thinking of him as a man: it was clear that never, not for a moment, had she done so. To that woman who makes a man feel for the first time that he is getting old is due a regard which is not so easily defined. He remembered the moment yesterday when she had leaned forward and asked emotionally why he cared about her; and thought of it as an opportunity lost. He knocked on the door of the flat, and waited, suitable remarks preparing themselves on his tongue.

Martha appeared at once, so that he was reminded he was late; and he apologized. He thought she looked very young, and rather appealing. He turned out the light for her, shut the door behind her, and, as they descended the broad stone stairs, tucked her arm under his. She suffered it to remain there a moment, then it dropped out from its own weight.

'You'll be cold,' he remarked. She wore one of her slips of coloured linen, arms and legs bare.

'But it's so hot,' she said.

He conceded to himself that for him a coat was something one put on when one went out in the evening. For Martha there was a different approach, apparently. He reflected that his wife had sets of clothes suitable for occasions; he could deduce from what she wore what she intended to do. That sage-green lace, for instance, was essentially for bridge with ulterior purposes; whereas, had she worn bunchy silver brocade, he would have diagnosed a late intimate call from the wife of the Prime Minister, or even the Governor's wife.

Whereas Martha might have been going shopping, for a picnic, or to the pictures.

She continued to walk beside him in silence. The moon was large, clear silver, directly above them. The little town was glaring white, black-shadowed, everything sharp and defined. The road glittered saltily. The street lamps were round bright-yellow globes.

'Do you often go to these meetings?' enquired Martha.

'Occasionally.'

'What are they talking about tonight?'

Mr Maynard considered. 'I don't know.' Then, seeing her surprise: 'The deficiencies of education, I believe.'

'Well, that should keep them busy.'

'Surely education's better than it used to be?'

She was puzzled. 'Oh, you mean in *England*.'

'You consider they should discuss education here?'

'We live here.'

Mr Maynard considered this in silence.

Aggressively she said, 'They just talk and talk.'

'I apologize,' he began, bringing unnecessary batteries of sarcasm to bear, 'for taking you to a function of which you disapprove so strongly.'

And now she slipped her arm into his. 'It's very sweet of you. It really is.'

At once he tightened the grip of his elbow intimately. She impatiently pulled hers away, then shot him an apologetic and embarrassed look. 'It's so hot,' she said again.

As they turned the corner of a street into that small area of the town which was the business area, she stopped and looked down a few hundred yards of shop fronts and office blocks. 'It's growing with the war, isn't it?'

He had never really considered it as a town at all; he tried to see it through Martha's eyes, and failed. 'You've never been out of the colony?' His voice was compassionate.

She burst out, 'I hate it. I loathe it. I wish I could take the first train out of it. It's like a – Victorian novel. They talk about their servants at tea parties, and say the lower orders are ungrateful. They even go so far as to pay them twelve pounds a year, like our grandmothers, and say they are spoilt. It's all so boring, things happen the same way over and over again. And in fifty years' time, people will be saying about now, 'How backward they were then!' But in the meantime, they fight and make speeches and write articles over every sixpence, and all the time with moral language, religion, and all the rest of it. What's it all about, that's what I want to know? It's all so stupid and unnecessary.'

'We'll be late,' he said, walking forward hastily – not away from the idea, which seemed to him sensible, but from the emotion she put into it. 'For a girl of your age, I can think of better things to care about.' There was no reaction to this. After a while he conceded, 'I admit that this place is only to be borne by those, like myself, who have had their fill of big cities and know that there is really very little difference – We turn in here, I believe.'

They were now in the street which lower down became very disreputable and petered out in the slums where the Coloured people lived. They entered a large old, ugly building, and began to mount a spiral iron staircase, that was lit by one dull-yellow electric bulb.

'I worked here once,' said Martha.

'When?'

'Oh, about two years ago.' Clearly, it might have been a decade.

'You know what's so awful about you?' she enquired angrily.

'I shall be pleased to be told.'

'You don't really care about anything.' She was sullen and aggressive. Then, looking at him, she was overcome with discomfort, and let out a short embarrassed laugh which was half flirtatious. 'Well, you don't, do you?'

They stood now on the second landing, which was in the darkness. Above them, over several twists of the iron stairway, came a glimmer of yellow. Doors stood shut and discreet all around them. There was a faint stale smell of urine.

Mr Maynard suddenly put his arms about Martha, kissed her, and said, 'So, I don't?'

She gave him a cold shocked look, pulled away, and went up the stairs in front of him. He followed resignedly.

On this third landing, the doors which studded the dim and dirty corridors stretching away all around them showed brown and peeling under that dingy yellow light. One door stood open, light spilled out, there were people inside. On the door was 'Contemporary Politics Discussion Circle' in small white letters on the cracked brown paint. They entered. The meeting had already begun. They slipped into empty spaces separated from each other. Martha looked around, and saw faces she had seen before.

It was a large room, with discoloured whitewashed walls, a bare board floor, yellow electric-light bulbs hanging from loosely knotted flex. There were rough wooden benches all around the walls. A plain wooden table stood at one end, and from behind it spoke a long, bony, bespectacled figure – Mr Pyecroft himself. He was speaking with great deliberation, mouthing over the long, many-syllabled words. There were about twenty people present, among them three young men in the grey-blue uniform.

On the walls hung two portraits, one of Mr Nehru and one of Lenin. She had never seen a picture of Lenin before, and the name had had a flavour of something unpleasant, furtive, shady. She saw a strong man, gazing calmly into the future over his little pointed beard. The contrast between the two images confused her. She began to listen to what was being said. Mr Pyecroft was talking about the provisions for education for village children in Wales in 1910; and although occasionally a match scraped or feet shifted, everyone was listening absorbedly. Martha thought that in 1910 Lenin was alive; she saw him against the background of Tolstoy and Chekhov; in 1910 children in Wales were suffering conditions not much better than Russian children – why, then, had there been no Lenin in Wales? And the way African children lived now . . . She looked around the room. If there existed a Lenin here, presumably he would be in this room? She looked from face to face, and her spirits sank; and she had again ceased to listen.

Opposite her she saw a small dark girl smiling, and recognized Jasmine. She smiled back. Jasmine's eyes turned with a look of enquiry towards Mr Maynard, and Martha felt herself grow hot. She saw Mr Maynard through Jasmine's eyes. She was embarrassed. He was seated on his part of the wooden bench stiffly, taking more room than anyone else, arms folded, legs stretched out in front, eyes lowered to the floor. The dark decided face showed no sign of emotion of any kind. Yet from time to time he lifted the bold hazel eyes and looked with a peculiar intentness at various people: Mr Pyecroft himself, Mr Perr, Mr Forester. This intent gaze made Martha uncomfortable, as if she were responsible for it; then, seeing a derisive, critical smile on Jasmine's face, and one that was meant to be noticed, she reacted in the other direction: in comparison with these careless, nondescript people, Mr Maynard was impressively dignified and sure of himself. If *he* were cut across, he would show solid clean grain right through; he was all of a piece.

But Mr Pycroft was still talking. He was now in Scotland and quoting a passage from Scott. People stirred and livened and laughed as Mr Pyecroft read; a fresh current of life ran through them, and they shifted themselves more comfortably for another effort at listening.

Then Martha saw everybody's eyes turn towards the door. A tall, stooping man stood there smiling; he was an African, dressed carefully in shabby clothes that had been darned and patched everywhere. He carried a briefcase under his arm. Mr Pyecroft stopped for him; he had continued talking as Mr Maynard and Martha came in.

Everyone nodded and smiled, made way for him beside them. Half a dozen packets of cigarettes were at once stretched out towards him. He seated himself between Jasmine, who smiled at him like an old friend, and a small fair woman whom Martha remembered seeing before somewhere. He accepted a cigarette, and looked towards the speaker; at once everyone, reminded of their obligations, did the same. But Martha continued to look at him. This was the first time in her whole life, and she was now twenty-one – the first time in a life spent in a colony where nine tenths of the population were dark-skinned – that she had sat in a room with a dark-skinned person as an equal. Again her spirits lifted, and she felt these were people to live and die for. She looked with envy at Jasmine, and at the fair woman on the other side, who had been whispering something to him. She was a tiny, thin creature, with fair braids wound around her head. She had a small, round bright-coloured face, small brown quick eyes, a big generous nose, a wide emotional mouth. On her other side sat a large, fattish young man, pale, with black-rimmed spectacles: Jewish obviously, and very much an intellectual. From her whispering to the African, she turned to him, the young man, and they exchanged a warm, intimate, deep smile. Martha saw they were in love; passion shone out all at once from the dingy room, and even from the measured sentences of Mr Pyecroft. Martha warmed to them, warmed to them all. Then, directed by another cautious sardonic look, this time from the tiny fair girl's young man, she looked towards Mr Maynard, who was steadily regarding the African under his heavy brows.

Martha caught a whisper from near her: some women were talking. One said, in a low humorous voice, 'That's Magistrate Maynard – he fined Mr Matushi two pounds or twenty days last week.' 'Dirty bastard,' came the reply. A great many eyes turned towards Mr Maynard, who was impervious to such atmospheres, obviously, for he remained calm and absent in his space of bench, a monument of detachment.

Mr Pyecroft had raised his voice. 'And now for my conclusions,' he said. He took off his spectacles, paused, laid down his papers. Eyes which had been directed at Mr Maynard, at Mr Matushi, centred on him again. Martha found herself gripped by what he was saying. The dead statistics, cautious assessments, hedged facts, were flowing together outwards on words that had the nobility that emanated from the picture of Lenin, from the couple in love, from Mr Matushi. She listened as if to her own deepest voice speaking. People, said Mr Pyecroft, were warped and twisted by the system; vast capacities for good lay in everyone; only the tiniest proportion of humankind had ever been given what was needed to raise them from brutes; he painted a picture of the world crowded with miserable, stunted, light-starved creatures, like animalculae writhing under a stone which needed only to be removed. But by Mr Pyecroft? If one shut one's eyes and listened to the words, then anything was possible, any belief, any vision of good; if one looked at him, that cautious lean gentleman, with his humorous, almost jaunty self-deprecation, the vision collapsed. He was finishing an extraordinarily moving description of new and ennobled humanity with the dry phrases, 'And so much for the set piece of the evening; now I'll leave the subject open for discussion.'

People stirred, and moved their limbs about: those benches were very hard. No one was eager to begin. After a long minute's silence, Mr Pyecroft remarked humorously that it appeared he had exhausted the subject. At once Mr Perr, in considered words, presented what he described as 'a small contribution'. It appeared that Mr Pyecroft had misquoted some figures from Scotland. Then the young pale Jew next to the fair girl began to speak. His English was slow, correct, and he would pause without embarrassment for as long as he needed to find the exact word. He asked them to consider the following proposition: In countries where there had been education for the working classes for any length of time, no revolution had been achieved. Revolutions occurred in countries where the masses had 'never been made –' he hesitated over the word – 'moulded – *formed*,' he brought out triumphantly, 'by the ruling classes.' Could there, then, be a case, he asked them to consider, for progressives such as themselves to fight against popular education instead of for it?

There was a small laugh around the room: it was an embarrassed one. Mr Pyecroft smiled indulgently, and asked their good friend Boris from Poland to remember that this was a general discussion on education; it was not in their province to discuss the techniques of revolution.

The young man Boris said sarcastically that he should have thought it was a key question. A short silence ensued; Martha saw that the fair girl looked with passionate support into his eyes, and even touched his hand with her own. He remained passive but bitter for a few moments, until he flashed out a warm, grateful smile at her. Various people looked at them tolerantly, but with a touch of malice, as Martha noted angrily.

Since there seemed to be no further contributions, Mr Pyecroft asked their good friends and visitors from the Air Force to contribute. Two looked at the floor to avoid the invitation. One, a bulky shockheaded mechanic, got up and said that he would like to take up Boris's argument, with which he disagreed, but he was forbidden while in uniform to discuss politics. Here he gave a rather sarcastic laugh, which provoked sarcastic laughter from everybody. He proceeded to describe his own education, which had finished at the age of fourteen, in London. When he modestly sat down, he was regarded with interest and compassion by them all: here was the subject of their discussion in person, the working man from England.

All this time, Mr Matushi had been listening intently. Now he stood up and asked leave to speak. They all leaned forward to listen. He began by saying that he had heard with gratitude the address given by Mr Pyecroft, he was sure everyone would be grateful to him for the trouble he had taken. But what had interested him very much was what the last speaker had said. Because it was always surprising and interesting to hear that white men were not always well educated and doing only nice work. (Here people looked at each other self-consciously, but with a certain satisfaction.) A great many of his people would not believe that in England white men lived in bad houses, and with not enough to eat, and had to dig coal and make roads. He wished very much that a great many of his people could hear what the last speaker had said. Then perhaps – he said this with a gentle humour – they might not be so hurt by the newspapers when they said all black men were centuries in evolution behind the white men. But what he really wanted to say was this: There was a problem that interested him even more than the wonderful and intelligent lecture of Mr Pyecroft. It was the question of the education that African children were given – if you could call it an education, he added apologetically. It would give him great pleasure, he would be very grateful, if that problem could be discussed.

He sat down and looked at them in his characteristic way: patient, dignified, but stubborn.

Mr Pyecroft at once rose, thanked Mr Matushi for his contribution, and said they would certainly have a discussion on African education very soon. Here he looked at Jasmine. 'In a month's time, Miss Cohen?'

Jasmine said it must be two months' time, since there was another meeting already arranged.

Mr Pyecroft looked around, his hand resting on the table before him. 'If no one wants to say anything?' he began; but Mr Maynard remarked, 'I should rather like to say something.'

Close attention was focussed on him. 'I will be brief. The assumption behind the speaker's very interesting address was this and I want to challenge it: that education is a good thing. There is no evidence at all that sow's ears can be made into silk purses. Popular education in Britain has existed, such as it is, for some decades; are the people better or happier as a result? I doubt it.'

There was a chorus of 'Oh! Oh! Oh!'

Mr Maynard waited until it had subsided, and said, 'Is there any evidence whatsoever that a person educated in one way rather than another will have different qualities, different abilities? And is there any evidence that the mass of human beings are better than brutes!'

He paused. Everyone exchanged ironical glances. There was also a feeling of discomfort, due to his repeated use of the word 'evidence': there was that gap between him and them that is always filled by silence; it was as if a peasant had asked them to prove that the world was round.

'I would be the first to admit that I am an avowed reactionary,' said Mr Maynard urbanely. There was a relieved laugh.

Mr Perr the statistician rose eagerly. 'This is my province,' he said, and they laughed again. He was a thin, dark man, with close gleaming black hair and pale gleaming cheeks with a ruddy patch on each. He held himself in such a way that he looked as if he might suddenly fold up like a hinged ruler. He quoted statistics plentifully from various countries, which – if it were necessary – proved to everyone that Mr Maynard was talking nonsense; Mr Maynard was obviously unimpressed, however. He smiled ironically until people began chanting all around him in lugubrious tones, 'The more things change the more they remain the same,' and 'Everything is the same under the sun.'

'That is my contention,' remarked Mr Maynard.

The deadlock might have been prolonged indefinitely, to peter out, as they do, in frustrated anger and hostility. But Mr Matushi, who had been regarding Mr Maynard with a sorrowful face, stood up and began passionately, in marked contrast with his controlled speech of a few minutes before, 'Our friend Mr Maynard says that people don't need to be educated. Well, I know that our people suffer from not being educated. Perhaps Mr Maynard has had too much education – then he doesn't want other people to be educated. All I know is that our children want to go to school, they want to learn, and they cannot because there are schools for a tiny number of them only.'

'You misunderstand me,' interrupted Mr Maynard.

'Oh, no, no, no, I don't misunderstand you, I understand you very well,' cried Mr Matushi.

'Mr Matushi . . .' said Mr Pyecroft urgently, half rising from his seat.

Mr Matushi hesitated, looking around him at faces which for the most part regarded him with interested compassion. He slowly seated himself. 'If I am out of order, I am sorry.'

'I think we should close the meeting,' said Mr Pyecroft. 'Are there any announcements?'

Jasmine rose, in her demure, self-contained way, and laid a slip of paper before him, and returned to her seat.

Mr Pyecroft read the slip, and then smiled in a way which prepared them all for a joke. 'The next meeting, which will take place here four weeks from tonight, will be addressed by Mr Dunhill.' There was a titter. 'Mr Dunhill, who, as we all know, is from the CID, has asked to address us on the comparative incidence of crime in industrial and agricultural areas in Britain.'

They all laughed loudly, and looked at a smooth clerkly man who sat, self-conscious, in a corner. 'It's a hobby of mine,' he muttered.

Could this be all that was meant by the gossip that the CID attended all their meetings? Martha felt indignant and let down.

'It is now ten o'clock,' said Mr Pyecroft. 'Before I close the meeting, there is the little matter of funds.'

Discreet tolerant smiles were held while Jasmine, who had apparently been secreting it about her person, produced a cocoa tin with a jagged rent in its lid. It went from hand to hand about the room, to the accompaniment of the small tinkling of falling coins. This incident, like every other, seemed to provide everyone here with the comforting sense of repetition, the safe, the familiar. These people, who all knew each other so well, who exchanged understanding glances at a word, who knew at once at which points to laugh in discussion – these people had been meeting once a month for years, to reassure themselves that their ideas were shared by enough others to make them valid; for years they had discussed education in Chile, or medicine in India; and for years respectable tea tables had been humming with talk of their dangerous activities. Martha found herself succumbing to something rather like fear: the old fear as if nets were closing around her, that particular terror of the very young. This was such a small town – the size of a small market town in England, so they said; and yet it was possible for so many different groups to form themselves, to lead their own self-contained lives, without affecting, or so it seemed, the existence of any other. She was instinctively shaking herself free of this mesh of bonds before she had entered them; she thought that at the end of ten years these people would still be here, self-satisfied in their unconformity, talking, talking endlessly.

All about her she heard small jokes, half-finished phrases that needed only an understanding laugh to complete them. People were rising, going to find particular friends, making plans to meet for sundowners, tea, or children's tea parties.

Jasmine had crossed the room and stood before her, smiling in her quiet friendly fashion. 'It's nice to see you here,' she began, and involuntarily shot a questioning look towards Mr Maynard, who was talking to Mr Perr the statistician. Mr Perr laughed; it had a note of flattered eagerness which Martha found unpleasant. She saw that Jasmine was observing the couple satirically.

'Did you enjoy it?' she enquired, turning her critical but patient attention back to Martha.

'Why England, why not Africa?' burst out Martha hotly.

Jasmine smiled her agreement, saying, 'Well, there are some of us who feel the same way . . .' She glanced round, looking at Boris. 'This crowd are a waste of time,' she added. Someone grasped her arm. She smiled hastily at Martha, saying, 'I'll get into touch with you,' and turned away, having thus dismissed the organization for which she had been acting as secretary for some years.

Her place was taken by the fair girl, Betty, who eagerly clasped Martha's arm, searching her face with warm brown eyes; behind her stood Boris, smiling.

'Well?' demanded Betty urgently. 'Jasmine's told us about you – we're pleased to see you here. How about coming to tea with us, and –'

'You are overwhelming the poor woman,' said Boris humorously, in his clear, correct voice. Betty fell back, laughing, looking at him with eyes full of love. For a moment they smiled at each other, in a way which isolated them from everyone else in the room. A pang of pure envy shot through Martha: she immediately saw their relationship as something lofty, beautiful, on a plane infinitely higher than anything she herself had ever known.

Boris withdrew his eyes from Betty with difficulty, and said with the slow humour which made him sound pompous, 'If you would care to come to tea with us and discuss certain matters? There might be a place, for instance, for a discussion group which is not quite so – cautious?'

'They're really too scared to live,' flamed Betty. 'They're so scared of the word "Left" that they won't even use it in their name, and –'

They both fell back as Mrs Perr came forward, shouldering them aside absently. Martha saw them exchange humorous glances.

Mrs Perr, a tall, thin dark woman, with hair cut straight around her face like a Dutch doll, loose straight discordantly coloured clothes, and a large dry orange mouth, looked closely at Martha and said, 'Oh – we've met before.'

'Yes, about two years –'

'Well, we're pleased to see you again. I'll ask Jasmine to send you notices of the meetings.'

'Thank you very much.'

Mrs Perr narrowed her eyes at her for a moment, in a way which suggested that she was mentally ticking off items on a list and said, 'And, of course, there's the Book Club, if you want to join that.' She glanced over her shoulder, frowned, then smiled with pleasurable malice. Betty and Boris were leaning against the wall on the other side of the room, talking in low voices, face to face. It was not only Mrs Perr who smiled in that discreet, faintly malicious way. 'Betty does the books, but since she's been in love they're neglected. Betty!' she called.

Betty slowly turned and blinked across at them, her small, warm, delicately pink face illuminated.

Martha saw that Mr Maynard was looking at her impatiently across the room, and said, 'I'll have to go, anyway.' She smiled apologetically at Mrs Perr, whom she disliked quite finally for being malicious about love, and joined Mr Maynard.

They went out into the long, dim, dusty corridor. The laughter and talk from the room they had left became a unit of cheerful sound, and Martha stopped, afflicted by the desire to return and belong to the warm community.

'And how did that strike you?' enquired Mr Maynard affably.

Martha was not going to confess to the criticism that was at the root of her confused disappointment: while they were a community, each of them seemed anxious to repudiate the others to an outsider at the first opportunity.

'That man Perr has real ability,' observed Mr Maynard. 'And so has Forester.'

'And not Mr Pyecroft?' Martha could see no difference between Forester, Perr and Pyecroft, all of them as far as she was concerned equally verbose, self-satisfied and elderly.

'Pyecroft has a head on his shoulders, but he's got bogged down in this talking shop. It's all very well as an amusement, but not as a lifework, after all.' He added, 'There is a certain type of man who leaves the common rooms and lecture halls of Britain simply because he will strike enlightened communities like this one as the last word in education and intellectual daring.'

Martha was digesting this when he said, 'I've never been able to understand why left-wing women choose to be so unattractive, a remarkable phenomenon.'

'They might have better things to do.'

'Conceivably.'

Martha was thinking of the imposing Mrs Maynard, who clearly regarded clothes as so many badges of office. She was wondering how Mr Maynard saw his wife, when feet hesitated behind them. It was Mr Matushi.

'Ah, Matushi,' exclaimed Mr Maynard. 'I'm glad of the opportunity to talk to you.'

They were on the dark platform of iron which was the landing on the second floor. This was where he had tried to kiss her. She would have liked to go quickly past it. But he waited calmly while Mr Matushi descended. She noted that Mr Maynard did not use the 'Mister,' which the others had been so careful to do; she most bitterly resented, on Mr Matushi's behalf, the casual, authoritative manner of Mr Maynard.

Mr Matushi was now standing quietly on the landing, drooping his length from his shoulders: he was a head taller than even Mr Maynard.

'I understand you regard yourself as a kind of leader of your – compatriots?' Mr Maynard enquired.

'Yes, I think that is so.' The voice was soft, firm, a little hesitant.

'Well, then – there's this question of the war. Would you like to represent your – followers, on a committee for raising funds, eh?'

Mr Matushi appeared to reflect. Then he said, 'Our people all support the war against fascism.'

Mr Maynard let out a surprised grunt. 'Eh?' It was the word 'fascism'; as far as he was concerned, England was fighting Germany again. 'So, you do, do you?'

'Our people are well aware of the danger Hitler represents to the civilized world.'

'I don't suppose that more than half of one per cent know who Hitler is.'

'In that case, it is not . . . democratic' – Mr Matushi hesitated delicately over the word – 'to make them soldiers in this war, is that not so, Mr Maynard?' He stooped before Mr Maynard, stubborn, gentle, expressing with every line of his body an infinite willingness to wait.

Mr Maynard looked at him heavily, and said, 'Be that as it may, it would be appreciated if a well-known and acknowledged leader – a man like yourself – would represent your people on the committee.'

Mr Matushi smiled gently. 'Perhaps there might be a better man for the position? A person like myself, fined in the courts, might not be – acceptable?'

Mr Maynard's black eyebrows shot up, and he said severely, 'Matushi, if you don't keep the law, it's my job to fine you. That's all there is to it.'

Mr Matushi was smiling, biting his lips, smiling again; he shook gently with laughter. 'But, Mr Maynard, you are a very good magistrate, we all know that; we all know you as a very just man.' There was no resentment in his manner, not even the impertinence which Mr Maynard was certainly looking for – nothing, apparently, but that genuine bubbling amusement. Suddenly he stopped his long body from the slight pervasive shaking, and said, 'Mr Maynard, our people will do everything they can in this terrible war. They will fight well. It is only fifty years since we were honourably defeated by your soldiers. Our soldiers have already gone to fight with your soldiers against fascism for democracy.' He waited, stooping and smiling.

'Good night, Matushi,' said Mr Maynard.

'Good night, sir.' He stood to one side while Mr Maynard and Martha went down the stairs before him, and then followed at a polite distance. They reached the street.

'What did you fine him for?'

'For not having a pass after nine o'clock.'

Martha was silent with hostility.

'I don't make the laws, I am their servant.'

Martha laughed angrily.

He looked at her in surprise. 'Personally I should be in favour of issuing educated men – comparatively educated, that is – with a special pass to exempt them from carrying other passes. I believe it is under consideration now.'

'Why not abolish passes altogether?'

'Why not? I suggest you put pressure on your Parliamentary representative to that effect.'

Martha laughed again.

'I am firmly of the opinion that the sooner a middle class with privileges is created among the Africans, the better it will be for everyone. Unfortunately, the majority of the whites are so bogged down in intelligent considerations such as that they wouldn't have their sisters marrying black men, that they are too stupefied to see the advantages of such a course.'

Martha was several years from understanding this remark, and felt herself to be as stupid as that majority he had dismissed so contemptuously.

They proceeded in silence down the empty moonlit street, Mr Maynard strolling along, putting one firm leg before the other under a heavy, massive body, hands behind his back, narrowed thoughtful eyes directed ahead. 'They are all the same, these African agitators. You can buy any one of them for ten shillings.'

'Has Mr Matushi been bought?'

'They all overreach themselves, if you give them time.'

'One of these days they'll fight you with their bare hands.'

'I don't doubt it. In the meantime I shall continue to do my duty in that station of life into which it has pleased God to call me.'

Martha considered this for a time; and then enquired, really wanting to know: 'I don't see why you go to these meetings?'

For the first time, Mr Maynard showed signs of discomfort. He said hastily, heavily humorous, 'I'm an interested observer of life.'

'You behave as if you were God,' said Martha at last.

They had reached the pavement outside the block of flats.

'If you are genuinely interested in uplifting humanity, which is right and proper at your age, then there are many things you could do.'

'Oh no you don't,' said Martha abruptly. Mr Maynard raised his brows. Martha was embarrassed because of the hostility that had sounded in her voice; she did not really understand what she had said. 'It was very sweet of you to take me out,' she said like a schoolgirl.

'So you have already said. Are you going to ask me up for a drink?' he enquired, facing her massively, so that she had to look up into his face. She felt him to be powerful and dangerous; she remembered him on the second landing. She said, 'Caroline wakes so early in the mornings.'

Up went those brows. 'But I thought Caroline was with your mother?' Then he said, 'Well, I won't obtrude myself. Good night.' He turned and went striding off along the street.

Martha went indoors in a ferment of embarrassment. He had made her feel gauche and unaccomplished. Yet there had been nothing of the ironical gentleman about him on the second landing among closed doors and the unpleasant, disreputable smell. She felt that that incident had been an insult to both of them. If she chose to remember it, she would never be able to feel liking for him again. She proceeded to forget it, with the vague thought, I suppose it's because he's so old; that generation – kissing hastily on staircases is the sort of thing they did.

She proceeded to think of Mr Matushi; she could not understand his extraordinarily gentle amusement. If I were Mr Matushi, she thought angrily, I would . . . But she could think of nothing but that she would have slapped Mr Maynard's face. Which would have earned him a sentence for assaulting a white man.

She went to bed in a mood of severe self-criticism.

As for Mr Maynard, he strolled through the moonlight, hands behind his back, and the memory of Martha's nervous hostility rankled. He felt he had been encouraged and then rebuffed. He proceeded to comfort himself by thinking of various romantic episodes. At the same time, he reflected on the meeting; he dwelt particularly on that moment when Mr Perr had laughed when he remarked that he could not understand why left-wing intellectuals always insisted on being so uncomfortable when they met. The grateful, almost obsequious note in that laugh caused another, but quite disconnected, image to float into his mind: the face of old Thompson-Jones, Minister for Finance, with whom he would be playing golf tomorrow.

2

The two rooms at the top of the block of flats were filled with light from the sky as soon as the sun, splendid, enlarged and red, swelled up over the horizon of suburb-clotted hills, pulling behind it filaments of rose-and-gold cloud. By half past five, fingers of warm yellow were reaching over the big bed, over Caroline's crib. Martha lay warm in the blankets, listening to Caroline wake. She always woke the moment the child first stirred, as if an alarm had gone off; she woke instantly if Caroline murmured in her sleep at night. Caroline gurgled, and strove with her limbs until the covers were off. She sat up. Martha, through eyes kept half closed, saw the tiny energetic creature in its white gown rolling over and stretching, two small rosy feet playing in the air, while the voice tried itself: a soft chuckle, then a deep, self-absorbed murmur; silence, and a sudden shriek of triumphant vitality as the cradle shook and rattled with her movements. The low meditative murmur began again; Caroline, crouching on all fours, looked steadily at the white blanket while she listened to her own voice; there was a look of thoughtful surprise on the small face. She dropped sideways, rolled to her back, her legs stuck straight up, she grunted and puffed while her face reddened. She lay there, rocking her legs from side to side, silent for the moment, apparently waiting with docile patience to hear what new sound her throat would bring forth. A high single note, like a bird's; another, a fifth lower; a long silence, and again a high triumphant yell. Caroline clambered resolutely to her feet, clutched the edge of the cradle, put her chin on it, and looked out of the window at the sun. The big yellow ball swam now in a clear sky. Caroline blinked at it; beads of sweat clung under her short black curls. She squeezed her eyes shut, and rocked, humming, from one foot to another, the sun sharply etching her rosy face with shadow and warm light. She opened her eyes cautiously; the sun filled her eyes with its dazzle. She turned her head slightly, and, frowning with determination, put up a clenched fist over one eye, and opened the other at the sun: it was still there, hanging in the blue square of the window. She stretched out one fist and spread it into a shaft of yellow light that swam with golden dust; the small fingers moved wildly, then clutch! they shut on nothing. Caroline looked down, puzzled, at her empty palm. She tried again; her hand went clutch! clutch! at the mote-filled sunlight. Then she stretched out both hands to the sun, a look of desperate desire on her face. She let out a high angry, baffled yell and shook the bars of her crib furiously. She lost her footing, rolled over, and lay on her back, legs waving comfortably in the warm sunlight, contentedly trying out her voice.

Martha shut her eyes and tried to sleep again. She could not. There was this band of tension, felt deeply as a web of tight anxiety, between her and the child. Every movement, every sound Caroline made reverberated through Martha. Relax! said Martha to herself, but she felt tension in every limb. She was waiting for that moment when Caroline's high shriek peremptorily sounded the summons for the day to begin.

And yct, during those three days while Caroline had been with her grandmother, Martha had slept, waked, gone about living as if Caroline did not exist, had never existed. Not for a moment had Martha felt anxiety; she had scarcely thought of the child. She came home; and again Martha was caught up into the rhythm of this other small life. Her long day was regulated by the clock to Caroline's needs; and she went to bed at night exhausted by Caroline's experience.

She lay now, eyes closed to a narrow slit, the sun making rainbows on her eyelashes, so that she might see it as Caroline had just seen it, and kncw that hcr rcluctance to get out of bed was simply boredom at the thought of the day ahead. She wished it were already the end of the day, and Caroline safely in bed and asleep. Then her, Martha's, life might begin. And yet the hours of evening were as restless and dissatisfied; she always went to bed early to put an end to them. Her whole life was a hurrying onwards, to get it past; she was back in the tension of hurry, hurry, hurry; and yet there was nothing at the end of it to hurry towards, not even the end of the war, which would change nothing for her.

At this point in her reflections, she again told herself to relax; her inability to enjoy Caroline simply filled her with guilt. Yet she could not relax into Caroline; that would be a disloyalty and even a danger to herself. Cycles of guilt and defiance ruled her living, and she knew it; she had not the beginnings of an understanding what it all meant.

Caroline was now chanting steadily, with a note of urgency in her voice that Martha knew. Her limbs involuntarily stiffened; she made them lie loose.

Caroline bundled herself over, dragged herself hand over hand up the bars of the crib, rested her chin on the rail and looked at her mother. Martha saw the small, white-gowned girl, her alert bright black eyes shrewdly watching her. Caroline let out a shriek of warning, and waited. Martha suddenly laughed, won over into tender amusement. Caroline surveyed her mother for a moment, and shook the bars like a monkey. In an instant, Martha had swung her legs over, lifted Caroline out and set her on the big bed.

The book prescribed rusk and orange juice. Martha fetched them. Caroline staggered around the room on her unsteady little legs, sucking the rusk into a sticky fawn-coloured paste.

The small white-painted room was filled with sunlight, like a glass bowl full of quivering bright water. Martha took a bath: the bathroom was shot with needles of sunlight; the water rocked in the white bath in spangles and opals of light. Then she dressed swiftly in one of the brief coloured dresses that gave her so much pleasure to wear. How lovely to wear so little, to feel her brown smooth limbs coming out of the slip of coloured linen; she was all free and her own again; she was light and supple, and the stains and distortions of pregnancy belonged to another epoch. How lovely then to wash the little girl, and see her in her fresh pretty cotton dress, the delicate pink feet balancing so surely and strongly over the floor.

By seven every morning Martha and her daughter were dressed and ready for the day, and they ate breakfast together; or rather, Martha drank tea and painfully did not care that Caroline would not eat.

Ever since the day Mr Maynard had entered on the unpleasant scene of Caroline being fed, when Martha had seen it sharply through his eyes, she had forced herself, and with an effort that exhausted her, *not* to care about Caroline's eating. She must break this bond! That was how she felt it: as something compulsive and deadly that would most certainly affect the child's whole future. So Martha no longer cared, on principle. But at the beginning it had not been so easy. She prepared the messes suitable for Caroline's age, set them on the wooden platform before the child, put a piece of linoleum under the high chair, and retired with a cup of tea and a book, forcing herself not to look at her.

And now what contests of will followed! Caroline had been used to a forceful pillar of a mother standing over her with a glinting hard spoon full of stuff that she *must* eat, no matter how she tightened her lips and turned away her face; now she saw this same woman – and from one day to the next – sitting away from her on the other side of the room, not listening to her cries of rage and shrieks of defiance. Caroline picked up the bowl of porridge and flung it on the floor so that the greyish mess splashed everywhere; Martha turned a page and did not look. Caroline sparked her black eyes at Martha, let out short sharp cries of anger to *make* her look; then she picked up a mug of milk and poured it all over herself. Martha remained indifferent in her chair; but there was a tight-lipped tension about her that Caroline knew. She paddled her hands in a lake of soiled milk and rubbed them in her hair, singing out her defiance. And suddenly Martha became a whirlwind of exasperation. She jumped up and said despairingly, 'Oh, Caroline! You are a naughty, naughty girl!'

The little girl, with blobs of porridge on her face, her hair plastered and dripping with milk, gurgled out triumphant defiance. Then she found herself lifted roughly from the chair; she yelled angrily while Martha held her kicking under her arm, and bent to fill the bath. She was dropped into the water, soaped hastily; she felt herself whirled into new clean clothes, and then she was dropped into her wooden pen, where she soon forgot all about it, and began playing with her toys.

In the meantime Martha was scrubbing porridge and milk off the floor, the furniture, herself. She was sick with disgust at the mess. She was asking herself why she had endured months of that other mess with only occasional lapses into distaste; a period when napkins and then clothes and blankets had been wet and dirty, without difficulty: the book had said so. The book and she had been admirably justified: Caroline was now, as the phrase went, perfectly clean. But that had been no problem; the battle centred on food. What is it all about? asked Martha in despair. She was furious with herself for losing her temper. She could have wept with annoyance. She was saying to herself, as she wiped off milk and grey pulp, Oh, Lord, how I do hate this business, I do loathe it so. She was saying she hated her daughter; and she knew it. Soon, the hot anger died; guilt unfailingly succeeded. Outside, on the little veranda which was like a wired cage projecting out into the sunlight – the sun was now pouring down from over the trees in the park – Caroline was cheerfully gurgling and singing to herself. Inside the room, Martha was seated, tired and miserable. Her heart was now a hot enlarged area of tenderness for the child whom she was so lamentably mishandling.

She went out onto the veranda. Caroline, in her short bright dress, looked up with her quick black eyes, and made an enquiring noise. She was snatched up and held against Martha's bosom. At once she began striving free; Martha laughed ruefully and put her down; she staggered around the room, singing to herself.

But she had eaten absolutely nothing. Martha produced rusks, and left them surreptitiously about the room. Caroline seized on them and began chewing vigorously.

'Oh, Caroline,' sighed Martha, 'what am I going to do with you?'

She was forming the habit of talking to the child as if to herself. The small brain was receiving the sound of a half-humorous, resentful, grumbling, helpless voice rumbling away over her head.

'My poor unfortunate brat, what had you done to deserve a mother like me? Well, there's no help for it, you'll just have to put up with it. You bore me to extinction, and that's the truth of it, and no doubt I bore you. But as far as I can make out, one of the most important functions of parents is that they should be suitable objects of hate: if psychology doesn't mean that, it means nothing. Well, then, so it's right and proper you should hate my guts off and on, you and I are just victims, my poor child, you can't help it, I can't help it, my mother couldn't help it, and her mother . . .'

After a silence the voice went on, rather like Caroline's own meditative experimental rumblings and chirpings: 'So there we are, and we'd better make the best of it. As soon as possible I'll send you to a nursery school where you are well out of my poisonous influence, I'll do that for you at least.'

By nine in the morning, it seemed always as if long stretches of the day had been lived through. And yet it was three hours till lunchtime. Martha sewed – she and Caroline had dozens of cheap pretty dresses. She watched the clock. She cooked little messes for Caroline. She leafed hopefully through the book – or rather, whichever one of them seemed most likely to provide what she wanted – to see if she had overlooked some pattern of words that might help her to feel better. And at the least she felt she was being honest, that virtue which she was still convinced was the supreme one. Somewhere at the bottom of her heart was a pleasant self-righteousness that while she was as little fitted for maternity as her mother had been, she at least had the honesty to admit it.

She would watch lunchtime approaching with helpless despair. But she was determined to break this cycle of determination, which always ended in her own violent anger and Caroline's rebellious screams.

She learned to put Caroline's food in front of her and then go out of the room altogether. When she came back, she forbade herself to notice the unpleasant fly-covered mess on the high chair. She quickly lifted the child out, and washed her, and set her back in her pen without saying a word. Day after day, Martha lay face down on the bed at every mealtime, her fingers stuck in her ears, reading, while Caroline yelled for attention next door. Slowly the yells lessened. There came a point where the child received her food and ate it. Martha returned from her exile in the bedroom, the victory won. She had succeeded in defeating the demon of antagonism.

And now she was able to cook the food and serve Caroline with it and not care if she ate it or not. And, of course, now it was eaten. And Martha existed on hastily cut slabs of bread and butter and tea. She could not be interested in food unless she was cooking it for someone with whom she would share it afterwards. Women living by themselves can starve themselves into a sickness without knowing what is wrong with them.

Then she became perversely sad because she had won the victory. It seemed that something must have snapped between her and her daughter. It increased her persistent uneasiness, which expressed itself in those interminable puzzled humorous monologues: 'It's all very well, Caroline, but there must be something wrong when you have to learn *not* to care. Because the trouble with me is not that I care too much, but that I care too little. You'd be relieved, my poor brat, if you knew that when you were with my mother I never thought of you at all – that's a guarantee of your future emotional safety, isn't it?' Silence, while Caroline pursued her own interests about the room; if the silence persisted, however, she cocked a bright enquiring eye towards her mother. 'But what I can't understand is this: Two years ago, I was as free as air. I could have done anything, been anything. Because the essence of the daydreams of every girl who isn't married is just that: it's the only time they are more free than men. Men *have* to be something, but you'll find when you grow up, my poor child, that you'll see yourself as a ballet dancer, or a business executive, or the wife of a Prime Minister, or the mistress of somebody important, or even in extreme moments a nun or a missionary. You'll imagine yourself doing all sorts of things in all sorts of countries; the point is, your will will be your limit. Anything'll be possible. But you will not see yourself sitting in a small room bound for twenty-four hours of the day – with years of it in front of you – to a small child. For God's sake, Caroline, don't marry young, I'll stop you marrying young if I have to lock you up. But I can't do that,' concluded Martha humorously, 'because that would be putting pressure on you, and that's the unforgivable sin. All I can promise is that I won't put any pressure on you of any kind. I simply *won't care* . . . But supposing that not caring is only the most subtle and deadly way of putting pressure on people – what then? . . . But what is most difficult is this: If you read novels and diaries, women didn't seem to have these problems. Is it really conceivable that we should have turned into something quite different in the space of about fifty years? Or do you suppose they didn't tell the truth, the novelists? In the books, the young and idealistic girl gets married, has a baby – she at once turns into something quite different; and she is perfectly happy to spend her whole life bringing up children with a tedious husband. Natasha, for instance: she was content to be an old hen, fussing and dull; but supposing all the time she saw a picture of herself as she had been, and saw herself as what she had become and was miserable – what then? Because either that's the truth or there is a completely new kind of woman in the world, and surely that isn't possible, what do you think, Caroline?'

All the morning, sunlight moved and deployed around the flat. After lunch the sun had moved away; the rooms were warm, airless, stagnant. And then Martha put Caroline into her push-chair, and filled in the time by wheeling her around the streets for an hour, two hours, three hours. Or she sat in the park under a tree with dozens of other young mothers and nannies, watching the children play. This period of the day seemed to concentrate into it the essence of boredom. It was boredom like an illness. But at six in the evening, Caroline was washed, fed, and put into her crib. Silence descended. Martha was free. She could go out, see people, go to the pictures. But she did not. She sat alone, reading and thinking interminably, turning over and over in her mind this guilty weight of thoughts, which were always the same. Those people who have been brought up in the nonconformist pattern may shed God, turn upside down the principles they were brought up to; but they may always be relied upon to torment themselves satisfactorily with problems of right behaviour. From these dreary self-searchings there emerged a definite idea: that there must be, if not in literature, which evaded these problems, then in life, that woman who combined a warm accepting femininity and motherhood with being what Martha described vaguely but to her own satisfaction as 'a person.' She must look for her.

Then one day she saw Stella in the street. They exchanged the gay guilty promises to come and see each other which people do who are dropping out of each other's lives. Afterwards Martha thought that Stella looked very contented. She had changed. Two years ago she had been a lithe, alive, beautiful young woman. Having a baby had turned her into a stout and handsome matron, very smart, competent and – this was the point – happy. Or so it seemed in retrospect. Thinking wistfully for several days about Stella's unfailing self-assurance, in whatever role life asked her to play, turned her, for Martha, into a symbol of satisfactory womanhood. On an impulse then she dropped Caroline in the house across the park with her mother, and drove out to the house in the suburbs where Stella now lived with her mother.

It was a very bright sparkling day, with a tang of chill in the air. The sky was glacially blue. The white houses in their masses of heavy green foliage shone in a thin clear light, with a remote, indrawn look, as if prepared to be abandoned by warmth for a short season. The wave of painful emotion that is a clearer sign of changing seasons than the loosening of a leaf or a clap of thunder after seven months' silence entered Martha suddenly with familiar and pleasurable melancholy – winter was coming. In such a mood, to enquire from Stella how one should live appeared absurd; nostalgia imposed different values – nothing mattered very much. Suppressing it, she drove on through the avenues, turned outwards over a narrow road through a shallow grass-filled vlei, and entered a new suburb; the town was spreading fast under the pressures of war. This suburb was a mile of new bungalows scattered hastily over a rock-strewn rise. Stella's mother's new house was at its limit; beyond stretched the unscarred veld; and the garden was bounded by heaps of granite boulders tangled over by purple bougainvillea. The bungalow was small, but no longer a Colonial bungalow. The veranda was a small porch, and there were green shutters to the windows, and there was a look of glossy smartness about it. Martha parked the car, went up prim steps, and rang the bell, feeling like someone paying a visit.

Stella appeared and cried out a gay welcome. She was wearing a handsome scarlet housecoat, and her dark braids fell down her back. In the living room her mother was playing with the baby. The room looked like an illustration from a magazine; it was all cream leather and red carpet. Through the cream-shaded windows a stretch of sere drying veld looked in and disowned the alien. Martha felt a sharp dislocation in her sense of what was fitting, as she always did with Mrs Barbazon, who, with her careful dark eyes, seemed a stray from the capitals of Europe.

Stella flung back her dark braids carelessly, and, with her new look of matronly contentment, sat down, watching her child – a little girl, dark-eyed, slender, pale. Both women were competing for Esther's attention. Mrs Barbazon was holding up her crystal beads and swinging them before the infant's moving eyes. Stella leaned forward and offered the end of one of her long thick plaits. Esther reached out for it, and with a satisfied smile Stella lifted her onto her own lap.

'How's Andrew?' asked Martha.

Without lifting her eyes from Esther's face, Stella said, 'Oh – I haven't had a letter recently. I don't know.' This was hard and careless.

'I heard from my brother that he'd met him somewhere up north.'

Stella looked up quickly, searched Martha's face, asked, 'What did he say he was doing?'

'Oh, nothing much, just that they'd met. My brother's with the South Africans.'

'This terrible, terrible war,' said Mrs Barbazon.

'Oh, they seem to be having a good enough time,' said Stella, with a careless laugh. Her face looked set for a moment; then she smiled at Esther, and began tickling her cheeks with the soft brush at the end of the braid.

'And how's Esther?'

Mrs Barbazon, smiling reminiscently, opened her mouth to give information. Stella cut in first with a story of how the child had crawled this morning across her bed. Mrs Barbazon said, 'You should let her sleep with me – you'd get some rest.'

'Oh, I've nothing else to do, and you're a good girl, aren't you, Esther?'

There was a silence. Martha felt the room oppressive. She could see that both women were devoting their lives to Esther; it was a close, jealous, watchful household.

'And are you having a good time?' asked Mrs Barbazon, in a way which told Martha they had been discussing her unfavourably.

'I've got my hands full with Caroline.'

'Oh, there's no time for anything else with a baby in the house.'

'I had a letter from Andrew last month,' said Stella casually. 'He says the boys up north are all demoralized because their wives and girl friends are unfaithful to them with the Air Force.'

'It's a terrible thing,' said Mrs Barbazon, 'when our men are sacrificing everything to fight, and the women have no loyalty.'

Here there was an inexplicable long look between Mrs Barbazon and Stella; the older woman rose, and said, 'I'll make some tea, the servants are out.' She left the room with a small wistful smile in the direction of Esther.

As soon as her mother had left the room, Stella set the child on the floor and gave her attention to Martha. She asked if Caroline was walking yet; when Martha said yes, she said quickly that a year was early to be walking, from which Martha deduced that Esther had fallen behind schedule in her achievements.

Martha looked at Esther with detached criticism, in which was concealed the distaste that women feel for other women's babies while they are still closely physically linked with their own. Esther, she decided, was listless and heavy compared to the ceaselessly mobile Caroline.

Stella began talking of how she had had to wean the child after three months; her health had not permitted her to stand the strain of breast feeding; as she spoke, she unconsciously felt her now plump breasts with both hands. 'Having babies ruins the figure, ruins it.' She looked over at Martha and said, 'You've lost the weight you put on.'

'I didn't lose it,' said Martha grimly, 'I starved it off.'

'Oh, I could never diet, I'm not strong enough. Anyway, Andrew always said he wished I was fatter.' Stella sighed, and her face fell into dissatisfied lines. The beautiful dark eyes looked strained and shadowed. The remote exotic gleam had gone; the seductive quality that Martha had so envied, that had showed itself in her every glance and movement, had completely vanished; she was a good-looking housewife, no more.

The doorbell rang. Stella's eyes gathered life; she half rose, then said, 'But I'm not dressed!'

'Leave it – I'll go,' said Mrs Barbazon from the kitchen.

Stella stood with her hands to her hair.

'You'd better get yourself dressed,' said Mrs Barbazon, as she came through to go to the door. There was a disapproving note in her voice which caused Martha to glance curiously at Stella.

A look of anger crossed Stella's face, then went. 'Oh, yes, I can't be seen like this,' she said, and went out quickly just before Mrs Barbazon came back with a young officer.

He was a big, bulky, fairheaded man, blue-eyed, Northern-looking. He sat down, while Mrs Barbazon moved and fussed about him. She sat down and began questioning him with the touching self-immolating devotion which was what she offered to her daughter, about how the flying had gone yesterday, had he been sleeping better?

'Stella's just getting dressed. You know what things are with a baby in the house.'

The newcomer, reminded of the household's obligations clucked at the baby. Mrs Barbazon, seeing him occupied, went out and quickly returned with a tea-waggon. She began pouring.

A gay voice was heard outside. 'Mother, where's my hairbrush?'

'I don't know.' Mrs Barbazon spoke sharply. She stood looking at the doorway, with the teapot held suspended in her hand. Stella, in a dress of apple-green linen which showed her apricot-coloured arms, was standing in the doorway, her loosened masses of hair about her face, apparently oblivious of the officer.

'Ah, there it is. Naughty Esther, you had it.' Stella reached for the hairbrush, holding back her heavy hair with one hand. 'Why, Rupert, is that you?'

Mrs Barbazon steadily poured tea, her lips compressed.

'You know how things get all over the place, with babies in the house,' said Stella with her jolly laugh. She stood in front of the big man, who had risen and was awkwardly facing her, and began brushing back the loads of glistening hair that slipped with a hiss over her shoulders. He could not keep his eyes off it. Her small smooth face emerged from the frame of falling hair, and Martha saw that the spirit of attraction had lit it again; Stella looked as she had done before the baby. She smiled and asked how he did, while he said, 'Fine, fine, thank you,' and his eyes followed the movement of the hair. She held the scene for a few moments longer; then, with a final swift toss of her head backwards, which flung the hair into an oiled, iridescent, dead-black curve, she said, 'Excuse me, I'll just finish dressing.'

The three sat and made conversation while the officer's eyes rested on the door through which Stella had gone. She returned in a few moments, the black hair done up demurely in its heavy knot, and sat down near him. Little Esther began tugging at the green linen. Stella put her hands down once or twice, and then said hastily, 'Let's call the nurse – she can go out for a bit.'

Mrs Barbazon rose, picked up Esther, and went out. She did not return.

Martha soon got up and said she must go and feed Caroline.

At once Stella said, 'Do come and see us again, Matty. You're a naughty girl, forgetting your friends like this.' But she was looking at the officer even as she spoke; Martha felt something like pity for the big likeable man with the candid blue eyes.

Stella came with her to the door. 'He's a nice boy,' she remarked. 'We try and make him feel at home. It must be hard for them, so far from their families.'

Martha laughed. Stella looked at her, puzzled.

'He's a really nice boy, Mother says she feels towards him like a son,' she went on, smiling a small, dreamy and quite unconscious smile.

Martha urged Stella with false animation to visit her soon. Stella again berated Martha for being so unsociable. They exchanged urgent invitations for a few moments, and parted, disliking each other.

Martha was feeling extraordinarily foolish as she drove home. The reaction against Stella sent her back to Alice. The two women had in common a basic self-absorption that made it possible to forget each other for weeks and meet again easily without any embarrassment. They understood each other very well. They would seek each other out for the sole reason that they needed a safety valve; they would discuss in humorous, helpless voices, for an hour or so, their boredom, the tediums of living alone, the unsatisfactory nature of marriage, the burden of bringing up children, and part in the best of humours with the unscrupulous and buccaneering chuckle that came of being so ruthlessly disloyal to everything they were.

Then each retired again into isolation. Alice was half crazy with being alone. She was very thin, her hair hung limp about her face, she neglected her clothes. From time to time she exclaimed defiantly, 'Oh, to hell with everything,' and rang up Martha to say she was going out with the Air Force. Martha always assured her that this was the least of her rights. Alice pulled out an old dance dress, combed her hair back, scrawled some lipstick across her face. She then set herself to be the life and soul of whichever party she happened to be at. Returned to her flat by some ardent young man, she allowed herself to be kissed and caressed for a while, as if she owed this to her self-respect, and then said, 'Oh, well, that's that – thanks for a lovely time.' With which she departed indoors, with a hasty apologetic wave. She never saw any young man for a second time. On these occasions Martha was likely to be rung up at three in the morning by Alice, who concluded her desperate, gay, rambling comments on the party by 'The point is, once you've been married there's no point in it, I don't enjoy anything any more.' And then, firmly: 'But if Willie thinks I'm going to sit at home weeping for him, he'd better think again, after what I heard he was up to!' With this, she let out her high fatalistic giggle, and wished Martha a good night.

3

The airstrip was an irregular stretch of glistening white sand in the
dull-green bush. As the aircraft turned in to land, the shadow of its
wings dipped over an acre or so of tin-and-brick bungalows. The
soldiers in the aircraft peered down past the tilting wings and suggested
Lower Egypt, Abyssinia, Kenya, Uganda. It seemed that they had all
seen this shantytown in the bush many times before.

The aircraft bounced a little as it landed, then slewed to a stop. A
thick cloud of white dust drifted up. The door was kept shut till it
cleared. Then they descended – half a dozen men on their feet. An
ambulance was already motoring across the half mile between here and
the red-brick shack that was an office, to pick up the stretcher cases.
The half dozen stood on one side hopefully while the stretchers were
slid inside the white car, but it drove off immediately. They walked
across the white glisten of the strip, sand giving with a silken crunch
beneath their boots, then through low dun-coloured bushes towards the
office. Small paper-white butterflies hovered over the bushes, or clung
with fanning wings. There was a hot, spicy smell of leaves. Over the
squashed remains of a chameleon, spreadeagled on the sand like a small
dragon's skin pegged out, was a thick black clot of ants. A stray kaffir
dog, his skeleton showing clear through tight skin, lay in the pit of blue
shade outside the veranda. They stepped over the dog and went in.

It was a single room. A South African sergeant sat behind a small deal
table. A black man in a sort of orderly's uniform stood at ease beside
him. The sergeant was pouring a glass of water from a bedroom
decanter. He tipped back his head, poured the water into his mouth,
wiped his hand across his mouth, looked at them and said, 'So there you
are.'

Douglas said half facetiously, 'Where are we, we'd like to know.'

The sergeant thought, concluded that the information could not
subvert the course of the war, and offered cautiously, 'Nyasaland.'

The men exchanged startled, bitter glances. 'Pretty far from the
front,' said Douglas, his face hard.

A quick glance from the sergeant. He said officially, 'Are you OK till you get into town? There's a car coming for you.'

He nodded at a bench set against the wall. They did not immediately sit down. They stood tense, looking at each other, at the sergeant.

'Sit down,' said the sergeant again, authoritative but uneasy.

They slowly walked over, dropped their packs by the wall, sat. Six men, all tough soldiers, very burnt, apparently fit for anything. Yet here they sat. They sat and waited with the patience which a year in the Army had taught them. Indeed, for that year they had done little else but wait. They had marched, drilled – and waited; slept under canvas or in the open – and waited; they had been told nothing, knew nothing. For the first time in their lives they had been *pushed around*; they were expected to wait. And now things were really happening up north, and they were back only a few hundred miles from home. They waited. The small brick room, unceilinged, was roofed with corrugated iron; the heat poured down. The brick at their backs burned through the thick khaki; they sat away and forward from the wall, looking out of the doorway into the sunlight. The aircraft looked like a small silver insect glittering off sunlight. It was apparently abandoned. A pair of hawks circled above on steady wings.

Douglas, at the end of the bench, blinked regularly out into the dazzle. Beside him sat Perry, legs sprawling in front of him, the big blond sun-reddened body tense. Douglas heard the breath coming fast and irregular, and glanced swiftly sideways; Perry was staring angrily at a map of Africa nailed to the brick wall opposite. Arrows of black ink showed the offensives and counteroffensives in North Africa. Their unit was – so they believed – combining with the Australians against Rommel at that moment. Perry's mouth, when closed, was a hard, lipless line; when slightly open, as now, it had a spoilt and peevish droop.

Douglas muttered with warning cheerfulness, 'Hey, take it easy, man.'

Perry moved his legs, showing mats of wet hair on reddened skin where they had adhered together. Sweat was dripping steadily off all of them. 'There's been a balls-up, a mucking balls-up.' The tone was one they all knew; legs shifted, bodies eased, all along the bench. The sergeant, seated behind his table, was writing a letter home, and did not look up.

Douglas got up, went to the table, reached out his hand, laid it on the decanter, and looked at the sergeant, who nodded briefly. Douglas took glass and decanter, and went along the line of men with it. Before he reached the end, the water was finished. He handed the decanter to the black orderly, who submerged it in a petrol tin covered with a wet sack that stood in a corner, and handed it back, dripping. The water hissed into the brick floor. Douglas returned the things to the table, and sat down again.

Perry's mouth and chin were wet with water. He raised his fist and rubbed it over the lower part of his face, then let it drop. The fist hung clenched. He banged it several times against the edge of the bench, and left it hanging. He looked at the map and said, 'They told us we'd be examined. They've balled us up. What are we doing in this God-damned dump?'

Douglas hastily agreed, 'Bloody mess,' and looked at him with entreaty.

Perry writhed his big body frustratedly and jumped up. He went rapidly to the table, snatched at the decanter as the sergeant instinctively jerked up his head, dived at the petrol tin, filled the decanter, and poured it all over his head and shoulders. The sergeant turned his head to watch, then went on writing. Perry dumped the decanter down under the man's nose.

'Oh, sit down, damn it,' the sergeant muttered uneasily.

Perry grinned slightly, and sat. They waited. The bricks hissed as the water sank in. Water dripped off Perry's neck and hair.

A lorry came bumping across the airstrip. But it swerved over to the aircraft. A couple of Africans got out, uncoiled a black hose, and began feeding petrol into it. The two hawks were now black specks high in the grey-blue air. The air between here and the aircraft swam in lazy hot waves. Then the aircraft began to shake. It turned, and trundled away up the strip for the take-off. They watched it turn and come roaring down the strip past them, and up. In a moment it was away over the trees, and its silver glitter was absorbed in the vast glitter of the sky. The two hawks continued to wheel on level wings.

'Mucking bastards, leaving us behind,' said Perry suddenly, and his voice cracked.

The sergeant's cheek muscles showed tense, but he went on writing fast.

Perry got to his feet with slow deliberation, and slouched over to the table. 'Sarge?'

The sergeant laid down his pen and looked at him. 'Steady on, man,' he said warningly, 'I'm not responsible for it.'

Perry, his face scarlet, his tunic soaked, drops of sweat and water scattering, leaned forward, suspending a big red hairy fist over the table. 'I'm not going to be messed up,' he said, in a quiet voice.

'I'm not messing you up,' said the sergeant steadily. He looked past Perry to the bench, where the men sat watching. There were half-grins on their faces. The man at the far end, nearest the door, a lanky youth with a bony freckled face, was smiling hilariously. He looked as if he were about to cheer.

Douglas remained seated for a moment, but then got up and came forward, laying his hand on Perry's shoulder. 'Now, come on, man, don't take it out on him.' He sounded embarrassed.

Perry kept his shoulder still, then flung off the hand with a sudden heave. Douglas stood back a pace, Perry leaned both his fists on the table, and stared straight into the sergeant's face. 'I'm going to break everything up if I don't get some sense out of you.'

The table leaned over, the sergeant put his hands down to steady it, it slid roughly over the lumpy brick tight against the sergeant's stomach. He was now pinned back against the wall. The orderly stood, arms folded, watching with interest.

Perry deliberately pressed the table forward against the sergeant, who was pale and gasping, and trying to push it back again. 'You mucking pen-pushing bastard . . .' Using all his strength, he forced the edge of the table into the sergeant. Ink, pens, paper, glass, decanter, went rolling and crashing.

Douglas made a movement of his head towards the others. After a hesitation, three of them rose, leaving the cheerful boy alone, and came over. 'Now stop it, damn it, man,' said Douglas.

Perry gritted his teeth, and heaved. The sergeant had lost his footing, and was pinned in mid-air against the wall, straining for breath. His boots scraped wildly at the floor. Douglas nodded at the three: all four gripped Perry by the shoulders, with a sort of weary good humour, and pulled him back. A moment's scrape, struggle, heave – then Perry came staggering back, the sergeant found his feet, the table shot away. The sergeant stood blinking, trying to get back his breath without showing he had lost it. He smoothed down his tunic, pulled up the fallen chair, and sat down. He nodded at the African, who began picking up things off the floor.

'Look at him,' gasped out Perry, 'sitting there on his fat arse, pushing a pen.' He shook off his captors, who had their hands laid warningly on various parts of his upper body. He looked at them, grinning. They grinned sheepishly back. Then they all turned suddenly at the sound of a wild cry of laughter from the youth who had remained sitting. His face was flushed and incoherent, his eyes lit with a blue glare. He stamped his boots a few times on the floor, let out a 'Hurray!' and all at once sat looking at them doubtfully, as if he did not know them.

'For God's sake,' said Douglas in a rapid warning undertone, 'he'll be off again.' Immediately all five returned to their places on the bench, leaving a small space between the youth and the man next to him. Perry leaned back against the burning wall, and began a low hissing whistle between his teeth, to the tune of 'Begin the Beguine.' From time to time he banged his big fists on his knees, in a considering way. His mouth drooped slightly open; but he looked cautiously over the youth, who was now staring straight in front of him, his clear blue eyes clouded with wonder, at the map on the wall. The African was sweeping the mess of glass, ink, and water from the brick with a fibre broom. The sergeant sat moodily, arms folded on the table.

'I could have you court-martialled,' he observed bitterly at last.

No one said anything. Perry continued to hiss out 'Begin the Beguine.'

'I'd be within my rights to have you court-martialled,' insisted the sergeant.

'Discipline,' said Perry. 'Discipline is what this war needs.' He turned his big head slowly towards the sergeant. He surveyed him steadily.

'Oh, for God's sake,' said Douglas impatiently. 'Don't start again.'

The sergeant glanced involuntarily through the square in the wall that called itself a window, and exclaimed, 'Your car's coming.' His voice was eager with relief.

Perry lapsed back against the wall, his lips stretched in a small ugly grin.

A large army lorry stopped outside. The soldiers stood up, stretching themselves. When the distracted youth did not move, the man nearest to him unceremoniously heaved him up: he stood for a while, vaguely looking, then began with hasty officious movements to straighten his clothes and arrange his pack.

A young woman leaped down from the driver's seat, landing with a skid in the white sand, and came forward. She was clumsy in khaki, her cap on the back of her head, wisps of pale damp hair hanging beside her face.

At once Douglas let out a whoop, and began thumping her on her shoulders, while she stiffened herself, laughing, saying, 'Hey, hey, steady now, boys.' They crowded around her; she was one of the girls from the Sports Club. They had played hockey with her, danced with her, made love to her all through their glorious youth. 'It's fine to see you here, Bobby,' said Douglas. She received their kisses on her offered cheek.

She was a rather tall, lumpish girl, with pale fatty cheeks which were stained wild pink in patches from the heat. Her grey eyes were slightly protuberant. She had acquired a mannish stride and a new hearty voice. 'Well, pile in, boys.' She made a half-serious salute to the sergeant – who returned a grin and a nod – and turned towards the lorry. 'Here, aren't you coming?' she shouted cheerfully at the youth, who had sat himself down again on the bench, and was watching the proceedings from a distance. Douglas significantly tapped his head, and she gave a stare of startled distaste at the youth. One of them went back, helped him to his feet, and came with him to the back of the lorry. He was heaved in. Bobby, Perry and Douglas stood beside the front seat.

'What the hell are you doing in this dump?' asked Douglas. 'We heard you'd got up north.'

'Join the Army and see the world. If I'd known I'd land in this mucking hole . . . But they're sending me up north next month, this bleeding place is being closed down.' This slightly hoarse, goodfellow's voice, the way she carefully seasoned in her obscenities, caused Douglas and Perry to involuntarily exchange a look.

Perry suddenly remarked, 'For Christsake, we haven't seen a woman in months.' He sounded injured.

Bobby's pale cheeks crimsoned irregularly. She looked at them in appeal. Douglas, embarrassed for her, said quickly, 'It's pretty good to see an old pal here, Bobby.' She looked now in gratitude, then turned away, and climbed up into the cab. Douglas was about to climb up beside her, when Perry laid his arm across, like a barrier, and grinned at him fiercely. For a moment Douglas glared. Then he smiled, let out a short laugh, and said, 'Go ahead.'

Perry hoisted himself up beside the girl, shouting down, 'You'll be seeing your wife tomorrow.'

Douglas looked annoyed. He said through his teeth, 'You'd better let up, Perry, I've just about had enough of you.'

Ever since Perry had been officially informed that he had an ulcer, he had been breaking out. Douglas had been watching over him like a father. It was his turn to feel injured. He walked moodily back to the end of the lorry, and jumped in. There was no window between the back of the lorry and the driver's seat. But they could all hear Bobby's loud boisterous laugh, increasingly uneasy, as the lorry turned, bumped across the bush-covered sand, found the strip, raced along it at sixty and, with a swerve that sent them sprawling, turned onto a rough track that wound through the bush. They were silent, crouching with their backs against the sides of the lorry, holding tight as it bounced and rocked. The youth with the wild eyes had stiffened himself and was glaring at them all in turn. They were all afraid of him and ashamed to be afraid. The trees were growing thinner, and shacks of brick and tin flashed past. Then it was a proper street, tarmac, where the heat oiled and quivered, and stretches of whitish sand on either side; then Indian stores and native eating houses. Now they were in a broad empty space of dust, whose surface eddied and stirred. There was a biggish new white building, with a couple of jacaranda trees shading it. The lorry stopped with a jolt. They swore angrily under their breaths as they banged themselves on the sides. Bobby's loud and boisterous voice invited them to descend. They did so in silence.

Under one of the trees a native woman sat in the dust, draped in red cloth. She was suckling her baby. She looked at them indifferently. Some dogs lay stretched under the other tree, looking as if they were dead. The men stood in a group around Bobby; she seemed hot and flustered, and would not look at Perry, who was grinning savagely.

'Now, who's got what wrong with them?' she enquired. 'We've got stomach and respiratory separate.'

They all laughed disgustedly.

'For crying out loud,' said Perry. 'What, two beds each?'

'Well, Perry,' said Douglas, 'we're together.' They stood off to one side.

Bobby looked at the other four, 'What's wrong with you?' Their faces tightened. 'Oh, very well,' she said hastily. 'I'll show you where to go. Perry and Douglas – over there, that house there. The doctor'll come over.' She quickly turned her back on Perry, and went off with her four into the big building, the youth lagging behind and looking around him suspiciously.

Perry and Douglas crossed the dust towards a small wire-enclosed house. 'Bloody skirts,' said Perry.

'Oh, go on,' said Douglas awkwardly. 'She's a nice kid.'

Perry spat and began whistling between his teeth.

The shack had a veranda closed in by greenish gauze. It was raised; three red cement steps led to the gauze door. On the steps sat a native orderly. He sprang up and stood to one side, quivering at attention. Perry heaved his shoulder dispassionately into the man's chest without looking at him, swung open the door and went in. The man saved himself from falling by clutching at the doorframe, nimbly straightened himself, and sat down on the steps, brushing whitish patches of dust from his khaki. He reached out for his hand piano where it had fallen beside the steps, and began playing it.

Inside on the veranda were four iron beds covered with neatly folded red blankets. There was no one in sight. Behind the veranda was a single room with a table and a chair in it. On the table stood a glass jar with some thermometers slanting up.

Douglas slung his pack onto one of the beds, took off his boots, and lay down on another, closing his eyes.

Perry heaved his pack beside the other, and let himself down flat on his back, his dusty boots side by side on the blanket. He waited, hands behind his head, a dangerous immobility about him.

It was about two in the afternoon. They had landed four hours ago. No one came. The expanse of dust outside the green gauze remained empty. Half a dozen native women came past with their children, chattering in their shrill voices. From a big msasa tree that shaded the veranda a pigeon was cooing regularly. The iron roof cracked in the heat. The hand piano tinkled.

'For crying out loud,' began Perry suddenly.

Douglas hastily opened his eyes, swung his legs down, said, 'I'll see if they can get us a bite.' He called the native orderly. 'Hey, Jim, where's the doctor?'

The orderly pointed at the other building cheerfully.

'Can you get us something to eat?'

'Yes, baas. Right away, baas.'

He went through into the inner room, through that into the back. Silence again. The pigeon cooed on and on.

He came back with a tin tray. Fried eggs, bacon, fried bread. Perry raised himself, looked at it, looked at him.

'We have ulcers,' he said. 'Ulcers – diet – no fat.' He flipped his hand up against the tray. It jerked, the plates slid, the orderly caught at it, steadied the plates into their pattern. Perry turned his back and was staring out through the green gauze at the sky.

'Can you boil us some eggs?' asked Douglas quickly.

'Boiled eggs? Yes, baas, right away, baas.' The orderly went out with the tray at a half-run.

Perry did not move. He was looking at an officer walking across the dust towards them, who came up the steps, pushed the door open impatiently, then carefully closed it behind him. Perry turned himself over in one movement, and lay looking at him. Douglas, who had been going to salute, stood up, then sat down again.

'You're the ulcers, are you?'

'That's me,' said Perry. 'Just one big ulcer.'

'Sorry I didn't get over before – was fixing those other chaps.' He sat down on the edge of Douglas's bed, and looked at them. He was rather slight, with rough fair hair, grey straight eyes. He was reddened and sweating.

'You're English,' remarked Perry.

'Yes, I am actually.'

Perry turned on his back and lay looking at the iron roof.

The doctor smiled rather tiredly and said, 'Well, how are things where you've come from?'

'Read the newspapers?' asked Perry.

'Pretty bad,' said Douglas.

The doctor glanced at Perry quickly, then more slowly at Douglas.

'When am I going to be examined?' asked Perry dangerously.

'There's been a bit of a balls-up,' said Douglas apologetically. 'We shouldn't be here.'

'What happened?'

'Well, it's like this –'

But Perry swung over again, and poked his head forward at the doctor: 'He got it in for me. I'll get him when the war's over, I'm warning you. Officer – well, he won't be an officer when the war's over, he'll be my junior clerk.' He dropped his head back again, and let his two fists dangle on each side of the narrow bed. They swayed back and forth over the floor.

'How about sleeping for a bit?' said the doctor. 'Then we'll talk about it.'

'I'm not going to sleep. I'm going to be examined – now.'

Douglas again smiled his small apology. Perry's sideways flickering eyes caught the smile. 'And I'll get you too, Douggie old pal. Arse-licker, that's all you are. Always were.'

Douglas yellowed, but kept his steady, rather nervous smile.

The doctor sat in thought. He sighed unconsciously. Of the four men in the other building, three had threatened him and the commanding officers, then broken down and wept. Secret cabals of influence worked against them; life itself had it in for them. But he, Doc, was a good type who understood them. He had given them sedatives, and tomorrow they would go home with battle fatigue. The crazy youth had been quite amenable, then suddenly had begun climbing out of the window, shouting that he would kill himself. He was now under guard. He was all in line with what the doctor knew and could handle. But he could not understand these colonials, so tough, masculine, violent – and then the sudden collapse into self-pity. It seemed a well of self-pity lay in all of them, ready to overflow at any moment. Caught by accident in South Africa at the beginning of the war, he had been with South Africans all the time. They every one of them got drunk or broke down at some stage or another and confessed to a vast grievance against life. Extraordinary, he thought, remarkable. He looked at Douglas, and considered. Douglas filled him with confidence. He looked a round, humorous, cheerful soldier of a man; the round good-natured face was frankly boyish. The doctor felt he could rely on him. He turned to him and asked, 'Tell me what happened?'

Perry stiffened, rolled his eyes sideways, but did not move.

'Well, I've had trouble with my stomach off and on for years,' said Douglas, with a wary look at the braced Perry. 'It flares up from time to time. I had a sudden bad go last week. Usually I just shut up about it and diet myself as well as you can on army food. But it was a really bad go – they got me into hospital. I'd only been there half an hour when orders came to evacuate. I was never examined. They flew a bunch of us down to the next town. We were evacuated from there again almost at once. The next thing was, we were all shoved onto a plane, and here we are. I'm sure I could carry on in the Army. I'm quite fit apart from the ulcer, and it's not bad.' He ended on a frank appeal.

'You can't feed an ulcer in the Army,' said the doctor pleasantly. 'And you're better out.'

Douglas's mouth was bitter. 'No one examined me, I was just pushed off.' Suddenly the lips quivered. He turned away, blinking. God help us! thought the doctor, astounded – here it is again.

Perry had slowly risen, was sitting on the edge of his bed. 'Hey, what about me? What about me, Doc?' He rose, fists clenched.

Deliberately ignoring him, the doctor said to Douglas, 'Get inside a minute, I'll call you.' He was embarrassed at what he was going to do.

Douglas hesitated, then rose, then stood still. He was staring like a child at the doctor. At last he turned and stumbled indoors.

Perry, crouching low, was on the point of springing at the doctor.

'Damn it,' said the doctor easily, 'take it easy, now.' His voice was deliberately kind, paternal.

Perry quivered all over, then sat. His lower lip, thrust out aggressively, worked. Tears sprang from his eyes. The doctor moved over and put a hand on his shoulder. Perry seemed to swell, then subsided. The doctor sat beside him, arm lightly across his shoulder, and began to talk, in a low, persuasive voice.

Douglas, standing behind the gauze door, looking suspiciously out, was amazed and upset at the scene. Then he turned away, and sat on the table inside. He could still hear the doctor's almost maudlin voice soothing Perry like a child. He could hear Perry heaving up great sobs and complaining that the officer had it in for him, the sergeant had it in for him, he'd never had a chance.

The back door cautiously opened; the orderly's head came around it. He came in with a tray of boiled eggs, and laid it before Douglas. Seeing a dangerous gleam in Douglas's fixed blue stare, he hastily slipped out again.

The sentimental murmuring had ceased. Douglas looked out. Perry was lying face down on the red blankets. His fists, hanging down each side of the bed, were being banged slowly and with method on the floor – there was a streak of blood on the knuckles. The doctor was standing upright, filling a syringe against the light. Then he swiftly bent, jabbed the needle into Perry's forearm, and moved quickly back: clearly, he expected Perry to attack him. But Perry was whimpering, face down, 'You're a good chap, Doc, thank you, Doc.'

Douglas saw the doctor shut his eyes, sigh, and open them again, as he stood motionless, syringe in hand. If he sticks that thing into me I'll kill him, thought Douglas. But the doctor dismantled the syringe and put it away. Then he stood up and braced himself: there was still Douglas. He came into the inner room. Douglas stood waiting for him belligerently.

'He'll sleep for a couple of hours and then he'll be all right,' said the doctor cheerfully.

'You're sending us home?' began Douglas, standing square in front of him.

The doctor suddenly snapped, 'Yes, I am. I'm sick to death of the lot of you. You've no right to be in the Army in the first place. How did you get in? Told a lot of lies, I suppose. Bloody clever.' He paused, and added, 'Hundreds of pounds spent on you, you crack at the first strain, and you have to be sent back home. What do you think this is, a picnic?'

Douglas looked at him incredulously. Seeing the familiar swelling and reddening, the working lower lip, the doctor snapped, 'Oh, shut up, shut up, shut up – go to hell and shut up.'

'Who's in charge here?' asked Douglas after a pause, the official in him coming to the rescue.

The doctor stared, laughed angrily, and said, 'You can go and see Major Banks if you like – he's over there.' He pointed at the building opposite, picked up his case, and went out past Perry without looking at him. He strode across the dust and vanished into the building. Douglas looked at the eggs; he was unconsciously grinding his teeth. Then he followed the doctor out.

A deep shady veranda surrounded the main building; off it rooms opened. Inside one of them sat Major Banks under a spinning electric fan, dealing with piles of papers. He looked up, irritated, as Douglas strode in, slamming the door. His eyes narrowed. Douglas stopped in the middle of the room, saluted hastily, came forward.

'Well, Doug, how are you?' said the Major, rising and holding his hand out over the table. Douglas shook it. They had known each other for years. 'Sit down.' Douglas sat. He was looking at the papers, the files, the ink banks, the paper clips: the fetters from which he had escaped.

'The doctor's been talking to me about you,' said Major Banks.

Douglas allowed himself a bitter smile. But he accepted a cigarette with a 'Thank you, sir.'

Major Banks was a lean, fibrous, olive-skinned man, with very keen, bright light-blue eyes: they looked odd in that burnt face. 'Active service's out, Doug,' he said finally. 'But if you want me to fix you up on the administrative side, I'll do it.'

'Thanks,' said Douglas with hostility.

'You're wise. I'll be spending the rest of the war in happy spots like this one – nice prospect.'

'If I've got to sit behind a desk I'd rather do it at home.'

'They should never have let you go, anyway. I know your chief was sick when you left.'

'They didn't let me go. I worked a point,' said Douglas, grinning proudly.

'So I gathered,' said the Major drily. He added, 'How's your wife – she'll be glad to see you.'

'Oh, she's fine, fine,' said Douglas proudly. 'We've a kid, did you know?'

'Lucky chap. Well – perhaps you'll join me for a drink later.'

'Alcohol's out – I've got an ulcer.'

'Bad luck.' The Major picked up some papers.

Douglas rose. He saluted; the Major casually, half jocular, returned it. As Douglas reached the swing doors, someone started shouting from a room nearby. He stopped. The sound was disturbing for a reason he could not define.

'That's your pal Simmons,' said the Major. 'He's gone clean off his rocker. Still, it's just as well to get the crocks out of the way before the fighting starts.'

Douglas went red. He looked with helpless affront at the oblivious Major, now bent over his papers. The shouting stopped. Silence. He slammed the door again, walked out across the square and entered the little gauze-covered house. Perry was lying face downwards, exactly as he had been, the unclenched hands knuckled loose on the floor. He was deeply asleep. The native orderly was back on the steps with his hand piano. The soft, brooding, tinkling melodies went on and on together with the pigeon's cooing. Douglas sat on the edge of his bed and sank into thought. His mouth was dry with loss. It seemed to him that everything he had ever wanted was being snatched from him. All his adult life he had sat in an office; now after a year's brief reprieve he was being sent back to it. He could see his future life stretching ahead, nothing unexpected, nothing new from one year's end to the next. Holidays every five years or so, retirement, death. He felt like an old man.

The year of discomfort and boredom in the Army was already arranging itself in a series of bright scenes, magical with distance. He thought of the men whom he had known all his life, been to school with,

worked with, played with, now up north in 'the real thing' at last. It
seemed that his whole life had led without his knowing it to the climax
of being with those men, his fellows, his friends, parts of himself, in real
fighting, real living, real experience at last. And he was out of it. A few
days before it started, he had been kicked out. A crock, he thought
bitterly.

His eyes rested on Perry, sprawled out loose a couple of feet away.
There was something childish about those big open fists resting on their
knuckles on the floor, something appealing and childish about the
closed lids fringed with sandy lashes. Tenderness, a warm protectiveness, filled him. He thought, He'll have a stiff neck lying like that. He
got up, and, using all his strength, turned the big man over on his back.
He was winded when he'd achieved it. He stood up, panting. His eyes
were wet; he'd be out of uniform in a couple of days. Never again would
he know the comradeship of men. Never. Never. He shut his eyes to
steady himself. He opened them at last and looked out. It was very still
out there. Thick black shadows lay stretched over the sand now. A
couple of scraggy hens scratched below the steps. The orderly had
dropped off to sleep, sprawled over the steps, the hand piano hanging
from his fingers.

The insignificant, dreary little dorp seemed to him what he was
returning to – this would be his life now. There stirred a small thought
of Martha; he let it die again, and a pang of fondness for her went with
it. What he felt for Martha was nothing, nothing at all compared with
his year among soldiers. Rage filled him. He was filled with a need to
tear, to destroy – he stood still, fists clenching and unclenching, his
mind teeming images of destruction. Next morning he would be put on
the plane home; he would step straight off the plane into domesticity
and the office from eight until four.

A sharp pain stabbed in his stomach; he remembered he had an
obligation towards himself. He went inside, and spooned out two of the
cold wet eggs onto bread, and began to eat the insipid mess with
disgust. He saw a pepper pot standing on the tray, and shook pepper
violently all over the eggs, with a savage delight in disobeying
prohibitions. Feeling slightly sick at last, he went back to the veranda,
thinking he might sleep. Then he saw across the square a black-lettered
sign on a small store: 'Joseph's Bar.'

He walked over and went in.

A fat, pale Greek youth was wiping glasses behind the bar. There was no one else in the place. Douglas asked for ginger beer and sat down. There was a single round table against the wall opposite the bar counter, with half a dozen upright wood chairs around it. In peacetime an occasional merchant or government official passed through; the bar was used by them and the local storekeepers.

Douglas took a mouthful of the prickly tepid ginger beer and let it stand. A loud offhand voice was heard just out of sight. Then Bobby came slowly past the open doorway. Her pale hair was now tidy, and bobbing up at the ends. She did not look in. Douglas called out, 'Hey there, Bobby.' She gave a start, but began to smile before she saw him. Douglas grinned proudly at the thought that she must have watched him enter the bar.

She came in and sat down. She was flushed with the heat. She asked for whisky, and Douglas's mouth filled unpleasantly as she began sipping it. Then she crossed her legs, blew out smoke, and fixed her pale-grey eyes attentively on him. The top buttons of her tunic were undone. Under it he could see a thin pink strap, rather grubby, loose on her shoulder. He felt a mixture of tenderness and repulsion at the sight.

'So you've had it – bad luck,' she remarked in the jocular loud voice which she had decided was suitable to her role as female soldier. But she looked sympathetic.

Douglas began to talk. After a while she asked after Martha. He produced photographs. Caroline stood on two sturdy legs smiling attractively up at her father from the small card square.

'That's a fine kid,' Bobby said sentimentally, and refixed her eyes on his at once. In her attitude was something touchingly devotional. She appeared to be saying that she was completely at his service.

She ordered a second whisky. His ginger beer was still nearly full. He almost succumbed, and then said, 'I'd better be strong-minded, hey?'

'That's the ticket,' she said. 'Mucking bad luck.'

It grated on him; he thought of Martha as a contrast. But the thought of Martha was not balm at all. The truth was, he had been relieved to get away from the atmosphere of bottles and napkins, and, more than this, from Martha's extraordinary tension during those months, when competent gaiety followed irritated exhaustion, and both seemed in some subtle way a criticism of him. But a more recent doubt was working in him. 'Heard any news from home?' he asked her casually.

'Lazy sods, they don't write. But I got a letter from Bogie – you remember Bogie? She says she's having a wonderful time with the boys from Home.'

Douglas said with a quick laugh, 'Yes, they all seem to be giving it stick, all right.' But his gaze still rested on her face with persistent suspicious enquiry, and she went on:

'I heard that Bella's marrying the Air Force, old Sam's breaking his heart over it.'

'Pretty bad show, that.'

'I heard news of Matty, come to think of it. She was at a dance at the air camp.'

'Oh, yes, she told me about it,' he said with an effort, frowning.

'Matty was always one for the boys. Lucky Matty, she hasn't got a figure like a sack of potatoes,' she said, and laughed painfully.

'Oh, you do fine,' he responded after a pause. He looked unhappily round. 'I think I'll be a devil and have a drink,' he said. He went over to the fat silent Greek, who polished glasses and watched these evidences of world war with an unquenchable curiosity. He fetched back two whiskies.

'Here's to the Army,' he said with quiet misery. He drained his down and sat grinning at her. 'Well, I'm all right, how are you doing, are you all right?'

She drained her third quickly, and responded to the rallying call. 'Oh, I'm all right, I'm fine, are you all right?'

He took the two glasses to the counter to be refilled. She watched him, smiling maternally. He came back and this time sat in the chair next to her. 'Let's give it a bang. Let's give it stick.'

'Oh, you're a crazy kid.'

She began questioning him again about up north, with an eager determination to hear every detail, prompting him when he hesitated on the edge of something he would normally gloss over for a woman. It was as if she were taking part by proxy. She listened, her pale-pink lips slightly open in a wistful greed. At first he was gruffly disapproving, then he let it go and softened to her. Poor old Bobby, she was having a bad time stuck in this dorp, she was a nice kid.

A shadow fell over them. Perry stood at the door, stooping inwards. Behind him the sun was sending up a last wild flare of red into the soft grey sky. The dust expanse had shrunk and dimmed. A group of Africans walking through had a soft and distant look in this thin light, and their voices were high and excited: they were hurrying to get indoors before the night came down.

Perry looked at them. Douglas noted that he was rather yellow, his eyes were inflamed, but he seemed quiet enough. He looked at the whiskies and said, 'That's an idea.' He went to the bar, nodded at the Greek, drained his glass with slow determined thirst, handed the glass back. He leaned on his elbow watching them. He took his second glass and stood there holding it for a while untasted, while the Greek took an oil lamp off the iron hook suspended from a rafter in the middle of the room, removed the glass funnel, lit the wick, fitted back the funnel, and hung the lamp up again. It swung steadily. A drop of paraffin dropped to the brick floor, then another. The smell of paraffin was strong.

The Greek returned to the other side of the counter. Perry still leaned there considering the seated couple, as if from a long distance. He looked very handsome beside the pale, fat youth with his sad olive-coloured eyes; conventionally handsome – square-jawed, hard-mouthed, strong. He was looking now direct at Bobby, and she shifted uncomfortably under it, fiddling with her bobs of pale hair.

'Come and sit down, man, damn it,' said Douglas.

Perry at once came across and sat down, as if he had needed an invitation. He gazed steadily at Bobby until she met his eyes.

'So you'll be going on up north?'

'Yes, next month.'

'Following the Army?'

'That's my job.'

'Nice work if you can get it.'

She gave a nervous look at Douglas, who laughed and said, 'Come off it, Perry man.'

Perry laughed, a calculated silent heave from his chest, and fingered his glass while he looked at Bobby. She had wriggled her chair an inch nearer to Douglas, but she was looking, fascinated, over at Perry and she was flushed.

The orderly came in, addressing Perry and Douglas equally. 'Baas, shall I bring your dinner here?'

'Get out,' said Perry.

'It's OK, Jim,' said Douglas quickly.

The man backed and vanished into the now thick dusk.

'What've you got to eat?' said Perry loudly to the barman.

'Wc don't cook.'

'So, you don't?'

'There's the mess. Since the war started there's been only the Army.'

Perry's jaw was thrust out. Seeing it, Douglas appealed, 'Couldn't you do us something? We're fed to teeth with army grub.'

The Greek hesitated.

'I want roast chicken, roast potatoes, vegetables, and some jam tart,' said Perry. He looked steadily over at the bar.

The Greek said, 'I'll go and ask my father.' He hurried out.

'Ruddy Dago,' said Perry. 'Bad as kaffirs.' He lifted his glass. 'Here's to Civvy Street.'

They all drank. Douglas looked over at Bobby with a tinge of grave reproach. The thread of sympathy that had held them was snapped. She could not take her eyes off Perry. Douglas moved his chair back to the wall, and comforted his glass between both hands. He was beginning to feel the alcohol.

Bobby took a moment's alarm at being left to Perry. She drank hastily, and spilled some. Perry reached out his large paw and brushed drops off her shoulders. She shrank away.

'Well, and how's the war been treating you?' he asked, on a personal, insulting note.

'Oh, fine, fine. But it's mucking boring here, though.'

'Mucking bad luck, muck everything, hey? You should meet the Ities. They've got a far wider range. You should hear their language when they get going. Shouldn't she, Douggie?'

Douglas looked away, dissociating himself.

'You mucking well should meet the bleeding Ities, then you wouldn't have to restrict yourself to bleeding mucking.'

She looked at him with a helpless fascination still, and let out her short gruff laugh.

'Let up, man,' said Douglas again, disgusted. 'Stop it.'

Perry took no notice. 'Still, you've not done too badly here, there's the Major and the doctor and the sergeant.'

She took his direct gaze and said, 'You don't do too badly, either. There's nothing you can tell me about what the boys do away from their wives.'

'But I'm not married, so that's all right. Thank God. She'd be lining the beds of the Air Force.'

She forced out another laugh. He leaned forward, gripped her wrist and said, 'Remember Christmas night three years ago at the Club – remember?'

'And so what?' she said, laughing.

He released her, frowned and said softly, 'We had a good time then, didn't we?'

'Those were the days,' said Douglas, half jocular, half wistful; they instinctively lifted their glasses to the good old days. Then Perry reached out his enormous arm over the bar, tilted the whiskey bottle standing on it, caught it as it heeled, and brought it triumphantly to the table.

The young Greek entered with a tray. Roast-beef sandwiches, mustard pickles, Marie biscuits, Cheddar cheese. He set it before them and retired silently behind the bar.

'Have some roast chicken,' said Douglas cheerfully.

They ate, Perry, steadily watching Bobby over his busy knife and fork, began reminiscing about the bang they'd had this night last week. Douglas played along with him. When it came to how Perry and half a dozen Australians had wrecked the brothel, Douglas smiled uneasily, but Bobby was laughing her good-fellow laugh. Perry stopped, and said disgustedly to Douglas, 'What do you think, she'd have liked to be there.' He leaned over, pushed his face against hers and said, 'So you'd have liked to be with us, hey?'

She pulled back her head, and said, 'Oh, cut it out, Perry, you're getting me down.'

'Nice girl,' he remarked companionably to the roof. 'Nice girl, this one.'

Douglas leaned over to her, and whispered, 'If you want to make your escape, then go, Bobby. He's been kicked out of the Army, that's all that's wrong with him.'

She returned a small, rather offended smile. 'I know, poor kid.' She at once drew back towards Perry. Her lips were parted. She passed the tip of a pink tongue across them.

Perry was looking at the doctor, who had just come in. The doctor nodded at them all, and stood by the bar.

'Come and join us, Doc,' said Douglas.

'Thanks, but I'm on duty.' He asked for a brandy, and stood leaning by the bar, watching Perry. He said nothing, however.

'How are the boys, Doctor?' asked Bobby, one professional to another.

'Bedded them all down for the night. The plane's leaving at six tomorrow morning.' He looked steadily at Perry and Douglas.

Perry ostentatiously tilted back his glass, emptied it, filled it again.

'Six o'clock,' said the doctor sharply. 'And anyone who's not ready can spend another three weeks here. If that tempts you.'

'We'll be ready, Doc,' said Douglas.

The three were set in hostile defiance against him; they were looking at him across a barrier of half-drunkenness.

'Parsons everywhere,' said Perry to Bobby intimately. 'Have you noticed it? Everywhere you go in this world – parsons. Hate their guts. Only to smell a parson half a mile away gives me guts-ache.'

She looked apologetically but defiantly at the doctor.

'An English parson – they breed them in England.' Perry jumped up, and grabbed her wrist. 'Coming for a walk?'

She hesitated, then rose, brushing down her tunic. He flung down four pound notes on the table, and pulled her by the wrist after him onto the veranda. Outside there was a steady beam of moonlight.

Douglas watched Perry and Bobby walk unsteadily over to that gauze veranda opposite, heard the gauze door slam. He looked pathetically at the doctor. 'Let's have a party, Doc,' he said. 'Come on, Doc, let's give it stick.'

'Sorry. I've got a raving lunatic on my hands tonight. I don't know quite . . . If I send him down on the plane with you tomorrow –' he looked, exasperated, at Douglas – 'surely five of you ought to be able to look after one boy like that. He'll be under drugs.'

'Oh, let him cut his ruddy throat,' said Douglas cheerfully. 'Who cares? Do you care? Do I care? No one cares.' He reached out his arm to stop the doctor as he went past. 'Come on, Doc, let's all cut our throats.'

'If I were you, I'd get myself to bed,' said the doctor from the doorway, with a harassed but pleasant grin. 'For God's sake – you'll be in hospital if you drink like that.'

'Who cares?' began Douglas again. 'Do you care . . .' But the doctor had gone. Douglas turned his head carefully and focussed at the Greek. 'Do you care?' he asked him.

The Greek grinned unhappily.

'Come and have a drink.'

The young man hesitated, then came over.

'Sit down, man, sit down.'

He sat, and poured himself a drink.

'Are you married?'

'No, I've got a girl at home.'

'Where's home?'

'Greece,' said the Greek apologetically.

'You don't want to get married – what do you want to get married for?' Douglas laid his fist on the shoulder opposite him and thumped it. The Greek continued to grin, watching him uneasily.

'Nothing but bitches, all of them.'

'I'm not married – sir.' In a country where all white men are equal there are perpetual problems of etiquette.

'Call me, Douggie.' He kneaded the fat young shoulder a little more, then held both hands around his glass and stared in front of him. 'What's your name?' he enquired at last, with difficulty.

'Demetrius.'

'Fine name, that, very fine name.' He lapsed away into a glass-eyed stare, then recovered himself. 'Let me show you my wife,' he said fumbling with his breast pocket. 'I've the finest wife in the whole of Africa.' He produced a wallet and dropped a bunch of snaps on the wet table. 'Tck, tck, tck,' he clicked his tongue reproachfully. 'Now, now, Douggie, that's very clumsy.' He fished a photograph of Martha out of a pool of whisky, and laid it before the Greek. Martha, in shorts and a sweatshirt, had the sun in her eyes and was trying to smile.

Demetrius courteously pulled out his wallet, and laid on the table a snap of a dark beauty sitting on a rock and dangling her feet in a pool. She and Martha lay side by side while the two men concentrated on them.

'You've got a fine wife, I've got a fine wife, we've both got fine wives,' pronounced Douglas. He hiccupped and said, 'Excuse me, I'm going to be sick.' He got up, and went out to the veranda, holding on to the wall.

When he came back, the Greek was back behind the counter, and the table in the corner was wiped clean. Douglas sat, looked about, finally located him and said, 'You've gone. They've all gone.'

'It's getting late, sir.'

'I want to have a party,' said Douglas obstinately. His eyes swam, focussed together on a bit of white on the floor. He bent, retrieved the snap of Martha from beside his feet, wiped it back and front on his tunic and put it into his top pocket. He remained sitting and swaying. He stared at the wall and blinked.

Demetrius wiped a few more glasses. Then he went out. In a moment he came back with himself twenty years older. The two Greeks conferred for a moment, then the father came over and said, 'You'd better get to bed, sir.'

'I'm staying here!' The table jumped as Douglas crashed his fist down.

'But we're closing the bar. I'll help you across to bed, sir.'

'I'm staying here. I can't go to bed, because my best friend is in bed with my wife.' His lower lip swelled and trembled.

The two men looked at each other, at him, and shrugged. Demetrius reached up and turned down the lamp. They went out. Douglas let his head fall forward onto his arms. His arms slipped forward until the upper half of his body lay over the table. It was now dark in the bar. A dim square of moonlight lay on the floor. It moved slowly back towards the door, slipped through the gauze and became one with the blaze of moonlight outside.

Later, Demetrius came in wearing striped pyjamas, carrying a candle. He shook Douglas twice. Then he left him, closing the gauze door with a simple hook on the inside, and sliding over a heavy door of wood.

A few minutes later Douglas sat up. It was very dark, and rather chilly. His head was clear again. He shook the wooden door in its groove, then went to the window. It was shut on the inside with a hasp and a hook. He fumbled at it a little; raised his fist and smashed it into the glass. A low tinkle came from outside. He heaved his shoulder into the pane; it flew out. He fell out with it and rolled over onto the earth four feet below. He got up unhurt under a big tree that filtered moonlight all over him. He turned himself till he faced the small gauze house, and concentrated on getting his feet to take him there. There was a small yellow glimmer coming from inside it. Overhead the moon was a great sheet of silver light. He gained the steps, climbed them, pulled open the gauze door, went in. It was light. Moonlight lay like white sand over his bed. On the one next to it he could see Perry's big body. It was in movement. He went through into the inner room.

The orderly was sitting drowsing at the table. His head was nodding and swaying over a book. Douglas focussed his aching eyes to see what the book was. It was a child's reading primer, soiled and dog-eared, open at a page with a cheap coloured picture of spring lambs frisking on an English meadow and a little yellow-haired girl offering them some pink flowers. The large clear print opposite said: 'Mai-sie is six. Mai-sie

likes to go for a walk in the spring mea-dow. She loves the lit-tle
lambs. They love her. When Mai-sie gets home, she will do her
lessons. Mai-sie works hard at her les-sons. She can read. She can
write. Mai-sie lives in a cot-tage on the hill near a sheep-fold. Her father is a police-man.'

'Poor sod,' remarked Douglas aloud, with a mixture of compassion,
contempt, and a sort of twisted envy.

A small cheap alarm clock on the table said it was half past eleven. He
had slept for about two hours.

He went back to the veranda. He sat on his bed. Perry was
murmuring with sentimental exasperation. 'Oh, come on, give us a
break, kid, give us a break, kid.' Bobby, invisible except for one
khaki-covered arm lying across his shoulder, was quite silent. A hand,
fat and very white in the moonlight, looked innocent and pathetic.

It gave Douglas vindictive pleasure that matters were not going
entirely to Perry's satisfaction.

After a while he felt his head roll; he let himself fall over on the bed
and was asleep at once.

He knew he was dreaming unpleasantly. There was danger in the
dream. He was in the aircraft with Perry. Perry was at the controls.
They were at an immense height. Looking down, he saw pretty rivers,
peaceful green fields. That was England. Then he saw a tall brown
purplish mountain. That was Africa. It was important to keep them
separate. He saw that Perry was hunched and straining over the
controls. The aircraft was slipping sideways through shrieking wind.
Perry was grinning and saying, 'Give us a break, give us a break, give us
a break.' The ground was slanting up and very near the purplish hairy
mountain. Douglas woke as they crashed, immediately rising on his
elbow and shaking his head clear of the dream. It was dawn. Through
the gauze a clear greyish sky lay like a stretched sheet. A few yellowish
streaks fanned out from the reddish hushed glow where the sun would
rise. Perry was lying on his back, asleep.

Inside the room the orderly moved about, and a Primus stove hissed.

A lorry stood outside the administration building opposite. Bobby
leaned beside it, apparently waiting. The white ambulance car came
driving around the edge of the building and parked beside the lorry.
Some native orderlies and the doctor came out and began sliding
stretchers into the ambulance with rolls of blanket on them that were
the casualties.

Douglas lay down again, rolling his dry and swollen tongue around his mouth. Today he would go home. He would walk into the flat and greet Martha. Tenderness for Martha and his small daughter filled him. The gay flat with its books and flowers seemed very attractive. And he would be back at his desk in Statistics in a week. They would be pleased to see him. He was a kingpin of his section, and everybody knew it. He dozed off for a moment, thinking of Martha and how that night he would be lying in bed with her. Voluptuous fantasies slid through his mind. He was asleep again; but almost at once someone shook him.

'Come on, get up, kids,' said Bobby's bluff voice.

Douglas sat up. Perry was leaning on his elbow looking at Bobby, who refused to meet his eyes. She said hurriedly, 'We're leaving in twenty minutes,' and went down the steps with her free manly stride, pale hair bobbing on her fat white neck.

'Mucking bitch,' said Perry dispassionately. He got up. Douglas was already stuffing things into his pack.

The orderly came out with boiled eggs on a tray. 'Good morning, baas, good morning, baas,' he said cheerfully. The reading primer was sticking up out of his breast pocket.

'Morning, Jim,' said Douglas, rubbing his hands. He felt elated and optimistic.

They were eating their eggs when the doctor came over.

'How are you feeling?'

'Fine, fine.'

'You don't deserve it.'

'Oh, come off it, Doc.'

The young English doctor smiled. 'If I put the schiz onto the plane, will you keep an eye on him? He's well and truly drugged.'

'The ulcers will look after the schiz,' said Perry. 'Leave it all to us.'

'Thanks. I've got to get him out somehow. There isn't even a nurse to send with the stretcher cases. They'll be all right. They're not bad. It's only a few hours. You'll be there before lunch. This place is packing up soon, anyway.'

'Bloody silly place for a hospital,' said Douglas.

'It isn't a hospital. It's a transfer casualty.'

'Whatever it is.'

'Well, I didn't choose it,' said the doctor, automatically clearing himself of responsibility like everybody else. 'Could you get yourselves into the lorry, gentlemen. Please.'

Douglas and Perry slung their packs on and flipped some silver to the orderly, who caught it with one hand.

'Thanks, baas, thanks, baas.'

They strolled over the dust to the lorry, which was now throbbing gently all over. Bobby was already in the driver's seat.

'You can have her,' said Perry to Douglas. 'I don't want her.'

Douglas hesitated. He did not want to drive the four miles with Bobby. But he went round to the front and climbed up beside her. She was being curt and official this morning, so he did not have to talk.

The lorry at once bounced off and away past the tin shanties into the bush. The sun was just coming up. A large red ball clung to the edges of the trees, stretched like a drop of water, then floated clear. By the time they reached the airstrip it had grown smaller, yellow, and was throwing off heat like a flame thrower. They were sweating already. Bobby drove them straight to the aircraft. The ambulance was driving away from it as they came up.

Bobby shook them all by the hand, Perry last, in an offhand, soldierly way. She at once got back into the lorry and drove off, shouting, 'Give my love to the home town.'

In the plane they had to wait. At the last moment a large saloon car drove up. The doctor got out, went round to the other door, and helped out the sleepy limp-looking youth. He half pushed him up the steps into Douglas's arms. Douglas and Perry hauled him in, and slumped him into the seat by Perry. He slept at once, looking very young and boyish, with his ruffle of damp fair hair on his forehead.

The doctor came in, took a last look at the stretcher cases, and said to Douglas, 'Keep an eye on them, there's a good chap.' He saluted and skipped thankfully down the steps and off to the car.

At once the plane swung round and began lumbering away to the end of the strip. It turned. Over the brick shack a funnel of white silk rippled out. As the aircraft roared past and up they could see a cloud of fluttering butterflies around it, like flying ants around a street lamp.

In a few minutes the bush was stretching empty beneath them. Perry was sitting beside the sick youth. He slipped sideways. Perry put his arm around him. The young flushed face was lying back on his shoulder.

Perry was watching a drift of wet cloud making rainbows in the bright sun, and humming 'Roll Out the Barrel' between his teeth, the shrewed hard blue eyes narrowed and abstracted, the mouth tight, the jaw solid. He shifted himself once or twice carefully to take the weight of the boy more comfortably, then settled down himself with his eyes shut. Douglas went back to talk to the stretcher cases.

About midday the plane touched down, and the boy was lifted, still fast asleep, onto the ambulance.

The Golden Notebook

[The black notebook now fulfilled its original plan, for both sides had been written on. Under the left side heading, *The Source*, was written:]

11th November, 1955

Today on the pavement a fat domestic London pigeon waddling among the boots and shoes of people hurrying for a bus. A man takes a kick at it, the pigeon lurches into the air, falls forward against a lamp-post, lies with its neck stretched out, its beak open. The man stands, bewildered: he had expected the pigeon to fly off. He casts a furtive look around, so as to escape. It it too late, a red-faced virago is already approaching him. 'You brute! Kicking a pigeon!' The man's face is by now also red. He grins from embarrassment and a comical amazement. 'They always fly away,' he observes, appealing for justice. The woman shouts: 'You've killed it – kicking a poor little pigeon!' But the pigeon is not dead, it is stretching out its neck by the lamp-post, trying to lift its head, and its wings strive and collapse, again and again. By now there is a small crowd including two boys of about fifteen. They have the sharp watchful faces of the freebooters of the streets, and stand watching, unmoved, chewing gum. Someone says: 'Call the R.S.P.C.A.' The woman shouts: 'There'd be no need for that if this bully hadn't kicked the poor thing.' The man hangs about, sheepish, a criminal hated by the crowd. The only people not emotionally involved are the two boys. One remarks to the air: 'Prison's the place for criminals like 'im.' 'Yes, yes,' shouts the woman. She is so busy hating the kicker she doesn't look at the pigeon. 'Prison,' says the second boy, 'flogging, I'd say.' The woman now sharply examines the boys, and realises they are making fun of her. 'Yes, and you too!' she gasps at them, her voice almost squeezed out of her by her anger. 'Laughing while a poor little bird suffers.' By now the two boys are in fact grinning, though not in the same shamefaced incredulous way as the villain of the occasion. 'Laughing,' she says. 'Laughing. You *should* be flogged. Yes. It's true.' Meanwhile an efficient frowning man bends over the pigeon, and examines it. He straightens himself and pronounces: 'It's going to die.'

He is right: the bird's eyes are filming, and blood wells from its open beak. And now the woman, forgetting her three objects of hatred, leans forward to look at the bird. Her mouth is slightly open, she has a look of unpleasant curiosity as the bird gasps, writhes its head, then goes limp.

'It's dead,' says the efficient man.

The villain, recovering himself, says apologetically, but clearly determined to have no nonsense: 'I'm sorry, but it was an accident. I've never seen a pigeon before that didn't move out of the way.'

We all look with disapproval at this hardened kicker of pigeons.

'An accident!' says the woman. 'An accident!'

But now the crowd is dissolving. The efficient man picks up the dead bird, but that's a mistake, for now he doesn't know what to do with it. The kicker moves off, but the woman goes after him, saying: 'What's your name and address, I'm going to have you prosecuted.' The man says, annoyed: 'Oh, don't make such a mountain out of a molehill.' She says: 'I suppose you call murdering a poor little bird a molehill.' 'Well, it isn't a mountain, murder isn't a mountain,' observes one of the fifteen-year-olds, who stands grinning with his hands in his jacket pockets. His friend takes it up, sagaciously: 'You're right. Molehills is murder, but mountains isn't.' 'That's right,' says the first, 'when's a pigeon a mountain? When it's a molehill.' The woman turns on them, and the villain thankfully makes his escape, looking incredibly guilty, despite himself. The woman is trying to find the right words of abuse for the two boys, but now the efficient man stands holding the corpse, and looking helpless, and one of the boys asks derisively: 'You going to make pigeon pie, mister?' 'You cheek me and I'll call the police,' the efficient one says promptly. The woman is delighted, and says: 'That's right, that's right, they should have been called long ago.' One of the boys lets out a long, incredulous, jeering, admiring whistle. 'That's the ticket,' he says, 'call the coppers. They'll put you down for stealing a public pigeon, mister!' The two go off, rolling with laughter, but fast as they can without losing face, because the police have been mentioned.

The angry woman, the efficient man, the corpse, and a few bystanders remain. The man looks around, sees a rubbish receptacle on the lamp-post, and moves forward to drop the dead bird into it. But the woman intercepts him, grasps the pigeon. 'Give it to me,' she says, her voice suffused with tenderness. 'I'll bury the poor little bird in my window-box.' The efficient man thankfully hurries off. She is left, looking down with disgust at the thick blood dropping from the beak of the pigeon.

12th November

Last night I dreamed of the pigeon. It reminded me of something, I didn't know what. In my dream I was fighting to remember. Yet when I woke up I knew what it was – an incident from the Mashopi Hotel week-ends. I haven't thought of it for years, yet now it is clear and detailed. I am again exasperated because my brain contains so much that is locked up and unreachable, unless, by a stroke of luck, there is an incident like yesterday's. It must have been one of the intermediate week-ends, not the climactic last week-end, for we were still on good terms with the Boothbys. I remember Mrs Boothby coming into the dining-room with a .22 rifle at breakfast and saying to our group: 'Can any of you shoot?' Paul said, taking the rifle: 'My expensive education has not failed to include the niceties of grouse and pheasant murder.' 'Oh, nothing so fancy like that,' said Mrs Boothby. 'There are grouse and pheasant about, but not too many. Mr Boothby mentioned he fancied a pigeon pie. He used to take out a gun now and then, but he's lost the figure for it, so I thought if you could oblige. . . ?'

Paul was handling the weapon quizzically. He finally said: 'Well, I'd never thought of shooting birds with a rifle, but if Mr Boothby can do it, so can I.'

'It's not hard,' said Mrs Boothby, as usual letting herself be taken in by the polite surface of Paul's manner. 'There's a small vlei down there between the kopjes that's full of pigeons. You let them settle and just pick them off.'

'It's not sporting,' said Jimmy, owlish.

'My God, it's not sporting!' cried Paul, playing up, clutching at his brow with one hand and holding the rifle away from him with the other.

Mrs Boothby was not sure whether to take him seriously, but she explained: 'It's fair enough. Don't shoot unless you're sure of killing, and then where's the harm?'

'She's right,' said Jimmy to Paul.

'You're right,' said Paul to Mrs Boothby. 'Dead right. We'll do it. How many pigeons for Host Boothby's pigeon pie?'

'There's not much use with less than six, but if you can get enough I can make pigeon pie for you as well. It'd make a change.'

'True,' said Paul. 'It *would* make a change. Rely on us.'

She thanked him, gravely, and left us with the rifle.

Breakfast was over, it was about ten in the morning, and we were glad to have something to fill our time until lunch. A short way past the hotel a track turned off the main road at right-angles and wandered ruttily over the veld, following the line of an earlier African footpath. This track led to the Roman Catholic Mission about seven miles off in the wilderness. Sometimes the Mission car came in for supplies; sometimes farm labourers went by in groups to or from the Mission, which ran a large farm, but for the most part the track was empty. All that country was high-lying sandveld, undulating, broken sharply here and there by kopjes. When it rained the soil seemed to offer resistance, not welcome. The water danced and drummed in a fury of white drops to a height of two or three feet over the hard soil, but an hour after the storm, it was already dry again and the gullies and vleis were running high and noisy. It had rained the previous night so hard that the iron roof of the sleeping block had shaken and pounded over our heads, but now the sun was high, the sky unclouded, and we walked beside the tarmac over a fine crust of white sand which broke drily under our shoes to show the dark wet underneath.

There were five of us that morning, I don't remember where the others were. Perhaps it was a week-end when only five of us had come down to the hotel. Paul carried the rifle, looking every inch a sportsman and smiling at himself in this role. Jimmy was beside him, clumsy, fattish, pale, his intelligent eyes returning always to Paul, humble with desire, ironical with pain at his situation. I, Willi and Maryrose came along behind. Willi carried a book. Maryrose and I wore holiday clothes – coloured dungarees and shirts. Maryrose wore blue dungarees and a rose-coloured shirt. I wore rose dungarees and a white shirt.

As soon as we turned off the main road on to the sand track we had to walk slowly and carefully, because this morning after the heavy rain there was a festival of insects. Everything seemed to riot and crawl. Over the low grasses a million white butterflies with greenish white wings hovered and lurched. They were all white, but of different sizes. That morning a single species had hatched or sprung or crawled from their chrysalises, and were celebrating their freedom. And on the grass itself, and all over the road were a certain species of brightly-coloured grasshopper, in couples. There were millions of them too.

'And one grasshopper jumped on the other grasshopper's back,' observed Paul's light but grave voice, just ahead. He stopped. Jimmy, beside him, obediently stopped too. We came to a standstill behind them both. 'Strange,' said Paul, 'but I've never understood the inner or concrete meaning of that song before.' It was grotesque, and we were all not so much embarrassed, as awed. We stood laughing, but our laughter was too loud. In every direction, all around us, were the insects, coupling. One insect, its legs firmly planted on the sand, stood still; while another, apparently identical, was clamped firmly on top of it, so that the one underneath could not move. Or an insect would be trying to climb on top of another, while the one underneath remained still, apparently trying to aid the climber whose earnest or frantic heaves threatened to jerk both over sideways. Or a couple, badly-matched, would topple over, and the one that had been underneath would right itself and stand waiting while the other fought to resume its position, or another insect, apparently identical, ousted it. But the happy or well-mated insects stood all around us, one above the other, with their bright round idiotic black eyes staring. Jimmy went off into fits of laughter, and Paul thumped him on the back. 'These extremely vulgar insects do not merit our attention,' observed Paul. He was right. One of these insects, or half a dozen, or a hundred would have seemed attractive, with their bright paint-box colours, half-submerged in thin emerald grasses. But in thousands, crude green and crude red, with the black blank eyes staring – they were absurd, obscene, and above all, the very emblem of stupidity. 'Much better watch the butterflies,' said Maryrose, doing so. They were extraordinarily beautiful. As far as we could see, the blue air was graced with white wings. And looking down into a distant vlei, the butterflies were a white glittering haze over green grass.

'But my dear Maryrose,' said Paul, 'you are doubtless imagining in that pretty way of yours that these butterflies are celebrating the joy of life, or simply amusing themselves, but such is not the case. They are merely pursuing vile sex, just like these ever-so-vulgar grasshoppers.'

'How do you know?' enquired Maryrose, in her small voice, very earnest; and Paul laughed his full-throated laugh which he knew was so attractive, and fell back and came beside her, leaving Jimmy alone in front. Willi, who had been squiring Maryrose, gave way to Paul and came to me, but I had already moved forward to Jimmy, who was forlorn.

'It really *is* grotesque,' said Paul, sounding genuinely put-out. We looked where he was looking. Among the army of grasshoppers were two obtrusive couples. One was an enormous powerful-looking insect, like a piston with its great spring-like legs, and on its back a tiny ineffectual mate, unable to climb high enough up. And next to it, the position reversed: a tiny bright pathetic grasshopper was straddled by, dwarfed, almost crushed by an enormous powerful driving insect. 'I shall try a small scientific experiment,' announced Paul. He stepped carefully among the insects to the grasses at the side of the road, laid down his rifle and pulled a stem of grass. He went down on one knee in the sand, brushing insects aside with an efficient and indifferent hand. Neatly he levered the heavy-bodied insect off the small one. But it instantly sprang back to where it was, with a most surprisingly determined single leap. 'We need two for this operation,' announced Paul. Jimmy was at once tugging at a grass-stem, and took his place beside him, although his face was wrenched with loathing at having to bend down so close to the swarm. The two young men were now kneeling on the sandy road, operating their grass-stems. I and Willi and Maryrose stood and watched. Willi was frowning. 'How frivolous,' I remarked, ironical. Although, as usual, we were not on particularly good terms that morning, Willi allowed himself to smile at me and said with real amusement: 'All the same, it is interesting.' And we smiled at each other, with affection and with pain because these moments were so seldom. And across the kneeling boys Maryrose watched us, with envy and pain. She was seeing a happy couple and feeling shut out. I could not bear it, and I went to Maryrose, abandoning Willi. Maryrose and I bent over the backs of Paul and Jimmy and watched.

'Now,' said Paul. Again he lifted his monster off the small insect. But Jimmy was clumsy and failed, and before he could try again Paul's big insect was back in position. 'Oh, you idiot,' said Paul, irritated. It was an irritation he usually suppressed, because he knew Jimmy adored him. Jimmy dropped the grass-stem and laughed painfully; tried to cover up his hurt – but by now Paul had grasped the two stems, had levered the two covering insects, large and small, off the two others, large and small, and now they were two well-matched couples, two big insects together and two small ones.

'There,' said Paul. 'That's the scientific approach. How neat. How easy. How satisfactory.'

There we all stood, the five of us, surveying the triumph of commonsense. And we all began to laugh again, helplessly, even Willi; because of the utter absurdity of it. Meanwhile all around us thousands and thousands of painted grasshoppers were getting on with the work of propagating their kind without any assistance from us. And even our small triumph was soon over, because the large insect that had been on top of the other large insect, fell off, and immediately the one which had been underneath mounted him or her.

'Obscene,' said Paul gravely.

'There is no evidence,' said Jimmy, trying to match his friend's light grave tone, but failing, since his voice was always breathless, or shrill, or too facetious: 'There is no evidence that in what we refer to as nature things are any better-ordered than they are with us. What evidence have we that all these – miniature troglodytes are nicely sorted out male above female? Or even' – he added daringly, on his fatally wrong note – 'male with female at all? For all we know, this is a riot of debauchery, males with males, females with females . . .' He petered out in a gasp of laughter. And looking at his heated, embarrassed, intelligent face, we all knew that he was wondering why it was that nothing he ever said, or could say, sounded easy, as when Paul said it. For if Paul had made that speech, as he might very well have done, we would all have been laughing. Instead of which we were uncomfortable, and were conscious that we were hemmed in by these ugly scrambling insects.

Suddenly Paul sprang over and trod deliberately, first on the monster couple, whose mating he had organised, and then on the small couple.

'Paul,' said Maryrose, shaken, looking at the crushed mess of coloured wings, eyes, white smear.

'A typical response of a sentimentalist,' said Paul, deliberately parodying Willi – who smiled, acknowledging that he knew he was being mocked. But now Paul said seriously: 'Dear Maryrose, by tonight, or to stretch a point, by tomorrow night, nearly all these things will be dead – just like your butterflies.'

'Oh no,' said Maryrose, looking at the dancing clouds of butterflies with anguish, but ignoring the grasshoppers. 'But why?'

'Because there are too many of them. What would happen if they all lived? It would be an invasion. The Mashopi Hotel would vanish under a crawling mass of grasshoppers, it would be crushed to the earth, while inconceivably ominous swarms of butterflies danced a victory dance over the deaths of Mr and Mrs Boothby and their marriageable daughter.'

Maryrose, offended and pale, looked away from Paul. We all knew she was thinking about her dead brother. At such moments she wore a look of total isolation, so that we all longed to put our arms around her.

Yet Paul continued, and now he began by parodying Stalin: 'It is self-evident, it goes without saying – and in fact there is no need at all to say it, so why should I go to the trouble? – However, whether there is any need to say a thing or not is clearly beside the point. As is well known, I say, nature is prodigal. Before many hours are out, these insects will have killed each other by fighting, biting, deliberate homicide, suicide or by clumsy copulation. Or they will have been eaten by birds which even at this moment are waiting for us to remove ourselves so that they can begin their feast. When we return to this delightful pleasure resort next week-end, or, if our political duties forbid, the week-end after, we shall take our well-regulated walks along this road and see perhaps one or two of these delightful red and green insects at their sport in the grass, and think, how pretty they are! And little will we reck of the million corpses that even then will be sinking into their last resting place all about us. I do not even mention the butterflies who, being incomparably more beautiful, though probably not more useful, we will actively, even assiduously miss – if we are not more occupied with our more usual decadent diversions.'

We were wondering why he was deliberately twisting the knife in the wound of Maryrose's brother's death. She was smiling painfully. And Jimmy, tormented continuously by fear that he would crash and be killed, had the same wry smile as Maryrose.

'The point I am trying to make, comrades . . .'

'We know what point you are trying to make,' said Willi, roughly and angrily. Perhaps it was for moments like these that he was the 'father-figure' of the group, as Paul said he was. 'Enough,' said Willi. 'Let's go and get the pigeons.'

'It goes without saying, it is self-evident,' said Paul, returning to Stalin's favourite opening phrases just so as to hold his own against Willi, 'that mine host Boothby's pigeon pie will never get made, if we go on in this irresponsible fashion.'

We proceeded along the track, among the grasshoppers. About half a mile further on there was a small kopje, or tumbling heap of granite boulders; and beyond it, as if a line had been drawn, the grasshoppers ceased. They were simply not there, they did not exist, they were an extinct species. The butterflies, however, continued everywhere, like white petals dancing.

I think it must have been October or November. Not because of the insects, I'm too ignorant to date the time of the year from them, but because of the quality of the heat that day. It was a sucking, splendid, menacing heat. Late in a rainy season there would have been a champagne tang in the air, a warning of winter. But that day I remember the heat was striking our cheeks, our arms, our legs, even through our clothing. Yes, of course it must have been early in the season, the grass was short, tufts of clear sharp green in white sand. So that week-end was four or five months before the final one, which was just before Paul was killed. And the track we strolled along that morning was where Paul and I ran hand in hand that night months later through a fine seeping mist to fall together in the damp grass. Where? Perhaps near where we sat to shoot pigeons for the pie.

We left the small kopje behind, and now a big one rose ahead. The hollow between the two was the place Mrs Boothby had said was visited by pigeons. We struck off the track to the foot of the big kopje, in silence. I remember us walking, silent, with the sun stinging our backs. I can *see* us, five small brightly coloured young people, walking in the grassy vlei through reeling white butterflies under a splendid blue sky.

At the foot of the kopje stood a clump of large trees under which we arranged ourselves. Another clump stood about twenty yards away. A pigeon cooed somewhere from the leaves in this second clump. It stopped at the disturbance we made, decided we were harmless and cooed on. It was a soft, somnolent drugging sound, hypnotic, like the sound of cicadas, which – now that we were listening – we realised were shrilling everywhere about us. The noise of cicadas is like having malaria and being full of quinine, an insane incessant shrilling noise that seems to come out of the ear-drums. Soon one doesn't hear it, as one ceases to hear the fevered shrilling of quinine in the blood.

'Only one pigeon,' said Paul. 'Mrs Boothby has misled us.'

He rested his rifle barrel on a rock, sighted the bird, tried without the support of the rock, and just when we thought he would shoot, laid the rifle aside.

We prepared for a lazy interval. The shade was thick, the grass soft and springy and the sun climbing towards midday position. The kopje behind us towered up into the sky, dominating, but not oppressive. The kopjes in this part of the country are deceptive. Often quite high, they scatter and diminish on approach, because they consist of groups or piles of rounded granite boulders; so that standing at the base of a kopje one might very well see clear through a crevice or small ravine to the vlei on the other side, with great, toppling glistening boulders soaring up like a giant's pile of pebbles. This kopje, as we knew, because we had explored it, was full of the earthworks and barricades built by the Mashona seventy, eighty years before as a defence against the raiding Matabele. It was also full of magnificent Bushmen paintings. At least, they had been magnificent until they had been defaced by guests from the hotel who had amused themselves throwing stones at them.

'Imagine,' said Paul. 'Here we are, a group of Mashona, besieged. The Matabele approach, in all their horrid finery. We are outnumbered. Besides, we are not, so I am told, a warlike folk, only simple people dedicated to the arts of peace, and the Matabele always win. We know, we men, that we will die a painful death in a few moments. You lucky women, however, Anna and Maryrose, will merely be dragged off by new masters in the superior tribe of the altogether more warlike and virile Matabele.'

'They would kill themselves first,' said Jimmy. 'Wouldn't you, Anna? Wouldn't you Maryrose?'

'Of course,' said Maryrose, good-humoured.

'Of course,' I said.

The pigeon cooed on. It was visible, a small, shapely bird, dark against the sky. Paul took up the rifle, aimed and shot. The bird fell, turning over and over with loose wings, and hit earth with a thud we could hear from where we sat. 'We need a dog,' said Paul. He expected Jimmy to leap up and fetch it. Although we could see Jimmy struggling with himself, he in fact got up, walked across to the sister clump of trees, retrieved the now graceless corpse, flung it at Paul's feet and sat down again. The small walk in the sun had flushed him, and caused great patches to appear on his shirt. He pulled it off. His torso, naked, was pale, fattish, almost childlike. 'That's better,' he said, defiantly, knowing we were looking at him, and probably critically.

The trees were now silent. 'One pigeon,' said Paul. 'A toothsome mouthful for our host.'

From trees far away came the sound of pigeons cooing, a murmuring gentle sound. 'Patience,' said Paul. He rested his rifle again and smoked.

Meanwhile, Willi was reading. Maryrose lay on her back, her soft gold head on a tuft of grass, her eyes closed. Jimmy had found a new amusement. Between isolated tufts of grass was a clear trickle of sand where water had coursed, probably last night in the storm. It was a miniature river-bed, about two feet wide, already bone dry from the morning's sun. And on the white sand were a dozen round shallow depressions, but irregularly spaced and of different sizes. Jimmy had a fine strong grass-stem, and, lying on his stomach, was wriggling the stem around the bottom of one of the larger depressions. The fine sand fell continuously in avalanches, and in a moment the exquisitely regular pit was ruined.

'You clumsy idiot,' said Paul. He sounded, as always in these moments with Jimmy, pained and irritated. He really could not understand how anybody could be so awkward. He grabbed the stem from Jimmy, poked it delicately at the bottom of another sand-pit, and in a second had fished out the insect which made it – a tiny ant-eater, but a big specimen of its kind, about the size of a large match-head. This insect, toppling off Paul's grass-stem on to a fresh patch of white sand, instantly jerked itself into frantic motion, and in a moment had vanished beneath the sand which heaved and sifted over it.

'There,' said Paul roughly to Jimmy, handing back his stem. Paul looked embarrassed at his own crossness; Jimmy, silent and rather pale, said nothing. He took the stem and watched the heaving of the minute patch of sand.

Meanwhile we had been too absorbed to notice that two new pigeons had arrived in the trees opposite. They now began to coo, apparently without any intention of co-ordination, for the two streams of soft sound continued, sometimes together, sometimes not.

'They are very pretty,' said Maryrose, protesting, her eyes still shut.

'Nevertheless, like your butterflies, they are doomed.' And Paul raised his rifle and shot. A bird fell off a branch, this time like a stone. The other bird, startled, looked around, its sharp head turning this way and that, an eye cocked up skywards for a possible hawk that had swooped and taken off its comrade, then cocked earthwards where it apparently failed to identify the bloody object lying in the grass. For after a moment of intense waiting silence, during which the bolt of the rifle snapped, it began again to coo. And immediately Paul raised his gun and shot and it, too, fell straight to the ground. And now none of us looked at Jimmy, who had not glanced up from his observation of his insect. There was already a shallow, beautifully regular pit in the sand, at the bottom of which the invisible insect worked in tiny heaves. Apparently Jimmy had not noticed the shooting of the two pigeons. And Paul did not look at him. He merely waited, whistling very softly, frowning. And in a moment, without looking at us or at Paul, Jimmy began to flush, and then he clambered up, walked across to the trees, and came back with the two corpses.

'We don't need a dog after all,' remarked Paul. It was said before Jimmy was halfway back across the grass, yet he heard it. I should imagine that Paul had not intended him to hear, yet did not particularly care that he had. Jimmy sat down again, and we could see the very white thick flesh of his shoulders had begun to flush scarlet from the two short journeys in the sun across the bright grass. Jimmy went back to watching his insect.

There was again an intense silence. No doves could be heard cooing anywhere. Three bleeding bodies lay tumbled in the sun by a small jutting rock. The grey rough granite was patched and jewelled with lichens, rust and green and purple; and on the grass lay thick glistening drops of scarlet.

There was a smell of blood.

'Those birds will go bad,' remarked Willi, who had read steadily during all this.

'They are better slightly high,' said Paul.

I could see Paul's eyes hover towards Jimmy, and see Jimmy struggling with himself again, so I quickly got up and threw the limp wing-dragging corpses into the shade.

By now there was a prickling tension between us all, and Paul said: 'I want a drink.'

'It's an hour before the pub opens,' said Maryrose.

'Well, I can only hope that the requisite number of victims will soon offer themselves, because at the stroke of opening time I shall be off. I shall leave the slaughter to someone else.'

'None of us can shoot as well as you,' said Maryrose.

'As you know perfectly well,' said Jimmy, suddenly spiteful.

He was observing the rivulet of sand. It was not hard to tell which ant-pit was the new one. Jimmy was staring at a largish pit, at the bottom of which was a minute hump – the body of the waiting monster; and a tiny black fragment of twig – the jaws of the monster. 'All we need now is some ants,' said Jimmy. 'And some pigeons,' said Paul. And, replying to Jimmy's criticism, he added: 'Can I help my natural talents? The Lord gives. The Lord takes. In my case, he has given.'

'Unfairly,' I said. Paul gave me his charming wry appreciative smile. I smiled back. Without raising his eyes from his book, Willi cleared his throat. It was a comic sound, like bad theatre, and both I and Paul burst out into one of the wild helpless fits of laughing that often took members of the group, singly, in couples, or collectively. We laughed and laughed, and Willi sat reading. But I remember now the hunched enduring set of his shoulders, and the tight painful set of his lips. I did not choose to notice it at the time.

Suddenly there was a wild shrill silken cleaving of wings and a pigeon settled fast on a branch almost above our heads. It lifted its wings to leave again at the sight of us, folded them, turned round on its branch several times, with its head cocked sideways looking down at us. Its black bright open eyes were like the round eyes of the mating insects on the track. We could see the delicate pink of its claws gripping the twig, and the sheen of sun on its wings. Paul lifted the rifle – it was almost perpendicular – shot, and the bird fell among us. Blood spattered over Jimmy's forearm. He went pale again, wiped it off, but said nothing.

'This is getting disgusting,' said Willi.

'It has been from the start,' said Paul composedly.

He leaned over, picked the bird off the grass and examined it. It was still alive. It hung limp, but its black eyes watched us steadily. A film rolled up over them, then with a small perceptible shake of determination it pushed death away and struggled for a moment in Paul's hands. 'What shall I do?' Paul said, suddenly shrill; then, instantly recovering himself with a joke: 'Do you expect me to kill the thing in cold blood?'

'Yes,' said Jimmy, facing Paul and challenging him. The clumsy blood was in his cheeks again, mottling and blotching them, but he stared Paul out.

'Very well,' said Paul, contemptuous, tight-lipped. He held the pigeon tenderly, having no idea how to kill it. And Jimmy waited for Paul to prove himself. Meanwhile the bird sank in a glossy welter of feathers between Paul's hands, its head sinking on its neck, trembling upright again, sinking sideways, as the pretty eyes filmed over and it struggled again and again to defeat death.

Then, saving Paul the ordeal, it was suddenly dead, and Paul flung it on to the heap of corpses.

'You are always so damned lucky about everything,' said Jimmy, in a trembling, angry voice. His full carved mouth, the lips he referred to with pride as 'decadent' visibly shook.

'Yes, I know,' said Paul. 'I know it. The Gods favour me. Because I'll admit to you, dear Jimmy, that I could not have brought myself to wring this pigeon's neck.'

Jimmy turned away, suffering, to his observation of the ant-eaters' pits. While his attention had been with Paul, a very tiny ant, as light as a bit of fluff, had fallen over the edge of a pit and was at this moment bent double in the jaws of the monster. This drama of death was on such a small scale that the pit, the ant-eater and the ant could have been accommodated comfortably on a small fingernail – Maryrose's pink little fingernail for instance.

The tiny ant vanished under a film of white sand, and in a moment the jaws appeared, clean and ready for further use.

Paul ejected the case from his rifle and inserted a bullet with a sharp snap of the bolt. 'We have two more to get before we satisfy Ma Boothby's minimum needs,' he remarked. But the trees were empty, standing full and silent in the hot sun, all their green boughs light and graceful, very slightly moving. The butterflies were now noticeably fewer; a few dozen only danced on in the sizzling heat. The heat-waves rose like oil off the grass, the sand patches, and were strong and thick over the rocks that protruded from the grass.

'Nothing,' said Paul. 'Nothing happens. What tedium.'

Time passed. We smoked. We waited. Maryrose lay flat, eyes closed, delectable as honey. Willi read, doggedly improving himself. He was reading *Stalin on the Colonial Question*.

'Here's another ant,' said Jimmy, excited. A larger ant, almost the size of the ant-eater, was hurrying in irregular dashes this way and that between grass-stems. It moved in the irregular apparently spasmodic way that a hunting dog does when scenting. It fell straight over the edge of the pit, and now we were in time to see the brown shining jaws reach up and snap the ant across the middle, almost breaking it in two. A struggle. White drifts of sand down the sides of the pit. Under the sand they fought. Then stillness.

'There is something about this country,' said Paul, 'that will have marked me for life. When you think of the sheltered upbringing nice boys like Jimmy and I have had – our nice homes and public school and Oxford, can we be other than grateful for this education into the realities of nature red in beak and claw?'

'I'm not grateful,' said Jimmy. 'I hate this country.'

'I adore it. I owe it everything. Never again will I be able to mouth the liberal and high-minded platitudes of my democratic education. I know better now.'

Jimmy said: 'I may know better, but I shall continue to mouth high-

minded platitudes. The very moment I get back to England. It can't
be too soon for me. Our education has prepared us above all for the
long littleness of life. What else has it prepared us for? Speaking for
myself, I can't wait for the long littleness to begin. When I get back –
if I ever do get back that is, I shall . . .'

'Hallo,' exclaimed Paul, 'here comes another bird. No it doesn't.' A
pigeon cleaved towards us, saw us and swerved off and away in mid-
air, nearly settled on the other clump of trees, changed its mind and
sped into the distance. A group of farm labourers were passing on the
track a couple of hundred yards off. We watched them, in silence.
They had been talking and laughing until they saw us, but now they,
too, were silent, and went past with averted faces, as if in this way they
might avert any possible evil that might come from us, the white
people.

Paul said softly: 'My God, my God, my God.' Then his tone changed,
and he said jauntily: 'Looking at it objectively, with as little reference as
we can manage to Comrade Willi and his ilk – Comrade Willi, I'm
inviting you to consider something objectively.' Willi laid down his
book, prepared to show irony. 'This country is larger than Spain. It
contains one and a half million blacks, if one may mention them at all,
and one hundred thousand whites. That, in itself, is a thought which
demands two minutes' silence. And what do we see? One might imagine
– one would have every excuse for imagining, despite what you say,
Comrade Willi, that this insignificant handful of sand on the beaches of
time – not bad, that image? – unoriginal, but always apt – this million-
and-a-little-over-a-half people exist in this pretty piece of God's earth
solely in order to make each other miserable . . .' Here Willi picked up
his book again and applied his attention to it. 'Comrade Willi, let your
eyes follow the print but let the ears of your soul listen. For the *facts* are
– the *facts* – that there's enough food here for everyone! – enough
materials for houses for everyone! – enough talent though admittedly so
well hidden under bushels at the moment that nothing but the most
generous eye could perceive it – enough talent, I say, to create light
where now darkness exists.'

'From which you deduce?' said Willi.

'I deduce nothing. I am being struck by a new . . . it's a blinding
light, nothing less . . .'

'But what you say is the truth about the whole world, not just this
country,' said Maryrose.

'Magnificent Maryrose! Yes. My eyes are being opened to – Comrade Willi, would you not say that there is some principle at work not yet admitted to your philosophy? Some principle of destruction?'

Willi said, in exactly the tone we had all expected: 'There is no need to look any further than the philosophy of the class struggle,' and as if he'd pressed a button, Jimmy, Paul and I burst out into one of the fits of irrepressible laughter that Willi never joined.

'I'm delighted to see,' he remarked, grim-mouthed, 'that good socialists – at least two of you call yourselves socialists, should find that so very humorous.'

'I don't find it humorous,' said Maryrose.

'You never find anything humorous,' said Paul. 'Do you know that you never laugh, Maryrose? Never? Whereas I, whose view of life can only be described as morbid, and increasingly morbid with every passing minute, laugh continuously? How would you account for that?'

'I have no view of life,' said Maryrose, lying flat, looking like a neat soft little doll in her bright bibbed trousers and shirt. 'Anyway,' she added, 'you weren't laughing. I listen to you a lot' – (she said this as if she were not one of us, but an outsider) – 'and I've noticed that you laugh most when you're saying something terrible. Well I don't call that laughing.'

'When you were with your brother, did you laugh, Maryrose? And when you were with your lucky swain in the Cape?'

'Yes.'

'Why?'

'Because we were happy,' said Maryrose simply.

'Good God,' said Paul in awe. 'I couldn't say that. Jimmy, have you ever laughed because you were happy?'

'I've never been happy,' said Jimmy.

'You, Anna?'

'Nor me.'

'Willi?'

'Certainly,' said Willi, stubborn, defending socialism, the happy philosophy.

'Maryrose,' said Paul, 'you were telling the truth. I don't believe Willi but I believe you. You are very enviable, Maryrose, in spite of everything. Do you know that?'

'Yes,' said Maryrose. 'Yes, I think I'm luckier than any of you. I don't see anything wrong with being happy. What's wrong with it?'

Silence. We looked at each other. Then Paul solemnly bowed towards Maryrose: 'As usual,' he said humbly, 'we have nothing to say in reply.'

Maryrose closed her eyes again. A pigeon alighted fast on a tree in the opposite clump. Paul shot and missed. 'A failure,' he exclaimed, mock tragic. The bird stayed where it was, surprised, looking about it, watching a leaf dislodged by Paul's bullet float down to the earth. Paul ejected his empty case, refilled at leisure, aimed, shot. The bird fell. Jimmy obstinately did not move. He did not move. And Paul, before the battle of wills could end in defeat for himself, gained victory by rising and remarking: 'I shall be my own retriever.' And he strolled off to fetch the pigeon; and we all saw that Jimmy had to fight with himself to prevent his limbs from jumping him up and over the grass after Paul. Who came back with the dead bird yawning, flinging it with the other dead birds.

'There's such a smell of blood I shall be sick,' said Maryrose.

'Patience,' said Paul. 'Our quota is nearly reached.'

'Six will be enough,' said Jimmy. 'Because none of us will eat this pie. Mr Boothby can have the lot.'

'I shall certainly eat of it,' said Paul. 'And so will you. Do you really imagine that when that toothsome pie, filled with gravy and brown savoury meat is set before you, that you will remember the tender songs of these birds so brutally cut short by the crack of doom?'

'Yes,' said Maryrose.

'Yes,' I said.

'Willi?' asked Paul, making an issue of it.

'Probably not,' said Willi, reading.

'Women are tender,' said Paul. 'They will watch us eat, toying the while with Mrs Boothby's good roast beef, making delicate little mouths of distaste, loving us all the more for our brutality.'

'Like the Mashona women and the Matabele,' said Jimmy.

'I like to think of those days,' said Paul, settling down with his rifle at the ready, watching the trees. 'So simple. Simple people killing each other for good reasons, land, women, food. Not like us. Not like us at all. As for us—do you know what is going to happen? I will tell you. As a result of the work of fine comrades like Willi, ever-ready to devote themselves to others, or people like me, concerned only with profits, I predict that in fifty years all this fine empty country we see stretching before us filled only with butterflies and grasshoppers will be covered by semi-detached houses filled by well-clothed black workers.'

'And what is the matter with that?' enquired Willi.

'It is progress,' said Paul.

'Yes it is,' said Willi.

'Why should they be semi-detached houses?' enquired Jimmy, very seriously. He had moments of being serious about the socialist future. 'Under a socialist government there'll be beautiful houses in their own gardens or big flats.'

'My dear Jimmy!' said Paul. 'What a pity you are so bored by economics. Socialist or capitalist – in either case, all this fine ground, suitable for development, will be developed at a rate possible for seriously undercapitalised countries – are you listening, Comrade Willi?'

'I am listening.'

'And because a government faced with the necessity of housing a lot of unhoused people fast, whether socialist or capitalist, will choose the cheapest available houses, the best being the enemy of the better, this fair scene will be one of factories smoking into the fair blue sky, and masses of cheap identical housing. Am I right, Comrade Willi?'

'You are right.'

'Well then?'

'It's not the point.'

'It's my point. That is why I dwell on the simple savagery of the Matabele and the Mashona. The other is simply too hideous to contemplate. It is the reality of our time, socialist or capitalist – well, Comrade Willi?'

Willi hesitated, then said: 'There will be certain outward similarities but . . .' He was interrupted by Paul and myself, then Jimmy, in a fit of laughter.

Maryrose said to Willi: 'They're not laughing at what you say, but because you always say what they expect.'

'I am aware of that,' said Willi.

'No,' said Paul, 'you are wrong, Maryrose. I'm also laughing at what he's saying. Because I'm horribly afraid it's not true. God forbid, I should be dogmatic about it, but I'm afraid that – as for myself, from time to time I shall fly out from England to inspect my overseas investments and peradventure I shall fly over this area, and I shall look down on smoking factories and housing estates and I shall remember these pleasant, peaceful pastoral days and . . .' A pigeon landed on the trees opposite. Another and another. Paul shot. A bird fell. He shot, the second fell. The third burst out of a bunch of leaves skywards as if it had been shot from a catapult. Jimmy got up, walked over, brought back two bloodied birds, flung them down with the others and said: 'Seven. For God's sake, isn't it enough?'

'Yes,' said Paul, laying aside his rifle. 'And now let's make tracks fast for the pub. We shall just have time to wash the blood off before it opens.'

'Look,' said Jimmy. A small beetle about twice the size of the largest ant-eater, was approaching through the towering grass-stems.

'No good,' said Paul, 'that is not a natural victim.'

'Maybe not,' said Jimmy. He twitched the beetle into the largest pit. There was a convulsion. The glossy brown jaws snapped on the beetle, the beetle jumped up, dragging the ant-eater halfway up the sides of the pit. The pit collapsed in a wave of white sand, and for a couple of inches all around the suffocating silent battle, the sand heaved and eddied.

'If we had ears that could hear,' said Paul, 'the air would be full of screams, groans, grunts and gasps. But as it is, there reigns over the sunbathed veld the silence of peace.'

A cleaving of wings. A bird alighted.

'No don't,' said Maryrose in pain, opening her eyes and raising herself on her elbow. But it was too late. Paul had shot, the bird fell. Before it had even hit the ground another bird had touched down, swinging lightly on a twig at the very end of a branch. Paul shot, the bird fell; this time with a cry and a fluttering of helpless wings. Paul got up, raced across the grass, picked up the dead bird and the wounded one. We saw him give the wounded struggling bird a quick determined tight-mouthed look, and wring its neck.

He came back, flung down the two corpses and said: 'Nine. And that's all.' He looked white and sick, and yet in spite of it, managed to give Jimmy a triumphant amused smile.

'Let's go,' said Willi, shutting his book.

'Wait,' said Jimmy. The sand was now unmoving. He dug into it with a fine stem and dragged out, first the body of the tiny beetle, and then the body of the ant-eater. Now we saw the jaws of the ant-eater were embedded in the body of the beetle. The corpse of the ant-eater was headless.

'The moral is,' said Paul, 'that none but natural enemies should engage.'

'But who should decide which are natural enemies and which are not?' said Jimmy.

'Not you,' said Paul. 'Look how you've upset the balance of nature. There is one ant-eater the less. And probably hundreds of ants that should have filled its maw will now live. And there is a dead beetle, slaughtered to no purpose.'

Jimmy stepped carefully over the shining round-pitted river of sand, so as not to disturb the remaining insects lying in wait at the bottom of their sand-traps. He dragged on his shirt over his sweaty reddened flesh. Maryrose got up in the way she had – obedient, patient, long-suffering, as if she had no will of her own. We all stood on the edge of the patch of shade, reluctant to plunge into the now white-hot midday, made dizzy and giddy by the few remaining butterflies who reeled drunk in the heat. And as we stood there, the clump of trees we had lain under sang into life. The cicadas which inhabited this grove, patiently silent these two hours waiting for us to go, burst one after another into shrill sound. And in the sister clump of trees, unnoticed by us, had arrived two pigeons who sat there cooing. Paul contemplated them, his rifle swinging. 'No,' said Maryrose, 'please don't.'

'Why not?'

'Please, Paul.'

The heap of nine dead pigeons, tied together by their pink feet, dangled from Paul's free hand, dripping blood.

'It's a terrible sacrifice,' said Paul gravely, 'but for you, Maryrose, I will refrain.'

She smiled at him, not in gratitude, but in the cool reproachful way she always used for him. And he smiled back, his delightful, brown, blue-eyed face all open for her inspection. They walked off together in front, the dead birds trailing their wings over jade-coloured clumps of grass.

The three of us followed.

'What a pity,' remarked Jimmy, 'that Maryrose disapproves so much of Paul. Because there is no doubt they are what is known as a perfectly-matched couple.' He had tried the light ironic tone, and almost succeeded. Almost, not quite; his jealousy of Paul grated in his voice.

We looked: they were, those two, a perfect couple, both so light and graceful, the sun burnishing their bright hair, shining on their brown skins. And yet Maryrose strolled on without looking at Paul who gave her his whimsically appealing blue glances all in vain.

It was too hot to talk on the way back. Passing the small kopje on whose granite chunks the sun was beating, waves of dizzying heat struck at us so that we hurried past it. Everything was empty and silent, only the cicadas and a distant pigeon sang. And past the kopje we slowed and looked for the grasshoppers, and saw that the bright clamped couples had almost disappeared. A few remained, one above another, like painted clothes-pegs with painted round black eyes. A few. And the butterflies were almost gone. One or two floated by, tired, over the sun-bleached grass.

Our heads ached with the heat. We were slightly sick with the smell of blood.

At the hotel we separated with hardly a word.

Briefing for a Descent into Hell

CENTRAL INTAKE HOSPITAL

Admittance Sheet   *Friday, August 15th, 1969*

Name . . .   Unknown
Sex . . .   Male
Age . . .   Unknown
Address . . .Unknown
General Remarks
. . . At midnight the police found Patient wandering on the
Embankment near Waterloo Bridge. They took him into the
station thinking he was drunk or drugged. They describe him
as Rambling, Confused and Amenable. Brought him to us at
3 a.m. by ambulance. During admittance Patient attempted
several times to lie down on the desk. He seemed to think it was
a boat or a raft. Police are checking ports, ships, etc. Patient was
well-dressed but had not changed his clothes for some time. He
did not seem very hungry or thirsty. He was wearing trousers
and a sweater, but he had no papers or wallet or money or marks
of identity. Police think he was robbed. He is an educated man.
He was given two Libriums but did not sleep. He was talking
loudly. Patient was moved into the small Observation ward as
he was disturbing the other Patients.

NIGHT NURSE   6 *a.m.*

Patient has been awake all day, rambling, hallucinated, animated. Two Librium three-hourly. Police no information.
Clothes sent for tracing, but unlikely to yield results: chainstore
sweater and shirt and underclothes. Trousers Italian. Patient
still under the impression he is on some sort of voyage. Police
say possibly an amateur or a yachtsman.

DOCTOR Y.   6 *p.m.*

*

I need a wind. A good strong wind. The air is stagnant. The current must be pounding along at a fair rate. Yes, but I can't feel it. Where's my compass? *That* went days ago, don't you remember? I need a wind, a good strong wind. I'll whistle for one. I would whistle for one if I had paid the piper. A wind from the East, hard on to my back, yes. Perhaps I am still too near the shore? After so many days at sea, too near the shore? But who knows, I might have drifted back again inshore. Oh no, no, I'll try rowing. The oars are gone, don't you remember, they went days ago. No, you must be nearer landfall than you think. The Cape Verde Islands were to starboard – when? Last week. Last *when*? That was no weak, that was my wife. The sea is saltier here than close inshore. A salt, salt sea, the brine coming flecked off the horses' jaws to mine. On my face, thick crusts of salt. I can taste it. Tears, seawater. I can taste salt from the sea. From the desert. The deserted sea. Sea horses. Dunes. The wind flicks sand from the crest of dunes, spins off the curl of waves. Sand moves and sways and masses itself into waves, but slower. Slow. The eye that would measure the pace of sand horses, as I watch the rolling gallop of sea horses would be an eye indeed. Aye Aye. I. I could catch a horse, perhaps and ride it, but for me a sea horse, no horse of sand, since my time is man-time and it is God for deserts. Some ride dolphins. Plenty have testified. I may leave my sinking raft and cling to the neck of a sea horse, all the way to Jamaica and poor Charlie's Nancy, or, if the current swings me south at last, to the coast where the white bird is waiting.

Round and round and round I go, the Diamond Coast, the Canary Isles, a dip across the Tropic of Cancer and up and across with a shout at the West Indies to port, where Nancy waits for her poor Charlie, and around, giving the Sargasso Sea a miss to starboard, with Florida florissant to port, and around and around, in the swing of the Gulf Stream, and around, with the Azores just outside the turn of my elbow, and down, past the coasts of Portugal where my Conchita waits for me, passing Madeira, passing the Canaries, always *en passant*, to the Diamond Coast again, and so around, and around again and again, for ever and ever unless the current swings me South. But that current could never take me South, not. A current is set in itself, inexorable as a bus route. The clockwise current of the Northern seas must carry me, carry me, unless . . . yes. They may divert me a little, yes they will, steering me with a small feather from their white wings, steadying me south, holding me safe across the cross not to say furious currents about

the Equator but then, held safe and sound, I'd find the South
Equatorial at last, at last, and safe from all the Sargassoes, the Scyllas
and the Charibs, I'd swoop beautifully and lightly, drifting with the
sweet currents of the South down the edge of the Brazilian Highlands to
the Waters of Peace. But I need a wind. The salt is seaming on the
timbers and the old raft is wallowing in the swells and I am sick. I am
sick enough to die. So heave ho my hearties, heave – no, they are all
gone, dead and gone, they tied me to a mast and a great wave swept
them from me, and I am alone, caught and tied to the North Equatorial
Current with no landfall that I could ever long for anywhere in the
searoads of all that rocking sea.

> Nothing from police. No reports of any small boats yachts or
> swimmers unaccounted for. Patient continues talking aloud,
> singing, swinging back and forth in bed. He is excessively
> fatigued. Tomorrow: Sodium Amytal. I suggest a week's
> narcosis.
> *August 17th*   DOCTOR Y.
>
> I disagree. Suggest shock therapy.
> *August 18th*   DOCTOR X.

Very hot. The current is swinging and rocking. Very fast. It is so hot
that the water is melting. The water is thinner than usual, therefore a
thin fast rocking. Like heat-waves. The shimmer is strong. Light.
Different textures of light. There is the light we know. That is, the
ordinary light let's say of a day with cloud. Then, sunlight, which is a
yellow dance added to the first. Then the sparkling waves of heat, heat-
waves, making light when light makes them. Then, the inner light, the
shimmer, like a suspended snow in the air. Shimmer even at night when
no moon or sun and no light. The shimmer of the solar wind. Yes, that's
it. Oh solar wind, blow blow blow my love to me. It is very hot. The salt
has caked my face. If I rub, I'll scrub my face with pure sea salt. I'm
becalmed, on a light, lit, rocking, deliriously delightful sea, for the
water has gone thin and slippery in the heat, light water instead of heavy
water. I need a wind. Oh solar wind, wind of the sun. Sun. At the end of
Ghosts he said the Sun, the Sun, the Sun, the Sun, and at the end of
When We Dead Awaken, the Sun, into the arms of the Sun via the solar
wind, around, around, around, around . . .

Patient very disturbed. Asked his name: Jason. He is on a raft in the Atlantic. Three caps Sodium Amytal tonight. Will see him tomorrow.

DOCTOR Y.

DOCTOR Y. Did you sleep well?

PATIENT. I keep dropping off, but I mustn't, I must not.

DOCTOR Y. But why not? I want you to.

PATIENT. I'd slide off into the deep sea swells.

DOCTOR Y. No, you won't. That's a very comfortable bed, and you're in a nice quiet room.

PATIENT. Bed of the sea. Deep sea bed.

DOCTOR Y. You aren't on a raft. You aren't on the sea. You aren't a sailor.

PATIENT. I'm not a sailor?

DOCTOR Y. You are in Central Intake Hospital, in bed, being looked after. You must rest. We want you to sleep.

PATIENT. If I sleep I'll die.

DOCTOR Y. What's your name? Will you tell me?

PATIENT. Jonah.

DOCTOR Y. Yesterday it was Jason. You can't be either, you know.

PATIENT. We are all sailors.

DOCTOR Y. I am not. I'm a doctor in this hospital.

PATIENT. If I'm not a sailor, then you aren't a doctor.

DOCTOR Y. Very well. But you are making yourself very tired, rocking about like that. Lie down. Take a rest. Try not to talk so much.

PATIENT. I'm not talking to you, am I? Around and around and around and around and around and around and around and around and around and around and around and around and . . .

NURSE. You must be feeling giddy. You've been going around and around and around for hours now, did you know that?

PATIENT. Hours?

NURSE. I've been on duty since eight, and every time I drop in to see you, you are going round and round.

PATIENT. The duty watch.

NURSE. Around and around what? Where? There now, turn over.

PATIENT. It's very hot. I'm not far away from the Equator.

NURSE. You're still on the raft, then?

PATIENT. *You* aren't!

NURSE. I can't say that I am.

PATIENT. Then how can you be talking to me?

NURSE. Do try and lie easy. We don't want you to get so terribly tired. We're worried about you, do you know that?

PATIENT. Well, it is in your hands, isn't it?

NURSE. My hands? How is that?

PATIENT. *You.* You said *We*. I know that 'We'. It is the categorical collective. It would be so easy for you to do it.

NURSE. But what do you want me to do?

PATIENT. *You* as *we*. Not you as *you*. Lift me, lift me, lift me. It must be easy enough for you. Obviously. Just use your – force, or whatever it is. Blast me there.

NURSE. Where to?

PATIENT. You know very well. Tip me South with your white wing.

NURSE. My white wing! I like the sound of that.

PATIENT. You can't be one of them. If you were, you'd know. You are tricking me.

NURSE. I'm sorry that you think that.

PATIENT. Or perhaps you're testing me. Yes, that's a possibility.

NURSE. Perhaps that is it.

PATIENT. It's just a question of getting out of the North Equatorial Current into the South Equatorial Current, from clockwise to anti-clockwise. The wise anti-clocks.

NURSE. I see.

PATIENT. Well, why don't you?

NURSE. I don't know how.

PATIENT. Is it a question of some sort of a password? Who was that man who was here yesterday?

NURSE. Do you mean Doctor Y.? He was in to see you.

PATIENT. He's behind this. He knows. A very kindly contumacious man.

NURSE. He's kind. But I wouldn't say contumacious.

PATIENT. I say it, so why shouldn't you?

NURSE. And Doctor X. was in the day before that.

PATIENT. I don't remember any Doctor X.

NURSE. Doctor X. will be in later this afternoon.

PATIENT. In what?

NURSE. Do try and lie still. Try and sleep.

PATIENT. If I do, I'm dead and done for. Surely you must know that, or you aren't a maid mariner.

NURSE. I'm Alice Kincaid. I told you that before. Do you remember? The night you came in?

PATIENT. Whatever your name, if you sleep you die.

NURSE. Well, never mind, hush. There, poor thing, you are in a state. Just lie and – there, there. Shhhhh, hush. No, lie still. Shhh . . . there, that's it, that's it, sleep. Sleeeeeeeep. Sle-e-p.

Patient distressed, fatigued, anxious, deluded, hallucinated.
Try Tofranil? Marplan? Tryptizol? Either that or shock.
August 21st DOCTOR X.

DOCTOR Y. Well, now, nurse tells me you are Sinbad today?

PATIENT. Sin bad. Sin bad. Bad sin.

DOCTOR Y. Tell me about it? What's it all about?

PATIENT. I'm not telling you.

DOCTOR Y. Why not?

PATIENT. You aren't one of Them.

DOCTOR Y. Who?

PATIENT. The Big Ones.

DOCTOR Y. No, I'm just an ordinary sort of size, I'm afraid.

PATIENT. Why are you afraid?

DOCTOR Y. Who are they, The Big Ones?

PATIENT. There were giants in those days.

DOCTOR Y. Would you tell them?

PATIENT. I wouldn't need to tell Them.

DOCTOR Y. They know already?

PATIENT. Of course.

DOCTOR Y. I see. Well, would you tell Doctor X.?

PATIENT. Who is Doctor X.?

DOCTOR Y. He was in yesterday.

PATIENT. In and Out. In and Out. In and Out.

DOCTOR Y. We think it would help if you talked to somone. If I'm no use to you, there's Doctor X., if you like him better.

PATIENT. Like? Like what? I don't know him. I don't see him.

DOCTOR Y. Do you see me?

PATIENT. Of course you are there.

DOCTOR Y. And Doctor X. isn't here?

PATIENT. I keep telling you, I don't know who you mean.

DOCTOR Y. Very well, then. How about Nurse? Would you like to talk to her? We think you should try and talk. You see, we must find out more about you. You could help if you talked. But try to talk more clearly and slowly, so that we can hear you properly.

PATIENT. Are you the secret police?

DOCTOR Y. No. I'm a doctor. This is the Central Intake Hospital. You have been here nearly a week. You can't tell us your name or where you live. We want to help you to remember.

PATIENT. There's no need. I don't need you. I need Them. When I meet Them they'll know my needs and there'll be no need to tell Them. You are not my need. I don't know who you are. A delusion, I expect. After so long on this raft and without real food and no sleep at all, I'm bound to be deluded. Voices. Visions.

DOCTOR Y. You feel that – there. That's my hand. Is that a delusion? It's a good solid hand.

PATIENT. Things aren't what they seem. Hands have come up from the dark before and slid away again. Why not yours?

DOCTOR Y. Now listen carefully. Nurse is going to sit here with you. She is going to stay with you. She is going to listen while you talk. And I want you to talk, tell her who you are and where you are and about the raft and the sea and about the giants. But you must talk more loudly and clearly. Because when you mutter like that, we can't hear you. And it is very important that we hear what you are saying.

PATIENT. Important to you.

DOCTOR Y. Will you try?

PATIENT. If I remember.

DOCTOR Y. Good. Now here is Nurse Kincaid.

PATIENT. Yes. I know. I know her well. She fills me full of dark. She darks me. She takes away my mind.

DOCTOR Y. Nonsense. I'm sure she doesn't. But if you don't want Nurse Kincaid either, we'll simply leave a tape recorder here. You know what a tape recorder is, don't you?

PATIENT. I did try and use one once but I found it inhibiting.

DOCTOR Y. You did? What for?

PATIENT. Oh, some damned silly lecture or other.

DOCTOR Y. You give lectures, do you? What sort of lectures? What do you lecture about?

PATIENT. Sinbad the sailor man. The blind leading the blind. Around and around and around and around and around and . . .

DOCTOR Y. Stop it! Please. Don't start that again. Please.

PATIENT. Around and around and around and around and . . .

DOCTOR Y. Around what? You are going around what? Where?

PATIENT. I'm not going. I'm being taken. The current. The North Equatorial, from the North African Coast, across, past the West Indies to the Florida Current, past Florida around the Sargasso Sea and into the Gulf Stream and around with the West Wind Drift to the Canaries and around past the Cape Verde Islands around and around and around and around . . .

DOCTOR Y. Very well, then. But how are you going to get out?

PATIENT. They. They will.

DOCTOR Y. Go on, now. Tell us about it. What happens when you meet them? Try and tell us.

He gives lectures. Schools, universities, radio, television, politics? Societies to do with? Exploration, archaeology, zoology? Sinbad. 'Bad sin.' Suggest as a wild hypothesis that just this once patient may have committed a crime and this not just routine guilt?

DOCTOR Y.

Accept hypothesis. What crime?

DOCTOR X.

Setting off from the Diamond Coast, first there is the southerly coastal current to get out of. Not once or twice or a dozen times, on leaving the Diamond Coast, the shore-hugging current has dragged us too far South and even within sight of that African curve which rounded would lead us in helpless to the Guinea Current to who knows what unwanted landfalls. But we have always managed just in time to turn the ship out and pointing West with Trinidad our next stop. That is, unless this time we encountered Them. Around and Around. It is not a cycle without ports we long to reach. Nancy waits for poor Charlie in Puerto Rico, George has his old friend John on Cape Canaveral, and I when the ship has swung far enough inshore wait to see Conchita sitting on her high black rock and to hear her sing her song for me. But when greetings and farewells have been made so many times, they as well as we want the end of it all. And when the songs have been heard so often, the singers no longer are Nancy, alone, poor Charlie, alone, or any of us. The last few journeys past the garden where Nancy waits, she was joined by all the girls in her town, and they stood along the wall over the sea watching us sail past, and they sang together what had so often called poor Charlie and his crew in to them before.

> Under my hand
>   flesh of flowers
> Under my hand
>   warm landscape
> You have given me back my world,
> In you the earth breathes under my hand.

> My arms were full of charred branches,
> My arms were full of painful sand.
> Now I sway in rank forests,
> I dissolve in strong forests,
> I am the bone the flowers in flesh.

> Oh now we reach it –
>   now, now!
> The whistling hub of the world.
> It's as if God had spun a whirlpool,
> Flung up a new continent.

But we men stood in a line all along the deck and we sang to them:

> If birds still cried on the shore,
> If there were horses galloping all night,
> Love, I could turn to you and say
> Make up the bed,
> Put fire to the lamp.
> All night long we would lie and hear
> The waves beat in, beat in,
> If there were still birds on the dunes,
> If horses still ran wild along the shore.

And then we would wave each other out of sight, our tears lessening with each circuit, for we were set for our first sight of Them, and they, the women, were waiting with us, for on us their release depended, since they were prisoners on that island.

On this voyage there were twelve men on board, with myself as Captain. Last time I played deckhand, and George was Captain. We were four days out from shore, the current swinging us along fair and easy, the wind coming from the North on to our right cheeks, when Charles, who was lookout, called us forward and there it was. Or, there they were. Now if you ask how it is we knew, then you are without feeling for the sympathies of our imaginations in waiting for just this moment. And that must mean that you yourselves have not yet learned that in waiting for Them lies all your hope. No, it is not true that we had imagined it in just such a form. We had not said or thought, ever: They will be shaped like birds or be forms of light walking on the waves. But if you have ever known in your life a high expectation which is met at last, you will know that the expectation of a thing must meet with that thing – or at least, that is the form in which it must be seen by you. If you have shaped in your mind an eight-legged monster with saucer eyes, then if there is such a creature in that sea you will not see anything less, or more – that is what you are set to see. Armies of angels could appear out of the waves, but if you are waiting for a one-eyed giant, you could sail right through them and not feel more than a freshening of the air. So while we had not determined a shape in our thoughts, we had not been waiting for evil or fright. Our expectations had been for aid, for explanation, for a heightening of our selves and of our thoughts. We had been set like barometers for Fair. We had known we would strike something that rang on a higher, keener note than ourselves, and that is why we knew at once that this was what we had been sailing to meet, around and around and around and around, for so many cycles that it might even be said that the waiting to meet up with Them had become a circuit in our minds as well as in the ocean.

We knew them first by the feeling in the air, a crystalline hush, and this was accompanied by a feeling of strain in ourselves, for we were not strung at the same pitch as that for which we had been waiting.

It was a smart, choppy sea and the air was flying with spray. Hovering above these brisk waves, and a couple of hundred yards away, was a shining disc. It seemed as if it should have been transparent, since the eye took in first the shine, like that of glass, or crystal, but being led inwards, as with a glass full of water, to what was behind the glitter. But the shine was not a reflected one: the substance of the disc's walls was itself a kind of light. The day was racingly cloudy, the sky half cloud, half sun, and all the scene around us was this compound of tossing waves and foam, and flying spray, of moving light, everything changing as we watched. We were waiting for strangers to emerge from the disc and perhaps let down, using the ways of humanity, a dinghy or a boat of some kind so that we, standing along the deck's edge, grasping fast to ropes and spars, might watch Them approach and take their measure – and adjust our thoughts and manners for the time. But no one appeared. The disc came closer, though so unnoticeably, being part of the general restless movement of the blue and the white, that it was resting on the air just above the waves a few paces off before we understood by a sinking of our hearts that we were not to expect anything so comfortable as the opening of a door, the letting down of a ladder, a boat, and arms bending as oars swung. But we were still not expecting anything in particular when it was already on us. What? What we felt was a sensation first, all through our bodies. In a fever or a great strain of exhaustion, or in love, all the resources of the body stretch out and expand and vibrate higher than in ordinary life. Well, we were vibrating at a higher pitch, and this was accompanied by a high shrill note in the air, of the kind that can break glasses – or probably break much more, if sustained. The disc that had been in our eyes' vision a few yards away, an object among others, though an object stronger than the others, more obliterating – seemed to come in and invade our eyes. I am describing the sensation, for I cannot say what was the fact. It was certain that this disc rose a little way up from the waves, so that it was level with our deck, and then passed over us, or through us. Yet when it was on us, it seemed no longer a disc, with a shape, but it was more a fast beating of the air, a vibration that was also a sound. It was intolerable while it lasted, as if two different substances were in conflict, with no doubt of the outcome – but it did not last more than a moment, and when my eyes had lost the feeling of being filled with a swift-beating light, or sound, and my whole body from having been stretched or expanded or invaded, as if light (or sound) had the capacity of passing through one's tissues, but in a shape as definite as one's own, then I looked to see if George, who stood nearest to me, was still alive. But he was gone, and when I turned in terror to see where he was, and where the others were, they weren't there. No one. Nothing.

The disc, which had again become a crystal disc, hovering over the waves on the other side of the ship, was lifting into the sky. It had swept away or eaten up or absorbed my comrades and left me there alone. All the ship was empty. The decks were empty. I was in terror. And worse. For all these centuries I had been sailing around and around and around and around for no other reason than that one day I would meet Them, and now at last we had indeed inhabited the same space of air, but I had been left behind. I ran to the other rail of the ship and clung there and opened my mouth to shout. I might indeed have shouted a little, or made some feeble kind of sound, but to what or to whom was I shouting? A silvery shining disc that seemed, as it lifted up and away into the air, that it ought to be transparent but was not? It had no eyes to see me, no mouth to acknowledge my shouting with a sound of its own. Nothing. And inside were eleven men, my friends, whom I knew better than I knew myself. Since we do know our friends better than we know ourselves. Then, as I stood there, gazing into the scene of blue and white and silver that tossed and sprayed and shook and danced and dazzled, sea and air all mixed together, I saw that I was looking at nothing. The disc had vanished, was no more than the shape of a cell on my retina. Nothing.

I was sickened with loss, with knowledge of an unforeseeable callousness on their part. To take them and to leave me? In all our voyagings we had never envisaged that we might simply be lifted up and taken away like a litter of puppies or kittens. We had wanted instructions, or aid, we needed to be told how to get off this endless cycling and into the Southern current. Now that this had not happened, and no instructions or information had been given, only a sort of kidnapping, then I wanted to scream against their coldness and cruelty, as one small kitten that has been hidden by a fold of a blanket in the bottom of a basket mews out in loneliness as it moves blindly about, feeling with its muzzle and its senses for its lost companions among the rapidly chilling folds of the blanket.

I stayed at the deck's edge. For while the ship needed steering and the sails setting, and for all I knew we had already swung about. I could not handle this ship by myself. I already knew that I must leave her, unless I was to choose to live on board her alone, on the small chance that the Disc would hover down again and discharge my companions in the same way it had taken them off. But I did not think this was likely to happen. And I was afraid to stay.

It was as if that Disc, or Crystal, in its swift passage across or through the ship, across or through me, had changed the atmosphere of the ship, changed me. I was shaking and shivering in a cold dread. I could hardly stand, but leaned clinging to a rope. When the shaking had seemed to stop, and I stood clenching my teeth and waiting for the puppy-warmth of life to come back, then the shaking began again, like a fit of malaria, though this was a sort of weakness, not a fever. Now everything in the ship was inimical to me, as if the Disc's breath had started a rot in its substance. To say that I had been terrified and was still terrified would be too much of an everyday statement. No, I had been struck with foreignness, I had taken a deep breath of an insupportable air. I was not at all myself, and my new loathing that was so much more than a fear of the ship was in itself an illness. Meanwhile the sails shook and flapped and bellied or hung idle above my head. Meanwhile the ship shuddered and swung to every new shift in the fitfully changing wind. Meanwhile she was a creature that had been assaulted and left to die.

I began making a raft, using timber from the carpenter's store. I worked feverishly, wanting to get away. It never crossed my mind to stay on her, so strong was my fear. Yet I knew that to set off by myself on a raft was more dangerous than staying. On the ship was water, food, some shelter, until it foundered or crashed on a rock. Until then, it would be my safety. But I could not stay. It was as if my having been ignored, left behind, out of all my old comrades, was in itself a kind of curse. I had been branded with my ship.

I worked for many hours and, when daylight went, I lashed a storm lantern to a spar and worked on through the night. I made a raft about twelve by twelve of balsawood poles. To this I lashed a locker full of rations, and a barrel of water. I fitted a sail on a mast in the middle of the raft. I took three pairs of oars, and lashed two spare pairs securely to the timbers of the raft. In the centre of the raft I made a platform of planks about four feet across. And all this time I worked in a deadly terror, a cold sick fear, attacked intermittently by the fits of shaking so that I had to double up as if in cramp, and hold on to a support for fear I'd shake myself to pieces.

By dawn my raft was done. The sky reddened in my face as I stood looking forward with the ship's movement, so I saw that the ship had already swung about and was heading back in the grip of the Guinea Current to the Cameroons or the Congo. I had to leave it as quickly as I could, and trust that I could still row myself out of this deadly shore-going current and back into the Equatorial stream once again. I put on all the clothes I could find. I let the raft fall into the sea, where it floated like a cork. And with all the sky aflame with sunrise like the inside of a ripening peach, I swarmed down a rope and swung myself on to the raft just as it was about to bob right out of my reach. I reached the raft still dry, though already beginning to be well-damped by spray, and at once began rowing with my back to the sunrise. I rowed as if I were making towards safety and a good dry ship instead of away from one. By the time the sun stood up in a clear summer-hazy sky three or four hands'-breadths from the horizon, our ship's sails were a low swarm of white, like a cluster of butterflies settled on the waves, and well behind me, and I was heading West on my real right course. And when I turned my head to look again, it was hard to tell whether I was looking at the white of the sails or at foam on a distant swell. For the sea had changed, to my advantage, and was rolling and rocking, and no longer chopping and changing. And so I rowed all that day, and most of that following night. I rowed and rowed and rowed, until my arms seemed separate from myself, they worked on without my knowing I was ordering them to. Then one day – I think it was three days after I last saw the sails of my ship vanishing East, there was sudden squally afternoon and my clothes got soaked, and I lost my spare oars. And two days after that, a heavy sea dragged my last oars from me and since then I've been trusting myself to the current that curves West and North. And now I have all the time in the world to reflect that I am still engaged in the same journey in the same current, round and round and round, with the West Indies my next landfall, and poor Charlie's Nancy and her song, just as if I had stayed on the ship with my comrades. And after the women's song, just as before, around and around, past the Sargasso Sea, and around in the Gulf Stream, and around in the swing of the sea past the coasts of Portugal and Spain, and around and around. But now I am not in a tall ship with sails like white butterflies but on a small raft and alone, around and around. And everything is the same, around and around, with only a slight but worsening change in the shape of my hope: will They, or the Disc, or Crystal Thing, on its next descent, be able to see the speck of my raft on the sea? Will they see me and find the kindness to give me a hail or a shout in reply when I ask them, How may I leave this Current, Friends, set me fair for that other coast, I pray you?

Yes, I'll hail them, of course, though now a new coldness in my heart tells me of a fear I didn't have before. I had not thought once, not in all those cycles and circles and circuits, around and around, that they might simply not notice me, as a man might not notice a sleeping kitten or a blind puppy hidden under the fold of his smelly blanket. Why should they notice the speck of a raft on the wide sea? Yet there is nothing for it but go on, oarless, rudderless, sleepless, exhausted. After all I know it would be a kindness to land on Nancy's coast and tell her that her Charlie has met up at last with – what? Them, I suppose, though that is all I can tell her, not even how he felt as he became absorbed into the substance of that shining Thing. Will she sing her song to me on my raft, drifting past, will the women line up along the walls of their summer gardens and sing, and shall I then sing back how the time is past for love? And then on I'll drift to George's friend and shout to him how George has – what? And where? And then on and on and on, until I see again my Conchita waiting, dressed in the habit of a nun, where all my wandering and sailing has put her.

> Man like a great tree
> Resents storms.
> Arms, knees, hands,
> Too stiff for love,
> As a tree resists wind.
> But slowly wakes,
> And in the dark wood
> Wind parts the leaves
> And the black beast crashes from the cave.
> My love, when you say:
> 'Here was the storm,
> Here was she,
> Here the fabulous beast,'
> Will you say too
> How first we kissed with shut lips, afraid,
> And touched our hands, afraid,
> As if a bird slept between them?
> Will you say:
> 'It was the small white bird that snared me?'

And so she sings, each time I pass, around and around, and on and on.

DOCTOR X. Well, how are you this afternoon?
PATIENT. Around and around and around . . .

DOCTOR X. I'd like you to know that I believe you could snap out of this any time you want.

PATIENT. Around and around and around . . .

DOCTOR X. Doctor Y. is not here this week-end. I'm going to give you a new drug. We'll see how that does.

PATIENT. In and out, out and in. In and out, out and in.

DOCTOR X. My name is Doctor X. What is your name?

PATIENT. Around and . . .

I think he may very well have reverted to age eleven or twelve. That was the age I enjoyed sea stories. He is much worse in my opinion. The fact is, he never acknowledges my presence at all. Doctor Y. claims he reacts to him.

August 24th   DOCTOR X.

DOCTOR Y. What is your name today?

PATIENT. It could be Odysseus?

DOCTOR Y. The Atlantic was surely not his sea?

PATIENT. But it could be now, surely, couldn't it?

DOCTOR Y. Well now, what's next?

PATIENT. Perhaps Jamaica. I'm a bit farther South than usual.

DOCTOR Y. You've been talking practically non-stop for days. Did you know that?

PATIENT. You told me to talk. I don't mind thinking instead.

DOCTOR Y. Well, whatever you do, remember this: you aren't on a raft on the Atlantic. You did not lose your friends into the arms of a flying saucer. You were never a sailor.

PATIENT. Then why do I think I'm one?

DOCTOR Y. What's your real name?

PATIENT. Crafty.

DOCTOR Y. Where do you live?

PATIENT. Here.

DOCTOR Y. What's your wife's name?

PATIENT. Have I got a wife? What is she called?

DOCTOR Y. Tell me, why won't you ever talk to Doctor X.? He's rather hurt about it. I would be too.

PATIENT. I've told you already, I can't see him.

DOCTOR Y. Well, we are getting rather worried. We don't know what to do. It's nearly two weeks since you came in. The police don't know

who you are. There's only one thing we are fairly certain about: and
that is that you aren't any sort of a sailor, professional or amateur.
Tell me, did you read a lot of sailing stories as a boy?

PATIENT. Man and boy.

DOCTOR Y. What's George's surname? And Charlie's surname?

PATIENT. Funny, I can't think of them . . . yes, of course, we all had
the same name. The name of the ship.

DOCTOR Y. What was the name of the ship?

PATIENT. I can't remember. And she's foundered or wrecked long ago.
And the raft never had a name. You don't call a raft as you call a
person.

DOCTOR Y. Why shouldn't you name the raft? Give your raft a name
now?

PATIENT. How can I name the raft when I don't know my own name.
I'm called . . . what? Who calls me? What? Why? You are Doctor
Why, and I am called Why – that's it, it was the good ship *Why* that
foundered in the Guinea Current, leaving Who on the slippery raft
and . . .

DOCTOR Y. Just a minute. I'll be away for four or five days. Doctor X.
will be looking after you till I get back. I'll be in to see you the
moment I'm back again.

PATIENT. In and out, out and in, in and out . . .

New treatment. Librium. 3 Tofronil 3 t.a.d.
August 29th   DOCTOR X.

The sea is rougher than it was. As the raft tilts up the side of a wave I see
fishes curling above my head and when the waves come crashing over
me fishes and weed slide slithering over my face, to rejoin the sea. As my
raft climbs up up up to the crest the fishes look eye to eye with me out of
the wall of water. There's that air creature they think, just before they
go slop over my face and shoulders while I think as they touch and slide,
they are water creatures, they belong to wet. The wave curls and furls in
its perfect whirls holding in it three deep sea fish that have come up to
see the sky, a tiddler fit for ponds or jam-jars, and the crispy sparkle of
plankton, which is neither visible nor invisible, but a bright crunch in
the imagination. If men are creatures of air, and fishes, whether big or
small, creatures of sea, what then are the creatures of fire? Ah yes, I
know, but you did not see me, you overlooked me, you snatched up my

comrades and let me lie squeaking inside my fold of smelly blanket. Where are they, my friends? Administering justice, are they, from the folds of fire, looking at me eye to eye out of the silkily waving fronds of fire. Look, there's a man, that's an air creature, they think, breathing yellow flame as we breathe H_2O. There's something about that gasping gape, they think – George? poor Charlie – that merits recognition. But they are beyond air now, and the inhabitants of it. They are flame-throwers. They are fire-storms. You think justice is a kindly commodity? No, it razes, it throws down, it cuts swathes. The waves are so deep, they crash so fast and furious I'm more under than up. They are teaching men – men are teaching men – to have fishes' lungs, men learn to breathe water. If I take a deep breath of water will my lung's tissues adapt in the space of a wave's fall and shout: Yes, yes, you up there, you, sailor, breathe deep and we'll carry you on water as we carried you on air? After all *They* must have had to teach my friends George and Charles and James and the rest to take deep lungfuls of fire. You're not telling me that when the Crystal swirl enveloped me with the others it was ordinary air we breathed then, no, it was a cool fire, sun's breath, the solar wind, but there are lungs attached to men that lie as dormant as those of a babe in the womb, and they are waiting for the solar wind to fill them like sails. Air lungs for air, but organs made of crystal sound, of singing light, for the solar wind that will blow my love to me. Or me onwards to my love. Oh, the waves rear so tall, they pitch and grow and soar, I'm more under than up, my raft is a little cork on the draughty sea and I'm sick, oh, I'm so sick, pitch and toss, toss and pitch, my poor poor head and my lungs, if I stay on this thick heavy slimy barnacled raft which is shrieking and straining as the great seas crash then I'll puke my heart out and fall fainting away into the deep sea swells. I'll leave the raft, then.

Oh no, no, no, I've shed my ship, the good ship *Why*, and I've clung like limpets to my new, hard bed the raft and now how can I leave, to go spinning down into the forests of the sea like a sick bird. But if I found a rock or an islet? Silly, there are no rocks or isles or islands or ports of call in the middle of the wide Atlantic sea here at 45 degrees on the Equator. But the raft is breaking up. It breaks. There were only ordinary sea ropes to fasten the balsa poles side by side and across and through, and what ropes could I ever find that could hold this clumsy collection of cross rafters steady in this sea? It's a storm. It's a typhoon. The sky is thunder black and with a sick yellowish white at the cloud's edge and the waves are blue Stephen's black and higher than the church tower and all the world is wet and cold and my ears are singing like the ague. And there goes my raft, splitting apart under me like bits of straw in the eddy of a kitchen gutter. There it goes, and I'm afloat, reaching out for straws or even a fishbone. I'm all awash and drowning and I'm cold, oh, I am so cold, I'm cold where all my own inside vital warmth should be held, there along my spine and in my belly but there it is cold cold as the moon. Down and down, but the corky sea upsends me to the light again, and there under my hand is rock, a port in the storm, a little peaking black rock that no main mariner has struck before me, nor map ever charted, just a single black basalt rock, which is the uppermost tip of a great mountain a mile or two high, whose lower slopes are all great swaying forests through which the sea buffalo herd and graze. And here I'll cling until the storm goes and the light comes clear again. Here at last I can stay still, the rock is still, having thrust up from the ocean floor a million years ago and quite used to staking its claim and holding fast in the Atlantic gales. Here is a long cleft in the rock, a hollow, and in here I'll fit myself till morning. Oh, now I'm a land creature again, and entitled to a sleep steady and easy. I and the rock which is a mountain's tip are solid together and now it is the sea that moves and pours. Steady now. Still. The storm has gone and the sun is out on a flat, calm, solid sea with its surface gently rocking and not flying about all over the place as if the ocean wanted to dash itself to pieces. A hot, singing, salty sea, pouring Westwards past me to the Indies next stop, but pouring past me, fast on my rock. Fast Asleep. Fast. Asleep.

NURSE. Wake up. Wake up, there's a dear. Come on, *no*, that's it. Sit up, all right, I'm holding you.

PATIENT. Why? What for?

NURSE. You must have something to eat. All right, you can go back to sleep in a minute. But you certainly can sleep, can't you?

PATIENT. Why make me sleep if you keep waking me up?

NURSE. You aren't really supposed to be sleeping quite so much. You are supposed to be relaxed and quiet, but you do sleep.

PATIENT. Who supposes? Who gave me the pills?

NURSE. Yes, but – well, never mind. Drink this.

PATIENT. That's foul.

NURSE. It's soup. Good hot soup.

PATIENT. Let me alone. You give me pills and then you keep waking me up.

NURSE. Keep waking you? I don't. It's like trying to wake a rock. Are you warm?

PATIENT. The sun's out, the sun . . .

....

> Who has not lain hollowed in hot rock,
> Leaned to the loose and lazy sound of water,
> Sunk into sound as one who hears the boom
> Of tides pouring in a shell, or blood
> Along the inner caverns of the flesh,
> Yet clinging like sinking man to sight of sun,
> Clinging to distant sun or voices calling?

NURSE. A little more, please.

PATIENT. I'm not hungry. I've learned to breathe water. It's full of plankton you know. You can feed your lungs as you feed your stomach.

NURSE. Is that so, dear? Well, don't go too far with it, you'll have to breathe air again.

PATIENT. I'm breathing air *now*. I'm on the rock, you see.

....

> See him then as the bird might see
> Who rocks like pinioned ship on warm rough air,
> Coming from windspaced fields to ocean swells
> That rearing fling gigantic mass on mass
> Patient and slow against the stubborn land,
> Striving to achieve what strange reversal
> Of that monstrous birth when through long ages
> Labouring, appeared a weed-stained limb,
> A head, at last the body of the land,
> Fretted and worn for ever by a mothering sea
> A jealous sea that loves her ancient pain.

NURSE. Why don't you go and sit for a bit in the day room? Aren't you tired of being in bed all the time?

PATIENT. A jealousy that loves. Her pain.

NURSE. Have you got a pain? Where?

PATIENT. Not me. You. Jealously loving and nursing pain.

NURSE. I haven't got a pain, I assure you.
PATIENT. He floats on lazy wings down miles of foam,
      And there, below, the small spreadeagled shape
      Clinging to black rock like drowning man,
      Who feels the great bird overhead and knows
      That he may keep no voices, wings or winds
      Who follows hypnotized down glassy gulfs,
      His roaring ears extinguished by the flood.
NURSE. Take these pills dear, that's it.
PATIENT. Who has not sunk as drowned man sinks,
      Through sunshot layers where still the under-
        curve
      Of lolling wave holds light like light in glass,
      Where still a jewelled fish slides by like bird,
      And then the middle depths where all is dim
      Diffusing light like depths of forest floor.
      He falls, he falls, past apprehensive arms
      And spiny jaws and treacherous pools of death,
      Till finally he rests on ocean bed.

      Here rocks are tufted with lit fern, and fish,
      Swim shimmering phosphorescent through the
        weed
      And shoals of light float blinking past like eyes,
      Here all the curious logic of the night.
      Is this a sweet drowned woman floating in her
        hair?
      The sea-lice hop on pale rock scalp like toads.
      And this a gleam of opalescent flesh?
      The great valves shut like white doors folding
        close.
      Stretching and quavering like the face of one
      Enhanced through chloroform, the smiling face
      Of her long half-forgotten, her once loved,
      Rises like thin moon through watery swathes,
      And passes wall-eyed as the long dead moon.

      He is armed with the indifference of deep-sea
        sleep

> And floats immune through sea-roots fed with
>   flesh,
> Where skeletons are bunched against cave roofs
> Like swarms of bleaching spiders quivering.
> While crouching engines crusted with pale weed,
> Their shafts and pistons rocking through the
>   green . . .

NURSE. Now do come on, dear. Oh dear, you are upset, aren't you? Everybody has bad times, everyone gets upset from time to time. I do myself. Think of it like that.

PATIENT. Not everyone has known these depths
> The black uncalculated wells of sea,
> Where any gleam of day dies far above,
> And stagnant water slow and thick and foul . . .

NURSE. It's no good spitting your pills out.

PATIENT. Foul, fouled, fouling, all fouled up . . .

,NURSE. One big swallow, that will do it, that's done it.

PATIENT. You wake me and you sleep me. You wake me and then you push me under. I'll wake up now. I want to wake.

NURSE. Sit up, then.

PATIENT. But what is this stuff, what are these pills, how can I wake when you . . . who is that man who pushes me under, who makes me sink as drowned man sinks and . . . ?

NURSE. Doctor X. thinks this treatment will do you good.

PATIENT. Where's the other, the fighting man?

NURSE. If you mean Doctor Y., he'll be back soon.

PATIENT. I must come up from the sea's floor. I must brave the surface of the sea, storms or no, because They will never find me down there. Bad enough to expect Them to come into our heavy air, all smoky and fouled as it is, but to expect them down at the bottom of the sea with all the drowned ships, no, that's not reasonable. No. I must come up and give them a chance to see me there, hollowed in hot rock.

NURSE. Yes, well, all right. But don't thrash about like that . . . for goodness' sake.

PATIENT. Goodness is another thing. I must wake up. I must. I must keep watch. Or I'll never get out and away.

NURSE. Well I don't know really. Perhaps that treatment isn't right for you? But you'd better lie down then. That's right. Turn over. Curl up. There. Hush. Hushhhhhhh. Shhhhhhhhhhhhhhhhhhhhhhhh

PATIENT. Hushabye baby
          lulled by the storm
          if you don't harm her
          she'll do you no harm

I've been robbed of sense. I've been made without resource. I have
become inflexible in a flux. When I was on the Good Ship *Lollipop* I
was held there by wind and sea. When I was on the raft, there was
nobody there but me. On this rock I'm fast. Held. I can't do more
than hold on. And wait. Or plunge like a diver to the ocean floor
where it is as dark as a fish's gut and there's nowhere to go but up.
But I do have an alternative, yes. I can beg a lift, can't I? Cling on to
the coat-tails of a bird or a fish. If dogs are the friends of man, what
are a sailor's friends? Porpoises. They love us. Like to like they say,
though when has a porpoise killed a man, and we have killed so
many and for curiosity, not even for food's or killing's sake. A
porpoise will take me to my love. A sleek-backed, singing, shiny,
black porpoise with loving eyes and a long whistler's beak. Hold on
there, porpoise, poor porpoise in your poisoned sea, filled with stink-
ing effluent from the bowels of man, and waste from the murderous
mind of man, don't die yet, hold on, hold me, and take me out of
this frozen, grinding Northern circuit down and across into the tender Southern-running current and the longed-for shores. There now.
Undersea if you have to, I can breathe wet if I must, but above sea if
you can, in case I may hail a passing friend who has taken the shape
of a shaft of fire or a dapple of light. There, porpoise, am I true
weight? A kind creature? Kith and Kind? Just take me South, lead
me to the warmer current, oh, now it is rough, we toss and heave as
it was in the Great Storm, when my raft fell apart like straw, but I
know now this is a good cross patch, it is creative, oh, what a
frightful stress, what a strain, and now out, yes out, we're well out,
and still swimming West, but South-West, but anti-clockwise,
whereas before it was West with the clock and no destination but the
West Indies and Florida and past the Sargasso Sea and the Gulf
Stream and the West Wind Drift and the Canaries Current and
around and around and around and around but now, oh porpoise, on
this delicate soap bubble our Earth, spinning all blue and green and
iridescent, where Northwards air and water swirl in time's direction

left to right, great spirals of breath and light and water, now, oh porpoise, singing friend, we are on the other track, and I'll hold on, I'll clasp and clutch to the last breath of your patience, being patient, till you land me on that beach at last, for, oh porpoise, you must be sure and take me there, you must land me fairly at last, you must not let me cycle South too far, dragging in the Brazil current of my mind, no, let me gently step off your slippery back on to the silver sand of the Brazilian coast where, lifting your eyes, rise the blue-and-green heights of the Brazilian Highlands. There, there, is my true destination and my love, so, purpose, be sure to hold your course.

There now, there's the shore. And now more than ever we must hold our course to true. There are no rocks, shoals or reefs here, porpoise, which could stub your delicate nose or take strips of blubber off your sleek black back, but there is the shining coast and of all the dangers of the Southern Current this one is worst, that if we keep our eyes on that pretty shore wishing we were on it, then the current will sweep us on in our cycle of forgetting around and around and around and around again back to the coasts of Africa with hummocks of Southern ice for company, so hold on now, porpoise, and keep your mind on your work, which is me, my landfall, but never let yourself dream of that silver sand and the deep forests there for if you do, your strength will ebb and you'll slide away southwards like a dead or a dying fish.

There. Yes. Here we are, close in, and the thunder of the surf is in us. But close your ears, porpoise, don't listen or look, let your thoughts be all of a strong purposeful haul. In. And in. With the wash of the south-dragging current cold on your left flank. In. Yes, and I'm not looking either, dear porpoise, for if I did not reach that shore now and if we did have to slide away falling South and around again and again and again then I think I'd ask you, porpoise, to treat me as men treat porpoises and carve me up for your curiosity. But there, closer. Yes, closer. We are so close now that the trees of the beach and the lifting land beyond the beach are hanging over us as trees hang over a tame inland river. And we're in. But will you come with me, splitting your soft fat shining tail to make legs to walk on, strolling up with me to the highlands that are there? No, well then, goodbye porpoise, goodbye, slide back to your playful sea and be happy there, live, breathe, until the poison man makes for all living creatures finds you and kills you as you swim. And now I roll off your friendly back, thank you, thank you kind fish, and I find my feet steady under me on a crunching sand with the tide's fringe washing cool about my ankles.

The Summer Before the Dark

The Holiday

On the 31st of July she walked out of the tall, gleaming, multi-national hotel in Istanbul, thus leaving, in one step, the world of international organization and planning, of conferences, of great Organizations – the atmosphere of money, invisible but so plentiful it is not important. The coffee and cakes she had eaten before leaving the hotel had cost two pounds, but she had never thought of asking the price. On the pavement, she was already in energetic altercation in three languages with the taxi-driver, who showed signs of wanting to overcharge her by a few pence.

She had with her one suitcase, for she was adept at packing in small spaces, because she had spent so many years buying and packing for four children of that class of the world's citizens who have the best of everything, and from all over the world, available on the counters of their local High Streets. She had given some of her new smart dresses to Ahmed for his wife, having ascertained they were the same size: from the trembling incredulity with which he handled these garments, mixed with only just-controlled resentment – not at her, she hoped, but against circumstances – she saw how much tact and self-control had gone into Ahmed's working with her for the past month.

She stepped on to the aircraft wearing a shocking-pink dress that was in discord to just the right degree with her dark-red hair, and with a white skin that could not tan – already provocative where everyone was brown by nature, or getting brown as fast as possible. She carried *Paris Match*, *Oggi*, the *Guardian*, *Time Magazine*, *Le Monde*. Jeffrey had the Paris *Tribune*, the *International Times*, the *Christian Science Monitor*.

By the time they had read their own and each other's newspapers, they were in Gibraltar, and in a couple of hours were sipping aperitifs in Malaga.

Again her ears were painfully reproached – the Spanish much worse than the Turkish, since she knew the language closest to it. All around

her were languages being spoken that found their way easily into her
understanding: outside this central stage of drinkers and waiters was
Spanish, but in offstage mutters again, noises off: the Spanish were
extras and bit-players on their own coasts.

Ever since early June that sun-loud coast had been filling. It was now
so loaded that one could easily imagine that if seen from the air the
peninsula must seem pressed down and the waters rising around it – the
blue of the Mediterranean on one side, the grey of the Atlantic on the
other. Soon these millions would submerge with their coloured clothes,
their umbrellas, their sunglasses; their hotels, night-clubs and restaurants.

At a table between a tall hibiscus bush and some plumbago that was
moth-grey and not blue in the artificial light, a couple who were turned
away from the crowd, and demonstrating their preference not to watch
it, from time to time touched hands, even held hands. Once or twice
they even kissed; but lightly, even humorously, certainly decorously.
They might have been observed, too, giving many glances and indeed
long looks away from each other, not into the crowd of which they were
a part, but away and down on to a beach where flocks of many-nationed
young people were playing. Not *in* the sea, no: that, alas, had become
too problematical a pleasure; the waters that glittered so appropriately
with moonlight held too many questions. Flesh was being withheld
from it. Or almost. One or two did swim there, making their statement
of confidence, or of indifference: to submit one's body to the waters of
this coast had become a manifesto; one could deduce people's attitudes
to the future by what they chose off a menu, or by whether they decided
to swim, or to let the children put their feet into the sea. In a restaurant a
man would order a dish of local fish with exactly the same largeness of
manner and a glance which circled the room, *I am feeling reckless tonight*,
that once would have gone with an order for champagne in a restaurant
that didn't take champagne for granted. A girl who walked into the sea
on a warm morning would draw glances and grimaces and shrugs: *She
isn't afraid, that one. But not for me, I wouldn't take the risk*. But if bodies
were being withheld from these warm waters where once people had
swum and played half the night, now the youth of a dozen countries
danced to guitars for hundreds of miles along their shores.

The glances of this couple were definitely wistful: he, because he
wished he was part of the scene; she, because she was thinking of her
children. She also watched the man, in the way one does watch someone

else's longing – only too ready to offer ointment and comfort, if one felt that could help.

He was a slightly built young man, good-looking but not remarkable, for his colouring classed him with the natives of this coast, brown eyes, sleek dark hair, olive skin. It did, that is, until he spoke.

The woman, older than he, was the more striking because he fitted so unobtrusively into the scene. She was category Redhead. She had dead-white skin. Her eyes were brown, like grapes or raisins. Her face was humorous and likeable, and around it her hair that was so beautifully cut and shaped and brushed lay in a solid sculptured curve, so thick that looking at it put a weight of reminiscent sensation in the palms of one's hands. Rather, that is what the amorist might have felt; the waiters knew what that haircut had cost, what her clothes had cost, and were automatically extending their expectations to a large tip.

This couple might have been observed . . . this couple were indeed being observed, closely, expertly. They had been minutely observed at the airport, when they descended from the plane, and then on the little bus where they had sat side by side among their fellow passengers from the plane, and then from the moment they booked in at the hotel – their room had been reserved by telephone from Turkey by Global Food. They had been examined, ticketed, categorized, docketed, by experts whose business during the summer months was to do nothing but observe and weigh their visitors.

Which visitors fell, roughly, into three categories. First the package tours, the groups that had been parcelled up in their home countries – Britain, France, Holland, Germany, Finland – had travelled as a unit by coach or plane, lived as a unit while here and would return as a parcel. These were the most predictable, financially and personally. It was enough for a hotel manager or waiter to give such a group five minutes' skilled attention to understand, and 'place', each individual in it. Then came the category International Youth, who moved up and down the coast in flocks and herds, like birds or animals, in an atmosphere of fierce self-sufficiency, of self-approval. These were decorative, always provocative of violent emotions – envy, disapproval, admiration and so on – but on the whole pretty non-rewarding financially: they could, however, be counted on to grow older and join Group One, or Three. The third and smallest class was that which once all travellers had been – the lone-wolves, or couples, or families travelling together and making their own arrangements, their passionately individual arrangements. These, for those experts in the tourist industry with the temperaments of philosophers or gamblers, were the most rewarding, because they might turn out to be anything, rich or poor, eccentric, criminal, solitary. It was among these, of course, that occurred most of the love-couples – that is, if you discounted 'the youth', who were by definition bound to be in a state of love, or sex. And, of course, the couples who travelled together without being married were more numerous than they had been. Just as, not much more than five, or ten, years ago, bikinis or even bare knees or bare shoulders had been banned, and by public notice and order at that, even on beaches and terraces – the *guardia civile* marching about to make sure these orders were being obeyed – and now all these don'ts and can'ts and prohibitions had melted away under the pressure of Money, so too had dissolved that silent NO which had made it difficult for unmarried couples travelling together to simply enter a hotel and order a room. It had been possible; it had been done, but with much discretion and often deception on the part of the unwed. Now, up and down that red-hot coast, during the months of bacchanalia, while 'the children' frolicked and loved on the sands – or, if they were gamblers by temperament, in the warm, treacherous, increasingly odiferous waters – sometimes copulating as openly as cats and dogs, it had become normal for a hotel manager, a good Catholic and a good family man, who would in his own life, from his own choice, refuse to speak to a woman suspected of such a crime, throw his own daughter out if she dishonoured him by making love unwed – this man welcomed into his clean and honourable premises, his beds, his bars, women with men not their husbands, would smile, bow, chat, wish them good day and good night and a good appetite, with never an inflection of disapproval, not a shadow of reproach – well, just the slightest shadow, perhaps, a *soupçon*, enough to suggest that the pressures of economics might be forcing this on him, but at least he (the manager) was still aware that it was immorality, even while he was housing and feeding it. So much honour and propriety remained to him – all this he might convey, in nuances so slight the couple could choose not to notice them at all.

This couple had been classified as an immoral one by these experts in the social condition.

They had also been classed as that time-honoured pair, older woman-younger man. The desk clerk at the hotel had been surprised at the large difference in age, when he had taken in the passports, to write down details for the police files. They were not a frivolous or an embarrassing couple; they behaved with taste and discretion. But there are conventions in love, and one is that this particular subclassification, older woman-younger man, should be desperate and romantic. Or, at least, tenderly painful. Perhaps – so those unwritten but tyrannical values of the emotional code suggest – a passionate anguish can be the only justification for this relationship, which is socially so sterile. Could it be tolerated at all in this form, which was almost casual, positively humorous – as if these two were laughing at themselves? They were indifferent to each other? – surely not! For their propriety was due to much more than good manners – so decided these experts, whose eyes were underlined with the experiences of a dozen summers, enabling them to flick a glance over such a couple just once, taking in details of class, sexual temperature, money. Perhaps this was, after all, not a pair of lovers? They could not be mother and son – no, impossible. Brother and sister? No, one could not believe that a single womb had produced two such dissimilar human types. They were an incongruous marriage? No, their being together lacked the congruence of mood and movement by which one recognizes the married – and then, there were the documents, at the desk. There was nothing else, they must be lovers.

So they were judged, as being in a category which demanded the utmost in tolerance from this country, whose own standards were still strict, men still owning women's sexuality; and as eccentrics within that category. They seemed to be non-loving lovers, though they did seem to pay homage to their condition by holding hands, or with a light kiss. It was this that caused the slight chilliness, the reproach, of the waiters (who were of course unaware that they showed these reactions) which was exacting from the lovers much larger tips than were necessary.

Jeffrey had been in Spain three times before. Once, at twenty, playing along the coast as were now playing 'the children' whom he was watching with such wistfulness that she, this mother with a quarter of a century of being attuned to other people's moods, felt it almost as her own. She watched him watch the very young girls, all beautiful, or seeming to be so because of the magicking light and the setting of highly tinted foliage, the sounding sea, visible as a solid moving glitter under the moon – all the atmosphere of the summer coast that was more poignant because of the general feeling that this coast-life, the migrations, the sun-worshipping, the sea-tasting was doomed, soon to be ended, and for good. She watched him as he longed for what he had lost – the young ones' freedom, their irresponsibility – and felt the pressures of his dilemma in herself. He could no longer be one with them. Last summer he had been – in Holland. But last summer he was already feeling wrongly placed, out of it. Because of last summer he knew he could not step down off this terrace and approach the singing, dancing group as he had 'when he was young' – as he was already putting it, though of course making fun of himself as he did so. But he was longing to do it, so dissolve himself into that friendly whole where so few demands are made. He was thinking, and saying, in his humorously self-demolishing way that was beginning to be painful, that perhaps he should decide to be a 'middle-aged hippie' – why not? One was bound to be ridiculous, out of place, whatever one did, so why not be a misfit in a way which he would enjoy. But of course he would not enjoy it. His upbringing would see to that. 'My conditioning, damn it, it's hanging me up!'

At twenty-five he had come to Spain having finished college and had lived up the coast in a cheap *pensión* for the long warm months, May to November, with a girl called Stephanie. They had been very happy, then less happy, then she had gone off with a German boy she met on the beach, and wrote to him that he was irresponsible, selfish, non-caring, conservative. After that she had married a man in her father's legal office in Cedar Rapids, Iowa.

He had come here two years ago for a summer and spent all the time in Córdoba and Seville, listening to and watching flamenco, for which he had a passion. He had dreamed of becoming a flamenco dancer, as some people dream of becoming bullfighters. Some do in fact become bullfighters; he had the build, and – he was convinced – the temperament, for flamenco. But a sense of the ridiculous or of the appropriate (or his conditioning, which could be described – and particularly by him, in bad moments – as cowardice) had stopped him. 'I can just see my parents! They'd turn up, and demand to be taken to the nearest gipsies. "Take me to the gipsies – they have stolen my little boy away!"'

And now he was here, for the fourth time, and in August – which was in itself enough to make him feel a foreigner, a greenhorn. For like everyone who has spent more than a month in a country, on his own steam, without much money, he felt like a native; and it was humiliating for him to be here at a time when every native – very properly of course – had only one thought, that his country was not his, was temporarily sold to tourism.

The country was corrupted, ruined, debased, compared with when he had first come here.

They discussed this at length, watching the golden boys and girls playing on the verges of the tainted sea.

When he had first come here, at the beginning of the 'sixties, there had been a pride, a dignity; there had been a readiness to proffer small services, unasked, without wanting money; there had been a dimension in the Spaniards, even on the already developed coasts, which went far beyond commercialism. There was a humanity in . . . a stature . . . a depth . . . He began to laugh at himself, when she did. There were tears in his eyes, certainly for the Spaniards.

As for her, she had come by car with her husband and the four children, for a prolonged camping holiday – she found this hard to say, but made herself – getting on for twenty years before. They had been among the very first tides of tourists. Along this coast, now loaded with hotels and holiday camps had been nothing – nothing at all. Sand in which some thin grass grew stretched from headland to headland; camping under the pines, they had seen no one for days at a time. She too had memories of all sorts of spontaneous kindnesses from the natives – she was more than able to match his words – dignity, pride, and so on and so forth.

She started to tell how, in those days, when the rare foreign car came into a town, an army of young men and boys would fight to earn sixpence for keeping watch on it for the night; how, when the Browns ate their frugal-enough meals in restaurants there would be a dozen hungry faces pressed to the glass, so that the Brown children had their fairy tales illustrated for them: those where the poor little boy gazes in at riches, but is noticed, and is brought inside by the kind family, or compensated by a fairy godmother – sometimes by being taken away altogether from his poor streets into heaven. She was telling him of children in rags and without shoes, children with sores and with flies crawling on their faces and into their eyes, children with the swollen bellies of malnutrition. But as she talked she was thinking how once and not so long ago these things had seemed like surface symptoms, soon to be corrected by the use of a general common sense, they had not yet presented themselves as the general condition of man which would soon worsen and darken everywhere. She was thinking how once talk of this kind sounded almost like a blueprint for a better world, or like a statement of concern. Now it sounded like callousness. In a moment they, Jeffrey and she, would be outbidding each other in that most common of middle-class verbal games: which of them had acquired more grace by being close to other people's sufferings.

That was not her own thought: it was her son James's. He got into a fury whenever poor people anywhere were mentioned – usually by Eileen, or by Tim, who engaged themselves in welfare work of different kinds. James saw the solution as simple: it was revolution. Anything less was insulting to the suffering poor, and a waste of time. The classic revolution – like Castro's.

But the four children had all evolved their own positions, quite different from each other. They had evolved, too, individual attitudes towards tourism, towards travelling so indefatigably in so many countries.

Stephen, the eldest, was in advance – it was a way of looking at it – of them all. His attitude that all governments were equally reactionary left him free to travel everywhere, exactly like the selfish and the indifferent, whom he spent much of his time attacking. Eileen, uninterested in politics, travelled without scruples of conscience, like Stephen. James had a more difficult time than any: for instance, he would not have visited Greece, but had visited Spain last year because he was, he had said, adding to his political education, regarded Israel as too fascist to enter, but had travelled with equanimity through the military dictatorships of the Near and Middle East. Tim believed the end of civilization was close, and that we should shortly be looking back from a world-wide barbarism formalized into a world-bureaucracy to the present, which would, from that nasty place in time, seem like a vanished golden age: he made journeys like someone tasting the last bottle of a rare vintage.

As for their mother, here she sat with (there was no other word for it, she supposed) a young lover, drinking aperitifs on a terrace in Spain: they were going to a bullfight tomorrow because he adored them. For aesthetic reasons.

Before the two went to their room, they descended to the beach along paths scented with oleander, sun-oil and urine, and stood on the same level as the throng of youngsters, their feet in churned sand. It being late, and the half-moon standing up high over the sea, and the crowds much thinner along the terraces, some of the young ones had put themselves to bed for the night and lay in each other's arms – anywhere, in the shelter of a rock, on a stretched towel, on sleeping bags. Reed mats had been laid on the sand, and on these some still danced, their hair flowing, their eyes gleaming and drowsy. Near the sea's edge a group sang to a guitar played by a girl who sat on a rock like a mermaid.

Kate was now careful not to look at her companion; she knew that he would certainly, in the state of emotional sensitivity he was in, resent it: already she was making comparisons with her own children's reactions. But she was remembering – not her youth, no, that was too far off and too different to be matched with this context. She was thinking of that time ten years ago when she had been in love with that boy. *That* pain, a longing after something beyond a barrier of time, matched with what he was now feeling. She had lived through and out the other side – well, she had had no alternative. So of course would he. But despite what people said about the poignancy of that class of experience, and what she said herself, she did not like remembering that time. It had been false memory again, she had dolled it up in her mind, making something presentable of it to fit the convention 'older woman-younger man'. But really it had been humiliating. Yes, looking at all these beautiful young creatures, all moving, or lolling, or sleeping in their postures of instant grace, she said to herself that that time had been horribly humiliating. The reason had been simple, and why old Goethe (or Mann) had talked of 'worming it'. Long marriage, long, gratifying sex, had absorbed sex, the physical, into the ordinary and easy expression of emotion, a language of feeling – but the boy had had practically no sexual experience, understood only fantasy, the romantic. Her sexuality for him had been horrifying – or would have been, she had of course damped it, learning that the conversations of the flesh were for the mature, learning, with the first inklings of unease, of her dependence on this long married conversation. She had felt when with him as if she had a secret or a wound that she must conceal. Young, as that girl in a white dress (another convention, like an old-fashioned portrait: 'Girl in a White Dress with Lilies'), a kiss had seemed a gateway into a world which had in fact turned out everything she had imagined – until she had had to look at it through the eyes of a twenty-year-old from public school and English university, a virgin as far as women were concerned.

She knew that she ought not to add to her companion's wild misery, which was mixed with so much animal shame – like her own with that boy – by letting him know how easily she was able to share what he felt.

As they stood there, not twelve paces from the young ones, but absolutely separated from them, a girl went past, smiling to herself, and dragging naked feet in the sand for the pleasure of the sensation. She glanced at Jeffrey; the smile was blotted out while she presented to him a blank face – and went on, smiling. Kate recognized that face: it was what one shows to someone outside one's own pack, herd or group. She tried to put herself in the girl's place – she was about seventeen, all long, thin, brown arms and legs and long black hair and what seemed like an absolute self-sufficiency – in order to see Jeffrey as a man old enough to be so looked at. She managed it with difficulty. So she herself had looked at men over twenty-five when she had been that age. She could just remember that the godlike creatures had had above all the glamour of responsibility, or power, in the adult world. Returning herself to her own stage or stratum in the human community, she could see only a young man whose strength was all going into recognizing his own weakness and not collapsing under it. He turned to her and said: 'Good thing you are here or I'd be dragged back into it again.'

At this most frank statement of why she was here, with him, her heart did give an obligatory gulp, or grimace, of pain – but nothing much, for it was much too occupied with painful reminiscence for small considerations: the official memories of all kinds were wearing thin, were almost transparent. If she had been asked, let us say in late May, on that afternoon when her husband's casually met acquaintance had come to her garden – when the series of chances which had brought her here had begun? – if she had been asked then what scene or set of circumstances would be best calculated to bring home to her a situation, a stage in life that she *must* recognize, no matter how painful, then she might have chosen this: to stand on the edge of a mile of soiled and scuffed sand that glittered with banal moonlight, watching a hundred or so young people, some younger than her own children, beside a young man who – it was no use pretending otherwise – made her feel maternal. Almost she could have said: There, there, it will be better soon, and hugged him. She was actually thinking, like a mother: Off you go then, you'll have to live through this, much better if I am not anywhere around – except, of course, that I have to be watching and guiding from somewhere just out of sight . . .

Their hotel was not in the glittering strip along the luxurious part of the little town. It was set back in the older part which in normal months was inhabited only by Spaniards. But they entered a foyer as lit and as lively as in day, for this was holiday month and sleep could be postponed. Couples of all nations sat about drinking. The dining-room was open, and people were still at dinner – it was past one o'clock. The desk clerk handed the key over to Mr Jeffrey Merton and Mrs Catherine Brown without any dimming of his smile, but his body expressed offended disapproval without knowing that it did.

They ascended to a bedroom which was not the best the hotel had: she had a lot of money because of the highly paid job, but was scaled down to him, who was making sure that his grandmamma's money would continue to preserve his independence for him – none of it was invested, he had insisted on putting it into jewellery and pictures, which were in a bank's keeping. It was the kind of hotel she and her family might have chosen: unpretentious, old-fashioned. The room had a balcony, which overlooked a little public garden; from it came a gay churning music, the sound of voices. She went to stand on the balcony. He joined her. They kissed, expert lovers. He departed to the bathroom. Down in the moon-whitened street people sat on doorsteps, talking. Their children, even small ones, sat with them, or played nearby. It was warm and soft and the small isolated music intensified a general stillness. People had slept all afternoon and would not go to bed until the sky lightened. The town felt more awake, more flowing and alert, than it ever did in the day. In the cities of southern Spain, at night, in the biting summer, another vitality awakes, holding together in a web of sociability that runs from street to alley to garden the cries of children, the barking of a dog, music, gossip. This is the time for sitting and watching, for talk, for living. From everywhere in the quiet dark, from the pools of light where the street was lit, arose voices.

Jeffrey had come back into the room. She left the balcony and went towards the bed to turn it back as he pitched forward on to it, prone. At first, her femininity rose and shouted that this was an insult: they had made love only once, and they were supposed to be lovers. Next, she found herself laying two fingers on his pulse and a hand on his shoulder, to assess his condition and his temperature. His flesh was hot, but then the air was. He looked exhausted. What she could see of his face was a beaded scarlet. His pulse was slow. She used all her strength to turn him over, to lay him in bed, to pull the sheet up. The flush was rapidly draining from his face: now he was pale, sallow. He might not have a temperature but he certainly wasn't well.

While her femininity continued to shout, or, rather, to make formal complaint, that it was outraged, and that she ought to feel insulted, she returned to the balcony, on the whole with relief. She fetched a straight chair from the room, which seemed stuffy as well as unwholesomely dark compared with this light airy night over a street that still moved and laughed, and she put the chair in the corner of the balcony, and sat herself there. She wore a white cotton robe that left her arms and neck bare to receive what breezes there were. There she sat, in that most familiar of all situations – alert, vigilant, while a creature slept who was younger than herself. The block of moonlight on the balcony soon shifted. She moved her chair out of it, in such a way that her legs and arms might lie in it but her head would stay in the shadow – exactly as if the moon were a sun.

Some fifty feet down, on the opposite pavement, two men were talking. They were two papas, stout men, in creased light summer suits that from here looked dazzling – like the sand on the beach in moonlight. The creases showed black. Beyond them boughs waved: the square where the music had stopped. Occasional cars went past, noisy, saying that the music had been louder than it had seemed. In the intervals between the roarings and hootings she could hear the men's voices quite clearly. The Spanish was coming into her ears in lumps or blocks – unassimilable. It was a veil between herself and Spain which she could not pull aside. But it was a semi-transparent veil, unlike the Turkish of only that morning. It had moments of transparence. The Portuguese that was in her, like an open door to half that peninsula, a large part of Africa and a large part of South America, sometimes fitted over the sounds she was listening to, sometimes not. A language she knew nothing of, like German, was all thick and impenetrable. But this listening to the Spanish was like seeing something through trees off a road one is rushing along. The conversation nagged, on the edge of meaning. When she leaned right over the balcony, receiving moonlight all over her, in a cool splash of white, so that she felt so prominent and self-displaying she could not prevent herself glancing this way and that along the face of this hotel – no, she was the only person out on the balconies – when she leaned right over so that she could see the gestures, the poses, the positions of the two portly bodies, then she was able to understand much more. A set of the fat shoulders, or a flinging open of a palm, added to the message sent out by the intonation – *almost* she was understanding Spanish. They were talking about business, that was clear. Yet she had not heard one word that told her this. Their voices were those of men talking about money; their bodies talked risk and gain. The shriek of a passing car swallowed the talk, spat it out again: it was a near-intelligibility, like windows paned with sheets of quartz instead of glass. The voices stopped. A smell of tobacco. She looked over and saw them lighting cigars. The smoke drifted away in small mists and sank into leaves. One fat man went away; the other lingered, looking about as if the night might offer him a postponement of sleep; then he went too. In a few minutes they would be in striped pyjamas. The pale suits would be heaped on a tiled bathroom floor, ready to be picked up by their wives and put into the wash. The men would be sliding into bed beside two fat pale women.

Darling! Chéri! Carissimo! Caro!

She inspected the bedroom, so dark because of this blaze of cold light outside. On the bed, her lover lay sprawled. She could hear his breathing. She did not like the sound of it. If he had been one of her sons, she would be thinking about calling the doctor in tomorrow – *she must stop this at once*!

It was getting on for four. At last the streets were emptying, though in the square people still reposed on benches, breathing in the night, dreaming, smoking. The steps below were empty now. But two children played quietly against the hotel wall, while their father sat by them on a stool, his back against bricks which were probably still warm. The mother came out and said the children should go to bed, and they set up a wailing protest; one did not need Spanish to understand what everyone was saying while Papa was being stern, Mamma exclamatory, the children clutching at the life their parents wished to bury in sleep. Then Mamma brought out a chair and sat by her husband; one child sat on her lap, the other on his. The children were drooping in sleep; the parents talked quietly: hotel employees, from the kitchens perhaps? The cars were few now. The town was as quiet as it could be in these frenetic months of the tourist.

Kate was far from sleep.

She was tempted to slide into the big bed and sleep simply to avoid – what she had to do, at some point.

Besides, she was still able to savour moments like those, without pressures of any kind, after the years of living inside the timetable of other people's needs. She could still hug to herself the thought: If I don't go to bed until the sun rises it doesn't matter. I needn't get up till midday if I don't choose.

It had not been until three years ago that this freedom had been regained by her – of course, that was where she was going to have to look, at the time of the children's growing up. But she could have claimed the right to freedom years before. Years before. What about Mary Finchley, for instance? If she felt like staying in bed till mid-afternoon she did, and shouted at the children to bring her food or tea. In between Kate the girl who had married Michael, and Kate of three years ago, which was when she had become conscious there was something to examine, the rot had set in.

The climactic moment of three years ago had been when Tim, then a tumultuous sixteen, had turned on her at the supper table and screamed that she was suffocating him. This had been wrenched from his guts, it was easy to see that. All the family were present, everyone was shocked – oh yes, they had understood that this was an event of a new quality, destructive, which announced a threat to that unit which they were: all had rallied into tact, smoothing this moment of real misery and fright for both herself and the boy. For it *had* been wrung out of him, and he was shocked at the hatred he had shown. Normally, in this well-tempered family – so they had thought of themselves, well-adjusted, with effort spent to keep them so – such conflicts were out in the open, discussed, bantered away. Sometimes brutally. It could be said that the spirit of the young couple's Phase Two – discussion to soften the painful limits of Phase One – had been taken into use by their growing family, years later. No one could have said – who? Kate was imagining some sort of critic, a welfare worker perhaps – that this was a family in which things were smothered, hidden, and had to go underground.

Yet that the boy had had to crack himself open in that way, before them all, and under pressure, showed that perhaps all the banter and psychologizing and criticism was not the healthy and therapeutic frankness she had imagined, they all had imagined, but a form of self-deception? A family *folie*, like the madness that encloses lovers who destroy themselves. If there is a *folie à deux* then there is certainly a *folie à* – as many as you like!

Looking back at a typical family scene, during the adolescence of her four, she saw herself at one end of the table, tender and swollen like a goose's fattening liver, with the frightful pressure of four battling and expanding egos that were all in one way or another in conflict or confluence with herself, a focus, a balancing-point; and her husband at the other end, being tolerant, humorous – a little weary. But not really implicated, not involved, for he worked so hard, had so little emotional energy left over to give to the family, to the four children – monsters. They called themselves so: we four monsters. Five monsters: she had been so involved with their growing, the continual crises, their drive up and out from herself, all the emotions, that she had found it hard to separate herself from them. She still did. Yet the monsters' pressure on her, the insistent demands, had ended. Well, nearly, except for the youngest, Tim.

On that particular occasion she had retired from the table as soon as she could without it seeming as if she were a little girl going off to sulk or weep. Even so she had been like a cat or a dog that has been kicked inadvertently by a friend. She knew that as she went, she was conscious of five pairs of eyes deliberately *not* looking at her. She had gone to her room while the boy fled in shame because he had shouted, having kept his head down over his plate to finish his pudding.

In her room she had sat and thought – had tried to think, while emotions rioted: she was feeling nearly crazy under the pressure of her old feeling: It's not fair, what do they expect of me?

It was her fault that Tim was very hard, on himself, on the others – on her? The three others had stepped imperceptibly from being 'children' into being adolescents. All stormy and problematical, certainly, but Tim's explosion into adolescence shook everybody. Everybody discussed, understood – much verbal display went on among these clever modern children. Tim was judged by them all to be more monstrous than any; and Kate as his victim. But the one thing that had *not* happened – she had to come back to this point again and again – was evasion, secrecy. During those years when she felt as if she were locked for ever in a large box with four perpetually exploding egos, she had consoled herself with: But nothing's being hidden, everything's being said. And she had compared her own family with others (not with the Finchleys, they were beyond comparison, they had their own laws), and all families with adolescents were like this. At the hub of each was a mother, a woman, sparks flying off her in all directions as the psyches ground together like pebbles on a beach in a storm. She had been over-anxious about dominating, controlling, keeping them younger than they should be? She had been as anxious about giving them too much freedom, treating them like adults too soon. But perhaps that was the fault, and Mary was right, who never gave a thought to *how* she should behave – she simply followed her mood. But it wasn't a question of domination or not. It was all to do with involvement. She had been too involved with everything, had sunk herself into it too far, so that the children had not had some strong fixed point to rely on? But surely the man, the father, should be that? Perhaps after all Michael had been right all the time, she had been wrong in criticizing him: his degree of involvement had been the right one. For why should it be necessary for a mother to be there like a grindstone at the heart of everything? Looking back it seemed as if she had been at everybody's beck and call, always available, always criticized, always being bled to feed these – monsters. Looking back at her own adolescence she could see nothing similar – of course, she had had a close, a very close, intimacy with her mother until she died, the year before the trip to Lourenço Marques, and her father had been away for most of the war, leaving the two, mother and daughter, together; but she could not believe it had been the same thing at all.

But what was the use of her sitting here balancing and sifting – making excuses? For Tim had cracked, shouting that she smothered him, she had made him into a baby, and the fact that this had not been just routine 'love-talk' – the family's own name for their criticisms of each other – was shown by everyone's reactions.

Very well then, she had been too dominant with him.

But the remarkable thing was that just as now, sitting on this moonlight balcony, she was quite aware of her current situation, standing as it were on a cliff with the north wind blowing straight into her face that would strip her of flesh and feature and colour, then, too, she had been aware, right from the start, of the danger to the last of a family when he was growing up. Clearly it was not enough to *know* a thing, otherwise he would not have screamed out: 'For Christ's sake leave me alone, you are suffocating me!'

All she had done was to tell him not to forget something, she couldn't now remember what . . . Had that been the point, it had been the *what*, and not the *how* of it? – but she couldn't remember, that had gone. Gone because she didn't want to remember, had arranged the incident so it could take its place among her official memories, memories that had stood in her mind for ten, fifteen, years; a quarter of a century? But certainly there *had* been a girl all vital energy and individuality, and much wider experience than most (for instance, there had been the year in Portuguese East Africa spent self-consciously, if not theatrically, as a *jeune fille*); a girl with the temperament that goes with being a redhead (she had been congratulated on possessing this temperament from her earliest childhood, *that* she could remember very clearly); a girl who had stood out, she knew she had, wherever she was, among others, not only by virtue of that dramatic colouring, but by her style and her manner – well, had any of that been untrue? She was deceiving herself in this description? – she did not think so. This girl, much coveted by a variety of men, had married her Michael. After first living together for a year (Phase One). They had become an attractive young couple, and a centre for others not yet married, or soon to be married, or married and lacking their – charm? Personality? This marriage had, however, been offered up as a charming, almost whimsical sacrifice to convention; they had continued to behave like a couple living together, in love, loving, lovable. The first baby had altered this, but not much. The baby (now Stephen) had been fitted into the life of an attractive young couple doing things rather more vitally than others. The baby accompanied them to parties, had travelled with them, had not prevented her from attending a course of lectures on Saracen influence in Provençal poetry. It was true that to continue living as if there had been no changes, with the wakings in the night, and the having to get up early, and the always being bound to the infant timetable, had been hard. But at the time this wrench in her habits had not seemed – as it did later – the important thing that was happening. When this first baby was a year old, she was pregnant. In the minds of both parents was the notion that they could continue living in this way with two children.

Anyone could have told them this was nonsense.

The real sharp change came not with the first, but with the second, baby. (Now a young woman called Eileen.) With one baby they had been a young married couple, still radiantly paying unforced tribute to foolish convention, to social demands. With the second the emphasis had sharply shifted. Seeing how different their life had become, they decided to have the third 'to get it over with' – a very different spirit; and they soon had a house, a mortgage, a small car, a regular charwoman, a regular life, all for the sake of the children. It was extraordinary for how long this couple continued to think of all these extraneous objects, car, house, and so on, as having nothing to do with them personally – not for their sakes at all, but only because of their children.

As for Kate, she was acquiring hard-to-come-by virtues, self-disciplines. Looking back now at the beautiful girl, indulged by her mother, indulged and flattered by her grandfather, treated always with that very slightly mocking deference which is offered to girls, and contrasting her with the same young woman of only five years later, she was tempted to cry out that it had all been a gigantic con-trick, the most monstrous cynicism. Looking back she could see herself only as a sort of fatted white goose. Nothing in the homage her grandfather paid womanhood, or in the way her mother had treated her, had prepared her for what she was going to have to learn, and soon.

With three small children, and then four, she had had to fight for qualities that had not been even in her vocabulary. Patience. Self-discipline. Self-control. Self-abnegation. Chastity. Adaptability to others – this above all. This always. These virtues, necessary for bringing up a family of four on a restricted income, she did slowly acquire. She had acquired the qualities before she had thought of giving names to them. She could remember very clearly the day when, reading certain words that seemed old-fashioned, in an old novel, she had thought: Well, that's what *this* is – getting up several times in a night for months at a time, and always good-temperedly; and that's what *that* is – not making love with Michael when a child was ill. And as for being a sponge for small wants year after year, so that anything that was not a child seemed a horizon too distant ever to be reached again – what was the word for that? She had been amused by big words for what every mother is expected to become. But virtues? Really? Really virtues? If so, they had turned on her, had become enemies. Looking back from the condition of being an almost middle-aged wife and mother to her condition as a girl when she lived with Michael, it seemed to her that she had acquired not virtues but a form of dementia.

On the morning after her youngest's outburst, it happened that she was out with a shopping-basket in the High Street, and she was held up in a brief traffic jam. She watched a young woman walk up the street with a baby in a push-chair. This girl, perhaps nineteen – about her own age when she had her first child – wore a brief skirt, had wild dark-red hair, green eyes, a calm energy. She looked, however, like a little girl playing at being Mum. She was pushing the baby along with one hand while she carried a vast bag of groceries in the other. She strode along like a viking's woman. From this girl Kate had turned her attention to others. It seemed as if the street was filled suddenly with young women, unmarried girls or girls with babies, and they all of them moved – yes, that was where you could see it, in how they moved – with a calm, casual, swinging grace, freedom. It was confidence. It was everything that she, Kate, had lost in excesses of self-consciousness, in awareness of the consequences of what she did.

Then, having most conscientiously absorbed the truth of these young women – it was painful, the contrasting of herself with them – she looked at the movements, at the faces, of her contemporaries. Twenty years was the difference, that was all it needed, to set these brave faces into caution, and suspicion. Or, they had a foolish good nature, the victim's good nature, and awful defenceless *niceness*, like the weak laugh that sounds as if it is going to ebb into tears. They moved as if their limbs had slowed because they were afraid of being trapped by something, afraid of knocking into something; they moved as if surrounded by invisible enemies.

Kate had spent the morning walking slowly up and down, up and down that long crammed street, taking in this truth, that the faces and movements of most middle-aged women are those of prisoners or slaves.

At one end of some long, totally involving experience, steps a young, confident, courageous girl; at the other, a middle-aged woman – herself.

Kate had then gone home and spent weeks watching herself move, talk, act, but from this other viewpoint, and had concluded, quite simply, that she was demented. She was obsessed, from morning till night, about management, about organization, about seeing how things ought to go, about the results of not acting like this or of acting like that. Watching herself, listening to herself, she turned her attention to the women of her own age, who were her friends. All, every one, had had a long education in just one thing, fussing. (Not Mary Finchley, of course. Not Mary. But she was going to have to understand what Mary meant to her, what she was standing for – obviously one couldn't simply exclude her from every normal category and leave it at that.) That was what all those years of acquiring *virtues* had led to: she and her contemporaries were machines set for one function, to manage and arrange and adjust and foresee and order and bother and worry and organize. To fuss.

Her family, she saw now, were quite aware of it. She was being treated by these independent individuals – husband, and young people only just free from the tyrannies of adolescent emotion and therefore all the more intolerant of other people's weakness – as something that had to be put up with. Mother was an uncertain quantity. She was like an

old nurse who had given her years to the family and must now be put up
with. The virtues had turned to vices, to the nagging and bullying of
other people. An unafraid young creature had been turned, through the
long, grinding process of always, always being at other people's beck
and call, always having to give out attention to detail, miniscule wants,
demands, needs, events, crises, into an obsessed maniac. Obsessed by
what was totally unimportant.

That realization had been three years ago. While continuing to run
the large and demanding house, running what she felt had become a
hotel or resthouse for the family and friends and friends' friends, she
tried to withdraw. It had been an inner withdrawal, since it was hardly
possible to announce her plan to do so without adding to the family's
irritation, to their feeling of being obligated to herself, the servant who
kept it all going. It was made harder because her efforts were not
noticed. Her husband had been particularly busy; and she could
understand that he was arranging to be, for in his position she would
take any chance to expand out, to go out and away from the narrowing
of middle age – he was older than she was, by seven years. The children
were quite naturally no more involved with her, her problems, than any
healthy young adults are with their parents. But she found that they
were always using mechanisms of defence against her in situations
where she had been trying to make them unnecessary. She had been
continually dragged back into – outgrown, she had hoped – patterns of
behaviour by people who still expected them of her.

But why should she not announce to the family that she was going to
change, was in the process of changing? She could not. They would see
it as a claim on their attention, their compassion. As she would have
done in their places – the point was, and here she was coming back to it
again, it was all nonsense, the out-in-the-open discussion and the talk
and the blueprinting and the making decisions to behave in this way or
that way. (That was not how people changed: they didn't change
themselves; you got changed by being made to live through something,
and then you found yourself changed.) But if all those years of 'love-
talk' had been any use at all, she now could have used it, could have
said: And now, enough. I'm like a cripple or an invalid after years of
being your servant, your doormat. Now help me. I need your help. But
she could not say this.

Soon after the incident of Tim's screaming at the supper-table, she had
gone away by herself to visit old friends. She left her daughter in charge.

She kept prolonging the visit, on all kinds of pretexts. She thought that if she could keep it up long enough, the pattern would be broken, the cage would be open . . . She went home earlier than she had planned, because Eileen decided to go off on a visit of her own.

Even though she had almost at once slid right back into what she had been flying from, she was able to look at herself, the worrying woman at whom the boy had shouted, as a creature who had been really mad. Crazy.

That summer, the scene at the supper-table, her going away, had been the begetter of this summer's event, for without them she would not have responded to Alan Post, not even with her husband's help – yes, his irritation with her for not leaping at the opportunity had been that. It is always a question, when in a cul-de-sac, a trap, of seeing what there is for you; one has to be listening.

But what had stopped her from saying that she wanted to take a room by herself somewhere in London for the months of summer? Nothing – except that it was inconceivable! It would have been so exaggerated a thing to demand that she wouldn't have thought of it; yet it was what, probably, she should have done.

She had needed a springboard.

She now sat on a balcony from which the moonlight had quite gone, looking up at a sky where stars stepped back into a cool grey, looking down into a street that was now really empty, at last. Now if she were alone, really alone, in this country, able to please herself . . . Yes, that is what she could have arranged for herself; it had never crossed her mind, of course.

She could have sat here while the dawn came up, then slept all day if she wanted, then wandered about this town, which was after all a Mediterranean port, as well as being a provider for tourists. She could have wandered on her own will, and returned home in two months' time, by herself, having been really alone – that is, a person operating from her own choices.

But now she sat in a cool dawn, thinking that she should go to bed because he would wake up fresh just as she was ready to collapse in sleep. And unless she was very much mistaken, she would be faced with a man on the defensive because he had keeled over the night before and gone to sleep and not made love as circumstances and convention demanded. Almost, she was able to hope that he was a little ill – not much, just a little.

At the end of the street a man came into sight. He was fair, a northern man – a tourist, like herself. He had been on the beach with the youngsters? Drinking? Dancing? He had been sitting talking in a café? In one of the cool, cellar-like bars? He came level with her balcony as the street lights went out. She saw him as a night figure caught out of his time by dawn: the sky was beginning faintly to flush and tingle. He was looking up at the sky. He was not young enough to have been with the young people. He was hard-bodied, in strong middle age, and his face was lined. No, he was older than that, his hair was quite white, it wasn't blond: he was a Spaniard, probably just finished with some night-work. He pushed his way through oleanders, and stopped at a fountain to splash water over his hands and face. He swallowed a mouthful or two by directing the flow with the edge of his palm straight to the back of his throat. Then he moved his hand so that the jet played on his lowered head. He shook his head energetically, and walked to a bench and lay on it, his face turned to its back, away from the street and from observers. He was a poor man then? Homeless? She was conscious of an upsurge of concern. This small spouting of emotion was like the falling tinkle of the fountain. Derisively she watched herself think, or feel, that she ought to go down into the square, and touch his shoulder – carefully of course, so as not to startle him – ask him if he needed something, offer help. In what language? She ought to learn Spanish!

The feeble spurt of emotion was the same as that which had led her, the winter after that dramatic scene with her son Tim, to take in a stray cat. Her emotions about this cat – while they had lasted – had been strong. She would not have been the product of all the years of 'love-talk' if she had not been able to say to herself: That cat represents me, is myself. I am looking after this poor cat because I feel I should be looked after. But by whom? By my family, of course! Who no longer need me, and who find me intolerable.

The family were aware of the cat's role, and her thoughts about it; aware of their part in it, their emotions. They had been humorous and indulgent. 'Oh, go on, you've taken in that smelly old cat just because we aren't being nice to you!'

'He's hit it on the head, Mother. You're just *showing* us, that's all.'

Sitting on that balcony, hundreds of miles away and over two years later, she wanted to spring up and shout out her rage and bitterness to them. At the time she had smiled, of course, been 'humorous'. Now she wished that she had slapped hard, her delightful daughter Eileen, her charming Michael, Tim – all of them. 'I wish I had hit him,' she heard herself mutter; 'I do, I wish I had hit them all hard!'

She had seen Mary Finchley scream abuse at her husband, at her children: afterwards she collapsed in laughter. Mary had done what she had felt like doing, at the time she felt like doing it.

The family had treated Kate like an invalid and the cat a medicine.

'Just the thing for the menopause,' she had heard Tim say to Eileen.

She had not started the menopause, but it would have been no use saying so: it had been useful, apparently, for the family's mythology to have a mother in the menopause. Sometimes she had felt like a wounded bird, being pecked to death by the healthy birds. Or like an animal teased by cruel children. And of course she felt she deserved it, because she disliked herself so much – oh, that had been an awful spring, to follow a bad winter. She had feared she was really crazy, she spent so much of her time angry. Then the two older ones had started to give their time entirely to university, to friends, and she had been delighted. Absolutely delighted, though of course she then felt guilty that she was delighted. Feeling guilty seems almost a definition of motherhood in this enlightened time. It was a lot of nonsense, it was all a lot of rubbish, all of it. Somewhere along the line they had gone wrong . . . Who? Herself? Not the children, of course not! Society? But *why* so much tension and antagonism and resentment? – it was over though. Eileen was busy with men; there was only Tim who still had his sights on her – that was how she felt it. So the nasty time was past. She looked back on it . . . But if that were really so, why was she here now, with this young man who Mary Finchley at least would have seen at first glance was going to offer her what she already knew, what she did not want . . . She did not leave the balcony until the sun's rim shot hot rays over the sea and into the town. She was really tired. Inside the room a blackness filled eyes that were adjusted to the day. Her eyes cleared and she saw that Jeffrey lay looking at her. She smiled, prepared for speech – saw that he was not really awake. He scrambled up, crouched on the bed, stared, a surprised animal, his dancer's limbs expressing the dream he must still be in, his face alert, suspicious, ready to turn itself aside. She said, carefully, 'Jeffrey!' – but he made a hot, confused, denying sound, and shot into the bathroom. She heard him being sick. She went on standing where she was, wondering if he would be awake when he came back. He came into the bedroom by dragging himself on the door frame, then the edge of a chest. He must feel himself alone, then; he saw her, lurched forward, clutched the bottom of the bed, stared. She was, she understood, outlined against the door on to the already dazzling balcony; she must seem a dark watching shape to him. At last he smiled: he knew he ought to know who she was. It was an effort, because he was three-parts asleep, but he was a polite person, he had been brought up to please, to offer courtesy. The smile was courtesy offered to a situation which demanded it and did not warm into pleasure. He manhandled himself into bed, and collapsed, asleep again immediately.

She sat by him in her white frilly robe that had on it the sweet coolness of the night air she had brought indoors away from this day's heat. She was swearing to herself that when she woke she would not be maternal, she would not suggest a doctor, she would not be concerned. Lying beside this young man, who she knew was at the least 'off-colour', if not ill, she tried to put herself into the frame of mind of a woman who had come here to be with him for love. Suppose that she were still 'a love woman' (this was how she put it) and not a maternal woman, as a result of a quarter of a century's nursery work – if she were this 'love woman', then how would she be feeling? That was easy – she had only to remember Michael. She would be waking Jeffrey to make love – she and her husband had enjoyed making love when she, but particularly he, had fever. He had tended to run temperatures for the least thing; and for years they had made the most of this condiment for eroticism – or so they had seen it. But she could not imagine approaching Jeffrey erotically. For one thing (as of course literature and all sorts of experts, marriage counsellors and the like, could have told her), if a woman is attuned well and truly to one man, then a new one doesn't come so easily. (For which reason she had never been able to believe in the easy pleasurability of wife-swopping and amiable adultery.) And, after all, her sexual experience had been with Michael – and, at second hand, through Mary.

Of course, if she had been madly in love, as the occasion de-manded, as even an aesthetic sense, a sense of the appropriate, demanded, she would not be lying here trying to imagine herself erotic.

She leaned on her elbow and examined him with all the caution of a mamma with sick child. He managed to suggest, even while his flesh flung out heat, that he was cold. There was a chill damp coming off his forehead. He smelled sickly. No, not even a woman madly in love could choose this moment to approach him. There was something about his present condition which was antipathetic to sex.

It was of course possible, indeed likely, that *he* was antipathetic to sex, at least in his present mood of worry about the future, or at least with her . . . The degree of her uninvolvement with him was confirmed by her coolness as she came to this conclusion.

She fell asleep and was at once on a rocky hillside. Yes, there was her poor seal, slowly, painfully, moving itself towards the distant, the invisible, ocean. She gathered the slippery creature up in her arms – oh, she ought not to have left it there. It was weaker; its dark eyes reproached her. Its skin was very dry; she must get some water for it. In the distance was a house. She staggered towards it. It was a wooden house, its roof steeply sloped for snow which – she knew – would soon fall, for it was already autumn. The house had no one in it, but people were living there, because, in a tiny fireplace, were embers of a fire that was going out. She laid down the seal on the stone before the fireplace and tried to blow the fire into life. There wasn't much wood, but she made the fire blaze at last. The seal lay quiet, its sides heaving painfully. Its eyes were closed. It needed water badly. She carried it to the bath-house and splashed water on it from the wooden buckets that stood along wooden walls – the dream's flavour was still, was more and more, that of another time; myth, or an old tale. The animal's eyes opened and it seemed to revive. She thought that there were many things she must do: she had to clean the house, to fetch wood for the fire from the forests before the winter snow came down, to get food, to take warm clothes out of the chests and lay them ready for herself and for the people in the house who, she knew, were her family, but transformed and transfigured into myth creatures, larger than themselves, representing more than they were in ordinary life. In an upper room of the house she saw a tall, fair young man with blue eyes. She knew him. He was her lover. He always had been. They made love. They had been waiting for years, and through waiting and wanting made this love perfect . . . She remembered the seal. The seal needed her, was lying abandoned on the floor of the bath-house, waiting for her. She left the fair young man, who was a nobleman of some kind, perhaps a prince, saying: 'I am sorry, I want to stay with you, but I must take the seal to the sea first.'

Shikasta

History of Shikasta, VOL. 3012, *The Century of Destruction.*
EXCERPT FROM SUMMARY CHAPTER.

During the previous two centuries, the narrow fringes on the north-west of the main landmass of Shikasta achieved technical superiority over the rest of the globe, and, because of this, conquered physically or dominated by other means large numbers of cultures and civilisations. The Northwest fringe people were characterised by a peculiar insensitivity to the merits of other cultures, an insensitivity quite unparalleled in previous history. An unfortunate combination of circumstances was responsible. (1) These fringe peoples had only recently themselves emerged from barbarism. (2) The upper classes enjoyed wealth, but had never developed any degree of responsibility for the lower classes, so the whole area, while immeasurably more wealthy than most of the rest of the globe, was distinguished by contrasts between extremes of wealth and poverty. This was not true for a brief period between Phases II and III of the Twentieth Century War. [SEE VOL. 3009, *Economies of Affluence.*] (3) The local religion was materialistic. This was again due to an unfortunate combination of circumstances: one was geographical, another the fact that it had been a tool of the wealthy classes for most of its history, another that it retained even less than most religions of what its founder had been teaching. [SEE VOLS. 998 and 2041, *Religions as Tools of Ruling Castes.*] For these and other causes, its practitioners did little to mitigate the cruelties, the ignorance, the stupidity, of the Northwest fringers. On the contrary, they were often the worst offenders. For a couple of centuries at least, then, a dominant feature of the Shikastan scene was that a particularly arrogant and self-satisfied breed, a minority of the minority white race, dominated most of Shikasta, a multitude of different races, cultures, and religions which, on the whole, were superior to that of the oppressors. These white Northwest fringers were like most conquerors of history in denuding what they had overrun, but they were better able than any other in their ability to persuade themselves that what they did was 'for the good' of the conquered: and it is here that the above-mentioned religion is mostly answerable.

World War I – to use Shikastan nomenclature (otherwise the First Intensive Phase of the Twentieth Century War) – began as a quarrel between the Northwest fringers over colonial spoils. It was distinguished by a savagery that could not be matched by the most backward of barbarians. Also by stupidity: the waste of human life and of the earth's products was, to us onlookers, simply unbelievable, even judged by Shikastan standards. Also by the total inability of the population masses to understand what was going on: propaganda on this scale was tried for the first time, using methods of indoctrination based on the new technologies, and was successful. What the unfortunates were told who had to give up life and property – or at the best, health – for this war, bore no relation at any time to the real facts of the matter; and while of course any local group or culture engaged in war persuades itself according to the exigencies of self-interest, never in Shikastan history, or for that matter on any planet – except for the planets of the Puttioran group – has deception been used on this scale.

This war lasted for nearly five of their years. It ended in a disease that carried off six times as many people as those killed in the actual fighting. This war slaughtered, particularly in the Northwest fringes, a generation of their best young males. But – potentially the worst result – it strengthened the position of the armament industries (mechanical, chemical, and psychological) to a point where from now on it had to be said that these industries dominated the economies and therefore the governments of all the participating nations. Above all, this war barbarised and lowered the already very low level of accepted conduct in what they referred to as 'the civilised world' – by which they meant, mostly, the Northwest fringes.

This war, or phase of the Twentieth Century War, laid the bases for the next.

Several areas, because of the suffering caused by the war, exploded into revolution, including a very large area, stretching from the Northwest fringes thousands of miles to the eastern ocean. This period saw the beginning of a way of looking at governments, judged 'good' and 'bad' not by performance, but by label, by name. The main reason was the deterioration caused by war: one cannot spend years sunk inside false and lying propaganda without one's mental faculties becoming impaired. (This is a fact that is attested to by every one of our emissaries to Shikasta!)

Their mental processes, for reasons not their fault never very impressive, were being rapidly perverted by their own usages of them.

The period between the end of World War I and the beginning of the Second Intensive Phase contained many small wars, some of them for the purpose of testing out the weapons shortly to be employed on a massive scale. As a result of the punitive suffering inflicted on one of the defeated contestants of World War I by the victors, a Dictatorship arose there – a result that might easily have been foreseen. The Isolated Northern Continent, conquered only recently by emigrants from the Northwest fringes, and conquered with the usual disgusting brutality, was on its way to becoming a major power, while the various national areas of the Northwest fringes, weakened by war, fell behind. Frenzied exploitation of the colonised areas, chiefly of Southern Continent I, was intensified to make up for the damages sustained because of the war. As a result, native populations, exploited and oppressed beyond endurance, formed resistance movements of all kinds.

The two great Dictatorships established themselves with total ruthlessness. Both spread ideologies based on the suppression and oppression of whole populations of differing sects, opinions, religions, local cultures. Both used torture on a mass scale. Both had followings all over the world, and these Dictatorships, and their followers, saw each other as enemies, as totally different, as wicked and contemptible – while they behaved in exactly the same way.

The time gap between the end of World War I and the beginning of World War II was twenty years.

Here we must emphasise that most of the inhabitants of Shikasta were not aware that they were living through what would be seen as a hundred-years' war, the century that would bring their planet to almost total destruction. We make a point of this, because it is nearly impossible for people with whole minds – those who have had the good fortune to live (and we must never forget that it is a question of our good fortune) within the full benefits of the substance-of-we-feeling – it is nearly impossible, we stress, to understand the mentation of Shikastans. With the world's cultures being ravaged and destroyed, from end to end, by viciously inappropriate technologies, with wars raging everywhere, with whole populations being wiped out, and deliberately, for the benefit of ruling castes, with the wealth of every nation being used almost entirely for war, for preparations for war, propaganda for war, research for war; with the general levels of decency and honesty visibly vanishing, with corruption everywhere – with all this, living in a nightmare of dissolution, was it really possible, it may be asked, for these poor creatures to believe that 'on the whole' all was well?

The reply is – yes. Particularly, of course, for those already possessed of wealth or comfort – a minority; but even those millions, those billions, the ever-increasing hungry and cold and unbefriended, for these, too, it was possible to live from meal to scant meal, from one moment of warmth to the next.

Those who were stirred to 'do something about it' were nearly all in the toils of one of the ideologies which were the same in performance, but so different in self-description. These, the active, scurried about like my unfortunate friend Taufiq, making speeches, talking, engaged in interminable processes that involved groups sitting around exchanging information and making statements of good intent, and always in the name of the masses, those desperate, frightened, bemused populations who knew that everything was wrong but believed that somehow, somewhere, things would come right.

It is not too much to say that in a country devastated by war, lying in ruins, poisoned, in a landscape blackened and charred under skies low with smoke, a Shikastan was capable of making a shelter out of broken bricks and fragments of metal, cooking himself a rat and drinking water from a puddle that of course tasted of oil and thinking 'Well, this isn't too bad after all . . .'

World War II lasted five years, and was incomparably worse in every way than the first. All the features of the first were present in the second, developed. The waste of human life now extended to mass extermination of civilian populations. Cities were totally destroyed. Agriculture was ruined over enormous areas. Again the armament industries flourished, and this finally established them as the real rulers of every geographical area. Above all, the worst wounds were inflicted in the very substance, the deepest minds, of the people themselves. Propaganda in every area, by every group, was totally unscrupulous, vicious, lying – and self-defeating – because in the long run, people could not believe the truth when it came their way. Under the Dictatorships, lies and propaganda *were* government. The maintenance of the dominance of the colonised parts was by lies and propaganda – these more effective and important than physical force; and the retaliation of the subjugated took the form, first of all and most importantly in influence, of lies and propaganda: this is what they had been taught by their conquerors. This war covered and involved the whole globe – the first war, or phase of the war, involved only part of it: there was no part of Shikasta by the end of World War II left unsubjected to untruth, lies, propaganda.

This war saw, too, the use of weapons that could cause total global destruction: it should go without saying, to the accompaniment of words like democracy, freedom, economic progress.

The degeneration of the already degenerate was accelerated.

By the end of World War II, one of the great Dictatorships was defeated – the same land area as saw the worst defeat in the first war. The Dictatorship which covered so much of the central landmass had been weakened, almost to the point of defeat, but survived, and made a slow, staggering recovery. Another vast area of the central landmass, to the east of this Dictatorship, ended half a century of local wars, civil wars, suffering, and over a century of exploitation and invasion by the Northwest fringes by turning to Dictatorship. The Isolated Northern Continent had been strengthened by the war and was now the major world power. The Northwest fringes on the whole had been severely weakened. They had to let go their grip of their colonies. Impoverished, brutalised – while being, formally, victors – they were no longer world powers. Retreating from these colonies they left behind technology, an idea of society based entirely on physical well-being, physical satisfaction, material accumulation – to cultures who, before encounter with these all-ravaging Northwest fringers, had been infinitely more closely attuned with Canopus than the fringers had ever been.

This period can be – is by some of our scholars – designated *The Age of Ideology*. [For this viewpoint SEE VOL. 3011, SUMMARY CHAPTER.]

The political groupings were all entrenched in bitterly defended ideologies.

The local religions continued, infinitely divided and subdivided, each entrenched in their ideologies.

Science was the most recent ideology. War had immeasurably strengthened it. Its ways of thought, in its beginnings flexible and open, had hardened, as everything must on Shikasta, and scientists, as a whole – we exclude individuals in this area as in all others – were as impervious to real experience as the religionists had ever been. Science, its basic sets of mind, its prejudices, gripped the whole globe and there was no appeal. Just as individuals of our tendencies of mind, our inclinations towards the truth, our 'citizens' had had to live under the power and the threat of religions who would use any brutalities to defend their dogmas, so now individuals with differing inclinations and needs from those tolerated by science had to lead silent or prudent lives, careful of offending the bigotries of the scientific global governing class: in the service of national governments and therefore of war – an invisible global ruling caste, obedient to the warmakers. The industries that made weapons, the armies, the scientists who served them – these could not be easily attacked, since the formal picture of how the globe was run did not include this, the real picture. Never has there been such a totalitarian, all-pervasive, all-powerful governing caste anywhere: and yet the citizens of Shikasta were hardly aware of it, as they mouthed slogans and waited for their deaths by holocaust. They remained unaware of what 'their' governments were doing, right up to the end. Each national grouping developed industries, weapons, horrors of all kinds, that the people knew nothing about. If glimpses were caught of these weapons, then government would deny they existed. [SEE *History of Shikasta*, VOLS. 3013, 3014, and CHAPTER 9 this volume, Use of Moon as Military Base.] There were space probes, space weapons, explorations of planets, use of planets, rivalries over their moon, about which the populations were not told.

And here is the place to say that the mass of the populations, the average individual, were, was, infinitely better, more sane, than those who ruled them: most would have been appalled at what was being done by 'their' representatives. It is safe to say that if even a part of what was being kept from them had come to their notice, there would have been mass risings across the globe, massacres of the rulers, riots . . . unfortunately, when peoples are helpless, betrayed, lied to, they possess no weapons but the (useless) ones of rioting, looting, mass murder, invective.

During the years following the end of World War II, there were many 'small' wars, some as vicious and extensive as wars in the recent past described as major. The needs of the armament industries, as much as ideology, dictated the form and intensities of these wars. During this period savage exterminations of previously autonomous 'primitive' peoples took place, mostly in the Isolated Southern Continent (otherwise known as Southern Continent II). During this period colonial risings were used by all the major powers for their own purposes. During this period psychological methods of warfare and control of civilian populations developed to an extent previously undreamed of.

Here we must attempt to underline another point which it is almost impossible for those with our set of mind to appreciate.

When a war was over, or a phase of war, with its submersion in the barbarous, the savage, the degrading, Shikastans were nearly all able to perform some sort of mental realignment that caused them to 'forget.' This did not mean that wars were not idols, subjects for pious mental exercises of all sorts. Heroisms and escapes and braveries of local and limited kinds were raised into national preoccupations, which were in fact forms of religion. But this not only did not assist, but prevented, an understanding of how the fabric of cultures had been attacked and destroyed. After each war, a renewed descent into barbarism was sharply visible – but apparently cause and effect were not connected, in the minds of Shikastans.

After World War II, in the Northwest fringes and in the Isolated Northern Continent, corruption, the low level of public life, was obvious. The two 'minor' wars conducted by the Isolated Northern Continent reduced its governmental agencies, even those visible and presented to the public inspection, to public scandal. Leaders of the nation were murdered. Bribery, looting, theft, from the top of the pyramids of power to the bottom, were the norm. People were taught to live for their own advancement and the acquisition of goods. Consumption of food, drink, every possible commodity was built into the economic structure of every society. [VOL. 3009, *Economies of Affluence.*] And yet these repulsive symptoms of decay were not seen as direct consequences of the wars that ruled their lives.

During the whole of the Century of Destruction, there were sudden reversals: treaties between nations which had been at war, so that these turned their hostilities on nations only recently allies; secret treaties between nations actually at war; enemies and allies constantly changing positions, proving that the governing factor was in the need for war, as such. During this period every major city in the northern hemisphere lived inside a ring of terror: each had anything up to thirty weapons aimed at it, every one of which could reduce it and its inhabitants to ash in seconds – pointed from artificial satellites in the skies, directed from underwater ships that ceaselessly patrolled the seas, directed from land bases perhaps halfway across the globe. These were controlled by machines which everyone knew were not infallible – and everybody knew that more than once the destruction of cities and areas had been avoided by a 'miracle.' But the populations were never told how often these 'miracles' had taken place – near-lethal accidents between machines in the skies, collisions between machines under the oceans, weapons only *just* not unleashed from the power bases. Looking from outside at this planet it was as if at a totally crazed species.

In large parts of the northern hemisphere was a standard of living that had recently belonged only to emperors and their courts. Particularly in the Isolated Northern Continent, the wealth was a scandal, even to many of their own citizens. Poor people lived there as the rich have done in previous epochs. The continent was heaped with waste, with wreckage, with the spoils of the rest of the world. Around every city, town, even a minor settlement in a desert, rose middens full of discarded goods and food that in other less favoured parts of the globe would mean the difference between life and death to millions. Visitors to this continent marvelled – but at what people could be taught to believe was their due, and their right.

This dominant culture set the tone and standard for most of Shikasta. For regardless of the ideological label attaching to each national area, they all had in common that technology was the key to all good, and that good was always material increase, gain, comfort, pleasure. The real purposes of life – so long ago perverted, kept alive with such difficulty by us, maintained at such a cost – had been forgotten, were ridiculed by those who had ever heard of them, for distorted inklings of the truth remained in the religions. And all this time the earth was being despoiled. The minerals were being ripped out, the fuels wasted, the soils depleted by an improvident and short-sighted agriculture, the animals and plants slaughtered and destroyed, the seas being filled with filth and poison, the atmosphere was corrupted – and always, all the time, the propaganda machines thumped out: more, more, more, drink more, eat more, consume more, discard more – in a frenzy, a mania. These were maddened creatures, and the small voices that rose in protest were not enough to halt the processes that had been set in motion and were sustained by greed. By the lack of substance-of-we-feeling.

But the extreme riches of the northern hemisphere were not distributed evenly among their own populations, and the less favoured classes were increasingly in rebellion. The Isolated Northern Continent and the Northwest fringe areas also included large numbers of dark-skinned people brought in originally as cheap labour to do jobs disdained by the whites – and while these did gain, to an extent, some of the general affluence, it could be said that looking at Shikasta as a whole, it was the white-skinned that did well, the dark-skinned poorly.

And this *was* said, of course, more and more loudly by the dark-skinned, who hated the white-skinned exploiters as perhaps conquerors have never before been hated.

Inside each national area everywhere, north and south, east and west, discontent grew. This was not only because of the gap between the well off and the poor, but because their way of life, where augmenting consumption was the only criterion, increasingly saddened and depressed their real selves, their hidden selves, which were unfed, were ignored, were starved, were lied to, by almost every agency around them, by every authority they had been taught to, but could not, respect.

Increasingly the two main southern continents were torn by wars and disorders of every kind – sometimes civil wars between blacks, sometimes between blacks and remnants of the old white oppression, and between rival sects and juntas and power groups. Local dictators abounded. Vast territories were denuded of forests, species of animals destroyed, tribes murdered or dispersed . . .

War. Civil War. Murder. Torture. Exploitation. Oppression and suppression. And always lies, lies, lies. Always in the name of progress, and equality and development and democracy.

The main ideology all over Shikasta was now variations on this theme of economic development, justice, equality, democracy.

Not for the first time in the miserable story of this terrible century, this particular ideology – economic justice, equality, democracy, and the rest – took power at a time when the economy of an area was at its most disrupted: the Northwest fringes became dominated by governments 'of the left,' which presided over a descent into chaos and misery.

The formerly exploited areas of the world delighted in this fall of their former persecutors, their tormentors – the race that had enslaved them, enserfed them, stolen from them, above all, despised them because of their skin colour and destroyed their indigenous cultures now at last beginning to be understood and valued . . . but too late, for they had been destroyed by the white race and its technologies.

There was no one to rescue the Northwest fringes, in the grip of grindingly repetitive, dogmatic Dictatorships, all unable to solve the problems they had inherited – the worst and chief one being that the empires that had brought wealth had not only collapsed, leaving them in a vacuum, but had left behind false and unreal ideas of what they were, their importance in the global scale. Revenge played its part, not an inconsiderable part, in what was happening.

Chaos ruled. Chaos economic, mental, spiritual – I use this word in its exact, Canopean sense – ruled while the propaganda roared and blared from loudspeaker, radio, television.

The time of the epidemics and diseases, the time of famine and mass deaths had come.

On the main landmass two great Powers were in mortal combat. The Dictatorship that had come into being at the end of World War I, in the centre, and the Dictatorship that had taken hold of the eastern areas now drew into their conflict most of Shikasta, directly or indirectly. The younger Dictatorship was stronger. The older one was already in decline, its empire fraying away, its populations more and more in revolt or sullen, its ruling class increasingly remote from its people – processes of growth and decay that had in the past taken a couple of centuries now were accomplished in a few decades. This Dictatorship was not able to withstand the advance of the eastern Dictatorship whose populations were bursting its boundaries. These masses overran a good part of the older Dictatorship, and then overran, too, the Northwest fringes, in the name of a superior ideology – though in fact this was but a version of the predominating ideology of the Northwest fringes. The new masters were clever, adroit, intelligent; they foresaw for themselves the dominance of all the main landmass of Shikasta, and the continuance of that dominance.

But meanwhile the armaments piled up, up, up . . .

The war began in error. A mechanism went wrong, and major cities were blasted into death-giving dusts. That something of this kind was bound to happen had been plentifully forecast by technicians of all countries . . . but the Shammat influences were too strong.

In a short time, nearly the whole of the northern hemisphere was in ruins. Very different, these, from the ruins of the second war, cities which were rapidly rebuilt. No, these ruins were uninhabitable, the earth around them poisoned.

Weapons that had been kept secret now filled the skies, and the dying survivors, staggering and weeping and vomiting in their ruins, lifted their eyes to watch titanic battles being fought, and with their last breaths muttered of 'Gods' and 'Devils' and 'Angels' and 'Hell'.

Underground were shelters, sealed against radiation, poisons, chemical influences, deadly sound impulses, death rays. They had been built for the ruling classes. In these a few did survive.

In remote areas, islands, places sheltered by chance, a few people survived.

The populations of all the southern continents and islands were also affected by pestilence, by radiations, by soil and water and contamination, and were much reduced.

Within a couple of decades, of the billions upon billions of Shikasta perhaps 1 percent remained. The substance-of-we-feeling, previously shared among these multitudes, was now enough to sustain, and keep them all sweet, and whole, and healthy.

The inhabitants of Shikasta, restored to themselves, looked about, could not believe what they saw – and wondered *why* they had been mad.

*   *   *

INDIVIDUAL FIVE (*Terrorist Type 12*)

X was the son of rich parents, business people who had made a fortune through armaments and industries associated with war: World War I provided the basis of this fortune. His parents had both been married several times, he had known no family life, had been emotionally self-sufficient since a small child. He spoke many languages, could claim citizenship from several countries. Was he Italian, German, Jewish, Armenian, Egyptian? He was any one of these, at his convenience.

A man of talent and resources, he could have become an efficient part of the machinery of death that was his inheritance, but he would not, could not, be any man's heir.

He was fifteen when he brought off several coups of blackmail – emotional legerdemain – among the ramifications of his several families' businesses. These showed the capacity to analyse; a cold far-sightedness, an indifference to personal feelings. He was one of those unable to separate an individual from her, his circumstances. The man who was his real father (though he did not think of him as such, claimed a man met half a dozen times almost casually, whose conversation had illuminated his life, as 'father'), this ordinary, harassed, anxious man, who died in middle age of a heart attack, one of the richest men in the world, was seen by him as a monster, because of the circumstances he had been born into. X had never questioned this attitude: could not. For him, a man or a woman *was* his, her circumstances, actions. Thus guilt was ruled out for him; it was a word he could not understand, not even by the processes of imaginative effort. He had never made the attempt to understand the people of his upbringing: they were all rotten, evil. His own milieu, the 'network,' was his family.

Meeting The Brand was important to him. He was twelve years younger than she was. He studied her adventures with the total absorption others might bring to 'God,' or some absolute.

First there had been that casually met man whose ruthless utterances seemed to him the essence of wisdom. Then there was The Brand.

When they had sexual relations – almost at once, since for her sex was an appetite to be fed, and no more – he felt confirmed in his deepest sense of himself: the cold efficiency of the business, never far from perversity, seemed to him a statement of what life was.

He had never felt warmth for any human being, only admiration, a determination to understand excellence, as he defined it.

He did not want, or claim, attention from the public or the press or any propaganda instrument: the world was contemptible to him. But when he had pulled off, with or without the 'network' (he often worked alone, or with The Brand), a coup that was always inside the empire of one of his families, he would leave his mark, so that they should know whom they had to thank: an X, like that of an illiterate.

In bed with The Brand, he would trace an X over the raised pattern of the concentration camp number on her forearm, particularly in orgiastic moments.

He was never caught. Later, he joined one of the international police forces that helped to govern Shikasta in its last days.

INDIVIDUAL SIX (*Terrorist Type 8*)

The parents of this individual were in camps of various kinds throughout World War II. The father was Jewish. That they survived at all was 'impossible.' There are thousands of documents testifying to these 'impossible' survivals, each one a history of dedication to survival, inner strength, cunning, courage – and luck. These two did not leave the domain of the camps – they were in a forced labour camp in the eastern part of the Northwest fringes for the last part of the war – until nearly five years after the war ended. There was no place for them. By then the individual who concerns us here had been born, into conditions of near starvation, and cold: *impossible* conditions. He was puny, damaged, but was able to function. There were no siblings: the parents' vitality had been exhausted by the business of setting themselves up, with the aid of official charitable organisations, as a family unit in a small town where the father became an industrial worker. They were frugal, careful, wary, husbanding every resource: people such as these understand, above all, what things cost, what life costs. Their love for the child was gratitude for continued existence: nothing unthinking, animal, instinctive, about this love. He was to them something that had been rescued – impossibly – from disaster.

The parents did not make friends easily: their experience had cut them off from the people around them, all of whom had been reduced to the edge of extinction by the war – but few had been in the camps. The parents did not often speak about their years in the camps, but when they did, what they said took hold of the child with the strength of an alternative vision. What did these two rooms they lived in, poor, but warm and safe, have to do with that nightmare his parents spoke of? Sometimes at this time of life, youngsters in the grip of glandular upheaval crystallise in opposition to their parents with a vigour that preserves opposition for the rest of their lives.

This boy looked at his parents, and was appalled. *How was it possible?* was his thought.

I digress here to the incredulity referred to in my report on Individual Three, who spent years examining the deprivations of the people around him with: *How is it possible? I simply don't believe it!* Meaning partly: Why do they put up with it? Meaning, too: That human beings should treat each other like this? I don't believe it!

In Individual Six this incredulity was wider far than that of Individual Three, who saw the streets around him, then a town, and could only with difficulty envisage the Northwest fringes, let alone the central landmass, the world: it took years of experience in the war to enlarge his boundaries.

But Individual Six felt *himself* to be the war, and the war had been a global event: had printed his vision of life as a system of interlocking, interacting processes.

From the time he first began to think for himself, he was unable to see the developments of events as the generation before his had done. There was no such thing as a 'guilty nation,' any more than there could be defeated or victorious nations. A single nation could not be solely responsible for what it did, since groups of nations were a whole, interacting as a whole. The geographical area called 'Germany' – it had become another name for wickedness – could not be responsible entirely for the mass murders and brutalities it had perpetrated: how could it be, when one day with the facts in a library was enough to show that 'World War II' was multicaused, an expression of the whole of the Northwest fringes, a development of 'World War I.' *How was it possible* that these old people saw things in this isolated piecemeal way, like children, or like idiots! They were simple-minded. They were stupid! Above all, *they did not seem to have any idea at all of what they were like*.

A boy of fifteen imposed on himself a regime completely distressing to his parents. He did not have a room of his own, but there was a folding bed in the kitchen, and this he covered with what they had been given in the camps: a single, thin, dirty blanket. He shaved his head, and kept it shaved. On one day a week he ate only the diet provided in the camp during the final days of the war: hot greasy water, potato peelings, scraps from rubbish bins. He was careful, not to say obsessed, in getting his 'food' for himself, and put the filthy stuff on the table at mealtimes, eating reverently – a sacrament. Meanwhile, his parents ate their frugal meals; their damaged stomachs could not absorb normal amounts of food. He read to them passages from biographies, accounts of conditions in camps, the negotiations or lack of them that led to 'World War II' – always stressing multicause and effect: if that nation had done that, then this would not have happened. If such and such warnings had been heeded . . . that step taken . . . that statesman listened to . . .

For these poor people it was as if a nightmare they had escaped from only by a miracle had returned and was taking over their lives. They had made for themselves a little sheltered place, where they could believe themselves kept safe, because evil was the property of that other place, or that other nation; wickedness was contained in the past, in history – terror might come again, but thank God, that would be the future, and by then with luck, they would be dead and safe . . . and now their refuge was being broken open, not by 'history' or 'the future,' but by this precious child of theirs, who was all they had been able to bring out from the holocaust.

The father begged him to take his truths elsewhere.

'Are they true or not?' the youngster challenged.

'Yes . . . no . . . I don't care, for *God's* sake . . .'

'You don't care!'

'Your mother . . . you don't know what she had to put up with, go easy on her!'

The boy added to his discipline by wearing, on certain days of the week, dirty rags and tatters. All over the walls of the kitchen, which after all was the only room he had, and he was entitled to consider them his, were a thousand pictures of the concentration camps, but not only those of the Northwest fringes: soon the pictured record of the atrocious treatment of man by man covered the walls.

He sat quiet at the table, his father and mother hastily eating their meal in a silence that was a prayer he would not 'begin again' – and then he *would* begin again, reciting facts, figures, litanies of destruction, deaths by ill treatment and torture in communist countries, non-communist countries, any country anywhere.

[SEE *History of Shikasta*, VOL. 3011, *The Age of Ideology*, 'Self-Portraits of Nations.' Geographical areas, or temporary associations of peoples for the purposes of defence or aggression. Such an entity capable of believing itself different, better, more 'civilised' than another, when in fact to an outside view there is nothing to choose between them. And VOL. 3010, *Psychology of the Masses*, 'Self-Protective Mechanisms.']

Through a series of chances, it had become impossible for this youngster to identify himself with national myths and self-flatteries. He literally could not understand how others did. He believed that they must be pretending, or were being wilfully cowardly. He was of that generation – part of a generation – who could not see a newspaper except as a screen for lies, automatically translated any television newscast or documentary into what the truth *probably* was, reminded himself all the time, as a religious person might remind himself of the wiles of the Devil, that what was being fed to the world or nation about any event was by definition bound to be only a small part of real information, knew that at no time, anywhere, was the population of a country told the truth: facts about events trickled into general consciousness much later, if ever.

All this was good, was a step towards freedom from the miasmas of Shikasta.

But it was useless to him, for he had no kindness.

He was intolerable to his parents. The mother, still only a middle-aged woman by ordinary reckoning, seemed old to herself, became ill, had a heart attack. The father remonstrated, pleaded, even used words like: Spare her, spare us.

The stern avenging angel of righteousness remained in the meagre rooms that held the family, his eyes fixed in unbelieving dislike on his parents: How is it possible that you are like this!

At last his father said to him that if he could not treat his mother – 'Yes, and me too! I admit it!' – more gently, then he must leave home.

The boy was sixteen. They are throwing me out! he exulted, for everything he knew was being confirmed.

He found himself a room in the home of a school friend, and thereafter did not see his parents.

At school he set himself to be an unsettling presence. It was an ordinary small-town school, providing nothing remarkable for its pupils in the way of teachers and teachings. He sat at the back of a class and emanated a punishing dislike, arms folded, legs stretched to one side, maintaining a steady unblinking stare first at one target, and then at another. He would rise to his feet, first having most correctly held his hand up to ask permission: 'Is it not a fact that . . . ? Are you perhaps unaware . . . ? You are of course familiar with Government Report No. XYZ . . . ? I take it that such and such a book will be part of the curriculum for this subject? No? But how can that be possible?'

He was feared by the staff, and by most of the pupils, but some of these admired him. At this time, when every kind of extreme political group tormented the authorities, and 'the youth' was by definition a threat, he had not reached his seventeenth year when his name was known to the police, for the headmaster had mentioned him to them with the air of one covering himself against future probabilities.

He drifted towards various groups first right-wing and unaffiliated to a political party, then fell in with a left-wing revolutionary group. But this had very specific allegiances: this country was good, that bad, this creed abhorrent, this one 'correct.' Again he was saying; 'But surely you must be aware . . . ? Have you not read . . . ? Don't you know that . . . ?' It was clear that he would have to form his own group, but he was in no hurry. To keep himself he pilfered, and took part in various petty crimes. He was indifferent about how he came by a couple of months in a flat somewhere, or free meals for a week, or a girlfriend. He was completely, even amiably, amoral. Accused of some lie or theft he might allow himself a smile that commented unfavourably on everything around him. His reputation among the political groups was still unformed, but on the whole he was seen as clever, as skilful at surviving in ways respected by them, but careless.

When his group of a dozen young men and women crystallised out finally it was not on the basis of any particular political creed. Everyone had been formed by experiences of emotional or physical deprivation, had been directly affected by war. None could do anything but fix the world with a cold, hating eye: *This is what you are like.* They did not dream of utopias in the future: their imaginations were not tuned to the future at all, unlike those of previous revolutionaries or religionists: it was not that 'next year, or in the next decade, or next century, we create paradise on earth . . .' only, '*This* is what you are like.' When this hypocritical lying, miserably stupid system was done away with, then everyone would be able to see . . .

It was their task to expose the system for what it was.

But they had a faith, and no programme. They had the truth – but what to do with it? They had a vocabulary, but no language.

They watched the exploits of guerrilla groups, the deeds of the terrorists.

They saw that what was needed was to highlight situations, events.

They staged the kidnapping of a certain politician who had been involved in some transaction they disapproved of, demanding the release of a man in prison who seemed to them innocent. They detailed the reasons why this imprisoned man was innocent, and when he was not released, shot their hostage and left him in the town square. *This is what you are like* was what they felt, as they murdered him, meaning, the world.

The murder had not been planned. The details of the kidnapping had been adequately worked out, but they had not expected they would kill the politician, had half believed that the authorities would hand over their 'innocent.' There was something careless, unthought-out about the thing, and several of the members of the group demanded a more 'serious' approach, analyses, reconsideration.

Our Individual Six listened to them, with his characteristic careless smile, but his black eyes deadly. 'Of course, what else can be expected from people like you?' he was communicating.

Two of the protesting individuals met with 'accidents' in the next few days, and he now commanded a group that did not think of him as 'careless' – or not as they had done previously.

There were nine of them, three women.

One of the women thought of herself as 'his,' but he refused to accept this view of the situation. They had group sex, in every sort of combination. It was violent, ingenious, employing drugs and weapons of various kinds. Sticks of gelignite, for instance. Four of the group blew themselves up in an orgy. He did not recruit others.

It was observed by the four remaining that he had enjoyed the publicity. He insisted on staging a 'funeral service' which, although police did not know which group had been responsible for this minor massacre, was asking for notice and arrest. Elegies for the dead, poems, drawings of a heroic nature were left in the warehouse where the 'socialist requiem' was held.

By then it had occurred to them that he was mad, but it was too late for any of them to leave the group.

They staged another kidnapping. The carelessness of it amounted to contempt, and they were caught and put on trial. It was a trial that undermined the country, because of their contempt for the law, for legal processes.

At that time, throughout the Northwest fringes, almost every person regarded the processes of the law as a frail – the frailest possible – barrier between themselves and a total brutal anarchy.

Everyone knew that 'civilisation' depended on the most fragile supports. The view of the older people of what was happening in the world was no less fearful, in its way, than that of the young ones like Individual Six and his group, or of the other terrorists, but it was opposite in effect. They knew that the slightest pressure, even an accident or something unintended, could bring down the entire fabric . . . and here were these madmen, these young idiots, prepared to risk everything – more, *intending* to bring it down, *wanting* to destroy and waste. If people like Individual Six 'could not believe it,' then ordinary citizens 'could not believe it' either: they never did understand each other.

When the five were brought to trial and stood in the dock loaded with chains, and behind barriers of extra bars, they reached their fulfilment, the apex of achievement.

'This is what you are like,' they were saying to the world. 'These brutal chains, these bars, the fact that you will give us sentences that will keep us behind bars for the rest of our lives – this is what *you* are like! Regard your mirror, in us!'

In prison, and in court, they were elated, victorious, singing and laughing, as if at a festival.

About a year after sentence, Individual Six and two others escaped. They went their separate ways. Individual Six got fat, wore a wig, and acquired a correct clerkly appearance. He did not contact either the escaped members of his group or those in prison. He hardly thought of them: that was the past!

He deliberately courted danger. He would stand chatting to policemen on the street. He went into police stations to report minor crimes, such as the theft of a bicycle. He was arrested for speeding. He actually appeared in court on one charge. All this with a secret glowing contempt: this is what you are like, stupid, incompetent . . .

He went back to the town he had grown up in, and got an undemanding job, and made a life for himself that lacked any concealment except for the change of name and appearance. People recognised him, and he was talked about. Knowing this gave him pleasure.

His father was now in an institution for the elderly and incapacitated, his mother having died, and, hearing his son was in town, he took to hanging about the streets in the hope of seeing him. He did, but Individual Six waved his hand in a jolly, friendly, don't-bother-me-now gesture, and walked on.

He was expecting from his inevitable rearrest a trial of the same degree of publicity as his first. He wanted that moment when he would stand chained, like a dog, behind double bars. But when he was arrested, he was sent back to jail to serve his sentence.

An elation, a lunacy – which had been carrying him up, up, up, from the moment of truth when he had first seen what the world was like, had 'had his eyes opened' – suddenly dissolved, and he committed suicide.

INDIVIDUAL SEVEN (*Terrorist Type 5*)

This was a child of rich parents, manufacturers of an internationally known household commodity of no use whatsoever, contributing nothing except to the economic imperative: thou shalt consume.

She had a brother, but as they were at different schools and it was not thought important that they should meet, she had little physical or emotional contact with him after early childhood.

She was unhappy, unnurtured, without knowing what was wrong with her. When she reached adolescence she saw there was no central place in the family, no place where responsibility was taken: no father, or mother, or brother – who never had any other destiny but to be his father's heir – imposed themselves on circumstances. They were passive in the face of events, ideas, fashions, expected conduct. When she had understood it – and she could not believe how she had taken so long – she saw that she was the only one of her family who thought like this. It occurred to none that it was ever possible to say 'no.' She saw them and herself as bits of paper or refuse blown along streets.

She did not hate them. She did not despise them. She found them irrelevant.

She went to university for three years. There she enjoyed the double life of such young people: democratic and frugal in the university, and the luxuriousness of an indulged minority to whom everything was possible, at home.

She was not interested in what she was taught, only in whom she met. She drifted in and out of political sects, all on the left. She used in them the cult vocabulary obligatory in those circles, the same in all of them – and they might very well be enemies at various times.

What they all had in common was that 'the system' was doomed. And would be replaced by people like themselves, who were different.

These groups, and there were hundreds of them in the Northwest fringes – we are not now considering other parts of the world – were free to make up their own programmes, frameworks of ideas, exactly as they liked, without reference to objective reality. (This girl never saw for instance that during her years among the groups she was as passively accepting as she had ever been in her family.) [SEE *History of Shikasta*, VOL. 3011, *The Age of Ideology*, 'Pathology of Political Groups.'']

From the time the dominant religions lost their grip not only in the Northwest fringes, but everywhere throughout Shikasta, there was a recurrent phenomenon among young people: as they came to young adulthood and saw their immediate predecessors with the cold unliking eye that was the result of the breakdown of the culture into barbarism, groups of them would suddenly, struck for the first time by 'truth,' reject everything around them and seek in political ideology (emotionally this was of course identical to the reaction of groups that continuously formed and re-formed under the religious tyrannies) solutions to their situation, always seen as new-minted with themselves. Such a group would come into existence overnight, struck by a vision of the world believed by them to be entirely original, and within days they would have framed a philosophy, a code of conduct, lists of enemies and allies, personal, intergroup, national, and international. Inside a cocoon of righteousness, for the essence of it was that they were in the right, these young people would live for weeks, months, even years. And then the group would subdivide. Exactly as a stem branches, lightning branches, cells divide. But their emotional identification with the group was such that it prohibited any examination of the dynamics which must operate in groups. While studies by psychologists, researchers of all kinds, the examiners of the mechanics of society, became every day more intelligent, comprehensive, accurate, these conclusions were never applied to political groups – any more than it had ever been possible to apply a rational eye to religious behaviour while the religions maintained tyrannies, or for religious groups to apply such ideas to themselves. Politics had joined the realm of the sacred – the tabooed. The slightest examination of history showed that every group without exception was bound to divide and subdivide like amoeba, and could not help doing this, but when it happened it was always to the accompaniment of cries of 'traitor,' 'treachery,' 'sedition,' and similar mindless noises. For the member of any such group to suggest that the laws known (in other areas) must be operating here, was treachery; and such a person would be instantly flung out, exactly as had happened inside religions and religious groups, with curses and violent denunciations and emotionalism – not to mention physical torture or even death. Thus it came about that in this infinitely subdivided society, where different sets of ideas could exist side by side without their affecting each other – or at least not for long periods – the mechanisms like parliaments, councils, political parties, groups championing minority ideas, could remain unexamined, tabooed from examination of a cool rational sort, while in another area of the society, psychologists and sociologists could be receiving awards and recognition for work, which were it to be applied, would destroy this structure entirely.

When Individual Seven left university, nothing she had learned there seemed of any relevance to her. Her family expected her to marry a man like her father or her brother, or to take a job of an unchallenging kind. It seemed to her, suddenly, that she was nothing at all, and nothing of interest lay ahead of her.

This was a time when 'demonstrations' took place continually. The populace was always taking to the streets to shout out the demands of the hour.

She had taken part in demonstrations at university, and, looking back on them, it seemed to her that during the hours of running and chanting, of shouting and singing, in great crowds, she had been more alive and feeling than ever in her entire life.

She took to slipping away from home when there were demonstrations for a few hours of intoxication. It did not matter what the occasion was, or the cause. Then, by chance, she found herself at the front of a crowd fighting the police, and soon she was engaged in a hand-to-hand struggle with a policeman, a young man who grabbed her, called her insulting names, and tossed her like a bundle of rags into the arms of another, who threw her back. She screamed and struggled, and she was dragged away from the police like a trophy and found herself with a young man whose name she knew as 'a leader'.

He was a common type of that time: narrow-minded, ill-informed, dogmatic, humourless – a fanatic who could exist only in a group. She admired him completely and without reservation, and had sex with him that night before returning home. He was indifferent to her, but made a favour of it.

She now set herself to win this youth. She wanted to be 'his woman.' He was flattered when it became known that this girl was the daughter of one of the city's – no, the Northwest fringes' – rich families. But he was stern, even brutal with her, making it a test of her devotion to the cause (and himself, for he saw these as the same) that she should engage herself more and more in dangerous activity. This was not the serious, well-planned type of feat, or coup planned by terrorists type 12, or 3. He demanded of her that she should be with him in the forefront of demonstrations, and fling herself at lines of police, that she should shout and scream louder than the other girls, that she should struggle in the hands of the police, who in fact enjoyed these hysterical women. He was demanding of her, in fact, an ever-increasing degree of voluntary degradation.

She enjoyed it. More and more her life was spent dealing with the police. He was always being arrested, and she was in and out of police stations standing bail, or going with him in police wagons, or handing out leaflets about him and associates. These activities came to the notice of her parents, but after consultation with other parents, they consoled themselves with the formula: young people will be young people. She was furious at their attitude: she was not being taken seriously. Her lover took her seriously. So did the police. She allowed herself to be arrested and spent some days in jail. Once – twice – three times. And then her parents insisted on bailing her out and so she was always leaving 'her man' and her comrades in police cells while she was being driven home behind a chauffeur in one of the family cars.

She changed her name, and left home, insisting that she should live with her man. Which meant, a group of twelve or so young people. She accepted everything, living in a filthy hovel that had been condemned years before. She exulted in the discomfort, the dirt. She found herself cooking and cleaning and waiting on her man and his friends. They took a certain pleasure in this, because of her background, but she felt she was taken seriously, even that she was being forgiven.

Her parents found her, came after her, and she sent them away. They insisted on opening bank accounts for her, despatching messengers with cash, food, artefacts of all kinds, clothes. They were giving her what they had always given her – *things*.

Her lover would sit, legs astraddle on a hard chair, arms folded on the back of it, watching her with a cold sarcastic smile, waiting to see what she would do.

She did not value what she knew had cost her parents nothing enough to return them: but dedicated all these things, and the money, to 'the cause.'

Her lover was indifferent. That they eat anything pleasant, wear anything attractive, care about being warm or comfortable, seemed to him contemptible. He and his cronies discussed her, her class position, her economic position, her psychology, at length, shuffling and reshuffling the jargon of the left-wing phrase books. She listened feeling unworthy, but taken seriously.

He demanded of her that at the next 'demo' she should seriously assault a policeman. She did it without question: never had she felt so fulfilled. She was three months in prison, where her lover visited her once. He visited others more often. Why? she humbly wondered. Not all of them were of the poor and the ignorant; one of his associates was in fact quite well off, and educated. But she was very rich, yes, that must be it. They were all more worthy than she was. In prison, among the other prisoners, most of them unpolitical, she radiated a smiling unalterable conviction which manifested itself as humility. She was always doing things no one else would do. Dirty tasks and punishment were food and drink to her. The prisoners christened her, disgusted, the Saint; but she took it as a compliment. 'I am trying to be worthy to become a real member of –' and she supplied the name of her political group. 'To become a real socialist one has to suffer and aspire.'

When she came out, her man was living with another woman. She accepted it: of course it was because she was not good enough. She served them. She waited on them. She crouched on the floor outside the room her lover and the woman were wrapped together in, comparing herself to a dog, glorying in her abasement, and she muttered, like the phrases of a rosary, I will be worthy, I will overcome, I will show them, I will . . . and so on.

She took a kitchen knife to the next 'demo' and did not even look to see if it was sharpened: the gesture of carrying it was enough. Intoxicated, lifted above herself, she fought and struggled, a Valkyrie with flying dirty blond hair, reddened blue eyes, a fixed, ugly smile. (In her family she had been noticed for her 'sweet gentle look.') She attacked policemen with her fists, and then took out the – as it happened – blunt knife, and hacked about her with it. But she was not being arrested. Others were. There was such a disproportion between the atmosphere, and even the purpose, of this demonstration, and her appearance and her frenzy, that the police were puzzled by her. A senior official sent the word around that she was not to be arrested: she was clearly unbalanced. Ecstatic with renewed effort, she yelled and waved the knife about, but perceived that the demonstration was ending and people streaming home. *She was not being taken seriously.* She was standing watching the arrested being piled into the police vans like a child turned away from a party, the knife held in her hand as if she were intending to chop meat or vegetables with it.

A group of people had been watching her: not only this day, but at previous demonstrations.

A girl standing like a heroic statue on the edge of the pavement with the knife at the ready in her hand, hair falling bedraggled round a swollen and reddened face, weeping tears of angry disappointment, saw in front of her a man waiting for her to notice him. He had a smile which she thought *kind*. His eyes were 'stern' and 'penetrating': he understood her emotional type very well.

'I think you should come with me,' he suggested.

'Why?' said she, all belligerence, which nevertheless suggested a readiness to obey.

'You can be of use.'

She automatically took a step towards him, but stopped herself, confused.

'What to?'

'You can be of use to socialism.'

Briefly on to her face flitted the expression that means: You can't get me as easily as that! while phrases from the *vocabulary* whirled through her brain.

'Your particular capacities and qualities are just what are needed,' he said.

She went with him.

This group was in a large shabby flat on the outskirts of the city, a workman's home, one of the refuges of these twelve young women and men whose leader had accosted her. While the circumstances – poverty made worse, and emphasised – of her previous living place had been of emotional necessity to the work of self-definition of her previous group, these people were indifferent to how they lived, and moved from opulence, to discomfort, to middle-class comfort in the space of a day, as necessary, without making anything of what they were surrounded by. The girl adapted herself at once. Although she had been lying, exulting in her misery, outside the door of her lover and his new woman, for days, now she hardly thought of that life – *where she had not been appreciated*. She did not immediately see what was to be asked of her, but was patient, obedient, gentle, doing any task that suggested itself.

These new comrades were engaged in planning some coup, but she was not told what. Soon she was taken to yet another flat, where she had not been before, and told that she was to strip and examine a young woman brought in for 'questioning.' This girl was in fact an accomplice, but just before the 'examination' began, Individual Seven was told that 'this one was a particularly hard case' and that 'there was no point in using kid gloves on her.'

Alone with her victim, who seemed dazed and demoralised, the girl felt herself uplifted by the same familiar and longed-for elation of her combats with the police, the atmosphere of danger. She 'examined' the captive, who, it seemed to her, had every mark of disgusting stupidity and corruption. It was not far off torture, and she enjoyed it.

She was complimented on the job she had done by this group of severe, serious, responsible young revolutionaries. Thus they described themselves. But she had not yet heard them define their particular creed or commitment. And in fact she was never to hear it.

She was told not to go out, to keep herself hidden: she was too valuable to risk. When the group moved, she was always blindfolded. She accepted this with a humble joy: it must be necessary.

This group added to the kidnapping of rich or well-known individuals a refinement, which was the kidnapping and torture, or threat of torture, of their relatives – mistresses, sisters, wives, daughters. Always women. The girl was given the task of torturing, first in minor ways, and then comprehensively, one young woman after another.

She looked forward to it. She had accepted her situation. Moments of disquiet were silenced with: They have more experience than I have, they are better than I am, and it must be necessary.

Reflecting that she did not know their allegiances, she was comforted by the phrases she was familiar with, and had been ever since – as she put it – she had become politically mature.

At moments when sharp pleasure held her in its power either because of some encounter just over or one promised her, she wondered if perhaps she had been physically drugged: whether these new friends of hers were feeding her stimulants, so alive did she feel, so vital and full of energy.

This group lasted three years before it was taken by the police, and the girl committed suicide when it was evident she could not avoid arrest. The impulse behind this act was a continuation of their dictate that she must not ever be visible – go out, be seen, or even know where she was. She felt that under torture – she now lived in her mind in a world where torture was not merely possible but inevitable – she would 'betray them.' Her suicide was, therefore, in her own eyes, an act of heroism and self-sacrifice in the service of socialism.

It will have been noted that none of the individuals categorised here was among those identified with a particular injustice, such as suffering under an arbitrary or tyrannous power, or being deprived of a country, or persecuted for being one of a despised or subjugated race, or kept in poverty by the thoughtless, the careless, or the cruel.

I could not contact the next individual through the Giants, or anything like them. I had been looking for someone suitable, and during my trips in and out of Shikasta, I had seen an old friend, Ranee, waiting on the margins of Zone Six at that place where the lines form for their chance of re-entry. I had told her that I needed very soon to spend time with her, and why. Now, searching up and down the lines I could not see her, and saw, too, that they were shorter and more sparse. I heard that there were rumours of an emergency, of frightful danger, in Zone Six, and all those able to understand had left to help people escape. The souls remaining in the lines were too fixed on their hope of an early re-entry, crowding forward each time the gates opened, jostling each other, their eyes only for the gates, and I could not get anything more out of them.

I walked on past them into the scrub and thin grasses of the high plateau, quite alone, as evening came on. I felt uneasy, and thought first this was because I had been told there was danger, but soon the sense of threat was so strong that I left the scrublands and climbed a small ridge, scrambling from rock to rock upwards, in the dark. I set my back to a small cliff, and my face to where I could expect the dawn. It was silent. But not completely silent. I could hear a soft whispering, like a sea . . . a sea where no sea was, or could be. The stars were crowding bright and thick, and their dim light showed low bushes and outcrops of stone. Nothing to account for this sound, which I could not remember ever hearing before. Yet it whispered danger, danger, and I stayed where I was, turning myself about and sensing and peering, like an animal alerted to some menace it cannot understand. When the light came into the sky and the stars went, the sound was there, and stronger. I descended from the ridge, and walked on, soon coming to the desert's edge, where I could hear the steady sibilant hissing. Yet there was no wind to blow the sand. Everything was quite still, and there was a small sweetness of dew rising from around my feet as I set them down on a crunchy surface. I walked on, every step slower, for all my senses shouted warnings at me. I kept close to my right the low ridge I had used for shelter the night before. It ran on in front of me until it joined black jagged peaks far ahead that were sombre and even sinister in the cool grey dawn. The rustling voice of the sands grew louder . . . not far from me I saw wisps of sand in the air, which vanished: yet there was no wind! The lower clouds hung dark and motionless, and the higher clouds, all tinted with the dawn, were in packed unmoving masses. A windless landscape and a still sky: and yet the whispering came from everywhere. A small smudge in the air far in front of me enlarged, and close to me the sands seemed to shiver. I left them and again climbed on the ridge, where I turned to look back at where I had been standing. At first, nothing; and then, almost exactly where I had been, I saw the sands shake. They lay still again. But I had not imagined it. At various places now over the plain of sands that lay on the left of the ridge I saw smudges of sand hanging. To the right of the ridge I had not yet looked, not daring to take my eyes away from the place I had been in, for it seemed essential to watch, as if something might pounce out like an animal, if I once removed my gaze. There was no reason in it, but I had to stand fixed there, staring . . . the place where the sands had moved, quaked again. They moved, definitely, and stopped. As if an enormous invisible stick had given half a stir . . . the soft whistling filled my ears and I could hear nothing else. I waited. An area I could span with my arms stretched wide was stirred again by the invisible stick: there was the slow, halting movement of a whirlpool, which stopped. Half a mile ahead I believed I could see a spinning underneath one of the air smudges. But I kept my eyes on the birth – for now I knew that this was what I was watching – of the sand whirlpool near to me. Slowly, creakingly, with halts, and new beginnings, the vortex formed, and then at various distances around it, the sand shivered, and lay still, and began again . . . Then the central place was in a slow regular spin, and grains of sand flung up and off to one side glittered as they fell. So the sun was up, was it? I looked, and saw all the sky in front a wild enraged red, shedding a ruddy glow down on to the gleam of the sands.

The whirlpool was now established, and steadily encompassing more and more of the sands around it, and the places near it where I had noted small movements, each were beginning to circle and subside, then start again as the new subsidiary pools formed. I saw that all the plain was covered with these spots of movement, and the air above them each showed a small cloud that hung there, enlarging but not drifting, because of the lack of wind. And now, with difficulty, I made myself look away from this dreadfully treacherous plain, and I gazed out to my right. Desert again, strething interminably, and I could see no movement here. The wastes lay quiet and still, inflamed by the wild scarlet of the skies, but then a desert fox came towards me, its soft yellow all aglow, and it trotted into the ridge of rocks and disappeared. Another came. Suddenly I saw that there were many animals in flight from some danger behind them. Far behind them: for I could see no movement in the sands on this side of the ridge, though on the other side all the plain was shaking and quivering between the whirlpools of sand. Far over this solid and ordinary plain, I could see that the sky, now fully light in a clear morning where the reds and pinks rapidly faded, was hung with a low haze, which I now understood.

I had taken in what was happening, was going to happen, and I ran clumsily forward along the rocky ridge, which I believed, or hoped, would not succumb to the movement of the sands, was solidly rooted.

I was looking for refugees from these terrible whirlpools who might have climbed to the safety of the rocks, but believed they were more likely to be on the mountains that still seemed to be such a distance from me. And then I did see a party of five approach, a woman, a man, and two half-grown children, and these were dazed and silly with the dangers they had survived, and could not see me. They were accompanied by someone whose face I knew from the lines at the frontier, and I stopped her and asked what was happening. 'Be quick,' she said, 'there are still people on the sands. But you must be quick' – and she went on along the ridge, calling to her charges to hurry. They were standing with their mouths hanging open, eyes fixed on the shivering and swirling sands of the plain to my left, their right, and seemed unable to hear her. She had to hustle them on, pushing them into movement. Again I ran onwards, clumsily, scrambling and falling over the rocks, and several times passed little groups, each shepherded by a person from the lines. The rescued ones shook and trembled, and stared at the liquid-seeming desert, and had to be continually reminded to move on, and to keep their eyes in front of them.

When at last I reached the beginnings of the mountain peaks, which rose straight up out of the sands, it was not too soon, for I had seen that if the great sands on my right were to dissolve into movement as they had on the other side, the ridge could not stand for long, but must be engulfed. I turned to look back from the mountain and saw that on the one side of the ridge there were no unmoving places left: all that desert was shivering, swirling, dissolving. On the other side, still, things seemed safe, yet, looking over those reaches of sands as far as I could, it was possible to see crowds of hopping, running, flying animals and birds. None looked back, none was panicky or stricken or had lost their senses, but purposefully and carefully picked their way through the dunes and hollows of the sands to the ridge, where they must all be working their way back through the rocks to the plateau I had come from. But from a certain point on that plain of sand, there was no movement of animals at all: I was seeing the last exodus of the refugees, and behind them the sands lay quiet. On the horizons, the dust clouds had risen higher into the cobalt blue of the morning sky.

I was not certain what I should do next. I had not met groups of refugees for some time now. Perhaps everyone had been rescued, there were none left? I went forward up the stony, cracked sides of the mountain, towards the right, and when I reached a small outcrop of young, harsh cracked rocks and dry bushes, I was able to see straight down into the plain where, ahead, suddenly, there were the beginnings of movement, the birth of sand whirlpools. And, at the same time, I saw down there a little bunching of black rocks, and on them two people. They had their backs to me, and they stood staring away across the plain. I seemed to know them. I ran down again towards them, with many thoughts in my mind. One, that a symptom of the shock suffered by these victims was that they were stricken into a condition where they could do nothing but stare, hypnotised, unable to move. Another, that I *could* get to them in time, but whether I could lead them out again was another matter . . . and I was thinking, too, that these were my old friend Ben and my old friend Rilla, together, and at least safe, if marooned.

As I reached the plain of the desert and ran forward I could feel the sands trembling under me. I staggered on, shouting and calling to them, but they did not hear me, or if they did, could not move. When I came up to their little outcrop, a whirlpool had formed not far away, and I jumped up onto the rock they stood on, and shouted, Rilla! Ben! They stood shivering like dogs that have got wet and cold and did not look at me, but stared at the liquefying whirling desert. I shouted, and then they turned vague eyes on me but could not recognise me. I grabbed them and shook them, and they did not resist. I slapped their cheeks and shouted, and their eyes, turned towards me, seemed to have in them the shadow of an indignant, What are you doing that for? But already they had turned to stare, transfixed.

I climbed around so that I stood immediately in front of them. 'This is Johor,' I said, 'Johor, your friend.' Ben seemed to come slightly to himself, but already he was trying to peer around me, so as to watch the sand. Rilla, it seemed, had not seen me. I took out the Signature and held it up in front of their staring eyes. Both sets of eyes followed the Signature as I stepped downwards, and they followed. They followed! – but like sleepwalkers. Holding up the Signature and walking backwards in front of them, I reached the desert floor, which was quivering everywhere now, with a singing hiss of sound, and I shouted, 'Now follow me! Follow me!' continuously moving the Signature so that it flashed and gleamed. I walked as fast I could, first backwards, and then, because I could see the terrible danger we were in, with the beginnings of vortexes everywhere around us, I turned myself half sideways and so led them forward. They stumbled and they fell, and seemed all the time drawn by a need to look back, but I pulled them forward with the power of the Signature, and at last we stood on the firm slopes of the mountain. There they at once turned and stood staring, clutching each other. And I stood with them, for I was affected, to, by that hypnotising dreadfulness. Where we had come stumbling to safety was already now all movement and shifting subsidence: as far as we could see, the golden sands were moving. And we stood there, we stood there, for I was lost as they, and we were staring at a vast whirlpool, all the plain had become one swirling centrifuge, spinning, spinning, with its centre deep, and deeper and then out of sight. Some appalling necessity was dragging and sucking at this place, feeding on the energies, the released powers, and I could not pull my eyes away, it seemed as if my eyes themselves were being sucked out, my mind was going away, draining into the spin – and then from the sky swooped down a black screaming eagle, and it was warning us: Go . . o . . o . . . Go . . o . . o . . . Go . . o . . o . . . and the clattering rush of its wings above my head brought me back into myself. I had even dropped the Signature, and I had to scramble and search for it, and there was its gleam under some rocks. I had to shake and slap and wake Ben and Rilla, and again move the Signature back and forth in front of their eyes to charm them away from their contemplation of the sands. Above, the eagle that had saved us swung in a wide circle peering to see if we were indeed safely awake, and then, when it knew we were watching, turned its glide so that it was off towards the east, where the ground climbed from the level of the sands, up into scrubland, grasses, low rocks, safe from the deadly plain which it was essential for us to get away from as soon as we could. Ben and Rilla were passive, almost imbecile, as I shepherded them on, the eagle showing the way. I did not try to talk to them, only wondered what to do, for we were walking in the opposite direction from the borders of Zone Six with Shikasta, which was where we all had to go. But I followed the eagle, I had to. If he had known enough to rescue me from my trance, then I must trust him . . . and after hours of stumbling heavy walk, beside my two dazed companions, the great bird screamed to attract my attention, and swung away leftwards in a deep and wide arc, and I knew that that was where we must make our way. And we travelled on all that day, until evening, trusting in the bird, for I did not know where we were. Rilla and Ben were talking a little now, but only clumsy half-phrases and random words. At night we found a sheltered place, and I made them sit quietly beside me and rest. They slept at last, and I got up and climbed to a high place where I could look back over the scrub of the plateau to the desert. Under the starlight I saw a single great vortex, which filled the whole expanse: the spine of the rocky ridge had been sucked down and had gone entirely. Nothing remained but the horizons-wide swirl, and the sound of it now was a roar, which made the earth I stood on shake. I crept back again through the dark to my friends and sat by them until the dawn, when the eagle, which was sitting on a high peak of rock, screamed a greeting to me. There was an urgency in it, and I knew we must move on. I roused Ben and Rilla, and all that day we followed the bird, through the higher lands that surrounded the sand plains, which we were working our way around. We could not see them, but we could hear, always, the roaring of the enraged and compelled earth. Towards evening I recognised where we were. And now I was thinking that I was late with my tasks on Shikasta, and that it was most urgent and necessary for me to get back to them. But I could not trust Ben and Rilla yet, to be alone. As they walked they kept turning their heads to listen to that distant roaring like a sea that keeps crashing itself again and again on shores that shake and tremble, and I knew that left alone they would drift back to the sands. I could not leave them the Signature: they were not reliable. After all, I had nearly lost it, and compared to them, my senses had been my own. I called up to the eagle that I needed its help, and as it circled above us, asked it to shepherd Ben and Rilla onwards. I held the Signature in front of them again, and said that the bird was the servant of the Signature, and they must do exactly what it told them. I said I would see them again on the borders of Shikasta, and they must not give up. Thus exhorting and pleading, I impressed on them everything I could, and then went on by myself alone, fast. I looked back later and saw them stumbling slowly forward, their eyes raised to the glide and the swerve and the balance of the eagle, who moved on, on, on, in front.

I found Ranee with a group she had saved from the whirlpools not far from the frontier. I asked if I might travel with her, so that I could make contact as I had to, and she agreed. So I went on with her. Her charges were as stunned, as lost to their selves, as poor Ben and Rilla.

But they did seem slowly to improve, while Ranee talked to them in a low steady compelling voice, as a mother talks a child up out of a nightmare, soothing, and explaining.

*   *   *

RACHEL SHERBAN'S JOURNAL

Our family has the four little rooms on the corner of this mud house, if that is the word for a building that is made of little rooms with doors out into the streets, inner doors opening in on to the central court. I can't imagine that one family could live here, not unless there were dozens of people in it, like those Russian families in novels. So it means the building was made to house a lot of poor families. Above our rooms is our patch of roof. There are six other families, each with its little patch of roof, separated from the other patches by low walls, which are high enough to hide you sitting or lying down but not standing. Mother and Father have one tiny room. Benjamin and George have another. There is a cubbyhole for me. Then the room we use for eating and sitting in if we aren't on the roof. The cooking place is outside. It is a sort of stove made of mud.

We are on good terms with all the families, but Shireen and Naseem are our particular friends. Shireen adores Olga. And Shireen's sister Fatima loves me.

Naseem went to school and did well. He is clever. He wanted to be a physicist. His parents did without everything so he could go on studying at college, but they did not stop him marrying, and so he had a wife and a baby before he was twenty. That is a western way of looking at things. He had to support them, so he works as a clerk. He says he is lucky to get this work. At least it is regular. I often wonder what he thinks about having to be a clerk, working seven a.m. to seven p.m., and with this wife and five children and he is twenty-four.

I spend quite a lot of time with Shireen and Fatima. When Naseem goes to work, and all the men leave the building, except for the old ones, the women are in and out of each other's homes, and the babies and children seem to belong to everyone. The women gossip and giggle and quarrel and make up. It is all very intimate. Sometimes I think it is awful. Like a girls' school. Women together always giggle and become childish and make little treats for each other. East or West. When Shireen has nothing in her rooms but two or three tomatoes and onions and a handful of lentils and has no idea what she is going to feed her family that day, she will still make a little rissole of lentils for a special friend across the court. And this woman puts some sugar on a bit of yoghurt and gives it to Shireen. It is always a feast, even with a spoon of yoghurt and seven grains of sugar. They spoil each other, caress each other, give each other little presents. And they have nothing. It is charming. Is that the word? No, probably it isn't.

Shireen is always tired. She has an ulcer on one breast that heals and breaks out again. She has a dropped womb. She looks about forty on a bad day. Naseem comes home tired and they quarrel and shout. She screams. He hits her. Then he cries. She cries and comforts him. The children cry. They are hungry. Fatima rushes in and out exclaiming and invoking Allah. She says Naseem is a devil. Then that Shireen is. Then she kisses them and they all weep some more. This is poverty. *Not one of these people has ever had enough to eat. They have never had proper medical care. They don't know what I mean when I say medical care. They think it means the big new hospital that is so badly organised it is a death trap and being treated like idiots. They don't go there. They can afford only old wives' tales when they are sick. A doctor that really cares about them is too expensive. Shireen is pregnant again. They are* pleased. *After they have quarrelled I hear them laugh. Then there is a sort of ribald angry good humour. This means they will make love. I've seen Shireen with bruises on her cheeks and neck from lovemaking, and then Fatima, the unmarried sister, has to blush and the married women tease Shireen. She is* proud. *Although she always has a backache and is tired she is good-humoured and wonderful with the children. Except sometimes. That is when she is so exhausted she sits rocking herself, crying and moaning. Then Fatima croons over her, and does more work than usual, though she always works very hard helping Shireen. Then Naseem caresses her and swears and is angry because she is so worn out. Then there is more laughing antagonism between them. This is mysterious, the ebbs and flows. I mean there is a mystery in it. I don't understand it at all. I watch them and I want to understand. They respect each other. They have a tenderness. Because their lives are so difficult and awful and he can't ever be a physicist, or anything but a little clerk. Often he goes mad thinking about it. And she will be an old woman at forty. And some of their children will be dead. Mother says that two are weak and won't live. Because not one of the children has had enough of the proper things to eat, they may have brain damage, Mother says.*

Sometimes I see an old woman, and I think she must be seventy at least, then I find out she is forty, and has had ten kids, four of them dead, and she is a widow.

I can't stand any of this. I can't understand it.

I am of the West and I believe in the equality of women. This is what I <u>am</u>. So does Olga. But when Olga is with Shireen and Fatima she is exactly like them. She laughs and is gay and intimate. These women have a marvellous time. They make fun for themselves out of nothing. I envy them. Believe it or not. They are supposed to be miserable and downtrodden. And they are. The dregs of the dregs. And so are their husbands. When you compare these lives, pared down to nothing, with what I can remember only too clearly of America I want to vomit. The fat vulgarity of it. When these women get hold of an old American magazine, a women's magazine, they all crowd around it and laugh and get such pleasure from it. One tattered old magazine, the sort of thing you leaf through at the dentist and think what a load of old rubbish, they handle with such respect. Each rubbishy advertisement gives them entertainment for days. They will take an advertisement, and go off and stand in front of the only mirror in the building. It is an old cracked thing and the woman who owns it takes it for granted everyone must use it. They pull some cheap dress around one of them, and match it with the advertisement, and laugh.

I watch and think of how we throw everything away and nothing is good enough.

Sometimes they say they are going to learn languages like clever me and they sit around and I start off with French or Spanish. They sit, with the children all crowding around wanting attention, then one has to go off and another. I am sitting there, handing out my marvellous phrases, while they repeat them. But the next time there is a lesson, there are fewer of them, and then only one or two. Fatima is learning Spanish from me. She says she could get a better job than she has. She is a cleaning woman. If you can call a seventeen-year-old girl that. The language lessons haven't come to much, but they made an occasion for fun while they lasted.

Shireen is delighted she is having a baby, though she is too tired to drag herself about, and it means even less food. And she worries all the time because it is time Fatima is married.

Fatima is very slim, and not pretty, but striking. She knows how to make herself attractive. She uses kohl and henna and rouge. She has two dresses. She washes and cares for them. Benjamin says they are fit for a jumble sale. But he would. I hate it when Benjamin comes anywhere near these people. They are all so slight and elegant and quick-moving. Like air, because of never having eaten enough. And then there is Benjamin, a great brown hairy bear. George fits in with them. He is like them. Quick and thin.

Benjamin knows he is out of place and that they find him amazing so he keeps away.

Shireen wants Fatima to marry a friend of Naseem, who is a clerk in the same office. Naseem thinks he will marry her. They joke about it. Naseem says, Have a heart, or words to that effect, why do you want the poor thing to be married and saddle himself with all this misery. Indicating Shireen and the five children. He laughs. She laughs. Fatima laughs. If I am there and I don't laugh, they all turn on me and tease me, saying I look so solemn and boring, until I do laugh.

And then there is a sudden wave of black bitterness. It is awful, an irritability that gets into Naseem and Shireen and they hate each other. The children whimper and wail. The two rooms seem full of children's dirt and vomit and worse. Flies. Bits of food. It is horrible, squalid and awful.

Naseem then jokes that perhaps his friend Yusuf would like me instead of Fatima because at least I am educated and can keep him in luxury. At which Fatima calls me into the cubbyhole she shares with the three older children, and she takes down her best dress from a hook in the mud wall. It is a dark blue dress, of a soft cloth, very worn. It smells of Fatima and of her perfume, heavy and languishing. The dress has beautiful embroidery on it in lovely colours. Fatima made the dress and did the embroidery. This dress is a big thing in her life. She puts on me gold earrings, long, to my shoulders, and then about a hundred bangles. Gold, glass, brass, copper, plastic. Yellow, red, blue, pink, green. The gold bangle and the earrings are precious to Fatima, they are her dowry. But she puts them on me and is delighted.

This has happened several times. She loves doing it. It is because she admires me for being so educated and able to do what I like. So she thinks. She thinks I am marvellous. My life seems quite beyond her and utterly amazing.

Yesterday afternoon she put all this on me and then made up my eyes. She made my lips a dark sultry red like a tart's. She stood me in front of the cracked glass in the neighbour's room, and the women came crowding around to watch. They were all excited and delighted. Then she took me back to her sister's rooms and sat me down to wait for supper. Yusuf was coming. I said to her she was mad. But it was the wrong note, I could see that. She had to do it. Meanwhile, Shireen was all worldly-wise and smiling. Naseem came home, worn out. Thin as a rake because he does not eat what little there is for him, he always gives it to the children. He laughs when he sees me. Then in comes Yusuf. He is handsome, with dark liquid eyes. A sheikh of Araby. He laughs. He pretends I am his bride. It is funny and sweet. As if everyone is forgiving everyone for something. I say to them, cross, that all this is silly because I have no intention at all of getting married. But I am quite wrong to say it, because it is a sort of game. They are making an alternative event. A possibility. Their lives are so narrow. They have so little. So here is this spoiled western girl Rachel. But they like her really. But they have to manage *her. And after all, she might marry Yusuf, who knows! Strange things do happen! Yusuf might fall in love with Rachel! Rachel might fall in love with Yusuf! A romance! But of course they don't believe this for a moment. And so it is a sort of acted-out possibility, no hard feelings. It was a feast. Vegetable stew and meatballs. They hardly ever eat meat. And I had insisted on bringing in a pudding Mother had made for us. It was a pudding of yoghurt and fruit. Shireen made sure the children stayed up to get some of it, after their share of the stew. She couldn't waste the chance of their getting some nourishment into them.*

There I sat, all dolled up, a sacrificial calf. It was a lovely meal. I adored it. All the time I was furious. Not at them. At the awfulness of this poverty. At Allah. At everything. And it was all ridiculous because Fatima and Yusuf might just as well be married already. There is that strong physical thing, and the antagonism. They quarrel as if they are married, and are sure of each other.

After the meal, the feast-feeling faded away. The children were excited and a nuisance. Everything was a mess. Naseem and Yusuf went to a café. Shireen put the kids to bed. Fatima cleaned things up. Then she sat with me and said, Do you like him Rachel? Quite seriously, but laughing. I said, Yes I like him and I shall have him! Oh, you are going to marry him then? Yes, I shall marry him, I said. She laughed, but looked grave, in case there was a chance in a thousand I might mean it. And I kissed her so she should understand of course I wouldn't marry her Yusuf. All the time I was wanting to howl and weep. But I personally think on reflection that I am extremely childish and they are not.

Then Fatima took me into the court.

It was a night with a moon, last night.

People were sitting around in the shadows of the court. We sat by the pool. It is a tiny rectangular pool. The lilies in the earth pot at one end were smelling very strong. Olga was there, sitting quietly in the dusk. She had one of the babies on her lap. It was asleep. I don't know where George was or Benjamin. Olga knew I was in with Shireen and Naseem and Fatima because I had asked to take the pudding. She knew about Yusuf. She was worried in case I hadn't behaved well. She didn't want me to have hurt their feelings.

When I came out and sat by the pool with Fatima she was looking at my face to see if I had behaved well. So I gave her a look which meant Yes I have.

The moon was overhead. It should have reflected in the pool. But there was this dust on the water. Also little bits of twig. Also bits of paper. The water is never clean. A woman will take a child that has made a mess and wash it there. Or someone will bend and spash water over his face, in the heat. Olga began by trying to stop people using the water but she has given up. She says by now they must be immune to any germs. Fatima leaned forward, and began carefully with the side of her palm to scoop the dust and rubbish off the water. Then Shireen came out from her quarters and she sat by Fatima and she too creamed off the dust. She knew what Fatima was up to, but I didn't. And Olga didn't. They were obviously up to something. This went on for some time. People sat quietly around, tired after the hot day, watching the sisters using the sides of their palms to scoop off the dust and wondering what would happen next.

Then Naseem came back from the café. He had been gone only an hour. He was tired, and kept yawning. He stood for a while leaning against a wall watching the sisters. Then he sat down by his wife, close but not too close, because they behave with dignity in public. He was close because he wanted to be. His leg and thigh was at least six inches from Shireen's folded-up leg, but I could feel the warmth of their being close. I could feel the understanding between them, in their flesh. They were conscious of every little bit of each other, even though they scarcely looked at each other and Shireen went on clearing the water. I was amazed by that thing between them. I mean the strength of it. If I could only understand it. Those two sitting there together in the dusk on the edge of the little pool, with the moon shining down – all the rest of us might just as well not have been there. I don't know how to say it. I was staring at them and trying not to.

And all the time Shireen went on competently scooping and skimming, and Fatima scooped and skimmed. And I was sitting there, all dolled up. Then the pool was clear. It was a little dark rectangle of water with a slit of moon shining brightly in it.

Then Fatima, smiling and delighted, and Shireen, smiling and pleased, came to me, one on either side, and gently pushed me forward to look in the pool.

I didn't want to. I felt ridiculous. But I had to. Naseem was sitting there, cross-legged, alert, watching, smiling, very handsome.

I was made to look at myself. I was beautiful. They made me be. I looked much older, not fifteen. I was a real woman, their style. I hated the whole thing. I felt as if Shireen and Fatima were holding me and dragging me down into a terrible snare or trap. But I loved them. I loved that strong physical understanding between Naseem and Shireen and I wanted to be part of it or at least to know what it was. It wasn't just sex, oh no.

The girls kept exclaiming over my reflection and softly clapping their hands, and making Naseem bend forward to look into the pool and then he clapped his hands, partly sardonic, and partly genuine. And the other people around the pool were smiling.

I was afraid of George coming in and seeing this charade going on. Because he hadn't seen what had led up to it. I could feel the tears start running and I hoped no one would notice. But of course Shireen and Fatima noticed. They exclaimed and kissed me and scooped the tears off my cheeks with the side of their palms that were still damp from the pool, and they said I was beautiful and lovely.

Meanwhile, Olga sat there watching, holding the sleeping baby. She did not smile. Nor did she not smile.

Olga, I will put down here as a fact, is not beautiful. This is because she is always tired and doesn't have time. Olga is English to look at, in spite of her Indian parent. She has the stubby solid look. She has dyed blond hair that is not always properly dyed. She has dark eyes that are sensible and considering. She is in fact too fat. This is because she forgets to eat sometimes all day, and then goes ravenous into the food cupboard and absentmindedly crams in bread or anything that is there to fill herself. She doesn't care. Or she will eat pounds of fruit or sweet stuff instead of a meal while she is writing a report.

She has nice clothes which she buys all at once to get it over with, but then she forgets about looking after them.

She sat there looking at this daughter of hers, who was so beautiful and exotic.

She was most interested in it all. I knew perfectly well she was thinking that all this would be good for me. Educational. Just as living in this poor building in this poor part of the town is good for us.

I could not stop crying. This disturbed the girls very much. Suddenly they did not understand it at all. Soon Naseem made them go off with him to their rooms, but first Shireen and Fatima hugged and kissed me, very affectionate and concerned, and I wanted to howl more than ever.

I stayed there on the edge of the pool. So did Olga. Then the others went off to sleep. They all had to get up early and they are tired with their hard lives.

That left Olga and me. I leaned forward and took a good look at the glamorous beauty. I have got thin in the last year. Sometimes I look at myself naked. The Queen of Sheba has nothing on me. Breasts and lilies and goblets and navel and the lot. But I don't want it. How could I want to be grown-up and marry and have six kids and know they are going to die of hunger or never have enough to eat.

When there was no one but me and Olga, and no chance of anyone coming out into the court, I did something I had been wanting to, but I couldn't while Shireen and Fatima were there. I loved them too much.

I took some sand from the pot around the lilies, and gently strewed it over the still surface of the gleaming water. Gently. Not too much. Just enough so that when I looked in I could no longer see the beautiful exotic Miss Sherban, Rachel the nubile virgin.

Olga watched me do this. She did not say a word.

I leaned over the pool, to make sure I couldn't see myself, only the blurred outline of the beautiful moon, shining down from the stars.

By the morning, if Shireen and Fatima remembered, and chanced to look, all they would think was that the winds had blown dust across the sky and some had fallen into the pool.

Olga got up and took the baby off to the room it belonged in. Then she came and put her arm around me and said, Now come on, go to bed. And she led me into our quarter. She hugged me and kissed me. She said, Rachel, it really isn't as bad as you think.

She said it humorous but a bit desperate.

I said, Oh yes, it is.

And she went off to bed.

I went through to my little mud room. I sat on the door-sill, with my feet in the dust outside, and I watched the night. I was still in Fatima's best dress of course, with her precious bits of gold. Being in that dress that she had been in a thousand times was something I can't describe. If there is a word, I don't know it. The cloth of the dress was full of Fatima. But that wasn't it. It smelled of her and of her skin and her scent. It was as if I had put on her skin over mine. No dress I have ever had in my life could possibly feel like that. It could never be that important. If I had a fragment of that cloth, wherever I was in the world, if I came on it in a drawer or a box, I would have to say at once, Fatima.

The feel of that warm soft cloth on my skin was burning me.

I understand that old thing, about a woman rending her bosom with her nails. If I had not been in Fatima's precious best dress that she would need to get married in, I would have raked my nails through the dress and into my bosom. And I would have raked my cheeks with my nails, too, but the blood would have hurt Fatima's dress.

I sat there all night until the light began to get grey. There were some dogs trotting about in the moonlight. The dogs were very thin. Three of them. Mongrels. So thin they had no stomachs, just ribs. I could feel their hunger. Living in this country I have a fire in my stomach which is the hunger I know nearly everyone I see feels all the time, all the time, even when they sleep.

Then I go into meals with the family and eat, because of course it is ridiculous not to. But each mouthful feels <u>heavy</u>, and too much, and I think of the people who are ravening. I am sure that even if I lived in a country where everyone had enough to eat all the time, and lived there for years, I would still have this burning in my stomach.

I did not go to bed last night. When the sun came up I took off Fatima's beautiful dress and folded it and put the earrings and the dozens of different bangles with it. Later I shall take these things over to her. One day soon I expect that I and Shireen will help Fatima into this dress so that she can marry Yusuf.

The Marriages Between Zones Three, Four and Five

Rumours are the begetters of gossip. Even more are they the begetters of song. We, the Chroniclers and song-makers of our Zone, aver that before the partners in this exemplary marriage were awake to what the new directives meant for both of them, the songs were with us, and were being amplified and developed from one end of Zone Three to the other. And of course this was so in Zone Four.

> *Great to Small*
> *High to Low*
> *Four into Three*
> *Cannot go.*

This was a children's counting game. I was watching them at it from my windows the day after I heard the news. And one of them rushed up to me in the street with a 'riddle' he had heard from his parents: If you mate a swan and a gander, who will ride?

What was being said and sung in the camps and barracks of Zone Four we do not choose to record. It is not that we are mealy-mouthed. Rather that every chronicle has its appropriate tone.

I am saying that each despised the other? No, we are not permitted actively to criticise the dispensations of the Providers, but let us say that we in Zone Three did not forget – as the doggerel chanted during those days insisted:

> *Three comes before Four.*
> *Our ways are peace and plenty.*
> *Their ways – war!*

It was days before anything happened.

While this famous marriage was being celebrated in the imagination of both realms, the two most concerned remained where they were. They did not know what was wanted of them.

No one had expected the marriage. It had not reached even popular speculation. Zones Three and Four were doing very well, with Al·Ith for us. Ben Ata for them. Or so we thought.

Quite apart from the marriage, there were plenty of secondary questions. What could it mean that our Al·Ith was ordered to travel to the territory of Ben Ata, so that the wedding could be accomplished on his land? This was one of the things we asked ourselves.

What, in this context, was a wedding?

What, even, a marriage?

When Al·Ith first heard of the Order, she believed it to be a joke. She and her sister laughed. All of Zone Three heard how they laughed. Then arrived a message that could only be regarded as a rebuke, and people came together in conferences and councils all over the Zone. They sent for us – the Chroniclers and the poets and the song-makers and the Memories. For weeks nothing was talked of but weddings and marriages, and every old tale and ballad that could be dug up was examined for information.

Messengers were even sent to Zone Five, where we believed weddings of a primitive kind did take place. But there was war all along their frontiers with Zone Four and it was not possible to get in.

We wondered, if this marriage was intended to follow ancient patterns, whether Zones Three and Four should join in a festival? But the Zones could not mingle, were inimical by nature. We were not even sure where the frontier was. Our side was not guarded. The inhabitants of Zone Three, straying near the frontier, or approaching it from curiosity as children or young people sometimes did, found themselves afflicted with repugnance, or at the least by an antipathy to foreign airs and atmospheres that showed itself in a cold lethargy, like boredom. It cannot be said that Zone Four had for us the secret attractions and fascinations of the forbidden: the most accurate thing I can say is that we forgot about it.

Ought there perhaps to be two festivals, simultaneously, and each would celebrate that our two lands, so different, could nevertheless mirror something, at least in this way? But what would be the point of that? After all, festivals and celebrations were not exactly pleasures we had to do without.

Should there then be small wedding parties among us, to mark the occasion?

New clothes? Decorations in our public places? Gifts and presents? All these were sanctioned by the old songs and stories.

More time passed. We knew that Al·Ith was low in spirits, and was keeping to her quarters. She had never done this before, had always been available and open to us. The women everywhere were out of temper and despondent.

The children began to suffer.

Then came the first visible and evident manifestation of the new time. Ben Ata sent a message that his men would come to escort her to him. This curtness was exactly what we expected from his Zone. A realm at war did not need the courtesies. Here was proof of the rightness of our reluctance to be brought low by Zone Four.

Al·Ith was resentful, rebellious. She would not go, she announced.

Again there was an Order, and it said, simply, that she must go.

Al·Ith put on her dark blue mourning clothes, since this was the only expression of her inner feelings she felt she still had the latitude to use. She gave out no instructions for a Grief, but that was what was being felt by us all.

Felt confusingly and – we suspected – wrongly. Emotions of this kind are not valued by us. Have not been for so long we have no records of anything different. As individuals we do not expect – it is not expected of us – to weep, wail, suffer. What can happen to any one of us that does not happen at some time to everyone? Sorrow at bereavement, at personal loss, has become formalised, ritualised, in public occasions seen by us all as channels and vehicles for our little personal feelings. It is not that we don't feel! – but that feelings are meant always to be directed outwards and used to strengthen a general conception of ourselves and our realm. But with this new dispensation of Al·Ith the opposite seemed to be happening.

Never had our Zone known so many tears, accusations, irrational ill-feelings.

Al·Ith had all her children brought to her and when they wept she did not check them.

She insisted that this much must be allowed her without it being considered active rebellion.

There were those – many of us – who were perturbed; many who began to be critical of her.

We could not remember anything like this; and soon we were talking of how long it had been since there had been any kind of Order from the Providers. Of how previous changes of the Need – always referred to by us simply, and without further definition, in this one word – had been received by us. Of why, now, there should be such a reversal. We asked ourselves if we had grown into the habit of seeing ourselves falsely. But how could it be wrong to approve our own harmonies, the wealths and pleasantness of our land? We believed our Zone to be the equal at least of any other for prosperity and absence of discord. Had it then been a fault to be proud of it?

And we saw how long it had been since we had thought at all of what lay beyond our borders. That Zone Three was only one of the realms administered generally from Above, we knew. We did think, when we thought on these lines at all, of ourselves in interaction with these other realms, but it was in an abstract way. We had perhaps grown insular? Self-sufficing?

Al·Ith sat in her rooms and waited.

And then they appeared, a troop of twenty horsemen, in light armour. They carried shields that protected them against our higher finer air which would otherwise have made them ill, and these they had to have. But why head protection, and the famous reflecting singlets of Zone Four that could repel any weapon? Those of us who were near the route chosen by our unwelcome guests stood sullen and critical. We were determined not to give any indications of pleasure. Nor did the horsemen greet us. In silence the troops made their way to the palace, and came to a standstill outside Al·Ith's windows. They had with them a saddled and bridled horse without a rider. Al·Ith saw them from her windows. There was a long wait. Then she emerged on the long flight of white steps, a sombre figure in her dark robes. She stood silent, observing the soldiers whose appearance in this manner, in her country, could only have the effect of a capture. She allowed plenty of time for them to observe her, her beauty, her strength, the self-sufficiency of her bearing. She then descended the steps slowly, and alone. She went straight to the horse that had been brought for her, looked into his eyes, and put her hand on his cheek. This horse was Yori, who became celebrated from this moment. He was a black horse, and a fine one, but perhaps no more remarkable than the others the soldiers were riding. Having greeted him, she lifted off the heavy saddle. She stood with this in her arms, looking into the faces of the men one after another until at last a soldier saw what it was she wanted. She threw the saddle to him, and his horse shifted its legs to adjust the weight as he caught it. He gave a comical little grimace, glancing at his fellows, while she stood, arms folded, watching them. It was the grimace one offers to a clever child trying something beyond its powers, yet succeeding. This was of course not lost on Al·Ith, and she now showed they had missed her real point, by the slow deliberation with which she removed the bridle and tossed that, too, to a soldier.

Then she shook back her head, so that the black hair that was bound lightly around it cascaded down her back. Our women wear their hair in many ways, but if it is up, in braids or in another fashion, and a woman shakes her hair loose, in a particular manner, then this means grief. But the soldiers had not understood, and were admiring her foolishly; perhaps the gesture had been meant for the onlookers who were by now crowding the little square. Al·Ith's lips were curling in contempt of the soldiers, and with impatience. I must record here that this kind of arrogance – yes, I have to call it that – was not something we expected from her. When we talked over the incident, it was agreed that Al·Ith's bitterness over the marriage was perhaps doing her harm.

Standing with loosened hair and burning eyes, she slowly wound a fine black veil around her head and shoulders. Mourning – again. Through the transparent black glowed her eyes. A soldier was fumbling to get down off his horse to lift her on to hers, but she had leapt up before he could reach the ground. She then wheeled and galloped off through the gardens in an easterly direction, towards the borders with Zone Four. The soldiers followed. To those of us watching, it looked as if they were in pursuit.

Outside our city she pulled in her horse and walked it. They followed. The people along the roads greeted her, and stared at the soldiers, and it did not look like a pursuit now, because the soldiers were embarrassed and smiling foolishly, and she was the Al·Ith they had always known.

There is a descent off the high plateau of our central land through passes and gorges, and it was not possible to ride fast, apart from the fact that Al·Ith stopped whenever someone wanted to talk to her. For when she observed this was so, she always pulled up her horse and waited for them to approach her.

Now the grimaces among the soldiers were of a different kind, and they were grumbling, for they had expected to be across their own frontier by nightfall. At last, as another group of her people waved and called to her, and she heard the voices of the soldiers rising behind her, she turned her horse and rode back to them, stopping a few paces before the front line of horsemen, so that they had to rein in quickly.

'What is your trouble?' she enquired. 'Would it not be better if you told me openly, instead of complaining to each other like small children?'

They did not like this, and a small storm of anger rose, which their commander quelled.

'We have our orders,' he said.

'While I am in our country,' said she, 'I will behave according to custom.'

She saw they did not understand, and she had to explain. 'I am in the position I hold because of the will of the people. It is not for me to ride past arrogantly, if they indicate they want to say something.'

Again they looked at each other. The commander's face showed open impatience.

'You cannot expect me to overturn our customs for yours in this way,' she said.

'We have emergency rations for one light meal,' he said.

She gave a little incredulous shake of her head, as if she could not believe what she was hearing.

She had not meant it as contempt, but this was what transmitted itself to them. The commander of the horsemen reddened, and blurted out: 'Any one of us is capable of fasting on a campaign for days at a time if necessary.'

'I hadn't asked as much,' she said gravely, and this time, what they heard was humour. They gratefully laughed, and she was able to give a brief smile, then sighed, and said, 'I know that you are not here by your own will, but because of the Providers.'

But this, inexplicably to her, they felt as insult and challenge, and their horses shifted and sidled as the emotions of their riders came into them.

She gave a little shrug, and turned and went to the group of young men who stood waiting for her at the road's edge. Below them now lay a wide plain, behind them were the mountains. The plains still lay yellowed by the evening sun, and the high peaks of the mountains sun-glittered, but where they were it was cold and in dusk. The young men crowded around her horse as they talked, showing no fear or awe, and the watching horsemen's faces showed a crude disbelief. When a youth put up his hand to pat the horse's cheek briefly, the men let out, all together, a long breath of condemnation. But they were in doubt, and in conflict. It was not possible for them to despise this great kingdom or the rulers of it: they knew better. Yet what they saw at every moment contradicted their own ideas of what was right.

She held up her hand in farewell to the young men, and the men behind her put their horses forward at this signal which had not been to them. She rode on, before them, until they were all on the level of the plain, and then turned again.

'I suggest that you make a camp here, with the mountains at your back.'

'In the first place,' said the commander, very curt – because he had been annoyed his soldiers had instinctively answered her gesture by starting again, instead of waiting for him – 'in the first place, I had not thought of stopping at all till we reached the frontier. And in the second . . .' But his anger silenced him.

'I am only making the suggestion,' she said. 'It will take nine or ten hours to reach the frontier.'

'At this pace it will.'

'At any pace. Most nights a strong wind blows over the plain from the east.'

'Madam! What do you take these men for? What do you take us for?'

'I see that you are soldiers,' said she. 'But I was thinking of the beasts. They are tired.'

'They will do as they are ordered. As we do.'

Our Chroniclers and artists have made a great thing of this exchange between Al·Ith and the soldiers. Some of the tales begin at this point. She is erect before them, on her horse, who hangs his head, because of the long difficult ride. She is soothing it with her white hand, which glitters with jewels . . . but Al·Ith was known for her simple dress, her absence of jewels and splendour! They show her long black hair streaming, the veil streaming with it and held on her forehead with a brilliant clasp. They show the angry commander, his face distorted, and the jeering soldiers. The bitter wind is indicated by flying tinted clouds, and the grasses of the plain lie almost flat under it.

All kinds of little animals have crept into this picture. Birds hover around her head. A small deer, a great favourite with our children, has stepped on to the dust of the road, and is holding up its nose to the drooping nose of Al·Ith's horse, to comfort it, or to give it messages from other animals. Often these pictures are titled 'Al·Ith's Animals.' Some tales tell how the soldiers try to catch the birds and the deer, and are rebuked by Al·Ith.

I take the liberty of doubting whether the actual occasion impressed itself so dramatically on the soldiers, or even on Al·Ith. The soldiers wanted to ride on, and get away from this land they did not understand, and which continually discomfited them. The commander did not want to be put into the position of taking her advice, but nor did he want to ride for hours into a cold wind.

Which in fact was already making itself felt.

Al·Ith was more herself now than she had been for many weeks. She was seeing that while she mourned in her rooms, there had been other things she should have done! Duties had been neglected. She remembered that messages had come in to her from all over the country, which she had been too absorbed in her fierce thoughts to respond to.

She was seeing in herself disobedience, and the results of it. This made her, now, more gentle with this troop of barbarians, and its small-boy commander.

'You did not tell me your name,' she asked.

He hesitated. Then: 'It is Jarnti.'

'You command the king's horses?'

'I am commander of all his forces. Under the king.'

'My apologies.' She sighed, and they all heard it. They thought it weakness. Throughout these experiences with her, they could not help feeling in themselves the triumph that barbarian natures show when faced with weakness; and the need to cringe and crowd together when facing strength.

'I want to leave you for some hours,' she said.

At this they all, on a single impulse, and without any indication from their leader, crowded around her. She was inside a ring of captors.

'I cannot allow it,' said Jarnti.

'What were your orders from the king?' she enquired. She was quiet and patient but they heard subservience.

And a great roar of laughter went up from them all. Long tension exploded in them. They laughed and shouted, and the crags behind them echoed. Birds that had already settled themselves for the night wheeled up into the skies. From the long grasses by the road, animals that had been lying hidden broke away noisily.

What Ben Ata had finally shouted at his commander of all the forces, was: 'Go and get that —— —— —— and bring her here. I'm for it if I don't —— ——' For while Al·Ith had been weeping and rebellious in her quarters, he had been raging and cursing up and down the camps of his armies. There was not a soldier who had not heard what his king thought of this enforced marriage, while the camps commiserated with him, drinking, laughing, making up ribald toasts which were repeated from one end of Zone Four to the other.

This scene is another favourite of our storytellers and artists. Al·Ith, on her tired horse, is ringed by the brutal laughing men. The cold wind of the plains is pressing her robe close around her. The commander is leaning over her, his face all animal. She is in danger.

And it is true that she was. Perhaps for the only time.

Now night had fallen. Only in the skies behind them was there any light. The sunset sent up flares high towards the crown of the heavens, and made the snow peaks shine. In front of them lay the now black plain, and scattered over it at vast distances were the lights of villages and settlements. On the plateau behind them that they had travelled over, our villages and towns were crowded: it was a populous and busy land. But now they seemed to stand on the verge of nothingness, the dark. The soldiers' own country was low and mostly flat, and their towns were never built on hills and ridges. They did not like heights. More: as we shall see, they had been taught to fear them. They had been longing for the moment when they could get off that appalling plateau lifted so high among its towering peaks. They had descended from it and, associating flat lands with habitation, saw only emptiness. Their laughter had panic in it. Terror. It seemed they could not stop themselves laughing. And among them was the small silent figure of Al·Ith, who sat quietly while they rolled about in their saddles, making sounds, as she thought, like frightened animals.

Their laughing had to stop at some point. And when it did nothing had changed. She was still there. They had not impressed her with their noise. The illimitable blackness lay ahead.

'What was Ben Ata's order?' she asked again.

An explosion of sniggers, but the commander directed a glance of reproof towards the offenders, although he had been laughing as hard as any of them.

'His orders?' she insisted.

A silence.

'That you should bring me to him, that was it, I think.'

A silence.

'You will bring me to him no later than tomorrow.'

She remained where she was. The wind was now howling across the plains so that the horses could hardly keep their footing.

The commander gave a brief order which sounded shamefaced. The posse broke up, riding about on the edge of the plain, to find a camping place. She and the commander sat on their tired horses, watching. But normally he would have been with his men who, used to orders and direction, were at a loss. At length he called out that such a place would do, and they all leapt off their horses.

The beasts, used to the low relaxed air of Zone Four, were exhausted from the high altitudes of this place, and were trembling as they stood.

'There is water around that spur,' said Al·Ith. He did not argue, but shouted to the soldiers to lead the horses around the spur to drink. He got off his horse, and so did she. A soldier came to lead both animals with the others to the water. A fire was blazing in a glade between deep rocks. Saddles lay about on the grass at intervals: they would be the men's pillows.

Jarnti was still beside Al·Ith. He did not know what to do with her.

The men were already pulling out their rations from their packs, and eating. The sour powdery smell of dried meat. The reek of spirits.

Jarnti said, with a resentful laugh, 'Madam, our soldiers seem very interesting to you! Are they so different from your own?'

'We have no soldiers,' she said.

This scene, too, is much celebrated among us. The soldiers, illuminated by a blazing fire, are seated on their saddles among the grasses, eating their dried meat and drinking from their flasks. Others are leading back the horses, who have drunk at a stream out of sight behind rocks. Al·Ith stands by Jarnti at the entrance to this little natural fortress. They are watching the horses being closed into a corral that is formed by high rocks. They are hungry, and there is no food for them that night. Al·Ith is gazing at them with pity. Jarnti, towering over the small indomitable figure of our queen, is swaggering and full of bravado.

'No soldiers?' said Jarnti, disbelieving. Though of course there had always been rumours to this effect.

'We have no enemies,' she remarked. And then added, smiling straight at him, 'Have you?'

This dumbfounded him.

He could not believe the thoughts her question aroused.

While she was still smiling at him, a soldier came out from the entrance of the little camp and stood at ease close to them.

'What is he standing there for?'

'Have you never heard of a sentry?' he enquired, full of sarcasm.

'Yes. But no one is going to attack you.'

'We always post sentries,' he said.

She shrugged.

Some soldiers were already asleep. The horses drooped and rested behind their rocky barriers.

'Jarnti, I am going to leave you for some hours,' she said.

'I cannot allow you.'

'If you forbid me, you would be going beyond your orders.'

He was silent.

Here again, a favourite scene. The fire roaring up, showing the sleeping soldiers, the poor horses, and Jarnti, tugging at his beard with both hands in frustrated amazement at Al·Ith, who is smiling at him.

'Besides,' he added, 'you have not eaten.'

She enquired good-humouredly: 'Do your orders include your forcing me to eat?'

And now he said, confronting her, all trouble and dogged insistence, because of the way he was being turned inside out and upside down by her, and by the situation, 'Yes, the way I see it, by implication my orders say I should make you eat. And perhaps even sleep, if it comes to that.'

'Look, Jarnti,' said she, and went to a low bush that grew not ten paces away. She took some of its fruit. They were lumpy fruits sheathed in papery leaves. She pulled off the leaves. In each were four segments of a white substance. She ate several. The tightness of her mouth showed she was not enjoying them.

'Don't eat them unless you want to stay awake,' she said, but of course he could not resist. He blundered off to the bush, and gathered some for himself, and his mouth twisted up as he tasted the tart crumbly stuff.

'Jarnti,' she said, 'you cannot leave this camp, since you are the commander. Am I correct?'

'Correct,' he said, in a clumsy familiarity, which was the only way he knew how to match her friendliness.

'Well, I am going to walk some miles from here. Since in any case you intend to keep that poor man awake all night for nothing, I suggest you send him with me to make sure I will come back again.'

Jarnti was already feeling the effects of the fruit. He was alert and knew he could not fall off to sleep now.

'I will leave him on guard and come with you myself,' he said.

And went to give orders accordingly.

While he did this, Al·Ith walked past the sleeping soldiers to the horses, and gave each one of them, from her palm, a few of the acrid fruits from the bush. Before she had left their little prison they were lifting their heads and their eyes had brightened.

She and Jarnti set off across the blackness of the plain towards the first of the glittering lights.

This scene is always depicted thus: there is a star-crowded sky, a slice of bright moon, and the soldier striding forward made visible and prominent because his chest armour and headpiece and his shield are shining. Beside him Al·Ith is visible only as a dark shadow, but her eyes gleam softly out from her veil.

It could not have been anything like this. The wind was straight in their faces, strong and cold. She wrapped her head completely in her veil, and he had his cloak tight about him and over the lower part of his face; and the shield was held to protect them both from the wind. He had chosen to accompany this queen on no pleasant excursion, and he must have regretted it.

It took three hours to reach the settlement. It was of tents and huts: the herdsmen's headquarters. They walked through many hundreds of beasts who lifted their heads as they went past, but did not come nearer or move away. The wind was quite enough for them to withstand, and left them no energy for anything else. But as the two came to within calling distance of the first tents, where there was shelter from low scrubby trees, some beasts came nosing towards Al·Ith in the dark, and she spoke to them and held out her hands for them to smell, in greeting.

There were men and women sitting around a small fire outside a tent.

They had lifted their heads, too, sensing the approach of strangers, and Al·Ith called out to them, 'It is Al·Ith,' and they called back to her to approach.

All this was astonishing to Jarnti, who went with Al·Ith into the firelight, but several paces behind.

At the sight of him, the faces of the fire-watchers showed wonderment.

'This is Jarnti, from Zone Four,' said Al·Ith, as if what she was saying was an ordinary thing. 'He has come to take me to their king.'

Now there was not a soul in our land who did not know how she felt about this marriage, and there were many curious glances into her face and eyes. But she was showing them that this was not her concern now.

She stood waiting while rugs were brought from a tent, and when they were spread, she sat down on one and indicated to Jarnti that he should do the same. She told them that Jarnti had not eaten, and he was brought bread and porridge. She indicated that she did not want food. But she accepted a cup of wine, and Jarnti drank off jugs of the stuff. It was mild in taste, but potent. He was showing signs of discomfort if not of illness: the altitude of our plateau had affected him, he had taken too many of the stimulant berries, and he had not eaten. He was cut through and through by the winds that swept over their heads where they all leaned low over their little fire.

This scene, too, is one much depicted.

It always shows Al·Ith, alert and smiling, surrounded by the men and women of the settlement, with her cup of wine in her hand, and beside her Jarnti, drowsy and drugged. Above them the wind has scoured the sky clean and glittering. The little trees are leaning almost to the ground. The herds surround the fireside scene, looking in and wondering, waiting for a glance from their queen.

She said at once: 'As I rode out from the capital today, and down through the passes, I was stopped by many of you. What is this that they are saying about the animals?'

The spokesman was an old man.

'What have they told you, Al·Ith?'

'That there is something wrong.'

'Al·Ith, we have ourselves sent in messengers to the capital, with information.'

Al·Ith was silent, and then said, 'I'm very much to blame. Messages came, and I was too much preoccupied with my own trouble to attend.'

Jarnti was sitting with a bent head, half asleep, but at this his head jerked up, and he let out a gruff triumphant laugh, and muttered, 'Punish her, beat her, you hear? She admits it!' before his head dropped again. His mouth hung open, and the cup was loose in his hand. One of the girls took it from him gently. He snatched at it, thrust forward his bottom lip and lifted his chin belligerently at her, saw she was pretty, and a female – and would have put his arms around her, but she swiftly moved back as he submerged again in drunkenness.

Al·Ith's eyes were full of tears. The women first, then the men, seeing this oaf and his ways, saw too what was in store for her – and they were about to raise their voices in lament, keening, but she lifted her hand and stopped them.

'There is no help for it,' she said, in a low voice, her lips trembling. 'We have our orders. And it is clear down in Zone Four they don't like it any more than we do.'

They looked enquiringly at her and she nodded. 'Yes. Ben Ata is very angry. So I understood today from something that was said.'

'Ben Ata . . . Ben Ata . . .' muttered the soldier, his head rolling. 'He will have the clothes off you before you can get at him with your magic berries and your tricks.'

At this, one of the men rose to his feet and would have dragged Jarnti off, with two hands under his armpits, but Al·Ith raised her hand to stop him.

'I am more concerned with the animals,' she said. 'What was in the messages you sent me?'

'Nothing definite, Al·Ith. It is only that our animals are disturbed in their minds. They are sorrowful.'

'This is true everywhere on the plains?'

'It is true everywhere in our Zone, or so we hear. Were you not told of it up on the plateau?'

'I have already said that I am much to blame. I was not attending to my duties.'

A silence. The wind was shrieking over them, but not as loud.

Jarnti was slumped, his cup leaning in his hand, blinking at the fire. Really he was listening, since the berries have the effect of preserving attention even while the muscles are slack and disobedient. This conversation was to be retold everywhere through the camps of Zone Four, and not inaccurately, though to them the emphasis must be that the queen of all the land was sitting 'like a serf' by the fire. And, of course, that 'up there' they spoke of animals as if they were people.

Al·Ith said to the old man, 'You have asked the animals?'

'I have been among the herds since it was noticed. Day after day I have been with them. Not one says anything different. They do not know why, but they are sad enough to die. They have lost the zest for living, Al·Ith.'

'They are conceiving? Giving birth?'

'They are still giving birth. But you are right to ask if they are conceiving . . .'

At this Jarnti let out a muttering, 'They tell their queen she is right! They dare! Drag them off! Beat them . . .'

They ignored him. With compassion now. He was sitting loose and rolling there, his face aflame, and they saw him as worse than their beasts. More than one of the women was weeping, silently, at the fate of their sister, as they watched him.

'We believe they are not conceiving.'

A silence. The wind was not shrieking now. It was a low wail. The animals that were making a circle all around lifted their muzzles to sniff the air: soon the wind would be gone, and their nightly ordeal over.

'And you, the people?'

They all nodded, slowly. 'We believe that we are the same.'

'You mean, that you begin to feel in yourselves what the animals feel?'

'Yes, Al·Ith.'

And now they sat quiet for a long time. They looked into each other's faces, questioning, confirming, allowing their eyes to meet, and to part, letting what each felt pass from one to another, until they all were feeling and understanding as one.

While this went on, the soldier was motionless. Later, in the camps, he was to say that 'up there' they had vicious drugs and used them unscrupulously.

The wind had dropped. It was silent. In a swept sky the stars glittered cold. But wisps of cloud were forming in the east, over the borders with Zone Four.

One of the girls spoke up at last. 'Al·Ith, some of us have been wondering if this new Order from the Providers has something to do with this sadness of ours.'

Al·Ith nodded.

'None of us remember anything like it,' said the old man.

Al·Ith said. 'The Memories speak of such a time. But it was so long ago the historians knew nothing about it.'

'And what happened?' asked Jarnti, suddenly finding his tongue.

'We were invaded,' said Al·Ith. 'By Zone Four. Is there nothing in your history? Your tales?'

At this Jarnti wagged his pointed beard at them, grinning – triumphant.

'Is there nothing you can tell us?' asked Al·Ith.

He smirked at the women, one after another, and then his head fell forward.

'Al·Ith,' said a girl who had been sitting, letting her tears run, 'Al·Ith, what are you going to do with such men?'

'Perhaps Ben Ata won't be so bad,' said another.

'This man is the commander of all the armies,' said Al·Ith, and could not prevent herself shuddering.

'*This* man? *This?*'

Their horror and shock made itself felt in Jarnti, and he would have punished them if he could. He did manage to raise his head and glare, but he was shaking and weak.

'He is going to have to get back to the camp at the foothills,' said Al·Ith.

Two of the young men glanced at each other, and then rose. They grasped Jarnti under the armpits, hauled him to his feet, and began walking him up and down. He staggered and protested, but complied, in the end, for his brain, clear all this time, told him it was necessary.

This scene is known as 'Jarnti's Walk,' and gives much opportunity for humour to our artists and tellers.

'I don't see that there is anything we can do?' asked Al·Ith of the others. 'If this is an old disease, nothing is known of it in our medicine. If it is a new disease, our doctors will shortly come to terms with it. But if it is a malady of the heart, then the Providers will know what to do.'

A silence.

'Have already known what to do,' she said, smiling, though not pleasantly. 'Please tell everyone on the plain that I came here tonight and we talked, and what we thought together.'

We will, they said. Then they all rose to their feet, and went with her through the herds. A young girl called three horses, who came and stood willingly, waiting, while the young man put Jarnti on one, and Al·Ith mounted another, and the girl herself got on a third. The animals crowded around Al·Ith on her horse, and called to her as the three rode past.

Out on the plain, headed back towards the camp, the grasses were now standing up grey in a dim light, and the eastern sky was aflame.

Jarnti had come awake, and was sitting straight and soldierly on his horse.

'Madam,' he asked, 'how do you people talk to your animals?'

'Do you not talk to yours?'

'No.'

'You stay with them. You watch them. You put your hands on them and feel how they feel. You look into their eyes. You listen to the tones of their cries and their calling to each other. You make sure that when they begin to understand that you understand them, you do not miss the first tones of what they say to you. For if you do not hear, then they will not trouble to try again. Soon you will feel what they are feeling, and you will know what they are thinking, even if they do not tell you themselves.'

Jarnti said nothing for a while. They had now left the herds behind.

'Of course we watch them and take notice of how they look, if they are ill or something like that.'

'There are none among you who know how to feel with your animals?'

'Some of us are good with animals, yes.'

Al·Ith did not seem inclined to say any more.

'Perhaps we are too impatient,' said Jarnti.

Neither Al·Ith nor the girl said anything to this. They trotted on towards the foothills. Now the great peaks of the high lands were pink and shining from the wild morning sky.

'Madam,' he said, blustering, because he did not know how to be on an equality with her, or with anyone, 'when you are with us, can you teach some of the soldiers who are in charge of the horses this way of yours?'

She was silent. Then: 'Do you know that I am never called anything but Al·Ith? Do you understand that I have never been called Madam, or anything like it before?'

Now he was silent.

'Well, will you?' he asked gruffly.

'I will if I can,' she said at last.

He was struggling with himself to express gratitude, pleasure. Nothing came out.

They were more than halfway between the herds and the camp.

Jarnti put his heels into his horse suddenly, and it neighed and bucked. Then it stood still.

The two women stopped too.

'Did you want to go on ahead?' asked the girl.

He was sullen.

'He won't carry you now,' she said, and slid off her horse. Jarnti got down from his. 'Now get on mine.' He did so. She soothed the bewildered horse he had kicked, and mounted it.

'*Think* that you want to go on in front of us,' said the girl.

He had an ashamed, embarrassed look. He went red.

'I'm afraid you will have to put up with us,' said Al·Ith at last.

When they were in sight of the camp, she jumped down from her horse. It at once turned and began cantering back towards the herds. Jarnti got off his. And this one too cantered back. He was standing looking in admiration at the lovely girl on her horse, who was turning around to go.

'If you ever come to Zone Four,' he shouted at her, 'let me know.'

She gave a long look of commiseration at Al·Ith, and remarked, 'Luckily for me I am not a queen.' And she sped off across the plain with the two other horses neighing and tossing up their heels on either side of her.

Al·Ith and Jarnti walked towards the camp with the sunrise at their backs.

Long before they reached the camp, the smell of burning meat was strong on the air.

Al·Ith did not say anything, but her face spoke.

'Do you not kill animals?' he asked, unwillingly but forced to by his curiosity.

'Only if it is essential. There are plenty of other foods.'

'Like those horrible berries of yours,' he said, trying to be good-humoured.

In the camp they had killed a deer. Jarnti did not eat any of it.

As soon as the meal was over, the horses were saddled, all but Al·Ith's. She stood watching the beasts adjust their mouths and their teeth uncomfortably as the bit went in.

She vaulted onto her horse, and whispered to it. Jarnti watched her, uneasy.

'What did you say to it?' he asked.

'That I am his friend.'

And again she led the way forward, into the east, back across the plain.

They rode to one side of the herds they had been with in the night, but far enough off to see them as a darkness on the plain.

Jarnti was riding just behind Al·Ith.

Now he was remembering the conversation around the fire last night, the tone of it, the ease of it. He yearned for it – or something in it, for he had never known that quality of easy intimacy. Except, he was saying to himself, with a girl, sometimes, after a good screw.

He said, almost wistfully, to Al·Ith, 'Can you feel that the animals out there are sad?' For she was looking continually towards them, and her face was concerned.

'Can't you?' she asked.

He saw she was weeping, steadily, as she rode.

He was furious. He was irritated. He felt altogether excluded from something he had a right to.

Behind them clattered the company of soldiers.

A long way in front was the frontier. Suddenly she leaned down to whisper to the horse and it sped forward. Jarnti and the company broke into speed after her. They were shouting at her. She did not have the shield that would protect her from the – to her – deadly atmosphere of Zone Four. She rode like the wild winds that scoured the plains every night until early dawn, and her long hair swept out behind her, and tears ran steadily down her face.

It was not for miles that Jarnti came up with her – one of the soldiers had thrown the shield to him, and he had caught it, and was now riding almost neck and neck with her.

'Al·Ith,' he was shouting, 'you must have this.' And held up the shield. It was a long time before she heard him. At last she turned her face towards him, not halting her mad pace in the slightest, and he wilted at the sight of her blanched, agonised face. He held up the shield. She raised her hand to catch it. He hesitated, because it was not a light thing. He remembered how she had thrown the heavy saddle the day before, and he heaved the shield towards her. She caught it with one hand and did not abate her pace at all. They were approaching the frontier. They watched her to see how she would be affected by the sudden change in the density of the air, for they had all been ill to some extent, the day before. She went through the invisible barrier without faltering, though she was pale, and did not seem well. Inside the frontier line were the observation towers, rising up at half-mile distances from each other, bristling with soldiers and armaments. She did not stop. Jarnti and the others fled after her, shouting to the soldiers in the towers not to shoot. She went between the towers without looking at them.

Again they were on the edge of a descent through hills and rocks above a wide plain. When she reached the edge of this escarpment she at last stopped.

They all came to a standstill behind her. She was looking down into a land crowded with forts and encampments.

She jumped down from her horse. Soldiers were running to them from the forts, holding the bridles of fresh horses. The jaded horses of the company were being herded off to recover. But Al·Ith's did not want to leave her. He shivered and whinnied and wheeled all about Al·Ith, and when the soldiers came to catch him, would not go.

'Would you like him as a present, Al·Ith?' asked Jarnti, and she was pleased and smiled a little, which was all she could manage.

Again she removed the saddle from this fresh horse, and the bridle, and tossed them to the amazed soldiers. And she rode forward and down into Zone Four, with Yori trotting beside her and continually putting up his nose to nuzzle her as they went.

And so Al·Ith made the passage into the Zone we had all heard so much of, speculated about, and had never been in.

Not even with the shield could she feel anything like herself. The air was flat, dispiriting. The landscape seemed to confine and oppress. Everywhere you look, in our own realm, a wild vigour is expressed in the contours of uplands, mountains, a variegated ruggedness. The central plateau where so many of our towns are situated is by no means regular, but is ringed by mountains and broken by ravines and deep river channels. With us the eye is enticed into continual movement, and then is drawn back always to the great snowy peaks that are shaped by the winds and the colours of our skies. And the air tingles in the blood, cold and sharp. But here she looked down into a uniform dull flat, cut by canals and tamed streams that were marked by lines of straight pollarded trees, and dotted regularly by the ordered camps of the military way of life. Towns and villages did not seem any larger than these camps. The sky was a greyish blue and there was a dull shine from the lines of water. A wide low hill near the centre of the scene where there seemed to be something like a park or gardens was all the consolation she could find.

Meanwhile, they were still descending the escarpment.

A turn in the road showed an enormous circular building of grey stone, squatting heavily between canals. It seemed recent, for rocks and earth near it were raw, broken. Her dismay that this might be where she was bound for brought her horse to a faltering stop. The company halted behind her, and she looked back to see a furtive triumph on every face. Jarnti was suppressing a smile as a leader does when he wishes to indicate he would like to join with his juniors in a show of emotion. Then as they remained there, with no sound but the horses shifting their hooves for relief, on the stony road, she saw that she had been mistaken: what she feared was not matched by the particular variety of triumph these captors of hers were showing.

'When may we expect to reach the king?' she asked, and Jarnti at once interpreted this as a reminder from her of higher authority. He rebuked his company with a strong look and adjusted his own face to obedience.

All this she watched, understood – and it came to her what a barbarous land this was.

They had imagined she had been intimidated by the sight of the rumoured 'round fortress of the deadly rays' as one of our songs described it.

She told herself, not for the first time, or the tenth, that she was not likely to adjust herself quickly to these people with their slavish minds, and to make a test of them, moved her horse on and towards the road that led to the building. At once Jarnti was beside her, and his hand was reaching out for her horse's head. She stopped. 'I would like to see into one of the famed round fortresses of your Zone,' she said.

'Oh, no, no, you must not, it is forbidden,' said he, still full of importance.

'But why? Your weapons are not directed against us, surely?'

'It is dangerous . . .' but at this moment, around the side of the building came some children running, and in scattering for some game, two of them darted into an open doorway.

'So I see,' she said, and rode on, without looking again at Jarnti or at the soldiers.

When nearly at the level of the plain, there were grazing cattle near the road, and a half-grown boy attending them.

Jarnti shouted at the boy to come forward, and the boy was already running towards them, before Jarnti said, 'You could teach him your ways with the animals,' and as the boy arrived at the roadside, pale and startled, Jarnti was shouting. 'Down on your face! Can't you see who this is we are taking to the king?'

The lad was face down, full length on the grass, and this was no more than a half-minute since he had first been hailed.

Jarnti was giving her half-pleading, half-commanding looks, and his horse was dancing under him, because of his master's eagerness to learn her lore.

'Well,' she said, 'I don't think we are likely to learn or teach anything in this way.'

But he had seen himself that he had mishandled the occasion and because of it was red and angry. He shouted, 'The lady here would like to know if your beasts are well.'

No reply, then a whimper which sounded like, 'Very well, yes, well, sir.'

Al·Ith slid down from her horse, walked over to the boy, and said, 'Stand up.' She made her voice a command, since commands were what he understood. He slowly shivered his way to his feet, and stood, almost collapsing, before her. She waited until she knew he had seen, from his furtive glances, that she was not so frightening, and said, 'I am from Zone Three. Our animals have not been well. Can you say if you have noticed anything unusual with yours?'

His hands were clenched at his chest, and he was breathing as if he had run several miles. Finally he brought out: 'Yes, yes, that is, I think so.'

From behind them Jarnti's voice, jocular and loud: 'Are they having sorrowful thoughts?' And the entire company sniggered.

She saw there was nothing that could be done, and said to the boy, 'Don't be frightened. Go back to your beasts.' She waited until he sped off, and she returned to her horse. Again, Jarnti knew he had behaved clumsily, and yet it had been necessary to him, for the sight of her, small, unarmed, standing rather below them near the defenceless and frightened boy, had roused in him a need to show strength, dominance.

She swung herself onto her horse and at once rode on, not looking at them. She felt very low, our poor Al·Ith. This was the worst time of all. Everything in her was hurt by the way the poor boy had been treated: yet these were the ways of this land, and she could not believe then, in that bad hour, that there could be any way of communicating with these louts. And of course she was thinking of what she was going to find when she was led to Ben Ata.

They rode on, through the middle of the day, across the plain, with the ditches and the lines of dull bunchy trees accompanying them all the way. She went first. Yori, the riderless horse, was just behind, with Jarnti, and behind them the company. They were all silent. She had not said anything about the incident of the boy, but they were thinking now that she would be soon with the king, and were not expecting she would give a good report of them. So they were sullen, sulky. There were few people on the roadside, or in the flat boats of the canals, but those who saw the little company go past reported that there was not a smile to be seen: this wedding party was fit for a funeral. And the riderless horse caused rumours to spread that Al·Ith had fallen and was dead, for the slight figure on the leading horse that they did see, had nothing about her to command their attention. She seemed to them a serving woman, or an attendant, in her plain dark blue, with her head in its black veils.

There was a ballad about how the horse of the dead Al·Ith had gone with the troop of soldiers to the king to tell him that there could be no marriage. The horse stood on the threshold of the wedding chamber and neighed three times, Ben Ata, Ben Ata, Ben Ata – and when he came out, said to him:

> Cold and dark your wedding bed,
> O King, your willing bride is dead.
> The realm she rules is cold and dark.

And this was popular, and sung when everyone knew that Al·Ith was not dead, and that the marriage was a fact. That it was not the smoothest of marriages was of course known from the beginning. How? But how do these things get themselves known? The song was always being added to. Here is a verse that came from the married quarters of the army camps:

> Brave King, your realm is strong and fine.
> Where beasts may mate, then women pine.
> I will be your slave, brave King.

Not anywhere with us, or at any time, have such verses as these been possible, though there were plenty of compassionate and tender ballads made up about Al·Ith. There are some who say that where there is rulership, there has to be criticism of this ribald kind, because no matter the level of the ruler, it is in the nature of the ruled to crave identification of the lowest sort. We say this is not so, and Zone Three proves it. To recognise and celebrate the ordinary, the day-to-day levels of an authority, is not to denigrate it.

Such Zone Four ballads, travelling upwards to us, found themselves transformed as they crossed the frontier. For one thing, there was no need of the inversions, the ambiguities, that are always bred by fear of an arbitrary authority.

We may almost say that a certain type of ballad is impossible with us: the kind that has as its ground or base lamentation, the celebration of loss.

In their Zone the riderless horse gave birth to songs of death and sorrow; in ours to songs about loving friendship.

The road, which cut straight across the plain, and was intersected at about the middle by one running equally straight, began to lift a little to reach the small hill that Al·Ith had seen with relief from the top of the escarpment. The canals were left behind, with their weight of dead water. There were a few ordinary trees, which had not been hacked into lumps and wands. At the top of the hill were gardens, and here the water had been forced into movement, for they rode now beside channels where it ran swiftly, fell from several levels to others, and broke into fountains. The air was lively and cool, and when she saw ahead of her a light pavilion, with coloured springing pillars and arches, she was encouraged. But there was no one to be seen. She was contrasting this empty garden and the apparently deserted pavilion with the friendly amplitude of her own courts, when Jarnti called an order, and the whole company came to a stop. The soldiers jumped off their horses, and surrounded Al·Ith, who, when she got down from her horse, found herself being marched forward in their midst, like a captive of war – and she saw that this was not the first time they had done this, from the ease of their arrangements.

But as they had enclosed her, Jarnti in front, she put out her hand to hold the horse she had been given, Yori, by the neck.

And this was how she arrived at the steps of the pavilion, when Ben Ata came out to stand in the doorway, arms folded, legs apart, a bearded soldier, dressed in no way different from Jarnti or the others. He was large, blond, muscular from continual campaigning, and burned a ruddy brown on the face and arms. His eyes were grey. He was not looking at Al·Ith but at the horse, for his first thought too was that his bride had been killed.

Al·Ith went quickly through the soldiers, suspecting that there were precedents here she might not want followed, and arrived in front of him, still holding the horse.

And now he looked at her, startled and frowning.

'I am Al·Ith,' said she, 'and this horse has been kindly given to me by Jarnti. Please, will you give orders for him to be well treated?'

He found himself speechless. He nodded. Jarnti then grasped the horse's neck and attempted to lead him away. But he reared and tried to free himself. Before he would allow himself to be taken away. Al·Ith had to comfort him and promise she would visit him very soon. 'Today, I swear it.' And, turning to Jarnti, 'So you must not take him too far away. And please see he is well fed and looked after.'

Jarnti was sheepish, the soldiers grinning, only just hiding it, because Ben Ata's face gave them no guidance. Normally, on such occasions, the girl would have been bundled across a threshold, or pushed forward roughly, according to the convention, but now no one knew how to behave.

Al·Ith said, 'Ben Ata, I take it you have some sort of place I can retire to for a time? I have been riding all day.'

Ben Ata was recovering. His face was hard, and even bitter. He had not known what to expect, and was prepared to be flexible, but he was repelled by this woman in her sombre clothes. She had not taken off her veil, and he could not see much of her except that she had dark hair. He preferred fair women.

He shrugged, gave a look at Jarnti, and disappeared into the room behind him. It was Jarnti then who led her into another room, which was part of a sct of rooms, and saw that she had what she needed. She refused food and drink, and announced that she would be ready to join the king in a few minutes.

And she did join him, emerging unceremoniously from the retiring rooms just as she had arrived, in her dark dress. But she had removed the veil, and her hair was braided and hanging down her back.

Ben Ata was lounging on a low divan or settee, in a large light airy room that had nothing very much in it. She saw that this was a bridal room, and planned for the occasion. Her bridegroom, however, sprawling on one edge of the divan, his chin on his hand, his elbow on his knee, did not move as she came in. And there was nowhere else to sit, so she sat down on the edge of the divan, at a distance from him, resting her weight on her hand in the position of one who has alighted somewhere for just a moment and has every intention of leaving again. She looked at him, without smiling. He looked at her, very far from smiling.

'Well, how do you like this place?' he asked, roughly. It was clear he had no idea of what to say or do.

'It has been built specially then?'

'Yes. Orders. Built to specification. Exactly. It was finished only this morning.'

'It is certainly very elegant and pleasant,' she said. 'Quite different from anything else I've seen on my way here.'

'Certainly not my style,' he said. 'But if it is yours, then that's the main thing.'

This had a sort of sulky gallantry, but he was restless, and sighing continually, and it was evident all he wanted to do was to make his escape.

'I suppose the intention was that it should be suited to us both?' she remarked.

'I don't care,' said he violently and roughly, his inner emotions breaking out of him. 'And obviously you don't either.'

'We're going to have to make the best of it,' she said, intending consolation, but it was wild and bitter.

They looked at each other with a frank exchange of complicity: two prisoners who had nothing in common but their incarceration.

This first, and frail, moment of tolerance did not last.

He had flung himself back on this marriage couch of theirs, arms behind his head, his sandalled feet dusty on the covers, which were of fine wool, dyed in soft colours, and embroidered. Nowhere could he have seemed more out of place. She was able to construct his usual surroundings by how he slouched there, gazing at the ceiling as if she did not exist.

She examined the place. This was a very large room, opening out on two sides into gardens through a series of rounded arches. The other two sides had unobtrusive doors leading – on one – to the rooms for her use where she had already been, and on the other, presumably, to his. The ceiling was rounded and high, fluted at the edges. The whole room was painted a softly shining ivory, but there were patterns of gold, soft red, and blue, and beside each archway embroidered curtains were caught back with jewelled clasps. The fountains could be heard, and the running of the waters. This was not far from the gaiety and freshness of the public buildings of Andaroun, our capital, though her own quarters were plainer than these.

The great room was not all one empty sweep of space. A column sprung up from its centre, and curved out, and divided into several, all fluted and defined in the same gold, sky blue, and red. The floors were of sweetly smelling wood. Apart from the great low couch, there was a small table near one of the arches, with two graceful chairs on either side of it.

A horse whinnied. A moment later, Yori appeared outside one of the arches, and would have come in if she had not run across and stopped him. It was easy to guess what had happened. He had been confined somewhere, and had jumped free, and the soldiers set to guard him did not dare to follow into these private gardens with the pavilion all the country had been talking of for weeks. She put her hands up to his cheeks, pulled down his head, whispered into first one ear, and then the other, and the horse swung around and went out of sight, back to its guard.

When she turned, Ben Ata was standing just behind her, glaring.

'I can see that it is true, what we have heard here. You are all witches in your country.'

'It is a witchcraft easy to learn,' she said, but as he continued to glare, her humour went, and now she crossed swiftly to the bed and, throwing down one of the big cushions, sat on it cross-legged. She had not thought that now he must do the same, or remain above her on the bed, but he was uncertain, seemed to feel challenged by her, and in his turn pulled a cushion off the bed, pushed it against a wall, and sat.

They sat opposite each other, on their two cushions.

She was at home, since this was how she usually seated herself, but he was uncomfortable, and seemed afraid to make any movement, in case the cushion slid about the polished floor.

'Do you always wear clothes like that?'

'I put this on especially for you,' she countered, and he reddened again: since her arrival she had seen more angry, embarrassed men than ever in her life, and she was on the point of wondering if they had some disorder of the blood or the skin.

'If I had known you were going to arrive like this I would have ordered dresses for you. How was I to know you'd turn up like a servant?'

'Ben Ata, I never wear elaborate clothes.'

He was eyeing the plain looseness of her robe with annoyance and exasperation.

'I thought you were supposed to be the queen.'

'You cannot be distinguished from one of your own soldiers.'

Suddenly he bared his teeth in a grin, and muttered something that she understood meant: 'Take the thing off, and I'll show you.'

She knew he was angry, but not how much. On their campaigns, when the army reached new territory, into his tent would be thrust some girl, or she was thrown down at his feet. She would nearly always be crying. Or she might be hissing and spitting. She might bite and scratch as he entered her. She could weep throughout and not cease weeping. A few gritted their teeth, and their loathing of him did not abate. He was not a man who enjoyed inflicting suffering, so these he would order to be returned to their homes. But those who wept or who struggled in a way he recognised he did enjoy, and would tame them, slowly. These were the conventions. These he obeyed. He had penetrated, and often impregnated, women all over his realm. But he had not married, he did not plan to marry, for the present arrangement did not come within his notions of marriage, about which he had the sentimental and high-flown ideas of a man ignorant of women. This woman with whom he was to be afflicted almost indefinitely, at least at intervals, was something outside his experience.

Everything about her disturbed him. She was not unbeautiful, with her dark eyes, dark hair, and the rest of the usual appurtenances, but there was nothing in her that set out to challenge him physically, and so he was cold.

'How long am I supposed to stay with you?' she enquired next, in exactly the cut-and-dried way he now – dismally – expected of her.

'They said, a few days.'

There was a long silence. The great pleasant room was full of water sounds, and watery reflections from the pools and fountains.

'How do you do it in your country?' he enquired, knowing this was clumsy but not able to think of anything else.

'Do *what*?'

'Well, we hear you have a lot of children, for a start.'

'I have five of my own. But I am the mother of many. More than fifty.'

She could see that everything she said put greater distance between them.

'It is our custom, if a child is left an orphan, that I should become its mother.'

'Adopt it.'

'It is not one of our words. I become its mother.'

'I suppose you feel about them exactly as you do about your own,' he said, and this was a mimicry. But of something she had not said.

'No, I did not say that. Besides, fifty children are rather more than one can keep very close to.'

'Then how are they your children?'

'They all have the same rights. And I spend the same time with each of them, as I am able.'

'It's not my idea of a mother for *my* children.'

'Is that what is expected of us, you think?'

This infuriated him! He had not *thought* very much at all about this appalling, affronting imposition, he had been too emotional. But at the least he had supposed that there would be children 'to cement the alliance' – or something of that sort.

'Well, what else? What did you have in mind? Amorous dalliance once every few weeks? *You!*' And he snorted out his disgust with her.

She was trying not to look at him too closely. She had seen that a close steady look – which was her way – discomfited him. And besides, he appealed to her less than she did to him. She found this great soldier gross, with his heavy overheated flesh, his hot, resentful eyes, his rough sun-bleached hair which reminded her of the fleeces of a much prized breed of sheep that flourished on a certain mountain.

'There's more to mating than children,' she observed.

And the commonsensicalness of this caused him to groan out loud and strike his fists hard on the floor beside him.

'Well, if so, one wouldn't think you knew much about *that*.'

'Indeed,' she retorted. 'But in fact it is one of the skills of our Zone.'

'Oh, no,' he said. 'Oh, no, no, no, no.' And he sprang up and went striding about the room, beating the delicate walls with his fists.

She, still cross-legged on her cushion, watched him, interested, as she would have done some strange new species.

He stopped. He seemed to make an effort. Then he turned, teeth gritted, strode across to her, picked her up, and threw her on the couch. He put his hand across her mouth in the approved way, twitched up her dress, fingered himself to see if he was up to it, thrust himself into her, and accomplished his task in half a dozen swift movements.

He then straightened himself, for he had not removed his feet from the floor during this process and, already embarrassed, showed his feeling that all was not right by a gesture of concern most unusual in him: he twitched her dress down again and removed his hand from her mouth quite gently.

She was lying there looking up at him quite blank. Amazed. She was not weeping. Nor scratching. Nor calling him names. Nor showing the cold relentless repulsion that he dreaded to see in his women. Nothing. It occurred to him that she was *interested* in a totally unsuspected phenomenon.

'Oh, you,' he groaned out, between his teeth, 'how did I get saddled with you.'

At which she suddenly let out a snort of something that was unmistakably amusement. She sat up. She swung her legs down over the couch, then she all at once burst into swift tears that shook her shoulders quite soundlessly, and then, just as suddenly, she stopped crying, and crept to her cushion, where she sat with her back to the wall, staring at him.

He noted that she was afraid of him, but not in any way that could appeal to him.

'Well,' he said, 'that's that.' He gave her uneasy sideways glances, as if waiting for a comment.

'Is that really what you do?' she enquired. 'Or is it because you don't like me?'

At this he gave her a look which was all appeal, and he sat on the bottom of the bed, and pounded it hard, with his fists.

She saw, at last, that he was a boy, he was not much more than a small boy. She saw him as one of her own half-grown sons, and for the first time, her heart softened.

Looking at him with the tears still full in her great eyes, she said, 'You know, I think there might be something you could learn from us.'

He gave a sort of shake of his great shaggy head, as if too much was reaching his ears all at once. But he remained leaning forward, not looking at her, but listening.

'For one thing, have you never heard that one may choose the times to conceive children?'

He winced. But only because again she talked of children. He pounded the bed with one fist, and stopped.

'You did not know that the nature of a child may be made by its conception?'

He shook his head and hung it. He sighed.

'If I am pregnant now, as I could be, then this child will have nothing to thank us for.'

He suddenly flung himself down on the bed, prone, and lay there, arms outstretched.

Again, a long silence. The smell of their coupling was a small rank reminder of lust, and he looked up at her. She sat leaning against the wall, very pale, tired, and there was a bruise by her mouth, where his thumb had pressed.

He let out a groan. 'It seems there is something I can learn from you,' he said, and it was not in a child's voice.

She nodded. Looking at each other, they saw only that they were unhappy, and did not know what to expect from the other.

She it was who got up, sat by him on the couch, and laid her small hands on both sides of his great neck as he still lay prone, chin on his fist.

He turned over. It was an effort for him to face her.

He took her hands, and lay there on his back, she sitting quietly close to him. She tried to smile, but her lips trembled, and tears rolled down her face. He gave an exclamation, and pulled her down beside him. He was astounded that his own eyes had tears in them.

He tried to comfort this strange woman. He felt her small hands on his shoulders, in a pressure of consolation and pity.

Thus they fell asleep together, worn out by it all.

This was the first lovemaking of these two, the event which was fusing the imaginations of two realms.

The Good Terrorist

She woke when Jasper did, at seven, but lay still watching him from nearly-closed eyes. His wiry body was full of the energy of expectation. Everything from his gingery hair (which she thought of privately as cinnamon-coloured) to his small deft feet, which she adored, because they were so white and slender, was alive. He seemed to dance his way into his clothes, and his pale face was innocent and sweet, when he stood momentarily at the window, to see what the weather was like for the day's picketing. There was an exalted dreamy look to him, as he went past the apparently sleeping Alice to the door. He did not look at her.

She relaxed, lay on her back, and listened. He knocked next door, and she heard Bert's reluctant response, and Pat's prompt, 'Right, we're awake.' Then the knock on Roberta's and Faye's door. Philip? Oh, not Philip, she needed him here! But there was no other knock, and then she began worrying: I hope Philip won't feel left out, despised? A knock on the door of the room immediately below this one; the big room that was Jim's, though it was really a living-room, and should perhaps be used as such . . . No, that was not fair. A startled shout from Jim; but she could not decide whether he was pleased to be roused, or not.

The sounds of the house coming to life. She could go down if she wanted, could sit with the cheerful group and send them on their way with smiles, but her mouth was dry and her eyes pricked. For some reason – a dream perhaps? – she wanted to weep, go back to sleep. To give up. She distrusted what she felt; for it had been with her since she could remember: being excluded, left out. Unwanted. And that was silly, because all she had to do was to say she was going too. But how could she, when their fate, the fate of them all, would be decided that morning at the Council, and it was by no means certain the house was theirs. When Mary had gone off saying, 'I'll do my best,' it meant no more than that. Alice brought Bob Hood to life in her mind's eye, and, staring at the correct, judicious young man, willed him to do what she wanted. 'Put our case,' she said to him. 'Make them let us have it. It's *our* house.' She kept this up for some minutes, while listening to how the others moved about the kitchen. Almost at once, though, they were out of the house. They were going to breakfast in a café. That was silly, raged Alice: wasting all that money! Eating at home was what they would have to learn to do. She would mention it, have it out with them.

Oh, she did feel low and sad.

For some reason she thought of her brother Humphrey, and the familiar incredulous rage took hold of her. How could he be content to play their game? A nice safe little job – aircraft controller, who would have thought anyone would choose to spend his life like that! And her mother had said he had written to announce a child. The first, he had said. Suddenly Alice thought: That means I am an aunt. It had not occurred to her before. Her rage vanished, and she thought, Well, perhaps I'll go and see the baby. She lay smiling there for some time, in a silent house, though the din from the traffic encompassed it. Then, consciously pulling herself together, with a set look on her face, she rolled out of the sleeping bag, pulled on her jeans, and went downstairs. On the kitchen table were five unwashed coffee-cups – they had taken time for coffee, so that meant they hadn't gone to the café; they would have a picnic on the train again; no, don't think about that. She washed up the cups, thinking, I've got to organise something for hot water – it used to come off the gas, but of course the Council workmen stole the boiler. We can't afford a new one. A second-hand one? Philip will know where and how . . . today he will fix the windows, if I get the glass. He said he needed another morning for the slates. Seven windows – what is that going to cost, for glass!

She took out the money that was left: less than a hundred pounds. And with everything to be bought, to be paid for. . . Jasper said he would get her Social Security, but of course, she couldn't complain, he worked really hard yesterday, getting all that good stuff from the skips. At this moment she saw, on the windowsill, an envelope with 'Alice' scribbled on it, and under that 'Have a nice day!' And under that 'Love, Jasper'. Her money was in it. She quickly checked: he had been known to keep half, saying: We must make sacrifices for the sake of the future. But there were four ten-pound notes there.

She sat at the table, soft with love and gratitude. He did love her. He did. And he did these wonderful, sweet things.

She sat relaxed, at the head of the great wooden table. If they wanted to sell it, they could get fifty for it, more. The kitchen was a long room, not very wide. The table stood near a window that had a broad sill. From the table she could see the tree, the place where she and Jim had buried the shit, now a healthy stretch of dark earth, and the fence beyond which was Joan Robbins's house. It was a tall wood fence, and shrubs showed above it, in bud. A yellow splodge of forsythia. Birds. The cat sneaked up the fence, and opened its mouth in a soundless miaow, looking at her. She opened the window that sparkled in the sun, and the cat came in to the sill, drank some milk and ate scraps, and sat for a while, its experienced eyes on Alice. Then it began licking itself.

It was in poor condition, and should be taken to the vet.

All these things that must be done. Alice knew that she would do none of them, until she heard from Mary. She would sit here, by herself, doing nothing. Funny, she was described as unemployed, she had never had a job, and she was always busy. To sit quietly, just thinking, a treat, that. To be by oneself – nice. Guilt threatened to invade with this thought: it was disloyalty to her friends. She didn't want to be like her mother who was selfish. She used to nag and bitch to have an afternoon to herself: the children had to lump it. Privacy. That lot made such a thing about privacy; 99 per cent of the world's population wouldn't know the word. If they had ever heard it. No, it was better like this, healthy, a group of comrades. Sharing. But at this, worry started to nibble and nag, and she was thinking: That's why I am so upset this morning. It's Mary, it's Reggie. They are simply not like us. They will never really let go and meld with us, they'll stay a couple. They'll have private viewpoints about the rest of us. Well then, that was true of Roberta and Faye, a couple; they made it clear they had their own attitudes and opinions. They did not like what was happening now, with the house. And Bert and Pat? No, they did not have a little opinion of their own set against the others; but Pat was only here at all because she actually enjoyed being screwed (the right word for it!) Jim? Philip? She and Jasper? When you got down to it, she and Jasper were the only genuine revolutionaries here. Appalled by this thought, she nevertheless examined it. What about Bert? Jasper approved of him. Jasper's attachments to men who were like elder brothers had nothing to do with their politics but with their natures; they had always been the same type, easy-going. Kind. That was it. Bert was a good person. But was he a revolutionary? It's unfair to say that Faye and Roberta are not real revolutionaries just because I don't like them, thought Alice . . . where were these thoughts getting her? What was the point? The group, her family, lay in its parts, diminished, criticised out of existence. Alice sat alone, even thinking, Well, if we don't get the house, we'll go down to the squat in Brixton.

A sound upstairs, immediately above. Faye and Roberta: they had not gone with the others. Alice listened to how they got themselves awake and up: stirrings, and the slithering sound the sleeping-bags made on the bare boards; a laugh, a real giggle. Silence. Then footsteps and they were coming into the kitchen.

Alice got up to put the saucepan on the heat, and sat down. The two smelled ripe; sweaty and female. They were not going to wash in cold water, not these two!

The two women, smiling at Alice, sat together with their backs to the stove, where they could look out of the window and see the morning's sun.

Knowing that she was going to have to, Alice made herself tell about last night, about Mary and Reggie. She did not soften it at all. The other two sat side by side, waiting for their coffee, not looking at each other, for which Alice was grateful. She saw appear on their faces the irony that she heard in her own voice.

'So the CCU has two recruits?' said Roberta, and burst out laughing.

'They are good people,' said Alice reprovingly. But she laughed too.

Faye did not laugh, but little white teeth held a pink lower lip, her shining brown brows frowned, and the whole of her person announced her disapproval. Roberta stopped laughing.

Hey, thought Alice, I've seen this before: you'd think it was Roberta who was the strong one; she comes on so butch-motherly, she's like a hen with one chick, but no, it's Faye who's the one, never mind about all her pretty bitchy little ways. And she looked carefully and with respect at Faye, who was about to pronounce. And Roberta waited too.

'Listen Alice, now you listen, you listen carefully, for I am about to say my piece . . .' And Alice could see it was hard for her to assert herself, that this was why she had so many little tricks and turns, little poutings and hesitations and small wary glances and little smiles at Roberta and at herself, but underneath she was iron, she was formidable. 'Once and for all, I do not care about all this domestic bliss, all the house and garden stuff . . .' Here she waited, politely, while first Roberta and then Alice – seeing that Roberta did – laughed. 'Well, for me it is all pretty classy stuff,' said Faye, 'this house would have seemed a palace to me once. I've lived in at least a thousand squats, dens, holes, corners, rooms, hovels and residences, and this is the best yet. And I don't care.' Here she pettishly, humorously, wagged a finger at Alice. Roberta had her eyes on her love's face, exactly like an elder sister; *is she going to go too far?* Too far, Alice knew, with all this presentation, the manner, the means that enabled Faye to say her piece. Roberta did not want Alice to think that this girl was frivolous or silly.

Well, she certainly did not.

'Any minute now we are going to have hot running water and double glazing, I wouldn't be surprised. For me this is all a lot of shit, do you hear? *Shit!*'

Alice got up, poured boiling water into the three mugs that already had coffee powder in them, set the mugs on the table, put the milk bottle and the sugar near Faye. She did this as something of a demonstration and saw that as Faye stretched out her hand for the coffee, which she was going to drink black and bitter, she knew it, and even appreciated it, judging from her quick shrewd little smile. But she was going on, with determination. She had also lost her cockney self, and the voice that went with it.

It was in all-purpose BBC English that she went on, 'I don't care about that, Alice. Don't you see? If you want to wait on me, then do. If you don't, don't. I don't care, either way.'

Roberta said quickly, protectively, 'Faye has had a terrible life, such an awful shitty terrible life . . .' And her voice broke and she turned her face away.

'Yes, I did,' said Faye, 'but don't make a thing of it. I don't.' Roberta shook her head, unable to speak, and put her hand, tentatively, ready to be rejected, on Faye's arm. Faye said, 'If you are going to tell Alice about my ghastly childhood then tell her but not when I am here.'

She drank gulps of the bitter coffee, grimaced, reached for a biscuit, took a neat sharp bite out of it, and crunched it up, as if it were a dose of medicine. Another gulp of caffeine. Roberta had her face averted. Alice knew that she was infinitely sorrowful about something; if not Faye's past, then Faye's present: her hand, ignored by Faye, had dropped from Faye's arm, and crept back into her own lap, where it lay trembling and pitiful, and her lowered head with its crop of black silvered curls made Alice think of a humbly loving dog's. Roberta was radiating love and longing. At this moment, at least, Faye did not need Roberta, but Roberta was dying of need for Faye.

Faye probably has times when she wants to be free of Roberta, finds it all too much – yes, that's it. Well, I bet Roberta never wants to be free of Faye! Oh God, all this personal stuff, getting in the way of everything all the time. Well, at least Jasper and I have got it all sorted out.

Faye was going on. Christ, listen to her, she could get a job with the BBC, thought Alice. I wonder when she learned to do it so well. And what for?

'I've met people like you before, Alice. In the course of my long career. You cannot let things be. You're always keeping things up and making things work. If there's a bit of dust in a corner you panic.' Here Roberta let out a gruff laugh, and Alice primly smiled – she was thinking of all those pails. 'Oh laugh. Laugh away.' It seemed she could have ended there, for she hesitated, and the pretty cockney almost reclaimed her, with a pert flirtatious smile. But Faye shook her off, and sat upright in a cold fierce solitude, self-sufficient, so that Roberta's again solicitous and seeking hand fell away. 'I care about just one thing, Alice. And you listen to me, Roberta, you keep forgetting about me, what I am, what I really am *like*. I want to put an end to this shitty fucking filthy lying cruel hypocritical system. Do you understand? Well, do you, Roberta?'

She was not at all pretty, nor appealing, then, but pale and angry, and her mouth was tight and her eyes hard, and this – how she looked – took sentimentality away from what she said next. 'I want to put an end to it all so that children don't have a bad time, the way I did.'

Roberta sat there isolated, repudiated, unable to speak.

Alice said, 'But Faye, do you think I'm not a revolutionary? I agree with every word you say.'

'I don't know anything about you, Comrade Alice. Except that you are a wonder with the housekeeping. And with the police. I like that. But just before you came, we took a decision, a joint decision. We decided we are going to work with the IRA. Have you forgotten?'

Alice was silent. She was thinking, But Jasper and Bert have been discussing things next door, surely? She said, carefully, 'I understood that a comrade at 45 had indicated that . . .'

'What comrade?' demanded Roberta, coming to life again. 'We know nothing about that.'

'Oh,' said Alice. 'I thought . . .'

'It's just amateurish rubbish,' said Faye. 'Suddenly some unknown authority next door says this and that.'

'I didn't realise,' said Alice. She had nothing to say. She was thinking: Was it Bert who led Jasper into . . . ? Was it Jasper who . . . ? I don't remember Jasper doing anything like this before . . .

After some time, while no one said anything, but sat separate, thinking their own thoughts, Alice said, 'Well, I agree. It is time we all got together and discussed it. Properly.'

'Including the two new *comrades*?' inquired Faye, bitter.

'No, no, just us. Just you and Roberta and Bert and Jasper and Pat and me.'

'*Not* Philip and *not* Jim,' said Roberta.

'Then the six of us might go to a café or somewhere for a discussion,' said Alice.

'Quite so,' said Faye. 'We can't have a meeting here, too many extraneous elements. Exactly.'

'Well, perhaps we could borrow a room in 45,' said Alice.

'We could go and have a lovely picnic in the park, why not?' said Faye, fiercely.

'Why not?' said Roberta, laughing. It could be seen that she was coming back into the ascendant, sat strong and confident, and sent glances towards Faye which would soon be returned.

Another silence, companionable, no hard feelings.

Alice said, 'I have to ask this, it has to be raised. Are you two prepared to contribute anything to expenses?'

Faye, as expected, laughed. Roberta said quickly, reprovingly of Faye – which told Alice everything about the arguments that had gone on about this very subject, 'We are going to pay for food and suchlike. You tell us how it works out.'

'Very cheaply, with so many of us.'

'Yes, said Faye. 'That's fair. But you can leave me out of all the gracious living. I'm not interested. Roberta can do what she likes.' And she got up, smiled nicely at them both, and went out. Roberta made an instinctive movement to go after her but stayed put. She said, 'I'll make a contribution, Alice. I'm not like Faye – I'm not indifferent to my surroundings. You know, she really is,' she said urgently, smiling, pressing on Alice Faye's difference, her uniqueness, her preciousness.

'Yes, I know.'

Roberta gave Alice two ten-pound notes, which she took, with no expression on her face, knowing that that would be it, and thanked

Roberta, who fidgeted about, and then unable to bear it, got up and went after Faye.

It was not yet ten. Mary had said, ring at one. Persuaded by the odours left on the air of the kitchen by Faye, by Roberta, she went up to the bathroom and forced herself into a cold bath where she crouched, unable actually to lower her buttocks into it, scrubbing and lathering. In a glow she dressed in clean clothes, bundled what she had taken off with Jasper's clothes that needed a wash – determined by sniffing at them; and was on her way out to the launderette when she saw the old woman sitting under the tree in the next garden, all sharp jutting limbs, like a heap of sticks inside a jumble of cardigan and skirt. She urgently gesticulated at Alice, who went out into the street and in again at the neat white gate, smiling. She hoped that neighbours were watching.

'She's gone out and left me,' said the old woman, struggling to sit up from her collapsed position. 'They don't care, none of them care.' While she went on in a hoarse angry voice about the crimes of Joan Robbins, Alice deftly pulled up the old dear, thinking that she weighed no more than her bundle of laundry, and tidied her into a suitable position for taking the air.

Alice listened, smiling, until she had had enough, then she bent down, to shout into possibly deaf ears, 'But she's very nice to bring you out here to sit in the garden, she doesn't have to do that, does she?' Then, as the ancient face seemed to struggle and erupt into expostulation, she said, 'Never mind, I'll bring you a nice cup of coffee.'

'Tea, tea,' urged the crone.

'You'll have to have coffee. We're short of a teapot. Now you just sit there and wait.'

Alice went back, made sweet coffee, and brought it to the old woman. 'What's your name?'

'Mrs Jackson, Jackson, that's what I am called.'

'My name is Alice and I live at 43.'

'You sent away all those dirty people, good for you,' said Mrs Jackson, who was already slipping down in her chair again, like a drunken old doll, the mug sliding sideways in her hand.

'I'll see you in a few minutes,' said Alice, and ran off.

The launderette used up three-quarters of an hour. She collected her mug from Mrs Jackson, and then stood listening to Joan Robbins, who came out of her kitchen to tell Alice that she should not believe the old lady, who was wandering; there was not one reason in the world why she, Joan Robbins, should do a thing for her let alone help her down the stairs to the garden and up again and make her cups of coffee and . . . the complaints went on, while Mrs Jackson gesticulated to both of them that her tale was the right one. This little scene was being witnessed by several people in gardens and from windows and Alice let them have the full benefit of it.

With a wave she went back into her own house.

It was eleven, and a frail apparition wavered on the stairs: Philip, who said, 'Alice, I don't feel too good, I don't feel . . .'

He arrived precariously beside her, and his face, that of a doleful but embarrassed angel, was presented to her for diagnosis and judgment, in perfect confidence of justice. Which she gave him: 'I am not surprised, all that work on the roof. Well, forget it today, I'd take it easy.'

'I would have gone with the others, but . . .'

'Go into the sitting-room. Relax. I'll bring you some coffee.'

She knew this sickness needed only affection, and when Philip was settled in a big chair, she took him coffee and sat with him, thinking: I have nothing better to do.

She had known that at some time she would have to listen to a tale of wrongs: this was the time. Philip had been promised jobs and not given them; had been turned off work without warning; had not been paid for work he had done; and this was told her in the hot aggrieved voice of one who had suffered inexplicable and indeed malevolent bad luck, whereas the reason for it all – that he was as fragile as a puppet – was not mentioned; could never, Alice was sure, be mentioned. 'And do you know, Alice, he said to me, yes, you be here next Monday and I'll have a job for you – do you know what that job was? He wanted me to load great cases of paint and stuff on to vans! I'm a builder and decorator, Alice! Well, I did it, I did it for four days and my back went out. I was in hospital for two weeks, and then in physio for a month. When I went to him and said he owed me for the four days he said I was the one in the wrong and . . .' Alice listened and smiled, and her heart hurt for him. It seemed to her that a great deal had been asked of her heart that morning, one poor victim after another. Well, never mind, one day life would not be like this; it was capitalism that was so hard and hurtful and did not care about the pain of its victims.

At half-past twelve, when she was just thinking that she could go to the telephone booth, she heard someone coming in, and flew to intercept the police, the Council – who, this time?

It was Reggie who, smiling, was depositing cases in the hall. He said that Mary had slipped out from the meeting to telephone him the good news. And she would be over with another load in the lunch hour. The relief of it made Alice dizzy, then she wept. Standing against the wall by the door into the sitting-room, she had both hands up to her mouth as if in an extreme of grief, and her tight-shut eyes poured tears.

'Why, Alice,' said Reggie, coming to peer into her tragic face, and she had to repel friendly pats, pushes, and an arm around her shoulders.

'Reaction,' she muttered, diving off to the lavatory to be sick. When she came out, Philip and Reggie stood side by side, staring at her, ready to smile, and hoping she would allow them to.

And, at last, she smiled, then laughed, and could not stop.

Philip looked after her; and Reggie, embarrassed, sat by.

And she was embarrassed: What's wrong with me, I must be sick too?

But Philip was no longer sick. He went off to measure up the broken windows for new glass, and Reggie climbed the stairs to look over the rooms. Alice stayed in the kitchen.

There Mary came to her with a carton of saucepans, crockery and an electric kettle. She sat herself down at the other end of the table. She was flushed and elated. Alice had heard her laughing with Reggie in the same way Faye and Roberta laughed; and sometimes, Bert and Pat. Two against the world. Intimacy.

Alice asked at once, 'What are the conditions?'

'It's only for a year.'

Alice smiled and on Mary's look, explained, 'It's a lifetime.'

'But of course they could extend. If they don't decide to knock it down after all.'

'They won't knock it down,' said Alice confidently.

'Oh, don't be so sure.' Now Mary was being huffy on behalf of her other self, the Council.

Alice shrugged. She waited, eyes on Mary who, however, really did not seem to know why. At last Alice said, 'But what has been decided about paying?'

'Oh,' said Mary, airily, 'peanuts. They haven't fixed the exact sum, but it's nothing, really. A nominal amount.'

'Yes,' said Alice, patient. 'But how. A lump sum for the whole house?'

'Oh no,' said Mary, as though this were some unimaginably extortionate suggestion – such is the power of an official decision on the official mind – 'Oh no. Benefit will be adjusted individually for every one in the house. No one's in work here, you said?'

'That isn't the point, Mary,' said Alice, hoping that Mary would get the point. But she didn't. Of course not; what in her experience could have prepared her for it?

'Well, I suppose it would be easier if it was a lump sum, and people chipped in. Particularly as it is so small. Enough to cover the rates, not more than £10 or £15 a week. But that is not how it is done with us.' Again spoke the official, in the decisive manner of one who knows that what is done must be the best possible way of doing it.

'Are you sure,' enquired Alice carefully, after a pause, 'that there really is no possibility of changing the decision?'

'Absolutely none,' said Mary. What she was in fact saying was: 'This is such a petty matter that there is no point in wasting a minute over it.'

And so unimportant was it to Mary, that she began to stroll around the kitchen, examining it, with a happy little smile, as if unwrapping a present.

Meanwhile Alice sat adjusting. Faye and Roberta would not agree, would leave at once. Jim, too. Jasper wouldn't like it – he would demand that both he and Alice should leave. Well, all right, then they would all go. Why not? She had done it often enough! There was that empty house down in Stockwell . . . Jasper and she had been talking for months of squatting there. It would suit Faye and Roberta, because their Women's Commune was somewhere down there. God only knew what other places, refuges, hideouts, they used. Alice had the impression there were several.

A pity about this house. And as Alice thought of leaving sorrow crammed her throat, and she closed her eyes, suffering.

She said, sounding cold and final, because of the stiffness of her throat, 'Well, that's it. I'm sorry, but that's it.'

'*What do you mean?*' Mary had whirled round, and stood, a tragedienne, hand at her throat. 'I don't know what you mean?' she demanded, sounding fussy and hectoring.

'Well, it doesn't matter to you, does it? You and Reggie can stay here by yourselves. You can easily get friends in, I am sure.'

Mary collapsed into a chair. From being the happiest girl in the world, she had become a poor small creature, pale and fragile, a suppliant. 'I don't understand! What difference does it make? And of course Reggie and I wouldn't stay here by ourselves.'

'Why not?'

Mary coloured up, and stammered, 'Well *of course* . . . it goes without saying . . . *they* can't know I am living here. Bob Hood and the others can't know I'm in a *squat*.'

'Oh well, that's it then,' said Alice, vague because she was already thinking of the problems of moving again.

'I don't understand,' Mary was demanding. 'Tell me, what is the problem.'

Alice sighed and said perfunctorily that there were reasons why some of them did not want their presence signposted.

'Why,' demanded Mary, 'are they criminals?' She had gone bright pink, and she sounded indignant.

Alice could see that this moment had been reached before, with Militant. Methods!

Alice said, sounding sarcastic because of the effort she was making to be patient, 'Politics, Mary. Politics, don't you see?' She thought that with Jim, it was probably something criminal, but let it pass. Probably something criminal with Faye and Roberta, for that matter. 'Don't you see? People collect their Social Security in one borough, but live somewhere else. Sometimes in several other places.'

'Oh. Oh, I see.'

Mary sat contemplating this perspective: skilled and dangerous revolutionaries on the run, in concealment. But seemed unable to take it in. She said, huffily, 'Well, I suppose the decision could be adjusted. I must say, I think it is just as well the Council don't know about this!'

'Oh, you mean you can get the decision changed?' Alice, reprieved, the house restored to her, sat smiling, her eyes full of tears. 'Oh, good, that's all right then.'

Mary stared at Alice. Alice, bashful, because of the depth of her emotion, smiled at Mary. This was the moment when Mary, from her repugnance for anything that did not measure up against that invisible yardstick of what was right, suitable and proper that she shared with Reggie, could have got up, stammered a few stiff, resentful apologies, and left. To tell Bob Hood that the Council had made a mistake, those people in No. 43 . . .

But she smiled, and said, 'I'll have a word with Bob. I expect it will be all right. So everyone will chip in? I'll get them to send the bills

monthly, not quarterly. It will be easier to keep up with the payments.'
She chattered on for a bit, to restore herself and the authority of the
Council, and then remarked that something would have to be done
about No. 45. There were complaints all the time.

'I'll go next door and see them,' said Alice.

Again the official reacted with, 'It's not your affair, is it? Why should
you?' Seeing that Alice shrugged, apparently indifferent, Mary said
quickly, 'Yes, perhaps you should . .'

She went upstairs, with a look as irritated as Alice's. Both women
were thinking that it would not be easy, this combination of people, in
the house.

Soon Mary went off with Reggie. He would drop her back at work,
and they both would return later with another load. They were bringing
in some furniture too, if no one minded. A bed, for instance.

Alice sat on, alone. Then Philip came to be given money for the glass,
and went off to buy it.

Alice was looking at herself during the last four days, and thinking:
Have I been a bit crazy? After all, it *is* only a house . . . and what have I
done? These two, Reggie and Mary – revolutionaries? *They* were with
Militant? Crazy!

Slowly she recovered. Energy came seeping back. She thought of the
others, on the battlefront down at Melstead. They were at work for the
cause; and she must be too! Soon she slipped out of the house, careful
not to see whether the old lady was waving at her, and went into the
main road, walked along the hedge that separated first their house from
the road, and then No. 45. She turned into the little street that was the
twin of theirs, and then stood where yesterday she had seen Bob Hood
stand, looking in that refuse-filled garden.

She walked firmly up the path, prepared to be examined by whoever
was there and was interested. She knocked. She waited a goodish time
for the door to open. She caught a glimpse of the hall, the twin of theirs,
but it was stacked with cartons and boxes. There was a single electric
bulb. So they did have electricity.

In front of her was a man who impressed her at once as being foreign.
It was not anything specific in his looks; it was just something about
him. He was a Russian, she knew. This gave her a little *frisson* of
satisfaction. It was power, the idea of it, that was exciting her. The man
himself was in no way out of the ordinary, being broad – not fat, though
he could easily be; not tall – in fact not much taller than herself. He had

a broad blunt sort of face, and little shrewd grey eyes. He wore grey
twill trousers that looked expensive and new; and a grey bush shirt that
was buttoned and neat.

He could have been a soldier.

'I am Alice Mellings. From next door.'

He nodded, unsmiling, and said, 'Of course. Come in.' He led the
way through the stacks of boxes into the room that in their house was
the sitting-room. Here it had the look of an office or a study. A table was
set in the bay window; his chair had its back to the window, and that
was because, Alice knew, he wanted to know who came in and out of the
door; he did not want his back to it.

He sat down in this chair, and nodded to another, opposite it. Alice
sat.

She was thinking, impressed: This one, he's the real thing.

He was waiting for her to say something.

The one thing she knew now she could not say was: Have you been
telling Jasper and Bert what to do? – which was what she wanted to know.

She said, 'We have just got permission from the Council, we are
short-term housing, you know.' He nodded. 'Well, we thought you
should do the same. It makes life much easier, you see. And it means the
police leave you alone.'

He seemed to relax, sat back, pushed a packet of cigarettes towards
her, lit one himself as she shook her head, sat holding a lungful of smoke
which he expelled in a single swift breath and said, 'It's up to the others.
I don't live here.'

Was that all he was going to say? It seemed so. Well, he had in fact
said everything necessary. Alice, confused, hurried on, 'There's the
rubbish. You'll have to pay the dustmen . . .' she faltered.

He had his eyes intent on her. She knew that he was seeing
everything. It was a detached, cold scrutiny. Not hostile, not unfriendly, surely? She cried, 'We've been given a year. That means, once the
place is straight, we can give all our attention to –' she censored 'the
revolution', but said, 'politics.'

He seemed not to have heard. To be waiting for more? For her to go?
Floundering on, she said, 'Of course not everyone in our squat . . . for
instance, Roberta and Faye don't think that . . . but why should you
know about them. I'll explain . . .'

He cut in, 'I know about Roberta and Faye. Tell me, what are those
two new ones like?'

She said, giving Reggie and Mary the credit due, 'They were once members of Militant, but they didn't like their methods.' Here she dared to offer him a smile, hoping he would return it, but he said, 'She works for the Council? On what sort of level?'

'She doesn't take decisions.'

He nodded. 'And what about him? A chemist, I believe?'

'Industrial chemist. He lost his job.'

'Where?'

'I didn't ask.' She added, 'I'll let you know.'

He nodded. Sat smoking. Sat straight to the table, both forearms on it, in front of him a sheet of paper on which his eyes seemed to make notes. He was like Lenin!

She thought: His voice. American. Yes, but something funny for an American voice. No, it was not the voice, the accent but something else, in *him*.

He didn't say anything. The question, the anxiety, that were building up in her surfaced. 'Jasper and Bert have gone down to Melstead. They went early.'

He nodded. Reached for a neatly-folded newspaper, and opened it in front of him, turning the pages. 'Have you seen today's *Times*?'

'I don't read the capitalist press.'

'I think perhaps that is a pity,' he commented after a pause. And pushed across the paper, indicating a paragraph.

> Asked whether they welcomed these reinforcements to the picket line, Crabit, the strikers' representative, said he wished the Trotskyists and the rent-a-picket crowd would keep away. They weren't wanted. The workers could deal with things themselves.

Alice felt she could easily start crying again.

She said, 'But this is a capitalist newspaper. They're just trying to split the democratic forces, they want to disunite us.' She was going to add: Can't you see that? but could not bring it out.

He took back the paper and laid it where it had been. Now he was not looking at her.

'Comrade Alice,' he said, 'there are more efficient ways of doing things, you know.'

He stood up. 'I've got work to do.' She was dismissed. He came out from behind the table and walked with her to the door and back through the hall to the front door.

'Thank you for coming to see me,' he said.

She stammered, 'Would there be a room in this house we could use for a – discussion? You see, some of us are not sure about – some of the others.'

He said, 'I'll ask.' He had not reacted as she had feared he would. Bringing it out had sounded so feeble . . .

He nodded, and at last, gave her a smile. She went off in a daze. She was telling herself, But he's the real thing, he *is*.

He had not told her his name.

She walked along the short stretch of main road slowly, because in front of her, in the middle of the pavement, was a girl with a small child in a pushchair. The child looked like a fat plastic parcel with a pale podgy spotty face coming out of the top. He was whining on a high persistent note that set Alice's teeth on edge. The girl looked tired and desperate. She had lank unwashed-looking pale hair. Alice could see from the set angry shoulders that she wanted to hit the child. Alice was waiting to walk faster when she could turn off into her own road, but the girl turned, still in the middle of the pavement. There she stopped, looking at the houses and, in particular, at No. 43. Alice went past her and in at her gate. She heard the girl say, 'Do you live here? In this house?'

'Yes, I do,' said Alice, without turning, in a curt voice. She knew what was coming. She walked on up the path. She heard the wheels of the pushchair crunch after her.

'Excuse me,' she heard, and knew from the stubborn little voice that she could not get out of it. She turned sharply, blocking the way to the front door. Now she faced the girl squarely, with a *No* written all over her. This was not the first time, of course, that she had been in this position. She was feeling: It is unfair that I have to deal with this.

She was a poor thing, this girl. Probably about twenty. Already worn down with everything, and the only energy in her the irritation she was containing because of her grizzling child.

'I heard this house is short-term housing now,' she said, and she kept her eyes on Alice's face. They were large grey rather beautiful eyes, and Alice did not want the pressure of them. She turned to the door, and opened it.

'Where did you hear that?'

The girl did not answer this. She said, '*I'm going mad*. I've got to have a place. I've got to find somewhere. I've got to.'

Alice went into the hall, ready to shut the door, but found that the girl's foot stopped her. Alice was surprised, for she had not expected such enterprise. But her own determination was made stronger by her feeling that if the girl had that much spirit, then she wasn't in such a bad way after all.

The door stood open. The child was now weeping noisily and wholeheartedly inside his transparent shroud, his wide-open blue eyes splashing tears on to the plastic. The girl confronted Alice, who could see she was trembling with anger.

'I've got as much right here as you have,' she said. 'If there's room I'm coming here. And you have got room, haven't you? Look at the size of this place, just look at it!' She stared around the large hall with its glowing carpet that gave an air of discreet luxury to the place, and to the various doors that opened off it to rooms, rooms, a treasury of rooms. And then she gazed at the wide stairs that went up to another floor. More doors, more space. Alice, in an agony, looked with her.

'I'm in one of those hotels, do you know about them? Well, why don't you, everyone ought to. The Council shoved us there, my husband and me and Bobby. One room. We've been there seven months.' Alice could hear in her tone, which was incredulous, at the awfulness of it, what those seven months had been like. 'It's owned by some filthy foreigners. Disgusting, why should they have a hotel and tell us what to do? We are not allowed to cook. Can you imagine, with a baby? One room. The floor is so filthy I can't put him to crawl.' This information was handed out to Alice in a flat, trembling voice, and the child steadily and noisily wept.

'You can't come here,' said Alice. 'It's not suitable. For one thing there's no heating. There isn't even hot water.'

'Hot water,' said the girl, shaking with rage. 'Hot water! We haven't had hot water for three days, and the heating's been off. You ring up the Council and complain, and they say they are looking into it. I want some space. Some room. I can heat water in a pan to wash him. You've got a stove, haven't you? I can't even give him proper food. Only rubbish out of packets.'

Alice did not answer. She was thinking, Well, why not? What right have I got to say no? And, as she thought this, she heard a sound from upstairs, and turned to see Faye, standing on the landing, looking down.

There was something about her that held Alice's attention; some deadliness of purpose, or of mood. The pretty wispy, frail creature, Faye, had again disappeared; in her place was a white-faced, malevolent woman, with punishing cold eyes, who came in a swift rush down the stairs as though she would charge straight into the girl, who stood her ground at first and then, in amazement, took a step back with Faye right up against her, leaning forward, hissing, 'Get out. Get out. Get out. Get out.'

The girl stammered, 'Who are you, what . . .' While Faye pushed her, by the force of her presence, her hate, step by step back towards the door. The child was screaming now.

'How dare you,' Faye was saying. 'How dare you crash in here, no one said you could. I know what you're like. Once you are in, you'd take everything you could get, you're like that.'

This insanity kept Alice silent, and had the girl staring open-eyed and open-mouthed at this cruel pursuer, as she retreated to the door. There Faye actually gave her a hard shove, which made her step back on to the pushchair, and nearly knock it over.

Faye crashed the door shut. Then, opening it, she crashed it shut again. It seemed she would continue this process, but Roberta had arrived on the scene. Even she did not dare touch Faye at that moment, but she was talking steadily in a low, urgent, persuasive voice:

'Faye, Faye darling, darling Faye, do stop it, no, you must stop it. Are you listening to me? Stop it, Faye . . .'

Faye heard her, as could be seen from the way she held the door open, hesitating before slamming it again. Beyond could be seen the girl, retreating slowly down the path, with her shrieking child. She glanced round in time to see Faye taken into Roberta's arms and held there, a prisoner. Now Faye was shouting in a hoarse, breathless voice, 'Let me go.' The girl stopped, mouth falling open, and her eyes frantic. *Oh no*, those eyes seemed to say, as she turned and ran clumsily away from this horrible house.

Alice shut the door, and the sounds of the child's screams ceased.

Roberta was crooning, 'Faye, Faye, there darling, don't my love, it's all right.' And Faye was sobbing, just like a child, with great gasps for breath, collapsed against Roberta.

Roberta gently led Faye upstairs, step by step, crooning all the way, 'There, don't, please don't, Faye, it's all right.'

The door of their room shut on them, and the hall was empty. Alice stood there, stunned, for a while; then went into the kitchen and sat down, trembling.

In her mind she was with the girl on the pavement. She was feeling, not guilt, but an identification with her. She imagined herself going with the heavy awkward child to the bus-stop, waiting and waiting for the bus to come, her face stony and telling the other people in the queue that she did not care what they thought of her screaming child. Then getting the difficult chair on to the bus, and sitting there with the child, who if not screaming would be a lump of exhausted misery. Then off the bus, strapping the child into the chair again, and then the walk to the hotel. Yes, Alice did know about these hotels, did know what went on.

After a while she made herself strong tea and sat drinking it, as if it were brandy. Silence above. Presumably Roberta had got Faye off to sleep?

Some time later Roberta came in, and sat down. Alice knew how she must look, from Roberta's examination of her. She thought: What she really is, is just one of these big maternal lezzies, all sympathy and big boobs; she wants to seem butch and tough, but bad luck for her, she's a mum.

She did not want to be bothered with what was going to come.

When Roberta said, 'Look, Alice, I know how this must look, but . . .' she cut in, 'I don't care. It's all right.'

Roberta hesitated, then made herself go on, 'Faye does sometimes get like this, but she is much better, and she hasn't for a long time. Over a year.'

'All right.'

'And of course we can't have children here.'

Alice did not say anything.

Roberta, needing some kind of response she was not getting, got up to fuss around with tea-bags and a mug, and said in a low, quick, vibrant voice, 'If you knew about her childhood, if you knew what had happened to her . . .'

'I don't care about her fucking childhood,' remarked Alice.

'No, I've got to tell you, for her sake, for Faye's . . . She was a battered baby, you see . . .'

'I don't care,' Alice shouted suddenly. '*You* don't understand. I've had all the bloody unhappy childhoods I am going to listen to. People go on and on . . . As far as I am concerned, unhappy childhoods are the great con, the great alibi.'

Shocked, Roberta said, 'A battered *baby* – and battered babies grow up to become adults.' She was back in her place, sitting, leaning forward, her eyes on Alice's, determined to make Alice respond.

'I know one thing,' Alice said. 'Communes. Squats. If you don't take care, that's what they become – people sitting around discussing their shitty childhoods. Never again. We're not here for that. Or is that what you want? A sort of permanent encounter group. Everything turns into that, if you let it.'

Roberta, convinced that Alice was not going to listen, sat silent. She noisily drank tea, and Alice felt herself wince.

There was something coarse and common about Roberta, Alice was thinking, too disturbed and riled up to censor her thoughts. She hadn't washed yet, even though water was running in the taps. There was the sharp metallic tang of blood about her. Either she or Faye, or both, were menstruating.

Alice shut her eyes, retreated inside herself to a place she had discovered long years ago, she did not know when, but she had been a small child. Inside her, she was safe, and the world could crash and roar and scream as much as it liked. She heard herself say, and it was in her dreamy abstracted voice:

'Well, I suppose Faye will die of it one of these days. She has tried to commit suicide, hasn't she?'

Silence. She opened her eyes to see Roberta in tears.

'Yes, but not since I . . .'

'All those bracelets,' murmured Alice. 'Scars under bracelets.'

'She's got one tiny scar,' pleaded Roberta. 'On her left wrist.'

Alice had shut her eyes again, and was sipping tea, feeling that her nerves would soon begin to stand up to life again. She said, 'One of these days I'll tell you about my mother's unhappy childhood. She had a mad mum, and a peculiar dad. Peculiar is the word. If I told you!' She had not meant to mention her mother. 'Oh never mind about her,' she said. She began to laugh. It was a healthy, even jolly laugh, appreciative of the vagaries and richnesses of life. 'On the other hand my father – now that was a different kettle of fish. When he was a child he was happy the whole day long, so he says, the happiest time in his life. But do we believe him? Well, I am inclined to, yes. He is so bloody *thick* and *stupid* and *awful* that he wouldn't have noticed it if he was unhappy. They could have battered him as much as they liked, and he wouldn't even have noticed.'

She opened her eyes. Roberta was examining her with a small shrewd smile. Against her will, Alice smiled in response.

'Well,' said Alice, 'that's that, as far as I am concerned. Have you got any brandy? Anything like that?'

'How about a joint?'

'No, doesn't do anything for me. I don't like it.'

Roberta went off and came back with a bottle of whisky. The two sat drinking in the kitchen, at either end of the big wooden table. When Philip came staggering in under the heavy panes of glass, ready to start work, he refused a drink saying he felt sick. He went upstairs back to his sleeping bag. What he was really saying was that Alice should be working along with him, not sitting there wasting time.

Roberta, having drunk a lot, went up to Faye and there was silence overhead.

Alice decided to have a nap. In the hall was lying an envelope she thought was junk mail. She picked it up to throw it away, saw it was from the Electricity Board, felt herself go cold and sick; decided to give herself time to recover before opening it. She went to the kitchen. *By hand*. Mrs Whitfield had said she came past on her way to and from work. She had dropped this in herself, on her way home. That was kind of her . . . Alice briskly opened the letter, which said:

> *Dear Miss Mellings, I communicated with your father about guaranteeing payment of accounts for No. 43 Old Mill Road, in terms of our discussion. His reply was negative, I am sorry to say. Perhaps you would care to drop in and discuss this matter in the course of the next few days? Your sincerely,*
>
> *D. Whitfield.*

This pleasant, human little letter made Alice first feel supported, then rage took over. Luckily there was no one to see her, as she exploded inwardly, teeth grinding, eyes bulging, fists held as if knives were in them. She stormed around the kitchen, like a big fly shut in a room on a hot afternoon, banging herself against walls, corners of table and stove, not knowing what she did, and making grunting, whining, snarling noises – which, soon, she heard. She knew that she was making them and, frightened, sat down at the table, perfectly still, containing what she felt. Absolute quiet after such violence, for some minutes. Then she whirled into movement, out of the kitchen and up the stairs, to knock sharply on Philip's door. Stirrings, movements, but no reply, and she called, 'Philip, it's me, Alice.'

She went in as he said, 'Come in,' and saw him scrambling up out of his sleeping-bag and into his overalls. 'Oh sorry,' she said, dismissing his unimportant embarrassment and starting in at once.

'Philip, will you guarantee our electricity bill?' As he stared, and did not understand: 'You know, the bill for this house? My mother won't, my father won't, bloody bloody Theresa and bloody bloody Anthony won't . . .'

He was standing in front of her, the late-afternoon light strong and yellow behind him, a little dark figure in a stiff awkward posture. She could not see his face and went to the side of the room, so that he turned towards her, and she saw him confronting her, small, pale but obstinate. She knew she would fail, seeing that look, but said sharply, 'You have a business, you have a letterhead, you could guarantee the account.'

'Alice, how can I? I can't pay that money, you know I can't.' Talking as though he would have to pay, thought Alice, enraged again. But had he heard her joke that the first payment would be the last?

She said, bossy, 'Oh, Philip, don't be silly. You wouldn't have to, would you? It's just to keep the electricity on.'

He said, trying to sound humorous, 'Well, Alice, but perhaps I would have to?'

'No, of *course* not!'

He was – she saw – ready to laugh with her, but she could not.

'What can I do?' she was demanding. 'I don't know what to do!'

'I don't think I believe that, Alice,' he said, really laughing now, but nicely.

In a normal voice, she said, 'Philip, we have to have a guarantor. You are the only one, don't you see?'

He held his own, this Petrouchka, this elf, with, 'Alice, no. For one thing, that address on the letterhead is the place I was in before Felicity – it's been pulled down, demolished. It isn't even there.'

Now they stared at each other with identical appalled expressions as if the floorboards were giving way; for both had been possessed, at the same moment, by a vision of impermanence; houses, buildings, streets, whole areas of streets, blown away, going, gone, an illusion. They sighed together, and on an impulse, embraced gently, comforting each other.

'The thing is,' said Alice, 'she doesn't want to disconnect. She wants to help, she just needs an excuse, that's all . . . Wait – wait a minute, I think I've got it . . .'

'I thought you would,' he said and she nodded and said excitedly, 'Yes. It's my brother. I'll tell Electricity he will guarantee, but that he's away on a business trip in – Bahrain, it doesn't matter where. She'll hold it over, I know she will . . .'

And making the thumbs-up sign she ran out, laughing and exultant.

Too late to ring Mrs Whitfield now, but she would tomorrow, and it would be all right.

No need to tell Mary and Reggie anything about it. Of course, if Mary was any good, she would be prepared to guarantee the account; she was the only one among them in work. But she wouldn't, Alice knew that.

She needed sleep. She was shaky and trembling inside, where her anger lived.

It was getting dark when Alice woke. She heard Bert's laugh, a deep ho, ho, ho, from the kitchen. That's not his own laugh, Alice thought. I wonder what that would be like? Tee hee hee more likely. No, he made that laugh up for himself. Reliable and comfortable. Manly. Voices and laughs, we make them up . . . Roberta's made-up voice, comfortable. And that was Pat's quick light voice and her laugh. Her own laugh? Perhaps. So they were both back and that meant that Jasper was too. Alice was out of her sleeping-bag, and tugging on a sweater, a smile on her face that went with her feelings for Jasper: admiration and wistful love.

But Jasper was not in the kitchen with the other two, who were glowing, happy, fulfilled, and eating fish and chips.

'It's all right, Alice,' said Pat, pulling out a chair for her. 'They arrested him, but it's not serious. He'll be in court tomorrow morning at Enfield. Back here by lunchtime.'

'Unless he's bound over?' asked Bert.

'He was bound over for two years in Leeds, but that ended last month.'

'Last month?' said Pat. Her eyes met Bert's found no reflection there of what she was thinking – probably against her will, Alice believed; and, so as not to meet Alice's, lowered themselves to the business of eating one golden crisp fatty chip after another. This was not the first time Alice had caught suggestions that Jasper liked being bound over – needed the edge it put on life. She said apologetically, 'Well, he has had to be careful so long, watching every tiny little thing he does, I suppose . . .' She was examining Bert who, she knew, could tell her what she needed to know about the arrest. Jasper was arrested, but Bert not; that in itself . . .

Pat pushed over some chips, and Alice primly ate one or two, thinking about cholesterol.

'How many did they arrest?'

'Seven. Three we didn't know. But the others were John, Clarissa and Charlie. And Jasper.'

'None of the trade union comrades?'

'No.'

A silence.

Then Bert, 'They have been fining people twenty-five pounds.'

Alice said automatically, 'Then probably Jasper will get fifty pounds.'

'He thought twenty-five. I gave him twenty so he'd have enough.'

Alice, who had been about to get up, ready to leave, said quickly, 'He doesn't want me down there? Why not? What did he say?'

Pat said, carefully, 'He asked me to tell you not to come down.'

'But I've always been there when he's been arrested. Always. I've been in court every time.'

'That's what he said,' said Bert. 'Tell Alice not to bother.'

Alice sat thinking so intently that the kitchen, Bert and Pat, even the house around her vanished. She was down at the scene of the picket. The van loaded with newspapers appeared in the gates, its sinister gleaming look telling everyone to hate it; the pickets surged forward, shouting; and there was Jasper, as she had seen him so often, his pale face distorted with a look of abstracted and dedicated hate, his reddish crop of gleaming hair. He was always the first to be arrested, she thought proudly, he was so dedicated, so obviously – even to the police – self-sacrificing. Pure.

But there was something that didn't fit.

She said, 'Did you decide not to get arrested for any reason, Bert?'

Because, if that had been so, one could have expected Jasper too to have returned home.

Bert said, 'Jasper found someone down there, someone who might be very useful to us.'

At once the scene fell into shape in Alice's mind. 'Was he one of the three you didn't know?'

'That's it,' said Bert. 'That's it exactly.' He yawned. He said, 'I hate to have to ask, but could you let me have the twenty pounds? Jasper said I should ask you.'

Alice counted out the money. She did not let her gaze rise from this task.

Pat said nicely, 'That little bundle won't last long at this rate.'

'No.'

Alice was praying: Let Bert go. Let him go upstairs. I want to talk to Pat. She was thinking this so hard that she was not surprised when he stood up and said, 'I'm going to drop around to Felicity's and get myself a real bath.'

'I'll come in a minute,' said Pat.

Bert went, and the two women sat on.

Alice asked, 'What is the name of that man next door?'

'Lenin?' said Pat. Alice gracefully laughed with her, feeling privileged and special in this intimacy with Pat that admitted her into important conspiracy. Pat went on, 'He says his name is Andrew.'

'Where would you say he was from?'

'Good question.'

'Ever such an American accent,' said Alice.

'The new world language.'

'Yes.'

They exchanged looks.

Having said all they needed to on this subject, they left it, and Alice said after a pause, 'I went round this afternoon. To ask them to do something about that mess.'

'Good idea.'

'What's in all those packages?'

'Leaflets. Books. So it is said.'

'But with the police around all the time?'

'The packages weren't there the day before yesterday. And I bet they'll be gone by tomorrow. Or gone already.'

'Did you actually see the leaflets?'

'No, but I asked. That's what he said – Andrew. Propaganda material.'

Again a subject was left behind, by unspoken consent.

Pat said, 'I gather Bert thinks this comrade – the one Jasper was talking to at Melstead – may have some useful leads.'

'You mean, for the IRA?'

'Yes, I think so.'

'Did you hear anything of what they said?'

'No. But Bert was there part of the time.'

At this Alice could have asked, What does Bert think of him? But she did not care what Bert thought. Pat's assessment, yes.

'What did he look like? Perhaps I know him,' she asked. 'He wasn't one of the usual crowd?'

'I've never seen him before, I'm sure. Nothing special to report.'

'Did – Comrade Andrew tell you to go down to the picket? Did he say anything about Melstead to you? How many times have you been next door?'

Pat smiled and replied, though she indicated by her manner that there was no reason why she should, 'I have been next door twice. Bert and Jasper have been over much more often. As for Melstead, I get the impression that Comrade Andrew . . .' and she slightly emphasised the 'comrade', as if Alice would do well to think about it, 'that Comrade Andrew is not all that keen on cadres from outside joining the pickets.'

Alice said hotly, 'Yes, but it is our struggle too. It is a struggle for all the progressive forces in the country. Melstead is a focal point for imperialist fascism, and it is not just the business of the Melstead trade unionists.'

'You asked,' said Pat. And then, 'In my view, Comrade Andrew has bigger fish to fry.' A thrill went through Alice, as when someone who has been talking for a lifetime about unicorns suddenly glimpses one. She looked with tentative excitement at Pat who, it seemed, did not know what she had said. If she had not been implying that they, the comrades at No. 43 Old Mill Road, had unwittingly come closer to great events, then what did she mean? But Pat was getting up. Terminating the discussion. Alice wanted her to stay. She could not believe that Pat was ready to go off now, at this thrilling moment when fabulous happenings seemed imminent. But Pat was stretching her arms about and yawning. Her smile was luxurious, and as her eyes did briefly meet Alice's, she seemed actually to be tantalising and teasing. She's so sensual, Alice indignantly thought.

But she said, 'I asked – Comrade Andrew, if we can use a room in that house for meetings. I mean, meetings of the inner group.'

'So did we. He said yes.'

Pat smiled, lowered her arms, and then stood looking at Alice, without smiling, saying with her body that she had had enough of Alice, and wanted to go. 'Where are our new comrades?' She was on her way to the door.

'They are upstairs.'

'I doubt whether we shall see much of them. Still, they are all right.' She yawned, elaborately, and said, 'Too much effort to go chasing out for a bath. Bert can put up with me as I am.'

She went, and Alice sat still until she had heard her go up the stairs, and the closing of her door.

Then she swiftly went out of the house. It was too early for what she was going to do. The street, though dark, had the feeling of the end of the day, with cars turning in to park, others leaving for the evening entertainments, a restlessness of lights. But the traffic was pounding up the main road with the intensity of daytime. She dawdled along to look into the garden of 45. It seemed to her that a start had been made on the rubbish; yes, it had, and some filled sacks stood by the hedge, the plastic gleaming blackly. She saw two figures bending over a patch towards the back; not far from the pit she and Pat and Jim had dug, though a big hedge stood between. Were they digging a pit too? It was very dark back there. Lights from Joan Robbins's top windows illuminated the higher levels of No. 45, but did not reach the thickets of the overgrown garden. Alice loitered around for a while, and no one came in or out, and she could not see Comrade Andrew through the downstairs windows, for the curtains were drawn.

She went to the Underground, sat on the train planning what she was going to do, and walked up the big rich tree-lined road where Theresa and Anthony had their home. She stood on the pavement looking up at the windows of their kitchen on the third floor. She imagined that they were sitting there on opposite sides of the little table they used when they were alone. Delicious food. Her mouth was actually watering as she thought of Theresa's cooking. If she rang the bell, she would hear Theresa's voice: Darling Alice, is that you? Do come in. She would go up, join them in their long comfortable evening, their food. Her mother might even drop in. But at this thought rage grasped her and shook her with red-hot hands, so that her eyes went dark and she found herself walking fast up the road, and then along another, and another, walking as though she would explode if she stopped. She walked for a long time, while the feeling of the streets changed to night. She directed herself to her father's street. She walked along it casually. The lights were on downstairs, every window spilled out light. Upstairs was a low glow from the room where the babies slept. Too early. She walked some more, around and back, past Theresa and Anthony, where kitchen windows were now dark, up to the top of the hill, down and around and into her father's street. Now the lights were dark downstairs, but on in the bedroom. An hour or so ago, she had seen a stone of the right size and shape lying on the edge of a garden, and had put it into her pocket. She looked up and down the quiet street, where the lights made golden leafy spaces in the trees. A couple, arm-in-arm, came slowly up from the direction of the Underground. Old. An old couple. They were absorbed in the effort of walking, did not see Alice. Who went to the end of the street, nevertheless, and came back briskly on the impetus of her need, her decision. There was now not a soul in the street. As she reached her father's house she walked straight in at the gate, which she hardly bothered to open quietly, and flung the stone as hard as she could at the glass of the bedroom window. This movement, the single hard clear line of the throw, with her whole body behind it; and then the complete turn in the swing of the throw, and her bound out to the pavement – the speed and force of it, the skill, could never have been deduced from how Alice was, at any other time of the day or night, good-girl Alice, her mother's daughter . . . She heard the shattering glass, a scream, her father's shout. But she was gone, she had run down in the thick tree shadows to a side street, was down that and in the busy main street within sixty seconds after she had thrown the stone.

She was breathing too hard, too noisily . . she stood looking into a window to slow her breath. She realised it was crammed full of television sets, and sedately moved to the next, to examine dresses, until she could walk into the Supermarket without anyone remarking her breathing. There she stayed a good twenty minutes, choosing and rejecting. She took the loaded wire basket to the outlet, paid, filled her carrier bags, and went homewards by Underground. Since the stone had left her hand she had scarcely thought about what might be happening in her father's house.

Now, seeing the sober blue gleam from the Police Station she went in. At the Reception Desk, no one, but she could hear voices from a part of the room that was out of sight. She rang. No one came. She rang again, peremptorily. A young policewoman came out, took a good look at her, decided to be annoyed, and went back. Alice rang again. Now the young woman, as tidy and trim in her dark uniform as Alice in hers – jeans and bomber jacket – came slowly towards her, an annoyed, decided little face showing that words were being chosen to put Alice in her place.

Alice said, 'It might have been an emergency, how were you to know? As it happens, it isn't. So you are lucky.'

The policewoman's face suddenly suffused with scarlet, she gasped, her eyes widened.

Alice said, 'I have come to report on an agreed squat – you know, short-term housing – surely you know . . .'

'At this time of night?' the policewoman said smartly, in an attempt to regain mastery.

'It can't be much more than eleven,' said Alice. 'I didn't know you had a set time for dealing with housing.'

The policewoman said, 'Since you're here, let's do it. What do you want to report?'

Alice spelled it out. 'You people were around – a raid, three nights ago. You had not understood that it was an agreed tenancy – with the Council. I explained the situation. Now I've come to confirm it. It was agreed at the regular meeting of the Council, today.'

'What's the address.'

'No. 43 Old Mill Road.'

A little flicker of something showed on the policewoman's face. 'Wait a minute,' she said and disappeared. Alice listened to voices, male and female.

The policewoman came back, with a man; Alice recognised him as one of those from the other night. She was disappointed it was not the one who had kicked in the door.

'Ah, good evening,' she addressed him kindly. 'You remember, you were in 43 Old Mill Road, the other night.'

'Yes, I remember,' he said. Over his face quivered shades of the sniggers he had just been enjoying with his mates. 'You were the people who had buried – who dug a pit . . .'

'Yes. We buried the faeces that the previous people had left upstairs. In buckets.'

She studied the disgusted, prim, angry faces opposite her. Male and female. Two of a kind.

She said, 'I really cannot imagine why you should react like this.

People have been burying their excrement in pits for thousands of years. They do now, over most of the world . . .' As this did not seem adequately to reach them, 'In this country, we have only generally had waterborne sewage for a hundred years or so. Much less in some areas.'

'Yes, well, we have it *now*,' said the policewoman smartly.

'That's right,' said the policeman.

'It seems to me we did the responsible and the hygienic thing. Nature will take care of it soon enough.'

'Well, don't do it again,' said the policeman.

'We won't have any need to, will we?' said Alice sweetly. 'What I came to say was, if you check with the Council, you will have confirmation: No. 43 is now an agreed squat. An agreed short-term tenancy.'

The policewoman reached for a form. Her colleague went back to join his mates. Soon there was a burst of loud scandalised laughter. Then another. The policewoman, diligently filling in her form, tightened her lips, Alice could not make out whether in criticism or not.

'Small things amuse small minds,' said Alice.

The policewoman shot her a look which said that it was not for her to say so, even if she, herself, had been thinking it.

Alice smiled at her, woman to woman. 'And so,' she said, 'that's it. No. 43 is now legal, and in order. Any more raids and you'll be stepping well over the line.'

'That's for us to say, I think,' said the policewoman, with a tight little smile.

'No,' said Alice. 'As it happens, no. I think not. There will certainly be no further complaints from the neighbours.'

'Well, we'll have to hope not,' and the policewoman retreated to join her own in the back room.

Alice, satisfied, went out, and home, directing herself to pass 45. No one in the garden now. But in the deep shade in the angle of the two hedges she could just make out that a pit had been dug. She could not resist. For the second time that night she slid silently in at a garden gate. 45 looked deserted; all the windows were dark. The pit was about four feet deep. There was a strong sweet earthy smell from the slopes of soil around its edges. The bottom looked very flat – water? She bent to make sure. A case, or carton, something like that, had been placed at the bottom. She swiftly straightened, looked around. Consciously enjoying her condition, the sense of danger, of threat, she thought: They will be watching from those curtains or upstairs – I would be, in their position. What a risky thing to do, though; she turned to examine the strategy of the operation. No, perhaps it was all right. Whereas the digging of their own pit on the other side of the hedge could have been observed by the occupants of three houses and by anyone about in Joan Robbins's house, here, two sides were tall hedge, the third the house. Between here and the gate were shrubs and bushes. Joan Robbins's upper windows were dark. Over the road, set back in its own garden, a house; and certainly anyone could see what they liked from the upstairs windows. Which were still dark; the people had not yet gone upstairs to bed. She had seen what she needed to see. She would have liked to stay, the sweet earthy smells and the impetus of risk firing her blood, but she moved, swift as a shadow, to the front door and knocked, gently. It was opened at once. By Andrew.

'I knew you must be watching,' she said. 'But I've come to say that I told the police station 43 is an agreed squat. So they will be quite prepared to accept it when you say you are.'

Her pulses were beating, her heart racing, every cell dancing and alert. She was smiling, she knew; oh, this was the opposite of 'her look', when she felt like this, as if she'd drunk an extra-fine distilled essence of danger, and could have stepped out among the stars or run thirty miles.

She saw the short, powerful figure come out of the dark of the hall, to where she could examine his face in the light from the streetlamps. It was serious, set in purpose, and the sight of it gave her an agreeable feeling of submission to higher powers.

'I've buried something – an emergency,' he said. 'It will be gone in a day or two. You understand.'

'Perfectly,' smiled Alice.

He hesitated. Came out further. She felt powerful hands on her upper arms. Did she smell spirits? Vodka? Whisky.

'I am asking you to keep it to yourself.'

She nodded. 'Of course.'

'I mean, no one else.' She nodded, thinking that if only one person was to know in 43, nevertheless in this house surely several must?

He said, 'I am going to trust you completely, Alice.' He allowed her his brief tight smile. 'Because I have to. No one in this house knows but myself. They have all gone out. I took the opportunity to – make use of a very convenient cache. A temporary cache. I was going to fill in another layer of earth, and then put in some rubbish.'

Alice stood smiling, disappointed in him, if not in her own state; she was still floating. She thought that what he had said was likely to be either partially or totally untrue, but it was not her concern. He still gripped her by her upper arms which, however, were on the point of rejecting this persistent, warning masculine pressure. He seemed to sense this, for his hands dropped.

'I have to say that I have a different opinion of you than of some of the others from your house. I trust you.'

Alice did not say anything. She simply nodded.

He went indoors, nodding at her, but did not smile.

She was going to have to think it out. Better, sleep on it.

Her elation was going, fast. She thought: But tomorrow Jasper and I are going out together, and then . . . it would be a whole evening of this fine racing thrilling excitement.

But poor Jasper, no, he would not feel like it, probably, if he had spent the night in the cells. What was Enfield Police Station like? She could not remember any reports of it.

From the main road she saw outside No. 43 gate a slight drooping figure. An odd posture, bent over – it was the girl of this afternoon, and she was going to throw something at the windows of the sitting-room. A stone! Alice thought: Throwing underhand, pathetic! – and this scorn refuelled her. Alive and sparkling, she arrived by the girl, who turned pathetically to face her, with an 'Oh'.

'Better drop that,' advised Alice, and the girl did so.

In this light she had a washed-out look: colourless hair and face, even lips and eyes. Whose pupils were enormous, Alice could see.

'Where's your baby?' hectored Alice.

'My husband is there. He's *drunk*,' she said and wailed, then stopped herself. She was trembling.

Alice said, 'Why don't you go to the short-term housing people? You know, there are people who advise on squats.'

'I did.' She began weeping, a helpless, fast, hiccuping weeping, like a child who has already wept for hours.

'Look,' said Alice, feeling in herself the beginnings of an all too familiar weight and drag. 'You have to do something for yourself, you know. It's no good just waiting for people to do something for you. You must find a squat for yourself. Move in. Take it over. Then go to the Council . . . Stop it,' she raged, as the girl sobbed on. 'What's the good of that?'

The girl subdued her weeping, and stood, head bent, before Alice, waiting for her verdict, or sentence.

Oh God, thought Alice, What's the use? I know this one inside out! She's just like Sarah, in Liverpool, and that poor soul Betty. An official has just to take one look, and know she'll give in at once.

An official . . . why, there was an official here, in this house; there was Mary Williams. Alice stood marvelling at this thought: that only a couple of days ago Mary Williams had seemed to hold her own fate – Alice's – in her hands; and now Alice had difficulty in even remembering her status. She felt for Mary, in fact, the fine contempt due to someone or to an institution that has given way too easily. But Mary could be appealed to on behalf of this – child. Alice again took in the collapsed look of her, the passivity, and thought: What is the use, she's one of those who . . .

It was exasperation that was fuelling her now.

'What is your name?'

The drooping head came up, the drowned eyes presented themselves, shocked, to Alice. 'What do you think I'm going to do?' demanded Alice. 'Go to the police and tell them you were going to throw a stone through our window?' And suddenly she began to laugh, while the girl watched her amazed; and took an involuntary step back from this lunatic. 'I've just thought of something. I know someone in the Council who might perhaps – it is only a perhaps . . .' The girl had come to life, was leaning forward, her trembling hand tight on Alice's forearm.

'My name is Monica,' she breathed.

'Monica isn't enough,' said Alice, stopping herself from simply walking away out of impatience. 'I'll have to know your full name, and your address, won't I.'

The girl dropped her hand, and began a dreary groping in her skirts. From a pocket she produced a purse, into which she peered.

'Oh never mind,' said Alice. 'Tell me, I'll remember.'

The girl said she was Monica Winters, and the hotel – which Alice knew about, all right – was the such-and-such, and her number, 556. This figure brought an image with it of concentrated misery, hundreds of couples with small children, each family in one room, no proper amenities, the squalor of it all. All elation, excitement gone, Alice soberly stood there, appalled.

'I'll ask this person to write to you,' said Alice. 'Meanwhile, if I were you, I'd walk around and have a look at what empty houses you can see. Take a look at them. You know. Nip inside, have a look at the amenities – plumbing and . . .' She trailed off dismally, knowing that Monica was not capable of flinging up a window in an empty house and climbing in to have a look, and that, very likely, her husband was the same.

'See you,' said Alice, and turned away from the girl and went in, feeling that the 556 – at least – young couples with their spotty, frustrated infants had been presented to her by Fate, as her responsibility.

'Oh God,' she was muttering, as she made herself tea in the empty kitchen. 'Oh God, what shall I do?' She could easily have wept as messily and uselessly as Monica. Jasper was not here!

She toiled up the stairs, and saw that a light showed on the landing above. She went up. Under the door of the room taken by Mary and Reggie a light showed. She forgot it was midnight and this was a respectable couple. She knocked. After stirrings and voices came, 'Come in.'

Alice looked in at a scene of comfort. Furniture, pretty curtains, and a large double bed in which Mary and Reggie lay side by side, reading. They looked at her over their books with identical wary expressions that said, 'Thus far and no further!' A wave of incredulous laughter threatened Alice. She beat it down, while she thought, These two, we'll see nothing of them, they'll be off . . .

She said, 'Mary, a girl has just turned up here, she's desperate; she's in Shaftwood Hotel, you know . . .'

'Not in our borough,' said Mary instantly.

'No, but she . . .'

'I know about Shaftwood,' said Mary.

Reggie was examining his hand, back and front, apparently with interest. Alice knew that it was the situation he was examining; he was not used to this informality, to group-living, but he was giving it his consideration.

'Don't we all? But this girl . . . her name is Monica . . . she looks to me as if she's suicidal, she could do anything.'

Mary said, after a pause, 'Alice, I'll see what there is, tomorrow, but you know that there are hundreds, thousands of them.'

'Oh yes, I know,' said Alice, and added, 'Good-night,' and went downstairs, thinking, I am being silly. It isn't as if I don't know the type. If you did find her a place, she'd muck it all up somehow.

Remember Sarah? I had to find her a flat, move her in, go to the Electricity Board, and then her husband . . . Monica's one of those who need a mother, someone who takes her on . . . An idea came into Alice's head of such beautiful and apt simplicity that she began laughing quietly to herself.

Now she was in their bedroom, Jasper's and hers. Alone. His sleeping-bag was a dull blue tangle, and she straightened it. She thought: It has been lovely, sharing a room with Jasper. Then she thought: But he's only here because Bert is just through that wall there. She listened: silence. Pat and Bert were asleep. This thought, of why Jasper consented to let her sleep here, instead of going up to another room, or asking her to go, made her mind swirl, as if it – her mind – was nauseous. She sat down on her sleeping-bag, stripped off her sweater, her jeans, pulled on an old-fashioned nightdress in scarlet Viyella which had been her mother's. She felt comfortable and comforted in it.

Again she began to laugh: her mother liked looking after people!

She was inside the sleeping-bag. Lights from the traffic fled across the ceiling. She thought with envy of Jasper in his cell. He would be with this mysterious new contact of his . . . well, she would hear about it all tomorrow. He would be here by lunchtime.

PART III

Going Home

11

A white trade-union leader came to see me, to put the white trade-union case. What he was saying in effect was: 'For God's sake! The white trade unionists are human, aren't they? What do you expect?'

All the time he was talking I was remembering the Whartons, who used to live opposite to us in the Mansions.

The Mansions had been built by a young architect who wanted to astonish the city with modern design. (That was fifteen years ago – now the city has fine modern buildings.) They were flats, shaped rather like a magnet standing on the closed end, with the open ends bent inwards.

We had a flat on the top, on one side, and the Whartons had the flat on the other. Between the flats was a gulf, crossed by a small iron stairway shaped like a rounded bridge.

We first got into acquaintance with the Whartons because they sacked their servant, Dickson, and he came to us. The Whartons never kept a servant longer than a month. Dickson was a gay and amiable person, who spent all his money on clothes. At any reference to the Whartons, or at the sound of the raised voices, the quarrelling, that came continuously from over the gulf, he would roll up his eyes, grimace, shrug deeply, and then laugh.

Sometimes Alice Wharton would yell across to him to bring in that cloth or keep an eye on her baby while he swept out our rooms, but he went on working as if he had not heard her. Alice Wharton shared the attitude that any black man in sight was available for doing odd jobs for her. Once she came across to complain that he was cheeky, just as if he had not stopped working for her weeks before. Alice Wharton's servants were always cheeky. One could hear her, or Bob Wharton, shouting to their servant. Their voices held that tense exasperation, that note of nagging despair, that means an obsession. In places like the Residence and the Mansion one heard that note often. Paternalism, that fine feudal kindness with one's servants, does not occur below a certain income level.

Bob Wharton came from England with his wife and two children in the hungry 'thirties. He was a bricklayer and a Socialist, interested in his trade union, and on his bookshelves were Keir Hardie, Morris, Shaw, the old stalwarts of British Socialism.

At first things went well with him. He rented a small house, the two children went to school, his head was well above water. He became an official of the trade union, and was well liked by his mates. And then there was a third child, a spastic; and it was too bad to be cured. Both parents adored this child; and soon, with hospitals and doctors and the illnesses that he kept having, their heads were no longer above water. They were in debt.

There was no sense in having a fourth child, but one was born, and Mrs Wharton, who was now a tired and harassed woman in her late thirties, swore that she would never, never have another child. She would no longer sleep with her husband, and went into the bed beside Robbie, the sick boy, as if she were married to him. And the marriage, which had been a good one, was full of bitterness. As for the two elder children, they were tender with the sick brother, but there was a terrible resentment in them. Deep down they felt as if they had done wrong in being born healthy and strong, for their mother's love went on the sick child, and she was only brisk and irritable with them. Bob Wharton began to drink, not heavily but enough to make a difference to the monthly bills. One night when he came home quite drunk he made a scene with his wife, and after the scene they broke down and wept together, and from this moment of warmth there began another child. But now Alice Wharton was determined. She used a knitting needle on herself, and killed the child, and nearly killed herself, but she could never have children again, and that, as she told me often, was the one bright thing in her life, the one weight off her shoulders. She used to say it loudly, and the elder children heard it, and they used to look at each other helplessly, trying to share the awful guilt of being born at all, and being such a burden to their parents.

After Alice Wharton came out of hospital, they could not pay the hospital bills, or the doctor. Bob Wharton was too proud to ask for the relief hospitals give to poor people. They sold what furniture they had, or nearly all of it, and they moved to the Mansions, which was cheaper, being only two small rooms, and they sold their little motor-car.

At this time, things were like this: Bob Wharton held his job steadily, and worked all the overtime he could get. He was not afraid for his job, for he was strong, not fifty yet, a tall man, rather thin, bent a little at the shoulders, with a way of poking his head forward, chin up, to look into your face with anxious, serious eyes, as if he might find a reason there why he had come to such a permanent morass of worry and unhappiness. He was still an official of his union, and this was what he was most proud of in his life.

Alice Wharton went out to work for a time, not as a cleaner or a charwoman, as she probably would have done in Britain, because here there were black people to do such work: she found a job as a saleswoman in one of the stores. But if she worked, she had to pay for someone to look after the sick child, who was inert all day, sitting where he was put. They would not let her take the child with her to the store: it might put customers off. So, finding that it cost more to pay for the child in a nursery than she earned, she stayed at home and earned a little extra making dresses for friends.

The baby was healthy, and no trouble to her. The two elder children were at school; and when they came home it was usually to go straight off to friends' houses, where they were not shouted and nagged at. Alice Wharton used to come crying across the iron bridge to me, saying she did not mean to shout and nag at the two children, but she could not help it, something got into her and she could not help it.

So the family all day was Alice Wharton, making dresses and underclothes on her sewing machine, and the sick boy, lying beside her in a wheeled chair, never speaking, never moving, his big, loose head swaying on the top of a long, skeleton neck, looking vaguely around him with large painfully bright blue eyes, and the baby, who rolled and staggered around the two rooms, and terrified the mother by trying to climb out over the edge of the small porch where it met the iron bridge that came over to us.

In the evenings the family was also Bob Wharton, doing his trade-union books at another table, and the two elder children, trying to find some space to do their homework in.

Alice used to complain all the time to Bob that he was mad to waste his time on the union; hadn't he got enough to do, didn't he care about his family; if he wanted to spend his evenings working, then he might just as well get work that was paid for. But Bob would not give up his union. It was the one thing that held him in his idea of himself, and connected him with Britain, where he had had such hopes for the future.

He used to work under the lamp, while Alice nagged and grumbled, a tired woman, chained every moment of her life to the sick boy, until he would fling down his things and bang out to the bar around the corner, or shout at the servant, and then the whole flat would ring with quarrelling and complaints, and the two elder children shrank away to their beds.

Things were bad. But they might get better. Why not?

They could at least not get worse, provided there was work. For Bob Wharton, with the memory of the 'thirties and unemployment behind him, there was always the terror of finding himself out of work.

And there was only one thing that could put him out of work, and that was if the blacks were allowed to do skilled work.

Of an evening he would come over to us, and say, 'We don't mind if the employers pay the blacks the same as us. That's fair, isn't it? Well, isn't it fair?' But he was always uneasy, always guilty about it. Here he was, a trade unionist with experience of trade unionism in Britain; and he was standing shoulder to shoulder with his white mates, keeping the black men out of skilled work. He knew it, and he was tormented by it. He would sit on our little porch, keeping an eye over on the windows beyond the gulf, where his wife sat sewing beside the sick child, her face rigid with hostility and bitterness, and he talked and talked endlessly about the native problem. 'After all, they aren't on our level, are they? It's not so bad as it is for us, being hard up: we're civilised, aren't we; they aren't civilised yet, are they? . . .'

That winter, the spastic child got pneumonia and went to hospital where he nearly died. Both parents were sick with worry, and good friends again because of it. Mrs Wharton visited the hospital three times a day, taking the baby with her.

When the spastic child came out, the bills were over £50, and now they really could not meet them. There was no money and Bob Wharton had to accept charity from a fund that existed for such needs, and to do it changed him in his own eyes from an independent man to a beggar.

But this was not the worst. During those weeks when the child was nearly dying, he neglected his trade-union work, and when it came to re-election, one of his mates got up at the meeting, and said that Brother Wharton was having too much personal trouble; he should be released from trade-union activities for the time being. And so Bob Wharton was no longer an official. He felt as if he had been condemned by his society.

He grew morose, and began to drink badly. Mrs Wharton nagged at him, and he shouted back; and they would sit together, frightened because they were hating each other. And things would be all right for a little while.

Then the eldest child, a girl, got ill for the first time in her life; and it was terrible, for there was no person in the family with the right to be ill but the spastic child. The bills were there again, the doctor's bills and the hospital bills. And when the girl came out, they said she must go for a holiday, so she went to the seaside on charity.

But Alice Wharton was saying to Bob that they could have paid for that holiday on what he spent on brandy.

They quarrelled and bickered, and Dickson, our servant, would stand on his broom listening, and say with a small shake of his head: 'That child it should die. That sick boy, it is no good for them.'

Which is how everybody in the Mansions felt, but no one dared to say it.

Bob used to come over the iron bridge to our porch and sit and talk, not about the native problem now, but about his own.

There were two solutions to his difficulties, as he saw them. First, since all their debts and troubles came from illness, they should go back to Britain. There was no unemployment in Britain now, and above all, there was the health service. Of course, one paid for the health service indirectly, but one could go to a hospital and have a doctor and not have to face these heavy bills afterwards. But to pay the fares back to Britain would cost over £300. He had not got it.

The second solution was this: Bob had worked out that during his ten years in this country he had spent enough on rent to have bought a house by this time. If he had had the capital to buy a house in the beginning, or to put down a payment on one, he would be out of the woods now.

Capital. Capital was what he needed. It was not fair that capitalists had capital and the working man had not.

It was extraordinary to hear Bob, a Socialist all his life, say those words, as if he had never heard them before, as if this was the first time he really understood them.

He would sit on our porch, railing against the capitalists like a man with a fresh vision.

And it was at this point that Mr McCarran-Longman came into our lives. Bob met him in the bar, and brought him up the long, winding stairs to meet Alice. She said to us that Bob was very taken with him. She said it drily, meaning us to understand that *she* was neither taken, nor taken in. And yet there was an uncertainty in her manner. Some time later Bob brought Mr McCarran-Longman to see us, with the manner of presenting something without prejudice for our judgment. And yet he was feverishly anxious to believe in Mr McCarran-Longman.

He was a man of 45 or so, heavily built, an open good-fellow's face. He was well dressed, very neat about the wrists and collar. He used to talk, without interest, of the weather and so on, until he was asked a direct question about himself, and then his polite eyes took fire and he shifted himself in his chair, to a talking position, and began.

It was a question of several people grouping together to buy a large piece of ground, and building houses on it instead of buying houses already built by a company. It would be cheaper this way. Why should one put money into the pockets of the capitalists? About ten people would be the right number. He knew of a good piece of ground, in the path of the town's growth, but one needed to raise at least £10,000. It was after the ground was bought that Mr McCarran-Longman's special talents would come into play. For he had thought of a wonderful invention. One took a large tank, which should be square, more like a swimming bath than a fish-pool, and one filled it with water. Then one shook into the water some chemicals, like shaking salt into soup. Then one stirred the mixture with a large stick or spoon, and behold, it would foam into a myriad of bubbles, like the baths of Hollywood film stars. This would set solid in about twenty-four hours, and one should cut it into suitable bricks or pieces with a very large sharp instrument. The resulting walls, or roofs, or portions of house would be rain-proof, dirt-proof, sound-proof, wear-proof – proof against any risk one might tentatively mention, only delicately, however, to Mr McCarran-Longman, who grew tense and uneasy when one made such suggestions.

Water, he said, would cost nothing, particularly if we were prepared to wait for a receptacle to fill with rainwater. And the chemicals were dirt-cheap. He would tell us the ingredients if it were not that he had applied for a patent. It wasn't that he didn't trust us, but it was a legal matter. The problem really wasn't the consistency of the bricks the houses would be built of, but the tanks to put the water and chemicals into.

He said he had considered having made several dozen shapes or forms, some ordinary brick-size, and some wall- or roof-shape, into which one could pour the water and then the chemical, so as not to have to cut the stuff with a knife or saw afterwards. But if you considered the thing practically, he said, perhaps fifty or a hundred receptacles, lying side by side in some barn or shed, or even in the open air, with water in them, and than shaking chemical in, it would be a tricky thing, and unless one was very careful, the stuff of the walls, roofs, etc., would come out a different consistency each time. Much better to have a large, square tank, big enough to give the stuff a thorough-going stir, and be done with it. So, in addition to the £10,000 needed for the ground for the building stands, and for the lawyers, one would need about £500 to buy or have made a really large square or perhaps oblong tank.

Having got the roofs and walls and floors ready – and the beauty of the thing would be that we could make our houses exactly to our own fancy, even colouring the foam mixture bright original colours, then one would need only to stick them together with a sort of glue. Mr McCarran-Longman was working on the glue now. It was quite good enough as it was, but scientists are never satisfied with less than the best. Another two weeks would see him through. He had the test-tubes on his washstand in the hotel; but the proprietor was getting unpleasant, and the sooner we all bought our bit of ground the better, so that he could build a little shed to do the research in.

So far, Mr McCarran-Longman had only found Bob Wharton and two other families interested, all people desperate to have homes of their own; but none of them had any capital at all.

I was fascinated by the thing, but it was a dilettante's interest. Having spent so much of my life moving from one place to the next, I had a natural inclination to schemes of this kind.

And besides, whereas it might be said that Mr McCarran-Longman was obviously a spiv, that is not altogether true.

Each country has its own type of rogue. Britain, for instance, has the spiv, and one has only to write the word to see him standing there. It was about this time that I got a letter from a friend in Britain saying: 'We have a new word. Spiv. I bet you don't guess what it is.'

I guessed it must be either a sort of meat-mixture, like Spam, or a detergent, but as soon as I heard about spivs, I asked my husband if he thought Mr McCarran-Longman was a spiv.

He said: 'No. Because a spiv is someone who consciously deludes his victims. But this man believes in every word he says.'

'Conscious or unconscious,' I said, 'I think a great many people are going to be very unhappy because of this man.'

'But,' said he, 'you will not be unhappier, because by now you have learned to take my advice. And you are being very bad for him, because you listen when he talks. You must not. And I shall tell Bob he must not. Yes.'

With this, he went across the iron bridge and knocked on Bob's door, and seeing that the living-room was so full of people, children and illness and the noise from the radio that one could not think in it, he invited Bob over for a drink.

For several hours he explained to Bob why he should not put any trust in Mr McCarran-Longman.

Bob listened, rather suspicious, as if he thought that he was being done out of something. It was this that made us worried for the first time about Bob, because he was not a suspicious person.

Then he said: 'Why shouldn't a man make bricks this way? Look what scientists do. They can do anything. So why shouldn't McCarran-Longman have invented something important?'

Then, his ears closed against everything that we said, he remarked finally that in any case nothing could be done until the ground was bought. After that evening he did not come near us for some days; he only nodded, rather stiff, from over the bridge.

We heard that he and another family and Mr McCarran-Longman had raised between them £500, borrowing it between them here and there. They were going to the big firms, who lend big sums of money, asking for £10,000 on the £500. All these firms wanted was some security. And there was not the vestige of security in the lives of the Whartons, the Strickmans, or, for that matter, Mr McCarran-Longman.

Weeks went by, and we hardly saw the Whartons. The elder daughter came back from her holiday, 14 years old now, and her horizons widened by the sea, and badly wanting some space to spread her soul in; and as a relief she took to dropping over to see me of an evening, and she talked steadily about her father, who was crackers, she said, and her mother, who couldn't manage her servant, and the baby –

she couldn't do her homework because the baby's things were everywhere. Not once did she mention that sick boy who sat in the middle of the family draining the life out of them. Her mother, she said, was learning shorthand in the evenings at the Polytechnic, between eight and ten, so she must stay in with the children. When we asked about Mr McCarran-Longman, she said: 'He's gone to see some friends in Portuguese East who will lend him the money for the project.' When she called it a project we could see that she believed in it, even though she had called her father crazy. She brought out the word delicately, with a respect for it.

And then nothing happened. Nothing. Mr McCarran-Longman did not come. But it was nothing sudden. It was not a question of saying: 'If Mr McCarran-Longman does not come back by the end of the month it means we have been made fools of.' For he had gone off, telling them reasonably that since none of them could raise enough money for the project, he would have to tap resources elsewhere, and that would naturally take some time. He even wrote a letter from Beira, saying he had great hopes of a certain man he had met.

And then the silence set in, and Bob Wharton did not even nod over the gulf, and Mrs Wharton pretended not to see her neighbours: her face was stiff, proud, angry.

Twice we were awakened early after midnight, hearing Bob Wharton, drunk, coming up the narrow stairway, arguing with someone he could not see. And then one morning he was found lying at the foot of the stairs, dead, where he had fallen down in the dark.

And now the Wharton family fell to pieces. The sick boy had to go to an institution at last; and the elder girl, the one who came to see us, was a salesgirl at the stores, though she had set her heart on going to university, and she lived in an institution that provided cheap accommodation for girls without proper homes. And Mrs Wharton moved into one room with the baby and the second child, the boy of twelve. She earned their living doing shorthand and typing.

Much later Mr McCarran-Longman did come back. And he had done very well for himself. He had sold a patent for a child's toy. One took a whole lot of fancy little shapes, fishes, dolls, flowers, birds, and poured water into them, and into the water one sprinkled chemical; and the stuff set solid and could be turned out. He made quite a lot of money out of it in the end. And so he was proved finally not to be a spiv, but a man of enterprise.

12

A Nyasaland congressman came to see me, very bitter about Federation.

We got on to the subject of the regiment of his people serving in the war in Malaya. He said: 'This is a terrible thing. They make us into slaves, and then they take our young men for their war in Malaya. They say we are fighting Communist terrorists. I don't know anything about Communism. I don't care about it. But they call *us* agitators and terrorists. We know that the people want only to have their own country back. Why should we fight them?'

I said: 'Why do the young men go to fight?'

He said: 'There are no industries in our country. If our young men want to earn money they must go to other countries. Ours is a very poor country. Our average income is £3 10s. a year. That is, for us Africans. And the recruiters come around to the villages, and the young men are excited at the idea of the uniform, and the pay is very high: it can be £15 a month. And it is a way of travelling and seeing another country. And they are made a great fuss of, with bands playing, and speeches on the wireless.'

I asked him: 'When they come home, what do they say?' 'They don't like it. They say: "What are we doing fighting those people for the white man? They are people with dark skins like our own."'

I said: 'You are a person involved in politics. Perhaps the young men who said that to you weren't ordinary people, but political people, friends of yours?'

He said: 'No, no, that is not true. They were ordinary young men, village boys. They had had time to think. When they come back they have all sorts of attentions paid them; they are asked to make speeches over the air, they are great heroes. But then they are back in the villages, and they start thinking.'

A great many Nyasaland Africans work in Southern Rhodesia. Dickson, the man who worked for me, came from Nyasaland.

I have often wondered what happened to him. He left us very suddenly at the time of the big strike in 1947.

This was the first strike in Southern Rhodesia. It began in Bulawayo and spread fast to all the towns. It was well organised and well disciplined. The most remarkable feature of this strike was this: that because, as always happens on these occasions, the white people got very angry, and armed themselves, so that bands of self-appointed custodians of order were roaming the streets armed to the teeth, looking for Africans to beat up and punish, the Government ordered all the Africans in the cities to get back into their locations and stay there. Troops and police saw that they stayed there. It was as if, in a big strike in Britain, the Government kept the strikers forcibly in their homes and prevented them from working. Because the Government's first fear was that the white defence committees and guardians of white civilisation would start racial battles in the streets. It is safe to say that probably most of the Africans in the country knew nothing about strikes, had possibly never heard the word before. Many were reluctant to leave work; they did not understand what was happening. But because they were forcibly locked into their townships for several days, with nothing to do but listen to the speeches of the strike leaders, they were all given a useful political education.

Dickson Mujani, our servant, was one of those who did not want to leave his work.

But he went, and he was away for five days. Then the strike was over, and the Africans coming back to work said that the Government spokesmen had promised them all a minimum wage of £4 a month. At that time the average was £1 a month.

But Dickson did not return. A week passed. Then, late one evening, long after the hour when Africans are legally forbidden the streets, Dickson came creeping up the narrow iron staircase that came to the back door of our flat. He looked ill and frightened. His polished black skin had a harsh, greyish look, and his eyes darted this way and that with a roll of frightened white eyeball.

He had under his arm a parcel of dirty, tattered paper.

First we made him eat. Then we tried to find out what had happened. But it was difficult; he was at first too frightened to tell us. He kept begging us to take the papers, because 'they' would kill him if they knew he had the papers. Who were *they*? When we had got the story more or less straight, we put him to sleep on a bed in the kitchen. He did not want to sleep. He said he must get away quickly before 'they' got him. We said there was nothing to fear, and in the morning we would take his story to the proper authorities and get justice done, if possible. But in the morning he had gone, vanished. And we never saw him again.

The story he had told us was not about himself but about his father. This was the story:

Long ago, he had forgotten how long, Samson Mujani came from Nyasaland south to find work. He was a young man then, with a wife and child in his village. In the big city he found work on the railways, at the station. He swept the platform, and ran errands for the white bosses, and was a messenger boy. He earned a few shillings a month, and he lived in the location. It was still called the location then. At first it was all frightening and difficult, after the peaceful green village he had known. He did not understand the money, he did not understand at all the customs of the white men, and he was puzzled and unhappy because of their rudeness and rough ways. After a while, he learned how to live, keeping quiet, dodging trouble and the police, keeping a smiling face always for his masters. The green village he had come from seemed a long way off, another world. He thought often of his wife and child, but the women in this town were not as he would wish his own wife to be, so he did not send for her. He took up with one of the women of the town and lived with her in a shack made of iron and brick on the borders of the location where the ground dipped towards the river. She bore him a child, and then another. It was at the birth of the second child that she died. It was then he sent a message to his wife, and after many months she came south, walking with some relatives who looked after her. She brought their own child, and so there was a family of three children in the little shack.

The years went past, and the town grew so that now instead of trains once or twice a week, they came every day, and then several times a day. Samson was a well-known figure on the station. White people who used the trains a great deal grew to know him, and used to give him bits of money, and call him by his name. His own people knew him, too, and when they found it hard to understand the business of buying tickets for a train, and the times of the trains, he would be called in to interpret. By now he was earning about 20s. a month, and it was hard to live with all the children, five of them now, so his wife went to work as a nanny at one of the white houses.

She was a good woman, strict with her children, and with her own behaviour in this city.

And now the elder children were growing up, and Samson thought hardly at all of the green village in the mountains. It was as if he had lived all his life here. But once, feeling tired, and sometimes dizzy, and sometimes with pains in him, he went home with his wife, and the younger children, this time on the big lorries that go to and fro over the long distance. He found the village hard now; he had grown away from it. He loved it, and he didn't love it. His wife would have stayed, but he fretted, and returned to the big city. His wife came with him. But he was growing to be an old man. He did not know how old he was, but it was harder to do the work, carrying messages around the offices on a bicycle, and the sweeping, and sometimes the moving of the luggage. And then there was a change in the way of work, for the union of the white men who worked on the railway was always very careful of what work the black men did. There was a reorganisation, and work like Samson's, which was neither one thing nor another, must be named and ordered. It was at this time that he changed from sweeping and running messages on the platforms, to becoming an assistant of one of the white men who tended the big engines. He might oil certain parts of the engine while the man watched him, or he might take tools and do small repairs under inspection. This was easier work for him, now that his back was stiffening. Also he had better hours. He was a real railway worker. And then the war came, and again it was as if the town had been fed with new life. It began to spread in all directions, and the trains were in and out all day, carrying troops wearing different coloured uniforms. That easy-going pace of the life along the platforms that he remembered was gone. Often he did not know the faces of the white men who drove and tended the trains. And only the older men in the offices of the station remembered him as a young man, the youth from Nyasaland.

In the location, too, things were changing. Instead of huts and shacks of all kinds, there were houses being built for the

Africans, and it was called the township. The Superintendent
of the township, who liked those he looked after to be willing
and cheerful and obedient, liked Samson, and he was given one
of the good houses for men with families. It had two rooms in it,
and a kitchen. They all lived in it, the mother and father, and
the oldest son, Dickson, who had been born in Nyasaland and
had come down with his mother, and the four younger
children, all of whom were working in the houses of the white
city.

But the new house cost more money than the old one, the rent
was higher, and because of the war, the prices of food and
clothing were rising all the time, and although everyone in the
family was working, it was hard to live, harder than it had ever
been.

Around him on the railway, his people were talking whenever they met of the difficulty of living. Often they would send a
spokesman to the management about their wages. But the
management now was not in the station buildings, it was as if
whenever they spoke to a white boss, he said he was not the real
boss, but there was another over him . . . they could never get
at this real boss to speak to him face to face, as had been possible
– so Samson told them – in the old days.

When the strike began, although there had been so much
discontent for so long, it was a surprising and troubling thing
even for those who had spoken most of it. To begin with, a
strike was not legal. And to one like Samson, who had spent all
his life avoiding trouble, learning the taboos that hedged his life
so as to respect them, to do something illegal was frightening.
But there came that evening when all about him walked off
from their work, saying it was a strike, and of course he went
with them.

There were no blacklegs in that strike.

And the white men, that is the white men who worked on the
railways as workers, wished them good luck as they went;
because although they were not on strike themselves, in their
capacity as workers they were sympathetic.

That first day on strike Samson stayed at home – by himself –
since everyone in the family was out at work in the city, and
knew very little about what was to happen. And then, on the

second day, he was not alone, for all the houseboys and cooks and messengers of the city struck, too: it was spreading. The last to come home was his wife; she stayed at home on the third day. There was little food in the location, or township, because the authorities, who were now very angry, were not bringing food in. All the Africans were in the townships of the city, and there was no food. And around the townships were cordons of police to prevent white men getting in, or Africans from getting out.

But the family stayed in their little house, and kept themselves out of trouble.

It was on the third day that a man came to Samson and said: 'May the committee of the strike come to your house tonight to discuss matters?'

'But why my house?' asked Samson, deeply troubled. And then he said yes, that they would be welcome.

As the time came near he sent his sons and daughters to a neighbour's house, and his wife went into the second room, leaving the front room free for the men who wished to talk.

When they came, they said that they moved from this house to that for their discussions, because even their talk was illegal, and they did not wish to remain always in one place, in case the police came to arrest them. Samson was old and he was respected, and his house was a good and respected house.

He received them politely and asked them to sit down, and the wife brought tea for them from the kitchen.

There were seven men, and Samson sat, saying little, while they talked. The matters which they discussed were difficult for him. Regulations and laws and prohibitions and white papers and blue papers and the reports of committees – these were what these men discussed. But at the end of all their talk was one fact only: the strike was not legal. Yet it existed. There were no Africans at work that day, none, in any place in the city, not for cooking, or for cleaning, or for digging gardens, or for looking after children, or for taking messages, or for driving cars or lorries. So what they had to say to the Government was only: 'Look, here is this strike. Here is this thing. And now what will you do?'

They talked for a long time, and again the wife made tea and brought it in, and the lights were going out in the houses around them.

Samson would have liked to say that it was getting late, and it would be wiser for them to go now; but he was proud they had chosen him, and so he said nothing.

Then there was a knock on the door, and through the small window they could see the shape of a policeman against the sky, and then another policeman. Four of the men in the room got up, and without a word ran out of the house by the back door into the night. For they were citizens of other countries, that is to say, they came from Nyasaland or from Northern Rhodesia, and even though they might have worked in this country all their lives, like Samson, they could be deported within a day.

When the two policemen came in there were only three men and Samson. But it could be seen that there had been more in the room. They asked to see the papers of the three men, and from these papers it could be seen that they were from this country. The three men wished Samson good night, like friends saying good night after a visit, and went out.

Then the two policemen went into the kitchen and saw Mrs Mujani sitting by her stove knitting a jersey for her daughter. She looked up and went on knitting, though it could be seen that her hands were trembling, and her knees were held together to keep them still. They left her, and went back into the other room, and Samson was straightening the chairs, like a host after his guests were gone. They stood for a moment, watching him, with their sticks in their hands, and then one saw a bundle of papers lying on the table, and he jumped forward for it.

'And what are these papers?' he shouted at Samson, unrolling them.

'I do not know,' said Samson. And then, thinking he might get his friends into trouble, he said: 'I found them lying on the ground.'

The two policemen, both tall, strong, fine fellows, spread the papers on the table, and looked at them, and then one turned to Samson, and said, 'Do you not know these papers are forbidden?'

'No,' said Samson. 'I know nothing.'

And now the two policemen came towards Samson, threatening. And the old man shrank back a little and then stood his ground. A timid man he had always been, a gentle man, a man who avoided trouble, and yet here he stood, in his own house with two big policemen standing over him. And his wife was crying in the next room. He could hear her.

'Where did you get these papers?' asked one of the policemen, and he hit Samson with his open hand across his head. Samson fell sideways a few steps, recovered, and said:

'I know nothing.'

And then the other policeman, grinning, moved across and hit Samson with his open hand on the other side of the head, so he staggered back to the first.

Now the wife was in the open door, wailing aloud.

The first policeman said: 'We will put you in prison, my fine fellow, you damn fool, you Kaffir.'

'What are you doing in my house?' asked Samson, breathing hard. 'This is my house.'

'Your house – you say that to the police?'

And he hit Samson again, with his closed fist, on the side of the head, and as Samson reeled across the room the other policeman hit him with his closed fist.

And now there was a silence, for instead of staggering back, to be hit again, Samson stood, his face screwed up, eyes shut, then his mouth dropped and his head fell sideways, and he slumped to the ground.

The wife wailed again.

The two policemen looked at each other, hurriedly bent over Samson who was lying on the ground motionless, and then ran out of the house into the night.

When Dickson came in from his friends', he found his mother sitting beside his father, swaying from side to side, moaning. His father was dead.

When the other sons and daughters came in, they talked over what to do.

Some said to go to the Superintendent. But the mother was frightened.

One said that policemen were not allowed to kill a man by

hitting him, but another that the policemen would lie and there would be trouble.

At last one ran for the nurse at the hospital, and men came with a stretcher and carried Samson away. They said he had fallen down dead suddenly.

He was an old man, and no one had eaten for two days.

On the next day the mother sat wailing in her kitchen, and the sons and daughters were with the crowds around the hall and the playing ground, listening to the talk about the strike, and to the men who were standing on boxes explaining about the strike. It was here that Dickson saw a policeman looking close at him. And the policeman came up to him through the crowd and stood by him and said: 'Where's your situpa?' Dickson produced his papers, and the policeman said: 'You'd better go home, you go to Nyasaland, before they catch you. I know you have those papers in your house.' Dickson looked at him, and then around for help, but the people about him had melted away to give distance to the policeman. He said nothing. Then the policeman went away, swinging his stick, and Dickson slowly went home.

'What is this about the papers?' he asked his mother.

She raised her voice and wept. He said: 'Mother, mother, it was those papers that killed him.'

She had put them in the back of the cupboard in the kitchen, and Dickson took them out and looked at them, and understood nothing. But he put them under his coat, and was going to find the men who had been there the night before to ask why these papers had killed his father, when he saw the policeman again, walking slowly past his house, looking at him, and then he turned and walked slowly back, looking at him all the time.

And now for the first time he listened to the wailing of the old woman, who was saying that she was alone, she was alone, and she wanted to go home. She meant to Nyasaland. In Nyasaland the police did not come into people's houses and hit them, there the police did not walk with sticks in their hands. She spoke as if she had come from there a week ago, instead of so many years. But Dickson listened, and he stood by the window and looked out and saw the policeman go past again, looking at him, fierce and threatening.

The papers were hot and uncomfortable under his coat. When at last the policeman went away, he left his mother and hastened to the house of one of the men who were directing the strike, but he was not there, and he did not like to leave these dangerous papers. He went to another house and another, but no one would tell him where the men were. So at last he returned to his own home, and all that night the mother and the children discussed what it was they should do. One of the daughters and one of the sons said they would stay in this city. Why go back home? There was nothing there, only the old people in the villages, and no work, and nothing to buy with money – no money even.

But Dickson and his youngest brother, who was only twelve years, and one sister said they would go with the mother.

But first they must get money from the people who employed them, and then there was the question of the papers.

On the next day the strike was finished. The mother and the youngest son, who worked as piccanin, or odd-job man in a house at the other end of the town, and the daughter, who was a nanny, went to tell their employers they must leave quickly, they must go home, their mother had died, or their father, or their child – anything, so as to leave quickly.

But Dickson, who had the papers under his coat and who seemed to see that policeman everywhere, waited until night came. When the dusk had fallen, he was hurrying out of the gate of the township, when he did indeed see the policeman, who fell into step beside him, and said, 'Where are you going?'

And Dickson said quickly, in a low voice: 'We are going to Nyasaland, we are going home . . .'

And then the policeman swerved off and away, on his own business, and Dickson came quickly through the streets to the Mansions, and up the narrow staircase and to the kitchen.

In the morning, when we went to look for him, and could not find him, we examined the bundle of wet and torn papers. In it were copies of the *World Federation of Trade Unions Journal* from Britain, which is banned, and other journals from down south. There was a copy of the Industrial Conciliation Act. There were also two pamphlets, very worn, as if innumerable hands had held them, one called *Peoples of Soviet Asia Awake!* and the other *Fight the Devil Drink.*

In Pursuit of the English

I

I came into contact with the English very early in life, because as it turns out, my father was an Englishman. I put it like this, instead of making a claim or deprecating a fact, because it was not until I had been in England for some time that I understood my father.

I wouldn't like to say that I brooded over his character; that would be putting it too strongly, but I certainly spent a good part of my childhood coming to terms with it. I must confess, to be done with confessions right at the start, that I concluded at the age of about six my father was mad. This did not upset me. For a variety of reasons, none of which will be gone into here, the quintessential eccentricity of the human race was borne in upon me from the beginning. And aside from whatever deductions I might have come to for myself, verbal confirmation came from outside, continuously, and from my father himself. It was his wont to spend many hours of the day seated in a rickety deck-chair on the top of the semi-mountain on which our house was built, surveying the African landscape which stretched emptily away on all sides for leagues. After a silence which might very well have lasted several hours, he would start to his feet, majestically splenetic in shabby khaki, a prophet in his country, and, shaking his fist at the sky, shout out: 'Mad! Mad! Everyone! Everywhere! Mad!' With which he would sink back, biting his thumb and frowning, into sombre contemplation of his part of the universe; quite a large part, admittedly, compared to what is visible to, let us say, an inhabitant of Luton. I say Luton because at one time he lived there. Reluctantly.

My mother was not English so much as British; an intrinsically efficient mixture of English, Scotch and Irish. For the purposes of this essay, which I take it is expected to be an attempt of definitions, she does not count. She would refer to herself as Scotch or Irish according to what mood she was in, but not, as far as I can remember, as English. My father on the other hand called himself English, or rather, an

Englishman usually bitterly, and when reading the newspapers: that is, when he felt betrayed, or wounded in his moral sense. I remember thinking it all rather academic, living as we did in the middle of the backveld. However, I did learn early on that while the word *English* is tricky and elusive enough in England, this is nothing to the variety of meanings it might bear in a Colony, self-governing or otherwise.

I decided my father was mad on such evidence as that at various times and for varying periods he believed that (*a*) One should only drink water that has stood long enough in the direct sun to collect its invisible magic rays. (*b*) One should only sleep in a bed set in such a position that those health-giving electric currents which continuously dart back and forth from Pole to Pole can pass directly through one's body, instead of losing their strength by being forced off course. (*c*) The floor of one's house should be insulated, probably by grass matting, against the invisible and dangerous emanations from the minerals in the earth. Also because he wrote, but did not post, letters to the newspapers on such subjects as the moon's influence on the judgement of statesmen; the influence of properly compounded compost on world peace; the influence of correctly washed and cooked vegetables on the character (civilized) of a white minority as against the character (uncivilized) of a black, indigenous, non-vegetable-washing majority.

As I said, it was only some time after I reached England, I understood that this – or what I had taken to be – splendidly pathological character would merge into the local scene without so much as a surprised snarl from anyone.

It is, then, because of my early and thorough grounding in the subject of the English character that I have undertaken to write about this business of being an exile. First one has to understand what one is an exile from. And unfortunately I have not again succeeded in getting to know an Englishman. That is not because, as the canard goes, they are hard to know, but because they are hard to meet.

An incident to illustrate. I had been in London two years when I was rung up by a friend newly-arrived from Cape Town. 'Hey, Doris, man,' she says, 'how are you doing and how are you getting on with the English?' 'Well,' I say, 'the thing is, I don't think I've met any. London is full of foreigners.' 'Hell, yes, I know what you mean. But I met an Englishman last night.' 'You didn't?' 'I did. In a pub. And he's the real thing.' At first glance I knew he was the real thing. Tall, asthenic, withdrawn; but above all, he bore all the outward signs of the inward, intestine-twisting prideful melancholy. We talked about the weather and the Labour Party. Then, at the same moment, and from the same impulse – he was remarking that the pub was much too hot, my friend and I laid delighted hands on him. At last, we said, we are meeting the English. He drew himself up. His mild blue eyes flashed at last. 'I am not,' he said, with a blunt but basically forgiving hauteur, 'English. I have a Welsh grandmother.'

The sad truth is that the English are the most persecuted minority on earth. It has been so dinned into them that their cooking, their heating arrangements, their love-making, their behaviour abroad and their manners at home are beneath even contempt, though certainly not comment, that like Bushmen in the Kalahari, that doomed race, they vanish into camouflage at the first sign of a stranger.

Yet they are certainly all around us. The Press, national institutions, the very flavour of the air we breathe indicate their continued and powerful existence. And so, whenever confounded by some native custom, I consider my father.

For instance. It is the custom in Africa to burn fireguards for dwelling-houses and outhouses against the veld fires which rage across country all through the dry season. My father was burning a fireguard for the cow-shed. It was a windless day. The grass was short. The fire would burn slowly. Yet it was in the nature of things that any small animal, grounded bird, insect or reptile in the two-hundred-yard-wide, mile-long stretch of fire would perish, not, presumably, without pain. My father stood, sombrely contemplating the creeping line of small flames. The boss-boy stood beside him. Suddenly there fled out from the smoke-filled grass at their feet, a large field-mouse. The boss-boy brought down a heavy stick across the mouse's back. It was dying. The boss-boy picked up the mouse by the tail, and swinging the still-twitching creature, continued to stand beside my father, who brought down his hand in a very hard slap against the boss-boy's face. So unprepared was he for this, that he fell down. He got up, palm to his cheek, looking at my father for an explanation. My father was rigid with incommunicable anger. 'Kill it at once,' he said, pointing to the mouse, now dead. The boss-boy flung the mouse into a nest of flames, and stalked off, with dignity.

'If there is one thing I can't stand it's cruelty of any kind,' my father said afterwards, in explanation of the incident.

Which is comparatively uncomplicated, not to say banal. More obliquely rewarding in its implications was the affair with the Dutchman. My father was short of money, and had undertaken to do, in his spare time, the accounting for the small goldmine two miles away. He went over three times a week for this purpose. One day, several hundred pounds were missing. It was clear that Van Reenen, who managed the mine for a big company, had stolen it, and in such a way that it looked as if my father had. My father was whitely silent and suffering for some days. At any moment the company's auditors would descend, and he would be arrested. Suddenly, without a word to my mother, who had been making insensitively practical suggestions, such as, going to the police, he stalked off across the veld to the mine, entered the Dutchman's office, and knocked him down. My father was not at all strong, apart from having only one leg, the other having been blown off in the First World War. And the Dutchman was six-foot, a great, red-faced, hot-tempered trek-ox of a man. Without saying one word, my father returned across country, still silent and brooding, and shut himself into the dining-room.

Van Reenen was entirely unmanned. Although this was by no means the first time he had embezzled and swindled, so cleverly that while everyone knew about it the police had not been able to lay a charge against him, he now lost his head and voluntarily gave himself up to the police. Where he babbled to the effect that the Englishman had found him out. The police telephoned my father. Who, even whiter, more silent, more purposeful than before, strode back across the veld to the mine, pushed aside the police sergeant, and knocked Van Reenen down again. 'How dare you suggest,' he demanded, with bitter reproach, 'how dare you even imagine, that I would be capable of informing on you to the police?'

The third incident implies various levels of motive. The first time I heard about it was, when very young indeed, from my mother, thus: 'Your governess is not suited to this life here, she is going back to England.' Pause. 'I suppose she is going back to that smart set she came from.' Pause. 'The sooner she gets married the better.'

Later, from a neighbour who had been confidante to the governess. 'That poor girl who was so unhappy with your mother and had to go back to England in disgrace.'

Later, from my father: '. . . that time I had to take that swine Baxter to task for making free with Bridget's name in the bar.'

What happened was this. My mother, for various reasons unwell, and mostly bedridden, had answered an advertisement from 'Young woman, educated finishing school, prepared to teach young child in return for travel.' The Lord knows what she, or my mother, expected. It was the mid-twenties, Bridget was twenty-five, and had 'done' several London seasons. Presumably she wanted to see a bit of the world before she married, or thought of some smart Maugham-ish colonial plantation society. Later she married an Honourable something or other, but in the meantime she got a lonely maize farm, a sick woman, two spoiled children, and my father, who considered that any woman who wore lipstick or shorts was no better than she ought to be. On the other hand, the district was full of young farmers looking for wives, or at least entertainment. They were not, she considered, of her class, but it seems she was prepared to have a good time. She had one, and danced and gymkhana'd whenever my parents would let her. This was not nearly as often as she would have liked. She was being courted by a farmer called Baxter, a tough ex-policeman from Liverpool. My father did not like him. He didn't like any of her suitors. One evening, he went into the bar at the village and Baxter came over and said: 'How's Bridget?' My father instantly knocked him down. When the bewildered man stood up and said: 'What the f—ing hell's that for?' my father said: 'You will kindly refer, in my presence at least, to an innocent young girl many thousands of miles from her parents and to whom I am acting as guardian, as Miss Fox.'

Afterwards he said: 'I must not allow myself to lose my temper so easily. Quite obviously, I don't know my own strength.'

When stunned by *The Times* or the *Telegraph*; when – yes, I think the word is interested, by the *Manchester Guardian*: when unable to discover the motive behind some dazzlingly stupid stroke of foreign policy; when succumbing to that mood which all of us foreigners are subject to: that we shall ever be aliens in an alien land, I recover myself by reflecting, in depth, on the implications of incidents such as these.

Admittedly at a tangent, but in clear analogy, I propose to admit, and voluntarily at that, that I have been thinking for some time of writing a piece called: In Pursuit of the Working-Class. My life has been spent in pursuit. So has everyone's, of course. I chase love and fame all the time. I have chased, off and on, and with much greater deviousness of approach, the working-class and the English. The pursuit of the working-class is shared by everyone with the faintest tint of social responsibility; some of the most indefatigable pursuers are working-class people. That is because the phrase does not mean, simply, those people who can be found by walking out of one's front door and turning down a side-street. Not at all. Like love and fame it is a platonic image, a grail, a quintessence, and by definition, unattainable. It took me a long time to understand this. When I lived in Africa and was learning how to write, that group of mentors who always voluntarily constitute themselves as a sort of watch committee of disapprobation around every apprentice writer, used to say that I could never write a word that made sense until I had become pervaded by the cultural values of the working-class. In spite of all the evidence to the contrary, these mentors claimed that not one truthful word could ever be written until it was first baptized, so to speak, by the working-class. I remember even now the timidity with which, just as I was about to leave Africa, I suggested that having spent twenty-five years of my life in the closest contact with the black people, who are workers if nothing else, some knowledge, or intimation, or initiation by osmosis must surely have been granted me. And I remember even now the indignant tone of the reply: 'The Africans in this country are not working-class *in the true sense*. They are semi-urbanized peasants.' I should have understood by the tone, which was essentially that of a defender of a faith, that I must stick by my guns. But it always did take me a long time to learn anything.

I came to England. Lived, for the best of reasons, namely, I was short of money, in a household crammed to the roof with people who worked with their hands. After a year of this I said with naïve pride to a member of the local watch committee that now, at last, I must be considered to have served my apprenticeship. The reply was pitying, but not without human sympathy: 'These are not the real working-class. They are the lumpen proletariat, tainted by petty bourgeois ideology.' I rallied. I said that, having spent a lot of my time with Communists, either here or in Africa, a certain proportion of whom, even though a minority, are working-class, surely some of the magic must have rubbed off on me? The reply came: 'The Communist Party is the vanguard of the working-class and obviously *not typical*.' Even then I didn't despair. I went to a mining village, and returned with a wealth of observation. It was no good. 'Miners, like dockworkers, are members of a very specialized, traditionalized trade; mining is already (if you take the long view) obsolete. The modes of being, mores and manners of a mining community have nothing whatsoever to do with the working-class as a whole.' Finally, I put in some time in a housing estate in a New Town, and everyone I met was a trade unionist, a member of the Labour Party, or held other evidence of authenticity. It was then that I realized I was defeated. 'The entire working-class of Britain has become tainted by capitalism or has lost its teeth. It is petit bourgeois to a man. If you really want to understand the militant working-class, you have to live in a community in France, let's say near the Renault works, or better still, why don't you take a trip to Africa where the black masses are not yet corrupted by industrialism.'

The purpose of this digression, which is not nearly so casual as it might appear, is to make it plain that when set on something I don't give up easily. Also to – but I must get back to why it took me so long to get started for England in the first place.

I can't remember a time when I didn't want to come to England. This was because, to use the word in an entirely different sense, I was English. In the colonies or Dominions, people are English when they are sorry they ever emigrated in the first place; when they are glad they emigrated but consider their roots are in England; when they are thoroughly assimilated into the local scene and would hate ever to set foot in England again; and even when they are born colonial but have an English grandparent. This definition is sentimental and touching. When used by people not English, it is accusatory. My parents were English because they yearned for England, but knew they could never live in it again because of its conservatism, narrowness and tradition. They hated Rhodesia because of its newness, lack of tradition, of culture. They were English, also, because they were middle-class in a community mostly working-class. This use of the word can be illustrated by the following incident. Scene: the local tennis club. The children are playing tennis, watched by their mothers. The hostess for the afternoon is a woman from the Cape, a member of an old Dutch family, newly married to a Scots farmer. She is shy, dignified, and on her guard. Mrs Mathews, a loquacious Scots farmer's wife attempts to engage her in conversation. She fails. She turns to my mother and says: 'That one's got no small-talk to change with a neighbour. She's too good for us. She's real English and that's a fact.' Then she blushes and says: 'Oh, but I didn't mean . . .' thus revealing how often she has made the criticism of my mother.

My parents were, now I come to think of it, grail-chasers of a very highly-developed sort. I cannot even imagine a country in which they would have been definitely ready to settle down without criticism. The nearest I can get to it would be a combination of the best parts of Blackheath or Richmond, merged, or mingled with a really large ranch, let's say about fifty thousand acres, in the Kenyan Highlands. This would have to be pervaded by a pre-1914 atmosphere, or ambience, like an Edwardian after-glow. Their Shangri-La would be populated thickly, for my mother, with nice professional people who were nevertheless *interesting*; and sparsely, for my father, with scamps, drunkards, eccentrics and failed poets who were nevertheless and at bottom *decent people*.

I would, of course, be the first to blame my parents for my own grail-seeking propensities.

England was for me a grail. And in a very narrowly-defined way. Not long ago people set foot for the colonies – the right sort of people, that is, in a spirit of risking everything and damning the cost. These days, a reverse immigration is in progress. The horizon conquerors now set sail or take wing for England, which in this sense means London, determined to conquer it, but on their own terms.

I have an anecdote to illustrate this. I had been in England for about five years, and was just beginning to understand that I had got the place whacked, when an old acquaintance telephoned to say that he had arrived in London to write a book. He had forever turned his back on his old life, which consisted of making enormous sums of money out of gold-mines, drinking a lot, and marrying a succession of blonde and beautiful girls. I visited him in his flat. It was in Mayfair, furnished at immense expense in the most contemporary taste, with two refrigerators. He was very excited that at last he had had the strength of mind to cut all his profits and tackle England. I remember, on the whole without regret, the strong, involuntary moral disapprobation that I radiated as he talked. Finally, and the remark welled up from the depths of my being, from the perfervid heart of the myth itself 'Do you mean to tell me that you are going to live in a flat that costs twenty-two guineas a week, in Mayfair, *with* a refrigerator, *to write a novel?*'

Looking back, I can see that there were several occasions when I could have come to England years before I did. For instance, there was talk of my being sent to school here. That would have meant my being taken on by a section of my family which I detested – I see now quite rightly – by instinct and without ever having met them. I used to get ill with mysterious spontaneity every time this plan was discussed. I would lie in bed and dream about England, which of course had nothing in common with that place inhabited by my cousins. That England was almost entirely filled with rather dangerous night-clubs, which had a strong literary flavour. I was then fourteen. I think the only person I would have allowed to bring me to England at that time was a father-figure in appearance like Abraham Lincoln, with a strong white-slaving propensity, yet fundamentally decent, and with an untutored taste for the novel *Clarissa*. My most powerful fantasy was of how I could gently release the captives, all of them misunderstood girls of about fourteen, all of them incredibly beautiful, but full of fundamental decency. I would press enough money into their hands (willingly given me by my master for this purpose) to enable them to find themselves, and set them free. At the same time I would be explaining to my master the real and inner significance of the novel *Clarissa*, while he gently toyed with my breasts, and, kissing me on the brow, willingly handed me large sums of money which would enable me to find myself.

The other occasions when nothing prevented me from coming to England but enough energy to do it, were the same: a powerful inner voice said it was not yet the time. The time, finally, was in 1949, when England was at its dingiest, my personal fortunes at their lowest, and my morale at zero. I also had a small child.

I have it on the highest secular authority that this propensity of mine to do things the hard way amounts to nothing less than masochism, but a higher authority still, the voice of the myth itself, tells me that this is nonsense.

By the time I came, things had been satisfactorily arranged in such a way that the going would be as hard as possible.

For instance. The ships for years after the war were booked months in advance. Yet I know now – and it would have been obvious to anyone but me, that the simple process of bribing someone would have got me a passage on one of the big regular boats. Instead I decided on a much cheaper, but slower, Dutch boat for which I would have to wait in Cape Town. Of course, by the time I had hung about in Cape Town, and spent money for four weeks on that terrible slow boat, it would have been much cheaper to fly.

The moment of arriving in England, for the purposes of the myth, would be when I got to Cape Town. This is because the Cape is English, or, as the phrase goes, is pervaded by the remnants of the old English liberal spirit.

It so happened that the first people I met in Cape Town were English. This was an immediately disturbing experience. They were a university professor and his wife, who had been, the last time I saw them, bastions of the local Communist Party. That had been eighteen months before. Now they had left the Communist Party. Things have now changed so that it is quite possible to leave the Communist Party and retain a sense of balance. In those days, one was either an eighteen-carat, solid, unshakeable red; or, if an ex-red, violently, and in fact professionally anti-Communist. The point was, that this *volte-face* had taken place about six weeks before, and in a blinding moment of illumination at that, like on the road to Damascus. I went into their beautiful house, which was on one of the hills overlooking the bay. I was full of comradely emotions. The last time I had seen it, it was positively the area office for every kind of progressive activity. I was greeted with an unmistakable atmosphere of liberal detachment, and the words: 'Of course we have left the Party and we are no longer prepared to be made use of.' Now I was hoping I might be asked to stay a few days while looking for a room; in fact I had been invited to stay any time I liked. I became even more confused as the conversation proceeded, because it seemed that not only had they changed, I had, too. Whereas, previously, I had been fundamentally sound, with my heart in the right place, yet with an unfortunate tendency towards flippancy about serious matters which ought to be corrected, now I was a dogmatic red with a closed mind and a dangerous influence on the blacks who were ever prey to unscrupulous agitators. I was trying to discuss this last bit reasonably, when I was informed that Cape Town was overflowing, that no one but a lunatic would arrive without arranging accommodation, and there was no hope of my finding a room. My situation was, in short, admirably deplorable. While my son has always been the most delightful, amiable and easygoing person, yet, being two years old, he needed to sleep and to eat. My total capital amounted to £47. I was informed that the prices for even bad accommodation were astronomical. They telephoned some boarding-houses which turned out, much to their satisfaction, to be full. They then summoned a taxi. On my suggestion.

The taxi-driver was an Afrikaner and he had an aunt who ran a boarding-house. He instantly took me there, refused payment for the trip, arranged matters with his aunt, carried in my luggage – which was extensive, because I had not yet learned how to travel – taught my son some elementary phrases in Afrikaans, gave me a lot of good advice, and said he would come back to see how I was getting on. He was a man of about sixty, who said he had forty-four grandchildren, but had it in his heart to consider my son the forty-fifth. He was a Nationalist. It was not the first time I had been made to reflect on that sad political commonplace that one's enemies are so often much nicer than one's friends.

Sitting in the taxi outside Mrs Coetzee's boarding-house, the mirage of England was still strong. While features like the white-slaving father figure and the night-clubs had disappeared, and it was altogether more adjusted to my age, it can't be said to have had much contact with fact – at least, as experienced. The foundation of this dream was now a group of loving friends, all above any of the minor and more petty human emotions, such as envy, jealousy, spite, etc. We would be devoted to changing the world completely, and very fast, at whatever cost to ourselves, while we simultaneously produced undying masterpieces, and lived communally, with such warmth, brilliance, generosity of spirit and so on that we would be an example to everyone.

The first thing I saw from the taxi was that the place was full of English. That is, English English, not South African British. Several English girls were sitting on the wooden steps, their famed English complexions already darkened, looking disconsolate. The boarding-house was on one of the steep slopes of the city, and overpowered by a great many dazzlingly new hotels that rose high above it on every side. It was very old, a ramshackle wandering house of wood, with great wooden verandas, a roof hidden by dense green creeper, and surrounded by a colourful garden full of fruit-trees and children. It had two stories, the upper linked to the lower only by an outside wooden staircase. The place was filthy, unpainted, decaying; a fire-trap and a death-trap – in short, picturesque to a degree. A heavy step upstairs made the whole structure tremble to its foundations. My room was in the front, off the veranda, and it had bare wooden floors, stained pink walls, stained green ceiling, a wardrobe so large I could take several strides up and down inside it, two enormous sagging double beds, and four single beds. My friend the grandfather had gone, so I went in search of authority, my feet reverberating on the bare boards. It was mid-afternoon. Towards the back of the house was a small room painted dingy yellow, and a broken wood-burning stove in it, a large greasy table dotted with flies, a hunk of cold meat under a great fly-cover, and the fattest woman I have ever seen in my life dozing in a straight-backed chair. It was as if a sack of grain was supported by a matchbox. Her great loose body strained inside a faded orange cotton dress. Her flesh was dull yellow in colour, and her hair dragged in dull strands on her neck. I thought she must be the coloured cook; but when I learned this was Mrs Coetzee herself, suppressed the seditious thought. I went back to my room, where a small, thin, chocolate-coloured girl who looked about twelve, but was in fact eighteen, was engaged in replacing the dirty sheets on the biggest of the beds with slightly less dirty sheets. She was barefooted, and wore a bright pink dress, rent under the arm. Her name was Jemima. She did all the housework of the boarding-house, which had between fifty and sixty people in it, and helped Mrs Coetzee in the kitchen. She earned three pounds a month, and was the most exploited human being I have known. To watch her do my room out was an education in passive resistance. She would enter without knocking, and without looking at me, carrying a small dustpan and brush, which she dropped on an unmade bed and did not use again. She would direct her small sharp body in a straight line to my bed, while her completely expressionless round black eyes glanced about her, but unseeing. With one movement she twitched the bedclothes up over the rumpled pillows. She then smoothed the surface creases of the faded coverlet out with the right hand, while already turning her body to the next bed, in which my son slept. She twitched up the bedclothes on that with her left hand, while she reached out the other for the dustpan and brush. She was already on her way to the door before her right hand, left behind, had picked up the dustpan. She then turned herself around in such a way, that at the door, she was facing into the room. She used the edge of the dustpan to pull the doorknob towards her. The door slammed. The room, as far as she was concerned, was done.

Mrs Coetzee and she carried on warfare in shrill Afrikaans, which I did not understand. But like all wars that have been going on for a long time, it sounded more like a matter of form than of feeling.

I got all the information I needed as soon as I approached the loaded staircase. A dozen resigned voices told me the facts. These were all brides of South African soldiers. They were all waiting for some place to live in. They had all arrived on recent ships. Mrs Coetzee was a disgusting war profiteer. For horrible food and conditions she charged the same as that charged by respectable boarding-houses on the beach.

If one could get into them. And if they would take children without making a fuss – which Mrs Coetzee did. But the fact that she was easy about the children did not outweigh her hatred of the English, about which she made no secret.

I rang up the shipping offices who said there was no sign of the ship, which was well known for taking its time at ports around the coast. It might be next week or the week after, but of course they would let me know. I was sitting on one of the beds, waving the flies off my cheerfully sleeping child, when a crisp white envelope slid under the door. It said: 'I and my husband would be very happy if you would care to join us for a drink after dinner. Yours sincerely, Myra Brooke-Benson. (Room 7.)' Room 7 was opposite mine, and I could hear English voices, male and female, from behind the closed door. A high voice, clearly at the end of its tether: 'But, my dear, I really do think that this DDT must have lost its strength.' And a low voice, firm and in command. 'Nonsense, my dear. I bought it this morning.'

Towards five in the evening I went again in search of the landlady. Mrs Coetzee was now awake, seated at the kitchen table, slicing pale yellowish slices off an enormous golden pumpkin. Her arms stuck out at her sides like wings, supported on wads of shaking fat. Great drops of sweat scattered off her in all directions. Jemima stood beside her, rapidly squeezing pale pink ground meat into flat cakes between her palms. I coughed. Mrs Coetzee nodded. She returned to her work. She had no English.

The supper was served in a room into which refinement had been injected in the shape of a dozen small tables that were covered with red tissue paper, and set with a knife, fork and spoon at each place. A coloured paper lantern was tied with string to the naked light bulb. We ate roast pumpkin, fried meat cakes, and fried potato hash. Afterwards, there were fried pumpkin fritters. Everyone was eating avidly from starvation. The portions were no larger than necessary to maintain life. I immediately pinpointed my hosts for after dinner. They were a small, fair pretty woman, looking incredibly clean and neat; and a bald fierce-looking man with a well-brushed moustache. I smiled at them, but as they stiffened and merely nodded back, I imagined I must be mistaken. When I presented myself at the door of No. 7, however, they were smiling and full of welcome. They had been here for three weeks, and were waiting for a flat to fall vacant in Ndola, where he was to work on the copper mines. 'I will not, I simply will not stay here, Timothy,' she kept saying, with crisp plaintiveness. And he kept saying, with bluff reassurance: 'But, my dear, of course we are going to stay here.' We drank brandy, and made small-talk. We offered each other many commiserations. We said goodnight, smiling. As far as I was concerned the evening had passed without any of that vital communication essential to real human relationships. I imagined it had been a failure.

Next morning, when I woke, the double bed opposite had two elderly women in it. They were asleep. I shushed my son and we waited. They woke, good-natured, smiling and unembarrassed when Jemima came in, without knocking, and slopped down four cups of tea on the floor just inside the door. They smiled and nodded. I smiled and nodded. Conversing in smiles and nods, we all dressed, and they departed in an ancient dust-covered car in the direction away from Cape Town.

I went into the kitchen. Mrs Coetzee was slicing pumpkin. Jemima was slicing beef into pale strips. I said: 'Mrs Coetzee, I would like to ask what those two strange women were doing in my room last night.' Jemima spoke to Mrs Coetzee. Mrs Coetzee spoke to Jemima. Jemima said: 'Says they are cousins from Constantia.' 'But why in my room?' 'Says boarding-house is full.' 'Yes, but it was my room.' 'Says you can go.'

I retired. Myra Brooke-Benson was just going into No. 7. She gave me a pretty but measured smile, appropriate to our having bumped into each other, with apologies, on the pavement a week ago. Nevertheless, I told her what had happened. 'My dear, anything is possible here,' she said. 'As for me, I simply will not have it. I have been trying to get her to give me a carafe for drinking water for a week, and if I don't get it, I shall report her to the city authorities.'

I gave the question of my correct relations with the Brooke-Bensons some thought, and at last hit upon the right mode, or method. I found a piece of writing paper, and a clean envelope, and wrote: 'Dear Mrs Brooke-Benson. I would be so happy if you and your husband would join me tonight after dinner for a drink. Yours sincerely.' This I pushed under her door. I was sitting on my bed waiting for her reply, in another envelope, to insinuate itself under my door, when she knocked, and said: 'Timothy and I would be delighted to accept your kind invitation for this evening. It is so very kind of you.'

Meanwhile, it was observable from my windows that a great deal of human energy was being misapplied. The deeply lush garden was teeming with small children, and about two dozen young mothers were perched on the outside stairs, on the front steps, or on the grass, each anxiously watching her own offspring. I knew that they were all waiting for that blessed moment when these children would be sleepy, so they could put them to bed and rush off down into the city in order to interview housing agents and employment agents. For my part, I wanted to look up friends. I therefore approached a woman sitting rather apart from the rest, a small, plump, dark, fiery-cheeked person, who was guarding a small girl, and said it would be a good idea if we all took turns to look after the children, thus freeing the others. 'You've just come,' she said. 'Yesterday,' I said. 'This is not a place I would leave my child alone in,' she said. 'But surely, they wouldn't be alone,' I said. She said: 'Some of these girls here I wouldn't trust a dog with, let alone a child.' I went to my room and considered this. It was only afterwards I realized she was middle-class and most of the other women were not. Believing that Myra Brooke-Benson's knock on my door entitled me to the same intimacy, I knocked on hers. She opened it with annoyance. 'Actually,' she said, 'I was trying to get the baby to sleep.' I apologized and withdrew.

After dinner, at what was the right time, I put my plan to her. She thought it was admirable. 'The trouble is, there's only one other woman here I'd trust with my poor little boy. She has a delightful little girl. Some of these women here are quite appallingly careless with their children.' I realized she meant Mrs Barnes, the red-cheeked woman in the garden. I still did not know what was the matter with the others, but suggested that in that case we three might take turns with the children. 'I should be quite delighted to keep an eye on your charming little boy,' she said, 'but I'm afraid that mine doesn't take easily to strangers.'

We spent the evening discussing the carafe. It turned out that Mrs Coetzee didn't have a carafe. Through Jemima, Mr Brooke-Benson had insisted she should buy one. Mrs Coetzee had said, through Jemima, that if Mr Brooke-Benson wanted a carafe so badly he could buy one for himself.

We all went to bed early. The boarding-house resounded until late every night with people coming in, going out, shouting goodbye and singing. Noises in the passage sounded as if they were in my room. I did hear furtive sounds in the night, but imagined they were made by some lucky reveller creeping in so as not to disturb the rest of us. As if this were likely. When I woke in the morning there was a young man asleep in the double bed opposite. My son was watching him with much interest. I got up, shook him, and demanded what he was doing in my room. He started awake, let out a furious exclamation in Afrikaans, shook his fist, exclaimed some more, and strode out to the bathroom. Luckily, the taxi-driver dropped in to see his aunt after breakfast, so I stopped him and explained what was happening. He sat on the edge of my unmade bed, picked up my son, set him on his knee and said: 'You have the best room in the house. It is too big for you and the child.' 'But I'd be quite happy to have a smaller one.' 'But there is no smaller one.' 'Well, that isn't my fault.' 'But my Aunt Marie has a kind heart and is not happy to turn away a man who has no place to sleep.' 'But you must see I can't go to bed every night not knowing who I'm going to find when I wake in the morning. Besides, it's not good for my son.' 'Ach, he is a very fine child, your son.' 'You must talk to your aunt.' 'Ya, man, but this terrible war we have had, the English started it, and now we are all suffering.' 'But please talk to your aunt.' 'Ach, Gott, she has had a hard life. Her husband – you've seen him by this time – he is no good for any woman.' I had seen a furtive little man around the back of the premises but not connected him with Mrs Coetzee. 'Ya, ya, God is unkind to many women sometimes. He could not even give her a child. Now your husband gave you a child. You should thank God for it.' 'Please will you speak to your aunt.' 'A poor woman, without a man to help her and without children. She is a brave woman and she works hard.' By this time my son was clambering all over him, and Mr Coetzee was chuckling and smiling with plesure. 'I will tell her what you said. But it is a hard world for a woman without a man. If you are uncomfortable, I have a cousin who keeps a boarding-house in Oranjezicht.' 'No, no, I'm very happy here, if you could just explain to your aunt.' 'This is a very good child you have here, and when he grows up he will be a good strong man.' With which we went into the passage, my son on his shoulder. There stood Mr Brooke-Benson, scarlet with anger, scarlet even over his bald pate. 'That bloody woman,' he said, 'She will not give me a carafe.' 'And what is this?' enquired Mr Coetzee. I explained. He nodded. 'Ach. Ya. I will speak to her.' That afternoon he came in with a carafe which he presented to the Brooke-Bensons. They were furious, and kept saying it was a question of principle. He suggested, with courtesy, that to buy a carafe was a small thing to do for a woman who had no man to look after her, and it was a pleasure for him to do things for his auntie. He gave me a great bag of peaches, and my son a pound of sweets. Then he took my son for a drive in his taxi to visit his cousin Stella.

That night, the envelope slipped under my door contained an invitation to morning tea next day. Myra Brooke-Benson was equipped with every kind of instinct for domesticity. She had a spirit lamp, a silver teapot, and some fine china teacups. Her room, every bit as unpromising as mine, had flowers, clean linen, even cushions. She said there was a most unfortunate misunderstanding which she felt bad about even having to mention. It appeared that Mrs Barnes said she was going to complain to Mrs Coetzee that I had been observed to have a man, not my husband, in my bedroom. She, Myra Brooke-Benson, had explained the situation to Mrs Barnes, but Mrs Barnes had said that if a strange man entered her room in the night she wouldn't have been able to sleep at all. Her sixth sense would have warned her. But the point was, any plan for guarding each other's children was now out of the question.

I now resigned myself. The days, and then the weeks passed. I wrote notes of invitation for after-dinner drinks and morning tea with the Brooke-Bensons, and they wrote them to me. We ate pumpkin and fried meat for every meal. Mr Coetzee came to see me and my son often, and we talked about his children and his grandchildren. I rang up the shipping agents daily. Only once was my room invaded again, and that was when a man and a wife and five children arrived, apologetically, at three one morning, explaining they were maternal relatives of Mrs Coetzee. Mrs Barnes coloured and stiffened whenever she saw me. She spoke only to the Brooke-Bensons. My son had a nice time playing in the garden. I found one of the English girls who was prepared to let her children out of her sight occasionally, and we took turns to relieve each other. The English girls continued to sit on the stairs and to talk, with bitter homesickness, about England. I was bored to death, but consoled myself by dreaming about England which I knew by now would not actually begin until the moment I set foot on its golden soil.

Suddenly I got a letter from an old friend, an Afrikaans painter, who had been out of Cape Town on a painting trip. While I was reading the letter he arrived in my room with flowers, fruit and an enormous fish, which he had just caught.

'Ya,' he said, looking at me severely, 'you must get the management to cook it for you. I can tell you, you need feeding up. I can see it. The English can't cook. They can't eat. You look very bad.'

'The management,' I said, 'is Afrikaans.'

'Wait,' he said. 'I will go and make enquiries.' I heard him stride over the bare boards of the passage. A silence. He came back, still swinging the fish by a loop of string through his forefinger. 'I can't give her this fish,' he said. 'She would not cook it as it should be cooked. And what are you doing here? This place is going to be pulled down, and instead we shall have a fine modern hotel with all conveniences for the tourists.' He laid the fish on the floor. The room was pervaded with a loud smell of salt, sea and fish. It was an extremely hot afternoon.

'Piet, I wish you'd take that fish away. People are very sensitive in this place. You'd be surprised.'

He nodded, with solemnity. 'I thought so,' he said. 'It's that English colony you've been living in. It makes people suspicious and conventional. In a minute you will be telling me not to speak so loudly.'

Piet did not look himself at all. Or rather, he was wearing his smug look, which went with his public personality. He was a tall man, rangy, with a high bounding stride. He had a long, pale portentous face. He wore his hair rather long. He also wore, for the benefit of his trade, flapping and colourful clothes. He had the ability to appear, by slightly tightening the muscles of his face, like a pale and enduring Christ. This is not at all what his character was. In fact I have never known a man who enjoyed himself more wholeheartedly than he did. He had a smile that spread, wicked and sly, from cheekbone to cheekbone, and eyes that crinkled amusement. Not, however, at the moment.

'You have come at a bad time,' he said. 'I'm not happy. I have realized that in three months I shall be forty. I have only ten years to live. I have always known that I shall die at fifty. It is a terrible thing to understand suddenly – death is approaching in great silent strides.' He smiled, slightly, sideways, his eyes narrowed, as it were listening to the footsteps of death. 'Ya,' he said. 'Ya. Ten years. So much to do, so little done.' With a great effort he prevented himself from laughing, and sighed deeply instead.

Piet is not the only man I've known who has sentenced himself to death in advance. I know a doctor, for instance, a man of the highest intelligence moreover, who decided when he was thirty-six that he had ten years to live, and planned his life accordingly. It seems the Medical Association, or some such body had announced that the average age for doctors to die was at forty-six, and from coronary thrombosis. Meeting this man after an interval, I pointed out that he now had only five years to live, and I trusted he was making good use of his time. But the BMA had meanwhile raised the statistical life of a doctor by ten years, and so things were not so urgent after all.

'But there will be a silver lining to my personal tragedy,' said Piet. 'When my death is announced in the Press, for the first time in her history South Africa will be united.'

'How is that?'

'Surely you can imagine for yourself? Ya, think of it. Think of that morning. It will be very hot. The pigeons will be cooing in the trees. Then the news will come. The pigeons will stop cooing. In every town, in every village, in every little dorp, there will be a silence like the end of the world. Then there will rise into the still air a single cry of agony. Then from every house will come wailing and weeping. From every house will rush weeping women, old women, young women, wives, mothers, the Mayor's daughter and the wife of the linesman. They will look at each other. By their tears they will know each other as sisters. They will run into each other's arms. English and Afrikaans, Jewish and Greek, they will weep and cry: Piet is dead. Our Piet is dead.'

'And the men?'

'Ya, the men. Well, they will be united by the inconsolable grief of the women.' He sighed again. 'I have been thinking of that day all the way back in my car. I have had a terrible trip this time, because of my new understanding of my approaching death. But I have made a lot of money this time. I have been painting pondokkies all over the Free State. Thank God, now I can pay my debts.'

Piet was a man of talent. He had even painted in Paris and London. But he had been unable to make a living in the Cape. Therefore, whenever short of money, he drove off into the interior, his clothing subdued and his expression mournful. He introduced himself to the Mayor or some bigwig in each city, as a sound son of the Afrikaans nation, and explained that it was a terrible thing that this great people should be so uncultured as not to support its talented child. He painted them, their houses, their children, and their wives. He also painted points of local interest, which, as he explained, always turned out to consist of pondokkies. In other words, African huts, slums, broken-down villages, shabby sheds and picturesque houses.

'And why do you come on holiday to Cape Town when I am not even here? My poor child, with no one to look after you. But as it happens now I must rush off, because I must take this beautiful fish home to my wife. I shall cook it myself. No woman can cook as well as I do. I caught it in a pool where I caught its brother last year. That is probably the most beautiful pool in the whole world. I'll take you there tomorrow.'

'I can't. My son isn't the right age for fishing.'

'A child? Of course, I forgot. Where is he.'

I pointed out of the window.

'A fine child.' He almost groaned. 'Ya, ya, and when I am dead he will be a fine young man, enjoying life, and I will be forgotten.'

'No, not that one, that one.'

'They are all fine children. And all of them, they will be fishing and – painting pondokkies when I am dead. But now you have this child you will be very dull and full of responsibility. Why is it, all women have children. Sometimes I think you do it to spite me.'

'All the same. And besides, my morale is very low due to living in this Afrikaans boarding-house. I am weak from malnutrition and haven't the heart for fishing.'

'And why do you put me and my nation at a disadvantage by taking a holiday in such a place?'

'I am not on holiday. I am waiting for my boat to England.'

He groaned. 'England. So that's it. Ya, that's it. Well, you'll be sorry, I am telling you. And what will you do, in a country full of those Englishmen? They are no good for women. I know this. When I arrived in London all those poor women, they rushed out with their arms extended saying: "Piet, Piet, is that you? Thank God you've come at last."'

'We shall see,' I said.

'Ya, it is a terrible thing.'

'It's a fact that men of all nations are convinced that men of any other nation are no good for women. I'm sure a statistically significant number of women would be able to vouch for this.'

'And listen to how you talk. You are bitter already. When I hear a woman use words like statistics, I know she is bitter. It is that English colony. It has very likely marked you for life. Ya. I shall come tomorrow and cheer you up. Now I shall take my fish. I have a very sensitive sense of smell, and I can tell it is time.'

With which he left, jerking the fish after him along the floor and saying: 'Come, come, little fish, come with me, come and leap into the great black pot where you will die another death for me.' Over his shoulder he said: 'And I shall bring you a real picture I have painted, to show you that all these pondokkies have not ruined my talent.'

Mrs Barnes knocked. 'Excuse me,' she said. 'I am afraid I really must ask you not to have fish in your room. This place is bad enough without fish as well.'

'It was caught this morning,' I said.

'The whole building smells.'

'I didn't invite the fish.'

'Is your friend a fisherman?' Her soft English cheeks were a clear red, and her full brown eyes, that had no whites to them, were glazed with suspicious fascination.

'He is a painter,' I said. 'He has won prizes in Paris, not to mention London.'

'How interesting,' she said.

Next day Piet arrived in a severe black suit. He looked like a predicant. His face was a solemn yard long. He carried a very large picture of a nude girl. He lifted it past the miserable English girls on the steps with an air of critical detachment. He put down the nude, and said: 'There, you see I can still paint. And what is more, this afternoon I have been furthering the cause of art in this continent. I am now, you must know, a leading representative of the Council for Art. I am very respectable. There is an exhibition on. It is by a homosexual poor boy. He wrote to me and asked for my encouragement and patronage. His pictures are all of male nudes and in very great detail. The arts teacher at the school here for nice English girls wrote to me and asked for my help and encouragement. So this afternoon I met this teacher, poor woman, at the door, wearing my beautiful black suit and an expression of cultural integrity. I lowered my voice to an official note. And I entered the hall followed by the teacher and a hundred and fifty pretty girls, all in search of artistic experience. And I escorted them around for an hour, all around those pictures of one subject only, pointing out the technique and the line and the quality of the paint. With severity. He is a bad painter. And not once did I smile. Not once did that poor English teacher smile. Not once did all those little girls smile. We were in the presence of art.' He flung himself across my bed and laughed. The whole building shook.

'For the Lord's sake,' I said, 'don't shout.'

'There, what did I tell you? Already you are asking me to lower my voice. The English will finish you, man. Ya.'

'All the same, I wish you could hurry on that boat. I've been here six weeks, and I'm very unhappy. Apart from anything else, there's an English couple across the passage and we have morning tea together all the time. And as soon as I say anything at all, about anything, they look very nervous and change the subject. It's a bad augury for my life in England.'

'Poor little one. Poor child. There, what did I tell you?' He roared with delight. I heard a door open on to the passage.

'*Piet*. And there's a woman called Mrs Barnes. She's very bad-tempered.'

'Poor woman,' he said. He took two large soundless strides to the door, opened it with a jerk, and there was Mrs Barnes in the passage. She frowned. He smiled. Slowly, unwillingly, and hating every second of it, she smiled. Then, furious, she went dark plum colour, glared at us both, and went into her room, slamming the door hard.

'It is a terrible thing,' said Piet sentimentally. 'A bad-tempered woman. It is all the fault of her husband. I suppose he's English.'

'Scotch.'

'It is all the same thing. That reminds me . . .' He told a story. By the time he had ended I was laughing too hard to ask him to lower his voice. He was rolling in an agony of laughter back and forth over the floor. The whole boarding-house was hushed.

'That reminds me,' said Piet again. He talked, listening with delight to the silence of his invisible audience. Then he told his story about his visit to a brothel in Marseilles. Unfortunately it is too indecent to write down. It was not too indecent for him to shout at the top of his voice. The end of the story was: 'Imagine me, in her room, in such a predicament, and the boat was leaving. It was giving out long, sad hoots of pain, to warn us all there was no time to waste. And there I was. My friends came in. They bandaged me. And I walked down to the ship through the streets of Marseilles, cheered on by the onlookers, with a bloodstained bandage a foot and a half long sticking out in front of me. I climbed up the gangway, supported on either side by my loyal friends, watched by the captain, a very fine fellow, and at least five thousand women. That was the proudest day of my life. That afternoon they gave me the gold medal for my artistic talent was nothing compared to it.'

Mrs Barnes came in. 'I am afraid I have to tell you that I have had no alternative but to complain to the management.' She went out.

'Poor woman,' said Piet. 'It is a very sad thing, a woman like that. Don't worry. I shall now go to Mrs Coetzee and tell her I'll paint a picture for her.'

Half an hour later I went to the kitchen. Mrs Coetzee was wheezing out helpless, wet laughter. Jemima, her face quite straight, her eyes solemn, had her hand cupped over her mouth, to catch any laughter that might well up and press it back again. Her narrow little body shook spasmodically. 'I told you,' said Piet. 'It is all right. I have explained to her that she must have a picture of this fine boarding-house. I shall paint it for her, at medium cost. I shall also make a copy and donate it to the city's archives, for the memory of a building such as this must not be lost to mankind. I feel it will be the finest pondokkie I have ever painted. Poor woman, she is very bitter. The war makes her unhappy.'

'She's doing very nicely out of it.'

'No, the Boer War. Those concentration camps you had. Ya, ya, the English were never anything but savages. Now, please, think no more about it. I have made everything right for you.'

He went. Almost at once Mrs Coetzee came in, with Jemima. It was a visit of goodwill. She was smiling. Then she noticed the picture, which unfortunately Piet had forgotten. Her face sagged into folds of disapproval.

She spoke to Jemima. Jemima said: 'Says will not picture her house.' 'Tell her it's not my picture.' 'Says take it away.' 'I'll tell my friend to take it tomorrow.' 'Says your picture, not his picture.' 'But it is his.' 'Says he is Afrikaans. A good boy.' 'It is a picture of his wife. She is a very good Afrikaans girl.' 'Says good boy does not make bad picture like that.' Jemima's face was expressionless, but her body shook. I tried to catch her eye. It was blank. Only her body was amused. 'Says you bad woman, says you go,' said Jemima.

That evening, the shipping agents rang to say the boat would be in tomorrow. As a favour, Mrs Coetzee allowed me to stay for the one night. Mrs Barnes came in to say she was sorry there had been this unpleasantness. *If she had known* she would not have complained to Mrs Coetzee. I have never been able to understand this. But my chief problem was to find the right way to say goodbye to the Brooke-Bensons. At last, my suppressed instinct for communication blossomed into a large bunch of flowers. I presented these, not so much to the Brooke-Bensons, as to a failed relationship. I shook hands. I noticed Myra's eyes were wet. She said, with formality: 'I will be so sorry when you've gone. I feel I have made a real friend in you.' Her husband said: 'And please keep in touch. Now that we've got to know each other.' I shook hands again and we said goodbye.

The boat was full of English. That is, South African British, going home. I had no time to meet them. My son was so excited by the experience of being on the boat that he woke at five every morning and did not sleep until eleven at night. In between, he rushed, hurled himself, bounded and leaped all over the boat. I arrived in England exhausted. The white cliffs of Dover depressed me. They were too small. The Isle of Dogs discouraged me. The Thames looked dirty. I had better confess at once that for the whole of the first year, London seemed to me a city of such appalling ugliness that I wanted only to leave it. Besides, I had no money, I could have got some by writing to my family, of course, but it had to be the bootstraps or nothing.

The first place I stayed in was a flat off the Bayswater Road. I passed the house the other day, and it now seems quite unremarkable. This is how it struck me at the time:

'A curving terrace. Decaying, unpainted, enormous, ponderous, graceless. When I stand and look up, the sheer weight of the building oppresses me. The door looks as if it could never be opened. The hall is painted a dead uniform cream, that looks damp. It has a carved chest in it that smells of mould. Everything smells damp. The stairs are wide, deep, oppressive. The carpets are thick and shabby. Walking on them is frightening – no sound at all. All the way up the centre of this immense, heavy house, the stairs climb, silent and ugly, flight after flight, and all the walls are the same dead, dark cream colour. At last another hostile and heavy door. I am in a highly varnished little hall, with wet mackintoshes and umbrellas. Another dark door. Inside, a great heavy room, full of damp shadow. The furniture is all heavy and dead, and the surfaces are damp. The flat has six rooms, all painted this heavy darkening cream, all large, with high ceilings, no sound anywhere, the walls are so thick. I feel suffocated. Out of the back windows, a vista of wet dark roofs and dingy chimneys. The sky is pale and cold and unfriendly.'

My arrangements for living here had been made with great intelligence by a friend. The idea was, I should share this flat with another woman, an Australian, who had a small child. We should share the rent and expenses, and the children would share each other.

They took to each other at sight and went off to play.

The Australian lady and I had now to make acquaintance.

She was a woman of inveterate sensibility. Her name was Brenda. She was sitting in a huddled mass in a deep chair by an empty grate. She was a large woman, of firm swarthy flesh. She had a large sallow face, and black hair cut doll-like across her forehead. She wore artistic clothes. She had been crying, and was still damp. Almost the first thing she said was, 'I do hope your child is sensitive. My Daphne is very sensitive. A highly-strung child.' I knew then that the whole thing was doomed.

Daphne was three, a strapping, lively-eyed child with a healthy aggressiveness. Peter was two and a half. They were well-matched. They began to fight, with much enjoyment. Brenda went next door, pulled Daphne to her, and said in a weak voice: 'Oh, darling, he's such a nice little boy, don't hit him.' She set Daphne in a chair with a picture book.

Then she said everything was too much for her, and so I went out and bought the rations and had some keys cut. While I did this, I reflected on the value of helplessness. During the next weeks I reflected about this often. Brenda was renting the flat for seven guineas a week. I don't know how she managed it. I've never since seen a flat of such size, class, and solid furnishing going at such a low rent. She had already let two rooms in it, at three and a half guineas each. That left four rooms. The largest room was her sitting-room, because she had to have privacy. The children had a room each, because Daphne could not sleep unless she was by herself. The largest room upstairs was Brenda's bedroom. That left one for me. She had put the dining-room table in it, where we would all eat, as she said this would be more convenient for all of us. She intended to charge me seven guineas a week. I did all the shopping and the washing-up and the tidying, because life was too much for her, particularly in England. Also I had to keep my son away from Daphne, because they would play together, and in the most insensitive manner.

I have often wondered about that remarkable phenomenon – that for sheer innate delicacy and appreciation of the finer sides of life, one has to seek for a certain type of Colonial.

Piet for instance. Robust is the word I would use to describe him. Yet his tastes in art, save when he was painting pondokkies were all exquisite. Corot he liked. Turner he liked. A passage of nature description in Chekhov would make him screw back the tears from his eyes. A couple of the more oblique sentences in Katherine Mansfield would send him into a melancholy ecstasy. But Balzac was coarse, and Rubens had no poetry. A letter from Piet would end something like this: . . . the exquisite veil of translucent twilight drawn gently down to the horizon, and I sit, pen in hand, and dream. The fire crepitates in the grate, and the shadows deepen on the wall. Ach, my God, and life is passing. Your old friend, Piet. PS – We went to the Bay this afternoon and swam and bought three crayfish for sixpence each. I boiled them till they squeaked and we ate them in our fingers with melted butter. My God, man, they were good. I bet you don't get crayfish in that godforsaken colony full of English. Christ but you're crazy, I'm telling you.

For real perception into the side-channels of British culture, one has to go to a university in Australia or South Africa. The definitive thesis on Virginia Woolf will come, not from Cambridge, but from Cape Town. Brenda was writing a thesis on: Proust – a nature poet manqué.

In short, we were temperamentally unsuited. I began looking for somewhere to live. Besides, I still had not met the English.

Piece Written for the Asia Society
July/August issue of *Asia*, 1982

People ask, 'When did you become interested in Sufism?' I give an exact reply, but feel the question is really a statement, 'I am surprised that you are the kind of person to become interested in mysticism.' This is because I am known to have been political. Yet from utopian politics to religion or mysticism is a short step: it is the same emotional 'set'. Not surprisingly it is now a sociological cliché that the psychological bases for socialism were laid down in the West (and in westernised people) during the two thousand years of Christianity. The earthly paradise of Communism is merely Paradise transposed. I was once an idealistic and utopian communist, and no, I am not proud of it. The real politicos are a very different kind of animal; now I am angry with myself for not having noticed that very evident fact. I had an inclination towards mysticism (not religion) even when being political. It is a not uncommon combination. People also are seldom all of a piece, even the bigots and fanatics, who are because of what they suppress. Their buried selves may surface in madness, in 'breakdowns'. This subject has always fascinated me. I've written about it in *The Golden Notebook*, in *Briefing for a Descent Into Hell*, and elsewhere.

I began this article with politics because so many people are political now, and for the same reasons I was: 'Society is intolerable, we must change it. To be political is to be on the side of the angels, it is the correct choice. If you are not political, you are a reactionary.' (If you are not God's child, you are the Devil's.) Everyone is preoccupied with politics and with sex; these are the imperatives of our time. A century ago it was religion – Christianity struggling to retain the total allegiance of flocks straying in all directions because of minds made freer by the opening up of the world, by science, by information. Religion and nationalism. Two hundred years ago? Three hundred? Every epoch has different preoccupations, judged by posterity as symptoms.

It was as a direct result of writing *The Golden Notebook* that I started an active study of mysticism. I was at a stage in my life when everything had to change: into my forties, and behind me battles about sex, about politics, fight, fight, all the way. I shaped that book to say (because it was what I had learned) that if one divided oneself up, lived with a compartmented mind, it was to invite disaster, which could be cured, sometimes, only by breakdown. I was surrounded by people in breakdown because of sex, because of politics. The book was taken as a trumpet for Women's Liberation. All right; fair enough; it was written by a woman. But the status of women was not, then, my priority. Because, while I wrote that book, I was thinking about my life so hard, and in a new way, all kinds of ideas not known to me before came flooding in. When I had finished it I knew I had either to pretend I had not had new ideas, intimations, experiences (and I am sure that a great many people, reaching this place in their lives, do close a door, do say, *No, this never happened*, because they can't face being called wrong-headed, eccentric, silly) or accept that I could no longer be the same person. To be precise: I could no longer accept the contemporary 'package'. This consists of materialism, socialism or an association with one of the many churches of Marxism; atheism, belief in material progress and that the betterment of society can come only through political action. Now I see this package as pitifully meagre and empty, but it was hard to jettison, because it is the current orthodoxy (which for some reason is able to see itself as fresh, original and brave) and because I did not know how to look elsewhere. I read and I read: the various kinds of Buddhism, the yogas, Christian mysticism, Hinduism, Islam. The libraries have it all, but you must find your own way, because current education excludes nearly everything that isn't part of the package. (One of the results of this vacuum in our education is that a highly-educated young person can be vulnerable to an encounter with a bogus cult. Even scientists are not immune.) I emerged with two main ideas. One, that all religions and types of mysticism say the same thing in different words: that it is possible for anyone to transcend the little cage which is how some people experience ordinary life, in an effort to come nearer to God, or Allah, or the Almighty, or The Other – that Power greater than ourselves Who is not to be made the property of any religion, or sect, or arrangement of words. Two, that in this area one should have a Guide, otherwise the journey can be dangerous.

At once I came up against a formidable barrier: in myself, in society. Everywhere in the world but those societies we call The West, or those that are western (probably temporarily) because they are communist, the idea of Exemplar or Teacher is a foundation of culture. Had I been in, let's say, India or Japan, to choose a teacher would have been what ordinary people did. But the West long ago outlawed this idea, making the Churches the sole road to God. I am of that (rapidly-increasing) number of people who see early Christianity as a history of power-lovers getting rid of any people or evidence that didn't suit their purposes: over 300 contemporary accounts of Jesus were destroyed by them. Jesus became God: unlike Islam, which does not claim divinity for Mahomed, but said he was the last in a long line of public Teachers, among them Jesus.

In the West, to accept a Teacher is to know you will be described as weakminded, easily influenced, in need of a father figure. It is hard on one's pride. And I had had more than enough of power-lovers, mostly male, in politics; as far as I was concerned, they were indistinguishable from priests. I disliked everything I heard or read about 'gurus'. I did not then know that Sufis regard the 'guru phenomenon' as a degeneration, and the people who pursue them as unfortunates. In the course of my search, I explored a number of sects and cults. Now I see this as a useful experience; then I was distressed and confused. So many obviously self-deluded or cynical 'teachers'. So many people joining this or that because, clearly, they needed a family or a tribe. So much weirdness, dottiness. Above all, these cults were all at a sharp angle to ordinary life, were cultural sidewaters.

I heard about Idries Shah during my enquiries, was told he was writing a book. What was said about him sounded sensible, not bizarre. I felt this book might turn out to be what I was looking for. It was *The Sufis*. I read it feeling it was for me; also, amazed at the robustness of its claims. I had had no idea how much Sufis had influenced the world, had helped to shape Western culture. How could I, when even an 'expert' like Bertrand Russell could write a History of Western Philosophy and never mention facts which were easily available for him to know, and part of credited and respectable scholarship? But my interest was not then, is not now, primarily academic. I mention this aspect of *The Sufis* because I feel it will turn out to have been one of the most remarkable books published in our time, with the potential for revolutionising several fields of study. I have friends who are historians, specialists in eastern studies, anthropologists, sociologists, who claim their ideas have been widened by this book, and others by Idries Shah.

That was twenty years ago. The stages of work under a Master are described in a thousand records, so I can say that nothing has been surprising. But can say, too, that every new stage is surprising, because the old phrases, terms, concepts, come to life in contexts where you don't expect them. An example. Having read *The Sufis*, several times and thought hard, I wrote to Idries Shah asking him to take me on as a pupil. I heard nothing for a long time: in my then state of mind it seemed for ever. But I reflected on all the old books I had read, and remembered that Teachers 'tested' potential pupils. An intriguing idea! When at last I did hear, it was the driest note, calculated to put off the most enthusiastic. And, indeed, I know people who, receiving this cold response, lost interest there and then, or were offended. What they had expected was to be treated as an important acquisition. It was months before I heard again. At last I saw that I was being taught, in the indirect way that is traditional, that I was approaching the subject in the wrong way; hot enthusiasm was not needed, but something cooler, quieter, more observant. When I actually did meet Shah, after all that impatience, I missed every opportunity I was given to ask real questions: thus making me think about the relationship between impatience, greed, heedlessness.

What strikes me now, when I read about other people's journeys into the mystical, is how vague and elevating it all is. Everything with Shah is on the contrary cool, exact, specific. If anything can be called exciting, it is the subtlety of the psychological understanding of people, groups, social developments, which is the Sufi age-old endowment, so much more advanced than anything we know in the West. But while this may be fascinating, as an intellectual interest, to keep up with it is very hard work.

It is easy to illustrate the Sufi claim that it is not possible to explain things beyond a certain point to someone outside the Sufi context. A person may ask: 'But what do you *do*?' When I tell them, the outside facts, the response is likely to be: 'But is that all?' But this can happen with people who have attended Shah's teaching sessions, even for some time. One man, when I asked why he had slept through a session, said, 'But Shah wasn't doing anything.' Shah teaches in subtle, sometimes difficult to observe ways. It may take a long time to see that something else is going on, and then, to stay with it. This is because we are accustomed, in ordinary meetings, political or otherwise, to look for emotional arousal, excitement; because in our culture we are continually assaulted by strong stimuli.

Twenty years can be regarded as a long time. Not when you have become attuned to the Sufi way of thinking in millenniums. The human community is evolving, all of us, whether we know it or not. We, the creatures of *now*, are in the caterpillar stage, are, if you like, 'the missing link'. The claim is that Sufis are aligned with the evolutionary drive. Students are not given the promise: 'You are Chosen to be Saved,' but, 'If you can learn to align yourselves with us, you can contribute to the real progress of humanity.'

For many people it happens that everything which took them to the Sufis in the first place is soon shed: the demand for instant 'enlightenment'; an appetite for 'secrets' and for exciting occasions, described by Shah as Thrills, Spills and Chills; the insistence, 'I want it now'. All the responses, in fact, of our having and wanting society. Or the hopeful student leaves because none of these desires are fed anywhere near a real Sufi.

Another difficulty: if it was hard to accept that one needed a Teacher, it was hard to accept one's fellow pupils. I remember the surprise on every face on a certain evening at a certain preparatory class. What! *These* people one's spiritual fellow aspirants! The thing is, we arrange our lives to exclude abrasive people, particularly those who do not share our opinions. I for one did not know that this was what I had been doing until I found myself with people chosen by a different measure; was made to see how very intolerant in fact we all tend to be. We were invited to study contemporary psychology, the information relating to the structure of groups: people put together with others they haven't chosen will react automatically with suspicion and dislike. It is the group animal in us. We were told that Sufis did not start at a level lower than had been attained by the society they were working in, and that if we wished to equip ourselves for more sophisticated information, we could begin by familiarising ourselves with available research in the fields of psychology, anthropology, sociology – on the shelves of any bookshop. We could first become adequately equipped people in terms of our own culture.

It will be seen that not everyone in pursuit of 'higher knowledge' will find this enticing fare. Other people, myself among them, were relieved that the real achievements of our own cultures were recognised. Sufis say that every new introduction of the Sufi tradition is always framed in contemporary terms, using the conventions of the society as a 'vehicle'. I have found this to be so. People with an appetite for the archaic or the bizarre have to leave.

As Richard Burton, the English Sufi, said a hundred years ago in his marvellous poem, *The Kasidah*, what we have to learn first is 'how to unlearn'. Unlearn thirst for sensations, flattery, attention; unlearn national, racial, class biases. Shah's pupils are of all religions, nationalities, races, classes, every type of education and experience. There are as many women as men. We all have to have a solid base in our own cultures, living as ordinary people, learning how to be really useful to humanity, aspiring one day to 'be in the world but not of it'. The human being is given by Nature little more energy than what is needed to maintain the species; to reproduce and to live out our (very short) spans. But if we want to be fit for the journey up and out of the limits of ordinary life, we have to learn not to waste energy. Which we do by busying ourselves too much with material things, and by using our minds in wasteful and damaging ways. You will have seen that I am describing concepts familiar to us from the religions, put here in a different context, rescued from being 'sins' or sources of guilt, reintroduced, simply, as tools. It is not 'wicked' to eat and drink too much, not a 'sin' to be envious; but gluttony makes 'The Way' difficult; and thoughts of enmity keep the mind in a seethe, making subtler inputs impossible. And, besides, laws operate that we have not been taught about, whether we have had the benefits of religion or not. Thoughts of anger, jealousy, enmity, revenge, bring retribution. There is nothing theoretical about this: slowly you learn to see patterns where before you saw nothing, because you were being over-emotional. Sufis say the division between theory and practice which is the basis of our education is a recent (historically speaking) distortion. Learning, with them, is to experience. The 'school' uses the processes of life, when the pupil is ready to see what is happening. The pupil has to study *Learning How to Learn* – the title of one of Shah's books.

You have to be able to concede that the Teacher is someone who is able to direct all this; to concede that there are those who are better and cleverer than oneself. This certainly does not mean the Holy-holy-holy, this-man (or woman) is-an-avatar approach, which leads to emotional afflatus and dulling of the mind. It means a readiness to watch what the Teacher is doing, and to reflect on it. (It may take a long time to understand what that word *teacher* means: not always or necessarily something personal). As an example: it took me some time to see, that Shah was using with me the 'mirror' technique, which I knew about in theory, because it is clearly described. He was using it in all kinds of ways. In letters for instance, where my faults of thought and application were copied with such insight that it was hard not to lose the determination to learn in admiration.

One of the first things we were told was that we all rush after leaders and gurus, political and religious, because we have been taught to admire leaders, to want to be given orders, to join groups, to submit ourselves to authority, to say that knowledge is 'beyond' and that at best we can have it only when we are dead. We have learned negative and defeatist attitudes through 2,000 years of an authoritarian religion which has left scars on our minds: we have internalised its rigidities. We have not been taught that this is what we are like: on the contrary, are told we are free, democratic, self-determined, individualistic; and as a result we are infinitely vulnerable to being conditioned, to tyrants, to propaganda, to gurus and leaders – priests of all kinds. But if you want to learn the Sufi Way, then all this must be left behind. The aim is to become, after a preparatory process, a person able to manage his or her own development. And it is not easy.

Throughout the preparatory process, you are expected to study the written material Shah makes available, most of it in his published books. There is a great deal of it, of infinite variety, from scientific information to poetry and jokes and tales, some of it new-minted, some of it old, and all together it is arranged to make a whole, right for this time, forming a matrix in which new outlooks, new experiences, can develop. It takes time and trouble to familiarise oneself with this material, but it is an essential basis for learning with Idries Shah. There are pupils all over the world who are not in groups, who have not met Shah, but who value this material as a means of self-development.

Finally. People ask, 'How can you, a feminist, have anything to do with an Islam-based study?' First, the real Sufis will say that Sufism is not more Muslim than Christian, that it pre-dated Islam and Christianity because it has always been in the world under one name or another or none, and cannot be equated with the temporary phase of any culture, though it found a home within conventional Islam for a time. Secondly: it is not enough for us to be concerned with the situation of women; it is the situation of humankind which should be our concern.

PART IV

Preface to
The Golden Notebook

The shape of this novel is as follows:

There is a skeleton, or frame, called *Free Women*, which is a conventional short novel, about 60,000 words long, and which could stand by itself. But it is divided into five sections and separated by stages of the four Notebooks, Black, Red, Yellow and Blue. The Notebooks are kept by Anna Wulf, a central character of *Free Women*. She keeps four, and not one because, as she recognises, she has to separate things off from each other, out of fear of chaos, of formlessness – of breakdown. Pressures, inner and outer, end the Notebooks; a heavy black line is drawn across the page of one after another. But now that they are finished, from their fragments can come something new, *The Golden Notebook*.

Throughout the Notebooks people have discussed, theorised, dogmatised, labelled, compartmented – sometimes in voices so general and representative of the time that they are anonymous, you could put names to them like those in the old Morality Plays, Mr Dogma and Mr I-am-Free-Because-I-Belong-Nowhere, Miss I-Must-Have-Love-and-Happiness and Mrs I-Have-to-be-Good-At-Everything-I-do, Mr Where-is-a-Real-Woman? and Miss Where-is-a-Real-Man?, Mr I'm-Mad-Because-They-Say-I-Am, and Miss Life-Through-Experiencing-Everything, Mr I-Make-Revolution-and-Therefore-I-Am, and Mr and Mrs If-We-Deal-Very-Well-With-This-Small-Problem-Then-Perhaps-We-Can-Forget-We-Daren't-Look-at-The-Big-Ones. But they have also reflected each other, been aspects of each other, given birth to each other's thoughts and behaviour – *are* each other, form wholes. In the inner Golden Notebook, things have come together, the divisions have broken down, there is formlessness with the end of fragmentation – the triumph of the second theme, which is that of unity. Anna and Saul Green the American 'break down'. They are crazy, lunatic, mad – what you will. They 'break down' into each other, into other people, break through the false patterns they have made of their pasts, the patterns and formulas they have made to shore up themselves and each other, dissolve. They hear each other's thoughts, recognise each other in themselves. Saul Green, the man who has been envious and destructive of Anna, now supports her, advises her, gives her the theme for her next book, *Free Women* – an ironical title, which begins: 'The two women were alone in the London flat.' And Anna, who has been jealous of Saul to the point of insanity, possessive and demanding, gives Saul the pretty new notebook, *The Golden Notebook*, which she has previously refused to do, gives him the theme for his next book, writing in it the first sentence: 'On a dry hillside in Algeria a soldier watched the moonlight glinting on his rifle.' In the inner Golden Notebook, which is written by both of them, you can no longer distinguish between what is Saul and what is Anna, and between them and the other people in the book.

This theme of 'breakdown', that sometimes when people 'crack up' it is a way of self-healing, of the inner self's dismissing false dichotomies and divisions, has of course been written about by other people, as well as by me, since then. But this is where, apart from the odd short story, I first wrote about it. Here it is rougher, more close to experience, before experience has shaped itself into thought and pattern – more valuable perhaps because it is rawer material.

But nobody so much as noticed this central theme, because the book was instantly belittled, by friendly reviewers as well as by hostile ones, as being about the sex war, or was claimed by women as a useful weapon in the sex war.

I have been in a false position ever since, for the last thing I have wanted to do was to refuse to support women.

To get the subject of Women's Liberation over with – I support it, of course, because women are second-class citizens, as they are saying energetically and competently in many countries. It can be said that they are succeeding, if only to the extent they are being seriously listened to. All kinds of people previously hostile or indifferent say: 'I support their aims but I don't like their shrill voices and their nasty ill-mannered ways.' This is an inevitable and easily recognisable stage in every revolutionary movement: reformers must expect to be disowned by those who are only too happy to enjoy what has been won for them. I don't think that Women's Liberation will change much though – not because there is anything wrong with their aims, but because it is already clear that the whole world is being shaken into a new pattern by the cataclysms we are living through: probably by the time we are through, if we do get through at all, the aims of Women's Liberation will look very small and quaint.

But this novel was not a trumpet for Women's Liberation. It described many female emotions of aggression, hostility, resentment. It put them into print. Apparently what many women were thinking, feeling, experiencing, came as a great surprise. Instantly a lot of very ancient weapons were unleashed, the main ones, as usual, being on the theme of 'She is unfeminine', 'She is a man-hater'. This particular reflex seems indestructible. Men – and many women, said that the suffragettes were defeminised, masculine, brutalised. There is no record I have read of any society anywhere when women demanded more than nature offers them that does not also describe this reaction from men – and some women. A lot of women were angry about *The Golden Notebook*. What women will say to other women, grumbling in their kitchens, and complaining and gossiping or what they make clear in their masochism, is often the last thing they will say aloud – a man may overhear. Women are the cowards they are because they have been semi-slaves for so long. The number of women prepared to stand up for what they really think, feel, experience with a man they are in love with is still small. Most women will still run like little dogs with stones thrown at them when a man says: You are unfeminine, aggressive, you are unmanning me. It is my belief that any woman who marries, or takes seriously in any way at all, a man who uses this threat, deserves everything she gets. For such a man is a bully, does not know anything about the world he lives in, or about its history – men and women have taken infinite numbers of roles in the past, and do now, in different societies. So he is ignorant, or fearful about being out of step – a coward . . . I write all these remarks with exactly the same feeling as if I were writing a letter to post into the distant past: I am so sure that everything we now take for granted is going to be utterly swept away in the next decade.

(So why write novels? Indeed, why! I supose we have to go on living *as if* . . .)

Some books are not read in the right way because they have skipped a stage of opinion, assume a crystallisation of information in society which has not yet taken place. This book was written as if the attitudes that have been created by the Women's Liberation movements already existed. It came out first ten years ago, in 1962. If it were coming out now for the first time it might be read, and not merely reacted to: things have changed very fast. Certain hypocrisies have gone. For instance, ten, or even five, years ago – it has been a sexually contumacious time –

novels and plays were being plentifully written by men furiously critical
of women – particularly from the States but also in this country –
portrayed as bullies and betrayers, but particularly as underminers and
sappers. But these attitudes in male writers were taken for granted,
accepted as sound philosophical bases, as quite normal, certainly not as
woman-hating, aggressive or neurotic. It still goes on, of course – but
things are better, there is no doubt of it.

I was so immersed in writing this book, that I didn't think about how
it might be received. I was involved not merely because it was hard to
write – keeping the plan of it in my head I wrote it from start to end,
consecutively, and it was difficult – but because of what I was learning
as I wrote. Perhaps giving oneself a tight structure, making limitations
for oneself, squeezes out new substance where you least expect it. All
sorts of ideas and experiences I didn't recognise as mine emerged when
writing. The actual time of writing, then, and not only the experiences
that had gone into the writing, was really traumatic: it changed me.
Emerging from this crystallising process, handing the manuscript to
publisher and friends, I learned that I had written a tract about the sex
war, and fast discovered that nothing I said then could change that
diagnosis.

Yet the essence of the book, the organisation of it, everything in it,
says implicitly and explicitly, that we must not divide things off, must
not compartmentalise.

'Bound. Free. Good. Bad. Yes. No. Capitalism. Socialism. Sex.
Love . . .' says Anna, in *Free Women*, stating a theme – shouting it,
announcing a motif with drums and fanfares . . . or so I imagined. Just
as I believed that in a book called *The Golden Notebook* the inner section
called the Golden Notebook might be presumed to be a central point, to
carry the weight of the thing, to make a statement.

But no.

Other themes went into the making of this book, which was a crucial
time for me: thoughts and themes I had been holding in my mind for
years came together.

One was that it was not possible to find a novel which described the
intellectual and moral climate of a hundred years ago, in the middle of
the last century, in Britain, in the way Tolstoy did it for Russia,
Stendhal for France. (At this point it is necessary to make the obligatory
disclaimers.) To read *The Red and the Black*, and *Lucien Leuwen* is to
know that France as if one were living there, to read *Anna Karenina* is to

know that Russia. But a very useful Victorian novel never got itself written. Hardy tells us what it was like to be poor, to have an imagination larger than the possibilities of a very narrow time, to be a victim. George Eliot is good as far as she goes. But I think the penalty she paid for being a Victorian woman was that she had to be shown to be a good woman even when she wasn't according to the hypocrisies of the time – there is a great deal she does not understand because she is moral. Meredith, that astonishingly underrated writer, is perhaps nearest. Trollope tried the subject but lacked the scope. There isn't one novel that has the vigour and conflict of ideas in action that is in a good biography of William Morris.

Of course this attempt on my part assumed that that filter which is a woman's way of looking at life has the same validity as the filter which is a man's way . . . Setting that problem aside, or rather, not even considering it, I decided that to give the ideological 'feel' of our mid-century, it would have to be set among socialists and marxists, because it has been inside the various chapters of socialism that the great debates of our time have gone on; the movements, the wars, the revolutions, have been seen by their participants as movements of various kinds of socialism, or Marxism, in advance, containment, or retreat. (I think we should at least concede the possibility that people looking back on our time may see it not at all as we do – just as we, looking back on the English, the French, or even the Russian Revolutions see them differently from the people living then.) But 'Marxism' and its various offshoots has fermented ideas everywhere, and so fast and energetically that, once 'way out', it has already been absorbed, has become part of ordinary thinking. Ideas that were confined to the far left thirty or forty years ago had pervaded the left generally twenty years ago, and have provided the commonplaces of conventional social thought from right to left for the last ten years. Something so thoroughly absorbed is finished as a force – but it was dominant, and in a novel of the sort I was trying to do, had to be central.

Another thought that I had played with for a long time was that a main character should be some sort of an artist, but with a 'block'. This was because the theme of the artist has been dominant in art for some time – the painter, writer, musician, as exemplar. Every major writer has used it, and most minor ones. Those archetypes, the artist and his mirror-image the businessman, have straddled our culture, one shown as a boorish insensitive, the other as a creator, all excesses of sensibility and suffering and a towering egotism which has to be forgiven because of his products – in exactly the same way, of course, as the businessman has to be forgiven for the sake of his. We get used to what we have, and forget that artist-as-exemplar is a new theme. Heroes a hundred years ago weren't often artists. They were soldiers and empire builders and explorers and clergymen and politicians – too bad about women who had scarcely succeeded in becoming Florence Nightingale yet. Only oddballs and eccentrics wanted to be artists, and had to fight for it. But to use this theme of our time 'the artist', 'the writer', I decided it would have to be developed by giving the creature a block and discussing the reasons for the block. These would have to be linked with the disparity between the overwhelming problems of war, famine, poverty, and the tiny individual who was trying to mirror them. But what was intolerable, what really could not be borne any longer, was this monstrously isolated, monstrously narcissistic, pedestalled paragon. It seems that in their own way the young have seen this and changed it, creating a culture of their own in which hundreds and thousands of people make films, assist in making films, make newspapers of all sorts, make music, paint pictures, write books, take photographs. They have abolished that isolated, creative, sensitive figure – by copying him in hundreds of thousands. A trend has reached an extreme, its conclusion, and so there will be a reaction of some sort, as always happens.

The theme of 'the artist' had to relate to another, subjectivity. When I began writing there was pressure on writers not to be 'subjective'. This pressure began inside communist movements, as a development of the social literary criticism developed in Russia in the nineteenth century, by a group of remarkable talents, of whom Belinsky was the best known, using the arts and particularly literature in the battle against Czarism and oppression. It spread fast everywhere, finding an echo as late as the fifties, in this country, with the theme of 'commitment'. It is still potent in communist countries. 'Bothering about your stupid personal concerns when Rome is burning' is how it tends to get itself expressed, on the level of ordinary life – and was hard to withstand, coming from one's nearest and dearest, and from people doing everything one respected most: like, for instance, trying to fight colour prejudice in Southern Africa. Yet all the time novels, stories, art of every sort, became more and more personal. In the Blue Notebook, Anna writes of lectures she has been giving: '"Art during the Middle Ages was communal, unindividual; it came out of a group consciousness. It was without the driving painful individuality of the art of the bourgeois era. And one day we will leave behind the driving egotism of individual art. We will return to an art which will express not man's self-divisions and separateness from his fellows, but his responsibility for his fellows and his brotherhood. Art from the West becomes more and more a shriek of torment recording pain. Pain is becoming our deepest reality . . ." I have been saying something like this. About three months ago, in the middle of this lecture, I began to stammer and couldn't finish . . .'

Anna's stammer was because she was evading something. Once a pressure or a current has started, there is no way of avoiding it: there was no way of *not* being intensely subjective: it was, if you like, the writer's task for that time. You couldn't ignore it: you couldn't write a book about the building of a bridge or a dam and not develop the mind and feelings of the people who built it. (You think this is a caricature? – Not at all. This *either* / *or* is at the heart of literary criticism in communist countries at this moment.) At last I understood that the way over, or through this dilemma, the unease at writing about 'petty personal problems' was to recognise that nothing is personal, in the sense that it is uniquely one's own. Writing about oneself, one is writing about others, since your problems, pains, pleasures, emotions – and your extraordinary and remarkable ideas – can't be yours alone. The way to deal with the problem of 'subjectivity', that shocking business of being preoccupied with the tiny individual who is at the same time caught up in such an explosion of terrible and marvellous possibilities, is to see him as a microcosm and in this way to break through the personal, the subjective, making the personal general, as indeed life always does, transforming a private experience – or so you think of it when still a child, '*I* am falling in love', '*I* am feeling this or that emotion, or thinking that or the other thought' – into something much larger: growing up is after all only the understanding that one's unique and incredible experience is what everyone shares.

Another idea was that if the book were shaped in the right way it would make its own comment about the conventional novel: the debate about the novel has been going on since the novel was born, and is not, as one would imagine from reading contemporary academics, something recent. To put the short novel *Free Women* as a summary and condensation of all that mass of material, was to say something about the conventional novel, another way of describing the dissatisfaction of a writer when something is finished: 'How little I have managed to say of the truth, how little I have caught of all that complexity; how can this small neat thing be true when what I experienced was so rough and apparently formless and unshaped.'

But my major aim was to shape a book which would make its own comment, a wordless statement: to talk through the way it was shaped.

As I have said, this was not noticed.

One reason for this is that the book is more in the European tradition than the English tradition of the novel. Or rather, in the English tradition as viewed at the moment. The English novel after all does include *Clarissa* and *Tristram Shandy*, *The Tragic Comedians* – and Joseph Conrad.

But there is no doubt that to attempt a novel of ideas is to give oneself a handicap: the parochialism of our culture is intense. For instance, decade after decade bright young men and women emerge from their universities able to say proudly: 'Of course I know nothing about German literature.' It is the mode. The Victorians knew everything about German literature, but were able with a clear conscience not to know much about the French.

As for the rest – well, it is no accident that I got intelligent criticism from people who were, or who had been, marxists. They saw what I was trying to do. This is because Marxism looks at things as a whole and in relation to each other – or tries to, but its limitations are not the point for the moment. A person who has been influenced by Marxism takes it for granted that an event in Siberia will affect one in Botswana. I think it is possible that Marxism was the first attempt, for our time, outside the formal religions, at a world-mind, a world ethic. It went wrong, could not prevent itself from dividing and subdividing, like all the other religions, into smaller and smaller chapels, sects and creeds. But it was an attempt.

This business of seeing what I was trying to do – it brings me to the critics, and the danger of evoking a yawn. This sad bickering between writers and critics, playwrights and critics: the public have got so used to it they think, as of quarrelling children: 'Ah yes, dear little things, they are at it again.' Or: 'You writers get all that praise, or if not praise, at least all that attention – so why are you so perennially wounded?' And the public are quite right. For reasons I won't go into here, early and valuable experiences in my writing life gave me a sense of perspective about critics and reviewers; but over this novel, *The Golden Notebook*, I lost it: I thought that for the most part the criticism was too silly to be true. Recovering balance, I understood the problem. It is that writers are looking in the critics for an *alter ego*, that other self more intelligent than oneself who has seen what one is reaching for, and who judges you only by whether you have matched up to your aim or not. I have never yet met a writer who, faced at last with that rare being, a real critic, doesn't lose all paranoia and become gratefully attentive – he has found what he thinks he needs. But what he, the writer, is asking is impossible. Why should he expect this extraordinary being, the perfect critic (who does occasionally exist), why should there be anyone else who comprehends what he is trying to do? After all, there is only one person spinning that particular cocoon, only one person whose business it is to spin it.

It is not possible for reviewers and critics to provide what they purport to provide – and for which writers so ridiculously and childishly yearn.

This is because the critics are not educated for it; their training is in the opposite direction.

It starts when the child is as young as five or six, when he arrives at school. It starts with marks, rewards, 'places', 'streams', stars – and still in many places, stripes. This horscrace mentality, the victor and loser way of thinking, leads to 'Writer X is, is not, a few paces ahead of Writer Y. Writer Y has fallen behind. In his last book Writer Z has shown himself as better than Writer A.' From the very beginning the child is trained to think in this way: always in terms of comparison, of success, and of failure. It is a weeding-out system: the weaker get discouraged and fall out; a system designed to produce a few winners who are always in competition with each other. It is my belief – though this is not the place to develop this – that the talents every child has, regardless of his official 'IQ', could stay with him through life, to enrich him and everybody else, if these talents were not regarded as commodities with a value in the success-stakes.

The other thing taught from the start is to distrust one's own judgement. Children are taught submission to authority, how to search for other people's opinions and decisions, and how to quote and comply.

As in the political sphere, the child is taught that he is free, a democrat, with a free will and a free mind, lives in a free country, makes his own decisions. At the same time he is a prisoner of the assumptions

and dogmas of his time, which he does not question, because he has
never been told they exist. By the time a young person has reached the
age when he has to choose (we still take it for granted that a choice is
inevitable) between the arts and the sciences, he often chooses the arts
because he feels that here is humanity, freedom, choice. He does not
know that he is already moulded by a system: he does not know that the
choice itself is the result of a false dichotomy rooted in the heart of our
culture. Those who do sense this, and who don't wish to subject
themselves to further moulding, tend to leave, in a half-unconscious,
instinctive attempt to find work where they won't be divided against
themselves. With all our institutions, from the police force to academia,
from medicine to politics, we give little attention to the people who
leave – that process of elimination that goes on all the time and which
excludes, very early, those likely to be original and reforming, leaving
those attracted to a thing because that is what they are already like. A
young policeman leaves the Force saying he doesn't like what he has to
do. A young teacher leaves teaching, her idealism snubbed. This social
mechanism goes almost unnoticed – yet it is as powerful as any in
keeping our institutions rigid and oppressive.

These children who have spent years inside the training system
become critics and reviewers, and cannot give what the author, the
artist, so foolishly looks for – imaginative and original judgement. What
they can do, and what they do very well, is to tell the writer how the
book or play accords with current patterns of feeling and thinking – the
climate of opinion. They are like litmus paper. They are wind gauges –
invaluable. They are the most sensitive of barometers of public opinion.
You can see changes of mood and opinion here sooner than anywhere
except in the political field – it is because these are people whose whole
education has been just that – to look outside themselves for their
opinions, to adapt themselves to authority figures, to 'received opinion'
– a marvellously revealing phrase.

It may be that there is no other way of educating people. Possibly, but
I don't believe it. In the meantime it would be a help at least to describe
things properly, to call things by their right names. Ideally, what
should be said to every child, repeatedly, throughout his or her school
life is something like this:

'You are in the process of being indoctrinated. We have not yet
evolved a system of education that is not a system of indoctrination. We
are sorry, but it is the best we can do. What you are being taught here is

an amalgam of current prejudice and the choices of this particular culture. The slightest look at history will show how impermanent these must be. You are being taught by people who have been able to accommodate themselves to a regime of thought laid down by their predecessors. It is a self-perpetuating system. Those of you who are more robust and individual than others, will be encouraged to leave and find ways of educating yourself – educating your own judgement. Those that stay must remember, always and all the time, that they are being moulded and patterned to fit into the narrow and particular needs of this particular society.'

Like every other writer I get letters all the time from young people who are about to write theses and essays about my books in various countries – but particularly in the United States. They all say: 'Please give me a list of the articles about your work, the critics who have written about you, the authorities.' They also ask for a thousand details of total irrelevance, but which they have been taught to consider important, amounting to a dossier, like an immigration department's.

These requests I answer as follows: 'Dear Student. You are mad. Why spend months and years writing thousands of words about one book, or even one writer, when there are hundreds of books waiting to be read. You don't see that you are the victim of a pernicious system. And if you have yourself chosen my work as your subject, and if you do have to write a thesis – and believe me I am very grateful that what I've written is being found useful by you – then why don't you read what I have written and make up your own mind about what you think, testing it against your own life, your own experience. Never mind about Professors White and Black.'

'Dear Writer' – they reply. 'But I have to know what the authorities say, because if I don't quote them, my professor won't give me any marks.'

This is an international system, absolutely identical from the Urals to Yugoslavia, from Minnesota to Manchester.

The point is, we are all so used to it, we no longer see how bad it is.

I am not used to it, because I left school when I was fourteen. There was a time I was sorry about this, and believed I had missed out on something valuable. Now I am grateful for a lucky escape. After the publication of *The Golden Notebook*, I made it my business to find out something about the literary machinery, to examine the process which made a critic, or a reviewer. I looked at innumerable examination papers – and couldn't believe my eyes; sat in on classes for teaching literature, and couldn't believe my ears.

You might be saying: That is an exaggerated reaction, and you have no right to it, because you say you have never been part of the system. But I think it is not at all exaggerated, and that the reaction of someone from outside is valuable simply because it is fresh and not biased by allegiance to a particular education.

But after this investigation, I had no difficulty in answering my own questions: Why are they so parochial, so personal, so small-minded? Why do they always atomise, and belittle, why are they so fascinated by detail, and uninterested in the whole? Why is their interpretation of the word *critic* always to find fault? Why are they always seeing writers as in conflict with each other, rather than complementing each other . . . simple, this is how they are trained to think. That valuable person who understands what you are doing, what you are aiming for, and can give you advice and real criticism, is nearly always someone right outside the literary machine, even outside the university system; it may be a student just beginning, and still in love with literature, or perhaps it may be a thoughtful person who reads a great deal, following his own instinct.

I say to these students who have to spend a year, two years, writing theses about one book: 'There is only one way to read, which is to browse in libraries and bookshops, picking up books that attract you, reading only those, dropping them when they bore you, skipping the parts that drag – and never, never reading anything because you feel you ought, or because it is part of a trend or a movement. Remember that the book which bores you when you are twenty or thirty will open doors for you when you are forty or fifty – and vice versa. Don't read a book out of its right time for you. Remember that for all the books we have in print, are as many that have never reached print, have never been written down – even now, in this age of compulsive reverence for the written word, history, even social ethic, are taught by means of stories, and the people who have been conditioned into thinking only in terms of what is written – and unfortunately nearly all the products of our educational system can do no more than this – are missing what is before their eyes. For instance, the real history of Africa is still in the custody of black storytellers and wise men, black historians, medicine men: it is a verbal history, still kept safe from the white man and his predations. Everywhere, if you keep your mind open, you will find the truth in words *not* written down. So never let the printed page be your master. Above all, you should know that the fact that you have to spend one year, or two years, on one book, or one author means that you are badly taught – you should have been taught to read your way from one sympathy to another, you should be learning to follow your own intuitive feeling about what you need: that is what you should have been developing, not the way to quote from other people.'

But unfortunately it is nearly always too late.

It did look for a while as if the recent student rebellions might change things, as if their impatience with the dead stuff they are taught might be strong enough to substitute something more fresh and useful. But it seems as if the rebellion is over. Sad. During the lively time in the States, I had letters with accounts of how classes of students had refused their syllabuses, and were bringing to class their own choice of books, those that they had found relevant to their lives. The classes were emotional, sometimes violent, angry, exciting, sizzling with life. Of course this only happened with teachers who were sympathetic, and prepared to stand with the students against authority – prepared for the consequences. There are teachers who know that the way they have to teach is bad and boring – luckily there are still enough, with a bit of luck, to overthrow what is wrong, even if the students themselves have lost impetus.

Meanwhile there is a country where . . .

Thirty or forty years ago, a critic made a private list of writers and poets which he, personally, considered made up what was valuable in literature, dismissing all others. This list he defended lengthily in print, for The List instantly became a subject for much debate. Millions of words were written for and against – schools and sects, for and against, came into being. The argument, all these years later, still continues . . . no one finds this state of affairs sad or ridiculous . . .

Where there are critical books of immense complexity and learning, dealing, but often at second or thirdhand, with original work – novels, plays, stories. The people who write these books form a stratum in universities across the world – they are an international phenomenon, the top layer of literary academia. Their lives are spent in criticising, and in criticising each other's criticism. They at least regard this activity as more important than the original work. It is possible for literary students to spend more time reading criticism and criticism of criticism than they spend reading poetry, novels, biography, stories. A great many people regard this state of affairs as quite normal, and not sad and ridiculous . . .

Where I recently read an essay about Antony and Cleopatra by a boy shortly to take A levels. It was full of originality and excitement about the play, the feeling that any real teaching about literature aims to produce. The essay was returned by the teacher like this: I cannot mark this essay, you haven't quoted from the authorities. Few teachers would regard this as sad and ridiculous . . .

Where people who consider themselves educated, and indeed as superior to and more refined than ordinary non-reading people, will come up to a writer and congratulate him or her on getting a good review somewhere – but will not consider it necessary to read the book in question, or ever to think that what they are interested in is success . . .

Where when a book comes out on a certain subject, let's say star-gazing, instantly a dozen colleges, societies, television programmes, write to the author asking him to come and speak about star-gazing. The last thing it occurs to them to do is to read the book. This behaviour is considered quite normal, and not ridiculous at all . . .

Where a young man or woman, reviewer or critic, who has not read more of a writer's work than the book in front of him, will write patronisingly, or as if rather bored with the whole business, or as if considering how many marks to give an essay, about the writer in question – who might have written fifteen books, and have been writing for twenty or thirty years – giving the said writer instruction on what to write next, and how. No one thinks this is absurd, certainly not the young person, critic or reviewer, who has been taught to patronise and itemise everyone for years, from Shakespeare downwards.

Where a Professor of Archaeology can write of a South American tribe which has advanced knowledge of plants, and of medicine and of psychological methods: 'The astonishing thing is that these people have no written language . . .' And no one thinks him absurd.

Where, on the occasion of a centenary of Shelley, in the same week and in three different literary periodicals, three young men, of identical education, from our identical universities, can write critical pieces about Shelley, damning him with the faintest possible praise, and in identically the same tone, as if they were doing Shelley a great favour to mention him at all – and no one seems to think that such a thing can indicate that there is something seriously wrong with our literary system.

Finally . . . this novel continues to be, for its author, a most instructive experience. For instance. Ten years after I wrote it, I can get, in one week, three letters about it, from three intelligent, well-informed, concerned people, who have taken the trouble to sit down and write to me. One might be in Johannesburg, one in San Francisco, one in Budapest. And here I sit, in London, reading them, at the same time, or one after another – as always, grateful to the writers, and delighted that what I've written can stimulate, illuminate – or even annoy. But one letter is entirely about the sex war, about man's inhumanity to woman, and woman's inhumanity to man, and the writer has produced pages and pages all about nothing else, for she – but not always a she, can't see anything else in the book.

The second is about politics, probably from an old Red like myself, and he or she writes many pages about politics, and never mentions any other theme.

These two letters used, when the book was as it were young, to be the most common.

The third letter, once rare but now catching up on the others, is written by a man or a woman who can see nothing in it but the theme of mental illness.

But it is the same book.

And naturally these incidents bring up again questions of what people see when they read a book, and why one person sees one pattern and nothing at all of another pattern, and how odd it is to have, as author, such a clear picture of a book, that is seen so very differently by its readers.

And from this kind of thought has emerged a new conclusion: which is that it is not only childish of a writer to want readers to see what he sees, to understand the shape and aim of a novel as he sees it – his wanting this means that he has not understood a most fundamental point. Which is that the book is alive and potent and fructifying and able to promote thought and discussion *only* when its plan and shape and intention are not understood, because that moment of seeing the shape and plan and intention is also the moment when there isn't anything more to be got out of it.

And when a book's pattern and the shape of its inner life is as plain to the reader as it is to the author – then perhaps it is time to throw the book aside, as having had its day, and start again on something new.

Doris Lessing
June 1971

From
A Small Personal Voice

My Father

We use our parents like recurring dreams, to be entered into when needed; they are always there for love or for hate; but it occurs to me that I was not always there for my father. I've written about him before, but novels, stories, don't have to be 'true'. Writing this article is difficult because it has to be 'true'. I knew him when his best years were over.

There are photographs of him. The largest is of an officer in the 1914–18 war. A new uniform – buttoned, badged, strapped, tabbed – confines a handsome, dark young man who holds himself stiffly to confront what he certainly thought of as his duty. His eyes are steady, serious, and responsible, and show no signs of what he became later. A photograph at sixteen is of a dark, introspective youth with the same intent eyes. But it is his mouth you notice – a heavily-jutting upper lip contradicts the rest of a regular face. His moustache was to hide it: 'Had to do something – a damned fleshy mouth. Always made me uncomfortable, that mouth of mine.'

Earlier a baby (eyes already alert) appears in a lace waterfall that cascades from the pillowy bosom of a fat, plain woman to her feet. It is the face of a head cook. 'Lord, but my mother was a practical female – almost as bad as you!' as he used to say, or throw at my mother in moments of exasperation. Beside her stands, or droops, arms dangling, his father, the source of the dark, arresting eyes, but otherwise masked by a long beard.

The birth certificate says: Born 3rd August, 1886, Walton Villa, Creffield Road, S. Mary at the Wall, RSD. Name, Alfred Cook. Name and surname of Father: Alfred Cook Tayler. Name and maiden name of Mother: Caroline May Batley. Rank or Profession: Bank Clerk. Colchester, Essex.

They were very poor. Clothes and boots were a problem. They 'made their own amusements'. Books were mostly the Bible and *The Pilgrim's*

Progress. Every Saturday night they bathed in a hip-bath in front of the kitchen fire. No servants. Church three times on Sundays. 'Lord, when I think of those Sundays! I dreaded them all week, like a nightmare coming at you full tilt and no escape.' But he rabbited with ferrets along the lanes and fields, bird-nested, stole fruit, picked nuts and mushrooms, paid visits to the blacksmith and the mill and rode a farmer's carthorse.

They ate economically, but when he got diabetes in his forties and subsisted on lean meat and lettuce leaves, he remembered suet puddings, treacle puddings, raisin and currant puddings, steak and kidney puddings, bread and butter pudding, batter cooked in the gravy with the meat, potato cake, plum cake, butter cake, porridge with treacle, fruit tarts and pies, brawn, pig's trotters and pig's cheek and home-smoked ham and sausages. And 'lashings of fresh butter and cream and eggs'. He wondered if this diet had produced the diabetes, but said it was worth it.

There was an elder brother described by my father as: 'Too damned clever by half. One of those quick, clever brains. Now I've always had a slow brain, but I get there in the end, damn it!'

The brothers went to a local school and the elder did well, but my father was beaten for being slow. They both became bank clerks in, I think, the Westminster Bank, and one must have found it congenial, for he became a manager, the 'rich brother', who had cars and even a yacht. But my father did not like it, though he was conscientious. For instance, he changed his writing, letter by letter, because a senior criticised it. I never saw his unregenerate hand, but the one he created was elegant, spiky, careful. Did this mean he created a new personality for himself, hiding one he did not like, as he did his 'damned fleshy mouth'? I don't know.

Nor do I know when he left home to live in Luton or why. He found family life too narrow? A safe guess – he found everything too narrow. His mother was too down-to-earth? He had to get away from his clever elder brother?

Being a young man in Luton was the best part of his life. It ended in 1914, so he had a decade of happiness. His reminiscences of it were all of pleasure, the delight of physical movement, of dancing in particular. All his girls were 'a beautiful dancer, light as a feather.' He played billiards and ping-pong (both for his county); he swam, boated, played cricket and football, went to picnics and horse races, sang at musical evenings. One family of a mother and two daughters treated him 'like a son only better. I didn't know whether I was in love with the mother or the daughters, but oh I did love going there; we had such good times.' He was engaged to one daughter, then, for a time, to the other. An engagement was broken off because she was rude to a waiter. 'I could not marry a woman who allowed herself to insult someone who was defenceless.' He used to say to my wryly smiling mother: 'Just as well I didn't marry either of *them*; they would never have stuck it out the way you have, old girl.'

Just before he died he told me he had dreamed he was standing in a kitchen on a very high mountain holding X in his arms. 'Ah, yes, that's what I've missed in my life. Now don't you let yourself be cheated out of life by the old dears. They take all the colour out of everything if you let them.'

But in that decade – 'I'd walk 10, 15 miles to a dance two or three times a week and think nothing of it. Then I'd dance every dance and walk home again over the fields. Sometimes it was moonlight, but I liked the snow best, all crisp and fresh. I loved walking back and getting into my digs just as the sun was rising. My little dog was so happy to see me, and I'd feed her, and make myself porridge and tea, then I'd wash and shave and go off to work.'

The boy who was beaten at school, who went too much to church, who carried the fear of poverty all his life, but who nevertheless was filled with the memories of country pleasures; the young bank clerk who worked such long hours for so little money, but who danced, sang, played, flirted – this naturally vigorous, sensuous being was killed in 1914, 1915, 1916. I think the best of my father died in that war, that his spirit was crippled by it. The people I've met, particularly the women, who knew him young, speak of his high spirits, his energy, his enjoyment of life. Also of his kindness, his compassion and – a word that keeps recurring – his wisdom. 'Even when he was just a boy he understood things that you'd think even an old man would find it easy to condemn.' I do not think these people would have easily recognised the ill, irritable, abstracted, hypochondriac man I knew.

He 'joined up' as an ordinary soldier out of a characteristically quirky scruple: it wasn't right to enjoy officers' privileges when the Tommies had such a bad time. But he could not stick the communal latrines, the obligatory drinking, the collective visits to brothels, the jokes about girls. So next time he was offered a commission he took it.

His childhood and young man's memories, kept fluid, were added to, grew, as living memories do. But his war memories were congealed in stories that he told again and again, with the same words and gestures, in stereotyped phrases. They were anonymous, general, as if they had come out of a communal war memoir. He met a German in no-man's-land, but both slowly lowered their rifles and smiled and walked away. The Tommies were the salt of the earth, the British fighting men the best in the world. He had never known such comradeship. A certain brutal officer was shot in a sortie by his men, but the other officers, recognising rough justice, said nothing. He had known men intimately who saw the Angels at Mons. He wished he could force all the generals on both sides into the trenches for just one day, to see what the common soldiers endured – *that* would have ended the war at once.

There was an undercurrent of memories, dreams, and emotions much deeper, more personal. This dark region in him, fate-ruled, where nothing was true but horror, was expressed inarticulately, in brief, bitter exclamations or phrases of rage, incredulity, betrayal. The men who went to fight in that war believed it when they said it was to end war. My father believed it. And he was never able to reconcile his belief in his country with his anger at the cynicism of its leaders. And the anger, the sense of betrayal, strengthened as he grew old and ill.

But in 1914 he was naïve, the German atrocities in Belgium inflamed him, and he enlisted out of idealism, although he knew he would have a hard time. He knew because a fortuneteller told him. (He could be described as uncritically superstitious or as psychically gifted.) He would be in great danger twice, yet not die – he was being protected by a famous soldier who was his ancestor. 'And sure enough, later I heard from the Little Aunties that the church records showed we were descended the backstairs way from the Duke of Wellington, or was it Marlborough? Damn it, I forget. But one of them would be beside me all through the war, she said.' (He was romantic, not only about his solicitous ghost, but also about being a descendant of the Huguenots, on the strength of the 'e' in Tayler; and about 'the wild blood' in his veins from a great uncle who, sent unjustly to prison for smuggling, came out of a ten-year sentence and earned it, very efficiently, along the coasts of Cornwall until he died.)

The luckiest thing that ever happened to my father, he said, was getting his leg shattered by shrapnel ten days before Passchendaele. His whole company was killed. He knew he was going to be wounded because of the fortuneteller, who had said he would know. 'I did not understand what she meant, but both times in the trenches, first when my appendix burst and I nearly died, and then just before Passchendaele, I felt for some days as if a thick, black velvet pall was settled over me. I can't tell you what it was like. Oh, it was awful, awful, and the second time it was so bad I wrote to the old people and told them I was going to be killed.'

His leg was cut off at mid-thigh, he was shell-shocked, he was very ill for many months, with a prolonged depression afterwards. 'You should always remember that sometimes people are all seething underneath. You don't know what terrible things people have to fight against. You should look at a person's eyes, that's how you tell . . . When I was like that, after I lost my leg, I went to a nice doctor man and said I was going mad, but he said, don't worry, everyone locks up things like that. You don't know – horrible, horrible, awful things. I was afraid of myself, of what I used to dream. I wasn't myself at all.'

In the Royal Free Hospital was my mother, Sister McVeagh. He married his nurse which, as they both said often enough (though in different tones of voice), was just as well. That was 1919. He could not face being a bank clerk in England, he said, not after the trenches. Besides, England was too narrow and conventional. Besides, the civilians did not know what the soldiers had suffered, they didn't want to know, and now it wasn't done even to remember 'The Great Unmentionable'. He went off to the Imperial Bank of Persia, in which country I was born.

The house was beautiful, with great stone-floored high-ceilinged rooms whose windows showed ranges of snow-streaked mountains. The gardens were full of roses, jasmine, pomegranates, walnuts. Kermanshah he spoke of with liking, but soon they went to Teheran, populous with 'Embassy people,' and my gregarious mother created a lively social life about which he was irritable even in recollection.

Irritableness – that note was first struck here, about Persia. He did not like, he said, 'the graft and the corruption'. But here it is time to try and describe something difficult – how a man's good qualities can also be his bad ones, or if not bad, a danger to him.

My father was honourable – he always knew exactly what that word meant. He had integrity. His 'one does not do that sort of thing,' his 'no, it is *not* right,' sounded throughout my childhood and were final for all of us. I am sure it was true he wanted to leave Persia because of 'the corruption'. But it was also because he was already unconsciously longing for something freer, because as a bank official he could not let go into the dream-logged personality that was waiting for him. And later in Rhodesia, too, what was best in him was also what prevented him from shaking away the shadows: it was always in the name of honesty or decency that he refused to take this step or that out of the slow decay of the family's fortunes.

In 1925 there was leave from Persia. That year in London there was an Empire Exhibition, and on the Southern Rhodesian stand some very fine maize cobs and a poster saying that fortunes could be made on maize at 25/– a bag. So on an impulse, turning his back forever on England, washing his hands of the corruption of the East, my father collected all his capital, £800, I think, while my mother packed curtains from Liberty's, clothes from Harrods, visiting cards, a piano, Persian rugs, a governess and two small children.

Soon, there was my father in a cigar-shaped house of thatch and mud on the top of a kopje that overlooked in all directions a great system of mountains, rivers, valleys, while overhead the sky arched from horizon to empty horizon. This was a couple of hundred miles south from the Zambesi, a hundred or so west from Mozambique, in the district of Banket, so called because certain of its reefs were of the same formation as those called *banket* on the Rand. Lomagundi – gold country, tobacco country, maize country – wild, almost empty. (The Africans had been turned off it into reserves.) Our neighbours were four, five, seven miles off. In front of the house . . . no neighbours, nothing; no farms, just wild bush with two rivers but no fences to the mountains seven miles away. And beyond these mountains and bush again to the Portuguese border, over which 'our boys' used to escape when wanted by the police for pass or other offences.

And then? There was bad luck. For instance, the price of maize dropped from 25/– to 9/– a bag. The seasons were bad, prices bad, crops failed. This was the sort of thing that made it impossible for him ever to 'get off the farm,' which, he agreed with my mother, was what he most wanted to do.

It was an absurd country, he said. A man could 'own' a farm for years that was totally mortgaged to the Government and run from the Land Bank, meanwhile employing half-a-hundred Africans at 12/– a month and none of them knew how to do a day's work. Why, two farm labourers from Europe could do in a day what twenty of these ignorant black savages would take a week to do. (Yet he was proud that he had a name as a just employer, that he gave 'a square deal'.) Things got worse. A fortuneteller had told him that her heart ached when she saw the misery ahead for my father: this was the misery.

But it was my mother who suffered. After a period of neurotic illness, which was a protest against her situation, she became brave and resourceful. But she never saw that her husband was not living in a real world, that he had made a captive of her common sense. We were always about to 'get off the farm'. A miracle would do it – a sweepstake, a goldmine, a legacy. And then? What a question! We would go to England where life would be normal with people coming in for musical evenings and nice supper parties at the Trocadero after a show. Poor woman, for the twenty years we were on the farm, she waited for when life would begin for her and for her children, for she never understood that what was a calamity for her was for them a blessing.

Meanwhile my father sank towards his death (at 61). Everything changed in him. He had been a dandy and fastidious, now he hated to change out of shabby khaki. He had been sociable, now he was misanthropic. His body's disorders – soon diabetes and all kinds of stomach ailments – dominated him. He was brave about his wooden leg, and even went down mine shafts and climbed trees with it, but he walked clumsily and it irked him badly. He greyed fast, and slept more in the day, but would be awake half the night pondering about . . .

It could be gold divining. For ten years he experimented on private theories to do with the attractions and repulsions of metals. His whole soul went into it but his theories were wrong or he was *unlucky* – after all, if he had found a mine he would have had to leave the farm. It could be the relation between the minerals of the earth and of the moon; his decision to make infusions of all the plants on the farm and drink them himself in the interests of science; the criminal folly of the British Government in not realising that the Germans and the Russians were conspiring as Anti-Christ to . . . the inevitability of war because no one would listen to Churchill, but it would be all right because God (by then he was a British Israelite) had destined Britain to rule the world; a prophecy said 10 million dead would surround Jerusalem – how would the corpses be cleared away?; people who wished to abolish flogging should be flogged; the natives understood nothing but a good beating; hanging must not be abolished because the Old Testament said 'an eye for an eye and a tooth for a tooth . . .'

Yet, as this side of him darkened, so that it seemed all his thoughts were of violence, illness, war, still no one dared to make an unkind comment in his presence or to gossip. Criticism of people, particularly of women, made him more and more uncomfortable till at last he burst out with: 'It's all very well, but no one has the right to say that about another person.'

In Africa, when the sun goes down, the stars spring up, all of them in their expected places, glittering and moving. In the rainy season, the sky flashed and thundered. In the dry season, the great dark hollow of night was lit by veld fires: the mountains burned through September and October in chains of red fire. Every night my father took out his chair to watch the sky and the mountains, smoking, silent, a thin shabby fly-away figure under the stars. 'Makes you think – there are so many worlds up there, wouldn't really matter if we did blow ourselves up – plenty more where we came from.'

The Second World War, so long foreseen by him, was a bad time. His son was in the Navy and in danger, and his daughter a sorrow to him. He became very ill. More and more often it was necessary to drive him into Salisbury with him in a coma, or in danger of one, on the back seat. My mother moved him into a pretty little suburban house in town near the hospitals, where he took to his bed and a couple of years later died. For the most part he was unconscious under drugs. When awake he talked obsessively (a tongue licking a nagging sore place) about 'the old war'. Or he remembered his youth. 'I've been dreaming – Lord, to see those horses come lickety-split down the course with their necks stretched out and the sun on their coats and everyone shouting . . . I've been dreaming how I walked along the river in the mist as the sun was rising . . . Lord, lord, lord, what a time that was, what good times we all had then, before the old war.'

Afterword to
The Story of an African Farm
by Olive Schreiner

A new novel, *The Story of an African Farm*, was being discussed around London in 1883. The writer, a Mr Ralph Iron, was unknown. South Africa was still a long way off, a land of native risings, kaffir wars, wild animals. Missionaries and explorers went there, and young men looking for adventure. Africa, large parts of it still unmapped, was the setting for tales of danger – and imagination. In his preface Ralph Iron wrote: 'It has been suggested by a kind critic that he would better have liked the little book if it had been a history of wild adventure; of cattle driven into inaccessible *kranzes* by Bushmen; "of encounters with ravening lions, and hair-breadth escapes." This could not be. Such works are best written in Piccadilly or in the Strand . . .' Also, and gently enough, he asked for a broader sympathy from a habit of criticism whose weakness was – and still is – a partiality for 'the charm that hangs about the ideal representation of familiar things.' One may profitably think about the nature of the society, safe, ordered, stable – or believed to be so by that part of it who so experience it; but more profitably about the writer who understood the readers, and the critics, he hoped to engage, so well that he could choose such apposite words, and who, in rejecting stronger ones, was already showing such strength and maturity.

The novel had had a hard birth, refused by one publisher after another. Not only was it about an Africa unfamiliar to England, but it had an unmarried mother whom the author refused to provide with a wedding ring. Then Chapman and Hall took it on the advice of George Meredith. Cuts and changes were suggested, and some made: it is said with resentment.

Soon it leaked out that Ralph Iron was a woman, and a young one: she was not yet thirty. She had been a governess in the Cape. She was lodging in London. She was very pretty and vivacious. Attractive female authors were then a rarity. She was around and about in London

society for a while. It was not only Meredith who recognised the novel.
An extraordinary assortment of the remarkable people of her time
praised it. It was one of the best novels in the English language. It was
greater than *The Pilgrim's Progress*. It had genius. It had splendour. For
the rest of her life she was the famous author of this novel that she had
written in her early twenties. And, until she died, people from every
part of the world would come up to her and say that it had changed their
lives. Some claim that it would have made no difference if she had never
written another word. This is true, from the point of view of literature;
but there were other sides to her.

Now I must write personally; but I would not, if I didn't know that
nothing we can say about ourselves is personal. I read the novel when I
was fourteen or so; understanding very well the isolation described in it;
responding to her sense of Africa the magnificent – mine, and
everyone's who knows Africa; realising that this was one of the few rare
books. For it is in that small number of novels, with *Moby Dick*, *Jude
the Obscure*, *Wuthering Heights*, perhaps one or two others, which is on a
frontier of the human mind. Also, this was the first 'real' book I'd met
with that had Africa for a setting. Here was the substance of truth, and
not from England or Russia or France or America, necessitating all
kinds of mental translations, switches, correspondences, but reflecting
what I knew and could see. And the book became part of me, as the few
rare books do. A decade or so later, meeting people who talked of
books, they talked of this one, mentioning this or that character, or
scene; and I discovered that while I held the strongest sense of the
novel, I couldn't remember anything about it. Yet I had only to hear the
title, or 'Olive Schreiner,' and my deepest self was touched.

I read it again, for the first time as an experienced reader, able to
judge and compare – and criticise. The first shock was that Olive
Schreiner, who had always felt so close, like a sister, could have been
my grandmother. The second was that, if I used the rules that turn out a
thousand good forgettable novels a year, let the book spread out from
the capsuled essence of it I had held, so that it became a matter of
characters and a plot, it was not a good novel. But, then, of course,
neither is *Wuthering Heights*. Well, then, what are these rules? Faced
with one of the rare books, one has to ask such questions, to discover,
again, that there aren't any. Nor can there be; the novel being that
hybrid, the mixture of journalism and the *Zeitgeist* and autobiography
that comes out of a part of the human consciousness which is always

trying to understand itself, to come into the light. Not on the level where poetry works, or music, or mathematics, the high arts; no, but on the rawest and most workaday level, like earthworms making new soil where things can grow. True lovers of the novel must love it as the wise man in the fable did the crippled beauty whose complaint against fate was that she was beautiful – for what use was her beauty? She was always trying for humanity and failing. And he replied that it was because of the trying that he loved her.

The true novel wrestles on the edge of understanding, lying about on all sides desperately, for every sort of experience, pressing into use every flash of intuition or correspondence, trying to fuse together the crudest of materials, and the humblest, which the higher arts can't include. But it is precisely here, where the writer fights with the raw, the intractable, that poetry is born. Poetry, that is, of the novel: appropriate to it. *The Story of an African Farm* is a poetic novel; and when one has done with the 'plot' and the characters, that is what remains: an endeavour, a kind of hunger, that passionate desire for growth and understanding, which is the deepest pulse of human beings.

There was nothing unconscious about Olive Schreiner's method, as this letter to Havelock Ellis shows. The book she discusses is her *From Man to Man*.

One thing I am glad of is that it becomes less and less what you call 'art' as it goes along. My first crude conceptions are always what you call 'art'. As they become more and more *living* and real, they become what I call higher art, but what you call no 'art' at all. I quite understand what you meant, but I cannot think that your use of the word in that sense is right, i.e., not misleading, and therefore *untrue*. If I understand what you mean, *Wilhelm Meister* is not art, one of Balzac's novels is. *Wilhelm Meister* is one of the most immortal deathless productions of the greatest of the world's artists, the result of twenty years labour, worth any six of Balzac's novels, great and glorious as Balzac is. Yet if you were writing of it, you would, ridiculous as it would seem, be *obliged* to call it 'not art'. You seem to say 'I will call "art" only that artistic creation in which I can clearly *see* the artist manufacturing the parts and piecing them together; when I cannot see that, though the thing be organic, true, inevitable, like a work of God's, I will not call it art; I must see the will shaping it (of course there always has been a will shaping it, whether it is visible or not) or I will not call it art.' This of course is not in justification of my method but touches what seems to me a weakness and shallowness in your mode of criticism. It *is* very valuable that the two kinds of art should be distinguished, but not that the one should be called art and the other not art. It would be better to call the one artificial and the other real art. But that wouldn't be just. I should rather call the one organic, and the other inorganic.

And in reply to his answer: 'No, I deny that you can see how *Wilhelm Meister* was made; you can see how it *grew*, not how it was *made* . . . It came like that, like a tree, not like a Greek temple. You never know where you are going to turn next in *Wilhelm Meister*. No more did Goethe – yet all was of necessity, nothing of chance.'

The 'plot'. On a Karroo farm in the second part of last century, lived a widowed Dutchwoman, Tant' Sannie. There is a daughter, Em, who will inherit the farm, and a niece, Lyndall. Em is sweet, gentle, humble, 'womanly'. Lyndall is all beauty, fire, and intelligence. She is an orphan. Lyndall dreams of an education: knowledge frees. She will make the Dutchwoman send her to school. The saintly German overseer has a son, Waldo. He and Lyndall love each other as prisoners may do. To the farm comes a mountebank, Bonaparte Blenkins, who tricks the rich Dutchwoman into wanting to marry him. While under his spell she treats Waldo and his father abominably: he wants to get rid of them. Also, he enjoys cruelty. He is afraid of Lyndall, who sees through him. Discovered by Tant' Sannie making love to her much richer niece, he leaves in disgrace. Time passes. The girls are grown to marriageable age: Em is a 'yellow-haired little woman of sixteen.' A new arrival, Gregory Rose, who had hired part of the farm, is in love with her. But Em tells him that when Lyndall arrives back from her boardingschool he will see a really beautiful woman, a princess, and change his mind. This happens. Lyndall despises the womanish Gregory, and spends her time with the 'low, coarse' fellow Waldo. He listens, she talks, mostly about the humiliating position of woman in her time. 'A little bitterness, a little longing when we are young, a little futile striving for work, a little passionate striving for room for the exercise of her powers – and then we go with the drove. A woman must march with her regiment. In the end she must be trodden down or go with it.' In her girls' school she had not learned what she had expected. 'I have discovered that of all cursed places under the sun, where the hungriest soul can hardly pick up a few grains of knowledge, a girls' boardingschool is the worst. They are called finishing schools and the name tells accurately what they are . . .' Olive Schreiner has been described as 'a suffragette before there were any.'

Waldo and Lyndall drive together over the veld. They sit on a kopje and talk. He takes her to a Boer dance. Then she goes away. Gregory Rose feels the first real emotion of his life: he goes in search of her, wants nothing but to serve her. Waldo leaves in search of wider experience. Em stays and suffers. Lyndall has become pregnant by a 'stranger, his tall slight figure reposing in the broken armchair, his keen blue eyes studying the fire from beneath delicately pencilled drooping eyelids. One white hand plays with a heavy flaxen moustache.' This figure, or a similar one, appears and reappears through Olive Schreiner's work. He is charged with the high tension of conflict, a man found overwhelmingly sexually attractive, but contemptibly wanting by a woman who demands moral and intellectual companionship, as well as physical, from her lover. The stranger wants to marry Lyndall. She will not: it will put her in his power, and he only decided to marry her when he realised that she might not want to. But she agrees to stay with him, unmarried, for the sake of the child. They travel around the Cape, but some quarrel occurs. She is left alone and ill. Gregory Rose tracks her down to a country hotel. She needs a nurse. He dresses himself in woman's clothes and looks after her. The baby dies soon after it is born. She dies too. Waldo returns to the farm, after eighteen months of every sort of degrading labour. He has learned that: 'You may work and work and work until you are only a body and not a soul.' Gregory returns with the news of Lyndall's death. He will marry Em because Lyndall has told him to. Em says: 'Why is it always so, Waldo, always so? We long for things and long for them and pray for them. Then at last, too late, when we don't want them any more, when all the sweetness is taken out of them, then they come.'

Waldo goes off to sit in the sunshine – and dies.

Lyndall is dead. Waldo is dead. The saintly old man is dead.

Gregory Rose lives to carry on the farm with gentle uncomplaining Em who, Lyndall says, 'is so much better than me that there is more goodness in her little finger than in my whole body.' Tant' Sannie, remarried, flourishes with her new husband.

Well, that's the story. Parts are well done by the conventional yard-stick: the scenes of rural Boer life; the dance, the scene where the young man comes in 'his hopeless resignation' to court Tant' Sannie; Tant' Sannie coming to visit with her new baby; Tant' Sannie on the joys of marriage; Tant' Sannie on progress: 'Not that I believe in this new plan of putting soda into the pot. If the dear Father had meant soda to be put into soap, what would He have made milkbushes for, and stuck them all over the veld, as thick as lambs in lambing season.' This woman, as near animal as they come, is written with love and with humour – a triumph. Em, too, the maiden dreaming of motherhood: 'I always come to watch the milking. That red cow with the short horns is bringing up the calf of the white cow that died. She loves it so – just as if it were her own. It is so nice to see her lick its little ears. Just look!' Now, these are characters that could have appeared in any good novel called *Scenes from the Karroo, 18 –*. It did not take Olive Schreiner to create them. The novel's great-ness lies precisely in where it breaks from 'lifelike' characters, and an easily recognisable probability.

There is the question of Bonaparte Blenkins, the charlatan. Later Olive said she was sorry that she had given him no real humanity, made him two-dimensional. But her first instinct was right. Evil is not personified in this book – neither is goodness. Human beings are small things in the grip of gigantic forces. They cry out and fight and struggle to understand the incomprehensible, which is beyond good and evil. Had Bonaparte been given depth and weight, we would have had to ask questions about the saintliness of the old German, Bonaparte's counter-weight, whom he has to destroy. He is saintly: but very silly. And Bonaparte is wicked – and silly. Not damaging? Indeed, yes: his persecution of the old German, his treatment of Waldo, the brutal beating he gave him, scarred Waldo, and taught him his helplessness; taught Lyndall her helplessness, and enforced her determination to free herself. But he was stupid, undid himself – and ran away. Wickedness is arbitrary, almost grotesque. And innocent childlike goodness is impo-tent. But – does it matter all that much? The sun burns down over the Karroo; the pitilessly indifferent stars wheel and deploy; and two young creatures look up at the skies where they see their unimportance written, and ask questions, can find no answers – and suffer most frightfully.

Lyndall and Waldo: Olive said that in these two she had put herself. They share a soul; and when Lyndall dies, Waldo has to die. But it is Waldo who is the heart of the book; a ragged, sullen, clumsy farm boy, all inarticulate hunger – not for education, like Lyndall, but for the unknown. And it is to Waldo that Olive gave the chapter that is the core, not only of this novel, but of all her work. It is called 'Waldo's stranger', and in it a man travelling through the Cape stops to rest on the farm for an hour. Waldo has carved a piece of wood. 'It was by no means lovely. The men and birds were almost grotesque in their laboured resemblance to nature, and bore signs of patient thought. The stranger turns the thing over on his knee . . .' and offers to buy it for £5. Waldo, whom he sees as 'a hind' says no: it is for his father's grave. The visitor is touched, presses the boy to talk, and finally, understanding his need, puts what Waldo has carved on the stick into a story. This is the legend of The Hunter. A version, or germ, of this tale appears in Attar's Parliament of the Birds. 'An astonishing thing! The first manifestation of the Simurgh' (God or what you will) 'took place in China in the middle of the night. One of his feathers fell on China and his reputation filled the world. Everyone made a picture of this feather, and from it formed his own system of ideas, and so fell into a turmoil. This feature is still in the picture gallery of that country: hence the saying: 'Seek knowledge, even as far as China.' But for his manifestation there would not have been so much noise in the world concerning this mysterious Being. This sign of his existence is a token of his glory. All souls carry an impression of the image of his feather. Since the description of it has neither head nor tail, beginning nor end, it is not necessary to say more about it. Now, any of you who are for this road, prepare yourself and put your feet on the Way.' The Hunter of the Stranger's tale has tried all his life to climb the mountains whose summits hold the Truth, cutting steps in the rock so that he, and others after him, can climb. He lies dying, alone. Long ago he has shed the childish arrogance that let him believe he could find Truth: what matters is that he has spent his life trying. Then: 'Slowly from the white sky above, through the still air, came something falling, falling, falling. Softly it fluttered down and dropped on to the breast of the dying man. He felt it with his hands. It was a feather. He died holding it.' What Olive makes of this tale is both all her own, and from that region of the human mind called Anon.

Lyndall, too, is visited by a stranger, who gave her, at just the time she needed that book, a book. In Olive's own life it was Spencer's First Principles, and she read it, sleepless, for the three days she was able to keep it. To us, the battle for education having been won, at least for this time and for the fortunate of the world, knowledge as it emerges filtered

through school and university is perhaps not as covetable as what Olive
Schreiner was able to make of books, by herself, using her own instinct
to find what she needed. But Lyndall's passion for an education would
be understood now by an African boy (or girl) who wants an education
so badly that he will walk or bicycle ten, fifteen miles, from a mud hut,
or a bunk in a shed in a shanty-town shared with half a dozen others, to
a day's hard labour; walk or cycle back; and then walk, bicycle, as many
miles in another direction to sit up till midnight in an ill-equipped
classroom run by a half-equipped teacher, so as to learn to read, write,
and do arithmetic. For which 'education' he will pay, or his parents
will, money he needs for food and clothes. There are millions of them in
Africa. To such people books, learning, are a key to freedom – as they
are to Lyndall, who, when she got them, discovered their limits.

But Waldo wanted a different kind of knowledge, and that is what he
was given by his stranger, to whom he says: 'All my life I have longed to
see you.' He was thinking: Ah, that man who believed nothing, hoped
nothing, felt nothing: *how he loved him*. And, when the stranger was
gone, he stooped and kissed passionately a hoof-mark in the sand.

Lyndall has given her name to dozens of little South African girls: the
beautiful young woman who chooses to die alone rather than marry a
man she cannot respect. Lyndall is that projection of a novelist created
as a means of psychic self-preservation. Olive, at that time, was very
much alone. If not estranged from her family, she could not get from it
the moral support she so badly needed. She was very young. She was ill:
was to be ill all her life. She had been through violent religious conflicts
that had left her drained, exhausted. She had been in love with, possibly
jilted by, a man who found her socially inadequate, and morally and
mentally his superior – or so the evidence suggests. That Olive should
have needed Lyndall is not surprising: she had to love Lyndall, and
stand by her, and protect her – and explain her; for Lyndall was the first
of her kind in fiction. Of her we can say: that kind of embattled woman
was the product of that kind of society, where women had a hard time of
it. But Waldo is the truth of Lyndall, and he is timeless.

Women novelists' men . . . Male novelists' women can be as
instructive, particularly in their archetypal state, like Haggard's *She* –
as the psychologists have pointed out. This 'she' is best studied in bad
novels, for in good novels she is a human being. And so with women
writers' men; the most useful exemplars we have being Rochester and
Heathcliff. They are the unregenerate strong man, the unfulfilled hero.

In the psyche of men, is the goddess, 'she'. In women, the hero; but it is as if women, looking for strength, the hero, the strong wise man who embodies humanity's struggle upwards, and not finding him, may take instead his failed brother, who at least has had potentiality; rather than a nothing-man who has never aimed at anything. Lyndall's lover, with his flaxen moustaches and his heavy eyelids; the rest of the attractive men who capture Olive Schreiner's heroines against their will – they are nothing-men, put there to be despised. But the hero, the strong man who challenges destiny: well, his place is of course with 'she' – in legend, myth, and magic. He cannot exist, in his pure form, in the novel, that struggling and impure art. He is out of place there, as 'she' is. You find her, him, only in romantic or second-rate novels. But Waldo is the first appearance in women's writing of the true hero, in a form appropriate to the novel; here a kind of Caliban who mysteriously embodies Prospero's spirit, or Faust's.

Waldo is the son of the old German, Otto, who is a portrait of Olive's father.

To the creation of a woman novelist seem to go certain psychological ingredients; at least, often enough to make it interesting. One of them, a balance between father and mother where the practicality, the ordinary sense, cleverness, and worldly ambition is on the side of the mother; and the father's life is so weighted with dreams and ideas and imaginings that their joint life gets lost in what looks like a hopeless muddle and failure, but which holds a potentiality for something that must be recognised as better, on a different level, than what ordinary sense or cleverness can begin to conceive.

Olive's mother was the daughter of a minister of religion destined for a good middle-class marriage. She met Gottlob Schreiner at a missionary meeting. He was a student, the son of a German shoemaker, in a family of peasants and preachers. At the wedding the minister tore the trimmings off Rebecca's hat, as unsuitable for the wife of a missionary. They went off together to the Cape, in a mood of high evangelical fervour, to convert the heathen. Gottlob never lost his sense of mission, but his wife later declared it was all 'claptrap and nonsense.' She tried to preserve some intellectual life, and the respectable standards of her upbringing, in isolation and in poverty, while he loved and idealised her as a being quite above him. She was educated, beautiful, clever – and frustrated. Olive, the sixth child, experienced her as cold and unloving. 'My mother has never been a mother to me. I have had no mother. She

is a brilliant, wonderful little woman, all intellect and genius. The
relation between us is a very curious one . . . she seems to me like a
favourite brilliant child of mine.' Olive was solitary, 'queer', and
fanciful in a way all the family found uncomfortable. She grew up on
poor mission stations, in close relationship with the wild untenanted
landscape of the Cape. This saved her: according to modern ideas, she
was brutally treated; but she escaped to the rocks, the bushes, the sun,
the stars. *Undine* describes her childhood. From the time she was a
baby playing with dolls, she was tormented by God, by hell, by
redemption – she was reading the Bible before she read anything – and
by her own passionate uncompromising temperament, and the conscience that was the product of her Lutheran, Wesleyan, heritage. In
crises of misery over God, there could be no comfort in her family: she
was locked up, punished. She was beaten: her worst was from her
mother, who gave her fifty strokes on her bare body with a bunch of
quince rods. This was for using a crude Dutch expression: she said
'Ach!' Rebecca and her fight for respectability emerges, in this
incident, as if into a spotlight. Olive was never able to forget this
experience. To read *Undine* is painful even now, not so much for the
punishings and the beating, but because of her hunger for love, for
understanding, and the mental anguish that she suffered for years.
Lying awake at night she listened to the clock tick: every tick meant
souls were being sent to hell by an unforgiving God. She cried out to be
given some burden or sacrifice so that even one soul might be spared
because of her. She staged sacrifices like Abraham, putting a mutton
chop saved from dinner onto a rock in the midday sun, and waiting for
the fire to come from heaven – for she had as much faith as Abraham.
But nothing happened, God was indifferent to her. She got up at night
to read the Bible by moonlight, to find some words that might comfort
her, and found: 'Strive to enter in at the strait gate, for many, I say
unto you, shall seek to enter in and shall not be able.' She flung the Bible
across the room and wept, and stared at the stars out of the window, and
was tormented by eternity and the littleness of human beings on their
earth. She lost her faith, and knew that she was wicked, and was
damned, but preferred the expectation of hell and rejection by God than
to accept God's injustice, which made some souls elect from the
beginning of time, and others inevitably damned. Many Victorians,
fighting a narrow and bigoted religion, lost their reputations, their jobs,
sometimes their reason: their conflicts are described in plentiful

memoirs from that time. But this frightful battle was fought out in a small girl, who had no one to help her. When still a girl she became 'a freethinker' and remained one, always contemptuous of conventional religion. Asked for help, much later, by a parson threatened with loss of faith, she wrote: 'If I must put it into words, I would say, the Universe is One, and It lives; or, if you would put it into older phraseology, There is NOTHING but God.' Sympathetic but not very insightful contemporaries defended her by saying she was a religious woman who did not believe in God. She said of herself that she had that deep faith that took the form of a lifelong battle with God, and which took for granted she would be forgiven: which is not the same thing at all. But to her, our almost casual rejection of God, an indifferent irreligiousness, would have been impossible. The Victorians who fought that battle carried their freethinking, their agnosticism, their atheism, like flags of faith in the free spirit of man. The question she makes us ask, as do all the great ones of the past, is: If she were alive now, what battle would she be fighting? The freedoms she fought for, we take for granted. Because of people like her. We tend to forget that. She never did; was searching literature and history for allies even as a child; and before she was twenty had read Darwin and Spencer, Montaigne, Goethe, Carlyle, Gibbon, Locke, and Lecky; J. S. Mill, Shakespeare, Ruskin, and Schiller. And had made amateur attempts, her mother aiding, at medicine and biology and anatomy. For poor Rebecca had once dreamed of studying medicine.

The family disintegrated in poverty, Gottlob was irremedially incompetent, and gave away what he possessed, often to rogues. He died, and the mother, extraordinarily, became a Roman Catholic, though according to the chapel creed, 'one of the three grand crimes was to believe in the possible salvation of a Roman Catholic.' Some of the children found it a crime; but not Olive, who continued to love her mother with that kind of love that is all a hopeful need. It was rewarded. As a woman she wrote, with deep emotion, how one night she woke to find her mother crying in her bed. Rebecca had read something Olive had written and was saying: 'Oh, my child, my wonderful beautiful child. Am I really your mother? Have I really given birth to a human being who could write like that? You could never have written this if you had not been thinking of your own childhood. Forgive me, please.'

At nineteen Olive became a governess, and taught for seven years in the families of Boer farmers. Here she learned 'to love and admire the Boer.' In one of her places her room was mud-floored, and when it rained

she had to put up an umbrella, because the roof leaked. The furniture
was a bed and a box for her clothes. There was no looking-glass, not
even a basin: she washed in the stream that ran past her door. But she
was content here, moved for health reasons: her asthma began at this
time. In these years she wrote drafts of *Undine*, *From Man to Man*, and
completed *The Story of an African Farm*. Because of 'the autobiograph-
ical element' she had affection for *Undine*, but she asked for it to be
destroyed. She was right: it is an undigested, mental book, in parts not
far away from the pathetic Victorian novel at its worst. Other people
knew better, and it was published. *From Man to Man* she cared for, and
worked on it all her life. But while it is full of plums, that fusing that
makes a work of art never took place. What, then, fused the *Farm*?
Possibly the unhappy love affair. We do not know. She did not care for
these emotions to be made public, and we should respect that. Though
certainly they scarred her, and she said so; but for her, pain was a
teacher, and painful experience necessary for growth.

After she became a literary figure in London, it is harder to see her
clearly. She appears in the reminiscences of other people, as in a series
of posed photographs. 'Distinctly pretty with large dark eyes and black
hair and the little square, strong figure.' That was Frank Harris. And
Havelock Ellis on their first meeting: '. . . the short sturdy, vigorous
body in loose shapeless clothes, sitting on the couch, with the hands
spread on her thighs and, above, the beautiful head with the large dark
eyes, at once so expressive and so observant.'

Her first desire to meet people was soon swallowed in the necessity
for privacy: she found she had no time to write or to study. She seems
always to be in flight – away from people, and towards some place where
at last she could feel well. There are letters; but letters, as I think
biographers tend to forget, are written to people, and reflect those
people, or the phase of a relationship, as much as they do the writer.
Letters to Havelock Ellis are best: she called him her other self, her
brother; and over the decades they were in correspondence there is
maintained the steady note of intellectual sympathy, even when in
emotional stress with each other. They might have married. He was
more explicit about his side than she about hers: she did not love him
enough, he said. But both were contradictory about each other, as they
were bound to be in a friendship that lasted till she died and survived
their marriages to other people. Her letters describe her conflicts over
marriage. 'I can't marry, Henry, I can't. And some awful power seems

to be drawing me on. I think I shall go mad. I couldn't. I *must* be free you know, I *must* be free . . .' 'Oh Henry, when passion enters a relationship it does spoil the holy sweetness. But perhaps those people are right who say no such thing as friendship is possible between man and woman, though I can't bear to think so.' 'The lesson of the last 5 years has been that there is no such thing as friendship, just as the lesson of the two before was that there is no such thing as sex-love, only sex-selfishness.' 'Please love me. I wish I could believe anything was real . . .' 'Life would be so perfect, so beautiful, so divine, but I think I'm reaching a kind of Nirvana. I can't feel much personally, nor desire much for myself . . . *Self* seems to be dead in me. Other people want to kill self, but I want so to wake mine to life again, but it won't wake. You know I didn't kill myself two years ago, but I really died then . . .' 'Sweet brother soul, don't feel far from me. I too am going through a very dark and bitter moment of my life . . .' '. . . for so many years I have longed to meet a mind that should understand me, that should take away from the loneliness of my life. Now I have found it . . .' 'In that you are myself, I love you, and am near to you, but in that you are a man I am afraid of you, I shrink from you.'

I think all this is simpler than it sounds. The 'anguish and ecstasy' of her childhood had burned her out emotionally before childhood had properly ended. She was tranquil – but dead. She was writing about such states before she was out of her teens, a kind of dark night of the emotions where she felt neither love, nor hate, nor hope, and would have welcomed even pain. Then she fell in love, came to life in hopes for the marriage that did not happen, and was again in the cold hell of no-feeling. Havelock Ellis could not free her from it, but later her husband did. Her letters to Ellis show the evasiveness of a woman who is fond of a man she does not find sexually compelling. She needed him, loved him; but could not respond as he wanted – and as she wanted.

She was in Europe, mostly England, for almost a decade. Through a fog of illness: asthma, heart trouble, neuralgia, which she knew to be what we call psychosomatic, though knowing it did not help her; through the confusion of her emotional conflicts; we can watch the growth of another side of Olive Schreiner. The social reformer was becoming a socialist. She met, became friends with, the socialists: Eleanor Marx was an intimate. And the feminist learned that what had been, in her girlhood, a solitary personal conviction, considered eccentric, was what the best men and women of her time were studying.

It was called The Woman Question. Always practical, always at the roots of any problem, she was helping poor women, prostitutes, women in every kind of trouble. She started work on a 'big scientific work' on sex, which she discussed with Havelock Ellis. It never saw the light; was destroyed in the Boer War. A pity; no one else could have written it so well, and no one can write it now. For sex changes, like everything else, must be part of a climate. Between that time, such a short time ago, and ourselves is such a gulf of experience that it is hard to imagine ourselves in an air where so much was twisted, dark, murky. For instance, part of her suffering was due to celibacy: she said it herself. But: 'I would so much like to have a child, but I couldn't bear to be married; neither could I bear any relationship that was not absolutely open to the world – so I could never have one.' This was written at a time she was being asked to leave lodgings by landladies who considered her immoral because she had single men and 'unrespectable' women visiting her. She continued to act as she believed she had the right to act; yet she was a woman so sensitive to notice she hated even to eat in public. There is one large lesson we can still learn from the battle over 'the woman question.' It is that a change in physical relations and conditions changes mental and emotional states beyond what even the most revolutionary of reformers can begin to foresee. Even Olive, considered wildly visionary about the future of women, was far from seeing how much that was considered innate, inherent, could disappear and how fast. None of them ever seemed far from a micro-climate of semi-invalidism. Take what used to be called 'the change of life,' which even our mothers faced and suffered like a dreaded illness. For most women now it doesn't exist, and for many it happens without the aid of drugs. Less than a hundred years has done it. How? Why? The book that was destroyed could have helped with these and with other questions that ought to be asked. But there is a generation of girls enjoying liberties won for them by women like Olive Schreiner and looking back with what seems to be patronage, amusement. It is really a shudder of terror at what they've escaped from – and it stops them thinking.

It was mostly South Africa's sun, which might help her health, that took her back there in 1889. She was now a public figure; and she took a stand on 'The Native Question' and on Rhodes' acquisition of what became Southern Rhodesia. At first she admired Rhodes, who always admired her. She became his enemy over his doubledealing in the

Jameson Raid; and wrote a novel called *Trooper Peter Halkett of Mashonaland*, which was good enough for its purpose: an effort to arouse public indignation. It did. But it didn't stop Rhodes from annexing Mashonaland. She continued to protest and to warn while the bases of modern South Africa and Rhodesia were being well and truly laid. If Africans were not admitted now, she said, into the fellowship of civilisation, it would soon be too late; and the future would be all bloodshed and misery. She was prophetic about this, as about so much else; and emotionally clear in a way that she must have found hard to achieve. It is difficult enough now for a white person brought up in white-dominated Africa to free himself, herself, from a prejudice that starts when, from the moment you see anything, you see Africans as inferiors. The child Olive was taught to despise 'kaffirs' and 'niggers'. Parts of *Undine* show an ignorance and prejudice that is now shocking. She was also taught to despise the Dutch. When she was four, a small Boer girl gave her some sugar. She accepted, 'not liking to refuse,' but dropped it afterwards, for one did not eat anything that had been held in the hand of a Boer child. She also had conventionally prejudiced ideas about Jews, though there is a possibility she was part Jewish. All this she had to fight in herself, to change, in order to become the champion of racial tolerance. Nor was she that kind of liberal that South Africa still produces, the paternalist who believes that the kindly-master-to-grateful-servant relationship is the only one possible, since it is the only one he has ever seen. Olive, a real revolutionary, knew that the dispossessed must always work for, and win, their own rights, their own freedom; because it is in the fighting, the working, that they grow and develop and learn their measure. She expressed this idea particularly well in her writing about women.

When she was nearly forty, this woman who said she could not marry married a South African farmer, rather younger than herself. There were times of great happiness, though the marriage was difficult, as it was bound to be. The much-longed-for child died, and particularly cruelly; it choked in its sleep the night after it was born. Her grief turned her again towards the dark, weakened her, and, it seems, the marriage which, however, continued to be buoyed by their common love for South Africa and by their sympathy over political questions. In the Boer War she championed the Boers against her own countrymen, by whom she was reviled. She loved England. She loved the Boers. She suffered acutely, but she kept her good judgement, as her book 'An

English South African's View of the Situation' shows. It throws light
even now, for the violent emotionalism of the time did not prevent her
from holding on to the essentials: that it was the black people who
would shape the future; and that in South Africa any conflicts were (and
are) bound to be over who owns the gold, the diamonds, the minerals.
In the bitter aftermath of the war she worked for an alliance between
British and Dutch that would include the black people. These views
were as unpopular then as they are now: but now she would be in exile
or in prison. Her husband always supported her, though some
sympathies were wearing thin. He had made sacrifices for the marriage.
The farm he loved (so did she) was given up: her health was bad there.
He had made another profession for himself, but there were money
shortages; and he complained that he had counted on her earning
money through books that in fact she did not get written. Above all, her
health grew worse. She spent nights without sleep, walking around the
house, talking to herself, fighting for breath. The drugs she took
affected her badly. Her behaviour, always 'free', was increasingly
unconventional, and Cronwright was upset by it. She had never cared
about her dress. At this time she is described as dowdy, unimpressive,
with none of her old fire and brilliance – until she stands up to address a
meeting, when she is electrifying. She is described as the sort of woman
who in an older society would have been made the prophetess of a tribe.
In short, being married to her must have been extremely uncomfortable; and the older she grew, the less important became the small
everyday things where a marriage has to live. She suffered, increasingly, from the states of mind we label, in one of our sterilising,
nullifying words, 'depressions'. She also had deeper, more frequent
glimpses into states of insight and ecstatic oneness that were for her the
meaning of life.

   In some ways, she narrowed; was finding far too many things, and
people, and kinds of writing 'coarse' or 'crude'. She sounded,
sometimes, like a prissy maiden aunt. Women as they get older seem
prone to this: witness Virginia Woolf on James Joyce. I think it is
because women find it hard to be public. If it is not against our deepest
nature, for what our deepest nature is seems a matter of doubt, when
things change so fast, it is certain that public women attract a certain
kind of spite, a bitchiness, from both men and women. Learning not to
care about this can create a reactive overemphasis: 'You say I am
unfeminine: look at my traditional female moral attitudes!' Olive

earned her share of spite; and she continued over-sensitive, an unfortunate trait for someone always in the public eye and always fighting on the unpopular side. She never grew a most essential protective skin: somewhere in her was the young woman who, like Charlotte Brontë, had chosen to be a young man, 'Ralph Iron', rather than expose herself to criticism, and this at a time when she was known as a feminist. But these are small faults in a big woman, whose essential self was generous and wide, whose scope was always enlarging, and who continued to work for women. Cronwright does not seem to have been as sympathetic over this as over her other crusades. At least, there is a note of tetchiness here. But he did support and help her; and in 1911 she published *Woman and Labour*, which had an immediate and extraordinary influence, became a kind of bible for the feminists. But, like all her social writing, it goes much deeper than the temporary conditions it describes.

The First World War interrupted the suffragettes' and Olive's work for women; Olive's work for South Africa – and for peace. She was a pacifist. She was in England during the war. Her husband stayed in South Africa. These years must have been bad ones for her. Most of the socialists and suffragettes who were her natural allies had swung into support of the war. Many of her oldest friends found her position unsympathetic. She hated all wars, for any reason, and this one seemed to her particularly wrong. The jingoist nationalism of the time was loathsome to her. She remained for the most part quiet and alone – when she was not being turned out of lodgings and reported to the police because of her German name. In 1917 she saluted the birth of communist Russia among a most remarkable assortment of people, in The 1917 Club: Ramsey Macdonald, Oswald Mosley, Bertrand Russell, E. M. Forster, H. W. Nevinson. But she had said for years that the future lay with Russia and with America: a view that seemed absurd. When the war ended, her husband did not recognise the old woman who answered the door to him. She asked him to go back to the Cape with her. But she sailed alone, seen off by him and by Havelock Ellis. She was very ill. Soon afterwards she died alone in a hotel in the Cape.

What is left of this wonderful woman is *The Story of an African Farm*. The great influence she had is hidden from us in the events she helped to shape. It is the right time for this book to be republished. There is an atmosphere that is sympathetic to it, particularly among young people.

It makes me very happy to introduce Olive Schreiner to a fresh generation of readers because:

> It seems to me more and more that the only thing that really matters in life is not wealth or poverty, pleasure or hardship, but the nature of the human beings with whom one is thrown into contact, and one's relation with them.

Allah Be Praised

Malcolm X's autobiography is not an autobiography. A ghost, Alex Haley, made this book – most of it approved by Malcolm X before he died – from speeches, articles, notes of interviews. Against difficulties. Haley is a Negro, but was first regarded by Malcolm X as 'a white man's tool sent to spy'. 'I trust you 70 per cent' was his way of announcing won confidence. Then, the Black Muslim section was done before the break, while Malcolm X was passionately identified with the movement and its leader, Elijah Muhammad. As any politician would, he glossed over the internal difficulties to which he was not deliberately blinding himself. Nor, after the break, could his loyalty to the Negro struggle allow him damaging admissions. So if you want facts about member-ship, hidden allegiances, military organisation and plans, this book is worthless. Worse: Malcolm X's viewpoint about himself and his ideas shifted during the writing of it. Which brings up again the point recently raised by Truman Capote and his murderers – a relationship between reporter and subject which is bound to be suspicious, resistant, hostile, then overconfiding. Malcolm X was alone, trusted no one, not even his wife, was paranoid. Like the hero of *Catch-22*, classified as paranoid for believing, a soldier in World War II, that people wanted to kill him.

Haley got nowhere until he carefully depth-bombed: 'I wonder if you'd tell me something about your mother.' 'After that night he never hesitated to tell me the most intimate details of his personal life.' 'It made me face something about myself,' said Malcolm X – and face himself he did, uncovering areas blocked off through misery, drugs, guilt, hate. Malcolm X was not by nature gifted with insight into himself. Learning it came hard. About what he learned he was immediately honest, with the kind of frankness which comes easiest to those who are able to see their lives impersonally, as representative of forces larger than themselves – in his case, the Negro struggle for freedom. His sharply shifting viewpoints about his past would have made this book an unsatisfactory patchwork even if it hadn't used the hypnotic rhetoric of the speeches, the provocative oversimplifications of the polemical writing, as if these were Malcolm X's considered voice. Much better to have had this as straight biography from the shrewd and compassionate Haley. *But*, should we really welcome books like these, where a man in such a prison is opened in trust for the first time to a reporter doing a job?

Malcolm X's father preached God and was an active follower of Garvey, who taught that Negroes must return to Africa since they could never achieve freedom in America. When Malcolm X's mother was pregnant with him, horsed and hooded Ku Klux Klansmen surrounded the house one night, brandishing guns and threats. His mother fended them off. When Malcolm X was four, the house was burned over the family's heads by two white men. The police did not catch the white men, but harassed the father about the gun he had used to try to defend himself. Malcolm's father had seen four of his six brothers die by violence, one by lynching. He was very black. Malcolm's mother was West Indian, her father a white man.

His father favoured Malcolm as the lightest child – he had red hair, was almost white – but the mother whipped him extra. It was a fighting marriage: she was educated and patronised her rougher husband. The family lived in poverty, mostly on prayer-meeting collections. The small boy admired his father because he was 'tough and scared the white folks to death.' When the child was six, the father was murdered by white men. The mother tried to keep eight children on charring jobs, which she lost when it was found she was the agitator's widow. She was proud, fought against charity, had to take it. The children were starving. Welfare people gave food, and patronage, which was bitterly resented. The children watched her slow breakup: she was committed to a mental hospital and they were boarded out. Malcolm was twelve. An intransigent child, he was sent to reform school. There, for once, he struck it lucky with the people who ran it, though he noted they would talk about 'niggers' in front of him, and 'it never dawned on them I wasn't a pet but a human being.' He was bright, worked hard, was elected class president. But his only period of social conformity ended when, asked by the white teacher what he planned for his future, he replied 'to be a lawyer' – which he was obviously born for – and was told that as a Negro he must be realistic and settle for carpentry. It should be noted that this was not in the South, but near Detroit, in 1940.

He went to Boston to stay with his formidable sister Ella, who planned respectability for him. He was sixteen. Within a year he was a criminal in Harlem, accepted by a fraternity that sounds as exclusive as a crafts union, because of his wits and courage. Also he had a status symbol, an upper-class white girl who was at his disposal for five years, whom he fleeced of money, and despised. He was revenging himself on the white race through sex. His voice, like Baldwin's, is theatrically accusing – but as long as there are white people who enjoy being trounced for their total inferiority, particularly sexual, I suppose we'll have to listen to it. He traded in drugs, liquor, gambling, sex; thieved, pimped – survived. These chapters should be required reading for our persistent sentimentalists about black slums. This is what it is really like to live on one's wits in Harlem: and presumably in any black ghetto in America. (And in South Africa, be it noted.) At last, demoralised by cocaine, opium, hashish, liquor, he was caught, his white mistress and another white woman with him. Because there were white women involved, the sentences were heavy for a first offence.

He was then twenty-one, and he served seven years. A fellow prisoner called Bimbi told him to use the prison correspondence courses and library. He impressed Malcolm X as 'the first man I'd known who commanded total respect – with his words.' Painfully, he rehabilitated himself by copying out the dictionary, word by word; learned Latin and grammar; read systematically. Still in prison, he heard of the Black Muslims and suffered a conversion, which he compares with St Paul's, to the 'true knowledge'. This truth was brought to America by a prophet as great as Jesus or Mohammed, called Mr Wallace D. Fard, from whom Elijah Muhammad learned historical facts hitherto concealed by the white man from the Negro. It seems that 6,000 yeas ago a mad scientist (in defiance of God and to punish the world) created the white race out of the black race, which is genetically the true one. The white man is the devil of the Bible and has deliberately corrupted the black man through slavery and Christian brainwashing. The only hope for the black man is total separation from the white, who is evil beyond redemption. Something like apartheid: the Black Muslim creed is the mirror image of the white racialist one. Malcolm X came out of prison into the arms of Elijah Muhammad, whom he believed to be an aspect of Allah, the black man's God. He had turned into his own opposite,

embracing puritanism with all the fervour of his nature. The Nation of
Islam don't smoke or drink; observe strict dietary laws; every hour of
the day is regulated by religious observance; their women wear a
uniform like a nun's dress; the penalties for not being chaste and
monogamous are expulsion and ostracism.

Whereas Malcolm X the Harlem hustler had gloried in the sexual
power-game of the race war's shadowlands, chalking up every white
man or woman attracted by black flesh as evidence of the white man's
corruption, now he preached against sex like a latter-day Calvin so that
the Brotherhood were always complaining to the leader that he was
anti-woman. Then he married, found happiness, and was able to admit:
'I guess by now I will say I love Betty.' Clearly, he loved her very much,
even if he was able to trust her only 75 per cent.

As for Elijah Muhammad, a man worshipped as God by a small,
manageable sect, he was embarrassed by his fanatical lieutenant, a
brilliant organiser, polemicist, politician, who wanted nothing less than
the total conversion of all the Negroes in the United States. In the
twelve years Malcolm X was a Minister, he transformed the black
Muslims into an efficient, growing, internationally-known organisation
which had America hopping – and all this in the name of his leader, to
whom, and to Allah, he gave the credit. Cassius Clay was a recruit and,
although a close friend of Malcolm's, he remained after the break.

Then Elijah Muhammad was publicly faced with two paternity suits
by ex-secretaries. Trying to save his world from crashing, Malcolm X
took precedents from the Bible to his leader, who said:

> Son, you always had such a good understanding of prophecy
> and spiritual things. I'm David, who took another man's wife.
> You read about Noah who got drunk – that's me. You read
> about Lot, who went and laid up his own daughters. I have to
> fulfil all these things.

Malcolm X was unable to turn his back on Muhammad, but Muhammad had decided to get rid of Malcolm X. Probably by murder:
Malcolm X thought so – he had himself trained the young men in the
military arts and had said, 'I know what they are capable of.' But he had
always known he would die by violence and 'tried to be ready for it.'
Meanwhile he went to Mecca on pilgrimage, and learned that what he
had been preaching as 'Islam' had little to do with the real Islam. Race

hatred, for instance, was no part of it. This section of the book, in which he is entertained by Islamic and nationalist leaders in the Middle East and in Africa, reads embarrassingly like Jennifer's Diary – as painful as the reminiscences of African Nationalist leaders who, taken to the MRA headquarters in Caux, may return converted because 'they treated me like a human being.' But they seldom stay converted.

Malcolm X came home with a new name, El-Hajj Malik El-Shabbaz (His 'X' had 'replaced the white slavemaster name of "Little" which some blue-eyed devil named Little had imposed upon my paternal forebears'). He came home, too, with considerably modified ideas. With his usual courage he said so: he was expecting assassination daily. His tactical sense was put to the service of new outlooks. If he had lived, his version of 'The Nation of Islam' would probably have manoeuvred usefully in conjunction with the moderate movements formerly described by him as 'Uncle Tom': as a Black Muslim lieutenant he had chafed because Muhammad would not allow collaboration. He was murdered in 1965 while addressing a meeting in New York.

The Black Muslim sect remains: so does Elijah Muhammad. Its value – apart from its work among ex-prisoners, junkies, prostitutes – has been largely propagandist. The moderate movements, 'the sit-downs, sit-ins and teach-ins', have achieved more in practical terms. If, as the Black Muslims believed, the devil white man can be terrified by threats of raw violence into parting with his privileges, then Los Angeles would be a better place for their race riots. I gather this is not the case. But what a pity he is dead. He was a most gifted man, and we don't know what he might have become.